2124.B3=27 C

0 4

IMMIGRATION IN CANADA

HISTORICAL PERSPECTIVES

NEW
CANADIAN
READINGS
SERIES EDITOR
J.L. GRANATSTEIN

Titles currently available

IMMIGRATION IN
CANADA
HISTORICAL PERSPECTIVES

EDITED BY

Gerald Tulchinsky
Queen's University

Copp Clark Longman Ltd.
Toronto

ISBN: 0-7730-5400-6

editing: Barbara Tessman, Andy Carroll
proofreading: Claudia Kutchukian
design: Susan Hedley, Liz Nyman
typesetting: April Haisell
printing and binding: Metropole Litho Inc.

Canadian Cataloguing in Publication Data

Main entry under title:

Immigration in Canada: historical perspectives

Includes bibliographical references.
ISBN 0-7730-5400-6

1. Canada – Emigration and immigration – History.
II. Canada – Emigration and immigration – Government policy – History.
3. Immigrants – Canada – History.
I. Tulchinsky, Gerald, 1933–

JV7220.I55 1994   325.71'09   C94-930540-5

Copp Clark Longman Ltd.
2775 Matheson Blvd. East
Mississauga, Ontario
L4W 4P7

associated companies: *Longman Group Ltd., London* •
Longman Inc., New York • *Longman Cheshire Pty., Melbourne*
• *Longman Paul Pty., Auckland*

Printed and bound in Canada

1 2 3 4 5   5400-6   98 97 96 95 94

FOREWORD

o

Immigration is today and has been for centuries a subject of contention in Canada. Much as their predecessors did, our current political parties take strong positions on the subject, sociologists and educators offer their views, and economists pronounce on the effect of newcomers on the nation's bottom line. Another constant is that the Canadian public, yesterday and today, seems largely hostile to immigration. In only one opinion poll since 1945, for example, has the majority of the respondents expressed support for the view that Canada needs more people. It sometimes does seem, to cite Irving Abella, that Canada is a nation of immigrants that does not want to take in any more immigrants. Still, Canada remains one of the very few nations at all receptive to the movement of large numbers of people to its shores, and the immigrants flood in. The policy of multiculturalism, adopted by the Canadian government in 1971, was one recognition of the impact immigration has had.

The phenomenon of immigration and the reaction of the receiving country clearly deserve study, and Canadian writers and scholars have paid substantial attention to the subject. Too often, regrettably, this takes the form of filiopietistic books that try to list all the firsts: the first Ukrainian to arrive; the first Jewish dentist in Moose Jaw; the first Somali in Toronto, and so on. While such works may be worthy, there are none of them in this volume. Instead, here are scholarly examinations of the reasons immigrants of different ethnicity came to Canada, where and why they settled as they did, how they lived, and how they were received. Here are analyses of government policy and of the impact of gender and class. The essays in this book, carefully selected by historian Gerald Tulchinsky of Queen's University, who has written extensively in the area, offer a clear view of the problems that have fascinated researchers in this burgeoning field of study. They demonstrate the sophistication of research already done, and they point to the issues that merit further study.

J.L. Granatstein
Series Editor

CONTENTS

o

INTRODUCTION

o

Canadian history has been shaped by the interplay between transcendent cultures and local context, between imported values, attitudes, and beliefs, and the local realities of Native peoples, geography, and climate. Out of such jostling, a nation was built, a constitution struck, a polity crafted, a community developed, and a national personality formed—all imperfectly, but nevertheless with a mixture of confidence and hope—in response to emerging crises and opportunities. This collection of articles on immigration in Canada attempts to explore that interplay.

It is, of course, a truism that, aside from Native peoples, everyone in Canada today is an immigrant or a descendant of immigrants. Some of the fathers of Confederation—John A. Macdonald, George Brown, Alexander Campbell, and d'Arcy McGee—were themselves immigrants. So were most of the country's tycoons of industry, commerce, transportation, and finance who shaped Canada's modernizing economy in the nineteenth and early twentieth centuries.[1] By contrast with the United States, where the top levels of political and economic life in the nineteenth century were occupied almost exclusively by native-born Americans, Canada's major institutions included many immigrants among their leading personnel. At the same time, immigrants were important participants in Canadian cultural institutions. In the United States, until relatively recently, immigrants were virtually absent from such institutions. Although nearly all of these influential Canadian migrants were from Britain, reflecting English Canada's colonial origins, the point is that these newcomers were prominent among Canada's recognized nation builders.

The peopling of Canada by immigrants from countries all over the world has been, and remains, one of the most important features of Canadian history and of the continuing evolution of its society, cultural institutions, and political life. As the origins of immigrants changed from the beginnings of permanent European settlement in the seventeenth century, the composition of Canada's non-Native population has been transformed. Until the mid-eighteenth century, immigrants were almost exclusively French. The arrival of Loyalists from the United States in the 1780s was part of a rapidly increasing British component. Waves of immigrants from the British Isles arrived throughout the nineteenth and early twentieth centuries, and a growing non-British element reached Canada after 1900, especially following the First World War. Indeed, by 1991 Canada's population of approximately 27 million was 23 percent French and 28 percent British, while 31 percent were neither. Another 19 percent reported multi-ethnic ancestry.[2] Canada is now, in fact as well as in theory, a multicultural society.

In studying immigration to Canada, we should remember that we are dealing with people who, for a wide variety of reasons, made individual, family, or group decisions to move from one country to another. The motives of some were undoubtedly intensely personal, like the romantic quest for adventure or perhaps the ignoble abandonment of family. Others could have been responding to poverty or revolution in the home country, taxes and impositions like military service, religious or political persecution, or the lure of economic opportunity in Canada. Marianne McLean's article in this collection describes the effect of declining economic conditions in the western Highlands in the late eighteenth and early nineteenth centuries, which drove many Scots to resettle in Upper Canada where they joined family and friends in Glengarry County. There were a multitude of such push-and-pull factors that helped to determine the peopling of Canada.

While immigrants came in response to such forces, they were governed by various state policies that attempted to regulate the flow of people. From the seventeenth century, governments attempted to assist these migrations and even employed private agencies to attract immigrants to Canada. With only minimally successful results, as Peter Moogk stresses in his article in this volume, the French government employed recruiters to draw peasants and artisans to New France. Inducements were offered to various groups: David Bell examines the provisions for the Loyalists in early New Brunswick while Robert Dilley studies policy regarding Mennonites in the eighteenth and early nineteenth centuries to settle parts of Upper Canada. Such efforts reflected the belief that Canada's attractiveness was less than fully apparent to the "most desirable" potential immigrants. Indeed, since the French regime, a significant number of people saw their migration to Canada as a sojourn of a few years before they returned to their homeland or moved to the United States.

To reach Canada immigrants travelled alone or with friends and family, usually over enormous distances. Inevitably they left relations and other friends behind, at the garden gate, the village boundary, the local railway station, or a seaport's dockside. Letters and, after the nineteenth century, photographs might be exchanged but, in most cases, it was unlikely that the immigrants would ever again see those they left behind. After leaving their loved ones, immigrants faced the challenges of travel to ports of embarkation. Sometimes their departures were illegal or clandestine and might involve bribes and additional dangers. Next came the hazards and discomforts of long sea voyages. The first sighting of the new land was often characterized by shock, loneliness, and ambivalence. Especially for immigrants who spoke neither French nor English, arrival at port meant confusion and anger at impersonal processing by officials. Such ordeals were followed by often lengthy and uncomfortable travel by various means to their new homes. These homes were often only temporary: for many, the migration process continued as they moved numerous times in search of a permanent place to settle. Anxiety and heartbreak were part of the migration process.

The history of Canadian immigration has not suffered from scholarly neglect. Earlier this century, the subject of immigration attracted the scholarly interest of historian Arthur Lower and social scientist Mabel Timlin. They and others expressed concern about Canada's capacity to effectively absorb large numbers of immigrants. Lower sounded warnings about the dangers he perceived in attempting to absorb non-Anglo-Saxons—mainly Slavs, whom he deemed to be unassimilable—into an overwhelmingly British-Canadian cultural milieu.[3] In a major critique of postwar immigration policy, Timlin raised important reservations about Canada's economic capacity to absorb large numbers of newcomers.[4]

Such appraisals reflected the doubts and outright racism expressed regarding the efficacy of Canada's early-twentieth-century "open-door" policy. Some of the arguments seem familiar as we witness increasingly widespread debate in the 1990s about the utility to Canada of even a humanitarian refugee immigration policy. These debates must raise serious doubts about the strength of Canada's commitment to multiculturalism, to the concept of the nation as a mosaic of many peoples, a peaceable community of different races, creeds, cultures, and religions.

Recent work on immigration history includes the volumes in the History of Canada's Peoples Series, edited by Jean Burnet and the late Howard Palmer, which were published under the auspices of the Multiculturalism Directorate, Department of the Secretary of State. (Some of these works—each with a substantial bibliography—are listed in the Further Readings section of this volume.)[5] Donald H. Akenson's *The Irish in Ontario: A Study in Rural History*,[6] along with his other outstanding works on the Irish in Canada—a sample of which is included in this collection— constitute a historiographical *tour de force* that should serve as an object lesson in what can be achieved in the field of Canadian immigration history. The current literature also includes two useful surveys: *Strangers at Our Gates: Canadian Immigration and Immigration Policy, 1540–1990*, by Valerie Knowles,[7] and *"Coming Canadians": An Introduction to a History of Canada's Peoples*, by Jean Burnet and Howard Palmer.[8] The secondary literature in books and articles on aspects of Canadian immigration is vast, and a systematic search in historical journals of national and regional scope would be amply repaid with a very large bibliography of useful articles, many of them excellent, on specific ethnic groups and their settlement. Given the size and quality of this literature, it has not been easy to select the pieces for this collection.

This group of essays attempts to cover aspects of the immigration experience of some of the people who came to Canada between the French regime and recent times. The literature covers many of the experiences of immigrants, ranging from their departures from their countries of origin to their transitions to life in Canada.

Several themes will become clear from reading the selections that make up this volume. One is that the question of immigration as a public issue and a matter of government policy dates back almost to the beginnings of European settlement. Given the perceived pressing need to people New France, and the practical matter of trying to ensure a gender balance to provide a natural increase in the Canadian population, as Peter Moogk explains, immigration assumed great importance to those making policy decisions about the colony's future. From that point forward, the immigration question was seldom dormant. The settlement of Upper Canada for a generation after the American Revolution was in large part determined on the basis of anticipated needs for the defence of that part of British North America. Such planning was evident in some of the immigration and settlement schemes. Development considerations also figured prominently in the nineteenth century and during the Laurier era when so many immigration initiatives were undertaken by the Dominion government to stimulate settlement and agriculture on the Prairies. John Lehr's article in this collection tells us that government officials tried to steer Ukrainian immigrants to settle in promising farming areas, usually without success.

It should be noted that immigration policy was not founded upon altruism. Canada was not then, as it now proclaims itself to be, a home for refugees from persecution in their own countries. In fact a more or less "open-door" immigration policy was accompanied by widespread and growing reservations among intellectuals and politicians, as Howard Palmer's article explains, about "the type of society that would emerge in English-speaking Canada." Immigration policy reflected the practical considerations and particular prejudices of the government. It routinely exercised what Reg Whitaker calls a "double standard." Those in power made concerted efforts to attract only people of preferred races and political stripes. After World War II, this meant that suspected communists, but not possible Nazi war criminals, were barred entry to Canada.

Allied to such planning is the theme of racial and religious exclusion. The attempt to keep out of Canada those who did not possess the right pedigree has been evident since the days of New France. Jews and Protestants were officially barred from the colony until the end of the *ancien régime*. Although immigration was more open during the nineteenth and early twentieth centuries, Asians were actively discouraged from entering Canada, and African Americans who sought entry received a very cold welcome. Those Asians, principally Chinese and Japanese, who did settle in Canada, especially in Vancouver, were the objects of powerful fear, flagrant discrimination, and bloody violence. Government policies abetted such racism. While Chinese single male immigrants were allowed into Canada in very limited numbers, and only after the payment of an enormous head tax, young British women were actively sought by both provincial and Dominion governments for positions as domestic servants.

By the early years of the twentieth century, a strong backlash of public sentiment against the "open-door" policy of the Laurier government towards non-English-speaking immigrants from Eastern and Southern Europe was apparent. Robert Harney's study of Italian workers demonstrates that immigration policies were based upon hard calculations of Canadian needs balanced against growing fears that Southern Europeans and others might endanger Canada's political equilibrium, cultural traditions, and racial purity. During the First and Second World Wars, hundreds of people were placed in prison camps because they were or had been citizens of countries with which Canada was at war. As Barbara Roberts explains, the Dominion was also prepared to deport many immigrants for political reasons, reflecting a deep-seated fear of dissent from established norms. During the 1930s and 1940s, widespread racism, reinforced by powerful antisemitism across the country, all but closed Canada's doors to European Jews trying to escape from persecution and death.

Another major aspect of the history of immigration in Canada is the response of immigrants to their own experiences. They were travellers through both space and time as they moved from a familiar culture to another geographical and social context. This transformation was easier for some than for others; perhaps a common language and institutions made it less difficult for immigrants from the British Isles and the United States to adjust to Canadian political and social norms. Most immigrants, nevertheless, tended to huddle together as a refuge from the strangeness of the new land, seemingly awestruck by its rawness, its size, and its simplicity.

Immigrants sought and found some solace with their own people. Highlanders from Inverness-shire insisted on settling near their kin in Glengarry County, where they formed a community of their own. Jews and Italians sought out their *landsmen* and *paesani* in cities like Montreal and Toronto; they congregated on streets, in stores, in restaurants, and on verandahs to exchange greetings, news, gossip, and reminiscences. German-speaking Mennonites, as we see in Robert Dilley's article, showed a very high propensity to remain in or very near their home community in nineteenth-century Waterloo County. In Vancouver's Chinatown, as Kay Anderson's article makes clear, there was not only a segregated Chinese geographical location, there was also social space in which Chinese could find familiar faces, language, foods, and associations. Such was the case with others as well. A familiar ethnic neighbourhood, whether rural or urban, was a powerful magnet for subsequent arrivals of these immigrant groups. As John Lehr informs us, many new Ukrainian immigrants, often against their own economic best interests, were determined to settle in areas offering what was to them suitable topography near fellow Ukrainians.

Many immigrants, even English-speaking arrivals from Scotland, Ireland, England, and the United States, set up associations to help their own people through the often painful process of adapting to Canadian conditions. Ross McCormack's article examines the importance of mutual assistance among immigrants from the British Isles living in Winnipeg. Despite their much greater familiarity with Canadian culture, they nevertheless felt the need for the comfort and utility of association with their compatriots. Thus, St Andrew's, St Patrick, Irish Protestant Benevolent, and Sons of England societies were formed—many of them with major women's auxiliaries—to attend to immigrants' special needs. The Sons of Italy and a multitude of groupings among Ukrainian, German, Chinese, and many other immigrant groups who arrived during the nineteenth and twentieth centuries performed the same vital functions. The discussion in Gerald Tulchinsky's article of the responses in the Montreal Jewish community to the challenges of immigration illustrates the strengths and weaknesses of this communal activity. The first generation, the immigrants themselves, generally had the hardest time, and these associations helped in many ways to ease the transition by providing material assistance, news, and, above all else, friendship and understanding to the bewildered immigrants. Associations helped those who were confused, astonished, and fearful at dockside after disembarking from the ship, at the railway station, in the immigration sheds, in the boarding houses, out on the busy streets. Ethnic associations also served a multitude of workers, from those hacking through the bush or laying the railroad, to others labouring endless hours in restaurant kitchens, city sweatshops, manufacturing establishments, or private homes.

The adjustment by women in their roles as wives and mothers, as domestic servants, and as wage earners points to the need to understand the immigration experiences that were specific to their gender. In her study of the Penman contract labour scheme, Joy Parr makes us aware of how some English women "came with common experience of wage work and the domestic dilemmas female employment engendered to a women's town [Paris, Ontario] . . . , where the numerical dominance of female wage earners offered a certain psychic and physical protection, a shelter for a woman-centred culture." A different form of accommodation is outlined in Franca Iacovetta's article, which examines the transformations in the lives of post-World War II southern Italian women immigrants to Toronto where they entered low-paid jobs—frequently in clothing factories—while maintaining their traditional notions of familial and motherly responsibility. The significance of imported cultures and local context on the immigrant experience is amply illustrated in the juxtaposition of these two studies.

This collection of essays demonstrates how complex an issue immigration has been in Canadian history. From the beginnings of European settlement, it has not been easy to populate this land. Yet immigrants able and willing to accept Canada's climatic limitations and rigours came in numbers, when beckoned by economic opportunities either in the form of arable farmland or the urban frontier of expanding cities. The immigrant imprint on Canadian society not only cannot be ignored, it must be actively investigated for the insights it will yield into the history of the Canadian people and how Canada got to where it is now.

NOTES

1. This pattern continued well into the twentieth century. Clarence Decatur Howe, a businessman and a leading member of the King and St Laurent governments between 1935 and 1957, was an American who immigrated to Canada in 1908. J.K. Johnson, ed., *The Canadian Directory of Parliament 1867–1967* (Ottawa: Public Archives of Canada, 1968), 279.

2. *Canada Year Book 1994* (Ottawa: Statistics Canada, 1993), 99.

3. See Welf Heick, *His Own Man: Essays in Honour of Arthur Lower* (Montreal: McGill-Queen's University Press, 1974), as well as Lower's *My First Seventy-Five Years* (Toronto: McClelland & Stewart, 1967), *Canadians in the Making* (Toronto: Longman, 1958); *Colony to Nation* (Toronto: Longman, 1944).

4. Mabel I. Timlin, *Does Canada Need More Immigrants?* (Toronto: Oxford University Press, 1951).

5. There are numerous volumes on many of Canada's ethnic communities in this series, which was published by McClelland & Stewart in association with the Multiculturalism Program, Department of the Secretary of State, and the Canadian Government Publishing Centre.

6. Montreal: McGill-Queen's University Press, 1984.

7. Toronto: Dundurn Press, 1992.

8. Toronto: McClelland & Stewart, 1988.

RELUCTANT EXILES:
EMIGRANTS FROM FRANCE
IN CANADA BEFORE 1760 ◇

PETER N. MOOGK

o

For the ambitious government administrator, wholesale merchant, or regular army officer, service in the colony of New France was a painful route to a desirable position in the mother country. The colony was seldom accepted as a home; life there was described as an "exile" or "purgatory." In 1707 a military engineer bemoaned his sojourn in Canada, "a wretched place [*triste Endroit*] where I am spending the best years of my life imperceptibly [*Insensiblement*]."[1] Earlier, an intendant observed that "Canada has always been regarded as a country at the end of the world, and as an exile that might almost pass for a [sentence] of civil death."[2] The revulsion felt by these emissaries from the metropolis for the cold and remote North American colony is understandable. What is surprising is that their inferiors, such as indentured servants or soldiers, were just as eager to return to France. Their attitude was eloquently expressed by their actions; they, too, were reluctant exiles. Recently, Mario Boleda concluded that "at least 27 000 French people came to Canada during the French regime." Of these, only 31.6 percent became permanent residents. Over two-thirds of the migrants returned to France.[3]

This astonishing flight back to the homeland helps to explain why New France had no more than 62 000 European inhabitants in 1755. There never was a sustained or large-scale movement of people from France to Canada, and most of those who came did not stay. Indentured workers and subsidized migrants were numerous in the 1650s and 1660s, but apart from the arrival of prisoners in the 1730s and the settlement of disbanded soldiers and Acadian refugees in the 1740s and 1750s, migrants were an incidental

◇ *William and Mary Quarterly*, 3rd series, 46, 3 (July 1989): 463–506. Reprinted with the permission of the author.

addition to the established population after 1673. There were rarely more than three hundred newcomers a year during the 1600s, and that number dwindled until the 1740s. It was natural increase, rather than migration, that increased the white population of the St Lawrence Valley sevenfold between 1681 and 1765. The total migration from France and then back home has been understated by historians of Canada, who relied on census returns and church registers. A "natural increase" was established by subtracting recorded deaths (including migrants) from the number of infant baptisms. The excess above this increase, recorded in censuses, was attributed to immigration. It was assumed that most migrants stayed. Thus traditional estimates of the migration from France between 1608 and 1760 varied from 7500 to 12 000.[4]

The fitful, small-scale migration to Canada and the high rate of returns to France reveal the influence of cultural attitudes. Human migrations are not fully explained by identifying the "push" of uncomfortable conditions at home and the "pull" of a new land's attractions. Between the "push" and the "pull" there must be mediating factors to produce a large and sustained movement of people over a long distance to a place where they will make a new home. Those factors include communal traditions, an emigrant recruiting system, favourable publicity about the new land, and commercial carriers who will transport numerous passengers. From 1600 to 1760 there was sufficient "push" to dislodge people from France, and life for the lower classes in Canada was sufficiently good to provide the "pull." But because the elements of linkage were deficient, there was no mass migration to French North America.

This article will emphasize popular resistance in France to overseas resettlement; it will also draw attention to the unwillingness of eighteenth-century French shipowners and merchant brokers to assist a large-scale migration of free migrants. High-seas traders decided that the modest profit from indentured workers did not justify the trouble involved in recruiting them. French traders preferred to carry goods and, by the mid-1700s, black slaves. This preference had a cultural as well as a commercial dimension, since contemporary merchants from Rotterdam willingly carried thousands of contract workers to British North America. What might the Netherlanders have done for Canada had they not been excluded from French colonial trade in the eighteenth century?

Apart from the prejudices of potential emigrants and merchant-shipowners, there were other serious impediments to a large-scale, voluntary migration to Canada before 1760. Little reliable information on the colony's assets was available to the lower classes in France. The Atlantic passage was costly and dangerous, and the maritime traffic to Canada, which might have carried migrants, was small.

In France, popular knowledge of the colonies depended more on hearsay than on publications or private letters. What little was heard was damning. Even in the literature of the early 1600s, "'Canada' was used only as a joke, a synonym for frightful exile."[5] In 1659, when the people of La Flèche heard that forty respectable women were departing for Canada, the townsfolk tried to prevent their departure because no one could believe that the women were going voluntarily. Pierre Boucher's *Histoire Véritable et Naturelle des Moeurs & Production du Pays de la Nouvelle France* (1664) was expressly written to improve the reputation of Canada. Boucher denied that ne'er-do-wells (*garnemens*) and prostitutes were exiled to New France but conceded that the colony had four great *incommoditez*: mosquitoes, long winters, rattlesnakes, and "the Iroquois our enemies."[6]

There were compensatory advantages to life in Canada for able-bodied members of the lower classes: obtainable land and material independence. Under seigneurial land tenure, uncleared land could be had for the asking; it cost the would-be tenant nothing. No direct taxes were paid to the crown—a wondrous situation for the peasantry of France. Seventeenth-century authors, such as Samuel de Champlain and the Jesuit missionaries, described the fertile soil, abundance of water, ample resources, and variety of wild game (which commoners could hunt!) in New France. Boucher also extolled these benefits but compromised his role as a recruiter of emigrants. Wanting to show that the Iroquois must be conquered, as well as to gratify European curiosity about the "wild people [*les sauvages*]" of the Americas, he devoted a quarter of his book to the native Indians, with a chapter on Iroquoian ritual torture and the eating of captives. Stories about such horrors had already been conveyed to France.[7] The impression of Canada left in the minds of those who read Boucher's book or heard it read aloud would have been contradictory: it was a fruitful land inhabited by cruel and barbarous natives.

Boucher's book and the annual *Relations* published by the Jesuits probably reached few potential settlers. The publications cost more than a manual worker's daily wage. In the *Relation* of 1636, Father Paul Le Jeune acknowledged that landless and ambitious members of France's lower orders were not his readers: "But to whom do I speak? To people who cannot know what I am writing, unless more capable ones than they tell it to them. These I beg to do so, in the name of God and of the King; for the interests of both are involved in peopling this Country."[8]

There was nothing in France to match the single-minded, effusive literature of seventeenth-century England that promoted emigration to the New World. Potential emigrants in France relied on hearsay and chance to learn about the colonies: one literate man obtained information about Canada and Louisiana from sailors, while another was told about New France by an officer visiting Paris.[9]

British colonization was spurred on by an army of pamphleteers *and* by private letters sent home by the immigrants. By this transatlantic correspondence the hesitant were informed, reassured, and encouraged to follow those who had gone ahead. The letter writers were familiar and trusted informants who frequently offered to help those who followed them to the New World. Two-thirds of Scottish emigrants bound for the Carolinas in 1774, when interviewed by customs officials at Lerwick, said they were induced to emigrate by letters from friends and kin in North America, as well as by hardships at home.[10] There is no evidence of a comparable network of correspondence to attract and assist emigrants to New France. Mail delivery in the French empire was informal and risky, and barely half the migrants in

Canada could sign their names.[11] Only one private letter to a relative recommending the colony as a place for settlement is known to exist: it was sent in 1651 by a gentleman at Quebec to his brother-in-law at Tours.[12] As we shall see, the French migrants were more likely to receive appeals to return home than to invite others to join them.

Can the royal government of France be blamed for hindering a large migration to North America? Some historians have argued that official preference for Roman Catholic settlers deprived New France of the addition of Huguenot fugitives from France.[13] The royal administration also feared that France would be weakened militarily and economically by the loss of any part of its population. In 1665, when Intendant Jean Talon offered to prepare homesteads in Canada for more than that year's quota of three hundred assisted emigrants, Secretary of State Jean-Baptiste Colbert refused the offer. He told Talon that the king regarded the increase as impractical and believed that "it would not be prudent to depopulate his kingdom to populate Canada."[14] Colbert expected New France's European population to grow by natural increase, once a nucleus of colonists had been established. Despite official religious prejudices and concern for maintaining the population of France, the government did not impede migration to the colony. The formal exclusion of Protestants and Jews from the French colonies was not strictly enforced, despite appeals from the Roman Catholic clergy. In the eighteenth century the crown approved the emigration of German-speaking Protestants to Louisiana, Cayenne, and Saint-Domingue.[15]

The six-to-nine-week voyage from France to Quebec could have been a deterrent to migration. The passage was longer than that to the British North American colonies, and the hazards were much the same. Some deaths en route were to be expected. The misfortunes afflicting passengers from France befell other transatlantic migrants: shipwreck, contrary winds, storms, seasickness, water damage to clothes and possessions, a tedious diet, foul drinking water, ship fevers, and surly crew members. Before 1760, piracy or attack by foreign warships was an additional risk.

For civilian passengers to Canada, shipboard conditions were usually better than those endured on immigrant ships going to the British possessions, because passengers on French merchant vessels were a small addition to the crew. Humble voyagers slept in hammocks on the gun deck and ate with the sailors—a situation to be envied by British immigrants traveling in steerage. When a vessel was packed with people as well as cargo, the crowding and unsanitary conditions bred maladies. Fatal epidemics sometimes broke out on French warships and royal transports carrying scores of soldiers and prisoners in addition to the usual complement of officers, government officials, and religious personnel.[16]

At the beginning of the Crown-subsidized migration in 1662–71, royal transports carried hundreds of workers and settlers. Without experience in caring for so many passengers and in the absence of health regulations, these vessels were death traps. Thirty-three percent of the passengers died en route in 1662. Of 300 persons embarked in France in 1663, nearly 60 perished at sea and a dozen more died in Quebec's hospital after arrival.[17] Thereafter, recruiting and transportation of the royal levies were entrusted to merchants with experience in the delivery of indentured labourers. In 1664 Dutch vessels were chartered, possibly because the Netherlanders knew how to keep passengers alive as well as being cheap and efficient mariners. A Dutch ship was retained in 1665 when the *Compagnie des Indes Occidentales* assumed responsibility for the royal program. The people transported by private vessels arrived in good health, and the death rates of 1662–63 were matched only in 1732, 1740, and 1757, when large numbers of soldiers, prisoners, and government workers were packed on royal vessels.[18]

Since religious and political dissidents from France tended to move to adjacent European countries rather than emigrate to the French colonies, secular migrants to Canada usually lacked ideological mettle to face the rigours of overseas settlement. Apprehension of the sea voyage and the Iroquois might explain the panic that swept one group. In the 1650s the *Société de Notre-Dame de Montréal* recruited batches of people in France for the Montreal Island settlement, which was frequently raided by the Iroquois. In 1653, 153 men were enticed to sign up for five years in the colony in return for good pay and a cash advance. Before boarding ship at Saint-Nazaire, 49 fled with the advance payment and one annulled his contract. The hulk bearing the remaining 103 took on so much seawater that it was forced back to France. The expedition's commander placed the migrant workers on an island off the French coast, "from which it was impossible to escape since, otherwise, not one of them would have remained." According to the same eyewitness, some were so desperate to escape that they jumped into the ocean to swim to the mainland "to save themselves, for they were like madmen and believed that they were being led to destruction."[19] That fear was vindicated: while crossing in a second ship, eight went to a watery grave and, in New France, another 24 were killed by Indians.

From this, it is evident that the "pull" of Canada was weak. The same could not be said of the "push" needed to dislodge people from home and familiar surroundings. If unemployment, famine, and hardship incline people to overseas migration, then France should have been an ideal recruiting ground for Canadian settlers. The entire seventeenth century and the early eighteenth century have been described as an era of crisis for all of France. In 1959, when Robert Mandrou sought the essence of Gabriel Debien's study of workers indentured at La Rochelle in 1634–1714 for service in the Americas, he saw an exact correlation between peaks in enlistments and periods of famine, hunger, and riot in western France. Mandrou concluded that "the emigration from La Rochelle is, therefore, largely due to misery. . . . The indentured workers were only willing [to sign up] in the port . . . during difficult years. In ordinary times, it was necessary to appeal to them, to go out and seek them, and often from very far away."[20]

There were major grain famines in northwestern France in 1660–62, 1675–79, 1692–94, 1698–99, and in 1709, when an excessively cold winter caused a general crop failure. Hunger and unemployment increased the wandering population. La Rochelle's civic authorities appointed *archers* in 1698 "to prevent itinerant beggars [*gueux forains*] and foreigners from entering the town."[21] Some of these starving wretches had traveled great distances: among the paupers who died at La Rochelle were a boy from Mons diocese, a young man from Maine province, a confectioner from Arles in Provence, as well as beggars from nearby Poitou.[22]

There was a connection between hard times in France and peaks in the recruiting of *engagés* (indentured workers) for the colonies. Famines in 1660–62, 1698–99, 1709–10, and 1721–23 aided recruiters in the ports of La Rochelle and Nantes.[23] There was *not* however, *an exact correspondence* between acute distress in France and the scale of recruiting.

By dealing with the "push" alone, Mandrou neglected the "pull" exerted by recruiters. The Montreal associates were responsible for the peaks in 1644 and 1659, and the royal program underlay the mass of contracts made in 1664–65 (see figure 1). Some regions may have been sheltered from the major demographic crises in France,[24] but La Rochelle was not one of them. The poor soil of its hinterland produced little grain; some inferior wines from the district were distilled into brandy for export. Distress in a region linked by trade with the American colonies did not automatically produce a wave of voluntary emigrants for the overseas possessions, as the table shows. A famine in the area around La Rochelle might displace farm workers and town artisans, but it did not follow that they would resettle in the colonies.

Most French migrants to Canada came from Paris and surrounding Île-de-France, Perche, and the coastal provinces of Saintonge, Aunis, Poitou, Brittany, and Normandy.[25] Recruiters concentrated on the hinterland of Atlantic seaports, such as St-Malo, Granville, and Dieppe. La Rochelle was the principal port of departure for New France during Louis XIV's reign. It was the natural outlet for Poitou, Aunis, Saintonge, and Angoumois, which, according to Stanislas A. Lortie and Adjutor Rivard, furnished 30 percent of Canada's French settlers in 1608–1700.[26] Thus La Rochelle is an appropriate choice for studying the migration from France to Canada.

The reluctance of the population to enroll for work in the colonies, even in times of distress, was common in France. Past overseas migration was geographically selective; regions accustomed to the departure of large portions of the population, whether as seamen or mercenary soldiers or migrant workers, always sent forth a disproportionately large number of emigrants. Areas of France that lost people by emigration, such as Normandy, lost them in internal migration to cities and other regions of France. Some wandered into neighbouring European kingdoms. Only a few thousand chose permanent resettlement in a distant colony. With a population four times England's five million and a history of demographic disasters, France sent out a much smaller number of contract workers to the colonies.

Contemporaries remarked on the paradox of rural folk who preferred a miserable, precarious existence in France to material security abroad. After the famine of the 1630s, Father Paul Le Jeune marvelled that "there are so many strong and robust peasants in France who have no bread to put in their mouths; is it possible they are so afraid of losing sight of the village steeple, . . . that they would rather languish in their misery and poverty, than to place themselves some day at their ease among the inhabitants of New France?"[27]

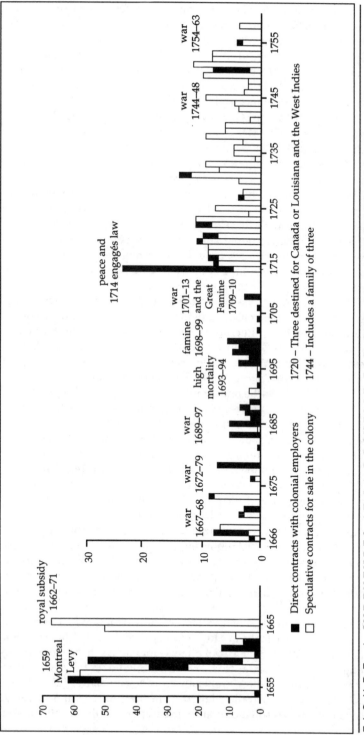

FIGURE 1 *INDENTURES AT LA ROCHELLE FOR THE ST LAWRENCE VALLEY, 1654–1760 (576 Contracts)*

The questions about Canada put to Pierre Boucher in the 1660s reveal that the enquirers were interested in emigration only if it allowed them to carry on their old way of life in greater comfort. Unlike the English Puritans, the French laity were seldom prepared to forego worldly comforts for spiritual ends. They were not escaping a detested liturgy and episcopacy to create a new Christian polity; they *had to be assured* that familiar religious institutions would be present. They also asked, "is wine dear there? . . . are there horses in the country?" and, most often, "what profit can be made there?" Boucher affirmed that "the land is good, and capable of producing all sorts of things as in France."[28]

Self-financed, independent newcomers were so rare in New France that they were noted in administrative records and in official correspondence.[29] They were usually gentlemen-travellers spying out the land; their social inferiors needed help to get to Canada. The fare, rations included, for a lower-class passenger sailing to New France in the second half of the seventeenth century was sixty to eighty *livres*.[30] It would take a skilled craftsman a year to accumulate enough money for a single fare.[31] French shipowners did not compete in offering cheap passages to the New World. The only alternatives for humble folk were indentured labour or a redemption contract. In the system of indentured or bond labour, the sponsor offered a passage to North America and material benefits in return for a few years of work in the colonies. In the case of families, the sponsor might demand a promise of repayment for the costs of transportation. This was the "redemption" system that brought so many German-speaking families to British North America's middle colonies. The French knew about redemptioning; they sometimes used it but preferred to indenture individual workers. Before 1663, when the Crown assumed direct administration of New France and ended the reign of the chartered companies, private interests sponsored the migration of most newcomers. Marcel Trudel estimates that 3106 migrants had arrived in 1632–62.[32]

In this period those making direct personal contracts with people in France were often recipients of seigneurial grants from *la Compagnie des Cent Associés*. Under its 1627 patent the company was to bring out 4000 emigrants over the next fifteen years.[33] English attacks on company ships and the loss of Quebec in 1629 so weakened the enterprise that it was unable to meet this requirement. After restoration of the colony to France in 1632, the company transferred part of its obligation to settle the land to those receiving estates from the venture. The recipients might be landless gentlemen or religious groups such as the pious founders of Montreal.

In 1634 the company granted Beauport seigneury to Robert Giffard, a surgeon from Mortagne in France. A condition of his grant was that "the men" he or his successors brought to Canada would be counted as part of the total the company had to transport to New France. In that year Giffard arranged to have forty-three people from the Mortagne district join his family in emigrating to the colony. A surviving contract made with a stonemason and a carpenter shows the high price he paid to overcome popular resistance to overseas migration. Giffard was to transport the two craftsmen to Canada and provide them with food, lodging, and maintenance "in all

their necessities" during the three years they helped him to clear and culti-
vate land. In addition, they would receive half the lands they cleared, not as
tenants but as subseigneurs, as well as another thousand acres of wild lands
close to the river. Giffard was to bring out their families two years later and
provide each family with two cows. The lord of Beauport kept his promise,
but his ungrateful workers claimed in 1637 that *all* of the lands granted
were noble estates and thus they owed him no tenants' dues. For the stonemason, these benefits and the presence of his children and fellow
Percherons did not cure his homesickness; he waited twenty years before
selling his house in Mortagne.[34]

Another colonizing seigneur, Noël Juchereau Des Chatelets, and his
brothers who recruited some forty workers in Perche in 1646–51, encountered the same reluctance to resettle permanently in Canada. All his recruits
received, in addition to food and wages, *the promise of a prepaid passage home*
at the end of their three or five years of service. Three made advance
arrangements for that return, and one manservant asked that his salary be
paid to his wife in France. Only a third of the workers became permanent
residents of Canada.[35]

The *Société de Montréal* was desperate to retain survivors of the 1653
levy in Canada; it offered them free land and settlement bounties to become
colonists. Those who accepted the offer had their service contracts annulled
in 1654 and were given credit and wages to assist their establishment, yet
only forty workers accepted this generous proposal.[36]

Immediate land grants and family ties were seen as effective in keeping
former indentured workers in the colony. The Montreal associates applied
the lesson in 1659 when they recruited 109 persons in France; 40 were
women (12 wives accompanied by single women and a few nuns). Eight
families had their passage paid in return for a redemption bond due in two
years. Thanks to the presence of relatives and marriageable females, most of
the 1659 recruits became *Canadiens*.[37] The value of bringing out entire families, as a sure way of fixing newcomers to the new land, was demonstrated.
The evidence, alas, was ignored by later recruiters.

Coincidental with the making of direct, personal contracts with workers in France by colonial employers or their agents, was a speculative trade
in impersonal contracts. From the mid-1650s, the merchants of La Rochelle
and other trading cities hired large numbers of workers with the intention
of selling the contracts in the Americas. The colonial buyer of the indenture
acquired the stated rights and obligations of the master. Before 1663 the
speculative trade brought 55 percent of the migrants to the St Lawrence
Valley—more than twice the number brought out by the *Cent Associés*.[38]

The trade in workers with Canada was a secondary branch of the large-
scale West Indian commerce. This is revealed by contracts that described
the labourer's destination as "the land of Canada in the said [Caribbean]
islands" and by eighteenth-century accords providing a salary payable in
sugar.[39] Over 900 people were indentured at La Rochelle for New France,
yet there were five times as many hired for the French West Indies.[40] This
matched the greater volume of maritime traffic between France and the
Caribbean islands, which were probably a more profitable market for work-

ers. By British North America's standard, it was still a small trade. Because of this dependency, the flow of indentured workers to Canada was influenced by the West Indian market for white labour.

From 1640 to 1670 the great demand in French America was for unskilled farm labourers; in Canada they were employed as land clearers (*défricheurs*). Among skilled occupations, the building trades attracted some interest.[41] By 1657 speculative contracts drawn up by French notaries no longer listed the worker's former trade; what counted were age and physique. Robust adult males were given a premium of ten to twenty *livres* above the base salary of sixty *livres* a year. Recruiters also began to restrict and then to omit the clause providing a prepaid return passage to France. This was an economy measure of employers, not an indication that *engagés* were willing to become colonists. The recruits still acted like migrant workers: fewer than a third of them became permanent residents of Canada.[42]

The program of subsidized emigration in 1662–71 continued the older, speculative indenturing system under the king's auspices. Royal officials used merchants as recruiters, who probably employed the customary forms of publicity: posters and criers in public places directing volunteers to a well-known inn or tavern to be enrolled. Recruits were given an advance of thirty to thirty-five *livres* to buy clothes and other necessities before their departure. They were quartered in quayside inns until a ship was ready for boarding. Any delay in sailing increased the chance of desertions.[43]

Under the royal program, the Crown paid merchant-recruiters for the indentured workers' transportation and for any cash advances. At Quebec the *Conseil souverain*, rather than the ship's master, arranged the sale of service contracts and the distribution of workers. Colonial employers of the king's *engagés* only had to pay the Quebec council for the advance given to the worker in France and, possibly, for his board in Canada if his indenture was not sold at once.[44]

Since the French Crown bore the cost of the passage across the Atlantic, these workers were cheaper than those supplied by independent merchants. This undermined the trade in speculative contracts with Canada. A comparison of lists of the king's *engagés* sent out in 1664–65 with the censuses of 1667–68 reveals that *Conseil souverain* members used their control over the distribution of workers to supply themselves and their friends with cheap labour. Councillors, seigneurs, merchants, Crown and company officials, as well as religious institutions, rather than simple colonists, profited from royal largesse.[45] Those who gained most from this program were the ones who had least need of a subsidy.

In the seventeenth century Boucher observed that "most of our settlers here [in Canada] are people who came as servants and, after serving a master for three years, set up for themselves."[46] The three-year term was just one of the favourable conditions offered to the poor and unemployed of France to get them to enroll as *engagés*. There were suggestions that the term of service be reduced further, but the *Conseil souverain* insisted that every *engagé* must serve a full three years to learn all the skills needed for survival in Canada. Other evidence and the rapid adaptation of later British immigrants show this to be a self-serving argument of the workers' employers.[47]

Three years became the standard term of indentured workers, who were later called *"trente-six-mois."* This period was short in comparison with seventeenth-century English colonial servants' bonds, which ran from four to seven years—four being customary for adult males. French *engagés* worked for a *shorter* term and *received a salary.* An unskilled man received at least sixty *livres* a year, in addition to food, shelter, and some clothing. Granted, that salary was often a credit against which the worker received liquor, personal articles, and services from the master.[48] English indentured servants generally received no salary beyond "meat, drink, apparel, and lodging." "Freedom dues" were a rare privilege consisting of tools, clothes, perhaps some land, and occasionally a small amount of money.[49] This reward at the end of service was to discourage runaways and to hold the labourer for the full contractual period; it was not a salary.

The benefits accorded a Canadian *"trente-six-mois"* did not end legal subjection. A governor defined an *engagé* as "a man obliged to go everywhere and to do whatever his master commanded like a slave."[50] Many were poorly fed and badly clothed. In 1737 a frozen body was identified as "a sailor or an *engagé*" because of its rough attire: brown vest and pants, grey outer vest, mittens, worn-out wool stockings, and sealskin moccasins.[51] In the brutal and exploited world of bond servants, however, the lot of the Canadian *engagé* was preferable to that of indentured workers in the British colonies; it was also superior to the fare of *engagés* in Louisiana and the French West Indies, where a white labourer's life was sickly and short.

Despite the advantages of service in Canada, recruiters never found volunteers in the numbers or of the quality desired. According to Quebec's *Conseil souverain*, those sent out by the crown in 1662–63 included "several persons unsuited for work or the clearing of land, whether because of their advanced age, infirmities, illnesses or because of ill-usage and misconduct while coming on the said vessels. Among their number are some discharged soldiers, all of whom are now public charges. . . . It would be appropriate to send them back to France." The healthy and well-inclined servants were mostly "young clerks, schoolchildren, or of that nature; the best part of whom have never worked."[52] Many had to be clothed at the council's expense. In 1667 Intendant Talon complained about the levy delivered by the *Compagnie des Indes Occidentales*: "instead of four hundred good men . . . I have received only one hundred and twenty-seven, very weak, of low age, and of little service."[53] In future, he asked that "passengers for Canada" be between sixteen and forty years of age and that no "idiot, cripple, chronically ill person or wayward sons under arrest" be sent, since "they are a burden to the land and degrade it."[54] Despite Colbert's repeated assurances that every care would be taken in selecting men, the quality of the king's *engagés* was never as good as in 1664, when nearly three hundred were delivered "ready to work upon landing."[55]

In 1682, a decade after the royal subsidy for transporting migrants to New France had lapsed, Intendant Jacques de Meulles asked for a restoration of the program since "we have an acute need for workers and day labourers."[56] The result was disappointing: the intendant wrote that the sixty *engagés* who arrived in 1684 were "little children" aged twelve to fourteen, "fit, at most, to tend cows." He permitted an extension in their period of service to four and five years to dispose of them.[57] Few mature and able-bodied men, it appears, would volunteer to work for an unknown master in New France.

From 1662 to 1671 almost 200 *engagés* were brought to Canada at the king's expense each year, except in 1666 when none arrived. The *Compagnie des Indes Occidentales* delivered 978 "*personnes*" in 1665–68; some were women. The Crown brought out an additional 180 men in 1668. Funds were provided for sending 500 people of both sexes in 1669 but their arrival was not acknowledged. An allocation for 100 was made in 1670 and 49 arrived.[58] Assuming that a third of the 2500 or more "*personnes*" delivered were females, the king's subsidy ought to have added 1700 males to the colony's population. A worker delivered, however, was not a settler established.

On average, the program had cost the Crown 25 000 *livres* a year; it did not produce a proportionate increase in the colonial population. By early 1666 the operation had transported 460 males to Canada, in addition to the workers hired by private individuals and religious orders. That year's census enumerated just 401 *engagés*. Colbert was surprised when the 1668 census of Canada listed only 1568 males capable of bearing arms.[59] In 1676 the king ordered the head count to be redone, "being unable to persuade myself that there are but 7832 persons . . . in the entire country, and having transported a larger number in the fifteen or sixteen years since I took charge."[60] This was an exaggeration, but the small number was remarkable since it included the native-born as well as settlers from other sources, such as the garrison troops. Marcel Trudel cautiously estimates that a third of *all* emigrants who came before 1660 re-embarked for France.[61] In the next decade that fraction increased as the proportion of single men whose contracts were to be sold to colonists grew. Over two-thirds of the king's *engagés* went home, just as the bachelors hired en masse by merchants had done.

Prevailing winds and the St Lawrence River's current made it easier and cheaper to sail eastward to France than to come to Canada. Former indentured workers, if not tied to the colony by marriage or a land grant, were wanderers. Their inclination was to go home, but since a governor's permit was required to leave the colony, they were not free to depart. In 1658 the governor noted with surprise that even workers whose services were in demand "all ask me for their permit [to leave]," once their contracts expired.[62] Quebec's *Conseil souverain* recorded in 1663 that "there are many working men who have served the time to which they are bound . . . [and] ask for the right to return to France."[63]

Intendant Talon opposed the liberal distribution of departure permits and warned Colbert that "while people return, this colony will scarcely grow stronger, whatever pains you take to increase it. . . . Several people returned this year, but a much larger number is still waiting to leave next year, thanks to the liberality in giving out permits."[64] Talon suggested that only prominent persons and those with an established home or family in the colony be allowed to leave "without difficulty," but that men who had just completed their indentured service be charged the equivalent of one transatlantic fare. An absolute denial would "dishearten those who might wish to come here . . . with the thought . . . that one never leaves when one is once here." In the meantime, Talon was endeavouring "to fix the single men and, by marriage, attach them to some community and so oblige them to work at the cultivation of the land."[65]

Tying bachelors to the colony by marriage was easier said than done. Eighty percent of the emigrants who arrived in 1632–62 were males.[66] Few European women were available as brides. In the 1660s there were more than twelve unmarried males, aged sixteen to thirty, for every eligible female in the same age group. This imbalance may have encouraged men to leave Canada. To provide wives for the surplus of bachelors, the French Crown assisted the emigration of 774 "filles du roi" in 1663–73. These women came from a charitable hospice in Paris and, to a lesser extent, from the countryside. A quarter were over age twenty-five, when most women were already married, and more than half had lost a parent.[67] For the filles du roi, overseas emigration led to marriage and, perhaps, a more honourable match than was possible at home. Unlike the engagés, these women were true immigrants: they came to Canada to wed an established colonist and to stay. The royal administration also nursed the hope that the missionaries' work would produce many Christian Amerindian brides for French settlers, but this was a false expectation.

The filles du roi and punitive measures against bachelors, such as Talon's 1670 interdict on trading and hunting by single men, did not eliminate by marriage the group that wanted to return to France. Devious methods were then used to hinder their departure. A dispatch in the king's name, sent to a governor in 1672, stated that "my intention is that you do not permit any Frenchman to return to my kingdom if he does not have a wife and children and a firm establishment in the said land of New France that will ensure his immediate return to the colony." The order was to be kept secret because, if widely known, it might discourage travel to Canada.[68] Migrant workers were to become settlers, whether they wished to or not. When the intendant was informed of this rule, he was advised to apply it discreetly, "it being important that the French should not feel themselves detained by force in the said country."[69]

Gentle firmness was again recommended to the governor of New France in 1675 when dealing with the persistent problem of people who wanted to leave the colony. "It would appear to me," wrote the king, "that a rather large number of residents, men and women, return to France. It is something you must prevent, as much as possible, by gentleness and by persuasion." Yet only those "who could never be suspected of deserting" would be permitted to leave Canada."[70] Unauthorized departures were indeed treated like military desertions. When one fugitive was sentenced to hang, the minister of maritime affairs reprimanded the governor for his excessive zeal.[71] If the rate of returns from New France was high, it would have been higher still had there been no restrictions on abandoning the colony.

The problem of retaining these unhappy exiles resulted from a short-sighted economy. Royal levies of migrants were recruited primarily from single males. In 1669 an official described the transportation of families as "a bad practice" since "one hundred persons, composing twenty-five families, will cost as much to the king as one hundred bachelors" who, presumably, would all be productive workers.[72] Bachelors' indentures would be easier to sell than contracts for families. The administration hoped that marriage *after* emancipation would convert migrant workers into settlers. In the seventeenth century, when voluntary civilian migration to the colony was greatest, most French *engagés* resisted settlement, whereas those coming with families almost always stayed in Canada.[73]

Emigration does not work out well for everyone; invariably, some retrace their steps in disappointment. In the seventeenth century many New Englanders lost heart and returned to old England, but they were a small fraction of the total migration.[74] This was equally true during the Great Migration from Britain in 1815–60. The numerous letters of their kin in Britain enquired about the prospects of life in North America. In the few hundred surviving letters to pre-1760 emigrants in French America, the theme is very different. Here we have evidence of a major cultural contrast; those left behind in France looked upon resettlement abroad as unnatural, even as selfish and immoral. Family obligations helped to call the emigrants home.

A worker hired in 1653 by the Montreal associates acquired land with the evident intention of becoming a colonist. In 1669 his distressed father wrote to remind the expatriate that filial duty and his material interests demanded his return to France. "I find it very strange," wrote the father, "to have a child whom I have cherished more than myself and who has no desire at all for me. I believed that I would have the happiness of seeing him within four or five years of his departure." Work in Canada was to be a temporary expedient, not a prelude to settlement there. In just three months, the son was told, he could be "in your good town of La Flèche, from which you come" and in possession of 800 *livres* from his late mother's estate, as well as "many other things that you only have to ask for." By the *droit de légitime*, every lawful child was assured of a share of the parental estate.[75] This may have enticed others home. As a final, persuasive flourish, the father conveyed the best wishes of the exile's kin "and all your good friends in this fine land of Anjou, where we drink good wine for a sou." The son returned to France for a decade, but then reappeared in Canada, where he married and died.[76]

Memories of friends and home were also skillfully evoked in 1756 for a Bayonne merchant living on Île Royale (Cape Breton). "Come back to your homeland [*Patrie*]," he was told, "here fine grapes are eaten.... Come and let us see if you have not lost your taste for them as well as for peaches, pears, and so on." The writer in France listed the daily amusements at Bayonne: skittles, *pelota*, and a card game for money. "This game, which will last all winter, will not ruin you," and "you might even win 800 *livres* for your bastard children while amusing yourself." The recipient in North America was addressed as "libertine" or "old sinner" and was advised that the "young lasses [*des jeunes tendrons*]" of Gascony would take his mind off his profits.[77]

One *fille du roi* sent to Canada to help secure the male population did the reverse. She married a Montreal joiner who, in 1680, unwisely let her depart with three of their children to visit her home in Paris. Once there she begged him in letters to join her with the other children. "It is something absolutely necessary; that is why I beg you in God's name, my dearest husband, not to delay in coming as soon as you can." He was to sell their house and possessions in the colony and to smuggle large fur muffs with their clothing, because "beaver and marten fur are extremely valuable in Paris." The joiner was assured of employment in France.[78] Church registers testify that the entire family, save one grown-up son, moved to France and stayed there.[79]

In a society built on networks of kinship and patronage, successful and well-connected individuals were expected to assist less fortunate relations. The widowed sister-in-law of the king's engineer in Canada offered in 1755 to attend to his affairs in France if he would obtain a clerical position in a government ministry for his fatherless nephew, who was unemployed.[80] Female relatives expected succour. There are innumerable letters from women that pray for the emigrant's good health and express hopes for his early return or, failing that, a remittance to aid family members in France.[81] The aid expected by relatives was best provided when the giver was in his place of birth; transatlantic communications were uncertain.

It was made emphatically clear to one absentee that the welfare of his widowed mother and unmarried sister demanded his return from New France; sending money was not enough. When this ship's captain married at Louisbourg, suggesting a desire to stay in North America, it was reported by a parish priest in France that the captain's mother

> was excessively afflicted to the point of dissolving into tears and of shrieking [*à jetter des hauts cris*] when she was given the news of your marriage at Louisbourg, but her pain ebbed slightly after receiving your two letters that inform her of your reasons binding you to establish yourself in this land [Gascony-Navarre] and, finally, she was almost entirely consoled upon learning that you had married a young lady of merit.

In short, the girl had property and respectable parents. Now that the captain and his bride had told the mother of their wish to come home "and live with her, she gives you both her blessing." The priest assured the newlyweds that "she ... only sighs ... to see you and embrace you. Therefore, come ... as soon as you can; come to console her and give her the satisfaction of spending her last days with you. Natural impulses, sentiments of honor and religion, gratitude for all the kind acts and for all the pains she took for your education—all cry out for that; all of them call you to her side." By corollary, his settlement in North America would be dishonourable, impious, ungrateful, and immoral. The *curé* suggested that the captain send some money to his mother and sister immediately "to ease thereby their discomfort."[82] An uncle made a similar suggestion.[83] The sickly sister informed the emigrant that her initial distress upon hearing of his marriage had been eclipsed by a belief that "my poor mother will have a peaceful and secure old age and I [will have] all the help and advantages that I ought to expect from a brother I love tenderly."[84] Such a consensus made establishment abroad impossible. If this were typical of the social pressure exerted on emigrants, one can readily understand their urge to return home.

The unwillingness of the French to come to New France and stay persisted after the danger of Iroquois attacks receded and the imbalance of the sexes was corrected. The 1701 peace treaty with the Five Nations Iroquois ended the threat of murderous incursions that had alarmed colonists.[85] By 1698, males no longer outnumbered females in the European population of Canada. This demographic change affected the market for indentured workers and reduced the flow of migrants from France. When it was easier to find a wife, concession farms became family-run operations. They produced enough to feed and maintain the family, with a small surplus to be bartered for manufactured goods. Canadian farms were not commercial enterprises; family self-sufficiency was all that was desired. Married tenant farmers did not want the costly services of an *engagé*. The potential employers of indentured workers were seigneurs with large *demesnes*, the administrative and mercantile elite, and religious houses. They still wanted cheap manual labourers and lamented the disappearance of the king's *engagés*.[86]

The market for indentured workers in Canada became more selective as well as smaller. Population growth and economic diversification produced skilled craftsmen who formerly had to be imported. The character of colonial workers was known, and they could be dismissed without financial loss if no longer wanted. For cheap domestic servants, *Canadiens* turned to the children of the poor, who would be bound until adulthood for their maintenance alone.[87] The cost of an indentured worker could be reduced by leasing the *engagé* out to other employers or by selling the contract before the term had expired, but hiring a stranger in Europe was a risky and expensive business. The cost and risk became less tolerable as the colony's labour supply developed.

After 1671 the flow of voluntary emigrants to Canada declined. Royal subsidies for transporting workers ended in 1672 when Louis XIV's war against the Low Countries diverted funds from colonial development. With the crown gone as a competitor, La Rochelle's merchant-shipowners resumed speculation in contract labour for the colonies but abandoned this commerce after 1673. In the French West Indies the shift to black slave labour explains the declining interest in European manual workers. Once again, the Caribbean trade may have determined the fate of commerce with Canada, but there were good local reasons for the decline in speculative contracts in the late seventeenth century (see figure 1).

Direct personal contracts with workers in France continued on a reduced scale. Colonial employers were always more selective than merchant-speculators; increasingly, they wanted skilled and experienced craftsmen. But such artisans were even more reluctant than unskilled youths to go overseas. In 1687 Canada's senior administrators were told that royal officials at La Rochelle had taken "all the pains in the world to find the [skilled] workers . . . asked for; there being scarcely one of them who would wish to leave his establishment to go to a country like Canada without some certainty of earning his living more richly than in France." The colonial officials were advised to keep the few being sent fully occupied and to pay them everything that had been promised, since it was agreed that the craftsmen "could return to France at any time they might please."[88]

Thirty years later, in an era of peace, the situation was no better. In 1720 Jean-Antoine, comte d'Agrain was commissioned to hire forty-eight masons, carpenters, and stonecutters to work on the fortifications of Île Royale and the Windward Islands. He traveled over 300 kilometres from Rochefort to the Auvergne, where, even with help, he obtained only twenty-five artisans, two of whom were limeburners accepted for want of the desired craftsmen. The workers insisted on a yearly salary, rather than payment by piecework, and a free return passage to France. All were given a cash advance and a travel allowance to get to the port of embarkation. One ingrate then tried to desert.[89] This affair led the maritime council to observe that it was very hard to find craftsmen for the colonies; it directed the intendant at Rochefort to keep all workers subsequently hired on Oléron Island "so they cannot escape."[90]

The Quebec Seminary's unhappy experiences with contract workers from France brought about a change in hiring policy. The seminary still wanted skilled specialists from France but had difficulty finding reliable and competent workers. When a brickmaker was wanted, the seminary's Paris agent (a priest) asked a brickyard owner, who came for confession, to find the craftsman. Months passed with no result. "I did not want one from the provinces, such as Normandy or elsewhere," wrote the agent, "but no one wanted to go to Canada. . . . It is no small difficulty to find a faithful and industrious man who is not immoral and who has a fear of God." A visiting builder-architect from Quebec considered himself "too great a lord to involve himself in this search" and refused to help.[91]

Qualified craftsmen, apart from textile workers and shoemakers, commanded yearly salaries of 75–120 *livres*. In addition, a man's food and lodgings cost the employer another 90–180 *livres* a year. There was also an initial expenditure of 70 or more *livres* to recruit and transport a worker from France. An employer counted on three years of labour to justify these expenses. Unfortunately for the seminary, some recruits turned out to be idlers, bunglers, drunkards, and runaways. Of thirty-two workers hired in France in 1671–76, seven had to be sent back before completing their term of service.[92] A gardener enrolled in 1673 for 75 *livres* a year was given clothing, a knife, and a comb on credit. After seven and a half months at Quebec he ran away. When he returned, he was sent to a new master on a distant estate. After a second flight, the seminary's account book recorded that the gardener was "sent back to France after five months in prison where he was fed [by the seminary] out of charity."[93]

Such experiences led the seminary's proctor to recommend in 1682 that, henceforth, colonial workers be hired "even if they are more costly . . . since one is often deceived in those who are sent from France" and because the value of the French *engagés'* work in the first year barely exceeded the cost of obtaining them.[94] From 1675 onward, the seminary relied increasingly on local men hired by the year or by the month. Some French recruits were kept at Paris for a probationary period to assess their nature because, as the bishop of Quebec observed in 1685, "it is very difficult to judge the character of all these people."[95]

Given the more selective market in Canada for French contract workers and their continuing reluctance to be enrolled, indentures for resale in the colony might have disappeared entirely. The absence of speculative contracts from 1696 to 1713 (figure 1) did not result solely from the buyers' wariness; the War of the Spanish Succession (1701–13) choked off the flow of workers, for the French navy was unable to protect merchant vessels in the colonial trade. The consequent shortage of labourers and servants inconvenienced Canada's gentry. In letters and memorials sent to the government in France, the colony's notables asked for a revival of the royal subsidy for *engagés*.[96] But because of the Crown's indebtedness at the end of Louis XIV's reign, the encouragement for sending workers to Canada would have to be legislative rather than financial.

Precedents existed for compelling shipowners or outfitters to carry workers on vessels sent to New France. The *Compagnie des Cent Associés* had a quota of one man for so many tons of cargo, and in 1664 the Quebec *Conseil souverain* wanted to insert a similar stipulation in its proposed landing permits.[97] The large number of workers then arriving in the colony made this provision unnecessary. In the West Indian trade, ships were obliged to carry a quota of specified commodities, livestock, or men, and one item could be substituted for another. By the 1680s blacks outnumbered Europeans on the French Caribbean islands, and the government became more insistent on the transportation of white workers because it feared a slave insurrection against the European minority. Indentured servants had to be carried on all ships sailing to "the American islands" and royal ordinances in 1699 and 1707 set minimum standards for the age and height of these men, who were to be inspected by admiralty officers. A wartime ordinance of 1706 allowed ship outfitters the option of paying a sixty *livres* fine for each worker not embarked, since recruits were difficult to find.[98] These provisions were incorporated into laws for vessels trading with Canada.

A royal ordinance of 20 March 1714, extended the requirement for carrying indentured servants to vessels sailing for France's North American colonies. The preamble spoke of the need of "the inhabitants of New France ... [for] *Engagés* to aid them ... whether for the cultivation of the land as well as for other tasks." Henceforth, passports would be issued to ships bound for Canada only on condition "that three indentured workers are carried there on those vessels of sixty tons or less; four for those ships of sixty to one hundred tons; and six for those over one hundred tons." The workers were to be "at least eighteen years old, and they cannot be older than forty, and they will be, at least, four *pieds* [four feet, four inches] tall." Port officials were to examine the men to see that they met these standards and were "of good complexion."[99] Shipowners were given the option of carrying two recruits for the colonial troops in place of each required *engagé*, and the ministry expected some captains to take this option, although there would be no indenture to be sold to pay for transportation costs.[100] More attractive was the provision of the 1714 ordinance allowing one craftsman to take the place of two unskilled labourers "in consideration of their [the artisans'] usefulness to the colony."

The La Rochelle indentures and official correspondence indicate that the 1714 ordinance was enforced and obeyed in that year and the following six. The merchant-shipowners' compliance was deceptively gratifying. When peace returned in 1713, the colonial market for workers was good because of the wartime interruption of trade. After a few years, however, merchants were trying to evade this new obligation. The profit in carrying *engagés* to New France was small in comparison with the gains to be made from delivering slaves to the West Indies. The overseas traders had frustrated an unpopular law in the past. To overcome the reluctance of workers in France to go to remote lands such as the Americas, Colbert in 1670 had unilaterally reduced the duration of unskilled *engagés'* contracts to eighteen months. Recruiters and employers ignored this law and had notaries draw up indentures for three years, as before. The administration backed down and reinstated the customary minimum term in 1672.[101]

After 1714, captains sailing to Canada declared that all the indentured workers on board were artisans, thereby cutting their quota in half. Merchants, familiar with their impecunious and extortionate government, regarded the sixty *livres* fine as a new tax. Since the mandatory *engagés* had been introduced into the West Indian trade as an alternative to certain goods, the merchants claimed that their obligation to transport workers had ended in February 1716, when the requirement to carry the enumerated commodities was lifted. A ruling of 16 November 1716 removed this misconception and identified the craftsmen who would be accepted in place of any two unskilled men: "mason, stonecutter, blacksmith, locksmith, joiner, cooper, carpenter, caulker, and other trades that can be useful in the colonies."[102] Textile workers were not listed, possibly because their products would reduce the colonial market for French cloth.

Between royal administration and merchant there was a recurrent cycle of a new legal imposition, evasion or noncompliance, followed by reassertion of the more precisely defined law. Merchants from Nantes, La Rochelle, and Bordeaux complained that it was difficult to find potential *engagés* and pleaded that they sometimes failed to meet the quota because hired men jumped ship before sailing. The government took them at their word. To ship outfitters [*armateurs*], a royal ordinance of January 1721 offered imprisoned "defrauders of the king's [fiscal] rights, vagabonds and others" to replace voluntary bond servants. The petty criminals would go to colonial employers for the cost of the passage. The malefactors' exile was not to end after three to five years of servitude; it was to be permanent. As for alleged escapes, a ship's crew was believed to be capable of preventing them, and, now, for every prisoner who fled, the shipowner would have to take on *two* more convicts as well as paying a sixty *livres* fine.[103] A supplementary ordinance granted exemptions—say, for fishing vessels—and allowed ships unable to meet the quota, when no prisoners were available, to sail after payment of the fines.[104]

There were always some petty criminals among the voluntary contract workers. Seventeenth-century writers noted the presence of fugitive rogues and villains among the *engagés*.[105] Villainy past and present brought an indentured journeyman-carpenter to the attention of Louisbourg's *Conseil supérieur* in September 1725. This eighteen-year-old was charged with steal-ing a piece of cloth from a merchant's garden. He admitted to the theft and said "his intention was to sell it [the cloth] to obtain some bread; that he had not eaten a full meal for four days." When asked "by what occasion had he come to this port?" the *engagé* replied that while

> working at his trade of joiner and turner in his father's house—his father being a [shipyard] foreman for the king at Brest—he unfor-tunately took from an adjoining storehouse . . . two cotton handker-chiefs that belonged to a merchant. The maidservant saw him and stopped him and, after having taken back the handkerchiefs, she and the merchant complained to the father of the accused. The father was outraged by this act. Since he [the son] was a wastrel [*libertain*], his father had him put on board the king's ship *Le Jason* to send him to this island. He arrived here in July of this year and was delivered by the ship's captain . . . to Mr de Bourville, the Town Major, to be employed at his trade for three years, and to be kept longer if he did not become well-behaved.

When asked "why would he wish to buy food, since he was fed at the major's house?, he replied that he was only given Canadian biscuits and some soup to eat."[106]

Like this joiner, most exiled prisoners were delivered to the colonies on the king's ships. French merchants were no more willing to transport petty criminals than the required *engagés*. In July 1721 the maritime council offered *to pay* shipowners sixty *livres* a head as well as a daily allowance for every prisoner carried in excess of the legal quota. La Rochelle's merchants promptly rejected this generous proposition.[107] After 1721, when the quota could be filled with involuntary exiles, French merchants still did not com-ply with the laws. In 1722 Louisbourg's administrators reported that "of all the ships that came last year . . . there was just one from Nantes that brought engagés." Other ships' captains pleaded ignorance of the 1721 ordi-nance.[108] There was no excuse in 1723, when only eight of thirty-five trad-ing vessels brought indentured servants to Île Royale.[109]

The king's ordinance of 15 February 1724, chronicled the deceptions used in France to evade the laws. "Most of the outfitters," it said, presented for the mandatory review "individuals that they would pass off as engagés . . . and whom they dismiss after having presented them for inspec-tion. To discharge themselves [from responsibility], they content themselves with bringing back certificates of desertion." As a result, "not a third of the indentured workers who were embarked in any one port of France went to the colonies last year." Moreover, "some of these outfitters presented people they said were craftsmen, even though they had no trade." Thereafter, documentary proof of desertions would not be accepted; there would be an automatic fine for each worker for whom there was no "certificate of deliv-ery" to a colony. The fine for a missing craftsman was 120 *livres*, and those presented as artisans required a certificate of competence from a master craftsman chosen by the administration.[110] A November 1728 ruling restated the 1716 regulations, but the official restatements, amplifications, and clarifications merely testify to the merchants' dogged resistance to carrying contract workers to the Americas.

Faced with this resistance, port officials lost heart and enforcement of the laws became haphazard. Exemptions were granted and fines accepted to allow ships to sail without *engagés*.[111] In 1742 Louisbourg's civil administrator reported that only vessels from Havre de Grace brought the required complement of workers; "those of Bordeaux and Nantes sometimes carry some, and those coming from other ports do not carry any at all."[112] The rarity of adult male servants at Quebec in 1744, in contrast to the numerous female and juvenile domestics, indicates that few *engagés* were arriving in that port too.[113] The number of imported workers would never have been great. For 1713–43, yearly arrivals from France at Quebec averaged nine or ten vessels. Although this traffic doubled and tripled in the next two decades,[114] full compliance with the regulations would have delivered fewer than one hundred craftsmen to Quebec annually. Had there been a great demand for passages and had shipowners seen a good profit in the passenger traffic, the number of vessels would have increased further. It did not.

War in 1744–48 led to a suspension of these laws and, when peace returned, merchants acted as if the regulations were still suspended. The intendant of New France had to ask for their formal reinstatement. Direct personal indentures were now rare, and speculative indentures for resale in New France were barely kept alive by the laws. Merchants were now able to obtain men for yearly salaries of fifty *livres* or less, indicating a willingness among the poor to come to the St Lawrence Valley. It was now the shipowners' reluctance to carry *engagés* that prevented a substantial migration. Île Royale's administrators were more interested in the enforcement of these laws than were the officials at Quebec, and in 1751 the island's governor wrote that "most of the outfitters coming here from France greatly neglect the obligation they are under to bring us indentured workers or *trente-six-mois*. Nevertheless, we have great need of them in this colony."[115]

Surviving embarkation lists give the impression that there was a steady flow of passengers, including *engagés*, to French North America. The 1749–58 register for Bayonne, a major port for the Île Royale and Newfoundland fishery, names seventy-four indentured workers who—if we believe it—went to Île Royale and Quebec.[116] The precision of the list, which gives age and occupation, makes it plausible evidence. Those familiar with French administration in the old regime, however, will be wary of any official's record of his fulfillment of royal directives.[117]

Chance revealed the falsity of this document. In March 1757 it recorded that, in compliance with the laws, a blacksmith and a joiner were taken on board the schooner *La Louise* as *engagés* for the colonies. The two artisans did not reach New France. The truth is revealed by one private letter among many from French vessels captured by the British and now in the Public Record Office at London. A Bayonne merchant wrote to his partner on Île Royale about *La Louise*'s cargo, which was to be sold for their joint profit. "Observe," wrote the merchant, "that there are two *Engagés* with trades on the crew list who will not be making the voyage at all. Do not fail to have them discharged on the roll as being disembarked, to avoid paying a fine of

80 *écus*." Another captain in their employ had returned to France without delivery receipts for his mythical workers; "I was obliged to pay that [fine] on your behalf" complained the writer.[118] This frank discussion about evading the laws indicates that there were admiralty officers who cooperated in the deception, undoubtedly for a consideration. Thus embarkation lists should be treated with caution. British reports on the personnel found aboard French ships captured in the 1740s and 1750s reveal that even notarial indentures and ships' rolls were falsified to appear to conform with the laws.[119]

What can be deduced from the reliable evidence on voluntary migration from France to Canada? Of those lay persons who could afford a transatlantic fare, fewer than 300 settled in the St Lawrence Valley. Independent emigrants who paid their own way were always rare. The colonization of New France depended on sponsored emigrants such as indentured servants. From the 1640s to the 1670s, commercial companies, seigneurs, religious groups, merchant-outfitters, and the Crown brought out about 4000 persons, male and female. Seventeenth-century recruiters met popular resistance to overseas emigration. They had to offer wages, a short period of service, and even prepaid return passages to obtain volunteers. Free emigrants, apart from women, were still reluctant to make a permanent home in Canada. Rough living conditions, the Iroquois threat, the shortage of marriageable European women, and strong ties to family and place of birth led most to abandon the colony. Over two-thirds of the single men brought out by merchant-speculators and the Crown returned home, and more would have gone if colonial officials had not hindered departures.

After the 1670s the shipowners' and outfitters' dislike for the trade in *engagés* meant that few workers' contracts were made for resale. Speculative indentures for the Americas were kept alive from 1699 onward by the force of law. The indentures' terms show that there was less popular resistance to overseas emigration in the 1700s. The merchants' attitude was now the major obstruction, but no document explains their disdain for the traffic in *engagés*. The merchants simply evaded the legal obligation to carry contract workers to the American colonies. Servants' indentures delivered thousands of potential settlers to British North America; they were unable to perform the same service for French North America in the eighteenth century.[120] After the 1670s most arrivals in New France were involuntary or unwitting immigrants.

Among the involuntary immigrants, the exiled petty criminals known as *faux-sauniers* have already been mentioned: about 720 poachers, smugglers, sellers of untaxed salt, and other minor offenders were exiled to Canada from 1721 to 1749. Only healthy men with useful skills were to be dispatched,[121] and most were countryfolk suited to farm work. In the 1720s some were "*fils de famille*," wayward sons sent abroad to save their families further embarrassment. Like the seventeenth-century *engagés*, the transported criminals tried to leave the colony: some fled to the English colonies while others stowed away on ships returning to France.[122] Gérard Malchelosse's careful study of the prisoners in the St Lawrence Valley concludes that, "like the prisoners and *fils de famille* of 1723–29, a very small number of the *faux sauniers* who came to Canada from 1730 to 1743 became established colonists." Of 648 faux-sauniers out in 1730–49, only 106 were noted in the colony's parish registers.[123]

Speaking of involuntary immigrants, let us not forget the 320 black slaves brought to the St Lawrence settlement from the French West Indies and the British colonies. There were twice as many Amerindian slaves in the colony. Most slaves arrived in the eighteenth century, long after the decline of colonial service indentures made in France, so there is no clear link between the appearance of slaves and the waning of white servitude.[124]

As numerous as these one thousand slaves, and equally unwilling immigrants, were the British captives seized by French and Indian raiding parties or taken off captured ships. Half were repatriated, and several hundred chose to remain in New France. The 126 who were granted French letters of naturalization in 1710–14 came primarily from New England and New York; some were Irish, and a few had German or Dutch surnames.[125] Hundreds more were brought to Canada during the War of the Austrian Succession (1744–48).[126] Over five hundred former captives elected to stay in New France, while one hundred other British subjects willingly removed to the French colony.[127]

The largest group of North American immigrants to Canada is the least documented one; they were indisputably reluctant exiles. When administrators in the British colony of Nova Scotia began to expel the French-speaking, Roman Catholic Acadians in 1755, many fled overland to the St Lawrence Valley settlements. After British forces captured Île Royale and Île Saint-Jean (Prince Edward Island) in 1758, mass deportations followed. Nearly two thousand Acadians sought refuge in Canada in the late 1750s.[128] At the 1760 capitulation of Montreal, Gen. Jeffrey Amherst refused the French governor's request that the refugees be safeguarded from a further expulsion.[129] Justifiably fearful of the British conquerors, the *Acadiens* submerged themselves in the Canadian population.

Last, there were soldiers sent to New France who chose to remain there; they were unwitting immigrants. Military garrisons in the French colonies were long regarded as a source of settlers. Beginning with the Carignan-Salières Regiment in 1665, soldiers who volunteered to become colonists were discharged and given settlement grants. From 1683 onward, the *Compagnies franches de la marine* were the garrison troops for the North American colonies and, in turn, provided settlers. Quartering soldiers in private homes and hiring them out to civilian employers helped to introduce the newcomers into colonial society. After 1698 a soldier marrying a woman of the colony was entitled to a discharge, his clothing, a year's pay, and land.[130] Over a thousand soldier-settlers made a home in New France during the seventeenth century, and more followed their example in the next century.

The marine soldiers enlisted for service in French ports, on ships, or in the overseas territories; they did not choose to come to Canada. According to one official, recruiting men for colonial garrisons was hindered by a popular belief in France that the soldiers never came home again.[131] Many were unemployed textile and clothing workers. To fill the ranks, standards were lowered, deceptive enlistments were used, and prisoners were conscripted.[132] The soldiers may have been social outcasts, but they, too, responded to the call of the homeland. In 1698 an intendant wrote of "the ardor that the greater part have to return to France in the hope of greater freedom."[133] A later memorialist regretted that too many soldiers were allowed to go home "under various specious pretexts."[134]

Despite opposition from the governors and military officers to a scheme that drew seasoned soldiers from the garrison troops and produced few good farmers,[135] soldiers were the principal source of immigrants for Canada in the eighteenth century. The exact number is open to conjecture. Yves Landry estimates that the battalions of French regulars sent out in the 1750s supplied 500 to 700 soldier-colonists.[136] The importance of military immigrants is evident in Mario Boleda's estimate of the gross recorded migration (*l'immigration observée*) from France to the St Lawrence Valley: soldiers—13 076; *engagés*—3900; women—1797; prisoners—716; male clergy—721. The net migration (*l'immigration fondatrice*) of those who settled permanently was said to be precisely 8527, although the varying retention rates for each category are not suggested.[137]

All estimates are open to dispute; for example, the figure for indentured servants is probably too high.[138] The exclusive focus on migrants from France and the implicit assumption that they were culturally French is also misleading. The soldiers and workers contained a seasoning of Flemings, Germans, Swiss, Italians, and Iberians. A more comprehensive estimate of the migrants who made a permanent home in Canada before 1760 would be: soldiers—3300; Acadians—1800; women from France—1500; indentured workers—1200; slaves—900; British subjects—600; male clergy—500; self-financed migrants—250; transported prisoners—200. Soldiers supplied a third of the estimated 10 250 colonists; their prominence was recognized by a writer in 1709 who grandly asserted that "soldiers populated this country," along with the women sent out by the Crown. This fact, he wrote, explained the "excessive pride and idleness" of the *Canadiens*.[139] The emphasis on the *filles du roi* was warranted. What this writer and subsequent historians failed to mention is that most of those who came to Canada did so unwillingly and with no intention of making a home there.

A study of migrants from France to Canada before 1760 reveals that large-scale emigration is not a simple mechanical process. The "push" of hardship at home, whether physical or mental, does not suffice to produce an overseas movement of humanity. The "pull" of opportunities in the New World must be publicized in print, through private letters or by emigrant recruiters. There was no effective campaign in France to counteract the colonies' low reputation in popular lore. Attractive publicity was one mediating factor needed to make a connection between the "push" and "pull." Other mediating factors were the volume of shipping, active recruitment, and the willingness of shipowners to transport large numbers of people paying low fares or traveling as redemptioners and indentured workers.

After the 1670s, French merchant-shipowners were indifferent to the passenger trade with Canada, and in the eighteenth century they evaded their legal obligation to carry a small quota of *engagés*. French skippers and *armateurs* were no longer willing to provide the transportation link required for an overseas exodus from France. As carriers of humans, they sought greater profits in the slave trade.

There was internal migration in France, some of it from the countryside to cities.[140] The origins of indentured workers and of beggars show that there was a large wandering population.[141] French artisans sought work in adjacent European states. Paul Le Jeune observed that "every year a great number of people leave France, and cast themselves, some here, some there, among foreigners, because they have no employment in their own country. I have been told ... that a large part of the artisans in Spain are Frenchmen."[142] France's army, which expanded from 20 000 in 1661 to 300 000 in 1710, [143] absorbed large numbers of unemployed craftsmen. Overseas emigration was not a popular answer to hardship. Despite the larger number of *engagés* going to Saint-Domingue, that French colony had only 20 000 white settlers in 1740. France's most valuable possession in the Americas seems to have been affected by the same reluctance to emigrate and the same resistance to resettlement. More needs to be known about the alternatives in old regime France to permanent relocation overseas. To say that because migration to Canada was so small, living conditions in France cannot have been bad, flies in the face of evidence of severe famines, unemployment, oppressive taxation, and social conflict during this period. Group migrations abroad are the result of a host of variable factors, such as religion, politics, historical experience, community traditions, recruiting, available information, financial assistance, and transportation facilities. To emphasize one impersonal factor, such as the land tenure system,[144] and to ignore cultural forces is to willfully misunderstand human behaviour because it is culture that shapes our choices.

There was nothing uniquely French in the reluctance to emigrate because the diverse subjects of His Most Christian Majesty were not yet a cultural nation. It would be anachronistic to refer to Bretons, Basques, Flemings, Alsatians, Provençaux, and speakers of French dialects as "the French people." The resistance to overseas emigration was probably normal for most peoples; willingness to relocate across the ocean was unusual, something that might develop over time with encouragement.

This account has emphasized the need for communities that are resigned to the continual and permanent departure of some members, who willingly accept settlement abroad as a prerequisite for a substantial, voluntary emigration. The emigrants to Canada left few literary sources, yet their behaviour makes it plain that most were reluctant expatriates from their provincial homeland or *patrie*. Single males left France unwillingly and with no intention of staying abroad. The high rate of returns from Canada proves this. Unlike the indentured workers going to the British colonies, the *engagés* were migrant workers rather than intending colonists. Soldiers stationed in the French colonies had the same outlook: they too were reluctant exiles. Nothing need be said about the intentions of the exiled prisoners and slaves; they had no choice in the matter. Only the families that came before 1663, the female migrants, and a handful of self-financed arrivals could be described as true immigrants—that is, people who intended to settle abroad and establish a new home. The rest of the migrants, the majority, saw absence from their birthplace as a banishment and yearned to return to their families and to France.

NOTES

1. Jacques Levasseur de Neré to the minister of maritime affairs, 12 Nov. 1707, MG 1, C11A series transcript, XXVII, 41, Public Archives of Canada (hereafter PAC).

2. Memorial of Intendant Jacques de Meulles to the minister, c. 1864, F3 Moreau de St-Méry, II-1, f. 198, Archives des Colonies, Archives nationales de France, Paris (hereafter AC). See also Jean Talon to Jean-Baptiste Colbert, 31 Oct. 1671, Archives nationales du Québec (hereafter ANQ), *Rapport de l'Archiviste de la Province de Québec* (Quebec, 1921–), 1930–31, 150 (hereafter *Rapport de l'Archiviste*), in which he begs to be allowed to return to France after "mes travaux dans un païs aussy rude qu'estoit celuy cy dans ses commencemens." Similar sentiments were expressed by eighteenth-century writers in the French West Indies: Intercepted letters, HCA 30, Public Record Office.

3. Mario Boleda, "Les Migrations au Canada sous le régime français" (PhD thesis, l'Université de Montréal, 1983), xxiv, 339. This estimate of the gross migration and the consequent deduction that about 70 percent of the migrants left the colony go beyond previous estimates. Hubert Charbonneau and Yves Landry speculate that 56 percent of all French emigrants to Canada in the seventeenth century became permanent residents: "La Politique démographique en Nouvelle-France," *Annales de Démographie historique* (1979): 29–57. Stanislas A. Lortie estimated 53.6 percent. See Hubert Charbonneau, *Vie et mort de nos ancêtres: Étude démographique* (Montreal, 1975), 39.

4. Boleda, "Les Migrations au Canada," 41–55, discusses these estimates with critical comments. The estimates, identified by author and date, were Edmé Rameau (1859) 9700–10 000; Benjamin Sulte (1907) 8000; Emile Chartier (1920) 12 012; Paul-Emile Renaud (1928) 10 126; Archange Godbout (1946) 7498; and the Programme de Recherche en démographie historique (c. 1982) 8527.

5. Morris Bishop, *Champlain: The Life of Fortitude* (New York, 1948), 362.

6. Boucher, *Histoire Véritable et Naturelle de Moeurs et Productions du Pays de la Nouvelle France . . .* (Paris, 1664), 149–55.

7. Marriage of Jacques Chaigneau and Louise Forrestier, 7 Jan. 1657, Mariages et inhumations de la paroisse Saint-Nicholas de La Rochelle, 1654–67, Registre 668, série E supplément, Archives de la Charente-Maritime. Witnesses in the French port testified beforehand that Chaigneau's first wife "had been killed by the Iroquois one league from Quebec."

8. Paul Le Jeune, "Some Advice to Those Who Desire to Cross Over into New France [1636]" in *The Jesuit Relations and Allied Documents: Travels and Explorations of the Jesuit Missionaries in New France, 1610–1791*, ed. Reuben Gold Thwaites, 73 vols. (Cleveland: 1896–1901), 9: 187. Le Jeune consistently promoted emigration to Canada. See his letter to Cardinal de Richelieu, Quebec, 1 Aug. 1635, ibid., 7: 238–45; the 1635 *Relation*, ch. 3, "How it is a benefit to both Old and New France, to send colonies here," 8: 8–15; and the *Relation* for 1659–60, ch. 1, 45: 189–95.

9. In 1752 a man who joined the colonial troops recalled "I sought information about the best country to live in; about Louisiana and Canada. . . . The sailors told me that Canada was more healthy, although its climate was colder." Sylvester K. Stevens et al., eds., *Travels in New France by J.C.B.* (Harrisburg, PA, 1941), 1–2. Inconsistencies in the story lead one to suspect that "J.C.B." was a transported convict and not a willing passenger. In a 1698 petition a servant at Quebec stated that at Paris, his birthplace, he met a minor port official from Quebec through a friend, "Et auroit pris Resolution Sur Le Recit que luy fit . . . De Ce Païs [Canada], dy passer." Petition of Etienne Courtin to Quebec's

Lieutenant général civil et criminel, 1698, 62e liasse, no. 3289, Collection de pièces judiciares et notariales, ANQ.

10. "Motives for Scotch emigration to America (1774)" in *English Historical Documents: American Colonial Documents to 1776*, ed. Merrill Jensen (New York, 1955), 9: 469–76.

11. The only way of measuring literacy in New France is by signatures on documents and by the legally required declaration that a party could not sign. Using this evidence, Marcel Trudel finds that 56.8 percent of the immigrants who came in 1632–63 could sign, males being more literate than females (62.2 percent as opposed to 34.4 percent): *Histoire de la Nouvelle France*, vol. 3, *La Seigneurie des Cent-Associés, 1627–1663*, pt. 2, *La Société* (Montreal, 1983), 51. Using parochial marriage registers from 1680 to 1699, Allan Greer finds that 44.1 percent of the male French immigrants could sign whereas 29 percent of the French-born females signed: "L'alphabétisation et son histoire au Québec: État de la question" in *L'Imprimé au Québec: Aspects historiques (18e–20e siècles)*, ed. Yvan Lamonde (Quebec, 1983), 42. It is evident from the crudeness of nearly a third of the signatures that signing one's name was the limit of the writer's literacy.

12. Lucien Campeau, S.J., "Un Témoignage de 1651 sur la Nouvelle-France," *Revue d'histoire de l'Amérique française* (hereafter *RHAF*) 23 (1970): 601–02. The author, Simon Denys, had come to Quebec from Acadia with his wife. He commended the fertility of the land and the virtues of the colonists. He too remarked on the prejudices in France: "Lorsqu'en France vous entendez parler du Canada, vous imaginez un désert inculte et plein d'horreur." As for him and his wife, they had decided to stay "sans renoncer toutefois à l'espérance de revoir la France" (ibid., 609, 611). This hope of seeing France again was typical of most emigrants.

13. Because the 1627 charter of the Compagnie des Cent-Associés specified that only Roman Catholic French subjects should be brought to New France, it has been suggested that the colony was deprived of a host of useful Protestant settlers by this requirement. This suggestion was first made by Louis-Armand de Lom d'Arce de Lahontan in 1703. See Reuben Gold Thwaites, ed., *New Voyages to North America, by the Baron de Lahontan*, 2 vols. (Chicago, 1905), 1: 392–93. François-Xavier Garneau repeated this idea in *Histoire du Canada*, 5th ed., 2 vols. (Paris, 1913–20) 1: 94.

14. Talon to Colbert, 4 Oct. 1665, *Rapport de l'Archiviste*, 1930–31, 36; Colbert to Talon, 5 Jan. 1666, ibid., 41. In 1666 Talon acknowledged Colbert's belief "qu'il n'y a pas dans l'ancienne France assez de surnuméraires, et de sujets ynutils po. peupler La Nouvelle" (Talon to Colbert, 13 Nov. 1666, ibid., 54).

15. Marc André Bédard has shown that the exclusion did not prevent a few hundred Protestants from entering or settling in the colony: "La présence protestante en Nouvelle-France," *RHAF* 31 (1977): 325–49. See his more detailed account, *Les Protestants en Nouvelle-France* (Quebec, 1978). In the more tolerant atmosphere of the eighteenth century, German-speaking Protestants were recruited by a private company as colonists for Louisiana in the 1720s, and in 1765 Rhineland Germans were sent by the Crown to Cayenne and Saint-Domingue. This underlines the resistance of the native French to overseas migration. Protestants and Jews were also formally excluded from the French West Indies, and there, too, secular officials quietly tolerated their presence. The Roman Catholic clergy, however, complained about heretics in the colonies. Mathé Allain, "Slave Policies in French Louisiana," *Louisiana History* 21 (1980): 127–37.

16. Gilles Proulx, *Entre France et Nouvelle-France* (Laprairie, PQ, 1984), 107–13.

17. *Jugements et Délibérations du Conseil souverain de la Nouvelle-France*, 6 vols. (Quebec, 1885–91), 1: 201–04; the passenger rolls appear in *RHAF* 6 (1952–53):

392–96. In 1663 a Dutch ship *Le Phoenix* (*de Feniks*) of Flushing, had been used to deliver the first contingent of *filles du roi* to Canada.

18. In 1740, just 81 of the complement of 270 on the king's ship *Le Rubis* arrived alive and well; 42 died en route to Canada. The passengers were military recruits, exiled prisoners, and workers for the royal shipyard at Quebec. Charles de Beauharnais and Gilles Hocquart to the minister, 27 Aug. 1740, MG 1, C11A series transcript, 73, 7, PAC.

19. Etienne Michel Faillon, *Mémoires particuliers pour servir à l'Histoire de l'Eglise de l'Amérique du Nord . . .*, 4 vols. (Paris, 1853), 1: 65. See also Roland J. Auger, *La Grande Recrue de 1653* (Montreal, 1955), 9–15. M. Auger introduced me to the genealogical sources that made it possible to trace the fate of individual immigrants.

20. Robert Mandrou, "Vers les Antilles et le Canada au XVIIe siècle," *Annales, Economies, Sociétés, et Civilisations* 14 (1959): 667–75. The study was Gabriel Debien, "Les Engagés pour les Antilles (1634–1715)," *Revue d'Histoire des Colonies* 38 (1951).

21. [Louis-Marie de] Meschinet de Richemond, *Inventaire sommaire des Archives départementales antérieures à 1790: Série E Supplément (archives communales). Ville de La Rochelle* (La Rochelle, 1892), 22–23.

22. Ibid., 277, 282, 290, 292, 326, 329, 450.

23. See graph in Mandrou, "Vers les Antilles," 671, covering indentures made for the West Indies as well as Canada. Gabriel Debien, "Les départs d'engagés par Nantes pour l'Amérique" (typescript, c. 1969), shows peaks in recruiting in 1698–1700, 1708, 1710, and 1713. Some of his findings are communicated in "Les Engagés pour le Canada partis de Nantes (1725–1732)," *RHAF* 33 (1980): 583–86. Among 6000 indentures made at Nantes in 1632–1732, he found just 18 contracts for Île Royale and the St Lawrence Valley.

24. Pierre Goubert's *La Vie quotidienne des Pays français au XVIIe siècle* (Paris, 1982), describes regional economies within France that operated independently of one another.

25. Observations made by Stanislas A. Lortie and Adjutor Rivard, *L'Origine et le Parler des Canadiens-français* (Paris, 1903) are confirmed by Mandrou, "Vers les Antilles," 667–75, and by Hubert Charbonneau and Normand Robert in *Historical Atlas of Canada*, vol. 1, *From the Beginning to 1800*, ed. R. Cole Harris (Toronto, 1987), plate 45.

26. Lortie and Rivard, *L'Origine et le Parler*, 11. Lortie made a meticulous study using Cyprien Tanguay's seven-volume digest of the surviving pre-1800 parish registers, *Dictionnaire généalogique des familles canadiennes depuis la fondation de la colonie jusqu'à nos jours* (Quebec, 1871–80), as well as the bishop of Quebec's confirmations register to identify the origins of 4894 French emigrants who settled in Canada in 1608–1700. Île-de-France (including Paris) and Normandy accounted for 32.3 percent of the newcomers, exceeding the group from Poitou-Aunis-Saintonge-Angoumois.

27. *Jesuit Relations*, 9: 187. In 1659–60 Fr. Le Jeune answered his question in part by acknowledging that fear of the Iroquois forced settlers to leave their lands and seek refuge in the towns (ibid., 45: 191–99).

28. Boucher, *Histoire Véritable*, 136–38.

29. *Jugements et Délibérations*, 1: 223; Talon to Colbert, 2 Nov. 1671, *Rapport de l'Archiviste*, 1930–31, 154–55; Talon to the king, 9 March 1673, ibid., 172.

30. Grand Livre: 1674–87, MS C2, Archives du Séminaire de Québec. There are four cases in which the passage from La Rochelle to Quebec cost 60 *livres*

(pp. 47–48, 188–89, 225, 242–43) and one in which the *engagé's* fare was 46 *livres*, 13 *sols*, 4 *deniers* (204–07); all are from the period 1675–76.

In a 1653 court case at Trois-Rivières it was claimed that the cost of bringing out an *engagé* from France was 110 *livres tournois* in beaver pelts; a witness suggested that 80 *livres* was a more reasonable charge. See cahier 4, 20 Nov. 1653, MG 8, D1 (Trois-Rivières), PAC.

In 1659 Jeanne Mance was charged 75 *livres* for the passage of each adult she had sponsored. Archange Godbout, *Les Passagers du Saint-André: La Recrue de 1659* (Montreal, 1964), 2. In peacetime, during the 1720s, the fare for those traveling on royal ships and eating with the crew, rather than at the captain's table, dropped to 30 *livres*. See Proulx, *Entre France et Nouvelle-France*, 108, and List of passengers embarked on the royal flute *Le Chameau*, 2 Nov. 1724, série 1E, CV, 323, Archives du Port de Rochefort. In 1749 passengers sailing from Bayonne to Île Royale paid 62 *livres* 10 *sols* "A la Ration ordinaire" or 150 *livres* to eat at the captain's table. See Bayonne: passengers for Île Royale, 1749, série F5B, art. 38, nos. 1 and 2, AC.

31. In northwestern France in 1693 rural weavers earned five or six *sous* a day while a good weaver in Beauvais might command nine *sous*. Carpenters and locksmiths in Rouen earned as much as fifteen or thirty *sous* in the same period. Fernand Braudel and Ernest Labrousse, *Histoire économique et sociale de la France*, 3 vols. (Paris, 1970), 2: 668–69. Allowing for compulsory days of rest, with no deduction for living expenses, even the Beauvais weaver would need almost a year to earn passage to Canada.

   Fares to British North America were slightly cheaper. According to Richard B. Morris, *Government and Labor in Early America* (New York, 1946), 319, in the seventeenth century "the average cost of transportation varied from £5 to £6 sterling."

32. Trudel, *Histoire . . . La Société*, 11, 22.

33. *Edits. Ordonnances royaux, déclarations et Arrêts du Conseil d'État du Roi concernant le Canada* (Quebec, 1854), 6–7 ("Acte pour l'établissement de la Compagnie des Cent Associés pour le commerce du Canada . . . 29 avril 1627"). The king's acceptance in March 1663 of the surrender of the company's charter claimed that the number of colonists established "étoit fort petit" (ibid., 32). In fact, over 3000 Europeans were living in New France in 1663.

34. Alfred Cambray, *Robert Giffard, premier Seigneur de Beauport, et les origines de la Nouvelle-France* (Cap-de-la-Madeleine, PQ, 1932), 34–39, 73–77. The transcription of the contract on pp. 34–39 does not conform to the facsimile on the pages opposite. The stonemason was Jean Guion (1588–1663) whose six grown children were present when he dictated his will in 1663. Greffes des notaires du régime francais, G. Audouart, 14 May 1663, ANQ. For more information on Guion see *Bulletin des Recherches historiques* 49 (1943): 268–72, and J-B Ferland, *Notes sur les Registres de Notre-Dame de Québec* (Quebec, 1863), 64–67.

35. Mme Pierre Montagne, *Tourouvre et les Juchereau: Un chapitre de l'émigration percheronne au Canada* (Quebec, 1965), 31–86, lists contracts and provides additional information on these people.

36. Auger, *La Grande Recrue*, 9–15; Gustave Lanctôt, *Montreal under Maisonneuve, 1642–1665*, trans. Alta Lind Cook (Toronto, 1969), 68–69.

37. Of those presumed to be alive in 1663, 70.8 percent (68 out of 96) became permanent settlers. This information was extracted from Godbout, *Les Passagers du Saint-André*, 11, 13–48; E.Z. Masicotte, "Les Colons de Montréal de 1642 à 1667," *Memoirs of the Royal Society of Canada* (1913), sec. 1, 16–22; and Masicotte, "Une recrue de Colons pour Montréal en 1659," *Canadian Antiquarian and Numismatic Journal*, 3d ser., 10 (1913): 171–91.

   The reaction rate for the 1659 levy was exceptionally high. In *Habitants et Marchands de Montréal au XVIIe siècle* (Paris, 1974), Louise Dechêne combines this group with the 1653 contingent to determine the proportion of survivors who became settlers. Her figure of 52 percent (74–75) only applies to this unusual sample and is atypical of the overall pattern for *engagés* going to seventeenth-century New France or even Montreal Island. Using other, equally limited samples of migrants from La Rochelle, Archange Godbout observes (without allowing for deaths in the colony) that "De 1642–1644, sur 147 engagés, ... 15% s'établissent et ... de 1655 a 1657, sur 42 engagés, ... 12% s'établissent" ("Familles venues de La Rochelle en Canada," *Rapport des Archives nationales du Québec* 48 (1970): 125). From my notes on 63 men indentured at La Rochelle for Canada in 1656–57 before the notary P. Moreau (MSS 1845, ff. 56VO–109, and MSS 1846, ff. 45VO–121VO, Bibliothèque de La Rochelle), I found 14, or 22.2 percent, still present in New France, according to the 1666–67 censuses. It seems reasonable to assume that a quarter of the surviving, single male workers remained in the colony after their term of service during the seventeenth century.

38. Trudel, *Histoire ... La Société*, 22.

39. Greffe de Pierre Moreau, Bibliothèque de La Rochelle. The phrase "Pays de Canada aux dittes Isles" appears in three contracts: MSS 1845, f. 56VO, MSS 1846, ff. 118–118VO, and 121VO, ibid. The Caribbean standard for indentured service was invoked in eighteenth-century contracts for Canada: in 1716 a Rochelais captain hired men "aux conditions des îles" and three others enrolled in 1733 were to be "nourris, logés sur le pied des engagés des îles," *RHAF* 13 (1959–60): 255; 14 (1960–61): 252.

40. Relying on surviving notarial indentures made at La Rochelle in 1634–1716, there were 943 departures for New France, including Acadia, as opposed to 4800 going to the West Indies. See Debien, "Les Engagés pour les Antilles," 142. This sum includes 15 more indentures for what is now Canada that my wife Susan and I found at La Rochelle. These do not appear in the total found by Debien (928) and later researchers. Debien also stated that of some 6000 *engagés* who sailed from Nantes in 1632–1732 only 18 went to Île Royale and the St Lawrence Valley (see above, n. 23). In the eighteenth century, Bordeaux became the principal port serving the American colonies, and the contracts made there for overseas *engagés* have yet to be inventoried. It is unlikely, however, that they will reveal a large-scale traffic in workers for Canada.

41. Occupational divisions among workers recruited for and resident in the St Lawrence colony were as follows:

Sector	New France, 1663 (526 persons)	Direct Indentures Made at La Rochelle for Canada, 1641–65 (224 contracts)
Agricultural and Domestic service	30.3%	38.8%
Food Trades	7.4%	5.3%
Building Trades	23.7%	20.8%
Clothing Trades	6.8%	2.2%
Toolmaking	7.4%	0.0%
Metalwork	0.0%	5.8%

42. The propensity of the single men hired by merchants under speculative contracts to go home is evident in Godbout's analysis of a 42 man sample 1655–57. "Familles venues de La Rochelle," *Rapport des Archives nationales du Québec* 48 (1970): 119–26.

43. Debien, "Les Engagés pour les Antilles," 69–72.

44. *Jugements et délibérations*, 1: 190–91.

45. Using the passenger roll for *Le Noir* in 1664 from Amirauté, B 5665, pièce 10, Archives de la Charente-Maritime (reprinted in *RHAF* 6 (1952–53): 392–93), I checked the names of 51 *engagés* listed against the nominal censuses of New France in 1666 and 1667. To make sure that the pattern for this group was not unique, I traced 66 other workers delivered by the other Dutch ship *Le Cat* (probably *De Kat*) in 1665, listed in ibid., 394–96, in the same fashion. After eliminating two duplications and one female, there remained 114 names. Of these, 57 could be found in the censuses; 38 were employed in Quebec town and the adjoining region. The masters were notable and wealthy colonials (23), tenant farmers (16), religious orders (10), and craftsmen (4). Ten indentured workers were employed as artisans, and 17 were living in towns.

46. Boucher, *Histoire Véritable*, 161–62. He added: "Ordinarily, they have little of anything and they later marry a woman who has nothing more. However, in less than four or five years you will see them at their ease, if they are fairly hard-working people." According to Le Jeune in 1659–60, many a diligent farmer with a family achieved self-sufficiency "in less than five or six years." *Jesuit Relations*, 45: 191–93. In 1665 Mother Marie de l'Incarnation wrote "when a family commences to make a habitation, it needs two or three years before it has enough to feed itself, not to speak of clothing, furniture." Joyce Marshall, trans. and ed., *Word from New France: The Selected Letters of Marie de l'Incarnation* (Toronto, 1967), 315.

47. *Jugements et Délibérations*, 1: 201–04. The hypocrisy of this claim is evident from the fact that 30 percent of the *engagés* were employed as servants in the towns, where life was little different from that in France. Moreover, in 1663 the council rejected a Sulpician priest's appeal that a former *engagé* who returned to New France on the king's ship be free to reenter the Sulpicians' service for a shorter term because "il ne seroit pas raisonnable qu'une personne qui auroit servy quatre ans dans le pais fust engagée comme les autres." The *engagé* had already been assigned to an officer and judge at Montreal. Ibid., 30.

48. Grand Livre: 1674–87, MS C2 passim. and Grand Livre: 1688–1700, MS C4 passim. Archs. du Séminaire de Québec. These account books list debits and credits under each employee's name, although continuing entries jump several pages before resuming. Subsequent account books are rough ledgers listing each transaction as it happened, without consolidating the entries for different creditors and debtors. They cannot be used to evaluate the treatment of employees. From the seventeenth-century account books, it appears that the Quebec Seminary tried to make each worker's debts equal any credit due him as if to avoid cash payments. For example, of 15 *engagés* in 1674–87, 7 had no outstanding balance, 5 were owed amounts from 6 to 195 *livres*, and 3 owed the seminary amounts from 42 to 115 *livres*. Typically, Julien Brûlé, a shoemaker whose annual salary was 150 *livres*, had a credit of only 6 *livres*, 3 *sols* at the end of his first year's service. He used the amount to pay off a 7 *livres* debt to another person. See MS C2, 250–51, ibid. His debts were for shoes, winter clothing, tobacco, beer, stockings, combs, fine shirts, a crucifix, laundry, and a tailor's services.

49. Bernard Bailyn, *Voyagers to the West: A Passage in the Peopling of America on the Eve of the Revolution* (New York, 1986), 167; David W. Galenson, *White Servitude in Colonial America: An Economic Analysis* (Cambridge, 1981), 5–10, 102–13; Robert Owen Heavner, *Economic Aspects of Indentured Servitude in Colonial Pennsylvania* (New York, 1978); Abbot Emerson Smith, *Colonists in Bondage: White Servitude and Convict Labor in America, 1607–1776* (Chapel Hill, NC, 1947), 17; Warren B. Smith, *White Servitude in Colonial South Carolina* (Columbia, SC, 1961), 72.

50. Marginal note to Gov. Buade de Frontenac's memorial on illicit fur traders, 1681, in *Rapport de l'Archiviste*, 1926–27, 123.

51. Kenneth Donovan, "Tattered Clothes and Powdered Wigs: Case Studies of the Poor and Well-To-Do in Eighteenth-Century Louisbourg" in *Cape Breton at 200: Historical Essays in Honour of the Island's Bicentennial, 1785–1985* (Sydney, NS, 1985), 7.

52. *Jugements et Délibérations*, 1: 29, 202.

53. Talon to Colbert, 27 Oct. 1667, *Rapport de l'Archiviste*, 1930–31, 81.

54. Talon to Colbert, 29 Oct. 1667, ibid., 87.

55. *Jugements et Délibérations*, 1: 201.

56. De Meulles to Colbert, 12 Nov. 1682, MG 1, C11A series transcript, VI, 116–17, PAC. In a 4 Nov. 1682 dispatch, de Meulles suggested that the holders of the export monopoly for beaver pelts be obliged to bring out fifty *engagés* yearly: ibid., 289.

57. De Meulles to Colbert, 12 Nov. 1684, série C11A, VI, f. 399, AC.

58. Talon to Colbert, 2 Nov. 1671, *Rapport de l'Archiviste*, 1930–31, 155.

59. Colbert to Talon, 20 Feb. 1668, ibid., 94.

60. The king to Louis de Buade, Comte de Frontenac, 15 April 1676, ibid., 1926–27, 87.

61. Trudel, *Histoire . . . La Société*, 71–73.

62. Voyer d'Argenson to Baron de Fancamp, 5 Sept. 1658, quoted ibid., 72.

63. *Jugements et Délibérations*, 1: 29.

64. Talon to Colbert, 11 Nov. 1671, *Rapport de l'Archiviste*, 1930–31, 164.

65. Memorial from Talon to Colbert, 2 Nov 1671, ibid., 152.

66. Trudel, *Histoire . . . La Société*, 37.

67. Silvio Dumas, *Les Filles du Roi en Nouvelle-France: Étude historique avec répertoire biographique* (Quebec, 1972), 35–60.

68. The king to Frontenac, 5 June 1672, *Rapport de l'Archiviste*, 1926–27, 8.

69. Colbert to Talon, 4 June 1672, ibid., 1930–31, 169.

70. The king to Frontenac, 22 Apr. 1675, ibid., 1926–27, 80. In a dispatch of April 1676, the monarch told Frontenac that exit permits must be issued sparingly, because of the loss of colonists and "parce qu'ils n'y repassent que par inquietude et pour venir consommer leur bien dans un voyage inutile" (ibid., 87).

71. Jean-Baptiste Colbert, Marquis de Seignelay, to François Charon de La Barre, 10 April 1684, in E.B. O'Callaghan, ed., *Documents Relative to the Colonial History of the State of New York*, 15 vols. (Albany, NY, 1853–87), 9: 221. The same volume contains the king's 1684 ordinance against removing to English and Dutch settlements and an edict to punish those who attempt to do so (224–25).

72. Acting Intendant Patoulet to Colbert, 11 Nov. 1669, série C11A, III, f. 61, AC.

73. Richard C. Harris, "The French Background of Immigrants to Canada Before 1700," *Cahiers de Géographie du Québec* 16 (1972): 313–24. The author, in using Fr. Archange Godbout's genealogical information published in *Rapport de l'Archiviste* from 1951 to 1965 under the title "Nos ancêtres au XVIIe siècle," assumed that the progenitors of Canadian families were representative of the entire migration. The bias of the evidence resulted in an erroneous conclusion that "the immigrants sent to Canada after 1662 usually came alone, and almost never returned to France." The propensity of single males to return to France is also neglected in Lucien Campeau, "Le peuplement de la Nouvelle-France, opération civilisée" in *La Vie quotidienne au Québec: Histoire, Métiers, Techniques*

et Traditions, ed. René Bouchard (Sillery, PQ, 1983), 107–23. Fr. Campeau has argued in this and in his previous work, *Les Cent-Associés et le peuplement de la Nouvelle-France (1633–1663)* (Montreal, 1974), that colonization before 1663 has been underestimated by historians, whereas the contribution of Louis XIV, Colbert, and Talon to the colony's settlement has been exaggerated. His evidence is the rate of population growth in the decades before and after 1663. Although the high proportion of single males in the post-1663 migration is noted, their tendency to return home is not related to the slower rate of population growth. A lower proportion of the Crown's recruits stayed in Canada because they were unmarried men.

74. Everett Emerson, ed., *Letters from New England: The Massachusetts Bay Colony, 1629–1638* (Amherst, MA, 1976), 65, 72. Those who returned are receiving scholarly attention; see Susan M. Hardman, "The Return of New England Settlers to England, 1640–60" (PhD thesis, Kent University, forthcoming).

75. Claude-Joseph de Ferrière, *Dictionnaire de Droit et de Pratique. . . ,* 2 vols. (Toulouse, 1779), 2: 104–06; *Ordonnances des Testamens du mois d'Août 1735, articles 51–53, in [Jacques-Antoine] Salle, L'Esprit des Ordonnances et des Principaux Edits et Déclarations de Louis XV* (Paris, 1771), 201–06.

76. Letter deposited in the file of the Montreal notary, Bénigne Basset, 25 March 1670, in Auger, *La Grande Recrue de 1653,* 103–04.

77. J. Barrère, cadet at Bayonne, to M. Laborde at Louisbourg, 23 Oct. 1756, HCA 30/264, 194.

78. Madeleine-Thérèse Sallé, Mme Raimbault, at Paris to Claude Raimbault, master joiner at Montreal, 15 March 1681, Centre régional de Montreal, Bailliages, feuillets séparés: 1681, ANQ. This letter is reprinted, with accents and punctuation added, in E.Z. Masicotte, "De l'usage du manchon autrefois," *Bulletin des Recherches historiques* 33 (1927): 325–27.

79. The makeup of the family and its members' fate are revealed by Tanguay, *Dictionnaire généalogique,* 1: 507–08; 6: 500; by E.Z. Masicotte in *Bulletin des Recherches historiques* 21 (1915): 78–81; and by Robert Lahaise in *Dictionary of Canadian Biography* (Toronto, 1969), 2: 541–42.

80. Irène Chaussegros, in France, to her brother-in-law, Joseph Gaspard Chaussegros de Léry, at Quebec, 13 May 1755, author's collection.

81. In addition to the letters referred to in notes 77, 79, 81, and 83, see Maria Pasqual to her father, Martin Pasqual, carpenter at Louisbourg, 12 March 1757 (HCA 30/264, 126); Catherine Valentin to Antoine Valentin, carpenter at Cap Français, 12 Nov. 1757, in which she assures him that upon his return "vous Seres Contan Come un Roy pour votre etat et vous metre[z] mon esprit an Repos" (HCA 30/265, 57), as well as a mother at Marseilles to Joseph Danillon at Cap Saint-Marc, 20 Oct. 1757, ibid., 58; Mme. Audileort at Aix to Joseph Audileort at Moka Neuf, Cap Français, 12 July 1757 (a mother's appeal to a military deserter to come home under an amnesty and restore "la tranquilité d'une pauvre mere qui ne feroit que plurer"), ibid., 63; Catherine Detchegaray at Ascain to Pierre Detchevery, shipbuilder on Martinique, 22 March 1757, ibid., 68; and passim. A sixth of the letters to Île Royale are in Euzkara/Basque, and seem to follow the same pattern. See Martin Larralde de Bastidaguerre at Saint-Pée to his nephew Saint-Martin de Duronea at Louisbourg, 16 March, 1757, in which he seeks aid for the recipient's mother (HCA 30/264, 68). Maria Urquidi of Vancouver translated this letter and the few other texts in Euzkara.

82. Father Behola at Saint-Pée to St Martin Duronea at Louisbourg, 14 Feb. 1757 (HCA 30/264, 122). A sailor from Saint-Jean de Luz, who had stayed on at Louisbourg, received a similar appeal from his mother in 1757: "Je suis Baucop Entristé de Votre part. . . . Je suis dans un age Comme Vous scavez La grasse

que Je vous demande [est] de vous Retirer ché Vous Mon cher fils pour Lamour de moy dans Letat que Vous Etes cert La grasse que Je demande avant ma mort que Je vous puisse vous Voir une fois au moins apres que Je vous E veu une fois Je ceRais content de moury." Here was a mother who knew how to exploit her son's conscience! Mariya Delapits at Saint-Jean de Luz to Pierre Laborde at Louisbourg, 2 April 1757, ibid., 130.

83. St Jean Mornigust at Ciboure to St Martin Duronea, 17 March 1757, ibid., 95.

84. Marie Martin Duronea to St Martin Duronea, 12 Feb. 1757, ibid., 104.

85. François Dupont, in a contract passed before the Quebec notary Guillaume Audouart, 24 Aug. 1661, sold his land to return to France because in Canada he was "sans assurance contre les incursions des Iroquois" (quoted in Trudel, *Histoire . . . Le Société*, 72). Cyprien Tanquay, *A travers les Registres* (Montreal, 1886), 36–90, 262–63, shows that attacks intensified in 1660–62, 1667, and reached a peak in 1687–94. John A. Dickinson, "La guerre iroquoise et la mortalité en Nouvelle-France, 1608–1666," *RHAF* 36 (1982): 31–47, argues that since some 190 colonists were killed by the Iroquois in this period and more people died by accident or by drowning, the murderous reputation of the Iroquois is undeserved. Perceived danger is not always based on statistical probabilities. The shocking and unusual nature of the killings would have made a greater impression on the colonists than a drowning.

86. Jean Bochart de Champigny to the minister, 1699, MG 1, C11A series transcript, XVII, 108, PAC. See also résumé of a letter from Mme Vaudreuil to the minister, *Rapport de l'Archiviste*, 1942–43, 415–16. Gedéon de Catalogne added his voice to the chorus in 1712; see his report of 7 Nov. 1712, in William Bennett Munro, ed., *Documents Relating to the Seigniorial Tenure in Canada, 1598–1854* (Toronto, 1908), 145, 149.

A 1687 memorial on the advantages that *engagés* would bring to neglected Acadia suggests that this region of New France no longer received indentured workers. Advantages to the state and to trade . . . to be procured by a company on the coast and land of Acadia, série C11D, II, ff. 67–75, AC.

87. Peter Moogk, "Les Petits Sauvages: The Children of Eighteenth-Century New France" in *Childhood and Family in Canadian History*, ed. Joy Parr (Toronto, 1982), 17–43.

88. Minister to de Champigny, 9 April 1687, B series transcript, XIII, 172–73, PAC. A letter of the same date to Gov. Jacques-René de Brisay de Denonville repeats this statement with the variation "pour aller dans un pais aussy esloigné que le Canada" (série B, XIII, f. 58, AC). This letter mentions the right of the workers to return whenever they please. In 1719 the king's engineer at Louisbourg noted "les bons ouvriers qui connoissent les Isles [American colonies] par experience ou par reputation demandent aujourd'juy 80#, de gages par mois" M. de Verville to the maritime council, 10 Aug. 1719, série C11B, IV, f. 235, ibid.

89. The story of d'Agrain's recruiting expedition comes from série B, XLII-1, ff. 58–58VO, 201VO–202, XLII-2, ff. 468–69, 485VO, AC, and from série IE (correspondence between the maritime council and the intendant at Rochefort), XCIV, 501–03, 621–25, XCV, 11–15, 57–58, C, 61, Archives du Port de Rochefort. The Crown paid out 2675 *livres* in expenses for the expedition; it gave the count a 400 *livres* bonus as well as a free passage with rations for eight workers destined for his Île Royale estate. These men murdered d'Agrain because of maltreatment and inadequate food. See série G2, CLXXVIII, ff. 78–85, AC.

90. Maritime council to the intendant at Rochefort, 22 Jan. 1721, série IE, XCVI, 69–70, Archives du Port de Rochefort.

91. Abbé Tremblay to François de Laval, 15 June 1703, Lettres, Carton N, No. 121, Archives du Séminaire de Québec.

92. Grand Livre: 1674–87, 41–412, MS C2, ibid. In 1634 a Jesuit father at Quebec reported, "last year they sent us a man as a carpenter who was not one" (*Jesuit Relations*, 6: 71).

93. MS C2, 47 [Jean Dubosq], Archives du Séminaire de Québec.

94. M. Dudouyt at Paris to Mgr de Laval at Quebec, 9 March 1682, Lettres, Carton N, No. 61, 10, ibid.

95. Mgr de Laval at Paris to the gentlemen of the Quebec Seminary, May 1685, *Rapport de l'Archiviste*, 1939–40, 263–65.

96. See above, n. 85.

97. *Jugements et Délibérations*, 1: 269, and Gabriel Debien, "Engagés pour le Canada au XVIIe siècle vus de la Rochelle," *RHAF* 6 (1952–53): 190. François Ruette d'Auteuil attributed the regulation that shipowners carry one man for every ten tons of cargo destined for Quebec to "le Conseil établi ensuite à Québec" (memorial of 12 Dec. 1715, in *Rapport de l'Archiviste*, 1922–23, 62–63). Paul-Emile Renaud, *Les Origines économiques du Canada: l'oeuvre de la France* (Mamers, 1928), 237, rephrases this as an enactment by "le Conseil qui fut alors institué à Québec (1647)" that shipowners must embark "un homme pour chaque tonneau [sic] de fret." Debien and later authors accepted Renaud's faulty paraphrase as a reference to a law made in 1647. D'Auteuil was referring to the August 1664 proposal of the Conseil souverain.

98. Debien, "Les Engagés pour les Antilles," 23–24; Lawrence C. Wroth and G.L. Annan, *Acts of French Royal Administration concerning Canada, Guiana, the West Indies, and Louisiana, prior to 1791* (New York, 1930), 36, 40.

99. Ordinance compelling captains of merchant vessels to transport indentured workers to New France, 20 March 1714, série B, XXXVI, ff. 336VO–337VO, AC.

100. Minister to Beauharnais, 28 March 1714, ibid., f. 149VO; the king to Vaudreuil and Michel Bégon, 19 March 1714, ibid., ff. 338–41.

101. Athanase Jourdan et al., eds., *Recueil Général des Anciennes Lois Françaises depuis l'an 420 jusqu'à la révolution de 1789, 29* vols. (Paris, 1821–33) 18: 370; Debien, "Les Engagés pour les Antilles," 64.

102. Ruling . . . concerning the *engagés* and muskets that must be carried to the French American colonies, 16 Nov. 1716, série A2, Art. 23, ff. 634–43, Archives de la Marine, AN. An earlier dispatch to the intendant of New France told him that the required *engagés* would be craftsmen and that he and the port captain were not to interfere in the sale of the workers' contracts. The freedom of ships' captains to sell to anyone at whatever price they pleased was said to be an established practice in the West Indies. Maritime council to Intendant Bégon, 16 June 1716, MG 1, B series transcript, XXXVIII-2, 379, PAC.

103. Royal ordinance concerning the prisoners who will replace the *engagés* to be transported to the colonies, 14 Jan. 1721, série B, XLIV, ff. 130–130VO, AC. Wroth and Annan, *Acts of French Royal Administration*, 53–54, lists a decree of 8 Jan. 1719, authorizing the dispatch of "les condamnés aux Galères, les Bannis, les Vagabons & les Gens sans aveu" to the colonies as *engagés*.

104. Royal ordinance concerning indentured workers, 20 May 1721, série B, XLIV, ff. 161VO–162VO, AC. Ships of the Compagnie des Indes going to Louisiana and those destined for Île Saint-Jean were also exempted.

105. Intendant de Meulles to the minister, 4 Nov. 1683, MG 1, C11A series transcript, VI, 290–91, PAC. Dom Guy Oury, ed., *Marie de l'Incarnation, Ursuline (1599–1672): Correspondance* (Solesmes, France, 1971), 863.
    Bishop de Laval described one case in 1687 when he sent a joiner to the Quebec Seminary. The joiner was a family man, and a decent person (*honnête*), but was obliged to leave France "à cause d'un accident qui luy est arrivé

d'avoir frappé un monopolier d'un coup de pierre dont il est mort" (Mgr de Laval to the directors of the Quebec Seminary, 9 June 1687, in *Rapport de l'Archiviste*, 1939–40, 279).

106. Interrogation of Jean Legouel in prison, 20 Sept. 1725, série G2 (Conseil supérieur de Louisbourg), CLXXVIII, ff. 831–835, AC.

107. Série B, XLIV, ff. 56VO–57, 191–191VO, 196VO–197, ibid. The per diem allowance was seven *sols*. In June 1721 printed copies of the offer were sent to Calais, Dieppe, Le Havre, Rouen, Honfleur, Saint-Malo, Morlaix, Brest, Nantes, La Rochelle, Bordeaux, Bayonne, and Marseille; these ports and Certe were the only ones authorized in 1717 to trade with the colonies. The resistance of La Rochelle's merchants was acknowledged in August and the council decided that acceptance of the prisoners would be voluntary: "l'Intention du Conseil n'est pas de les y contraindre" (ibid., f. 197).

108. Maritime council to the intendant at Rochefort, 9 April 1722, série IE, XCIX, 381–82, Archives du Port de Rochefort.

109. Jacques-Ange Le Normant de Mézy to the minister, 28 Dec. 1723, série C11B, VI, ff. 257–257VO, AC.

110. Royal ordinance concerning indentured servants, 15 Feb. 1724, série A1, Art. 62, pièce 11, Archives de la Marine.

111. Maurice Filion, *La Pensée et L'Action coloniales de Maurepas vis-à-vis du Canada: 1723–1749* (Montreal, 1972), 376.

112. François Bigot to the minister, 29 Sept. 1742, série C11B, XXIV, ff. 103–103VO, AC. See also Bigot to the minister, 7 Oct. 1744, ibid., XXVI, ff. 101–102VO, when he anticipated the wartime suspension of the regulations, which happened in 1748.

113. "Le recensement de Québec, en 1744," *Rapport de l'Archiviste*, 1939–40, 3–153, shows that in the town there were 27 white male *domestiques* or *ouvriers*, older than 19 years, as opposed to 137 miscellaneous female servants and 89 juvenile or adolescent male servants, including slaves. There may have been more adult male *engagés* in the rural areas, even though craftsmen tended to work in the towns. The use of indirect evidence is necessary because the Quebec admiralty registers have been lost and there are few sales of French *engagés*' contracts in the files of Canadian notaries. Greffes des notaires, L. Chambalon, contains one such sale (12 Aug. 1715), and some other possible sales (20 Dec. 1693, 29 March 1701, 30 Oct. 1706, 10 Aug. 1713), ANQ.

114. James S. Pritchard, "The Pattern of French Colonial Shipping to Canada before 1760," *Revue française d'Histoire d'Outre-Mer* 63 (1976): 189–210. In 1853 Quebec received 1351 ships of 570 738 tons in total; in 1753 only 25 vessels of 4959 tons left France for Quebec.

115. Jean Louis, Comte de Raymond to the minister, 4 Nov. 1751, série C11B, XXXI, ff. 50VO–51, AC.

116. Classes: Bayonne, Passengers going to the colonies, 1749–77, f. 72 (2 March 1757: *La Louise*), série F5B, Art. 30, ibid. Previous voyages of this schooner are noted on ff. 53–54, 58, and a later trip on f. 75.

117. On the deliberate falsification of statistics by government officials see Peter Moogk, "Beyond the C11 Series: Approaches and Sources for the Social History of New France," *Archivaria* 14 (1982): 53–62.

118. B. Duvergé at Bayonne to M. Imbert at Louisbourg, 10 March 1757, HCA 30/264, 186.

119. Dale Miquelon found that the rolls of vessels contracted to Dugard of Rouen in 1731–55 carefully listed *engagés*, and muskets carried in compliance with the

laws (private correspondence). Series HCA 32 (papers of prize vessels) in the Public Record Office provides an opportunity to compare the numbers of crew-men and indentured workers on the ships' rolls with the number of men found on board by British captors. Evidence that *La Louise* was not the sole delinquent is contained in the following examples: 1744: *Le Saint Marc* of Olonne via Bordeaux destined for Canada, crew 15, no *engagés* carried (Box 130-1); 1745: *La Gracieuse* of Bayonne, 122 tons, destined for Quebec, crew 22 with 3 *engagés* aged 32, 29, and 22; when captured, the ship had 23 mariners and 4 "boys" on board (Box 113-1); 1747: *La Fleur du Jour* of La Rochelle, 102 tons, destined for Quebec, 12 crew on roll, one extra sailor found on board when captured but not the 3 *engagés* declared upon departure (Box 112-1); 1747: *Le Fortuné* of Bordeaux, 200 tons, destined for Quebec, crew 28 with one shoemaker-*engagé* in place of the required 4 by special permission of the admiralty. English captors reported that the ship had 26 live crewmen and 2 dead on board when taken (Box 112-2); 1757: *L'Acadie* of Bordeaux, 160 tons, destined for Quebec and the West Indies, crew 22 and 3 *engagés*; the English report reads "there was Twenty Two Mariners officers included on board" (Box 161-1); and 1757: *L'Aigle* of Bordeaux, 200 tons, destined for the West Indies, crew 33 and 2 *engagés* (in place of 3), had 36 persons aboard when captured! (Box 161-1). There were indentures for *engagés* among the ship's papers of *La Fleur du Jour* and *L'Acadie* but none on board *L'Aigle*, which shows the false contracts were made to sat-isfy the authorities.

120. Jack and Marion Kaminkow, *A List of Emigrants from England to America 1718–1759* (Baltimore, 1964), names 3122 persons indentured at London for serv-ice in the British American colonies. Galenson's *White Servitude in Colonial America* is based on a sample of 16 847 indentured servants going to the British American colonies in 1654–75. Morris speaks of 10 000 emigrants from the port of Bristol alone, and of 6000 leaving England from December 1773 to October 1775; he also quotes an estimate of 43 720 departing from 5 Irish ports in 1769–74 (*Government and Labor*, 315, n. 2).

121. President of the maritime council to Gov. Beauharnais and Intendant Hocquart in Canada, 8 May 1743, série B, LXXVI, ff. 70–70VO, AC. In 1731 these officials expressed satisfaction with the *faux-sauniers* as useful workers and potential settlers, in contrast to the worthless characters sent in the previous year. See série C11A, LII, ff. 83–85, LIV, ff. 77–78VO, ibid. The ideas of exiling petty crim-inals to New France had been discussed in 1715–16 but was put off without explanation. See MG 1, B Series transcript, XXXVIII-2, 356, PAC. Série B, XLIV, ff. 130–267VO, AC, contains letters and documents about the first shipment of petty criminals in 1721. The difficulty of preventing escapes by *faux-sauniers* is mentioned in 1735 in Beauharnais and Hocquart to the minister, 5 Oct. 1735, MG 1, C11A series transcript, LXIII, 18–19, PAC. In that year 54 men arrived in Canada of whom 5 joined the troops and the remainder were distributed to colonists to work for 100 *livres* a year (ibid., LXIII, 26–27, 89–93).

122. A royal ordinance to prevent the return to France or escape to the English colonies "faux sauniers et Contrebandiers déserteurs" exiled to Canada and Île Royale, dated 25 May 1742, is in série A1, Art. 78, pièce 44, Archives de la Marine, and also in série B, LXXIV, ff. 538–538VO, ibid. The continuing escapes on English colonial ships are mentioned in a dispatch from Jean-Baptiste-Louis Le Prévost Duquesnel and Bigot to the minister, 14 Oct. 1742, série B, XXIV, ff. 22–22VO, AC.

123. Malchelosse, "Faux sauniers, prisonniers et fils de famille en Nouvelle-France au XVIIIe siècle," *Cahiers des Dix* 9 (1944): 161–97. See also his "Les Fils de famille en Nouvelle-France, 1720–1750," ibid., 11 (1946): 261–311, in which he says that only 10 out of 68 *fils de famille* became permanent settlers.

124. Marcel Trudel, *L'esclavage au Canada français: Histoire et conditions de l'esclavage* (Quebec, 1960).

125. Pierre-Georges Roy, "Les Lettres de Naturalité sous le régime français," *Bulletin des Recherches historiques* 30 (1924): 225–32. One hundred twenty-six letters are listed in Pierre-Georges Roy, ed., *Inventaire des insinuations du Conseil souverain de la Nouvelle-France* (Beauceville, 1921), 119–21. In 1705–07 there was a long correspondence about a list of "Anglais, Ambourgois et Flamans qui sont establis en ce pays" who desired letters of naturalization as well as many female converts to Roman Catholicism who wanted to remain in Canada (*Rapport de l'Archiviste*, 1938–39, 83, 110, 158, 169; 1939–40, 366). This may be the origin of the large number of letters of naturalization in 1710–13. Since the letters cost 100 *livres* after 1722 (while also requiring proof of Catholicity), they are not a complete record of those who stayed in Canada.

126. See a 1747 report on those who returned to Boston and on those left behind in Emma Lewis Coleman, *New England Captives Carried to Canada between 1677 and 1670 during the French and Indian Wars*, 2 vols. (Portland, ME, 1925), 1: 107. More captives were taken before the war ended. For example, 20 Irish and Scottish girls destined for Virginia were captured with a prize vessel in 1748 and became domestic servants in Canada. See O'Callaghan, ed., *Documents*, 10: 172. After the war 33 "English deserters" also chose to remain in New France. Jacques-Pierre de Taffanel de La Jonquière and Bigot to the minister, 23 Oct. 1750, série C11A, XCV, ff. 102–103, Archives des Nationales. James Axtell, *The Invasion Within: The Contest of Cultures in Colonial North America* (New York, 1985), 289–92, gives a total of 1641 for persons captured between 1675 and 1763 and analyzes the nature of those who remained in Canada.

127. Maritime council to M. Dupuy, 14 May 1728, B series transcript, L-2, 79 (ff. 498–498VO), PAC, mentions the "great number of Englishmen" living at Montreal said to be smugglers posing as merchants, craftsmen, or settlers. The activities of "the great number of English artizans, merchants and others established at Montreal" was also discussed in 1727 in the light of a law forbidding intercolonial trade by foreigners. O'Callaghan, ed., *Documents*, 9: 985. In 1753 the "prodigious number of English deserters" being maintained at French posts on the frontiers of Canada was reduced by shipping off 45 to France. The governor complained that deserters employed as servants were more adept at thievery than honest labour. Ange Duquesne de Menneville to the minister, 18 Aug. 1753, série C11A, XCIX, ff. 7–9, AC.

128. Michel Roy estimates that 1800 fled to New France, *L'Acadie des origines à nos jours: Essai de synthèse historique* (Montreal, 1981), 133. Some estimates are higher and, indeed, a higher estimate is justified if we add fugitives from Île Royale and Île Saint-Jean.

129. Adam Shortt and Arthur G. Doughty, eds., *Documents Relating to the Constitutional History of Canada, 1759–1791* (Ottawa 1907), 27. See articles 38, 39, and 41 of the 1760 capitulation.

130. Ordinance of 21 May 1698, série B, XXVII (Canada, 1706), ff. 89VO–90, AC. The law's text did not reach New France until 1706, and war delayed its implementation. In 1716 the intendant's subdelegate on Île Royale was told not to hinder soldiers' marriages "dans une Colonie qu'il faut peupler et surtout dans les Commencemens." Maritime council to de Soubras, 22 April 1716, MG1, B series transcript, XXXVIII-2, 556, PAC. The secondary role of the French soldiers as settlers is evident in the king's instructions not to accept *Canadiens* into the ranks of the garrison troops. That would deprive the colony of "des hommes capables de contribuer a Son Etablissement." Memorial of the king to Beauharnais and Hocquart, May 31, 1743, série B, LXXVI, ff. 95VO–96, AC.

131. In 1753, Gov. Raymond of Île Royale wrote that it was widely believed in France that "lorsqu'un Soldat . . . est engagé [pour les colonies], il n'en peut plus revenir." This quotation from série C11B, XXXIII, f. 89, AC, appears in T.A. Crowley, "The Forgotten Soldiers of New France: The Louisbourg

Example," French Colonial Historical Society, *Proceedings of the Third Annual Meeting* (1978): 55.

132. These points are made by Crowley ibid., 52–69, and by Allan Greer, "Mutiny at Louisbourg, December 1744," *Histoire sociale/Social History* 10, 20 (1977): 305–36. Although it is not possible to measure the moral quality of the recruits, the physical standards were certainly low. Looking at a list of 585 recruits on the Île de Ré in 1753, I found that 170 were under the minimum height of "5. pieds 2. pouces" and "Sans Espérence de croistre." See Review of recruits destined for the colonies, Île de Ré citadel, Feb. 1753, série 1R, No. 20, Archives du Port de Rochefort. Although recruits were described in 1685 and 1698 as being very young and of deplorable quality, in 1706 and 1728 officials praised the soldiers received. See série B, XI, f. 3, AC, and MG 1, C11A series transcript, XV, 38, XXIV, 8, L, 114, PAC.

133. Intendant Bochart de Champigny, 14 Oct. 1698, quoted in Dechêne, *Habitants et Marchands*, 87.

134. Ruette d'Auteuil, 1715, Rapport de l'Archiviste, 1922–23, 64.

135. The process by which experienced soldiers were released to marry and were replaced by new recruits, leaving many unfit soldiers in the ranks, was described by Chaussegros de Léry in October 1720, in Pierre-Georges Roy, ed., *Inventaire des Papiers de Léry*, 3 vols. (Quebec, 1939–40), 1: 62.
   Gov. Duquesne claimed that soldiers married sluts and wine-sops in order to get a settler's discharge, and that these men were more likely to become tavern-keepers rather than successful farmers. Duquesne to the minister, 26 Oct. 1753, série C11A, XCIX, f. 98vo, ACs. On Île Royale it was alleged that, except for the Germans (Swiss?) who were "plus laborieux et plus patiens Cultivateurs," soldiers were hopeless as farmers. See Augustin de Boschenry de Drucour to the minister, 27 June 1756, série C11B, XXXVI, ff. 61VO–62, ibid. An earlier dispatch argued that to expect a soldier to become a farmer was unrealistic: "aussytost qu'il a gousté La vie du Soldat jl n'est plus propre a labourer la terre." See Joseph de Mombeton de Saint-Ovide de Brouillon and Le Normant de Mézy to the minister, 28 Nov. 1726, ibid., VIII, ff. 16VO–17.

136. Landry, "Mortalité, nuptialité et canadianisation des troupes françaises de la guerre de Sept Ans," *Histoire sociale/Social History* 12 (1979): 298–315.

137. Boleda, "Les Migrations au Canada," 112, 339. This hypothetical total and a conjectural breakdown of net migration from France by decades is presented as fact in Harris, ed., *Historical Atlas of Canada*, plate 45.

138. Mario Boleda reached the figure of 3900 for indentured workers by deducing that La Rochelle supplied 23.1 percent of the *engagés* for New France and then by multiplying the 922 indentures for "Canada" found by Debien and others by 4.23 to achieve a total number of *engagés* sent from France. The problems with this computation are that La Rochelle was probably the port of departure for at least 30 percent of all indentured workers going to New France, the figure 922 (which misses some deeds) is for "Canada" in the modern sense (including Acadia and French settlements on the Atlantic coast and Gulf of St Lawrence), and no allowance is made for fraudulent indentures after 1716. There are at least 709 indentures made at La Rochelle for the St Lawrence Valley and, allowing for a loss of a fifth of the indentures as well as falsification of a tenth of the post-1716 contracts, one comes up with 820 for La Rochelle and a possible total of 2733 coming from all French ports to the St Lawrence Valley. A cautious estimate might be 3000. Boleda's total figure for female migrants is a compromise between four different estimates by earlier researchers. See Boleda, "Les Migrations au Canada," 105.

139. Camille de Rochemonteix, ed., *Relation par Lettres de l'Amérique Septentrionale* (Paris, 1904), 4. The author is probably the co-Intendant Antoine-Denis Raudot.

140. Migration within France and into its neighbours is described in Michael W. Flinn, *The European Demographic System, 1500–1820* (Baltimore, 1981), ch. 5, "The Movement of Population."

141. Two-thirds of the men indentured at La Rochelle for Canada before 1716 came from this port, its immediate neighbourhood, and the provinces of Aunis and Saintonge. The balance, and especially the unskilled men hired speculatively by merchants, came from distant cities. The patterns for all the men indentured at La Rochelle for the Americas are discussed in Debien, "Les Engagés pour les Antilles," and are displayed on the maps accompanying Mandrou, "Vers les Antilles," *Annales* 14 (1959): 667–75.

142. *Jesuit Relations*, 7: 243; this observation is confirmed in Fernand Braudel, *Civilization and Capitalism, 15th–18th Century*, vol. 1, *The Structures of Everyday Life: The Limits of the Possible*, trans. Siân Reynolds (New York, 1981), 54–55, which mentions the migration from France into Spain, which is the subject of J. Nadal, *La Population catalane de 1553 à 1717: L'immigration francaise et les autres facteurs de son développement* (Paris, 1960).

143. André Corvisier, *Armies and Societies in Europe, 1494–1789* (Bloomington, IN, 1979), 113.

144. Roberta Hamilton argues that the small migration to New France, which she underestimates at 10 000, was due to the "feudal" nature of French society, which gave the peasant more secure land tenure than was known in rural England. As "the world's first capitalist country," England had "a surplus population [displaced by commercial farming], surplus capital accumulated through capitalist agriculture, rapidly expanding internal markets, and the potential for the development of external markets." These, she says, were the preconditions for successful, large-scale colonization: *Feudal Society and Colonization: The Historiography of New France* (Ganonoque, ON, 1988), 59. This is a rhetorical argument drawing on secondary studies and theoretical works; it is not based on the primary evidence and ignores the problem of emigrants who returned to France.

EARLY LOYALIST SAINT JOHN[*]

D.G. BELL

○

> They have no other country to go to—no other asylum.
>
> *Robert Morse, 1783*

When news of Britain's decision to concede independence to all the rebelling colonies reached New York in the summer of 1782 Loyalists reluctantly turned their mind to the possibility of exile as the ultimate safeguard against retaliation by the victorious Patriots. For the wealthy the mother country was the destination of choice. For the especially adventurous remote Quebec was one possibility; the West Indian colonies were another. But for the great majority of those trapped in the former asylum of loyalty at the mouth of the Hudson the only feasible avenue of escape was Nova Scotia. Although that northern outpost of New England had never enjoyed a favourable reputation in the older colonies it had the great advantage of being relatively close to New York and it was known to be habitable. Since Nova Scotia's population was small there would likely be large tracts of vacant land in good situations.

Initial arrangements on behalf of New York area Loyalists indicating interest in evacuation were made by private associations in negotiation with the commander-in-chief and the governor of Nova Scotia. There were several such associations. The Westchester Refugees, one of the elements of the paramilitary Associated Loyalists, decided to settle in the Fort Lawrence region at the head of the Bay of Fundy. Another association, composed of Baptist and Quaker refugees, made its way to Beaver Harbour in the future Charlotte County. Many officers and men in the provincial corps formed an association of their own. The great majority of the civilian refugees joined either the Port Roseway Associates (proposing to settle what became Shelburne in peninsular Nova Scotia) or the Bay of Fundy Adventurers (proposing to settle the River St John and the environs of Annapolis Royal).

[*] *Early Loyalist Saint John: The Origin of New Brunswick Politics, 1783–1786* (Fredericton: New Ireland Press, 1983), 14–33. Reprinted with permission.

THE BAY OF FUNDY ADVENTURERS

In mid-1782 the earliest group of "refugees" (as civilian Loyalists were called, to distinguish them from "provincial" or military Loyalists) to join the Bay of Fundy Adventurers met to elect a board of agents (collectively known as the "New York Agency"), of which the Rev. Samuel Seabury became president.[1] The agency drew up a list of the forms of assistance needed for resettlement and presented it to the commander-in-chief. Included among the requests were transportation to Nova Scotia, provisions for one year, clothing, medicine, building material, farm utensils, mill equipment, and weapons. All this Carleton was willing to grant, as supplies permitted. But in response to the agency's central request for 300 to 600 acres of surveyed land for each family he could only commend their petition to the favourable attention of Nova Scotia's civilian governor, John Parr.[2] Still, Carleton's response had been warmly supportive, and with this assurance the Bay of Fundy Adventurers were ready to begin an active campaign for members. One of their subscription forms read as follows:

> We whose names are hereunto subscribed do agree to remove to the province of Nova Scotia, . . . with our families, in full reliance on the future support of Government, and under the patronage of the following gentlemen as our agents, they having been approved of as such by his Majesty's Commissioner for restoring Peace [Sir Guy Carleton].[3]

The first group of Bay of Fundy Adventurers left New York for Nova Scotia as early as the autumn of 1782. Because the agency had not yet sent forth explorers to spy out eligible locations for settlement this first party was sent to the relatively civilized environs of Annapolis Royal in peninsular Nova Scotia. Numbering between four and five hundred they arrived off the colony's ancient capital in a fleet of eleven sail on 19 October 1782.[4]

With this unfortunate multitude, for whom little advance preparation had been made, came three representatives of the New York Agency— Amos Botsford, Frederick Hauser, and Samuel Cummings. This trio was charged with exploring the colony for sites of future settlement and with soliciting assistance from Parr's administration at Halifax. Their tour brought them to the River St John at the end of November, and in early 1783 they transmitted enthusiastic findings to the main body of the agency at New York. The St John waterway, they exulted,

> is a fine river, equal in magnitude to the Connecticut or Hudson. At the mouth of the river is a fine harbour, accessible at all seasons of the year—never frozen or obstructed by the ice, which breaks in passing over the falls. . . . [The river] is navigable for vessels of seventy or eighty tons burthen, for about eighty miles up the river, and for boats much farther.

Their attention was transfixed by the lushly fertile intervale land of the Maugerville area. It produced "crops of all kinds with little labour; and vegetables in the greatest perfection; parsnip of great length, &c. . . . These intervals would make the finest meadows."[5]

This rich description delighted the agency at New York, which pub-lished "large Extracts . . . in the Newspapers here, which have done much good."[6] Yet there are indications that the agency's hopes were fixed on the empty St John Valley even before it received the praise of the three explor-ers. Seabury had already written from New York that the agency could not but think "that a Settlement on St Johns River will be preferable to any other, on account of the soil, the lumber and the fur trade [sic]." In another early letter the agency declared itself

> anxious to hear from you respecting S. Johns River—the degree of cold this winter—the Number, Situation and Temper of the Indians, &c. . . . We hear that . . . [the Port Roseway Associates] are turning their attention to St. Johns River. As they have declined being connected with us, we thought it right to give you this Notice, that you may act accordingly in fixing your location as soon as can conveniently be done.[7]

It was this predisposition in favour of the St John, confirmed by the agents sent northward to explore, which channelled much the greater number of Bay of Fundy Adventurers to the region, which was to become New Bruns-wick, rather than to peninsular Nova Scotia. Although the agency had dis-patched one fleet of exiles to Annapolis and would continue to do so on a small scale, their focus was from early 1783 on the River St John.

Because the evacuation of civilian New York was a co-operative effort between the several private Loyalist associations and the British military the refugees had to both join an organization like the Bay of Fundy Adventurers and conform to various regulations imposed by military authorities. The evacuees of the spring 1783 fleet were, for example, cautioned that "[N]o Person is permitted to Embark who has not resided twelve months within the British Lines, without a Special Passport from the Commandant." "It is also recommended to the Refugees to take Care no Person of bad Character is suffered to embark with them."[8] Those Loyalists who claimed to be free blacks were subject to special control. Nearly all had obtained manumission by responding to the British invitation to desert their rebel owners, many of whom tried to reclaim them at war's end. While the British military reso-lutely refused to surrender any who had achieved their freedom in that man-ner they did promise patriot authorities to prevent any other escaped slaves from fleeing to Nova Scotia. Consequently a board was appointed, including representatives of the rebel Congress, to examine all embarking blacks. At least three thousand civilian negroes were inspected in this manner.[9]

There were also restrictions on the type of goods Loyalists could carry with them into exile. Under the provisional terms of peace, for example, no one could take away public records of any of the rebelling colonies or any other rebel property. There was a particular concern that evacuees would carry off bricks secured by demolishing patriot-owned houses. A commit-tee was appointed to inspect every transport ship for improper cargo of this kind.[10]

How much property were departing Loyalists allowed to carry with them on public transports? One historian, noting that shipping was in short supply and that New York newspapers for 1783 are full of auction notices, concluded that the British would not allow the exiles to ship much in the way of household goods.[11] This reasoning seems sound and would in part account for the fact that about 10 percent of the civilian Loyalists going to Saint John preferred to hire passage on private ships.[12]

Six major fleets of government-provided vessels carried loyal exiles from New York to the mouth of the River St John in 1783. Five of these were composed primarily of refugees of the Bay of Fundy Adventurers. The sixth fleet was composed almost entirely of disbanding provincials and their families. The remainder of this chapter will sketch this massive process of evacuation. The sources on which it is based are those generated by various branches of the British military, in their attempt to exercise control of the enormous issue of rations and other forms of royal bounty to the exiles. In the aggregate their numbers confirm the well-established estimate of about 10 000 Loyalist arrivals in the St John Valley. Analysed with careful scepticism they also provide a sensitive statistical profile of the various Loyalist fleets.

THE SPRING FLEET

The spring fleet of Bay of Fundy Adventurers to Saint John was more fully under the direction of the New York Agency than the British military would subsequently allow. The agency, having decided to focus its efforts on the River St John, began preparations in February 1783 to send a fleet northward as soon as weather permitted. To promote the little-known St John region—and perhaps in a spirit of rivalry with the Port Roseway Associates—the agency publicized its venture in the press and by personal representations. One passenger in the spring fleet later recalled that the Rev. John Sayre so effectively combined his pastoral office with boosterism that he enrolled most of his congregation at Eaton's Neck, the future settlers of Kingston, Kings County.[13]

Embarkation of some thousands of refugee and provincial families, many with small children, and their baggage from all parts of the government-controlled New York region destined to four separate points in Nova Scotia was a massive undertaking. The loading process began as early as 1 April 1783 and lasted a good three weeks. With some vessels bound for Halifax, some for Shelburne, some for Annapolis, and some for Saint John there was great congestion and disarray as evacuees for each port were collected at the several loading points. To facilitate embarkation of those refugees under its direction the Port Roseway Association sensibly divided its party into manageable companies. The directors of the Association nominated the chief men in each unit to be its officers, the companies ratified this choice, and Sir Guy Carleton confirmed the structure by commissioning them militia officers.[14]

The New York Agency did not at first adopt this shrewd pattern of authority for the Fundy Adventurers. Its attempt at internal co-ordination consisted merely of sending one of its number, Agent James Peters, forward with the fleet and in designating leading refugees on each of its transport ships as a deputy-agent. Thus attorney Fyler Dibblee was so designated on the *Union*, Solomon Willard on the *Ariel*, Christopher Jenkins on the *Aurora*, Benjamin Anderson on the *Brothers*, Anthony Ferril on the *Camel*, George Leonard and William Tyng on the *Grand Duchess of Russia*, Jonathan Ketchum on the *Hope*, Ebenezer Foster and Richard Bowlby on the *Mars*, and Andrew Ritchie and Thomas Gilbert Jr on the *Spencer*. Fyler Dibblee styled himself as, "appointed to have the Care of the People in the Union." This suggests his role was simply to treat with the ship's captain on the refugees' behalf and to superintend internal distribution of the various sorts of donated provisions. Similarly Solomon Willard described himself as "Sup[erintenden]t [of] Refugees on board the Ariel."[15] Although refugees under the care of these deputy-agents were not divided into companies in the same sense as were the Port Roseway Associates,[16] it is likely that groups of old or new friends, drawn together at New York by common misfortune, arranged to take passage in the same vessel. If there were more detailed passenger lists for the spring fleet like the one for the future inhabitants of Kingston on the *Union*, one would undoubtedly see many patterns of acquaintance formed in New York reflected in the arrangement of farm lots in early New Brunswick.

Nearly fifty sail left Sandy Hook for Nova Scotia on Sunday, 27 May 1783, in a flotilla commodored by Captain Henry Mowat.[17] Eighteen transports of refugees were destined for Shelburne; a further eleven carried civilian exiles to the Bay of Fundy (ten to Saint John, one to Annapolis). Also destined for Saint John were a number of provincials and dependants, mostly of the King's American Dragoons. Several smaller vessels brought baggage, provisions, and horses. On the fourth day out the fleet was much scattered off the Nantucket Shoals, so that when the *Union* sailed into Saint John harbour 10 May she was alone. Two days later, however, most had caught up and the Loyalists were anxiously preparing for their first poignant encounter with the inhospitable Saint John landscape.

The Commissariat Department of the British military at New York reported that it victualled about 2400 civilians destined for the River St John in the spring fleet and that statistic has entered all the books.[18] In its typical gnat-straining methodology the military bureaucracy even produced an alphabetical register of the intending exiles.[19] Unfortunately for genealogists this remarkable document lists only those who *said* they would go to Saint John in the first fleet, not those who actually did so.

There is, however, a reliable way to ascertain how many refugees did embark for Saint John. Two sources are of great value: the record (Captains' Certificates) of the number of refugees on the various public transports from New York to Saint John,[20] and an alphabetical list (Victualling Return) of all refugee households provisioned through the Fort Howe commissariat at Saint John, commencing a fortnight after the fleet's arrival.[21]

The Captains' Certificates are accounting forms submitted by the commanders of the vessels hired by the military to carry refugees and provincials from New York to Nova Scotia. The captains were obliged to supply each passenger with seventy days' rations and, at the end of the voyage, to submit a statement showing how many Loyalists had been victualled in this manner. Accordingly the certificates, abstracted in table 1, yield a sensitive estimate of just how many of the 2400 refugees planning to go to the River St John in the spring fleet actually took ship.

Analysis of the Victualling Return for the spring fleet at Saint John yields a similar result. On 25 May 1783 the local commissary, William Tyng (who had himself arrived in the spring fleet), commenced the enormous task of issuing the royal bounty of provisions to his fellow exiles. In doing so Tyng produced a nominal list of the householders he was victualling. This invaluable enumeration indicates Tyng victualled 1682 souls, composed of 562 adult males, 300 adult females, 368 children aged ten and over, 342 children under ten, and 110 servants.[23] (Tyng later abstracted this return as 566, 300, 367, 343, and 110, totalling 1686, but did not account for the discrepancy.)

The variation between Tyng's total and that of the Captains' Certificates is relatively minor in view of the fact they measure different aspects of the migration: the former, those who took ship, the latter, those who remained at Saint John long enough to be victualled. A few refugees who made the voyage to Saint John must have surveyed the desolate scene and retreated southward on the ships that brought them. In other cases we know some Loyalists went upriver so soon after arrival that they missed Tyng's initial issue of provisions.[24] There are also two or three instances of households who may have arrived but to whom rations were not issued (perhaps because they had come over from Annapolis where they had drawn the previous fall). These considerations in the reconciliation of Tyng's account with those of the captains are recited to emphasize how remarkably precise one can be in discussing the composition of the spring fleet. The two sets of statistics show quite definitively that the Loyalist experiment on the River St John was begun by a band of about 1700 civilian refugees.

Also arriving in the first fleet from New York was a number of provincial troops and their dependants. They came (in the first instance) not as settlers but to strengthen the garrison of Royal Fencible Americans at Fort Howe. As a practical matter they spent the summer of 1783 engaged largely in land clearing and road building.

TABLE 1 REFUGEES IN THE SPRING FLEET

Ship	Number Aged Ten and Over	Number Under Ten	Total
Ariel	153	32	185
Aurora	173	39	212
Brothers	108	31	139
Camel	110	25	135
Grand Duchess of Russia	101	12	113
Hope	124	43	167
Mars	160	48	208
Sovereign	151	94	245
Spencer	107	32	139
Union[22]	128	36	164
	1315	392	1707

TABLE 2 *PROVINCIALS IN THE SPRING FLEET*

Unit	Men	Women	Children	Servants	Total
King's American Dragoons	295	52	34	40	421
2nd DeLancey's	4				4
2nd New Jersey Volunteers	21				21
Royal Fencible Americans	2				2
					448

A few of the military arrivals sailed from New York on the same ships as refugees but the great majority came on the *Lady's Adventure*. The statistics on this provincial migration, like those for the refugees, are best viewed comparatively. They indicate that approximately 450 soldiers and dependants went to Saint John in the spring fleet.[25]

THE JUNE FLEET

Preparation for a second major exodus to Nova Scotia commenced even as the spring fleet sailed from New York. The Agency for the Bay of Fundy Adventurers warned those of its number already in the northern colony that the new swarm of refugees would again be a large one, and that the greater number would again go to the River St John rather than Annapolis. To simplify control over this and future embarkations the agency—probably at the instance of the British military, which was footing the bill for the evacuation—organized those who applied for passage under its aegis along the plan already in use by the Port Roseway Associates. All Bay of Fundy Adventurers would now, as they came forward for the monthly embarkations, be divided into companies of thirty households, averaging 125 souls. (In the event the companies were much larger.) Each unit elected a captain, who appointed two lieutenants. All received commissions from the commander-in-chief as militia officers.[26] The essential terms of one such appointment are as follows:

> I do hereby constitute and appoint you to be Captain of a Company of Militia, No 18, destined for the District of St. John's in the Province of Nova-Scotia; you are therefore to take the said Company into your care and charge, and duly to exercise as well the Officers, as command them to obey you as their Captain. . . . This Commission [is] to be in force until Directions shall be given by the Governor of the Province of Nova-Scotia, for the Regulation of the Militia.[27]

This mode of organization was adopted for convenience in embarking a large number of refugees in an efficient manner and to ease the process of issuing and accounting for the various forms of royal bounty. Collaterally the company system provided the refugees with a popularly-elected leadership which would continue to be recognized in Nova Scotia. The militia companies were thus both a means of hierarchical control and a potential forum for articulation of grievances.

The second fleet was supposed to leave New York at the end of May 1783. Sarah Frost recorded in her journal that she, her family, and about 250 other refugees boarded the *Two Sisters* for Nova Scotia on Sunday, 25 May. There they impatiently remained for three tedious weeks while other vessels were readied. Not until 7 June did the agency give notice that it was "absolutely necessary" for members of the various militia companies to board by the following evening, but it proved a false alarm. Frost's frustration at the continued delay was relieved by teas, card playing, buying expeditions on shore, berry picking, and visiting friends. But overcrowding on the ship (there were seven families in the Frost cabin), confusion, constant howling by infants, oppressive heat, and nausea from riding at anchor were a slow torture for the refugees. "Our people seem cross and quarrelsome today," Frost wrote. Only on 16 June could she exclaim that they were "Off at last! We weighed anchor about half after five in the morning, with the wind North Nor'West, and it blows very fresh. . . . We have now got all our fleet together: We have thirteen Ships, two Brigs, one Frigate."[28]

The largest component of the June fleet was fifteen militia companies in ten transports bound for the River St John. One additional company of Bay of Fundy Adventurers was destined for Annapolis. (The fleet also included a company of the Port Roseway Associates, and several hundred of the paramilitary Westchester Loyalists bound for the Cumberland region.) Soon after their departure several smaller vessels also started for Saint John with officers seconded from provincial units. They were being transferred northward to man small craft for use in transporting Loyalists upriver. The June fleet made a general landing on 5 July.

Various branches of the British military bureaucracy generated at least six different statistics on the number of exiles intending to leave New York for Saint John in the June fleet, or the number sailing on the public transports, or the number landing. Most are without value. They are based on the same false assumption that invalidates most statistical data for the spring fleet: that the number of refugees who said they were going to Saint John was the same as the number who subsequently took ship. The estimate of "between 1500 and 1600 passengers" in E.C. Wright's *Loyalists of New Brunswick* is of this character.[29] There are, however, two sources of statistical information which, as for the spring fleet, are reasonably reliable: the surviving Captains' Certificates and William Tyng's nominal list of those victualled from the June fleet.[30]

It will be noted that Tyng's figures in table 3, while consistent with, are often slightly higher than those on the corresponding Captain's Certificate. While neither record, especially a return copied out in Tyng's hard-pressed commissariat office, can be thought perfectly exact, such differences as do exist will be due largely to the fact that some refugees in each company were now endeavouring to go to Saint John in private vessels.[34] Those who arrived privately before Tyng commenced victualling the June fleet would presumably show up on his provision list but not, of course, on a certificate from a captain of one of the public transports. Accepting, then, the general accuracy of Tyng's figure of 1169, the total of arrivals with the June fleet was less than three-quarters of the number that has generally been supposed.

	Militia Company	Ship	Captains' Certificates	Victualling Return
1	Sylvanus Whitney	*Two Sisters*	} 193[31]	130
2	Joseph Gorham	*Two Sisters*		94
3	Henry Thomas	*Hopewell*		105
4	John Forrester	*Symmetry*		147
6	Thomas Elms	*Generous Friends*		49
8	John Cock	*Thames*		92
9	Joseph Clark	*Bridgewater*	40	39
10	James Hayt	*Bridgewater*	29	40
11	Thomas Welsh	*Amity's Production*		62
12	Oliver Bourdett	*Tartar*		77
13	Asher Dunham	*Duchess of Gordon*	63	63
18	Abiathar Camp	*Duchess of Gordon*	26	34
20	Christopher Benson	*Bridgewater*	41	46
21	Peter Berton	*Littledale*		81
23	Joseph Forrester	*Bridgewater*	44	47
	Seconded Officers	various[32]		58
	miscellaneous			5
				1169[33]

TABLE 3 REFUGEES AND PROVINCIALS IN THE JUNE FLEET

THE JULY FLEET

The third major wave of Loyalists destined for the River St John took ship at the end of June, departing New York about 8 July 1783. Although the size of the July fleet was comparatively small, it patterned the June exodus in that almost all the companies it embraced went to Saint John rather than Annapolis or Shelburne. The first ship to reach port, the *Ann*, arrived by 24 July, and the others soon followed.[35]

Many statistics on the size of the July fleet to Saint John might be cited, but most are inflated for the same reason most statistics on earlier fleets are wide of the mark. Recognizing how inexact previous methods of accounting had been, the military now began to have refugee companies mustered on board their transports soon before departure. (The mustering was done, it would seem, by members of the New York Agency rather than the military.) But because these embarkation returns were made when there was still time for refugees to embark and disembark and because they are subject to other variables difficult to eliminate consistently for comparative purposes, it is more convenient to gauge the size of the July fleet with reference to ship Captains' Certificates and Commissary Tyng's victualling data (see table 4).[36]

There is notably less consistency between these two prime sources than was the case for the May and June fleets. One can suggest several reasons for this. Tyng's figures are higher than many corresponding Captains' Certificates because they include an ever increasing number of arrivals in private vessels.[38] Tyng's figures will also occasionally be higher because

T A B L E   4   *R E F U G E E S ,   P R O V I N C I A L S ,   A N D   O T H E R S*
IN THE JULY FLEET

Militia Company	Ship	Captains' Certificates	Victualling Return
5 Richard Hill	*Elizabeth*	13	
7 Peter Huggeford	*Commerce*	112	} 211
	Montague	105	
11 Thomas Welsh	*Grace*	2	
14 Thomas Huggeford	*Three Sisters*	72	38
15 William Wright	*William*	85	127
16 John Mersereau[37]	*Lord Townsend*		56
17 Donald Drummond	*Joseph*	43	47
19 William Perrine	*Aurora*	63	43
21 Peter Berton	*Commerce*	8	
22 Nathaniel Horton	*Elizabeth*	70	81
24 John Menzies	*Sovereign*	44	44
28 Robert Chillas	*Ann*	81	103
Jacob Cook[37]	*Lord Townsend*		60
31 John Oblenis	*Aurora*	52	53
32 William Olive	*Three Sisters*	38	} 39
	Elizabeth	3	
34 Richard Squires	*Grace*	18	19
35 Daniel Fowler	*Grace*	34	36
King's American Regiment			10
1st NJ Volunteers	*Commerce*	10	7
Adjutant-General's Department	*Elizabeth*	1	
Lt.-Col. Thomas Rogers	*Aurora*	14	_15_
			989

some transports dropped passengers at Annapolis or the Passamaquoddy islands; in the case of Annapolis this was rather common. Theoretically this ought to be evidenced in Captains' Certificates but one cannot be sure it always was. In the context of the July fleet one notes that although Captain Hill's company may have arrived at Saint John it was likely carried across the Bay of Fundy without being victualled. Although this variety of circumstances somewhat inhibits conviction one may take Tyng's victualling account of a thousand arrivals as fundamentally accurate.

THE AUGUST FLEET

The fourth fleet from New York to the River St John set sail about 4 August 1783. The first of its number arrived in port ten days later. Among the passengers was the Rev. John Sayre, secretary to and *de facto* head of the Bay of Fundy Adventurers' New York Agency.

After producing his July nominal victualling return Tyng had warned his superiors he was too busy to continue the practice. Consequently the single most valuable source of statistics for the first three Loyalist fleets is unavailable for the last three. One is reduced to the surviving Captains'

TABLE 5   REFUGEES AND PROVINCIALS IN THE AUGUST FLEET

	Militia Company	Ship	Captains' Certificates or DeLancey
30	Joseph Cooper	*Peggy*	58
33	Peter Grim	*Spencer*	87
		Sally	22
36	William Grey	*Fishburn*	130
37	William Walker	*Polly* to *Peggy*	53
40	Robert Campbell	*Sally*	77
41	John Cluett	*Mary*	77
	Nathaniel Chandler[40]	*Grand Duchess of Russia*	12 (+ 20?)
	King's American Dragoons	*Sally*	18

Certificates supplemented by a set of statistics produced by Oliver DeLancey of the British military bureaucracy showing the number shipped to Saint John at public expense.[39] This latter source, which for the earlier fleets was grossly inflated, is now in such agreement with the Captains' Certificates that it had evidently come to be based on musters taken on board the transports just before they left New York (see table 5).

The *Clinton* arrived at Saint John on 30 August, so soon after the fourth fleet that it is convenient to notice it in this context. Its human cargo was four companies of free black refugees. We have only a general idea of their number. Oliver DeLancey reported that the ship was thought to carry 253 free blacks, but this included those destined to both Annapolis and Saint John. On the other hand it is also known that by the spring of 1784 the five (one more had arrived) black companies mustered only about 175 souls. Probably, then, the number of arrivals in August 1783 was closer to the lower figure than the higher.

Another uncertainty in connection with the August fleet is the role of the brig *Hesperus*. DeLancey lists it as carrying eighty-three passengers for the River St John and Commissary Tyng's correspondence indicates that it did, indeed, arrive.[41] But there is no indication whether it left passengers or who they were. In the whole story of the evacuation to Saint John this is one of the few instances where such elementary data are wholly lacking. Despite uncertainty over the *Hesperus* and the *Clinton* it is safe to suppose that the August fleet brought in the order of 800 Loyalists to the River St John.

THE FALL FLEET

When it became plain, late in 1782, that many Loyalists in and around New York would not be suffered to be reconciled with the victorious patriots, the provincial military, like the refugees, formed an organization to spy out land in Nova Scotia. One of their agents, Edward Winslow Jr, went forward to Annapolis with the spring fleet, later inspecting the St John more than once. The agents seem to have accomplished little, however, perhaps because the provincials' fortunes depended closely on the disposition of their superiors in the British military.

Although Sir Guy Carleton, the commander-in-chief, had contemplated a large exodus of provincials to Nova Scotia as early as April 1783, it was 17 August before he gave them permission to evacuate and 27 September when they actually arrived on the River St John. This was too late in the season for them to get to their promised land (even had detailed surveys been made) or to erect substantial shelters against the approaching winter. The provincials may have been kept at New York in part to safeguard its security and internal order. But it is more likely that Carleton so delayed their evacuation because, with an acute shortage of transports, he thought it better to give priority to removal of the less manageable civilian Loyalists.

A substantial portion of two provincial units was already on the St John: a detachment of the Royal Fencible Americans had garrisoned Fort Howe for some years, and most of the King's American Dragoons had gone to Saint John in the spring fleet. Now it was intended to send to the river all those in major British American units remaining at New York who wished to accept the King's offer of land grants, remitted quit rents, a bounty of provisions, and retention of their arms.[42] The relative few (so late in the season) who wished to stay behind and come later were to be accommodated in the civilian militia companies. In addition to the units sailing from New York, the King's Orange Rangers stationed in peninsular Nova Scotia were also ordered to Saint John (Quaco) to be disbanded and settled. The offer of land and bounty was also extended to those of the regular army who wished to settle in Nova Scotia, but none went to Saint John in the September embarkation.[43]

Since the British military bureaucracy produced such a plenitude of (generally inaccurate) statistics on the refugee exodus to Saint John it is surprising that relatively few are to be found on the provincial evacuation. Table 6 gives a statistical profile of the provincials from three perspectives: DeLancey's account of the number embarking at New York, Captains' Certificates of the number victualled on the journey, and Commissary Tyng's account of the number victualled on arrival.[44]

Despite their disparate appearance these various totals are in general agreement. The figure shown for Captains' Certificates appears anomalous only because at least three are missing: for the *Martha* (which sank en route, carrying families of the Maryland Loyalists and the 2nd DeLancey's[46]), for the *Esther* (carrying part of the 3rd New Jersey Volunteers and probably some of other units) and for whatever ship(s) carried the Queen's Rangers and part of the Prince of Wales' American Regiment. As well, the Captains' Certificates for that part of the King's American Regiment on the *William* and for the 3rd New Jersey Volunteers on the *Ranger* (and perhaps for the 2nd DeLancey's on the *Pallisar*) underestimate the number actually carried in those units by including only one-half of the children aged under ten. Moreover, the great majority of the King's American Dragoons will not be on a Captain's Certificate (or on the DeLancey list) because that unit was already on the river. A less substantial reason why Captains' Certificates will show less than Tyng's figures is that, as it was subsequently discovered, many officers in the provincial corps drew provisions for servants who did not exist, and all ranks claimed for family members who had not yet arrived.[47] With these glosses on the Captains' Certificates one can say

TABLE 6   PROVINCIALS IN THE FALL FLEET

Unit	Ship	DeLancey	Captains' Certificates	Tyng
American Legion	*Elizabeth*	140	140	112
1st DeLancey's	*Sovereign*	266	199	243
2nd DeLancey's	*Pallisar*	334	162	215
Guides and Pioneers	*Ann*	203	204	204
King's American Dragoons	*Apollo*	17	7	316
King's American Regiment	*William*	279	161	345
	King George		140	
Loyal American Regiment	*Apollo*	263	187	289
	Ann		74	
Maryland Loyalists	*Martha*	122		72
1st NJ Volunteers	*Duke of Richmond*	330	342	371
2nd NJ Volunteers	*Duke of Richmond*	272	281	298
3rd NJ Volunteers	*Commerce*	490	153	189
	Elizabeth		1	
3rd NY Volunteers	*Ranger*	186	199	217
North Carolina Volunteers		25		
1st Pennsylvania Loyalists	*Commerce*	80	75	73
Prince of Wales'				
American Regiment	*Montague*	330	168	355
	Elizabeth		78	
Queen's Rangers		399		397
Royal Garrison Battalion	*King George*	15	16	
Unattributable passengers	*Martha*[45]		[70]	
		3751	2657	3696

with some confidence that about 3050 British American troops and dependants arrived at Saint John in the September fleet. There they met 400 King's
American Dragoons, 160 Royal Fencible Americans, and about 40 in miscellaneous provincial units already on the river. They would soon be augmented by the arrival from Halifax of the King's Orange Rangers.[48]

A number of refugees also sailed from New York to Saint John in
September although not, it would seem, as part of the provincial fleet. The
transport *Camel* brought companies of Baptists, Quakers, and a few others,
totalling 260 souls, into Saint John harbour at mid-month; but only two of
the religious and three ordinary refugees disembarked. The others took on
three months' provisions and sailed to Beaver Harbour.[49]

With the *Camel* came the transport *Cyrus*. According to its embarkation
muster of 29 August it was supposed to carry seventy-five refugees in
Militia Company 43 (Captain James Dickinson's) and sixty-five of Militia
Company 44 (Captain Nathaniel Merritt's). Evidently more boarded after
the muster, however, as the ship's muster book (one of the few available for
Loyalist transports) shows that on 19 September the *Cyrus* discharged 195
souls at Saint John. Since all are named there is no possibility of error.[50]

The third transport known to have brought refugees in September was
the *Eagle* (*L'Aigle*). According to DeLancey's embarkation profile it was to
carry 240 members of Captain John Smith's Militia Company, a statistic
which exactly accords with the relevant Captain's Certificate.[51]

THE OCTOBER FLEET

The final Loyalist fleet from New York arrived on the River St John about 17 October. Eight ships carried refugees in eleven militia companies. The statistics in table 7 are based on musters on board the named ships taken between 29 September and 7 October.[52] (They largely accord with statistics on the refugee exodus compiled by the British military bureaucracy except where the latter are incomplete.[53]) Table 8 provides statistics on the number of regular army soldiers arriving at Saint John to accept the British invitation to become settlers in Nova Scotia.[54]

TABLE 7 REFUGEES IN THE OCTOBER FLEET

Militia Company	Ship	Embarkation Muster
40 Robert Campbell	*John & Jane*	43 +?
45 John Ford	*Mary*	106
46 James Thorne	*John & Jane*	134
47 Samuel Dickinson	*Mercury*	147
48 Thomas Spragg	*Jason*	76
49 Thomas Wooley	*Nancy*	121
50 Thomas Fairchild	*Neptune*	36
51 Joseph Ferris	*Neptune*	61
52 William Lewis	*Neptune*	51
53 Bartholomew Crannell	*Alexander*	116
54 John Wetmore	*Sally*	144
		1035 +?

TABLE 8 BRITISH AND GERMAN REGULARS IN THE OCTOBER FLEET

Unit	Ship	Number
7th Regiment	*John & Jane*	8
17th Regiment	*John & Jane*	18
37th Regiment	*John & Jane*	9
38th Regiment	*John & Jane*	20
	Nancy	5
40th Regiment	*Nancy*	45
	Neptune	24
42nd Regiment	*Mercury*	50
	Jason	48
Regiment du Corps	*Nancy*	4
		231

FURTHER ARRIVALS

Royal forces finally quit New York on 25 November 1783. Although the October fleet was the last large-scale evacuation to the River St John there were several small accessions of Loyalists lasting into 1784. Beginning on 14 December, for example, the *Camel* was back at Saint John with a cargo of latecomers. Thirteen souls were landed on that date. Mercifully the others were allowed to remain on board throughout the winter. It was not until early March that the *Camel* deposited another thirty-one passengers at Saint John and the remaining sixty-eight at various points in Passamaquoddy.[55]

Among other late arrivals were thirteen attached to Captain John Wetmore's Militia Company (54). Some of these had made it as far as Campobello by 26 January 1784, where they remained on this first outpost of British government until they could move on to Saint John in the spring.[56]

Another late accession was a party of sixteen regulars connected with the 42nd Regiment, evidently forwarded from Halifax.[57] It was at this time also that about 180 of the King's Orange Rangers finally arrived at Quaco, near the river's mouth. In the spring of 1784 a further 124 recent civilian arrivals were added to the Fort Howe victualling lists.[58]

DEPARTURES

In surveying the number of refugees and provincials known to have arrived at Saint John in the year commencing 10 May 1783 one must also be aware that some quickly left. Among the data on Commissary F.W. Hecht's victualling returns for the spring and early summer of 1784 are a miscellany of references to Loyalists said to have departed the colony: some on business, some to fetch their families, some to pass the winter in a more temperate climate. Most never returned.

We know of a few refugees who departed Saint John almost immediately after arrival. On 31 July 1783 Commissary Tyng provided his superior with a list of nine heads of household who had just returned to New York on public transports.[59] They assigned an interesting variety of reasons.

Benjamin Robson, 6 in family, all except one son going on pretense of purchasing small vessels, to return again soon

James Morrel returning for his family, leaves two servants

Nicholas Howell returning for his family; has built a small house

Robert Tongate and wife returning as they say to collect small debts, but the truth is he is turned out of the society for stealing from some persons in Captain Elm's company; he belongs to that company

Richard Penny, ten in family, returns because he cannot support his family through the winter, has drawn no provisions, says he has a house building in the town at St. Johns

Benjamin Haywood returns on account of getting no employ—intends to come back in the spring

Theodorick Bland, for trade

Capt'n [George] Bennison, for trade—has a good character

Miss Katy Hawser, returns (as she says) for a husband

There is no way to estimate how many Loyalists returned to the old colonies in the 1780s, or when the return migration reached its peak. Here is how one Saint John Loyalist explained the exodus to a London correspondent in 1787.

The report you mention of all the Refugees going back as fast as they get [Loyalist Claim] compensation is groundless and false. Many its true have gone back to the States, some from one cause, some from another; but generally speaking those that have gone back were a set of poor wretches that had they staid here must have been supported by the publick at least every winter. Very few people of any consequence have left us.[60]

These remarks are too defensive to be very reassuring; but the very obscurity of the "poor wretches" who slipped back into the new republic means we are unlikely ever to have more than this general impression of the exodus from the St John Valley in the 1780s.

NOTES

1. Initially the agents were: for the Bergen County, NJ, Loyalists—Samuel Seabury, Thomas Ward, William Harding, George Harding, Frederick Hauser, and Joshua Pell; for those of Queens County—Joshua Chandler and Samuel Seabury; and for those at Lloyd's Neck—Benjamin Thompson, Edward Winslow, S.S. Blowers, John Sayre, Amos Botsford, and John Mosley. Membership fluctuated. Among the additions were James Peters, Abijah Willard, John Wardel, and Joshua Upham.

2. The text of the "Articles of Settlement" is printed in W.O. Raymond, *The River St John* (Saint John, 1910), 507–08; Seabury to Botsford et al., 24 Jan. 1783: Botsford Papers, Public Archives of Canada (hereafter PAC).

3. Raymond, *River St John*, 508.

4. I have seen no definitive statistics for this migration. The rector of Annapolis noted this fleet as numbering about 500: William Bartlet, *The Frontier Missionary: A Memoir of the Life of the Rev. Jacob Bailey* (Boston, 1853), 193. The New York Agency requested clothing for 437 (120 men, 83 women, 152 "grown children," 82 "small children"): Upham to Coffin, 27 Sept. 178, WO60/27. Another document suggests that 106 intended to go on the *Three Friends*, 82 on the *William*, 76 on the *Happy Couple*, and 70 on the *Escape*: Upham, "Return of Persons to be victualled for Nova Scotia," 26 Sept. 1782, WO60/32 pt. 2.

5. Botsford et al. to NY Agency, 13 Jan. 1783, quoted in Beamish Murdoch, *A History of Nova-Scotia* (Halifax, 1867), 3: 13–15.

6. Seabury and Sayre to Botsford et al., 23 April 1783, Botsford Papers, PAC. The River St John was being given unfavourable publicity at the same time: Seabury and Peters to Botsford et al., 24 Jan. 1783, Botsford Papers, PAC.

7. Seabury and Peters to Botsford et al., 24 Jan. 1783, Botsford Papers, PAC.

8. General Orders, British Headquarters, New York, 18 April 1783, WO28/9. The stringent one-year requirement was intended to confine the considerable benefits offered evacuees to bona fide Loyalists and to deny them to mere speculators who might flock in from the country to seize the opportunity of bettering their condition in a new land.

9. James Walker, *The Black Loyalists* (New York, 1976), 10–12. Loyalists were, of course, allowed to embark with their own slaves. Walker estimates that 10 percent of Maritime Loyalists were black.

10. General Orders, British Headquarters, New York, WO28/9.

11. Oscar Barck, *New York City During the War for Independence* (New York, 1931), 214.

12. There is, however, considerable evidence that some cattle and horses of refugees and provincials were shipped to Nova Scotia.
    The only account I have found of effects shipped by a Loyalist family in public transportation states that the Ingraham family (headed by a provincial rather than a refugee) transported 5 wagon loads of baggage to Saint John, including 20 bushels of wheat, tubs of butter and pickles, and "a good store of potatoes." They killed their cow just before departure. "Narrative of Hannah Ingraham" in *The Price of Loyalty: Tory Writings from the Revolutionary Era*, ed. Catherine Crary (New York, 1973), 401.

13. W.O. Raymond, ed., *Kingston and the Loyalists of the "Spring Fleet" of 1783* (Saint John, 1889), 12.

14. Joseph Durfee et al. to Watson, 27 March 1783, WO60/33 pt. 2.

15. Captain's Certificate, WO60/23 pt. 1; Captain's Certificate, WO60/33 pt. 1.

16. There is only one indication that refugees in the spring fleet to Saint John were divided into companies. Commissary William Tyng's initial victualling return at Fort Howe refers to the provisioning of "Loyalists in 25 companies." Whatever this may mean, the abundant source material on the first fleet nowhere else hints of any subdivision of the refugees into companies analogous to the militia companies that were to follow in subsequent fleets. So lamentably free from close organization were the refugees of the spring fleet that Tyng was moved to protest "the irregular manner in which they were put on board the ships, (having no captains to give an account or return of them)": Tyng, "Abstract of the number of Men, Women and Children Victual'd from . . . Fort Howe between 25th May and the 24th June 1783," WO60/33 pt. 2; Tyng to Watson, 4 July 1783, WO60/33 pt. 1.

17. I use the departure date given two weeks after the event by James Peters (Peters to Botsford and Hauser, 12 May 1783, Botsford Papers, PAC) rather than the 26 May date recorded by Walter Bates late in his life: Raymond, *Kingston and the Loyalists*, 13.

18. Various officials at the British Military Headquarters at New York put into circulation three similar figures as to the number of refugees taking ship for Saint John: 2384, 2434, and 2437. Probably the first of these was the most official: Oliver DeLancey, "Return of Loyalists and Troops sailed for the undermentioned Places," 10 Oct. 1783, WO60.27.

19. "Return of the Bay of Fundy Adventurers, for Cloathing &ca," WO60/33 pt. 2.

20. The Captains' Certificates are in WO60/22, WO60/23 pts. 1 and 2, WO60/25 pts. 1 and 2, WO60/32 pt. 2, and WO60/33 pt. 1. It will be noted that these statistics relate only to refugees in the spring fleet; the provincials are discussed separately.

21. Tyng, "Return of Loyalists who have drawn provisions from his Majesty's stores at Fort Howe from 25th May to 24th June 1783," WO60/33 pt. 1.

22. This account of the passengers of the *Union* differs substantially from the total shown on the muster printed in Raymond, *Kingston and the Loyalists*, 14. While this printed passenger list impliedly shows 209 souls on board on 16 April ready to sail to the River St John, there were actually only 164 passengers when the transport finally lifted anchor 9 days later. Possibly the others disembarked in

the interim, but the experience of working with dozens of similar lists suggests the "missing" refugees had not boarded at all.

23. For clarity of exposition the practical complexity of Tyng's documentation has been somewhat simplified. A minor arithmetical error has been corrected and a few arrivals in the spring fleet whom Tyng (for technical reasons) included only in his second victualling return have been treated as though they were on the first.

24. Tyng to Watson, 4 July 1783, WO/33 pt. 1. Weighted against this, however, would be the unknown number of refugees (led, it would seem, by Andrew Ritchie) who, having apparently been victualled at Saint John, were carried over to Annapolis on the *Spencer*: Captain's Certificate, WO60/33 pt. 1.

25. At first it was intended to send the King's American Dragoons to Cumberland but none seems to have reached there.

The principal statistical source for this account is Tyng, "Abstract of Provisions . . . Issued from His Majesty's Stores at Fort Howe between the 25th May & the 24th June 1783," WO60/33 pt. 1. Other sources are Captains' Certificates for the *Ariel*, *Mars*, and *Sovereign*, the "Embarkation Return of Troops &c going from New York to Nova Scotia," 23 April 1783, CO5/109 and Oliver DeLancey, "Return of Loyalists and Troops sailed for the undermentioned Places," 10 Oct. 1783, WO60/27. William Tyng himself was technically another military arrival.

Those pursuing these references should be aware that, in general, only 8 dependent women for every 100 soldiers were allowed victuals by the British military. In fact, however, the actual number of women with the King's American Dragoons was allowed to draw victuals at Saint John, but only by special permission: DeLancey to Watson, 18 April 1783, WO60/27. This may account for some of the discrepancies between the number of provincials and dependants projected in New York as going forward to Saint John in the spring fleet and the (larger) number actually provisioned by William Tyng. There may be an analagous reason for the discrepancies among the various statistical reports as to the number of servants attached to the provincials.

26. Sayre to "Gentlemen," 2 May 1783; Sayre to Botsford et al., 25 May 1783, Botsford Papers, PAC.

27. 1 June 1783, in Camp to Treasury, 31 March 1788, T1/655.

28. Frost journal, W.O. Raymond Transcript Book 1, New Brunswick Museum (hereafter NBM). Raymond's well-known edition of the Frost journal in *Kingston and the Loyalists*, 29–32, is a remarkable instance of myth making. Whole sentences are invented. Most genuine passages have been amended to turn Frost into one of those women "delicately reared" who still dominate the public's image of the Loyalists. In apology for Raymond it will be noted that *Kingston and the Loyalists* (1889) was his first publication. Twenty-one years later when he printed part of the journal in *River St John* (1910) he silently corrected some of the infidelities.

29. Wright, *The Loyalists of New Brunswick* (Moncton, 1955), 78. With three unexplained changes Wright's statistics are from George Robertson, "A List of Transports Appointed to Receive Refugees going to Nova Scotia from New York in June 1783 of which Lieut. George Robertson had the Direction as Agent," nd, AD49/9.

30. These Captains' Certificates are in WO60/22 and WO60/25 pt. 2. Tyng's "List of Associated Loyalists victualed from his Majesty's Stores at Fort Howe from 25 June to 24th July 1783" is in WO60/33 pt. 2.

31. The Captain's Certificate for the *Two Sisters* actually attributes the 142 adults and 51 children entirely to Sylvanus Whitney's Militia Company. It is probable, however, that the figure also includes passengers in Joseph Gorham's Company,

which also travelled on the *Two Sisters* but is not mentioned on the Certificate. A total of 193 for Whitney's Company alone would be implausibly high.

32. The Seconded Officers and their dependants came in the *Three Friends*, *Phebe*, *Kingfisher*, *Ann*, and *Samuel*: "Return of Seconded officers & their families, who embark on board the following Vessels for Saint John's," 23 June 1783, WO60/32 pt. 1.

   The *Thetis* and the *Nicholas and Jane* in the same fleet carried refugees of the Westchester Loyalists to Cumberland. The former landed 195 souls there in mid-July. The total of Westchester Loyalists embarked at New York was about 500, but one or more were landed at Annapolis. There is no evidence that either of these transports called at Saint John.

33. Tyng's victualling return also includes 211 of Dr Peter Huggeford's Company (7), commencing on 3 July, as if they had arrived in the second fleet. Other evidence puts it beyond doubt that no significant part of Huggeford's Company arrived before the last week of July. The most plausible explanation for Tyng's conduct is that Huggeford's Company had been inadequately victualled on the voyage from New York and was being retrospectively compensated.

34. While the available statistics for those who said they would leave New York in private vessels are no more reliable than for those who said they would go in public transports, the relevant numbers ("Return of the Number of Persons who follow the Fleet in Private Vessels," nd, WO60/33 pt. 2) show that in many cases one-third and more of a refugee militia company contemplated making the voyage northward by private arrangement at their own expense.

35. Tyng to Watson, 24 July 1783, WO60/33 pt. 1.

36. The Captains' Certificates are in WO60/22, WO60/23 pts. 1 and 2, WO60/25 pt. 1 and WO60/33 pts. 1 and 2. The Tyng data on the refugees come from his nominal "List of Associated Loyalists victualed from His Majestys Stores at Fort Howe from the 25th of July and the 24th of August 1783," WO60/33 pt. 1. Tyng's data on Peter Huggeford's Company come from his previous victualling return. The relevant figures in Wright, *Loyalists of New Brunswick*, 80, are, with a few unexplained deviations, from Captains' Certificates.

37. The Captain's Certificate for the Lord Townsend shows that the equivalent of 47 adults were victualled in John Mersereau's Company and 50 adults in Jacob Cook's. The figures are, however, somewhat short of the actual number transported in these companies because they take into account only one-half of the number of children aged under 10.

38. Those who came in private vessels were not victualled by Tyng immediately on their arrival but only when their militia company next drew provisions. Only in this way could Tyng keep his work manageable and ensure that those who arrived privately were bona fide refugees. This helps guarantee that Tyng's overall victualling statistics include virtually all refugees, not merely those who arrived in public transportation.

39. The Captains' Certificates are in WO60/22, WO60/23 pts. 1 and 2, and WO60/32 pt. 1. The DeLancey figures are from his "Return of Loyalists and Troops sailed for the undermentioned Places," 10 Oct. 1783, WO60/27.

40. Chandler's was one of the (unnumbered) Annapolis companies. The statistics represented here are for the Rev. John Sayre and his party who journied with the majority of Chandler's people to Annapolis before being carried across to Saint John.

41. Tyng to Watson, 26 Aug. 1783, WO60/33, pt. 1.

42. Although all the major provincial units at New York were originally destined for Saint John, the British Legion and the South Carolina Loyalists went elsewhere and 36 of the 1st New Jersey Volunteers said they were going to Annapolis on the *Olive Branch*.

43. It is possible that the 4th Battalion of the 60th Regiment was first intended to go to Saint John, but the *Aurora* took it to Halifax.

44. DeLancey, "Return of Loyalists and Troops sailed for the undermentioned Places," 10 Oct. 1783, WO60/27; Captains' Certificates in WO60/22, WO60/23 pts. 1 and 2, and WO60/32 pt. 1. The statistics I have presumed to be Tyng's are printed in *RWP*, 245. Due to the scattered nature of the provincial settlements, the victualling statistics in use before Deputy-Commissary Knox's massive revision were likely the ones originally obtained at Saint John in the fall of 1783.

It may be noted that the first row of figures for each unit in the comparative table printed in Wright, *Loyalists of New Brunswick*, 247–49, is from an early version of the DeLancey statistics and that the second row reproduces what I have called the Tyng statistics.

45. In fact about 70 of the *Martha's* unfortunate passengers did survive to reach Saint John, but one cannot distribute them as between the two provincial units on board: Tyng to Watson, 11 Oct. 1783, WO60/33 pt. 1. See also *Halifax Gazette*, 28 Oct. 1783.

46. The *Martha* sank near Yarmouth amid scenes of great anguish and inhumanity. W.O. Raymond made an official account of the sinking available in *RWP*, 137–38. Less well-known is the narrative of Elizabeth Woodward, wife of a soldier in the Maryland Loyalists. "[S]he embarked on board a transport, with part of [2nd] DeLancey's and Chalmer's troops [Maryland Loyalists], was shipwrecked on Seal Island, in the Bay of Fundy, when near three hundred men, and numbers of women and children were lost—that she suffered unparalleled hardships, being pregnant, and with a child in her arms, remained three days on the wreck, was taken up with her husband and child by fishermen, off Marble Head, and shortly after being landed, delivered of three sons." (Petition of Elizabeth Hopkins, 12 April 1816, in *Carleton Sentinel*, 17 Sept. 1850.)

47. Knox to Campbell, 3 Nov. 1784; *RWP*, 243.

48. The figures last given are based on Tyng's "Abstract of the number of Men, Women and Children Victualed at Fort Howe between the 25th of July and the 24th of August 1783," WO60/33 pt. 1 (which does not include servants) and (for the King's Orange Rangers) on Roger Johnson, "Abstract of Provisions . . . Issued from His Majestys Storehouses in Halifax . . . from the 8th October to the 17th December 1783," WO60/25 pt. 1. It does not include servants.

49. Camel Muster Book: AD36/9430; Tyng to Watson, 18 Sept. 1783, WO60/32 pt. 1.

50. "Return of Captain James Dickinson's Company of Loyalists actually embarked on board the Cyrus armed Ship bound for St. Johns River in Nova Scotia," 29 Aug. 1783, WO60/33 pt. 2; ibid for Captain Nathaniel Merritt's Company; Cyrus Muster Book, AD10.

51. DeLancey, "Return of Loyalists and Troops sailed for the undermentioned Places," 10 Oct. 1783, WO60/27; Captain's Certificate, WO60/33 pt. 1.

No one, including the victualling authorities at Fort Howe, seems to have known the number of John Smith's Militia Company. Possibly it was the last company created and did not receive one. Wright, *Loyalists of New Brunswick*, 247, gives Smith's Company number as 40, but this is mistaken.

52. WO60/32 pt. 2. A few of the number in James Thorne's company shown on the *John & Jane* may have come on other ships.

53. DeLancey, "Return of Loyalists and Troops sailed for the undermentioned Places," 10 Oct. 1783, WO60/27.

54. General Orders, British Headquarters, New York, 26 Sept. 1783, WO28/9.

55. Camel Muster Book, AD36/9430.

56. Victualling returns of Jacob Bell et al. and John White et al., 28 April 1784, T1/609.

57. Roger Johnson, "Abstract of Provisions . . . Issued from His Majesty's Storehouses in Halifax . . . from the 8th October to the 17th December 1783," WO60/25 pt. 1. This same source also shows the following units going from Halifax.

To Passamaquoddy

84th Regiment and other corps	60
Royal Fencible Americans	46
South Carolina Regiment	2
Sundry Corps	14
King's Orange Rangers	21
Royal Nova Scotia Volunteers	4

To Beaver Harbour

Royal Nova Scotia Volunteers	105

58. Knox to Campbell, 24 June 1784, *RWP*, 212.

59. Tyng to Watson, 31 July 1783, WO60/33 pt. 1.

60. Jarvis to Jarvis, 25 Oct. 1787, Jarvis Transcripts, NBM. On 22 December 1784 the *New Jersey Gazette* reported the recent arrival of 17 Loyalist families from "Nova Scotia." On 24 March 1785 it reported 30 recent arrivals at New York. On 12 October 1785 it noted that New Jersey "swarms" with returned Loyalists. See Henry Onderdonk, *Revolutionary Incidents in Queens County* (New York, 1846), 256.

PEOPLING GLENGARRY COUNTY: THE SCOTTISH ORIGINS OF A CANADIAN COMMUNITY⬦

MARIANNE McLEAN

o

INTRODUCTION

A generation ago, American historian Mildred Campbell commented that very little was actually known of the identity of the emigrants to colonial America, and the same point can be made concerning the people who settled in Upper Canada. Campbell's own work signalled the blossoming of considerable interest in the British origins of colonial American immigrants.[1] Yet in 1973, two American historians could still complain of the dearth of studies which began "with the English origins of the migrants" and followed "them through their experience in the New World." Such an approach was of interest since "divisions within the colonies may have owed much to divergences between the various regions of the mother country."[2] While Canadian historians have analysed the European background of late nineteenth and early twentieth century immigrants, little attention has been paid to the origins of those who arrived before Confederation.[3] This paper examines in detail the Scottish origins of the migrants who settled one Upper Canadian county between 1784 and 1815.

Superficially, the Scottish Highlanders who came to Glengarry County are among the best-known settlers of Upper Canada. One of their religious leaders, Bishop Alexander Macdonnell, was a brilliant polemicist who never failed to sing the praises of the loyal Glengarrians to colonial and imperial officials. The comments of army officers and travellers who passed

⬦ Canadian Historical Association *Historical Papers* (1982): 156–72. Reprinted with the permission of the Canadian Historical Association.

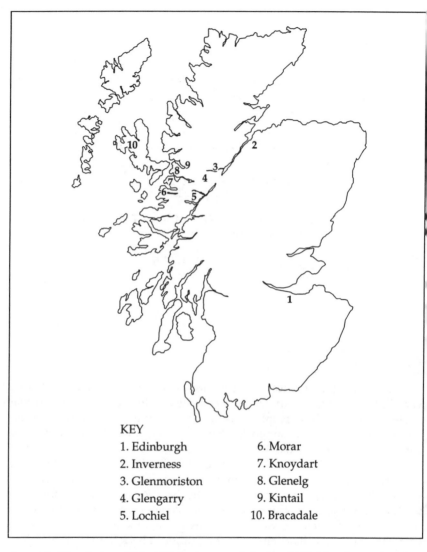

KEY

1. Edinburgh
2. Inverness
3. Glenmoriston
4. Glengarry
5. Lochiel

6. Morar
7. Knoydart
8. Glenelg
9. Kintail
10. Bracadale

through Glengarry reinforced the image of the loyal Highlander and added to it that of the backward farmer.[4] Canadian historians writing about Highland emigrants have seemingly taken their approach from this literature. Thus H.C. Pentland relies on British travellers for his statement that Highlanders were vain, unhandy, and unco-operative, while K.J. Duncan erroneously suggests that the Glengarry immigrants were principally military settlers. Local county histories are unfortunately just at their weakest in describing the origin of the Highlanders who settled in Glengarry.[5] A considerable gap now exists between traditional accounts of the Glengarry immigrants and the knowledge needed to assess the economic and social origins of these Highland settlers.

In the following paper, a detailed look is taken at the circumstances surrounding the Glengarry emigrations. The first part of this study involves a general overview of the Highlands, in particular of western Inverness-shire, in the eighteenth century and of the effects of political and economic change during that period. The second section presents an analysis of the origins of the Glengarry emigrants, of their reasons for departure, and of the character of their emigration and settlement. Finally, I have made certain observations concerning Highland emigration to Glengarry and emigration to British North America in general.[6]

○

The picture commonly drawn of the Scottish Highlands in the eighteenth century is one of social disintegration and decline. Beset by military defeat and subject to cultural assimilation, the Highlanders are presented as the hapless victims of an alien political and economic order. While this account of events in the Highlands is superficially correct, it fails to reflect either the persistent strength of traditional Gaelic social structures or the degree of control which the clansmen continued to exert over their daily life. In fact, popular Gaelic culture flourished and some of the greatest Gaelic poets wrote during the eighteenth century. It is against this backdrop of an embattled, but resilient culture that Highland emigration to Upper Canada must be viewed.

By 1700 Highland society represented an anomaly in the complex, commercial society of England and southern Scotland. Throughout the late Middle Ages, the north had remained outside the control of the Scottish government in Edinburgh, and it maintained its independence from the government in London during the troubled years of the seventeenth century. Social organization in the Highlands was still clearly tribal in origin, justice was local and personal, and agriculture operated at a subsistence level. The emigrants to Glengarry County came principally from the estates of Cameron of Lochiel, Macdonnell of Glengarry and Knoydart, and MacLeod of Glenelg at the geographic heart of the Highlands in western Inverness-shire. Although surrounded by other Gaelic-speaking districts and thereby insulated from the immediate influence of southern Britain, western Inverness was nonetheless in a vulnerable position, particularly after the defeat of the Jacobites in 1745. Its location at the western end of the Great Glen and across the road to the Isles, as well as the ardent Jacobitism of its Catholic and its Protestant inhabitants alike, made western Inverness an important centre for southern efforts to "improve" or "civilize" the Highlands.

At mid-eighteenth century, society in western Inverness consisted of a number of kin-based, hierarchical communities. At the head of each group of communities was the clan chief, a paternal ruler around whom revolved economic affairs, the right to justice, and much social life. The clan gentlemen, many of whom were close relations of the chief, received large land holdings from him and assisted in leading the clansmen. Perhaps a majority in the community were tenants, but they varied in status from substantial farmers with a large number of cattle, to joint-tenants who shared a farm, to sub-tenants who paid rent to another tenant. Below these were the cottars and servants, who had no direct share at all in the land. In spite of these differences of economic and social status, traditional Gaelic society, in western Inverness and elsewhere, can be best described as of a whole or one piece. While men held different amounts of land or fulfilled various functions, the people saw themselves as members of a single community. This single identity is reflected in the unity of Gaelic literature, whose aristocratic works were known by the people and whose popular works were sometimes created by the gentry.[7]

The economic backbone of this traditional social order was subsistence agriculture based on cattle. Blackadder's description of the economy of Skye and North Uist in 1799 could be applied equally well to western Inverness at the time of the Rebellions:

> At present every Family in the Country is a Kind of independent Colony of itself, They turn up what part of the soil is necessary to support them with Meal, . . . take their own Fish, Manufacture, and make the most of their own cloaths and Husbandry utensils. Their cows supply them in Summer with Butter and Milk, after which a few of them are sold to pay for the small spot on which they live.

Large estates were divided into farms of varying sizes and quality; a farm could be held by one man, or, more commonly, be shared by a number of tenants. Few of the western Inverness farms had more than five acres of land suitable for growing grain. The remaining acreage was given over to pasture, including summer grazings known as sheillings located in the hills some distance from the farmhouses.[8]

The tenants of western Inverness were good farmers, making skilled and balanced use of available resources. Archibald Menzies, General Inspector of estates annexed to the Crown after 1745, noted with approval the manner in which the Barisdale tenants in Knoydart managed their farms. The tenants moved their cattle regularly from one pasture to another, ensuring that the land was used to greatest advantage: milk cows were first, store and yeld cattle next, and horses and sheep last in grazing over any particularly good field. The Barisdale tenants were experts in cattle-breeding and in the treatment of animal disease; they even took into account the nutritional value of various grasses when pasturing their livestock.[9] The agricultural skill which the Barisdale clansmen demonstrated to Menzies was shared by most of the tenants in western Inverness.

Traditional Highland agriculture has too often been judged by the standards of eighteenth century improvers. As Scottish economic historian Malcolm Gray pointed out, traditional agricultural practices represented a balance between the physical environment and possible farming techniques on one hand, and social considerations on the other. Since a large population was a military necessity until 1750, labour-saving practices were pointless in an area with no alternate employment. Instead, "any device, however laborious, that would increase...yield was justified."[10] The land itself provided no large areas of fertile ground that might serve as an enticement to improved agrarian practices, and the climate, varying from the overwhelmingly wet and mild to the sub-arctic, set further limitations on agricultural techniques. Highland agriculture had achieved a relatively successful balance between the needs of the people and the availability of resources.

The basis of traditional society in the Highlands was the community's right to land. Although in the eye of southern Scottish law, land belonged to the chief who had legal title to it, the clansmen firmly believed that they were entitled to a share in the land. Ownership of land in the modern sense of an individual's exclusive right to it was quite foreign to Highland tenants at mid-eighteenth century. Rather the tenants believed that the community which for generations had maintained itself on the land, had an enduring right to the land. This age-old principle, never conceded by the tenants, was nonetheless denied by the British government after 1750 when the Highlands first passed under southern domination.

The half century following the Jacobite defeat on Culloden Moor witnessed radical change in western Inverness that was only partly the result of the Hanoverian victory. Government regulations designed to inculcate southern values and norms of behaviour in the clansmen, and particularly in the Highland gentry, predate the 1745 rebellion by more than a century. Similarly, the penetration of modern commercial attitudes towards the land dates to the early eighteenth century, at least on the periphery of the Highlands, and to a growing involvement in the market economy. The principal effect of the Uprising was to intensify the process of integrating the Highlands into British society and to commit government resources and authority to that task. The simplest, and yet most far-reaching, achievement of government was its successful imposition of southern law and order across the Highlands. Until mid-eighteenth century in western Inverness, justice was administered through local, heritable jurisdictions, and traditional clan military organization was essential to the protection of life and property. Within a dozen years following the suppression of the rebellion, parliamentary laws were enforced in the Highlands—as illustrated by the tragic end of several infamous cattle lifters—and the defensive raison d'être of the clan had disappeared.

The extension of southern rule into the Highlands made possible the introduction of improved agriculture there. In the aftermath of the rebellion, the British government made a determined effort to develop the infrastructure necessary for a modern economy in the north. Numerous roads and bridges greatly improved communication within western Inverness and provided access to southern Britain; similarly, schools and churches were established in districts not previously well served by these institutions. Two distinct stages are apparent in the improvement of agriculture in western Inverness. During the thirty years from 1750 to 1780, landlords and government officials introduced such reforms as better housing, the fencing of fields, and new crops so as to increase production on traditional joint-tenant farms. In the second stage following 1780, landlords completely reorganized clan estates with the creation of large-scale sheep farms and separate crofting townships.

The first stage of agricultural improvement was compatible with the clansmen's traditional belief in the community's right to land and generally most tenants were able to maintain their usual share in a farm. However, in certain Highland districts, including Glen Garry, rent increases were extremely high in the late 1760s and 1770s; tenants here had sometimes to choose between a reduced income and the loss of their farm. The second stage of improvement completely ignored the community's right to clan lands. Highland landlords took advantage of their exclusive legal title to their estates and accepted the modern concept that land should be put to the most commercially viable use. In the years after 1780, landlords rapidly adopted large-scale sheep farming, which doubled or quadrupled their income, at the expense of denying their clansmen a reasonable living from the land. The flood of emigration that followed from western Inverness was the clansmen's response to this denial of the community's right to land.

o

The Highlanders who emigrated to Glengarry County were a remarkably homogeneous group who came to Canada by choice. These clansmen originated in the same geographic district, leaving Scotland with their neighbours in extended family groups; the emigrants were relatively prosperous farmers led by clan gentlemen. They left the Highlands because increasing rents and large-scale sheep farming destroyed the community's right to a living from the land. The emigrations to Glengarry were generally organized by the clansmen themselves and they departed from the Highland port nearest their home. The coherent identity of the Glengarry settlers was the result of the community motivation for and control of the emigration.

Nine major emigrations of some 2500 people substantially settled Glengarry County, Upper Canada. The first emigrants left Scotland in 1773, but were resettled in Canada as Loyalists in 1784. Other clansmen followed in 1785, 1786, 1790, 1792, 1793, in two sailings in 1802, and in 1815.[11] A majority of the Glengarry immigrants came from neighbouring districts in western Inverness: Glen Garry, Lochiel, Knoydart, and Glenelg all sent successive groups of emigrants to the Upper Canadian county. There were departures from Glen Garry in 1773, 1785, 1792, and 1802, from Lochiel in 1792 and 1802, from Knoydart in 1786, 1802, and 1815, and from Glenelg in 1793, 1802, and 1815. In addition adjacent districts with political or kinship ties to this region provided a further number of emigrants. Thus the Grants, Camerons, and Macdonells of Glenmoriston joined the 1773 emigration from nearby Glen Garry, and families from Kintail and Glenshiel were part of the large sailing from Glenelg and Knoydart in 1802. Even individual emigrations, both during and after the group departures, left chiefly from this same geographic heartland or its immediate vicinity.

The Glengarry emigrants left Scotland chiefly in family groups, which included a large number of children. A passenger list survives for the 1790 emigrant party, describing the age and family structure of that group. Aside from four servants and four single adults, the remaining seventy-nine passeners travelled with family members. Families with young children were over-represented in the 1790 party since 42 percent of the passengers were twelve years and under, in contrast to 34 percent of the Scottish population as a whole.[12] The less detailed information available concerning the remaining Glengarry emigrants suggests that families, often with young children, also dominated other departures.[13] But if most emigrants arrived in Glengarry accompanied by their family, they also travelled with or joined related families in the New World. For instance among the 1786 emigrants were the first cousins Angus Ban Macdonell, Malcolm Macdougall, and Allen Macdonald, who were met in Glengarry by Angus Ban's brother Finan, uncle John, and cousin Duncan. Similarly the families of John Roy Macdonald and brother Angus left Scotland in 1786 to join their Loyalist cousins, Alex and John Macdonald; other related families emigrated sixteen years later in the 1802 party. The limited number of Gaelic Christian names and the overwhelming number of Macdonalds, or even MacMillans, makes tracing family relationships among the emigrants a frustrating experience. Nonetheless, the available evidence strongly suggests that most emigrants to Glengarry County were bound by family ties to several other emigrant or settler families.[14]

The great majority of Glengarry emigrants came from the broad middle rank of Highland society and as would be expected from the agrarian basis of traditional Highland life were predominantly farmers. Only in the 1815 party were 40 percent of the heads of household craftsmen and labourers. These men emigrated chiefly from Perthshire in the southern Highlands where the land-holding reorganization that accompanied the new agricultural economy was oldest and had had most effect.[15] Neither the very rich nor the very poor are evident among the emigrants to Glengarry during this period. Although there were obvious distinctions of wealth and status among the many farmers who emigrated, the majority seem to have been tenants with a right to a share in the land. Even the craftsmen and labourers in the 1815 party were men of more than subsistence income since they were able to pay the deposit for their passage to Canada.[16]

Perceptions of the social and economic status of the Glengarry emigrants have differed on opposite sides of the Atlantic. Scottish sources make clear the relative prosperity of the emigrants in comparison to the clansmen who remained in the Highlands. Thus in 1785, the Highland Catholic bishop Alexander MacDonald reported that the 300 emigrants leaving Glen Garry and Glen Moriston were "the principal tenants" and "the most reputable Catholics" of the two districts. Similarly when 520 clansmen left Knoydart in 1786, the Catholic hierarchy explained that "those who emigrate are just the people who are a little better off." Few of the Glengarry emigrants were servants or cottars, from the bottom one-third of Highland society; most were tenants, which in the Scottish context of the time implied a middling social and economic status.[17] In contrast, Canadian sources generally emphasize the poverty of the Highland emigrants arriving at Quebec. The same emigrants, who in July 1786 were described as "a little better-off" in Scotland, landed at Quebec in September in a "very destitute and hopeless situation."[18] In October 1790, Lord Dorchester felt obliged to give assistance to another group of Highland emigrants to prevent "their becoming a burden to the public or the Crown," and in 1802 a public subscription was opened in Quebec for the indigent Highlanders who arrived on the *Neptune*.[19]

These apparent contradictions between Scottish and Canadian descriptions of the Glengarry emigrants arise from the different vantage points of the observers, and from the effects of emigration on the clansmen. When the emigrants were compared to the population of the Highlands as a whole, it is evident that they were relatively well off, comprising somewhat more than the middle one-third of local society. Most of the Glengarry emigrants were able to leave Scotland because they were tenants: unlike servants or cottars, tenants could realize a small capital sum through the sale of their stock. However, as the second stage of agricultural improvement took root in the north, the tenants' financial position generally worsened and fewer, or poorer, tenants found it possible to leave Scotland after 1800. When the Glengarry emigrants reached Quebec, many had little more than the fare needed to travel on to Upper Canada. From a Canadian perspective, Highland tenants were never very well off, but at this point in their journey, the Glengarry emigrants were particularly poor in comparison to the inhabitants of Canada. Some had exhausted their resources in the major capital investment of emigration. Yet it remains extremely important not to confuse the financial condition of the emigrants on arrival in Canada with their actual social and economic standing in Highland society in the generation before departure.

In social background, the leaders of seven Glengarry emigrant groups differed somewhat from the majority of clansmen emigrants. The leaders of the emigrant groups can be identified as Highland gentlemen, whose families had traditionally played an important role in clan life. Thus the various Macdonell gentlemen who organized the 1773, 1785, 1786, 1790, and 1792 emigrations were all cousins (and in the Highlands a fourth cousin is a close relation) of the Glengarry chief.[20] Similarly Alex McLeod, leader of the 1793 emigration and Archibald McMillan of Murlaggan, organizer of the 1802 departure from Fort William, were related to Glengarry and to Lochiel respectively.[21] Other men, not as closely connected to the chief but rather men of standing in their local communities, also played a significant role in organizing the emigrant groups. Angus Ban Macdonell of Muniall was a well-established Knoydart tenant in the 1786 party, and he is described by Glengarry County tradition as a "leading man" of the group. Archibald McMillan named eight men from across Glen Garry and Locheil who helped him "in preserving good Order among the People" during their 1802 voyage. The other sailing that year, made by the *Neptune*, had no gentlemen leaders; instead the emigrants appointed Duncan McDonald, Murdoch McLennan, and Norman Morrison to speak for them. These men seemingly represented the three districts from which the emigrants were drawn, and McLennan at least had been a prosperous tenant in his community.[22] Neither clan chiefs nor major landlords participated in the Glengarry emigrations but the second level of traditional community leaders, including both gentlemen and locally respected tenants, were represented in them.

The Glengarry emigrants left the Highlands by choice in face of the rapid transformation of traditional Gaelic society under the impact of commercial land development. The first, underlying cause of this emigration was the economic squeeze which struck the tenants of western Inverness in the late eighteenth century. While tenants' incomes rose slowly, rents increased rapidly, particularly after 1780 when competition from sheep farmers for Highland farms drove rents up 400 percent and more over twenty years.[23] In many instances, the clansmen found their holdings reduced and in others, tenants put themselves in debt competing with sheep farmers for long-term leases. Bishop MacDonald's description of a new "Set" or rental of farms on Clanranald's property illustrates the financial quandary faced by tenants in the west Highlands:

> The Set has turned out more favourable to the small tenants than what we were at first given to understand would be the case. Every Body was allowed to overbid each other, notwithstanding the former possessors had preference, & got, some of them, a considerable deduction of the offers made by better Bets than themselves. The rents are however exorbitantly high & great numbers will not be able to make them good for any length of time, unless divine providence will interfere.[24]

The nine Glengarry emigrant groups left Scotland over a forty-year period that spanned the intensification of this financial squeeze and saw the beginning of the disappearance of the traditional Highland tenant. The tenants who put off their departure for several decades after the introduction of sheep farming paid an increasing price for their delay and often emigrated "with sadly reduced possessions."

Farm rents rose in Glen Garry by 130 to 170 percent in 1772, and the 200 clansmen who left the area for America in 1773 gave high rents as the cause of their departure.[25] The Highlanders in the 1785, 1786, 1790, 1792, and 1793 parties emigrated shortly after the introduction of sheep farming broke up their traditional communities.[26] Other western Inverness clansmen attempted to adapt to the new agricultural economy but found themselves impoverished by their efforts. In 1802 close to four hundred of Glengarry's tenants and their families refused to pay yet another rent increase and emigrated instead, while emigrants from Glenelg and Kintail also left communities threatened by sheep farms. The 1815 emigrants from the same districts witnessed a further decline in their land and fortunes before they too abandoned the Highlands.[27] The nine group emigrations from western Inverness to Glengarry County were the result of the landlords' denial of reasonably priced land to their tenants.

Although the tenants of western Inverness faced a financial crisis as a result of the loss of traditional farm lands, this loss did not compel them to emigrate. In spite of the forcible introduction of sheep farming and its accompanying evictions, emigration was not the only option open to the clansmen. Some tenants were able to maintain a share in a traditional farm, albeit smaller and at a higher rent. Others acquired a croft, a piece of land individually held, but too small to support a family; the crofters were employed at estate improvements, kelping, or fishing.[28] The remainder of the tenants became labourers, congregating in the small villages that appeared for the first time in the Highlands, or migrating south, ultimately to Glasgow and Edinburgh.[29] The Glengarry settlers chose emigration over these other options available to the tenants of western Inverness.

The reason for the clansmen's decision in favour of emigration and hence the second fundamental cause of the departures was their desire to live in a community of kin and friends. Economic pressures alone were not sufficient to bring such a conservative people suddenly to abandon a much-loved native land for the sparsely settled wilderness of Upper Canada. But the commercialization of land holding in the Highlands and particularly the adoption of large-scale sheep farming not only damaged the tenants' financial well-being, but also broke apart traditional Highland communities. In some cases several adjacent farm settlements were cleared, while in others high rents forced a number of tenants to surrender their holdings. The tenants of western Inverness could not accept this destruction of local communities and many preferred to emigrate to Canada where they could both satisfy their desire for land and re-establish kin and neighbourhood groups. In 1790 when tenants from Eigg and the west coast of the mainland "heard from their friends & relatives settled in the upper parts of . . . [Quebec] that upon removing to this Country they would be able to obtain portions of the waste lands of the Crown contiguous to them, they were glad to embark for Canada."[30] The composition of the emigrant groups, the organization of the departures, and the nature of the settlement in Upper Canada confirms the importance of community in sending the clansmen to Glengarry County.

The identity of the Glengarry emigrants has already been established, and that analysis points out the significance of family and friends in the formation of the emigrant groups. In addition eight of the nine departures were organized and controlled by the Highlanders themselves; only the 1815 emigration, a government sponsored sailing, broke this pattern. Between 1773 and 1802, however, no emigrant agent was needed in western Inverness to drum up dissatisfaction with home and enthusiasm for North America. The decision to emigrate was taken within the local community, although kin and friends from neighbouring estates were sometimes asked to join a group. The emigrants often appointed a gentleman from among their number to go south to Glasgow to hire a ship for the voyage. Thus Lieut. Angus Macdonell and Father Alexander Macdonell travelled to Greenock to charter a ship for the 1786 emigrants, and Archibald McMillan went to Glasgow on the same business in 1802.[31] The Glengarry emigrants, seemingly with the exception only of the 1815 party, did not leave Scotland from a Lowland port. In a reflection of the community control of the emigration, the clansmen sailed from the port nearest their home, Fort William in 1773, 1792, and 1802; Loch Nevis in Knoydart in 1786 and 1802; Culreagh in Glenelg in 1793; and from Eigg or Arisaig in 1790.[32] This local control of the departure underlines the continuing vitality of community, in spite of the tenants having apparently chosen a course of action destructive of traditional community ties.

The pattern of settlement of the nine emigrant groups from western Inverness emphasizes the clansmen's pre-eminent interest in acquiring land within a Highland community. The re-location of the 1773 emigrants in

Upper Canada as Loyalist refugees led another five groups to join them over an eight year period. Each successive group of emigrants received Crown land in a body, distinct from but generally adjacent to previous arrivals.[33] While most clansmen thereby settled in close proximity to those kin and neighbours who had accompanied them to Canada, a few took up land near friends who had emigrated some years earlier. Thus four families of the 1785 emigrant party from Glen Garry and Glenmoriston settled in the front of Charlottenburgh, among Loyalists born in the same Scottish districts.[34] Within a brief ten years, some three hundred western Inverness clansmen and their families had obtained land and created a new Highland community in Glengarry County.

The same determination to acquire land in the company of family and friends also marked the settlement of the three large emigrant groups that reached Glengarry after 1800. However, changes in land granting regulations, the limited number of lots then available in the county, and the very modest financial resources of the clansmen meant that few of the 1802 emigrants received a Crown grant in Glengarry.[35] Several gentlemen offered the emigrants land elsewhere in the Canadas, but such schemes were not attractive to the Highlanders who preferred to live in the vicinity of their friends. Thus General Hunter's attempt to settle the 1802 emigrants near York failed, because "they would not agree to go so far out of the world."[36] Instead the 1802 emigrants stayed with friends, rented and ultimately bought land in Glengarry, or in a few instances in the adjacent counties of Soulanges and Stormont.[37] The 1815 settlers were given one-hundred-acre lots as assisted emigrants; these lots were Crown reserves mostly located in the north-eastern quarter of the county, which enabled the emigrants to settle in reasonable proximity to one another.[38] The choice made by one of the 1815 emigrants is indicative of the way in which family ties were more often significant than economic considerations in the settlement of Glengarry. After Duncan McDonell rejected the rear half of lot 2 in the fourth concession of Lochiel as "bad land," John McRea asked to be given the same lot. McRea explained that since "no other vacant lot was to be had in the settlement," he was anxious to acquire this land and "be settled along with his Brothers and names sakes who were located on adjoining lots."[39]

○

This examination of the origins and character of Highland emigration to Glengarry County gives several insights into early immigration to Upper Canada that are of interest to both Canadian and Scottish historians. First, a knowledge of the emigrants' background underlines the remarkable degree of control which the Highlanders exercised over their departure. In spite of economic pressures and the narrowing of options open to Highland tenants, many western Inverness clansmen were able to choose a course of action that satisfied traditional aspirations for land and community. Secondly, the confusion which has existed over the social and economic origin of the Highland settlers reveals the importance of first looking at any group of emigrants in context of the society which they left behind. In the case of the Glengarry emigrants, their strained resources on arrival at Quebec or in the early years of settlement by no means reflected their previous position of modest consequence in the Highlands. These two points emphasize the value of a knowledge of the British, or European, communities which the emigrants left for Upper Canada.

Thirdly, Highland emigration in this period can well be seen as an act of protest against the radical transformation of Highland social and agrarian structures in the late eighteenth century. While the clansmen reluctantly accommodated themselves to the commercialization of the Highland economy and the shift of power to southern authorities, they resolutely maintained their right to obtain a living from the land in a Gaelic community. When that right was denied, in a minor degree by large rent increases, and then overwhelmingly by the creation of sheep farms, many of the people of western Inverness emigrated to Upper Canada. The kin and neighbourhood base of the emigration and the eager acquisition of land within a Gaelic settlement are evidence of the emigrants' continuing commitment to those traditional values.[40] Between 1784 and 1803 emigration, particularly from Knoydart, Glen Garry, and Glenelg, seems to have been limited almost solely by the cost of a passage across the Atlantic. Large numbers of emigrants left western Inverness, including close to 25 percent of the population of Knoydart in one sailing in 1786. A more profound, better-organized protest against the creation of sheep farms and the loss of traditional lands and community cannot easily be imagined.[41]

Finally, the origins and experience of the Glengarry immigrants can be compared to other British immigrant groups in pre-Confederation Canada. Highland settlers in the Maritimes were often linked by a common origin in Scotland and displayed the same dense pattern of settlement evident among the clansmen of Glengarry.[42] The Irish emigrants studied by J.J. Manion were also principally small farmers from adjacent districts, squeezed out of their traditional holdings by a shift to pastoral farming. However, these Irishmen emigrated as young, unmarried individuals or in nuclear families and took up land in settlements which were Irish, but not kin-based. The key to the difference between Irish and Highland emigration might be in the weakening of traditional Gaelic communities in Ireland before departure overseas. Most Irish settlers were already bilingual, and Manion describes emigration as a "highly individualistic solution to the economic and social ills that encumbered the Irish peasant."[43] In contrast emigration to Glengarry County was a communal solution to the problems facing the clansmen of western Inverness.

Several small emigrant groups also displayed a pattern of emigration which in some ways mirrored the experience of the Glengarry settlers. Similarities are evident between the Glengarry immigrants and the Yorkshire settlers of Cumberland County, Nova Scotia. Many of these Englishmen were prosperous tenant farmers who left the north and east ridings in family groups between 1772 and 1774, because enclosures and rising rents threatened their possession of the land.[44] The ballad of the *Albion*, which describes a party of Welsh emigrants to New Brunswick, points to several tantalizing resemblances between them and Glengarry settlers. The 150 Welsh-speakers were "not a desperate and dispossessed rabble" but farmers who "possessed a powerful and coherent sense of community identity."[45]

What these cases do is to suggest that the individual elements of the pattern of emigration to Glengarry County were not uncommon in the Canadian experience. In particular farming families from a middling level of society in regions across Britain and Ireland were likely to emigrate, quite often in the company of friends. These people left their homes in response to the actual or feared loss of social and economic status that followed on agricultural improvement and the commercialization of land-holding in the eighteenth and nineteenth centuries. In the exceptional case of the Glengarry immigrants, circumstances favoured the departure of some three thousand people in a series of community based emigrations to a single destination over more than sixty years. It is this intense and sustained character that makes Highland emigration to Glengarry County exceptional and explains the overwhelmingly Scottish origin of the new community.

NOTES

1. For Campbell, see "English Emigration on the Eve of the American Revolution," *American Historical Review* 61 (1955), esp. 2, and "Social Origins of Some Early Americans" in *Seventeenth Century America: Essays in Colonial History*, ed. James Smith (Chapel Hill, NC, 1959), 63–89. Carl Bridenbaugh re-examined English emigration in *Vexed and Troubled Englishmen, 1590–1642* (New York, 1968). Campbell's work was recently attacked in David Galenson, "'Middling People' or 'Common Sort?': The Social Origins of Some Early Americans Reexamined," *William and Mary Quarterly* 35 (1978).

2. T.H. Breen and Stephen Foster, "Moving to the New World: The Character of Early Massachusetts Immigration," *William and Mary Quarterly* 30 (1973): 190, 209.

3. The Eastern and Southern European origins of post-Confederation immigrants have been studied in detail. See, for instance, Robert Harney, "The Commerce of Migration," *Canadian Ethnic Studies* 9 (1977): 42–53, and "Men Without Women: Italian Migrants in Canada, 1855–1930," *Canadian Ethnic Studies* 11 (1979): 29–47. J.J. Manion's *Irish Settlers in Eastern Canada* (Toronto, 1974) was exceptional since it examined the material culture of Irish settlers with reference to its Irish antecedents. Very recently Donald Akenson and J.M. Bumsted have re-examined Irish and Highland immigration in attempts to redefine who the immigrants were. See Donald Akenson, "Ontario: What Ever Happened to the Irish?" *Canadian Papers in Rural History* 3 (Gananoque, ON, 1982), and J.M. Bumsted, "Scottish Emigration in the Maritimes, 1770–1815: A New Look at an Old Theme," *Acadiensis* 10 (1981).

4. For Bishop Macdonell's arguments in favour of the loyal Glengarrians, see for instance Public Archives of Canada (hereafter PAC), Upper Canada Sundries (hereafter UCS), reel C-4504, 2872–75, Rev. McDonell to Wm. Halton, 31 Jan. 1808, and UCS, reel C-6863, 45301, Rev. McDonell to Hillier, 2 April 1827. For travellers, see John Howison, *Sketches of Upper Canada* (Edinburgh, 1821, reprint 1965), 18–24; John McGregor, *British America* (Edinburgh, 1832), 530; and Adam Fergusson, *Tour in Canada* (Edinburgh, 1833), 85.

5. H.C. Pentland, *Labour and Capital in Canada, 1650–1860* (Toronto, 1981), 93–94. Kenneth Duncan, "Patterns of Settlement in the East" in *The Scottish Tradition in*

Canada, ed. W.S. Reid (Toronto, 1976). J.A. Macdonell's *Sketches of Glengarry in Canada* (Montreal, 1893) focussed on the Glengarry gentlemen who led several of the migrations. Ewen Ross and Royce MacGillivray in their *History of Glengarry* (Belleville, ON, 1979) describe the emigrants only in very general terms.

6. This paper is drawn from the writer's 1982 University of Edinburgh doctoral thesis. "'In the New Land a New Glengarry': Migration from the Scottish Highlands to Upper Canada, 1750–1820." Chapters 2–5 of the thesis include a detailed examination of economic and social life in western Inverness in the period up to and during the emigrations, only a summary of which is presented here in section 1. Chapters 6–12 of the thesis deal extensively with the process of emigration and settlement, an outline of which is found in the second section of this paper.

7. Derick Thomas, quoted in Kenneth Mackinnon, *Language, Education and Social Process in a Gaelic Community* (London, 1977), 10.

8. Scottish Record Office (hereafter SRO), RH2/8/24, pp. 107–8, Blackadder's Survey, 1799. Only 3 of Cameron of Lochiel's 36 farms produced enough corn to support their inhabitants and provide a surplus for sale; most farms yielded only enough for 6 or 9 months' subsistence.

9. Virginia Willis, ed., *Reports of the Annexed Estates* (Edinburgh, 1973), 100.

10. Malcolm Gray, *The Highland Economy* (Edinburgh, 1957), 35.

11. For 425 emigrants in 1773, see Public Record Office (hereafter PRO), TI/499, Campbell & McPhail, 13 Dec. 1773; for 300 emigrants in 1785, see Scottish Catholic Archives (hereafter SCA), Blairs papers, Bishop A. MacDonald, 5 Aug. 1785; for 520 in 1786, see *Quebec Gazette*, 7 Sept. 1786; for 87 in 1790, see PAC, reel B-48 CO42/71, p. 82, *British Queen*; for some 150 emigrants in 1792 see *Quebec Gazette*, 27 Sept. 1792; for some 150 emigrants in 1793, see PAC, RG1 L3. Upper Canada Land Petitions (hereafter UCLP), Mc21 (1837–39), no. 46, Capt. Alex McLeod; for some 750 emigrants in 1802, see *Selkirk's Diary* (Toronto, 1958), 199, and also *Quebec Gazette*, 25 Aug., 5 and 15 Sept. 1802; for 363 emigrants in 1815, see PAC, MG11, CO385, vol. 2 and compare to Ontario Archives (hereafter OA), RG1 C-1-3, vol. 101, March 1816.

12. For the 1790 passenger list, see PAC, reel B-48, CO42/71, p. 82. For estimates of the Scottish populations, see Michael Flinn, *Scottish Population History* (Cambridge, 1977), 263, 445.

13. Thus in 1773, 47 percent of the 425 emigrants leaving Fort William were children; not all of these emigrants however necessarily settled in Glengarry (PRO, T1/499, Campbell and McPhail to Nelthorpe, 13 Dec. 1773). Among 52 families in the 1786 group, there were "many children" (PAC, "S" Series, reel C-3001, 9909–15, John Craigie to Stephen Delancey, 4 Sept. 1786). Reference is made to 27 families in the 1792 group (OA, RG1, A-1-1, vol. 49, Richard Duncan, 6 Nov. 1792). In the 1802 McMillan emigration, 30 percent of the group was 12 and under, while in the 1802 west coast emigration, 43 percent of the group was 16 and under (*Parliamentary Papers*, 1802–3 [80] 4: 41). In 1815, 61 families and 8 bachelors emigrated to Glengarry; each family had an average of 5.7 members (PAC, MG11, CO385, vol. 2 compared to OA, RG1 C-1-3, vol. 101, Return of Locations, March 1816). No account has been found of the family relationships of the 1785 emigrant party.

14. Information concerning John Roy Macdonald was obtained from Alex Fraser, Lancaster, Ontario; Mr Fraser has an extensive genealogical chart of John Roy's family, the Macdonalds of Loup. For Angus Ban's cousins, see PAC, MG29 C29 Notebook . . . 1st page blank, Interview with James Duncan Macdonald, age 92; also my interview with Mrs Florence Macdonell of the Glen Road, Williamstown, Ontario. For the 1802 arrivals, see OA, Father Ewen John

Macdonald Collection, Box 8, C-1-2, Typescript: Copy of letter from Angus McDonald (John Roy's son) to Roderick McDonald, 14 Oct. 1804.

15. Of the 69 heads of household in the 1815 party, 20 were craftsmen and 16 were labourers. Many of the latter were young men, not long in the labour force.

16. Numerous labourers and craftsmen wanted to participate in the assisted emigrant scheme that brought the 1815 group to Glengarry, but could not afford the deposit. See PAC, MG11 Q135 pt. 2, Memorial of Allan McDonell, etc., Fort Augustus, March 1815.

17. For Bishop A. MacDonald, see SCA, Blairs papers, Bishop Alexander MacDonald, 5 Aug. 1785. For Catholic hierarchy in 1786, see OA, Father Ewen J. Macdonald Collection, box 8 B-7, Two extracts from a letter written by Bishops Hay, MacDonald, and Geddes, 28 July 1786. The 1773 emigrant party was made up of the "best" of Glengarry's tenants; see SCA, Blairs papers, Bishop John MacDonald, 10 Feb. 1773. For the tenant status of the 1790 emigrants, see PAC, "S" Series, Reel C-3006, 15917, Report. For the tenant status of the 1802 McMillan emigrants, see Glengarry's offer to them in SRO, RH2/4/87, f. 151, 21 March 1802. The 1815 emigrants, farmers, craftsmen, and labourers alike, possessed financial resources not shared by the entire population; see note 16.

18. PAC, "S" Series, Reel C-3001, 9909-15, Hope to McDonell, 25 Sept. 1786.

19. For the 1786 emigrants in Quebec, see PAC, "S" Series, Reel C-3001, 9909–15, Craigie to Delancey, 4 Sept. 1786. For Dorchester's comments, see PAC, reel B-48, CO42/72, pp. 57–58, Dorchester to Grenville, 10 Nov. 1790. For subscription in 1802, see *Quebec Gazette*, 16 and 30 Sept. 1802.

20. Macdonell of Aberchalder, Collachie, & Leek were fourth cousins, and Macdonell of Scotus, a second cousin, of Glengarry; these men led the 1773 group. Allan Macdonell, who headed the 1785 group, was descended from a seventeenth-century Glengarry chief. Father Alex Macdonell of the 1786 party was a first cousin, Miles Macdonell of the 1790 group a third cousin, and Alexander Macdonell of Greenfield of the 1792 party a second cousin, of Glengarry.

21. For Murlaggan, see Rev. Somerled MacMillan, *Byegone Lochaber* (Glasgow, 1971), 66–79. For McLeod, see Clan MacLeod, *The MacLeods of Glengarry* (Iroquois, ON, 1971), 37 and 63–66.

22. For Angus Ban, see SRO, GD128/8/1/5 for Ranald McDonell of Scotus' comments describing Angus Ban as a man of consequence; see also PAC, MG29, C29 Notebook: Family I from R.S., question 2, "Col. James' father was a leading man." For men helping McMillan, see PAC, LCLP, reel C-2545, 66478, Petition of Arch McMillan, 6 Aug. 1804. For *Neptune* spokesmen, see *Quebec Gazette*, 16 Sept. 1802; also John McLennan, "The Early Settlement of Glengarry," *Transactions of the Celtic Society of Montreal*, 113–21.

23. For instance, on McDonell of Scotus' small property in Knoydart, rents rose by 687 percent from £56 to £385 between 1773 and 1785; see Charles Fraser-Macintosh, "The Macdonells of Scotos," *Transactions of the Gaelic Society of Inverness* 16: 88.

24. SCA, Blairs papers, Bishop MacDonald, 20 April 1789.

25. PRO, T1/499, Campbell & McPhail to Nelthorpe, 13 Dec. 1773.

26. Glengarry's plans for sheep farming resulted in his ordering the removal of tenants in Glen Garry and Knoydart in 1785; see SRO, GD128/65/12, Precept of Removing, 1 April 1785; also SRO, GD128/7/1/39, 41, 45, Ranald McDonell, 26 and 30 Nov. 1785 and 13 Feb. 1786. The 1792 emigrants from Glen Garry were doubtless affected by Glengarry's improvements. Lord Dorchester reported that the 1790 emigrants had lost their holdings to sheep farmers; see PAC, "S" Series,

reel C-3006, 15917. The 1795 Statistical Account of Glenelg reported that emigration had followed the introduction of sheep farms there; this would include the 1793 Glengarry immigrants.

27. For the 1802 emigration from Glengarry's property, see SRO, RH2/4/87 f.151, Letter from Alex McDonell, 21 March 1802. For other 1802 emigrants, see McLennan, "Early Settlement of Glengarry." For Glenelg and Knoydart emigrants in both 1802 and 1815, see *New Statistical Account of Scotland*, vol. 9, Glenelg, 136. That the clansmen who emigrated were not completely impoverished is evident in their ability to pay their fare (or deposit in the case of the 1815 group) to Canada.

28. In spite of evictions, some tenants remained in Glengarry, even on the farms from which they were supposedly cleared; compare SRO, GD128/65 12, Precept of Removing, 1 April 1785, with MacMillan, *Byegone Lochaber*, 89, 236–39. In Knoydart, the south coast was seemingly left to "the remains" of the "antient tenants of Glengarry"; see Fraser-Macintosh *Antiquarian Notes*, 2nd Series (Inverness, 1897), 134–35. Some kelping was carried out on the coasts of Knoydart and Glenelg.

29. Father Ranald McDonald reported that many of Glengarry's tenants had settled in Fort Edinburgh and Glasgow, SCA, Blairs papers, Ranald McDonald, 23 June 1789.

30. PAC, "S" Series, Reel C-3006, 15917, Report to Dorchester.

31. For 1786, see SRO, GD128/8/1/3, Charles McDonell, 1 April 1786. For 1802, see PAC, MG24 I 183, Account Book of Voyage to America, 44–45.

32. For 1773, see PRO, T1/499, Campbell & McPhail, 13 Dec. 1773. For 1786, see SCA, Blairs papers, Alexander McDonald, Keppoch, 23 May 1786. For 1790, see SCA, Blairs papers, James MacDonald, 12 Oct. 1790; MacDonald reports that a "King's Ship was ordered to the coast" to impress men and thereby prevent emigration, a fact which clearly suggests that the emigrants were intending to leave from the Highland coast. For 1792, see SCA, Blairs papers, Ranald MacDonald, 16 July 1792. For 1793, see PAC, UCLP Reel C-2139, Mc(1837-9), no. 46, Alex McLeod. For 1802, see *Quebec Gazette*, 25 Aug., 5 and 15 Sept. 1802.

33. The Loyalists settled in the 1st to 3rd concessions of Lancaster and the first 5 concessions of Charlottenburgh; see PAC, RG1 L4, vol. 12, and McNiff's Map of the New Settlements, 1784. The 1785 and 1786 emigrants arrived in Canada within 6 months of each other and were generally settled together in the 5th to 8th concessions of Lancaster and the 7th to 9th concessions of Charlottenburgh; see PAC, RG19, vol. 4447, parcel 3, no. 7, Sundry persons . . . located by Mr James McDonell. The 1790 emigrants were located in the 12th concession of Lancaster since the 10th and 11th had been set aside as additional Loyalist lands; see PAC, RG1 L4, vol. 10, 107a, and Government of Ontario, Department of Lands and Forests, Plan of Lancaster by James McDonell. The 1792 emigrants were located in the 13th & 14th concessions of Lancaster; see PAC, RG1 L4, vol. 15, List of applicants, 18 and 26 March, 1 and 16 April 1793 compared to OA, RG1 A-1-1, vol. 49, 327, Return of Sundry persons. The 1793 emigrants were placed in the 15th and 16th concessions of Lancaster; see OA, RG1 C-1-4, vol. 9, Return, Glengarry, 10 Oct. 1794.

34. PAC, MG29, C29 Notebook . . . 1st page blank, Capt Grey, age 93. There were Arch Grant, Alex Roy, and Kenneth and Alex Macdonell, who settled near Summerstown.

35. I have not found any reference to Crown grants to 1802 emigrants in Glengarry; a small number may have acquired such grants. Government officials planned to settle the 1802 emigrants in a body, as had been the case with earlier Highland emigrant groups, in Finch township, in northwest Stormont. When that land was

finally made available in 1805, only 29 emigrants from western Inverness took locations there. A lack of cash to pay fees, and perhaps for the Knoydart and Morar emigrants (none of whom settled in Finch), the distance from numerous relatives in Glengarry, prevented three-quarters of the 1802 emigrants from accepting a grant in the western township.

36. For General Hunter, see T.D. Selkirk, *Selkirk's Diary* (New York, 1969), 200. Selkirk himself tried to recruit some of these recent arrivals for his Baldoon settlement in 1804; see ibid., 342. Arch McMillan, leader of one 1802 group, later attempted to organize a group settlement in Argenteuil, Lower Canada, but few of the emigrants were willing to leave Glengarry and district.

37. The 1802 emigrants settled in all 4 Glengarry townships, albeit often in local concentrations. Some obtained land in the 1st of Lancaster (*Selkirk's Diary*, 198), the 9th of Lancaster, and the 4th to 9th of Lochiel (PAC, MG29 C29). Ten families settled in the 3rd concession Indian Lands in western Charlottenburgh. Others are found in scattered lots in Charlottenburgh and Kenyon. At least 4 families settled in Soulanges (PAC, MG24 I 183, Templeton, etc.); the parents of a Hugh McDonell settled in the 9th of Cornwall township (PAC, Reel C-2200, UCLP, M11 (1811–19), no. 316).

38. PAC, Reel C-4547, USC, p. 12906, Abstract of Locations.

39. PAC, Reel C-2208, UCLP, M14 (1821–26), no. 540, esp. n-q.

40. Those who stayed in the Highlands, becoming crofting tenants, were also still committed to the right of the community to the land. Although these clansmen lost their farms, they built new communities and continued to press their right to the land. The tension thus engendered culminated in the "Crofters' Wars" of the late nineteenth century; see James Hunter, *The Making of the Crofting Community* (Edinburgh, 1976).

41. In "How Tame Were the Highlanders During the Clearances?" *Scottish Studies* 17 (1973), Eric Richards refers to a minimum of 40 instances of a pre-industrial type of violent response to the Clearances. Clearly, if emigration is also viewed as a protest, the level of violence was much more substantial.

42. Charles Dunn, *Highland Settler* (Toronto, 1953), 26.

43. Manion, *Irish Settlement in Eastern Canada*, 16–18.

44. Campbell, "English Emigration," 10–13.

45. Peter Thomas, introduction to "The Ballad of the Albion," *Acadiensis* 11 (Autumn 1981): 83.

ONTARIO: WHATEVER HAPPENED TO THE IRISH?[*]

DONALD H. AKENSON

o

PART I

To anyone interested in the history of the Irish and of their diaspora in the
nineteenth and twentieth centuries, their settlement in Ontario is doubly
fascinating: in the first instance because their settlement and assimilation
indicate that the American pattern of urban concentration cannot be taken
as the North American norm and that the American pattern almost certainly was a result of factors peculiar to that country rather than of cultural
determinants set down in the Old World. Second, the paucity of historical
literature on the subject is noteworthy and, indeed, strange. Once one has
referred to Nicholas Flood Davin's *The Irishman in Canada* (1878) and to John
J. Mannion's *Irish Settlements in Eastern Canada: A Study of Cultural Transfer
and Adaptation* (1974), one has mentioned all of the books and monographs
which deal directly with the Irish in Ontario as an ethnic group. Fortunately,
there are several monographs available which deal with the Irish as a political group and others that deal with institutional matters, but these skirt the
central issue of ethnicity. The dearth of studies on Irish ethnicity in the
region that is now Ontario is underscored when one makes the natural comparison to the Irish Americans. In the nineteenth century, they wrote massive volumes memorializing the Irish contribution to the rise of urban
America and to their part in the creation of American democracy and,
sometimes, put forth a modest claim for the Hibernian basis of all western
civilization. Further, in recent times there has developed a corpus of scholarship tracing in depth and detail the history of the Irish as an ethnic group
in the United States. There are no cognate bodies of literature for the Upper
Canadian Irish.[1]

[*] Donald H. Akenson, ed., *Canadian Papers in Rural History*, vol. 3 (Gananoque, ON:
Langdale Press, 1982), 204–56. Reprinted with the permission of the publisher.

These lacunae become all the more striking when one realizes that the Irish in Upper Canada (later called Canada West and, later still, Ontario) were much more important to Canadian society than the American Irish were to that of the United States. For most of the nineteenth century the Irish were the single largest European group in Upper Canada. This point with regard to Upper Canada will be developed in the text which follows. Here, one should note as demographic context for that later discussion that the Irish were the largest ethnic group throughout British North America in the nineteenth century. From the end of the Napoleonic Wars until the mid-1860s, emigrants from Ireland to all parts of British North America exceeded those from England and Wales and from Scotland in almost every single year and, indeed, until the mid-1850s, usually exceeded the *combined* total from the rest of the British Isles. Not surprisingly, when the censuses of 1841–42, '51, '61, '71, and '81 tallied the birth place of all persons in British North America, Ireland was the most common homeland of those born outside the country. Not until 1891 were there more English-born than Irish-born in British North America.[2]

One wonders what, in fact, happened to the Canadian Irish and to their history. Especially, one would like to know why so little is known about them in Upper Canada, where they settled in the largest numbers.[3]

o

Part—but only part—of the explanation for the lack of documentation is that our information on the movement of the Irish to Upper Canada is fragmentary, at least before the mid-nineteenth century. (For convenience, "Upper Canada" will be used in Part I of this study to denominate the area first called Upper Canada, and, later, Canada West.) As a start, then, it is appropriate to sort out what we know and what we do not know about this great Irish migration.

Initially, one should note that the post-1815 migrations from the British Isles were the by-product of a series of population explosions that remain to this day among the most perplexing phenomena in modern history. Firm population figures are not available for Great Britain before 1801, or for Ireland before 1821, but it is clear that during the eighteenth century and the first half of the nineteenth century, population in the British Isles grew at a rate as fast as that which presently holds for many "third-world" countries, and which we now view as a portent of inevitable disaster for the nations involved. The causes of the population explosions were not everywhere the same throughout the British Isles, and, indeed, must have varied from region to region within each country. Nor were the results everywhere the same; in Ireland, for example, the population boom in the region of industrializing Belfast produced radically different social configurations than in deepest Connaught. As a whole, however, it is undeniable that the Irish population was growing faster than was the nation's economic production.[4]

Second, one should not ignore the seemingly obvious point that there were three major Irish migrations to British North America. The first, from 1815 to 1845 inclusive, consisted chiefly (but by no means entirely) of individuals who were above the subsistence line and who came to the new world with resources and ambitions intact. The second migration, from 1846 to 1854, inclusive, stemmed from the starvation and social dislocation caused by the Great Famine. During these years, the flow of migrants was a veritable flood. Third, from 1855 onward, migration from Ireland to British North America continued at a reduced, but substantial rate for the rest of the century.

T A B L E   1   *EMIGRATION FROM THE BRITISH ISLES TO MAJOR EXTRA-EUROPEAN COUNTRIES, (unrevised data) 1815–45*

Year	British North America	United States	Australasia
1815	680	1 209	N/A
1816	3 370	9 022	N/A
1817	9 797	10 280	N/A
1818	15 136	12 429	N/A
1819	23 534	10 674	N/A
1820	17 921	6 745	N/A
1821	12 955	4 958	320
1822	16 013	4 137	875
1823	11 355	5 032	543
1824	8 774	5 152	780
1825	8 741	5 551	485
1826	12 818	7 063	903
1827	12 648	14 526	715
1828	12 084	12 817	1 056
1829	13 307	15 678	2 016
1830	30 574	24 887	1 242
1831	58 067	23 418	1 561
1832	66 339	32 782	3 733
1833	28 808	29 109	4 093
1834	40 060	33 074	2 800
1835	15 573	26 720	1 860
1836	34 226	37 774	3 124
1837	29 884	36 770	5 054
1838	4 577	14 332	14 021
1839	12 658	33 536	15 786
1840	32 293	40 642	15 850
1841	38 164	45 017	32 625
1842	54 123	63 852	8 534
1843	23 518	28 335	3 478
1844	22 924	43 660	2 229
1845	31 803	58 538	830

Source: N.H. Carrier and J.R. Jeffery, *Studies on Medical and Population Subjects, No. 6: External Migration, a Study of the Available Statistics, 1815–1950* (London: HMSO, 1953), 95.

Given the distinction between these Irish migrations, I wish to concentrate for the moment on the first, that which took place between 1815 and 1845, inclusive. And immediately the trouble begins, for one discovers that the data are distressingly flawed.[5] Before 1825, emigrants from the British Isles were not recorded in any systematic way as to their provenance, and from 1825 to 1853, inclusive, records dealt only with points of embarkation, not actual home country of the migrants.[6] Despite a considerable number of flaws, the raw data presented in table 1 at least define the rough dimensions of emigration from the British Isles and the destination of the migrants.

In respect of the key question of the Irish and their move to North America, table 2 indicates the number of individuals migrating from Irish ports, beginning in 1825, the first date for which we have even a rough approximation.

But sailing from an Irish port did not mean that the individual migrant actually was an Irishman, any more than sailing from a British port made one a Scotsman or an Englishman. Actually, the number of Irish migrants was even greater than the tally of the numbers leaving Irish ports would indicate, because many Irishmen sailed from ports in Great Britain, and

TABLE 2 MIGRATION FROM IRISH PORTS TO NORTH AMERICA, (*unrevised data*) 1825–45

	To British North America		To the United States	
	From Irish ports	As percent of UK total to BNA	From Irish ports	As percent of UK total to US
Year		(percent)		(percent)
1825	6 841	78.3	4 387	79.0
1826	10 484	81.8	4 383	62.1
1827	9 134	72.2	4 014	27.6
1828	6 695	55.4	2 877	22.4
1829	7 710	57.9	4 133	26.4
1830	19 340	63.3	2 981	12.0
1831	40 977	70.6	3 583	15.3
1832	37 068	55.9	4 172	12.7
1833	17 431	60.5	4 764	16.4
1834	28 586	71.4	4 213	12.7
1835	9 458	60.7	2 684	10.0
1836	19 388	56.6	3 654	9.7
1837	22 463	75.2	3 871	10.5
1838	2 284	49.9	1 169	8.2
1839	8 989	71.0	2 843	8.5
1840	23 935	74.1	4 087	10.1
1841	24 089	63.1	3 893	8.6
1842	33 410	61.7	6 199	9.7
1843	10 898	46.3	1 617	5.7
1844	12 396	54.1	2 993	6.9
1845	19 947	62.7	3 708	6.3

Source: Carrier and Jeffery, 95.

relatively few Britishers sailed from Irish ports. In particular, two British ports were attractive and accessible to the Irish: Liverpool, which in the 1830s was the third leading English port of emigration, and Greenock, in Scotland, which in the same period was the leading Scottish emigration port.[7]

Further, it is clear that the number of actual Irish migrants was underestimated for two additional reasons: because there was a substantial illegal migrant trade and because children were counted (or discounted) in an eccentric fashion. The matter of the children is especially confusing since, from 1817 to 1833, inclusive, children coming to British North America were counted as one-half, one-third, or not at all, according to their age. Thereafter, they appear to have been counted as adults.[8]

The most successful attempt at resolving all these difficulties is William Forbes Adams' classic study (1932). Given in table 3 are Adams' final figures, indicating his upward revision of Irish estimates of the Irish migration to North America.[9] When combined with the raw data in tables 1 and 2, the conclusion dictated by these data is inescapable: well before the Great Famine, the Irish were the single most important group of migrants to British North America.[10]

Having obtained a responsible estimate of the actual magnitude of Irish emigration to North America, we must now find, if possible, three crucial fractions of that total: first, the proportion of migrants to British North

TABLE 3 *ADAMS' REVISED ESTIMATE OF IRISH EMIGRATION TO BRITISH NORTH AMERICA FROM ALL UNITED KINGDOM PORTS*

Year	Figures
1825	8 893
1826	13 629
1827	11 969
1828	8 824
1829	10 148
1830	25 679
1831	54 514
1832	50 305
1833	23 139
1834	32 315
1835	10 764
1836	22 528
1837	26 102
1838	2 908
1839	10 943
1840	28 756
1841	30 923
1842	42 884
1843	14 668
1844	17 725
1845	26 708

America who disembarked at Quebec or Montreal; second, the proportion who eventually settled in Upper Canada; and third, the breakdown of these settlers as to the proportions that were Catholic and Protestant.

More problems arise. Obviously, not every ship sailing to British North America discharged its passengers only in Quebec or Montreal, the western terminus of the emigrant trade. Ships often docked at St John or Halifax, or at various small ports in the Maritimes, but records for such ports are too fragmentary to be satisfactory.[11] Fortunately, an emigration agent, A.C. Buchanan, was sent to Quebec City in 1828, and from 1829 onwards, he compiled a set of records which include figures for passengers from Irish ports being discharged at Quebec City and Montreal. Like the emigration figures collected in the United Kingdom, this series probably somewhat underestimated the actual number of Irish, for Buchanan did not take into account the Irish coming to these ports from Greenock and Liverpool, and, in addition, there was some immigrant smuggling and also considerable under-reporting (it was common for ships that were overloaded to land a number of their passengers below Quebec and thus to come into harbour with only their legal complement of passengers). Once again, it is William Forbes Adams who gives us a sensible, if not necessarily irreproachable, revision of Buchanan's figures, taking into account the various probable errors in the original data (table 4).[12]

What happened before 1829? The best raw data available were collected by Adams from reports in Quebec newspapers concerning ships arriving from Irish ports for 1818–24, inclusive. The reports seem to be trustworthy (before 1818 the newspaper accounts were incomplete, and for 1825–28,

TABLE 4	REVISED ESTIMATE OF IRISH PASSENGERS WHO DISEM-BARKED AT QUEBEC AND MONTREAL, 1829–45
Year	Figures
1829	10 575
1830	19 476
1831	39 053
1832	32 502
1833	13 581
1834	21 836
1835	8 078
1836	16 335
1837	17 490
1838	1 847
1839	6 437
1840	20 125
1841	22 145
1842	31 867
1843	11 094
1844	16 293
1845	21 138

inclusive, Adams did not collect data). If one corrects for under-reporting of illegal migrants and for Irish migrants shipping out from English and Scottish ports, by adding 10 percent to the raw data (as was done above in the case of Buchanan's data), one arrives at the following estimates of Irish landing in Quebec City and Montreal (table 5).[13] Ideally, one could take the revised version of the Quebec shipping figures as representing the annual population pool of Irish who settled in Upper and Lower Canada. Alas, there were three sources of leakage from this pool, the first two being minor, the third being disastrous for the purposes of this study. First, there were undoubtedly a few individuals who returned to the United Kingdom, their numbers being unrecorded, but doubtless minimal. Second, a small percentage of those who disembarked at Quebec City may have found their way to the Maritimes: emigrant ships were not always available to every destination and some Irish passengers may have taken the Quebec-bound ships as their only chance of emigration, intending later to move to join family and friends in the east. Third, and crucially, a very sizeable proportion of the Irish who landed in Montreal and Quebec City made their way to the United States. And, to complicate matters further, there was a counterflow of Irish migrants who landed in the States and later came north.

At this point one has reached a dead end, for there is no acceptable method of estimating how many Irishmen went to the United States to settle after landing in Quebec City or Montreal. In 1831, A.C. Buchanan estimated that in the years 1816–28, an average of two-thirds of all emigrants arriving in Lower Canada passed on to the United States, but this is merely an informed guess, made without the aid of dependable records.[14] Rather more precise estimates are possible for 1824, '25, and '26, when it was found that 40 percent, 42 percent, and 32 percent, in respective years, landed in Lower Canada and then went on to the state of New York.[15] It was estimated in 1828 that fully one-half of those who landed in Quebec City or Montreal went on to the United States, but that the proportion was considerably lower in the following year and was well under one-quarter in 1830.[16] The figure for 1832 was officially estimated at some 6.4 percent of total migration into Quebec[17] and for 1833 as 11.3 percent.[18] What these disparate figures add up to is even more confusing. There was no system of

TABLE 5	REVISED ESTIMATE OF IRISH PASSENGERS WHO DISEMBARKED AT QUEBEC AND MONTREAL, 1818–24
Year	Figures
1818	5059
1819	6568
1820	6138
1821	4455
1822	9211
1823	9254
1824	5685

ascertaining where people actually settled, and the wide range of estimates of the pass-through population merely indicates the lack of trustworthy information.

Statistics concerning the counterflow—that is, the stream of United Kingdom migrants who landed in the United States and then proceeded north—are virtually nonexistent. There are lists of the "passes" given by James Buchanan, the United Kingdom consul general in New York, to emigrants from the British Isles who wished to travel from New York to settlement in Upper Canada, but these cover only the years 1817–19.[19] In what smacked of a counsel-of-despair, the Quebec authorities in the late 1820s and early '30s claimed that the inflow and outflow almost matched each other. Although lacking accurate data on either flow, the *Quebec Official Gazette* stated that "Upon information derived from Upper Canada and other places, it is fair to presume that a reflux of British settlers from the United States has entered these Provinces, amounting to but few short of the number admitted to have passed through the Canadas, on their way to settle among our republican neighbours."[20] And, in the absence of evidence, the governor of Lower Canada gamely contended that "it might be considered as a reasonable approximation to the truth, that the number of emigrants when finally settled and form part of the resident population of Canada do not fall very short of the numbers who arrive at the port of Quebec."[21] Perhaps these claims are correct, but given the lack of systematic information on migrants from the United States, and considering that the interests of the governmental officials in Quebec were served by minimizing the loss of British subjects to the American republic, the conclusion must be "not proven." Thus, at present there is no way to employ migration data to determine the actual pattern of settlement in Upper Canada of the Scots, English, and Irish.

We can escape from this *cul de sac* (albeit only in the 1840s) by examining the Upper Canada census data. The various censuses of Upper Canada were not nearly as accurate or as probing as one would wish, but the 1842 enumeration inquired into place of birth of the province's residents. In that year, Upper Canada had 78 255 Irish-born inhabitants, making the Irish by far the largest non-indigenous group.[22]

In interpreting table 6, the crucial point to note is that, large though the immigrant numbers were, the enumeration procedures radically underrepresented the extent of new additions to Upper Canadian society. This occurred because the census authorities recorded only the birth place, not the ethnic background of each individual. Thus, although the mother and father in a family of recent arrivals were enumerated as being of European birth, their children, so long as they were born in Canada, were recorded as native Canadians, with no distinctions in the records between them and the children of, say, third-generation loyalists. At minimum, one should define as members of an identifiable ethnic group not only those born abroad, but at least the first generation born in Canada; indeed, in many groups the sense of identifiably ethnic identity has run considerably longer. Thus, the magnitude of the native-born Canadian population was a statistical chimera, not one reflective of the actual ethnicity of the people.

TABLE 6   *BIRTHPLACES OF UPPER CANADIAN
            POPULATION, 1842*

Country of Birth	Numbers	Proportion of UC population (percent)
Canadian-born		
English Canadian	247 665	50.8
French Canadian	13 969	2.9
Subtotal Canadian-born	261 634	53.7
Foreign-born		
British Isles		
Ireland	78 255	16.1
England and Wales	40 684	8.4
Scotland	39 781	8.1
Subtotal British Isles	158 720	32.6
United States	32 809	6.7
Continental Europe	6 581	1.4
Subtotal Foreign-born	198 110	40.7
Not known	27 309	5.6
Total population	487 053	100.0

Source: Derived from 1842 census, as found in *Census of Canada, 1871*, 4: 136.

Ideally, the 1842 census should be reprocessed in its entirety. Failing that, there are three methods of redacting the 1842 data, each helpful in part, but none totally satisfactory. First—Revision A—one can begin with the base population of Upper Canada before heavy emigration started and define this group, plus the numbers accruing to it by natural increase, as the "native Canadian" population. This figure will be less than the native-born category as defined in the 1842 census. The difference between the two numbers, presumably, will consist of the first generation of offspring of foreign-born parents, and their grown children, in cases of early migrants. Then, one adds this ethnic figure to foreign-born populations as shown in the 1842 census, to obtain an aggregate total of the foreign-born and their offspring. Next, one adds a portion of this corrected ethnic figure to each ethnic group in proportion to its existence in the population in 1842, and in theory, obtains a more accurate indication of the relative numerical importance of each group than is provided in the original census data. Specifically, *if* one takes the base population of Upper Canada to have been 100 000 in 1812[23] and the rate of natural increase to have been 30 percent per decade, [24] *then* the "true" native indigenous population in Upper Canada in 1842 would have been approximately 219 700. One could then estimate the ethnic derivation as in table 7.

For many reasons (in particular, the shakiness of the estimate of the base population—in 1812 it may well have been closer to 70 000 than to 100 000—and the arbitrary nature of the percentage of rate of natural increase) these estimates are highly questionable.

T A B L E 7 R E V I S I O N A	
Ethnic Derivation	Percentage
Indigenous Canadian	45
Irish	18
English and Welsh	10
Scottish	10
United States	8
Continental Europe	2
Unknown	7

Thus, we abandon Revision A and attempt Revision B. Fundamentally, this is an attempt to estimate the first-generation ethnic population and to add this number to the figures for the foreign-born and thus to provide an indication of ethnicity over two generations. Here we (1) "correct" the raw population data for 1842 by distributing the "unknown" category amongst the various ethnic categories in proportion to the relative size of each group. This is not unreasonable—they were, indeed, born somewhere, and a proportional distribution makes more sense than any alternative allocation.[25] (2) We now determine the hypothetical number of families in Upper Canada (an actual number was not enumerated). We do this by dividing the number of married people—155 304—by two and then multiplying by 1.028 to take into account single-parent families (this multiple is derived from the 1848 census, as comparable information was not available for 1842).[26] This yields us an estimate of 79 826 family units in Upper Canada in 1842. (3) We assume that both the propensity to marry and family size does not vary by ethnic group. Actually, this assumption is conservative, because in most societies immigrant groups have larger families than do long-established residents. The conservative procedure guarantees that our revision will, if anything, err on the side of caution. (4) To obtain the average number of children in each family, we divide the number of children fourteen years of age and under—224 023—by the estimated number of families and obtain 2.8 children per family. The reader will recognize that this too is a highly conservative procedure as far as estimating ethnicity is concerned, both because many children stayed en famille beyond age fourteen, and because the completed family size (the total number of children born in the lifetime of a marriage) is greater than the actual number in the family at any given time. (5) Finally, we subtract the imputed number of first-generation born in Canada from the "Canadian" total and add it to the appropriate ethnic total. These procedures yield the following estimate (table 8) of the ethnicity of Upper Canada's population in 1842. The revisions suggested are conservative in part because they were based on an assumption of average family size—2.8 children per family—that is very small indeed. This figure comes from a statistical definition of family size as including only children fourteen years of age or younger.

Let us turn to Revision C. In making it, we will follow the same procedures and make the same assumptions as for Revision B, with one exception: instead of taking 2.8 as the average number of children in each family,

TABLE 8 *REVISION B*

Ethnicity	Estimate	Percentage
Born in Ireland or born in Canada of Irish-born parentage	120 949	24.9
Born in England or Wales or born in Canada of English- or Welsh-born parentage	62 884	12.9
Born in Scotland or born in Canada of Scottish-born parentage	61 480	12.6
Subtotal for British Isles	245 313	50.4
Born in the United States or born in Canada of American-born parentage	50 720	10.4
Born in Continental Europe or born in Canada of European-born parentage	10 169	2.1
Canadian—defined as all second and succeeding generations born in British North America	180 851	37.1
Grand total	487 053	100.0

we will take 5.76 as the average family size (including parents). This figure comes from the census of 1851 which enumerates as family members all those living in the family unit, regardless of their age. (The 1851 census was the first to collect data permitting this kind of calculation.)[27]

Whereas Revision B was a conservative recension of the ethnicity data, Revision C probably goes too far: when transposed to the 1842 data, the average family size calculable from the 1851 census leaves too few single people in the society. Taking Revision B and Revision C together, however, we have a set of bracketing figures. These can be considered the boundaries of probability and somewhere between them will be found the truth of the matter.

The long paperchase through the extant statistical sources leads to two sets of conclusions. The first of these indicates that even if ethnic identity is defined very narrowly (as lasting through the first generation born in Canada, and no longer) only a moiety, or less, of the Upper Canada population in the early 1840s can be considered native Canadian. The constellation of ethnic groups from the British Isles constituted, at minimum, half of the population, and, amongst all ethnic groups, the largest was the Irish: a quarter of the population, at the least, and probably more. This was *before* the massive Irish migrations of the Famine years.

Second, the necessity of making long skeins of calculations, of employing unverifiable (albeit reasonable) assumptions on a number of points, and the complete lack of data on other matters (such as the absence of data on

TABLE 9 REVISION C

Ethnicity	Estimate	Percentage
*Born in Ireland or born in Canada of Irish-born parentage	134 363	27.6
Born in England or Wales or born in Canada of English- or Welsh-born parentage	69 859	14.3
Born in Scotland or born in Canada of Scottish-born parentage	68 298	14.0
Subtotal for British Isles	272 520	55.9
Born in the United States or born in Canada of American-born parentage	56 348	11.6
Born in Continental Europe or born in Canada of European-born parentage	11 296	2.3
Canadian—defined as all second and succeeding generations born in British North America	146 889	30.2
Grand total	487 053	100.0

place of birth before the year 1842), helps to explain why the history of the Irish in Upper Canada has been largely avoided—avoided by all but a few Canadian social historians, by historians of the Irish in America, and by historians of the Irish nation and its diaspora.

○

Here it would be comforting to introduce a simplification—to claim that the main reason that the historical literature on the Irish in Upper Canada is so thin is that the Irish who migrated there were predominantly of the "wrong sort," in the sense that they were not from the Catholic majority of the Irish population. From that Catholic majority arose Irish nationalism and it was this nationalism that not only triumphed in the home country but was celebrated by the predominantly Catholic Irish who settled in America. Historians love winners, but the Protestant Irish who predominated in Upper Canada were not part of the romantic, victorious, and memorable tradition of Irish nationalism, and are hence easily (although wrongly) consigned the role of reactionary, uninteresting, and, in the context of Irish historiography, forgettable losers.

This explanation actually is more plausible than stating it in so bold a fashion may imply, as it is based on some sensible observations about the general nature of large migrations. That the major causes of human migrations are economic was of course the observation that underlay Ravenstein's classic Laws of Migration, formulated in the 1870s and '80s.[28] This is not merely a truism, but an important operational point in analyzing Irish migration, for economically induced or motivated migration—as distinct from compelled migrations, such as, for example, the expulsion of almost the entire Acadian population—is selective.[29] And, crucially, this selectivity, taking all migrants together, almost always tends to be bimodal. Specifically, in most societies from which migrants issue, there is a sharp distinction between those who leave because of "plus factors" (such as, say, a young shopkeeper who leaves to seek better commercial opportunities in another city) and those who respond chiefly to negative factors (as, say, the herdsmen of Eretrea, forced to move by dearth of vegetation). The one group is positively selected, the other negatively, and if one plots the characteristics of migrants using almost any index, whether education, class, or financial position, one can expect to get a J-shaped or U-shaped curve.[30]

It is possible to argue that this bimodality would be interesting in any population, but that, concerning the Irish, it is absolutely pivotal, for Irish society in the first half of the nineteenth century was itself rent by a series of social dichotomies: the Catholics and Protestants were virtually endogamous tribal groups; economically, the distinction between the agricultural subsistence sector and the rest of the economy was severe; and the northeastern quarter of the country (roughly equivalent to present-day Northern Ireland) was geographically, socially, and economically distinct from the rest of Ireland. These various Irish dualities were not coterminous, but they did overlap. As related to Irish migration to Upper Canada, the Irish dichotomies might be taken to imply that not merely was there a radical change in the character of Irish migration consequent upon the Famine, but the pre-Famine migration to Canada was overwhelmingly Protestant and that occurring thereafter, mostly Catholic.

But reality intervenes. Neither the pre- nor post-Famine emigration fits neatly into this pattern. Granted, it is well known that the Irish port from which, in most pre-Famine years, the largest number emigrated to British North America was Belfast;[31] and it is undeniable that the Protestants were predominant in Ulster. But it is a long way from these two points to conclude solidly that the bulk of the pre-Famine emigrants were Protestants or, indeed, that most migrants actually hailed from Ulster—as distinct from embarking there—whatever their religion.

S.H. Cousens has made a remarkable series of studies of the pre-Famine Irish demographic data, for our purposes the most important being a discussion of regional variations in emigration from 1821 to 1841. In the absence of trustworthy direct emigration figures, he has calculated reliable indirect indicators of emigration before the Famine, region by region, through analysis of population change in each census district. His research reveals that migration came mostly from the northern half of Ireland (from Ulster and the neighbouring parts of Leinster and Connaught) and least from the south. Specifically, counties Longford, Westmeath, Londonderry, and

Donegal had the highest pre-Famine rates of outward migration. Cousens notes that emigration was especially strong in areas in which there was a domestic textile industry: this domestic industry was severely hurt by the post-Napoleonic slump, combined with the spread of textile mechanization. (That the fringe areas of the domestic textile industry were hurt more than the central Lagan valley industry is a reasonable assumption; the rise of mechanical production in Belfast and environs absorbed thousands of otherwise displaced textile workers). In the southern half of Ireland, emigration was especially strong in small pockets (in particular, parts of counties Limerick, King's, Queen's, Wicklow, and Cork), from which small Protestant minorities engaged in weaving had a high emigration rate. In contrast, the subsistence agricultural areas of Connaught and Munster produced relatively few emigrants. (Counties Clare, Kerry, and Galway had the lowest emigration rates, 1821–41.) Thus, it is fair to assess the pre-Famine emigration as comprised largely of migrants who were in reduced circumstances, but well above the poverty line.[32]

Thus, from Irish data we know that (1) in most pre-Famine years, Belfast was the most common port of out-migration; (2) that most migrants came from the northern half of Ireland; (3) that most came from the relatively prosperous areas of the country, not from the subsistence regions; and (4) that Protestants had a higher propensity to emigrate than did Catholics.

Yet, in the absence of direct data on out-migration, we can *not* conclude (1) that most migrants came from Ulster. The northern half of Ireland and the province of Ulster are not at all the same thing, and it was the Leinster and Connaught counties which border on Ulster that had the highest out-migration rates. And parts of Ulster (in particular, County Antrim) had very low emigration rates; (2) *nor* can we conclude that the bulk of pre-famine migrants necessarily were Protestants. Although Protestants certainly had a higher propensity to emigrate than did the Catholics, there were fewer of them in the general population. As far as Irish sources are concerned, we can go no further.

In trying to escape from this trap, one might be tempted to posit that, as far as Upper Canada was concerned, a socio-religious filter operated and that Irish Catholics tended to go to the United States and Irish Protestants to Upper Canada. This would fit well with the traditional notion that Protestants, being loyal to the Crown, wished to continue to live under the Union Jack, and that Catholics, being instinctively nationalist and therefore republican, chose to live in the republic to the south. For such a comforting simplicity, I can find no convincing evidence, at least as relates to the pre-Famine migration. And I suspect that most people who migrated before the Famine—mostly individuals with some financial resources, with information on alternate economic opportunities, and with the will to act decisively to better their chances in life—found the constitutional niceties and geopolitical boundaries to be a virtual irrelevance.

In the absence of Upper Canadian data bearing directly on the issue of ethnicity and religious affiliation (the 1842 census tallied both country of birth and religious affiliation, but did not cross-tabulate these categories) what can one do? The answer is: quite a bit, provided one proceeds with a large degree of humility and sedulously avoids the "fallacy of false precision." Ideally, one would like to see a complete retabulation of the 1842 census for the entire province, but that would be so expensive a proceeding as to be chimerical. Failing that, a random sampling, comprising several thousand cases would be desirable, and perhaps some day that will be done. For the present, however, one must be satisfied with employing accounting procedures which permit a reformulation of the aggregate data. The reformulation detailed below, which gives an estimate of the Protestant–Catholic breakdown amongst the Irish, should be read as being the most likely division within a possible range of two to three percentage points either way. Given the assumptions which one must make in the reformulation process and given the shaky nature of the 1842 census, to claim any greater degree of precision would be to invite hubris.

The Right Reverend Alexander Macdonnell, the Catholic bishop of Kingston and one of the best-informed observers of the Upper Canadian religious situation, stated in 1838 that "the Catholics, who compose a great proportion of the population of Upper Canada, are either Irish emigrants, Scots highlanders, or French Canadians."[33] This can be employed as the basis for a formula for estimating the religious composition of the Irish, as follows: (1) begin with the Catholic population as reported in 1842—65 203; (2) from this, subtract the total of French Canadians;[34] (3) doubtless there were some French-Canadian Protestants, but assume that their numbers equal those of Catholics born in Continental Europe, England, Wales, and the United States, or those of the first generation of such parentage; (4) assume that 3 percent of the Scots-born and of the first generation born in Canada of Scots parentage and 3 percent of the second generation Canadian-born inhabitants of non-French origin were Catholics and subtract these figures from the preceding subtotal (actually, this probably underestimates somewhat the Catholic proportion of the Scots-born and first generation Scots populations, and overstates that of the non-French, second generation Canadian-born group);[35] (5) the remaining number of Catholics can be taken to equal the number of Irish inhabitants (either Irish-born, or first generation) who were Catholics. This number is slightly under 44 000; (6) finally, by comparing this figure to the inferred total for Irish ethnicity,[36] one has a figure for the Catholics amongst the Irish-born and first-generation Irish in Upper Canada in 1842 of 34.5 percent.

Forget now all the procedures and the individual numbers. Instead, focus on the two key points that have emerged; (1) that before the Famine, the Irish population in Upper Canada was mostly Protestant, but (2) that the Irish-Catholic minority was formidable, indeed, much larger than was supposed by contemporaries and by later historians. The Protestant–Catholic split is best described as roughly 2:1. One can accept this with considerable confidence. Changes in detail of our calculations would budge the results a percentage point or, at most, two or three, either way, but the historian who is content to deal in words can be confident in accepting that there were about twice as many Protestants as Catholics amongst the Irish in Upper Canada.

o

Remember that this was *before* the Famine. And then recognize how complicated the picture has now become. Instead of a simple dichotomy between
early arriving Protestants and later Famine-starving Catholics, one must
instead deal amongst the Irish with two groups of early emigrants,
Protestant and Catholic, each of whom had emigrated with resources in
hand and with aspirations intact, and each of whom would have relationships with the later arrivals. (Implicit in this observation is the point that
most pre-Famine Catholics were not pauper peasants, although, undeniably, there were pauper emigrants amongst both Catholics and Protestants.)
The problems of the early-arrived and relatively prosperous Catholics in
dealing with their post-Famine coreligionists was infinitely more difficult
than that posed for the early-arrived Protestants, who treated the Famine
Catholics as members of a lower and alien order.

Indirectly, by establishing that the Catholics comprised such a large
proportion of the pre-Famine population, one opens the door to another
level of understanding—and of complication. If one compares the probable
religious persuasion of those of Irish derivation in 1871 with that calculated
for 1842, one discovers that the Catholic proportion of the Irish in Upper
Canada has stayed virtually constant—*not* risen as one might expect following the Famine: it was approximately 34.5 percent in 1842 and 33.8 percent
in 1871.[37] Either there was a high degree of apostasy amongst Irish
Catholics (a suggestion that cannot be considered even remotely possible)
or, *despite* the Famine in Ireland generally having affected the Irish
Catholics more severely, the stream of migrants was still a dual stream and
the bulk of the emigrants to Upper Canada continued to be Protestant.

Thus, the complexity of relationships within the Irish ethnic community
increases almost exponentially. Not only must a history of the Irish in
Upper Canada take into account the relationship to each other of the relatively well-off Protestants and Catholics who migrated before the Famine;
not only must it indicate how each group dealt with the post-Famine
expelled Catholics; the social history of the Irish must show how the later,
post-Famine Protestants related to both sets of earlier pre-Famine settlers;
and, of course, how the Protestant and Catholic Irish of the Famine and
post-Famine years related each to the other in the New World. All this must
be taken into account in addition to defining the relationships of these several sectors to the outside society.

o

Not only do we actually know very little about the Irish in Upper Canada,
but most of what we think we know is wrong. To take one example: the classic article by H.C. Pentland on the development of a capitalistic labour market in Canada managed to be simultaneously a masterpiece of compact
Marxist social history and of inaccurate ethnic observation.[38] The piece has
obtained the virtual status of holy writ amongst many labour historians. Yet,
without offering any documentation, Pentland states that it was Ulstermen

(by whom he means Protestants from Ulster) who almost exclusively comprised the migrants to Upper Canada in the 1820s and who predominated until about 1835. Then, says he, they were gradually supplanted by Roman Catholic peasants, a group whom he believes were subsistence tenant farmers from Munster and Connaught. Further, Pentland states, the great flood of these poor Catholic Irishmen began in the 1840s, before the Famine.

Pentland's work implies several observations that probably are inaccurate. First, the equation of Ulster emigrants with Protestant emigrants is untenable. Second, as Cousens' study indicated, the majority of migrants, even in the 1820s, were not from Ulster; they were from the northern half of Ireland, something quite different. Third, the equation of Roman Catholicism with subsistence farming is not justified. Catholicism cannot be used as a synonym for abject poverty. Fourth, there is no justification in equating Catholic migration with a geographic origin in Munster or Connaught. And, fifth, the pre-Famine flight of large numbers of impoverished Irish Catholics should not be vaguely dated as beginning in the 1840s before the Famine, but with the Famine itself. To view the 1840s as a decade having some kind of historical unity in this matter is fanciful. There was not a natural flow of pauperized Irish peasants that was "especially large in the 1840s and reached its peak with the Famine flight in 1847,"[39] but instead a radical break caused by the Famine in the numbers of migrants and the immediate economic situation from which they came.

This is not to gainsay the fact that the Irish migrants, like those of most migrating groups, did have their bimodal characteristics. Yes, the Irish did follow an archetypal J-curve: most of the pre-Famine migrants were individuals of some resources who probably were attracted by the opportunities of betterment in the new land; a minority were paupers who were virtually expelled from their homeland (by emigration-aid groups, by parish aid, or by clearing landlords). They fetched up in the Canadas with few skills and fewer resources and became, at least for a time, part of the emerging wage proletariat. But just because someone was poor and had to take wage labour, one should not assume that he was a Catholic, or from the subsistence areas of Ireland. As Pentland himself admitted, the men who dug the Lachine Canal in the 1820s were probably mostly Ulster Protestants.[40]

Such faulty religious and geographical equations are relatively easy to correct. Much more difficult to deal with are mistaken or misleading points of emphasis in the literature dealing with the Irish migrants. This problem is well illustrated by Michael Cross's often brilliant work on the social concomitants of the Upper Canadian lumber trade.[41] Cross shows how the Irish Catholics in the "Lower Town" of Bytown in the 1830s formed a ghetto community that was physically violent, culturally defensive, and economically vulnerable. The picture is convincing; the problem is that this community, while real, was highly atypical of the settlement locations of most Irishmen. Although one cannot fault Cross for not emphasizing how unusual the Bytown area was—what author will preface an article by telling the reader of the *un*importance of the subject at hand?—it is very easy to misread his work because he is dealing with the abnormal tip of the J-curve, not the stem which represents the bulk of the Irish ethnic population.

This leads to a warning about studies of the Irish in ghetto areas or in urban concentrations: because such studies are relatively easy to do (urban populations produce newspapers and municipal records in bulk) and because the Irish conflicts with other urban groups were often dramatic (and thus attractive to the historian looking for a saleable topic) the Irish urban experience has been—and doubtless in future studies will continue to be—magnified out of all proportion to its historical reality. Thus, Kenneth Duncan, in a widely reprinted and highly misleading article on the Irish settlement in Canada West after the Great Famine, argues two major points, each without a shred of demographic evidence: that even before the Famine, the Irish showed a "preference for urban life," and that during and after the Famine, in Canada West, "the Irish peasant became a city man," preferring "an urban slum to an independent farmstead."[42] Actually, as I will argue later (a) it is certain that most Irishmen who arrived before the Famine did not settle in urban areas; (b) even after the full effects of Famine migration were felt, most people of Irish descent lived in rural areas; (c) even if one limits one's definition of "Irish" to mean Roman Catholics (and this is *not* an acceptable limitation), most of them settled in the countryside; and (d) if one went even further and defined "Irish" to mean Roman Catholics from the subsistence sector of the Irish economy, *even then* it is unlikely that most of them settled in cities.

Note that in referring to Pentland, Cross, and Duncan, I have not been picking on academic weak sisters. Their comments on the Irish are quoted extensively and often are taken as the most authoritative judgements on the Irish in Upper Canada. That their works include factual errors and evidentiary shortcomings is irritating but not serious; those errors are easily correctable. What is not so easily put right is a set of fallacious ways of thinking about the Irish in Upper Canada which are more pernicious and much more likely to do lasting harm. Unless one can scrub these fallacies from the minds of young scholars taking up the study of the Irish as an ethnic group, the work by the next generation of historians will be worth little; even if they get the facts right, misleading modes of thought will preclude proper explication. Specifically, one finds amongst the three sages the following fallacious ways of thinking.

First, and most embarrassing, but inherent to all three writers, is a racism that, although doubtlessly unconscious and unintentional, is incompatible with responsible scholarship. Thus, Pentland stereotypes the Irish as follows: "The Irish peasant was hard-working for others, indolent for himself, ignorant, superstitious, fervent, belligerant [sic], loyal, sociable,"[43] a characterization that might well have been used by a Cracker describing an American black, had he added that they sure had a good sense of rhythm. Similarly, Cross notes that the Lanark County Irish were "an uncivilized group of semi-savages; indigent, ignorant of any but the most primitive agricultural techniques." He adds that the "lawlessness" of the Irish terrorized "the honest settlers and good folk,"[44] a duality which reminds one of all those good folk and honest settlers being terrorized by all them evil men in them black hats in all them westerns. Least offensive is Kenneth Duncan, who, with the social scientist's sensitivity to racial stereotypes, merely assumes that the Irish had an inherent cultural drive to live in slums, be often unemployed, and frequently diseased.

Second, the fallacy of floating terminology is endemic to the three authorities, who might in exculpation plead that it is prevalent in the contemporary sources as well. In particular, the term "Irish" is sometimes used to refer to all migrants from Ireland. (This is the only sense in which the term has any operational meaning.) At other times, "Irish" means "Irish Catholic," and at still other times, it means an Irish Catholic from the poorest areas of Ireland who himself was poverty stricken.

Floating terminology, of course, is based on the failure of specificity. The remedy is simple enough: always make it clear that Irish Catholics and Irish Protestants are part of a larger general ethnic body—the Irish—and let us know which segment you are talking about. And, among both Irish Catholics and Irish Protestants, make it clear that there are poverty stricken emigrants and those of at least moderate means, and, again, let us know which ones you are discussing.

Third, "Irish peasant" appears in all three students' works as a prime example of the fallacy of false specificity. It is used in each of the studies to mean a Catholic from Ireland who was sufficiently pauperized to fit into the social stereotyping involved in each of the three men's work. The specificity is invalid, for pauperized peasants of the Protestant faith emigrated, and, conversely, many of the Catholic small tenant farmers who left before the Famine, though undeniably peasants, were well above the poverty line.

Fourth, the tendency to project the atypical (but dramatic, readable, and politically agreeable) as the general, in portraits of the Irish in Upper Canada follows almost inevitably from fallacies one through three, listed above.

Fifth, all of the works, but especially that of Michael Cross, show an unremitting desire to explain (at least in part) the behaviour of various Irishmen in Upper Canada in terms of their background in Ireland. That is fine, indeed, admirable. However, one can*not* explain the behaviour of any special group of individuals as directly derivative from the general condition of the country from which they came. Moreover, individuals often leave their homeland with the desire to repudiate, not replicate, its central characteristics. Thus, Cross's analysis of the Lanark County Irish Catholics in the 1820s is causally absurd: he notes that they were termed "little better than banditti" by the commandant of the Lanark settlement, and then explains, "but they were so because they were uncivilized and lazy, because they came from a dislocated society."[45]

Sixth, both Pentland and Duncan illustrate the fundamental fallacy of letting one's framework dictate one's data. In Pentland's case, he is committed to an ideologically mounted explanation of the creation of a capitalistic labour market in Canada that requires a surplus labour force if the model is to function. The Irish migrants fill that need nicely, at least if bent to his purposes. Concerning the "Irish peasant" (that phrase again) Pentland asserts:

> Unlike all earlier arrivals in North America, he never wanted to be
> an independent farmer. Whether because of his remoteness from
> the Protestant ethic, or because the countryman's position was so

hopeless in Ireland where wage employment offered the only chances, the Irish peasant clung to wage work in spite of every hazard of low pay, uncertain employment and abominable conditions. This attitude made Wakefield class these peasants, scathingly, as his fourth category of slaves—voluntary ones. But it was this attitude that made possible the capitalistic market, as far as unskilled labour is concerned, in which employers could take or reject labour at will, always confident of a reserve to cushion their needs.[46]

Thus, the needs of Pentland's model dictate the characteristics ascribed to the Irish.

Kenneth Duncan engages in a similar fallacy, but in his work the framework which dictates the data is not ideological, but cultural: he takes the experience of the Irish in the United States as his model and, although he questions the applicability of the explanatory system of Oscar Handlin to the Upper Canadian data, he implicitly accepts the American urban experience as the norm. But the Upper Canadian data fit the American pattern only if they are grossly distorted. As will be shown in Part II, unlike the American Irish, those in Upper Canada were not ghettoized and, indeed, not even chiefly urbanized.

PART II

We know so little about the Irish in Upper Canada, therefore, in part because the information on the Irish migration is scanty before mid-century, and in part because Canadian scholars, in the few instances when they have addressed the Irish as an historical group, have been remarkably wrongheaded. In fact, they have done more harm than good.

But there is more to the problem than that. We have little accurate information because the Irish in Upper Canada are devilishly elusive. Even after making allowances for the thinness of early sources, one almost feels that most of them made an effort to become historically invisible.

Let me pursue this point, limiting discussion here to the pattern of migration during and after the Famine. Data on this migration has import for our viewpoint on both Protestants and Catholics, but is especially important to a proper understanding of the settlement pattern of the Irish Catholics. Later, in Part III, I will touch directly on the problems of chronicling the Irish Protestant population. (For the sake of convenience, from now onward, I shall refer to the territory involved as "Ontario": although the official name for Upper Canada became "Canada West" at the union of the Canadas, and stayed so until Confederation, the name was not fully adopted by contemporaries, and since most of the important data concerning the Irish was collected soon after Confederation, "Ontario" is quite appropriate.)

The Great Famine of 1846–49 is the one event in modern Irish history that is presently familiar to the educated layman throughout the English-speaking world.[47] Within Irish society, the Famine effected a social, cultural, and economic upheaval more thoroughgoing than could conceivably be produced by a merely political revolution. The bulk of the Irish population completely redefined its marriage and inheritance patterns and its agricultural practices. That was at home. Abroad, the English-speaking colonies and the United States received the Irish outpouring which, at times, was more of a flood than a diaspora. Crucially, the Irish outflow did not end with the passing of the Famine. The new Irish social and economic arrangements that came in train of the Famine (in particular, the replacing of partible with impartible inheritance of land and the increase of pastoral farming at the expense of intensive tillage) meant that for a full century after the Famine, Ireland extruded sons and daughters for whom there was no place at home. At least 3 million persons left Ireland between 1845 and 1870, and another 1.1 million emigrated between 1871 and 1891. In 1891, 39 percent of all Irish-born individuals in the world were living outside their homeland.[48]

Until 1853 the figures for Irish migration to British North America are less than completely reliable. (Table 10 gives the total British Isles emigration figures as a context for viewing the Irish pattern; the table is a continuation of table 1).[49] The unrevised figure for migrants from Irish ports to

TABLE 10	TOTAL MIGRATION FROM THE BRITISH ISLES TO MAJOR EXTRA-EUROPEAN COUNTRIES, (unrevised data) 1846–71		
Year	British North America	United States	Australasia
1846	43 439	82 239	2 277
1847	109 680	142 154	4 949
1848	31 065	188 233	23 904
1849	41 367	219 450	32 191
1850	32 961	223 078	16 037
1851	42 605	267 357	21 532
1852	32 873	244 261	87 881
1853	31 779	190 952	54 818
1854	35 679	153 627	77 526
1855	16 110	86 239	47 284
1856	11 299	94 931	41 329
1857	16 803	105 516	57 858
1858	6 504	49 356	36 454
1859	2 469	57 096	28 604
1860	2 765	67 879	21 434
1861	3 953	38 160	20 597
1862	8 328	48 726	38 828
1863	9 665	130 528	50 157
1864	11 371	130 165	40 073
1865	14 424	118 463	36 683
1866	9 988	131 840	23 682
1867	12 160	126 051	14 023
1868	12 332	108 490	12 332
1869	20 921	146 737	14 457
1870	27 168	153 466	16 526
1871	24 954	150 788	11 695

Source: Carrier and Jeffrey, 95.

North America, 1846–52, inclusive, are in table 11.[50] These figures, however, do not include any indication of the large numbers of Irish who embarked from British ports, especially Liverpool, and make no provision for illegal passengers. For the sake of comparability to pre-1846 data, I am employing William Forbes Adams' formula to revise the data (table 12).[51] This accomplished, one can present a numerical outline of Irish migration to British North America and to the United States from the beginning of the Famine through 1871 (see table 13).

So cataclysmic was the Irish Famine and so forceful was the resultant tidal wave of migration that it is easy to misinterpret the pattern of Irish migration insofar as Ontario is concerned. Specifically, it is tempting, but wrong, to infer either that the Famine-induced migration completely changed the character of the human flow between Ireland and Ontario or that the Famine sent to Ontario a group of humans so pulverized by poverty as to be as socially indistinguishable as storm-tossed stones upon a shingle beach. Such a lack of discrimination is easy enough to fall into because both contemporary observers and later historians often did so themselves. For example, writing in the autumn of 1847, the chief emigration agent for Canada West noted that three-quarters of the immigrants in that year were Irish, "diseased in body and belonging generally to the lowest class of unskilled labourers."[52] And, in 1931, Gilbert Tucker employed an oft-quoted phrase in the pages of the *American Historical Review*: "during that baleful

TABLE 11

Year	To British North America	To the United States
1846	31 738	7 070
1847	71 253	24 502
1848	20 852	38 843
1849	26 568	43 673
1850	19 784	31 297
1851	23 930	38 418
1852	17 693	23 371

TABLE 12

Year	To British North America	To the United States
1846	40 667	68 730
1847	104 518	119 314
1848	24 809	157 473
1849	33 392	181 011
1850	26 444	183 672
1851	31 709	219 453
1852	23 389	194 874

year, 1847, there poured into Canada the most polluted as well as relatively the most swollen stream of immigration in the history of that country."[53]

Whatever the Irish multitudes may have seemed to contemporary observers (one can readily understand their being overwhelmed by the unprecedented influx) there is no excuse for present-day historians treating the Irish immigrants as a faceless lumpenproletariat. As the work of S.H. Cousens clearly has demonstrated, the Irish who emigrated were *not* by-and-large the decimated paupers of the poorest regions of Ireland: the inhabitants of the most cruelly-affected regions of the country, the west and south-west, if they escaped starvation and epidemic, were far too poor to migrate. Of course, few migrants were people of significant means: emigration was lowest in the areas of Ulster where the Famine had the least effect. Actually, by-and-large, the Irish migrants came from the same areas and from the same economic strata that had been the source of migration before

TABLE 13 IRISH MIGRATION TO NORTH AMERICA FROM ALL PORTS IN THE UNITED KINGDOM, 1846–71 (including revised data: 1846–52)

Year	Total to North America	To USA	To British North America
1846	109 397	68 730	40 667
1847	223 832	119 314	104 518
1848	182 282	157 473	24 809
1849	214 403	181 011	33 392
1850	210 116	183 672	26 444
1851	251 162	219 453	31 709
1852	218 263	194 874	23 389
1853	179 361	156 970	22 391
1854	134 004	111 095	22 900
1855	63 270	57 164	6 106
1856	63 131	58 777	4 354
1857	70 516	66 060	4 456
1858	33 656	31 498	2 158
1859	42 271	41 180	1 091
1860	53 318	52 103	1 215
1861	30 054	28 209	1 845
1862	36 628	33 521	3 107
1863	98 424	94 477	3 947
1864	99 978	94 368	5 610
1865	89 274	82 085	7 189
1966	90 515	86 594	3 921
1867	84 153	79 571	4 582
1868	61 354	57 662	3 692
1869	69 776	66 467	3 309
1870	70 768	67 891	2 877
1871	68 652	65 591	3 061

Source: Carrier and Jeffrey, 95, and revised estimate for 1846–52, given in table 12.

the Famine: the areas of Leinster, southern Ulster, and northern Connaught that can be denominated "north-central Ireland." These were areas in which the increase in poor rates (caused by local destitution consequent upon the potato failure) was most pronounced. These rates fell most heavily upon the small tenant farmers. It was these small farmers who led the flight from Ireland, exchanging the proceeds of their last cash crop in Ireland for a ticket to a New World. The emigration rate in the commercial farming areas of north-central Ireland, where most families operated small tenant farms, was two to three times as high as in the counties such as Cork, Kilkenny, Waterford, and Tipperary, which had the highest proportion of landless labourers. To the extent that landless labourers could afford to migrate, they went largely to England. North America was for the relatively well-off.[54]

Physically, the Irish migrant to Ontario arrived in terrible condition, but his bodily emaciation should not be equated with cultural impoverishment or with technological ignorance. Typically, he had not been a landless labourer and he did not now become a lumpenprol. Instead, he had been the manager of a small-scale commercial farming enterprise, one which had been scuttled, not by his own ineptitude, but by a natural disaster of overwhelming magnitude. As will be seen in a moment, in Ontario, he passed through the cities on the way to settling successfully in the commercial farm economy of small towns and isolated farmsteads.

The pattern of geographic provenance within Ireland and the economic background of the overseas emigrants from Ireland were remarkably similar before and during the Great Famine, and a parallel continuity can be discerned in the religious composition of the group who migrated to Ontario. Here, recall the calculations from Part I which indicated that the religious divide in the Irish ethnic population was close to the same in 1871 as it had been in 1842: the Catholics composed approximately 34.5 percent of the Irish ethnic population in 1842 and 33.8 percent in 1871.

Certainly, the continuity in patterns of origin, both geographic and economic, amongst Irish migrants, and the remarkably stable pattern of religious distribution should give some pause to anyone who wishes to view the Irish (in Ontario) as some great engine, by which at mid-century, the world began to be turned upside down.

o

The question in dealing with the Irish who came during and after the Famine is: where did they settle? In cities, towns and villages, or on farms? This question is applicable to all Irish migrants, but is especially pertinent to the Catholics. The dominant view of what happened to the Famine and post-Famine Irish migrants is expressed most clearly by Kenneth Duncan:

> To sum up, disease, ignorance, and poverty made the entry into agriculture exceedingly difficult for the famine migrants and they became, it would appear, urban by compulsion.
>
> Later, however, when circumstances altered, the Irish remained urban.[55]

Urban? Let us see.

The censuses of 1851 and 1861 tallied the birthplace of all inhabitants of Ontario and also indicated whether the populace lived in cities, towns and villages, or in the countryside. These enumerations had their flaws, but are quite serviceable for defining the fundamental characteristics of the population. Irritatingly, however, the census authorities did not cross-tabulate place of birth and place of residence, so one must do this task oneself. The job is clerical and tiresome, but not methodologically controversial. The results: in 1851, 14.0 percent of the inhabitants of Ontario who had been born in Ireland lived in cities (the average size of which was 14 253 inhabitants); in 1861, 13.6 percent of the Irish-born lived in cities (the average size of which had risen to 20 777).[56] A group urban by compulsion? Hardly.

But let us be generous and include as urbanites all those who lived in incorporated towns and villages, irrespective of how small those settlements were. We find then that an additional 7.1 percent of the Irish-born are included as of the 1851 census (living in towns and villages, the average size of which was 2111). And, in 1861, 12.0 percent of the Irish-born in Ontario resided in towns and villages (whose average size was 1957).[57] Now, it is hard to see how living in a town of 2000, in the typical case, can be viewed as an urban experience, but if one wishes to accept it as such and to add these town and village residents to the inhabitants of the cities, one still finds that in 1851 only 21.1 percent of the Irish-born in Ontario lived in cities, towns, and villages (averaging 4030 residents in size) and in 1861 the proportion was 25.6 percent (living in towns, villages, and cities whose average size was 3077).

The unavoidable fact is that, even employing the broadest possible definition of "urban," one has to conclude that the overwhelming majority of the Irish migrants to Ontario settled in the countryside. In 1851, 78.9 percent of the Irish-born lived in rural areas, and in 1861, the percentage was 74.4 percent, and that by the most narrow of definitions of rural.

Those figures deal with the Irish-born. Perhaps their children drifted to the cities and perhaps the real urban predisposition of the Irish only came out in the first and second generations born in North America. The 1871 census provided a self-definition question in which each individual's national descent was to be recorded "as given by the person questioned."[58] In modern terms, this is a subjective ethnicity item, one which is dependent wholly upon the self-perception of the individual tallied. Of the individuals in Ontario who reckoned themselves as being of Irish descent (whether Irish-born, first generation, second, or subsequent), their place of residence was as in table 14.[59]

TABLE   14

Place of Residence	Percentage
Cities (average size: 26 517)	9.5
Towns and villages (average size: 2148)	13.0
Total urban (including all cities, towns, and villages (average size: 3266)	22.5
Total rural	77.5

Clearly, actually to describe the experience of the Irish migrants and their descendants in Ontario as having been an urban one requires an act of faith sufficient to move mountains.[60]

o

There may be a plausible explanation. Possibly, just possibly, the Roman Catholics amongst the Irish-born or Irish-descended lived in urban areas, and thus underwent the Handlinesque trauma of being a religious minority and an impoverished immigrant group in an urban society—or so one could argue.

Here, the available data present us with a double difficulty: not only was there no cross-tabulation relating to the urban–rural breakdown to ethnicity in the 1871 census, but no attempt was made to cross-tabulate religious persuasion and ethnic origin. (And, of course, before 1871, ethnicity was not dealt with at all). However, a reasonably simple two-stage redaction of the 1871 data permits us to view the Irish-descended Catholics as a distinct group: first, one does a simple bit of bookkeeping, tallying the residence pattern of each of the major ethnic groups; second, one then employs the equation developed in Part I to distinguish the imputed number of Roman Catholics amongst the Irish in each major type of residential area.[61] The results for 1871 are as in table 15. Given that only one in three Irish Catholics in Ontario settled in areas that can even remotely be considered urban—and given the fact that only one in seven settled in cities—it is impossible to apply the American model to the Canadian situation, either as it involves Catholics or Protestants.[62] We must deal with the Canadian Irish on their own, not on borrowed terms.

This is inconvenient, first, because that means we must now discard all the analogies so easily drawn from the American literature and the Canadian studies which were based, either directly or indirectly, on that American material. Second, it is clear that we desperately need studies of Ontario Irish, both Protestant and Catholic, in typical places where they settled—not in cities, or even towns and villages—but in rural areas. We need to reconstruct

TABLE 15	
Place of Residence	Percentage
Catholics of Irish descent, living in cities (average size: 26 517)	14.7
Catholics of Irish descent, living in towns and villages (average size: 2148)	19.0
Total urban Catholics of Irish descent (including all cities, towns, and villages) (average size: 3266)	33.7
Total Catholics of Irish descent living in rural areas	66.3

several representative rural townships, farm by farm, family by family, correlating data of ethnicity and religion with records of landholding and with economic data from the assessment rolls. This is a difficult and time-consuming task, and the cumulative results will emerge only after many scholars have put in years of work. But to proceed any other way would be to cheat—and to risk a return to the misinformation and misinterpretation that has characterized most modern studies of the Irish in Canada.

Third, we must face the inconvenience of jettisoning most of our preconceptions about the Irish process of settlement in Ontario. No more can we accept the easy, lazy phrases, such as H.C. Pentland's, that the Irish "[were] left as sediment on the seaboard."[63] Of course, the newly arrived Irish were debouched in the major cities and towns—communication links end in cities and towns, after all, not in the middle of the countryside—but eventually most of them settled in rural areas. Thus, in all probability, a multi-stage (and in some instances, multi-generational) migration occurred from the points of disembarkation to the farmsteads. The technical problems in tracing this multi-step Irish migration to the backwoods are immense, but, like the micro-studies of individual townships, the work must be done.[64]

Although the aggregate census data indisputably establishes that the vast majority of both Catholic and Protestant Irish settled in rural areas, they do not establish that the great bulk were farmers: only township-by-township studies, or a large-sample survey will settle that point for certain. But, for the moment, I think we can posit that it is very highly probable that farming was the most common occupation amongst Irishmen and that an additional segment became farm labourers:[65] in the rural areas in nineteenth-century Ontario, there were relatively few non-farm occupations. And even if one accepts (which I do not) that the Irish probably became ancillary personnel—such as blacksmiths and small traders—out of all proportion to their numbers in the rural population, most Irish still would have to have been farmers.

And here arises another series of scholarly inconveniences. In most of the literature concerning the settlement and assimilation of the Irish in North America, an invisible syllogism reigns:

1. It is implicitly accepted that pioneering farming was a skilled and complex task.

2. It is usually stated, or at least implied, that the Famine and post-Famine Irish were technologically backward and culturally unadaptable.

3. And, therefore, had they settled in rural areas, they would have been unsuccessful as farmers.

As applied to the United States of America, this syllogism at least has the virtue of being merely meaningless: since most of the Irish migrants settled east of the Alleghenies and had little contact with the farming frontier, the assertion is virtually untestable, and, therefore, without significance.

However, when applied to Canada, and in particular to Ontario, the syllogism is pernicious in the extreme. To begin with, the romantic chronicle of early agriculture, so beloved by pioneer historians, has obscured the fact that the initial stages of settlement required relatively little skill. Brute strength and energy achieved more than agricultural expertise, as many transplanted English semi-gentry discovered, to their own discomfiture. Certainly, as farms emerged into the commercial wheat economy, increased technical skill was required, but nothing beyond the ken of an individual of average intelligence. (The quite justified wonder with which enthusiasts view late-nineteenth century barns and hand-forged implements of the same era is irrelevant. They were made by skilled artisans after long years of apprenticeship; in contrast, harrowing behind an ox is a skill learned by a strong lad in a week). It is quite clear that the Irish migrants of both religious persuasions possessed the necessary technical adaptability to cope with this kind of agriculture. Remember here the crucial point established by S.H. Cousens: that the bulk of the Famine-forced migrants came not from the totally pauperized or the landless labourers, but from amongst the small tenant farmers, individuals whose holdings, though small, were part of the cash economy and who already possessed at least minimal commercial skills. These people when they emigrated were broke, not culturally broken.

They could adapt, and in rural Canada, they did. The Irish became farmers and successful ones. Precisely how successful awaits intensive local study. The only direct approach to this question of which I am aware, Guy Ferguson's study of the Peter Robinson settlers in Emily township, reveals both a high degree of continuity on their original farmsteads and a standard of agricultural achievement comparable to that of neighbours of other ethnic backgrounds. Specifically, Ferguson's work on a group of pauper Catholic settlers from the Blackwater River Valley in County Cork (a group probably less technically advanced than the dispossessed tenant farmers of the Famine era), showed that about 45 percent of the farms settled in the mid-1820s were still held in 1861 by the original owners or their descendants, a strikingly high degree of continuity as compared to the mobility which held for pioneer settlements in general. And, despite initial disadvantages, by 1861, the Irish Catholics had the same levels of capital accumulation and were as firmly committed to mixed commercial agriculture as were their non-Catholic and non-Irish neighbours.[66]

Obviously, one cannot generalize from a single study (especially because the Robinson settlement was unusual in its origin), but, from aggregate census data, one can infer that the Irish, both Catholic and Protestant, were successful farmers—at least in the sense of their surviving and making a livelihood in the activity—from the fact that they did not pour back into the cities, towns, or villages. In 1871, when 78.0 percent of the population of Ontario was rural, 77.5 percent of those of Irish descent lived in rural areas. In 1901, when 57.1 percent of Ontario's inhabitants were rural, 58.4 percent of those of Irish descent lived in the countryside.[67] If anything, it may be argued that the Irish were slower to drift to the cities, towns, and villages than was the general population.

To return to the larger question of what happened to the Irish Catholics in Ontario, it is clear why they became, if not historically invisible, at least thoroughly camouflaged. Unlike the American situation, the Irish Catholics in central Canada dispersed amongst the larger rural population, and in all probability, their economic activities were fundamentally no different from those of their neighbours. Of course, they were distinguished by their religion, and consequent upon their faith followed certain political controversies (especially concerning education); and to this day, party political lines in rural Ontario follow religious lines.[68] Yet these divisions were formed by the practical politics of a group which was not prepared to be shoved about in their new homeland and not by the embittered, buy-the-dynamite, God-free-Ireland nationalism with which so many Irish-Americans reacted to the harsh experience of the American urban ghetto. As far as Irish nationalism was concerned, few Irish-Canadian Catholics could be bothered. And, thus, few historians of Ireland have bothered themselves about them.[69]

One can well argue that to the historian of the nineteenth century, the near-invisibility of the Irish Catholics is itself a prime indication of their success in adapting to life in this part of the New World.

o

A final, seemingly incongruous, note is in order concerning the Irish (and especially the Irish Catholics) and the cities. Although it is clear that the first step in dealing with the historical experience of the Irish in nineteenth-century Ontario is to deal with them in their predominantly agrarian setting, the Irish in cities will demand special study. (By cities, I refer to Hamilton, Kingston, London, Ottawa, and Toronto, jurisdictions which had an average size in 1851, '61, and '71 respectively of 14 253, 20 777, and 26 517.)

At first, the Irish were overrepresented in the cities,[70] but by 1871, the Irish as a group seemed to have settled in. The great Famine-induced flood was over, subsequent migration had gradually been reduced, and the Irish migrants and their offspring had completed their trek to the Canadian farm-steads: in 1871, 9.5 percent of persons of Irish descent were living in the five major cities. The comparable statistics for the entire population was strikingly similar—8.2 percent. Thus, the Irish, generally, were no longer a new and deviant immigrant group, but a part of the majority pattern. The consistency of the Irish pattern in the overall pattern is noteworthy; in 1871, 13.0 percent of those of Irish descent lived in small towns and villages, and 77.5 percent were rural residents. The figures for the overall population were, respectively, 13.8 percent and 78.0 percent, a virtually identical profile.[71]

This profile, however, masks an internal distinction amongst the Irish. Although both Catholics and Protestants became predominantly rural, the Catholics were somewhat more apt to linger behind in the cities. This point can be illustrated in two ways in table 16 (the data are for 1871, the first year when one can distinguish between Protestants and Catholics of Irish descent).

In attempting to explain this difference between the Protestants and Catholics, it is tempting to grab on to the simplistic notion that Catholics in Ireland lived in densely populated agricultural areas and that this predisposed them to live in cities; the Protestants, on the other hand, came from isolated farmsteads and were predisposed to become agricultural isolates in the New World. Possibly. But there is as yet no evidence to back up these

TABLE 16

			Percentage
I	A.	Proportion of all Irish-descended Catholics who lived in the five major cities	14.5
		Proportion of all Irish-descended Protestants who lived in the five major cities	6.9
	B.	Proportion of all Irish-descended Catholics who lived in rural areas	66.3
		Proportion of Irish-descended Protestants who lived in rural areas	83.2
II	A.	Irish-descended Protestants as proportion of total population of Ontario	22.9
		Irish-descended Protestants as proportion of total population of the five major cities	19.3
	B.	Irish-descended Catholics as proportion of total population of Ontario	11.6
		Irish-descended Catholics as proportion of total population of the five major cities	20.7

Source: Compiled and computed from *Census of Canada, 1870–71*, 1: 86–145, 252–81.

ideas, and one must be highly skeptical. In particular, one must be cautious because the areas of the classic isolated Protestant farmstead, Antrim and Down, were the very regions wherein the rate of emigration was lowest. It is likely that most Protestant emigration came from the north-central region (and was especially high in the "border" counties of Monaghan and Cavan). Probably, landholding in these areas was not signally different from Catholic landholding in the same region and in the contiguous midland areas. In other words, there is at present no compelling evidence that Catholics and Protestants who migrated to the New World came from residential backgrounds in Ireland sufficiently distinct as to explain their residential patterns in Ontario.[72]

Instead of casting about in the Old World for some vague cultural factor that would explain the differing Protestant and Catholic settlement patterns, it would be more sensible to look to more mundane reasons. Two possible explanations occur on examination: first, in terms of skills and experience as farmers, the Famine migrants by-and-large were considerably better off than were those that followed in the decade after the Famine. The Famine migrants to North America were mostly small tenant farmers who were especially hard hit by poor rates. They left, but the really poor, the landless labourer and the Galetacht peasant could not. After the Famine, poor rates dropped and the economic position of the small farmer improved, so he was less apt to leave Ireland. Simultaneously, the position of the landless labourer improved enough so that he could scrape together sufficient money to leave. These processes especially affected the character of Catholic migration. The post-Famine emigration contained a higher proportion of people from the south and west than previously, a small proportion of individuals who had operated their own farms, and a large proportion of single men (the Famine migration had largely been a family affair). All of these characteristics were of the sort that would naturally bear the new arrivals towards life in cities.[73]

A second explanation is closer at hand. Specifically, it is helpful to ask who, in Ontario, was the greater deviant from a "normal" pattern—the Catholics who were proportionately overrepresented in the cities or the Protestants who were underrepresented? The answer is: the Protestants. Why so? Because it is natural to expect that any group of relatively recent immigrants will be represented in the cities, for that is where they disembark, and even in a predominantly rural society, such as Ontario, the move to the countryside often takes years. Thus, in the decade 1871–81, when the English overtook the Irish as the largest in-coming group in Ontario, they showed the same basic pattern of overrepresentation in the cities that had prevailed amongst the Irish Catholics in 1871 (see table 17). Hence, any explanation of the difference between Catholics and Protestants must not only take into account matters that influenced the Catholics to be overrepresented in the cities (such as the changing character of migration from Catholic areas of Ireland after the Famine was over), but also those that influenced the Protestants to be underrepresented.

My own guess (and at this stage of our knowledge, it can scarcely be more than that) is that institutions and practices peculiar to Ontario rather than factors relating to the Irish homeland influenced the Protestants. One can account for their being underrepresented in the cities in 1871 only by assuming either (1) that, in general, the Protestants arrived earlier than did the Catholics: there is as yet no demographic evidence to suggest that this was indeed the case, and the constancy of the religious proportions of the Irish ethnic population as between 1842 and 1871 implies that the Protestants and Catholics actually came in relatively constant dual streams; or (2), more likely, that the Protestants possessed organizational mechanisms for speeding their migration to rural areas. The Orange Order comes immediately to mind. The question is an open one, however; especially because it is not yet

T A B L E 1 7		
	1881	Percentage
A.	English-born as proportion of total population of Ontario	7.2
	English-descended as proportion of total population of the five major cities	14.1
B.	English-descended as proportion of total population of Ontario	27.8
	English-descended as proportion of total population of the five major cities	35.8

Source: Compiled and computed from *Census of Canada 1880–81*, 1: 58–93, 262–95, 360–94.

lear if the Protestants moved out of the cities and into the countryside pro-
•ortionately more often than did the Catholics—or simply that they did so
nore quickly.

Just as one cannot convincingly argue, on the basis of present evidence,
hat the Irish Catholics were culturally predisposed to live in cities, one can-
ot argue that those who did live in cities (only one-seventh of the Irish
Catholic ethnic group in 1871) were alienated from the general population
nd ghettoized in the same way as were the Irish Catholics in the eastern
eaboard cities of the United States. There is a vast gap in the historical liter-
ture on this point and, until a direct study of the Irish in the various major
ities of Canada is undertaken, the case will remain open. In a report on his
esearch in progress on the adjustment of the Irish immigrants in Toronto,
840–60, the Reverend D.S. Shea stated that the "Boston model" did not fit
oronto. The Irish were not perceived as an economic threat—although the
rish tended to concentrate in specific neighbourhoods, the availability and
ccessibility of building land and rental accommodation prevented the
oronto Irish from becoming enclosed in a ghetto. Single-family residences,
ather than multiple-family tenements, prevailed. The newcomer faced
ome discrimination, but it was relatively mild when compared to the
American situation, and upward occupational mobility was commonplace.
hea concluded that there was enough evidence to "suggest that the Irish
ever remained a massive lump in the Toronto community, undigested and
ndigestible."[74] (Studies of Montreal and Halifax dictate much the same
onclusion, that the Irish Catholics faced hardship, but that they found
nany avenues to upward mobility and that they did not undergo an embit-
ering ghetto experience.)[75]

This returns us to our final incongruity. The Irish (Protestant and
Catholic taken together), formed the largest ethnic group in the cities of
Ontario: the Irish-born comprised 34.7 percent of the populace of the five
najor cities in 1851 and 25.1 percent in 1861; 40.0 percent of the residents of
he five major cities in 1871 were of Irish descent. Yet for both Protestants and
Catholics, the city life was a relatively minor part of their collective experi-
•nce: only 14.5 percent of Catholics of Irish descent lived in cities in 1871, and
•ven a smaller proportion of Protestants of Irish descent—6.9 percent—lived
n the cities.[76] Thus, one might well reverse the usual arguments which pre-
•ent urban societies as forces that acted upon the Irish and instead concen-
rate upon the Irish as major causal factors in determining the shape of the
Canadian cities. Or, to put it another way, the Irish were more important to
he cities than the cities were to the Irish.

PART III

f one accepts that the Irish were the largest ethnic group in Ontario for
nuch, or most, of the nineteenth century (at minimum, from 1842 to 1881,
ut probably from at least the early 1830s to the late 1880s, and, quite possi-
ly, from the late 1820s to the mid-1890s)[77] and if one accepts that roughly
wo-thirds of the Irish were Protestants, then one has every reason to expect
a rich and varied literature on the Irish Protestants.

Yet I can find only a single modern published article which deals directly with the Irish Protestants as a cultural and social group whose interplay and integration with the wider population in Ontario is dealt with at a satisfactory scholarly level.[78] One article. Certainly, there must be more but where? Of course, there are references to the Irish Protestants in histories of the province. Most are casual and stereotypic, although a few (as in A.R.M. Lower's work) are at least thought-provoking. And political histories often introduce the Irish Protestants, especially the Orangemen, as explanatory factors, in the same way that the Greeks introduced mechanical devices to resolve dramatic improbabilities. But studies which look straight at the Irish Protestants on their own historical terms. Where?

This is more than merely remarkable, for the Irish Protestants were among the most assertive people to colonize the New World. Unlike most other groups, long before they moved to North America the Irish Protestants were old hands at being colonists. Whatever their individual background, almost all of the Protestants knew what it was like to live amidst a hostile indigenous population and to seize and to hold on to the means of livelihood by an act of will—backed by the threat of physical force. Many families migrating to British North America already had two centuries or more of tradition as frontiersmen or as conquerors in an alien land. This held for the descendants of the Cromwellians, it was true for the Scots settlers in Antrim and Down, and for the English Protestants in Armagh; it characterized the pockets of Protestant small farmers in the south of Ireland and the Protestant farmers of Scots and English origin who infiltrated the border lands of Ulster and spread into the north-central region of Ireland. They took, had, and held.

As applied to the New World, Irish Protestant assertiveness had three primary dimensions. First, in the old country, they had acquired a noteworthy aggressiveness in the acquisition of land. They were land hungry. In the society from which they came, clear title to land was not merely a positive economic benefit (something that could make one comfortable, if not rich), but was a bulwark against the hostile natives who surrounded them. Thus, their desire for land was intense, single-minded, and beyond mere economic calculation. Second, despite their preternatural urge to acquire land, the Irish Protestants were experienced in asserting themselves in commercial ventures: in the eighteenth and early nineteenth centuries, many of the Protestant small farmers in the north of Ireland engaged in weaving, an activity which even in its rudimentary stages of evolution involved a complex commercial network. Finer textile work was carried out in pockets of Protestant settlements in the south of Ireland. In any case, most Protestant farmers operated in the commercial, not the subsistence, sector of agriculture. And, as the nineteenth century wore on, the economy of the north of Ireland, centred on Belfast, became the only part of the Irish economy to adhere to the world of the English industrial revolution; this affected everyone, Protestant and Catholic alike, but the Protestants, because of their social hegemony, were more able to benefit from the commercial economy than were the Catholics.

Neither their hunger for land nor their commercial assertiveness was
apt to cause the Irish Protestants difficulty in British North America.
Indeed, these were adaptive traits for migrants to a new world and would
seem to lead them directly and efficiently to economic success. Their third
single characteristic, however, was potentially maladaptive: they were very
assertive politically and thus potentially contumacious in governmental
eyes. The political activities and attitudes of the Irish Protestants in the eighteenth and nineteenth centuries are immensely complicated, but for the purposes of understanding their behaviour in Ontario, it is sufficient to note
that (1) Protestants of all stripes were predisposed to use legislative bodies
to further their own ends and, if possible, to do down their enemies. (2) The
Protestants of the north of Ireland, and especially the Scots Presbyterians,
were politically radical in the sense that they favoured democratic forms of
government far in advance of those provided by the Irish or British consti-
tutions of the time. (3) There was a Protestant predilection for paramilitary
activity in support of political ends.

Obviously, these characteristics were in constant conflict, the one with
the other, the legislative with the paramilitary, the constitutional with the
democratic, and when combined with the general assertiveness in political
matters, produced extraordinary volatility. For example, in the 1798 Rising,
one finds that Ulster Protestant democrats, losing hope of reform through
Parliament, joined an attempted paramilitary revolution. Simultaneously,
other Ulster Protestants, mostly Orangemen and sympathizers, who were
frightened of a Catholic upsurge (which, in a democratic revolution, would
be a normal result) formed militia units to suppress the Rising. Strongly
assertive politically, yet at war with their own conflicting urges, the Irish
Protestants were like a cocked gun, always ready to go off. But in which
direction? No one could tell, either in Ireland or in British North America,
because the Irish Protestants shared no consistent ideology, but instead, an
attitude, one of assertion. Thus, they were as capable of being left-wing as
right, democratic as authoritarian, revolutionary as reactionary. The one
thing they were not likely to be was quiet.[79]

o

In a sense, we know too much about one institution of Irish Protestant culture in Ontario: the Orange Order. Not that all the secrets of the Order have
been fully plumbed; they have not. But the quantity of work done on the
Order is too much in the sense that its bulk is out of all proportion to that
done on other aspects of Irish Protestant life. Thus, good as much of this
institutional literature is, through no fault of the authors concerned it invites
a double distortion: because the institutional material is perforce presented
against a bare backdrop, it is difficult to obtain a perspective of the overall
context of Irish Protestant social and cultural life. And, simultaneously, it is
easy for readers of the studies of Orangeism to latch on to a false equation of
Orangeism with Irish Protestantism. This equation is particularly tempting

for historians who wish to find a short-cut method of grouping all Irish Protestants, for, unlike the Irish Catholics, they did not belong to a single denomination, and therefore one cannot turn to denominational data as a convenient method of sorting and grouping them. There is no short cut Until we know for several communities who belonged to the Order and how these individuals fitted into the economic and social profile of their specific communities, we cannot safely generalize about the meaning of the Orange Order to the large number of Protestant migrants from Ireland.[80]

When an adequate corpus of local studies finally is assembled, it probably will become clear that the Order was not an institution, but instead is best understood as a set of local agencies that operated differently in different communities. Further, it probably will be found that the Orange constituency varied greatly by social class, occupational status, and by Protestant denominations in the various locales that it served.

The local Orange lodges served as social clubs, immigrant aid organizations, benevolent societies, and economic nexuses, as well as well-publicized political lobbies. In particular, the economic importance of the Order has been virtually ignored; like the Freemasons, they undoubtedly served as commercial conduits. But how all these activities were carried on and which received the greatest emphasis at what time in the Order's history and in what specific areas, demands not speculation, but investigation. And in studying the actual membership of local lodges, historians would do well not only to chart who belonged, but who did not.

o

Woven throughout this survey of what we know and do not know about the Irish in Ontario is the simple observation that we know so little because, as historians, we have studied a dispersed population as if it were concentrated. The Irish migrants to Ontario, Protestant and Catholic, Orange and Hibernian, mostly lived on farms and in rural hamlets, and there is no sense in looking for them on street corners when they were more apt to be found at rural crossroads.

The antidote to our remarkable ignorance concerning the Irish in the nineteenth century is equally simple to formulate: we should start doing micro-studies, chiefly (but not entirely) of farming areas and small towns, where most of the Irish actually were. And instead of generalizing first and investigating later (the dominant practice in Canadian social history, at least so far as the Irish have been concerned), we should wait until a score or more of careful local studies have been completed before trying to draw anything but the most tentative generalizations. Granted, proceeding lot-by-lot, farmer-by-farmer, labourer-by-labourer, through a township or county is extremely hard work, and sometimes the conclusions derived from a complete study may be of less than dramatic result. But at least such studies will have the virtue of being based on real data.

Considering the magnitude of the job at hand, it is time we got down to work.

NOTES

1. Unhappily, demographers have largely evaded the question of ethnicity in nineteenth-century Ontario. This is especially disappointing as the numerical contours of an ethnic population must be determined before one can speak of their secondary cultural characteristics with much certainty. One can look forward, however, to the work of the sociologists A. Gordon Darroch and Michael D. Ornstein. Some of their early material is found in "Ethnicity and Occupational Structure in Canada in 1871: the Vertical Mosaic in Historical Perspective," *Canadian Historical Review* 61 (Sept. 1980): 303–33. This article stands in impressive contrast to the slighting treatment of ethnicity in, for example, *The Demographic Bases of Canadian Society*, 2nd ed., by Warren E. Kalback and Wayne W. McVey (Toronto: McGraw-Hill Ryerson, 1979).

   For reasons of space, I am not able to discuss in detail the various books about the political or institutional life of the Ontario Irish. See particularly the books by Senior and by Houston and Smyth, cited below, note 80.

2. See *Census of Canada, 1870–71*, vol. 4; *Census of Canada, 1665 to 1871*; M.C. Urquhart and K.A.H. Buckley, *Historical Statistics of Canada* (Toronto: Macmillan, 1965), 20.

3. There is, of course, a mass of material in the parliamentary papers of the United Kingdom which relates to Irish emigration to British North America. For the pre-Famine period, the most useful of these are as follows (in chronological order as they appear in the papers): *Report from the Select Committee on Emigration from the United Kingdom*, H.C. 1826 (404), iv; *Estimate of the sum required for facilitating emigration from the South of Ireland to the Canadas and the Cape of Good Hope*, H.C. 1823 (491), xiii; H.C. 1825 (131), xviii; H.C. 1826–27 (160), xv; *Report from the Committee appointed to inquire into the expediency of encouraging emigration from the United Kingdom*, H.C. 1826–27 (88), v; 1826–27 (237), v; 1826–27 (550), v; *Report from the select Committee appointed to take account of the state of the poorer classes in Ireland and the best means of improving their condition*, H.C. 1830 (667), vii; *Reports from the commissioners for emigration to the colonial secretary*, H.C. 1831–32 (724), xxxii; *Emigration, North America and Australia*, H.C. 1833 (141), xxvi; *Emigration. Return . . . 1833*, H.C. 1833 (696), xxvi; *Emigration. Return . . . 1835*, H.C. 1835 (87), xxxix; *Report from the agent-general for emigration from the United Kingdom*, H.C. 1837–38 (388), xl; *Number of persons who have emigrated from the United Kingdom . . . between 1832 and 1836*, H.C. 1837–38 (137), xlvii; *Emigration. Return . . .*, H.C. 1839 (536-I), xxxix; *Correspondence relative to emigration to Canada*, H.C. 1841 (298), xi; *Emigration. Return . . .*, H.C. 1841 (61), iii, sess. 2; *Emigration and Crown Lands*, H.C. 1842 (231), xxxi; *Despatch from the governor-general of British North America to a transmitting of the annual reports of the agents for emigration in Canada* [373], H.C. 1842, xxxi; H.C. 1843 (109), xxxiv; H.C. 1844 (181), xxxv; *Reports by the emigration agents of Canada, etc.*, H.C. 1843 (109), xxxiv; *General report of the colonial land and emigration commissioners*, H.C. 1842 (567), xxv; H.C. 1843 (621), xxix; H.C. 1844 (178), xxxi; H.C. 1845 (617), xxvii.

4. The basic English census data from 1801 onwards are most conveniently available in *Abstract of British Historical Statistics*, by B.R. Mitchell and Phyllis Deane (Cambridge: Cambridge University Press, 1962). The pre-1801 estimates of population which were cited so confidently as recently as fifteen years ago, have been shown to have been untrustworthy and of necessity have been abandoned. With them have gone the several complex explanations of the eighteenth-century demographic explosion. What remains is the certain knowledge that there was an extraordinary boom in England and Wales in the eighteenth century, but its exact magnitude is now highly problematic. See M.W. Flinn, *British Population Growth 1700–1850* (London: Macmillan, 1970) for a compact summary of the problems with the data.

For the Scottish situation see Michael Flinn, ed., *Scottish Population History from the 17th Century to the 1930s* (Cambridge: Cambridge University Press, 1977).

The standard study of eighteenth and early nineteenth century Irish population growth remains K.H. Connell's *The Population of Ireland, 1750–1845* (Oxford: Clarendon Press, 1950). See also Connell's "The Population of Ireland in the Eighteenth Century," *Economic History Review* 16 (1946): 111–24, and Michael Drake's "Marriage and Population Growth in Ireland, 1750–1845," *Economic History Review* 2 ser., 16 (Dec. 1963): 301–13.

5. The most complete compendium of the data on emigration from the British Isles, which includes both the actual data and a discussion of the limits on its reliability, was compiled for the General Register Office of the United Kingdom, as *Studies on Medical and Population Subjects, No. 6: External Migration, a Study of the Available Statistics, 1815–1950* (London: HMSO, 1953), by N.H. Carrier and J.R. Jeffery.

   Two older works are still highly serviceable: Stanley C. Johnson's *A History of Emigration from the United Kingdom to North America, 1763–1912* (1913; reprint, London: Frank Cass and Co., 1966), and William Forbes Adams' *Ireland and Irish Emigration to the New World from 1815 to the Famine* (New Haven: Yale University Press, 1932). A considerably less sophisticated volume from the same era is Helen I. Cowan's *British Emigration to British North America, 1783–1837* (Toronto: University of Toronto Library, 1928). This was later revised (1961), but not greatly improved. A precis of this work is *British Immigration before Confederation*, by Helen I. Cowan (Ottawa: Canadian Historical Association, 1968). Norman MacDonald's *Canada, 1763–1841, Immigration and Settlement: The Administration of the Imperial Lands Regulations* (London: Longmans, Green and Co., 1939), is chiefly descriptive and is imprecise on numerical matters.

   H.J.M. Johnston's *British Emigration Policy, 1815–1830* (Oxford: Clarendon Press, 1972), deals chiefly with pauper emigration, but includes some shrewd redactions of emigration statistics. And, although Lynn Hollen Lees' *Exiles of Erin, Irish Migrants in Victorian London* (Ithaca: Cornell University Press, 1979) deals primarily with intra-British migration, it assesses data that are relevant to external migration as well.

   A convenient compendium of Irish data is *Irish Historical Statistics. Population, 1821–1971*, edited by W.E. Vaughan and A.J. Fitzpatrick (Dublin: Royal Irish Academy, 1978).

   The data on Scottish migration are discussed in Flinn's *Scottish Population History*, 91 ff. See also the precis of James M. Cameron's PhD thesis (University of Glasgow, 1970), "Scottish Emigration to Upper Canada, 1815–55: A Study of Process," in W. Peter Adams and Frederick Helleiner, eds., *International Geography 1972* (Toronto: University of Toronto Press, 1972), 1: 404–6. See also Cameron's "The Role of Shipping from Scottish Ports in Emigration to the Canadas, 1815–55," in Donald H. Akenson, ed., *Canadian Papers in Rural History* 2 (1980): 135–54.

   On the migration by the lowland Scots before the time of their move to Upper Canada, see *The Scottish Migration to Ulster in the reign of James I*, by M. Perceval-Maxwell (London: Routledge and Kegan Paul, 1973), and *Ulster Emigration to Colonial America, 1718–1755* (London: Routledge and Kegan Paul, 1966) by R.J. Dickson. Dickson's "Critical Note on Authorities" deals succinctly with the available data and published work for the American colonial period.

6. See Carrier and Jeffery, *Studies on Medical and Population Subjects*, 17–18, 137–39.

7. For statistics for all United Kingdom emigration ports, 1831–34, see *Report on Canadian Archives, 1900*, "Emigration," 58–59. The statistical series is continuous through 1860, in C.M. Godfrey, *The Cholera Epidemics in Upper Canada, 1832–1866* (Toronto: Secombe House, 1968), 70–72.

8. Adams, *Ireland and Irish Emigration*, 411–13.

9. Ibid., 413–14. Although the best available revision, Adams' material is not above reproach. In particular, he seems somewhat cavalier in his treatment of migra-

tion from Greenock. I have interpolated the estimate for 1836 myself, from data found in Carrier and Jeffery, *Studies on Medical and Population Subjects*, 95. It should be added that Adams believed the original data for 1827 to have been seriously below the true situation.

10. The reader may notice that for 1825 and 1826 Adams' revised estimates of Irish migrants to British North America exceeds the unrevised official emigration figures for all of the British Isles. It would be natural—but quite wrong—to see this as indicative of a flaw in Adams' procedures. Actually, Adams made allowances for children and for illegal migrants, which the official version of the figures did not do. A "true" version of the official figures would have to include the same compensations to figures for all of the British Isles which Adams made only for the Irish.

Strictly speaking, then, the data in table 1 and those in Adams' work are incompatible, but as confirming the point made in the text about the prepotence of Irish migration, they are more than adequate.

11. See Adams, *Ireland and Irish Emigration*, 422–23.

12. Ibid., 415. Note that Adams' corrected estimate for passengers disembarking at Quebec City in 1829 (10 575), drawn from information given by Buchanan in Quebec City, seemingly does not mesh with the corrected estimate (based on information at points of migration in the United Kingdom) of 10 148 total Irish migrants to British North America.

Incidentally, Adams' sources for the 1829 and 1830 Quebec City and Montreal data (an enclosure by A.C. Buchanan to Lord Aylmer, of 7 May 1831, in Aylmer to Viscount Goderich, 12 May 1831) is slightly, maddeningly, miscited. It is PRO, C.O. 42/233, not C.O. 42/223.

13. The newspaper estimates are found in Adams, *Ireland and Irish Emigration*, 421. On the basis of his comments upon the unreliability of the news reports before 1818, I have excluded his 1815–17 data.

These estimates of Irish migration have a rough comparability to inferences dictated by other sources. Specifically, there are two series of figures on total UK migration to Quebec and Montreal. One of these was made by A.C. Buchanan by going through the records of the harbour master at Quebec. Lord Aylmer, governor of Lower Canada, took these returns sufficiently seriously to refuse at first to vouch for them, as he had not seen an official and authentic register (copy, Aylmer to Viscount Goderich, 12 May 1831, PRO, C.O. 42/233), and then, after investigating Buchanan's source of information, changed his mind, concluding that "I have now reason to believe that his return may be considered approximately the truth as nearly as may be necessary for all purposes . . . " (Lord Aylmer to Goderich, 18 May 1831, PRO, C.O. 42/233). The estimates are found in "Report of Mr. Buchanan . . . of the number of emigrants arrived within the Province of Lower Canada by sea since the year 1790 to 10th May, 1831," PRO, C.O. 42/233.

The other series for total migration was produced by Robert J.W. Horton, an MP with an informed interest in the subject, and was reported in the 1826 Select Committee on Emigration. *Report from the Select Committee on Emigration from the United Kingdom*, H.C., 1826 (404), iv, 394. Given these numbers, one could do as Adams does (*Ireland and Irish Emigration*, 421) and take as being applicable to any given year Horton's statement that "three-fifths of these were Irish." And, indeed, these numbers are found to be roughly comparable in most years to the newspaper data. As long as one limits one's conclusion thereon to stating that this helps to confirm the newspaper estimates, all is well. However, one should not make the mistake of taking Horton's three-fifths figure as literally applicable to any specific year. Instead, the direct evidence of the newspaper reports is preferable, and, therefore, that is the material on which the revised estimate given in the text is based.

Year	Buchanan	Horton
1815	(no figures: reports total emigration, 1790–1815, as 5000)	5 500
1816	1 250	5 500
1817	6 796	6 796
1818	8 400	8 221
1819	12 809	12 907
1820	11 239	11 239
1821	8 050	8 056
1822	10 468	10 470
1823	10 258	10 258
1824	6 515	6 515
1825	9 097	N/A
1826	10 731	N/A
1827	15 802	N/A
1828	12 697	N/A

14. (Copy), A.C. Buchanan to Lord Aylmer, 7 May 1831, PRO, C.O. 42/233.

15. Derived by comparing official migration statistics (Carrier and Jeffery, *Studies on Medical and Population Subjects*, 95) with data in *Appendix to the Third Report from the Select Committee on Emigration from the United Kingdom, 1827*, H.C., 1826–27 (550), vi, 574.

16. From *Quebec Official Gazette*, quoted in *Montreal Gazette*, 13 Dec. 1830, reproduced in H.A. Innis and A.R.M. Lower, eds., *Select Documents in Canadian Economic History, 1783–1885* (Toronto: University of Toronto Press, 1933), 104–5. Almost certainly, this report was written by A.C. Buchanan.

17. Derived from *Emigration. North America and Australia*, H.C., 1833 (141), xxvi, 195.

18. Derived from *Emigration. Return . . . 1835*, H.C. 1835 (87), xxxix, 11.

19. PAC, RG 5, A 1, Upper Canadian Sundries. Professor Brian Osborne kindly called this material to my attention. See also, A.R.M. Lower, "Immigration and Settlement in Canada, 1812–20," *Canadian Historical Review* 3 (1922): 45.

20. Reproduced in Innis and Lower, *Select Documents in Canadian Economic History*, 105.

21. (Copy), Aylmer to Goderich, 12 May 1831.

22. The 1842 census is found in *Appendix (F.F.)* to the *Journals of the Legislative Assembly, 1843*. It is reprinted in altered form, in *Census of Canada, 1870–71*, vol. 4, *Censuses of Canada, 1665 to 1871*, 134–40. The reprint is preferable, as arithmetical errors in the original are corrected in the reprint. The differences, however, are relatively small.

23. The two relevant estimates are those by Michael Smith, of 95 000, and of Joseph Bouchette, of 135 000, which, though published three years apart, can be taken as co-equal in time, as they both deal with the situation before heavy trans-Atlantic immigration began (Michael Smith, *A Geographical View of the Province of Canada . . .* , 1813, and Joseph Bouchette, *Topographical Description . . .* , 1815). Most observers have taken the lower estimate as most likely to be closer to the truth. Professor George Rawlyk has kindly communicated to me the results of his unpublished work which suggest that 75 000 is a realistic figure for the loyalist base pattern. George A. Rawlyk, "The Fathers and Founders of our Native Country? The Loyalists and Evolving Conservatism in English-Speaking Canada," (unpublished paper, presented at Columbia University, 14 Oct. 1980).

24. I am here following the procedure and, in the absence of Upper Canadian figures, the usage of a rate of natural increase taken from the United States, as found in Johnston, *British Emigration Policy*, l, n. 1.

25. Because of the arithmetical corrections necessary in the 1842 census, one cannot accept their proportional distribution of the "unknown" category, but must do it oneself.

26. Census of 1848, in *Census of Canada, 1870–71*, vol. 4, *Censuses of Canada, 1665–1871*, 164. The multiplier obviously is low, but I suspect that any error is self-correcting. Many widows and widowers probably were tallied (incorrectly) as being married, even though they had no spouse. Thus, the married figure probably is artificially high, and the multiplier artificially low. The final result of the estimates of total families, however, should be reasonably accurate.

27. *Census of Canada, 1851–52*, 1: 308, shows 152 336 families, comprising 863 971 members actually resident and an additional 13 651 family members temporarily absent, for a total of 877 622 family members.

28. For a useful formulation of Ravenstein's laws in modern terms, see D.B. Grigg, "E.G. Ravenstein and 'the Laws of Migration,'" *Journal of Historical Geography* 3 (1979): 41–54.

29. On the various forms of migration, see "A General Typology of Migration," by William Petersen, *American Sociological Review* 23 (June 1958): 256–66.

30. Everett S. Lee, "A Theory of Migration," *Demography* 3 (1966): 56.

31. Adams constructs a set of interesting tables on emigration ports in the years immediately after the Napoleonic Wars (*Ireland and Irish Emigration*, 420–25). On later emigration to Upper Canada from specific Irish ports, see: *Report on Canadian Archives, 1900* ("Emigration," 58–59); *Second Report from the Select Committee on Emigration from the United Kingdom*, H.C., 1826–27 (237), v, 70; *Emigration. Return..., 1833*, H.C., 1833 (696), xxvi, 3; *Emigration... Return...*, H.C., 1839 (536-I), xxxix, 34.

32. S.H. Cousens, "The Regional Variation in Emigration from Ireland between 1821 and 1841," *Institute of British Geographers. Transactions* 37 (Dec. 1965): 15–30.
    There are several studies of the Irish textile industry, of which the most important segment in relation to emigration in this period is the linen industry. An admirably succinct summary is W.H. Crawford, *Domestic Industry in Ireland. The Experience of the Linen Industry* (Dublin: Gill and Macmillan, 1972).

33. Alexander Macdonnell to Lord Durham, 22 June 1838, reproduced in Lord Durham's *Report on the Affairs of British North America*, vol. 3, *Appendixes*, ed. C.P. Lucas (Oxford: Clarendon Press, 1912), 20.

34. Two points: (1) one employs the number of native-born French Canadians as given in the 1842 census, without any redaction for first-generation immigration (this is not a methodology incompatible with Revisions B and C, as it is assumed that the first-generation ethnic populations all were tallied in the census as part of the non-French, native-Canadian category); (2) the French-Canadian native-born numbers must be slightly augmented, however, to distribute the "unknown" category, as was done in estimating the total ethnic population.

35. Here let me reemphasize the need for humility in interpreting the data and also the necessity of keeping in mind the arithmetic of the formula employed. As discussed below, the Catholic percentages employed are highly problematical, but they deal with a very small percentage of subcategories of the total population so that the effect of any error in the data would be very small on the final result.
    That said, one is dealing in each instance with speculation, albeit of an informed sort. Intentionally, I have probably somewhat overestimated the Catholic percentage of the non-French second-generation Canadian-born population. That a number as high as 3 percent is even within the bounds of possibility rests on the fact that amongst the earliest settlers (whose descendants by 1842 often were second-generation born in Canada) were the considerable numbers of Glengarry Fencibles.

The probable overestimation should compensate for any underestimation of the Catholic proportion of the Scots-born and first-generation Scots, for I have opted for the low end of the possibility range in dealing with the Scots Catholics. Unfortunately, the only data on Scots which I can find indicates that in 1871 (a very late date for my purposes), 10 percent of the Scots throughout Canada were Roman Catholics (Darroch and Ornstein, "Ethnicity and Occupational Structure," 312). This figure can be taken as the top edge of the possibility range for Upper Canada in 1842. But I am loath to project a national figure for the 1870s onto this province for the 1840s, especially in view of the relatively large communities of Scottish-derived Catholics in various parts of the Maritimes.

What do the contemporary data for Upper Canada suggest? Unfortunately, one cannot deal with data on Scottish religious persuasion by reference to the Upper Canada census data of 1842. It would be temptingly simple to determine the actual number of Scots Catholics by subtracting the number of adherents of the Church of Scotland from the Scots ethnic total (taken to be the average of that given in Revisions B and C, tables 8 and 9 in the text). However, because of adhesions from other ethnic groups in Canada, the membership of the Church of Scotland in 1842 *exceeded* the Scots ethnic population!

Thus, we must turn to religious data from the home country. This is such a vexed matter that even Flinn's massive work on Scottish demography (*Scottish Population History*) virtually avoids the entire religious question. The earliest information we have comes from the religious census of 1851, with its well-known shortcomings and double-counting.

But, our problem is even worse, as we know that the Scots who emigrated did not form a representative profile of the entire population, and, in particular, one needs to know more about the position of highlanders' emigration (for, as Bishop Macdonnell suggested, highland Catholics were an important element of his flock).

"Which part of Scotland supplied the most emigrants?" Scotland's most distinguished demographer recently has asked. His reply: "On this point the available records are at their most intransigent" (Flinn, *Scottish Population History*, 453).

The most careful and useful studies are by James Cameron (see above, n. 5). If one takes Cameron's data on emigration from Scottish ports to the St. Lawrence for 1831–37, inclusive, and also takes into account the proportion of highlanders sailing from the Clyde, then it appears that roughly (very roughly) 44 percent of those emigrating in that period were highlanders (derived from Cameron, "The Role of Shipping," figures 2 and 3). For an array of non-statistical data, see *First Report from the Select Committee on Emigration, Scotland*, H.C. (82), 1841, vi and *Second Report from the Select Committee on Emigration, Scotland*, H.C. 1841 (333), vi. Also helpful is Ronald Sunter's "The Scottish Background to the Immigration of Bishop Alexander Macdonnell and the Glengarry Highlanders," *Study Sessions 1973, The Canadian Catholic Historical Association*, 11–20.

Now, if one tallies the number of attendants at public worship on Sunday, 31 March 1851, and assumes that because the Protestant practice in many parishes of holding two services a day led to a one-third over-counting of Protestants, one finds that the proportion of Catholics in the highlands was approximately 5.5 percent (calculated from *Census of Great Britain, 1851. Religious Worship and Education, Scotland* [1764], H.C., 1854, lix, 6–20).

Juxtaposing this with Cameron's data, and assuming that all the Catholic Scots came from the highlands, then a reasonable estimate is that 2.4 percent of all Scots emigrants were Catholic.

Unfortunately, for our purposes, the Catholics were not distributed evenly over the population, but were found in pockets. Moreover, Scottish emigration was noted for being highly localized, large numbers of whole parishes emigrating together or within a year or two of each other. Upper Canada was especially attractive to some of these groups. Thus, in employing 3 percent, I am trying to minimize any underestimating of the numbers of Scots Catholics. Further, in cognizance of Darroch and Ornstein's work, I have built in further compensation for possible underestimation of the Scots Catholics when dealing with the second-generation non-French cohort born in Canada (see above).

36. In all the calculations above, the ethnic estimates used are the mean of those shown in Revisions B and C (tables 8 and 9) in the text.

37. The 1871 religious estimate is based on data in the *Census of Canada*, 1870–71, 1: 142–44, 280–81, 364–65.

Of necessity, the religious–ethnic proportions are derived differently than those for 1842, but the data and procedures are sufficiently comparable to support strongly the conclusion argued in the text. The 1871 census was the first to provide data not only on place of birth but on the ethnic origin of all respondents. This was basically a self-definition item, and as such, it defined ethnicity in a manner that varied according to each individual's perception; thus, for example, a third-generation Scot might define himself as Scots, while a first-generation individual of another ethnic group might refuse any ethnic label at all. This apparent messiness was actually the strongpoint of the ethnicity census, for it employed self-definition rather than arbitrary and imposed external criteria.

As for the calculation, it was derived by (1) taking the total Roman Catholic population as a starting figure; (2) subtracting the number of French-derived ethnicity, under the presupposition that the French Canadians were overwhelmingly Catholic; and (3) assuming that whatever number of French Canadians had turned Protestant were equalled by Catholics in the English, American, and Continental European-derived population; then (4), as was done in the calculation for 1842, assuming that 3 percent of the Scots in Canada were Catholic and subtracting from the previous total. This leaves 188 912 Catholics amongst a total Irish ethnic population of 559 442.

My figure of 33.8 percent is close to that of William J. Smyth, who calculated that, in 1871, "thirty-six per cent represents the absolute maximum proportion of Irish who could have been Catholics." (William J. Smyth, "The Irish in mid-Nineteenth Century Ontario," *Ulster Folk Life* 23 (1977): 100).

In their excellent recent book, *The Sash Canada Wore. A Historical Geography of the Orange Order in Canada* (Toronto: University of Toronto Press, 1980), Houston and Smyth estimate that there were in 1871, 182 000 persons in Ontario of Irish Catholic background (p. 186, n. 27). This estimate, which equals 32.5 percent of the Irish ethnic population, well may be more accurate than mine as my formula may have underestimated the number of Scots Catholics and, unlike the case of 1842, there is no item in the 1871 formula to compensate for such overestimation. This said, my point in the text is buttressed, not weakened, by Houston and Smyth's work, as, if they are accurate, it would mean that there were slightly fewer Catholics than I posit. And if true, my point that the post-Famine migration to central Canada was not composed wholly, or even chiefly of Catholics, is strengthened.

38. H.C. Pentland, "The Development of a Capitalistic Labour Market in Canada," *Canadian Journal of Economics and Political Science* 25 (1959): 459, 460.

39. Ibid., 460.

40. Ibid., 459. If the reader thinks that I am being too hard on Pentland's brief article, he can find the same points in Pentland's PhD thesis, "Labour and the Development of Industrial Capitalism in Canada" (University of Toronto, 1960). I am not competent to judge his argument about the development of industrial capitalism in Canada (although, the vigour of his argument is certainly attractive), but on migration and upon the Irish in general, three characteristics of the thesis deserve note. First, in his general discussion of immigration (pp. 144–207) he is remarkably trusting in his use of disparate (and, in my judgement, highly unreliable) immigration data. Second, in his discussion of the Irish (pp. 208–81), his generalizations on Protestant–Catholic differences in Ireland are so simplistic as to be racialist and highly objectionable. Third, his assertions on the changing

characteristics of Irish migration to Upper Canada before the Famine are virtually without evidence, although not entirely without citation. As far as the Irish
are concerned, Pentland's work is an example of a strong theory and a vivid
imagination overcoming a proper sense of evidence.

41. The most relevant of Cross's several pieces for our purpose is "The Shiners' War:
Social Violence in the Ottawa Valley in the 1830s," *Canadian Historical Review* 54
(March 1973): 1–26. His PhD thesis repays reading: "The Dark Druidical Groves:
The Lumber Community and the Commercial Frontier in British North America
to 1854" (University of Toronto, 1968), especially the chapter, "The Day of the
Shiner," upon which the *Canadian Historical Review* article is based.

42. Kenneth Duncan, "Irish Famine Immigration and the Social Structure of Canada
West," originally published in the *Canadian Review of Sociology and Anthropology*
(1965): 19–40, reprinted in *Studies on Canadian Social History*, edited by Michiel
Horn and Ronald Sabourin (Toronto: McClelland & Stewart, 1974), 140–63. The
quotations are from this reprint, 140 and 153, respectively. The article is also
reprinted in *Canada: A Sociological Profile*, edited by W.E. Mann (Toronto: Copp
Clark, 1968), 1–16.

43. Pentland, "The Development of a Capitalistic Labour Market," 460.

44. Cross, "The Dark Druidical Groves," 251.

45. Ibid., 253. Although not a fallacious way of reasoning—but rather an insufficient
examination of evidence—Cross's attempt to fix the Shiners geographically is
instructive as to how not to proceed. In his *Canadian Historical Review* article
("The Shiners' War," 4), Cross confidently indicated that most of the Irish immigrants in the Ottawa Valley were drawn from counties Limerick and Tipperary.
However, in the thesis upon which the article is based, Cross states (p. 294) that
the origin of the immigrants was difficult to determine because they arrived as
anonymous individuals, "however, local historians *seem* agreed that most of the
Shiners came from the *vicinities* of Limerick and Tipperary . . . " (emphasis
mine). He added that this conclusion "*seems* to be verified by a survey of the origins of Irish on the Ottawa *whose birthplace can be determined*" (again, the emphasis is mine). Cross adds, "most derived from the Irish southwest." (This is not at
all the same thing as coming from counties Limerick and Tipperary.)
    Even after all this retreating, his footnotes indicate that, in reality, only a very
few birthplaces actually can be determined and further, that his two local histories "are unreliable sources" (p. 327, nn. 148, 149). All in all, this is a fascinating
example of the process whereby scanty data (the "unreliable" local histories and
a few available local biographies) made their way into a tentative and hedged
statement in a thesis, and thence into an authoritative statement through publication in the senior journal in the field of Canadian history.
    For a contrasting example, in this case illustrating the standard of evidence
and documentation required concerning geographic linkages if one is to make
statements concerning cultural transfer from specific geographic districts in
Ireland to the New World, see J. Richard Houston, *Numbering the Survivors: A
History of the Standish Family of Ireland, Ontario and Alberta* (Agincourt, ON:
Generation Press, 1979). Essentially, if one is to make statements concerning
transfer from specific geographical locations (as distinct from general matters of
cultural transfer), one must use the tools of the too-often despised genealogists.

46. Pentland, "The Development of a Capitalistic Labour Market," 460.

47. From an historical viewpoint, the most striking thing about the Famine is that
there has been so very little scholarly work done on it. One can cite only two
major volumes: R. Dudley Edwards and T. Desmond Williams, eds., *The Great
Famine. Studies in Irish History, 1845–52* (Dublin: published for the Irish
Committee of Historical Sciences by Browne and Nolan, 1956), and Cecil

Woodham-Smith, *The Great Hunger, Ireland, 1845–9* (London: Hamish Hamilton, 1962).

48. Robert E. Kennedy, Jr., *The Irish, Emigration, Marriage and Fertility* (Berkeley: University of California Press, 1973), 27.

49. From 1846 onwards, the material in the United Kingdom parliamentary papers concerning emigration is copious and does not bear direct listing here. The following items, however, are especially useful: The annual *General Report* of the Colonial Land and Emigration Commissioners; *First Report from the Lords Select Committee on Colonization from Ireland*, H.C., 1847–48 (415), xvii; *Second Report*, H.C., 1847–48 (593), xvii; *Third Report*, H.C., 1849 (86), xi; *Papers relative to Emigration to the British Provinces in North America* [777] and [824], H.C., 1847, xxix; [932], [964], [971], and [985], H.C. 1847–48, xlvii; H.C. 1847–48 (50), xlvii; [1025], H.C. 1849, xxxviii; H.C., 1851 (348), xl; [1474], H.C., 1852, xxxiii; *Despatch transmitting report . . . showing the facilities afforded to Emigrants from Europe for reaching the interior by the completion of the St. Lawrence Canals*, H.C., 1850 (173), xl; *Report from the Select Committee on the Passenger Acts*, H.C. 1851 (632), xix.

50. Carrier and Jeffery, *Studies on Medical and Population Subjects*, 95.

51. Adams never stated his formula except in round-about literary terms, but it can be expressed as follows: Migration to either BNA or USA = official migration figure to BNA or to USA + 10 percent of official figure to account for illegals + 90 percent of Liverpool embarkations to BNA or USA. See Adams, *Ireland and Irish Emigration*, 412–13. Adams suggested that the 90 percent Liverpool figure probably was too high, but that it was compensated for by the numbers which sailed to North America from other British ports, especially Greenock and Glasgow.

I employ Adams' formula with some hesitation since it seems to be more accurate for the 1840s than for the early 1850s. In particular, I suspect that its use overestimates, by a tenth to a fifth, the Irish figures for the early 1850s.

The Liverpool data which is necessary for employing Adams' formula is found in: *Appendix to the Seventh General Report of the Colonial Land and Emigration Commissioners*, 36 [809], H.C., 1847, xxxii; *Eighth General Report of the Colonial Land and Emigration Commissioners*, 36 [961], H.C., 1847–48, xxvi; *Ninth General Report of the Colonial Land and Emigration Commissioners*, 32 [1082], H.C., 1849, xxii; *Tenth General Report of the Colonial Land and Emigration Commissioners*, 36 [1204], H.C., 1850, xxiii; *Eleventh General Report of the Colonial Land and Emigration Commissioners*, 32 [1383], H.C., 1851, xxii; *Appendix to the Twelfth General Report of the Colonial Land and Emigration Commissioners*, 74 [1499], H.C., 1852, xvii; *Appendix to the Thirteenth General Report of the Colonial Land and Emigration Commissioners*, 66 [1647], H.C., 1852–53, xl.

52. A.B. Hawke to the Civil Secretary, 20 September 1847, quoted in Gilbert Tucker, "The Famine Immigration to Canada, 1847," *American Historical Review* 36 (April 1931): 537.

53. Ibid.

54. S.H. Cousens, "The Regional Pattern of Emigration during the Great Irish Famine, 1846–51," *Institute of British Geographers Publications* 29 (1968): 119–34, is a brilliantly succinct clarification of the entire issue of Irish migration. Also relevant is his "Regional Death Rates in Ireland during the Great Famine, from 1846 to 1851," *Population Studies* 14 (1960–61): 55–73, and "The Regional Variation in Mortality during the Great Irish Famine," *Proceedings of the Royal Irish Academy* 63: sec. C, 127–49.

See also, *Report of the Commission on Emigration and Other Population Problems* (Dublin: Stationery Office, 1955) and Lynn Hollen Lees, *Exiles of Erin*, 39–41. See also, Oliver MacDonagh, "The Irish Famine, Emigration to the United States," *Perspectives in American History* 10 (1976): 409, 414, 418–26.

55. Kenneth Duncan, "Irish Famine Immigration and the Social Structure of Canada West," reprinted in Horn and Sabourin, *Studies on Canadian Social History*, 146.

56. Computed from *Census of the Canadas, 1851–52* 1: 4–37, and from *Census of the Canadas, 1860–61*, 1: 48–80, and cf. 128–60.

57. Ibid. The concept of an urban–rural breakdown of population data is a relatively new one and was not used by the census authorities for the three censuses (1851, '61, and '71) with which I deal in Part II. In employing incorporated cities, towns, and villages as the unit whereby to compute "urban" populations, I am following the example of the historical analysis done in the 1920s and published in *Seventh Census of Canada, 1931* (see vol. 1: 81 and 154, for a justification of this procedure). This procedure will underestimate all urban percentages to the extent that (a) urban areas were unincorporated or (b) the extent whereby two separately incorporated areas merge physically into each other but remain distinct municipal entities. Point (b) is a serious problem in evaluating twentieth-century census data, but had little import in the nineteenth. And, although there were unincorporated towns of two to three thousand, the inclusion of villages as small as four to five thousand as urban, more than offsets the potential underestimation on this account.

I should warn any reader who wishes to do a similar calculation for another ethnic group of a vexing problem: one cannot relate one's totals for the cities, towns, and villages as shown in the 1851 and 1861 enumerations to the overall figures of urban life as given in the historical sections of the 1931 census. The reason is that the census authorities, in doing their historical work, "corrected" the 1851 and 1861 returns but did not indicate where, why, or how they did this. As a result, the urban total given in the historical section of the 1931 census (see vol. 1: 366) is higher than that reported district-by-district in 1851, but lower than 1861. Fortunately, in many cases for 1851, and in most for 1861, one can infer what the 1931 investigators did, and proceed according to their pattern. Even so, the figure one derives for 1851 is 3.5 percent less than that in the historical section of the 1931 census, and that for 1861 is one-tenth of one percent higher. Because returns for cities seem to have been unambiguous and thus not needing "corrections" by the historical census workers for the 1931 volume, it is clear that most of the changes were made in the figures for the towns and villages.

For the purpose of the argument put forward in the text, the possible under-enumeration of "urban" Irishmen is not serious: it amounts only to a possible 3.5 percent in 1851 and then consists almost entirely of individuals who lived in small towns and villages, whose claim to be urban would be dubious at best.

For those working on other ethnic groups, however, it means that they must (as I have done in this study) calculate not only the city, town, and village components of their respective populations, but must also calculate by exactly the same criteria the total urban segments of the entire population of the province so that valid comparisons can be made to the general population. If the 1931 data is used as a shortcut, the comparisons will be invalid.

58. *Manual containing "The Census Act" and Instructions to Officers employed in taking the First Census of Canada (1871)* (Ottawa: Queen's Printer, 1871), 23.

59. *Census of Canada, 1870–71*, 1: 86–145, cf. 252–81.

60. In attacking the dominant view in Canadian historical writing that the Irish were an urban group, I do not wish to tar all commentators with the same brush. There have been several scholars who have gotten the basic facts straight, no small achievement. Of the older generation, see the article by Frances Morehouse, "Canadian Migration in the Forties," *Canadian Historical Review* 9 (1928): 309–29. During the 1950s and '60s, Professor John Irwin Cooper of McGill University, supervised a number of graduate theses that were sensible. Mostly, these dealt with Quebec, but not entirely. Cooper's own view was that "the bulk of the Irish who remained in Canada chose a predominantly rural world. Those

who emigrated to the United States, if they joined their brethren, entered the era of greatest urban concentration" (John Irwin Cooper, "Irish Immigration and the Canadian Church before the Middle of the 19th Century," *Journal of the Canadian Church Historical Society* 2 (May 1955): 5). More recently, three articles of diverse topic and approach have each dealt with the Irish as a rural people: "The Irish in Mid-Nineteenth Century Ontario," by William J. Smyth, in *Ulster Folk Life* 23 (1977): 97–105; "The Settlement of Mono Township," by R. Cole Harris, Pauline Roulston, and Chris de Freitas, in *The Canadian Geographer* 19 (1975): 1–17; and "The Welcome and the Wake. Attitudes in Canada West toward the Irish Famine Migration," by G.J. Parr, in *Ontario History* 66 (1974), 101–13.

61. The source of the raw data is the *Census of Canada, 1870–71*, 1: 86–145.
     Because the basic argument of this section is that most Irish Catholics did not live in cities and were not socially acclimatized in Ontario in the same urban experience as in the United States, the formula used to estimate the number of Irish Catholics in cities, towns, and villages is biased so as to err, if at all, in the direction of overestimating their urban numbers: In particular, it may do so by underestimation of the number of Scots Catholics. In other words, the case against the Irish Catholics being an urban people could easily have been made even stronger.
     The formula is as follows: Irish-born urban Catholics = total or urban Catholics – 100 percent of urban French Canadians – 3 percent of urban Scots. This is the same formula used for the general population (see note 37 above).
     Note that this formula should be used only with aggregate populations and not to calculate the Irish Catholics in any specific municipality.

62. For purposes of comparison, the reader may wish to note the residential pattern of the Protestants of Irish descent for 1871.

Protestants of Irish descent living in cities (average size: 26 517)	6.9 percent
Protestants of Irish descent living in towns and villages (average size: 2148)	9.9 percent
Total urban Protestants of Irish descent (including all cities, towns, and villages, average size: 3266)	16.8 percent
Total Protestants of Irish descent living in rural areas	83.2 percent

63. H.C. Pentland, "The Lachine Strike of 1843," *Canadian Historical Review* 29 (Sept. 1948): 257.
     Incidentally, as a footnote to the same page, Pentland states: "Oscar Handlin's Boston Immigrants, 1790–1815 (Cambridge, Mass. 1941), provides an excellent discussion on the character of Irish immigration into America. Most of the findings for Boston apply equally to Irish immigration into Canada."

64. I am heartened to read the research reports of Darrell A. Norris, for the projected *Historical Atlas of Canada* [which has since been published by The University of Toronto Press in three volumes]. Norris is doing remarkable work on what he calls the "step wise" migration pattern into Euphrasia Township, Canada West. Many of the settlers in that township were Irish.
     The reader may be familiar with the multi-stage migration of Wilson Benson, an Ulster Protestant whose peregrinations were the heart of the chapter on "Transiency and Social Mobility," in Michael B. Katz, *The People of Hamilton, Canada West. Family and Class in a mid-Nineteenth-Century City* (Cambridge: Harvard University Press, 1975), 94 ff. Since Katz was interested only in a single urban area, he rather obscured the central fact that despite sixteen moves in residence and approximately two-and-a-half dozen changes of occupation and location, Benson spent most of his mature years as a farmer, and most of that working the same farmstead.

65. Certainly the early work of Darroch and Ornstein tends to confirm this specula-
    tion (see especially "Ethnicity and Occupational Structure," 326).

66. Guy R. Ferguson, "The Peter Robinson Settlers in Emily Township, 1825 to 1861"
    (MA thesis, Queen's University, 1979).

67. Computed from *Seventh Census of Canada, 1931*, 1: 716.

68. See John Meisel, *Working Papers on Canadian Politics* (Montreal: McGill-Queen's
    University Press, 2nd edition, 1975).

69. For a preliminary survey, useful not only on Fenianism, but on the general char-
    acter of Canadian-Irish nationalism, see Hereward Senior, *The Fenians and
    Canada* (Toronto: Macmillan, 1978). Also interesting is D.C. Lyne and Peter M.
    Toner, "Fenianism in Canada, 1874–84," *Studia Hibernica* 12 (1972): 27–76.

70. In 1851, 14.0 percent of the Irish-born lived in cities as compared to 7.5 percent of
    the overall population. The parallel figures for 1861 were 13.6 percent and 7.4
    percent. Compiled and computed from *Census of the Canadas, 1851–52*, 1: 4–37
    and *Census of the Canadas, 1860–61*, 1: 48–80 and cf. 128–60.

71. Compiled and computed from *Census of Canada, 1870–71*, 1: 86–145 and 252–81.

72. The misreading and misuse of the data of Irish agricultural settlement patterns
    before the Famine is widespread. A particularly interesting example is Duncan
    (in Horn and Sabourin, *Studies on Canadian Social History*, 155–56), who sets out
    to explain why most Famine-migrated Irishmen in Ontario were urbanized (!) by
    reference to settlement patterns in the southwest of Ireland—from which most
    Famine migrants did not come. Cousens, "The Regional Pattern of Emigration
    during the Great Irish Famine, 1846–51" is a vital antidote to such vapouring.

73. See S.H. Cousens, "Emigration and Demographic Change in Ireland, 1851 to
    1861," *Economic History Review*, 2 ser., vol. 14 (August 1961): 275–88, and David
    Fitzpatrick, "The Disappearance of the Irish Agricultural Labourer, 1841–1912,"
    Irish Economic and Social History 7 (1980): 66–92.

74. D.S. Shea, "The Irish Immigrant adjustment to Toronto: 1840–1860," *Study
    Session, 1972 . . . The Canadian Catholic Historical Society*, 55.
        Susan E. Houston, in "The Impetus to Reform: Urban Crime, Poverty, and
    Ignorance in Ontario, 1850–1875" (PhD thesis, University of Toronto, 1974)
    includes an interesting case study (186–226) of the Famine Irish and their impact
    upon welfare resources in Toronto. She correctly emphasizes that strenuous
    efforts were made to move the Irish out of the main port towns of Toronto,
    Hamilton, and Kingston. In the summer of 1848, for example, only about 200 of
    the 4219 Irish who arrived in Toronto stayed on (196). As for the larger issue of
    whether or not the Catholic Irish became ghettoized and alienated from the gen-
    eral population, the impressionistic nature of the demographic data in
    Houston's study are too limited to permit any conclusion being drawn about
    social mobility in Toronto.
        Much the same evaluation holds for Murray W. Nicholson's interesting, "The
    Irish and Social Action in Toronto, 1850–1900" (paper given at the convention of
    the Canadian Historical Association, 1980).
        On the other hand, Darroch and Ornstein's study ("Ethnicity and Occupational
    Structure") of a 10 000 case study for 1871 for all of Canada (including a large
    sample from Ontario) is unambiguous. It argues strongly against the historian's
    usual notion that occupational status and ethnicity were closely related. In par-
    ticular, they found a striking range of occupations and of occupational status
    amongst Irish Catholics. Because of the nature of their sample, however, it
    remains to be seen whether or not, within a pattern of general occupational
    mobility, there were pockets of intransigence and insuperable discrimination in
    specific cities.

Paul C. Appleton's, "The Sunshine and the Shade: Labour Activism in Central Canada, 1850–60" (MA thesis, University of Calgary, 1974), indicates that the urban Irish were successful in penetrating the "middle rank trades" and were very active in the unions of their day. He argues against a simple two-tier model of the urban labour pool, with the Irish on the bottom.

75. See especially, Dorothy S. Cross, "The Irish in Montreal, 1867–1896" (MA thesis, McGill University, 1969), and also, George R.C. Keep, "The Irish Migration to Montreal, 1847–1867" (MA thesis, McGill University, 1948). Also relevant is Daniel C. Lyne, "The Irish in the Province of Canada in the decade leading to Confederation" (MA thesis, McGill University, 1960). On Halifax, see Terence Punch, "The Irish in Halifax, 1836–71. A Study in Ethnic Assimilation" (MA thesis, Dalhousie University, 1976).

There is a good deal of valuable material about the Irish in Michael Katz's *The People of Hamilton, Canada West. Family and Class in a mid-Nineteenth Century City*, but it is hard to know what to make of it, as the study's numbers are presented in a virtual historical vacuum. The Irish Catholics, it is clear, had a harder time of it than did most ethnic groups and had a more difficult time rising from the lower rungs of the social ladder. On the other hand, Katz denies that there were ghettos in Hamilton and argues that the anti-immigrant Know-Nothingism of American politics did not have a counterpart in Hamilton.

76. Compiled and computed from *Census of Canada, 1870–71*, 1: 86–145 and 252–81.

77. See Part I, Revisions B and C (tables 8 and 9), and the surrounding discussion of the early data and see also, *Census of Canada, 1931*, 1: 716.

Unhappily, the data are muddy at both ends of the time period.

A comparison of the revised emigration figures, with both the total base population of Upper Canada in 1815 and the total migration from the British Isles, makes it inevitable that, by the early 1830s, the Irish were the largest group in Upper Canada, but precisely when this pre-eminence began is impossible of determination. They well may have been the largest group by the mid to late 1820s.

As for the terminal data, the unfortunate fact is that the Irish-descended were clearly dominant in 1881, and the English-descended were dominant in 1901; the 1891 census, however, did not ask or process the ethnic descent question in a manner comparable to 1881 or to 1901, so all that is certain is that between those two dates, the Irish were passed by the English. Relation of the census data to immigration figures suggests, however, that this should not have occurred before the late 1880s and, quite possibly, later (see *Census of Canada, 1890–91*, 1: 340 ff. for the 1891 material, such as it is).

78. I am referring to "The Settlement of Mono Township," by R. Cole Harris, Pauline Roulston, and Chris de Freitas, in *The Canadian Geographer* 19 (1975): 1–17.

William J. Smyth's "The Irish in mid-Nineteenth Century Ontario" deserves mention as a succinct introduction to the position of the Irish, Protestant and Catholic, in the province. It is found in *Ulster Folk Life* 23 (1977): 97–105.

79. If the reader wishes to escape from the generalizations in the text, he will find relevant material, tied to two specific Protestant communities, in Donald H. Akenson, *Between Two Revolutions: Islandmagee, Co. Antrim, 1798–1920* (Toronto: P.D. Meany Co.; Dublin: Academy Press; Hamden, CT: Shoestring Press, 1979) and (with W.H. Crawford), *Local Poets and Social History: James Orr, Bard of Ballycarry* (Belfast: Public Record Office of Northern Ireland, 1977).

80. For a sophisticated discussion of the Orange Order in Ontario dealing with its urban manifestations, see "The Orange Order in Toronto: Religious Riot and the Working Class," by Gregory S. Kealey, in Gregory S. Kealey and Peter Warrian, eds., *Essays in Canadian Working Class History* (Toronto: McClelland & Stewart, 1976), 13–35, and 195–99. Kealey's argument is reproduced, substantially

unchanged, in chapter 7 of his *Toronto Workers Respond to Industrial Capitalism, 1867–1892* (Toronto: University of Toronto Press, 1980.) Also valuable is Cecil Houston and William J. Smyth, "The Orange Order and the expansion of the frontier in Ontario, 1830–1900," *Journal of Historical Geography* 4 (1978): 251–64. In *The Sash Canada Wore. A Historical Geography of the Orange Order in Canada* (Toronto: University of Toronto Press, 1980), Cecil J. Houston and William J. Smyth provide a great deal of data relevant to Ontario. Their material on the distribution of the lodges is especially valuable.

Earlier work concerning the Order in Ontario was done by Hereward Senior: *Orangeism in Ireland and Britain, 1795–1836* (London: Routledge and Kegan Paul, 1966); "The Character of Canadian Orangeism," in *Thought from the Learned Societies of Canada, 1961* (Toronto: W.J. Gage, 1961), 177–89; *Orangeism: The Canadian Phase* (Toronto: McGraw-Hill Ryerson, 1972); "The Genesis of Canadian Orangism," *Ontario History* 60 (1968): 13–29; "Orangeism in Ontario Politics, 1872–1896," in Donald Swainson, ed., *Oliver Mowat's Ontario* (Toronto: Macmillan, 1972), 136–53; "Ogle Gowan, Orangeism, and the Immigrant Question, 1830–1833," *Ontario History* 66 (1974): 193–206; "Ogle Robert Gowan," in *Dictionary of Canadian Biography*, vol. 10.

A good deal of work of a less scholarly sort was done by W.B. Kerr. See his "When Orange and Green United, 1832–9: the Alliance of MacDonell and Gowan," *Ontario Historical Society Papers and Records* 36 (1944): 34–42, and fugitive historical pieces found in the Orange paper, the *Sentinel*, 19 Jan., 2 Feb., 16 Feb., and 2 March 1939. (Microfilm, TPL.)

Amongst unpublished material, see: V.M. Nelson, "The Orange Order in Canadian Politics" (MA thesis, Queen's University, 1950); W.J.S. Mood, "The Orange Order in Canadian Politics, 1841–1867" (MA thesis, University of Toronto, 1950); and Sean Conway, "Upper Canadian Orangeism in the Nineteenth Century: Aspects of a Pattern of Disruption" (MA thesis, Queen's University, 1977).

MIGRATION AND THE MENNONITES: NINETEENTH-CENTURY WATERLOO COUNTY, ONTARIO[✦]

ROBERT S. DILLEY

o

The use of aggregate population data has long been commonplace in the work of both geographers and historians, though only recently have systematic attempts been made to trace the demographic histories of individuals and families from the last century. Such work as has been published relating to migration within North America points to the conclusion that movement from one location to another was a regular occurrence for a large proportion of the population. "The internal movement from place to place within past societies was astonishingly high; it was not an urban phenomenon, nor one restricted to the nineteenth century, nor limited to Anglo-Saxon countries."[1]

Particularly relevant to this study is the description by Gagan and Mays of transiency rates in a part of Peel County, Ontario, a little to the east of Waterloo County: "It would seem that one of the most pervasive and persistent characteristics of nineteenth-century Ontario was the relentless movement of people in and out of this society at every stage in its development. From first to last, the landscape of Toronto Gore must be described in terms befitting a way station of a busy highway."[2]

In most migration studies, the total population of the area in question, or a representative sample thereof, is analyzed. In this paper, I have isolated a particular subset of a population on the basis of ethnic identity. In his study of nineteenth-century Hamilton, Ontario, Katz concludes that ethnicity "exerted no independent influence whatever" and that "All ethnic groups,

[✦] Donald H. Akenson, ed., *Canadian Papers in Rural History*, vol. 4 (Gananoque, ON: Langdale Press, 1984), 108–29. Reprinted with the permission of the publisher.

it is abundantly clear, were on the move to a roughly similar extent."[3] It is worth investigating whether this statement also holds for rural Ontario. In an urban area it is often difficult for a minority ethnic group to maintain more than a superficial grasp on its cultural identity: the enforced proximity of peoples of other origins and the day-to-day needs of urban life tend to break down barriers. In a rural setting such a group has a better chance of holding on to its own peculiar characteristics, since it is more isolated and, if sufficiently large in numbers, much of its business can be retained within the ethnic community.[4]

o

Of the various groups which settled Ontario in the nineteenth century, one of the most distinctive in language, religion, and general way of life, and one which retained those distinctions longer than most (to some extent to the present day) is the Mennonite community of Waterloo County.

The Mennonite Church was founded in Switzerland in 1525, as a Protestant sect favouring plain dress and plain living and opposing military service and the taking of oaths. Unable to find a secure home in Europe, many took up William Penn's offer of land in Pennsylvania, where they enjoyed the religious liberties granted by the British government to the similar English Quaker sect. However, by the end of the eighteenth century, land in and around the principal Mennonite settlements of Montgomery County was becoming prohibitively expensive. Moreover, many were becoming doubtful about the continuation of their freedom under the new government: already some had been persecuted by rebels for refusing to participate in the revolutionary war. These pressures led to a large-scale migration from Pennsylvania to Upper Canada, as Ontario was then known.[5]

The Pennsylvania Mennonites went to several different parts of the province, including the Niagara district and York County, but their main centre was Waterloo County.[6] They had Waterloo to themselves for only a few years. In the 1820s and 1830s there was an influx of non-Mennonite Germans from the United States, and from 1826 migration directly from Germany began. At about the same time a number of Amish began to arrive: members of a closely related sect who were mostly German-speakers from Alsace-Lorraine. Other nineteenth-century settlers included Highland Scots from New York State, Lowland Scots from Scotland, English from England, and Canadians from elsewhere in the country. There was even an influx of Russian Mennonites in the 1920s.[7]

Despite this multicultural settlement, the Mennonites were long the dominant force in Waterloo County: "The early history of Waterloo is essentially linked with the history of the Mennonites. The Mennonite church was at first and for many years the supreme power in the colony. All were not members of the church, but as a rule those who were not members were adherents, and under the influence of the church. We might call the colony a moderate theocracy."[8]

The consciousness of the Mennonites of their group identity is widely stressed in the literature: their traditions of mutual aid, their tendency to ntermarriage, and their rejection of outside influences are all documented.[9] Although their numerical dominance passed, the sense of a separate identity persisted: "Waterloo, the last area to receive settlers from Pennsylvania, s interestingly enough now the only locality in Ontario to retain the ethnic characteristics of its early settlers."[10]

The source used to trace the movements of the Waterloo County Mennonites is a late nineteenth-century work by Ezra Eby entitled, in the discursive style typical of Victorian scholarship, *A Biographical History of Waterloo Township and other Townships of the County, being a History of the Early Settlers and Their Descendants, mostly all of Pennsylvania Dutch origin, as also much other Unpublished Historical Information chiefly of a Local Character*.[11] This work was published in two volumes in 1895 and 1896, the whole being reprinted, with additions and annotations, in 1971. As the title implies, it does not give an exhaustive listing of all Waterloo Mennonites. It covers only the families of those Pennsylvania Germans (including some of Swiss, Dutch, and French origin, provided they came from the German-speaking districts of Pennsylvania) who played a role in the early settlement of Waterloo County. Thus, the forebears of the Waterloo pioneers are included, as are family members who never came to Canada or who arrived later in the century; but settlers from Germany who did not live in Pennsylvania are excluded, as are non-Mennonite German-speakers and those among the early settlers whose families left early or died out before making much of a mark.

Within the chosen population, individual biographies are organized by family. The amount of information on each individual varies considerably; from detailed life histories to nothing more than a name. Not surprisingly, there is usually more detail available for those who stayed in Waterloo County than for those who migrated elsewhere or who never even came.[12] In all, Eby gives separate biographies for 8473 individuals from 143 families.

In order to study the migratory patterns of this group, individuals were selected from among Eby's biographees if they met the following criteria:

(1) They were male. Since each family's entry is organized by male descent, this greatly simplified the task of tracing relationships. Moreover, this was a highly patriarchal society and it is likely that most females migrated because their fathers or husbands did so.[13]

(2) They were born in Waterloo County. The fact of having migrated to Waterloo from Pennsylvania may have had an effect on future decisions whether to migrate. For someone born locally, any move out of the county was a first migration.

(3) They were eighteen years old or more. Since the latest information in Eby is for 1894, this means including individuals born in 1876 or earlier and surviving eighteen years. With few exceptions, younger boys would not have been making independent decisions about migration. By eighteen, most males would have been fully economically active, as the older Mennonite

sects were and are opposed to higher education.[14] The few eighteen-year-olds still in school were excluded, as were all those described as mentally deficient, it being assumed that these were not in charge of their own futures.[15]

(4) Their biographies included at least their date of birth, evidence of birth in Waterloo County, and place of death or of latest residence.

These selection criteria reduced the numbers to be studied considerably. In all, 1684 individuals were analyzed. Given that about half the 8473 in Eby were female, and that about half were born before coming to Waterloo County or after their parents had left, it can be seen that 1684 represents a respectable proportion of the adult males born in the county.

Of the 1684 Waterloo-born Mennonites studied, 533 (32 percent) by 1894 were living, or had died, outside the county.[16] These figures are not directly comparable with those published for other groups, but the migration of less than a third of the population in three-quarters of a century hardly suggests that transiency was a "way of life" with the Mennonites.

In order to provide somewhat more comparable figures, an attempt was made to measure rates of migration between 1850 and 1860, a statistic available for a number of other populations. In all, 903 individuals were alive in both 1850 and 1860; of these, 314 (35 percent) had migrated by the time of Eby's compilation. However, many of those 314 would already have left Waterloo County and been resident elsewhere *before* 1850; others would not have migrated until *after* 1860. The actual rate of persistence is clearly higher than 65 percent. Unfortunately, Eby almost never gives the date for a migration; but if it is assumed that the mean age at which migration takes place is twenty, then any migrant born before 1830 may be considered to have left the county by 1850; any born in 1840 or later may be considered still to be resident locally in 1860. Given this assumption, then 76 of these migrants would have left the county before 1850. Of the 828 individuals still in the county at that date, only 91 would have left by 1860; a persistence rate of 89 percent. When this is compared with figures for persistence over the same period elsewhere—39 percent in Boston; 32 percent in Philadelphia; 35 to 40 percent in Hamilton; and 48 percent in Toronto Gore—the sheer stability of the Waterloo Mennonite population becomes apparent.[17]

One important caveat must be borne in mind when making these comparisons. For the purpose of this study, *migration* is defined as moving to live outside Waterloo County. Since it is being argued that living among other Mennonites was a major element in the lives of these people, moving from one area of the county to another involves no cultural break and is not considered migration. Therefore comparison with the figures for Toronto Gore, which are specific to one township, is not strictly valid.[18]

Another feature stressed in the literature is the frequency with which each migrant moves.[19] The group studied in this paper hardly conforms to that image. In addition to the twelve who left Waterloo County and returned (eight having gone no further than one of the neighbouring counties), sixteen migrants moved twice (eight first to neighbouring counties and then to the United States); two moved three times; two, four times; and

ne was more-or-less continuously on the move. In all, thirty-three of those
tudied migrated twice or more: 2 percent of the total. Twelve of those
hirty-three ended up back in Waterloo.

o

Analysis of the destinations of the migrants reveals a distinctive pattern (see
igures 1 and 2). The largest proportion (39 percent) migrated to other parts
of Ontario, and a further 29 percent went to Michigan. No other state or
province comes anywhere near these two in attracting Waterloo Mennonites:
Kansas, with 4 percent of the total, is next. Only one individual is noted as
eaving North America (for Australia).

Within Ontario, migration is strongly directed to the immediate north
and west: six counties in this area account for well over a quarter of all
migrants.[20] In many cases these migrations consisted of the overspilling of
Mennonite farmers into land just beyond the Waterloo boundary, and, by
the definition used here, should not be considered "leaving home" at all.
Few moved any distance east in Canada, even within Ontario, Toronto representing the eastern limit of all but a handful of migrants. Rather more
went to the western provinces, especially to Manitoba but, in all, less than
5 percent of the migrants went to parts of Canada outside Ontario.

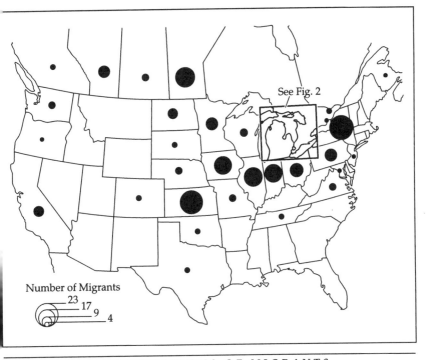

Number of Migrants

FIGURE 1 *DESTINATIONS OF MIGRANTS*

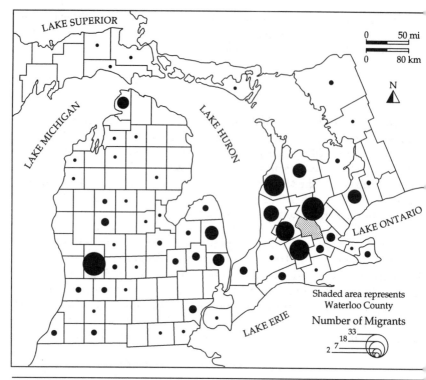

FIGURE 2 *DESTINATIONS OF MIGRANTS: MICHIGAN AND SOUTHWESTERN ONTARIO*

The United States proved to be a more popular destination than Canada, taking 55 percent of those who left Waterloo County and 90 percent of those who migrated out of Ontario. Michigan was by far the most attractive state, accounting for almost as many migrants as all the other states together.[21] Migration was generally concentrated in a belt from New York State to Kansas and the Dakotas. None went to New England, none to the deep south, and few to the Rockies or the west coast.

This pattern strongly suggests that the Mennonites were attracted above all to developing farming areas. Some ended up in the cities (Toronto with twelve, Buffalo ten, and Chicago nine were the most popular); but fewer than one in six of the migrants went to anything bigger than a small town. The Mennonites seemed prepared to settle on relatively poor land if it was close to home; otherwise they looked for good farmland in Michigan, on the plains, and on the prairies. The mountains were avoided and the west coast seems to have been considered too far away. Areas of strong religious feeling different from their own were clearly shunned; notably Quebec, the Bible belt, and the Mormon region. Surprisingly few went to Pennsylvania, considering that most would still have had close relatives there. Presumably, there, as with New England and the Atlantic provinces, good land was just too scarce or too expensive.

Since proximity to other Mennonites and the preservation of traditional ways seem to have been important factors weighing against migration, one would expect to find those who did migrate clustering in a few centres to recreate as much as they could of their old lifestyle. This clearly did not happen. Apart from Michigan, no real concentrations seem to have developed outside Ontario. Fifteen individuals ended up in Marion County, Kansas, but no other rural county attracted as many as ten. Even in Michigan, the 130 individuals whose precise destination is known were spread around thirty-five different counties, with only Kent (including the town of Grand Rapids) forming a very strong concentration. It appears that once a Waterloo County Mennonite decided to migrate, he decided also to do without the company of other Mennonites: or, more likely, that many, if not most of those who did migrate, were not firmly attached to their cultural and economic milieu. It seems that the description used of the initial settlement of Waterloo—"The initiative in emigration was, in most cases, individual, or in small groups"—is equally applicable to later migrations.[22]

Any attempt to chart changing patterns over time is handicapped by the lack of data on the actual date of most migrations. Using birthdate as the most convenient surrogate, a slow but steady increase over time in the rate of migration can be seen, from 23 percent of those born between 1800 and 1809 to 38 percent of those born between 1840 and 1849 (see table 1). There would have been some migration out of Waterloo from the very beginning, by those searching for better opportunities elsewhere, but the pressures for migration undoubtedly increased as land became scarcer and as the prospects of new lands further west became more appealing. "The question of available land for future generations became more serious after 1835 as settlement by non-Mennonite farmers caused a rush for lots and a rise in prices,"[23] though for a while much of the pressure was released by the development of the other townships in the county, outside the original Waterloo Township settlement, and by movement into farmland in the adjacent counties.

The percentage migrating appears to have dropped sharply for those born in the 1860s and 1870s. In part this can be explained as a genuine lessening of the pressures to migrate, associated with the development of more marginal lands for farming, improvements in agricultural techniques allowing the further subdivision of farms, and the growth, with growing urbanization, of job opportunities outside farming.[24] In part, this apparent drop in migration is caused by the nature of the data: some of the younger Mennonites still at home at the time of Eby's compilation are likely to have migrated later.

Changes in destinations over time are noticeable, but not particularly striking. The United States was consistently slightly more attractive than Canada. In each case the western parts of the country became relatively more important over time as more land became available there, though this trend was to some extent countered by an increase in the number of non-farming Mennonites seeking work in the urban areas of the east.[25]

TABLE 1   *DESTINATION OF MIGRANT BY DATE OF BIRTH*

Destination of Migrant	Date of Birth								
	1800–09	1810–19	1820–29	1830–39	1840–49	1850–59	1860–69	1870–76	Total
Ontario	1	8	24	34	58	50	28	4	207
Western Canada	—	—	1	3	6	10	8	1	29
Michigan	3	5	12	27	38	27	24	2	138
Eastern United States◊	1	4	10	11	11	19	20	3	79
Western United States	—	2	7	16	14	25	12	2	78
Total✦	5	19	54	91	128	131	93	12	533
Persisters	17	59	103	170	213	258	251	80	1151

Source: Eby, *A Biographical History.*

Notes:

◊ Those states east of the Mississippi-St Croix rivers, except for Michigan.
✦ Includes one migrant to New Brunswick and one to Australia.

TABLE 2 *DESTINATION OF MIGRANT BY OCCUPATION*

Destination	Professional	Business	Clerical	Category of Occupation Skilled	Unskilled	Farming	Total[◇]
Ontario	13	32	2	21	7	96	171
Western Canada	1	8	–	–	3	13	25
Michigan	8	12	4	16	3	59	102
Eastern United States [✦]	9	17	2	16	4	7	55
Western United States	5	5	–	12	–	36	58
Total[†]	36	76	8	65	17	211	413
Persisters	38	90	31	116	45	683	1003

Source: Eby, *A Biographical History.*

Notes:

◇ Those migrants whose profession is not known are omitted.

✦ Those states east of the Mississippi-St Croix rivers, except for Michigan.

† Includes one migrant to New Brunswick and one to Australia, both in the business category.

o

Marriage might be expected to play a role in decisions whether to migrate, especially among people accustomed to large families: "People with families usually are more settled."[26] Unmarried sons are likely to be more foot-loose, while couples just married may wish to move to establish a new home for themselves before starting a family. Again, the lack of dates of actual migration makes conclusions difficult to reach. In all, 88 percent of migrants and 89 percent of persisters married, and these percentages would certainly have been even higher if those born in the 1860s and 1870s were traced later in life.[27]

The relative dates of marriage and migration were determined for only thirty-one cases, and in twenty-nine of those, marriage preceded migration. No conclusions can be drawn from such a small sample, though it may be significant that the average age of marriage for migrants was actually slightly lower than for persisters.[28] If a substantial number were migrating as bachelors and marrying later, then a higher median age of marriage for migrants would be expected.

An investigation of the ethnicity of the marriage partner was carried out. In an intensely ethnocentric group such as the Mennonites, marriage to another member of the same group would be likely to reinforce community and cultural ties, while marriage to an "outsider" might lessen local ties and make migration seem less of a break. First marriages only were studied. There were many cases of multiple marriage, but the first was the most likely to influence migration one way or another.[29]

Strikingly, 54 percent of those studied had first marriages to women also given individual biographies in Eby, and a further 31 percent married women with distinctly German names.[30] Also notable is that persisters were almost twice as likely to have married another biographee as migrants, while migrants were more than twice as likely to have married non-German wives. It is not possible to determine, however, whether men were more likely to migrate because their wives were not from the pioneer group, or whether many migrated as bachelors and were therefore less likely to marry other pioneer descendants because there were fewer around for them to choose from.

Marital partner seems to be unrelated to direction of migration. Only the prairies are anomalous, being particularly attractive to bachelors and particularly unattractive to those married to Eby biographees. It may, of course, simply have been that wives were more difficult to obtain there, especially wives from pioneer families.

o

Most of Eby's biographees have their occupation described; this information is given for 1416 of the 1684 studied, including 413 of the 533 migrants. Nearly 100 different occupations are mentioned; for convenience of analysis these have been grouped into six categories: professional, business, clerical, skilled, unskilled, and farming.[31]

Not surprisingly, by far the largest category of occupation is that of farmer, with 63 percent of the total (see table 2). Farming has always been the principal activity of the Mennonites, at least in North America: "the care of the soil, animals, and property generally has been considered not only a right but a duty."[32] Nonetheless, 37 percent of the population worked in occupations other than farming. Groh specifically points out that the pioneers worked in trades and commerce as well as on the land, and certainly the most populous categories after farming are skilled worker (13 percent) and business (12 percent).[33] Unskilled labourers were few, presumably because most of those capable only of manual work stayed on the farm: cities and factories were never very attractive to the Mennonites. Neither were there very many professionals—evidence of the general distrust of higher education among the Mennonites, and their low regard of "book-learning." This predilection is also reflected in the small number following clerical careers.[34]

Work on nineteenth-century Hamilton has shown that "Occupation is no help in estimating the probability with which any given person might remain . . . there was virtually no pattern in the differing rates of persistence among people in the common occupations;" moreover, "most studies report rather small differences in the rates of migration for various occupation groups."[35] The Waterloo Mennonites certainly did not conform to these findings, and significant differences can be noted in both the rates and the direction of migration for various occupational groups.

The lowest rates of migration occurred among the farmers and the two small categories of clerical and unskilled workers. That farmers should be persistent is not surprising: not only was farming a particularly strong element of Mennonite culture, but farmers generally tend to be more stable than most. In Toronto Gore, farmers were almost always below average in transience, if landowners, and always well below average, if landless.[36] In Toronto Gore, though, "the most mobile householders were the unskilled labourers," and Katz remarks that "historical studies of nineteenth century places prior to industrialization show . . . it was the semiskilled and unskilled manual workers who moved more frequently than men in more rewarding and prestigious callings."[37] In Waterloo the reverse was the case: only 27 percent of the unskilled migrated, compared with nearly 50 percent of the professionals.[38] It would seem that the highly-rural, self-sufficient nature of Waterloo County at that time offered few suitable openings for professionals. Possibly, also, an educated Mennonite would feel out of place in the community. The few manual workers, however, clearly had little difficulty in finding off-farm work locally and presumably felt no social stigma for their lack of accomplishments.

The lack of urban opportunities in Waterloo County may also be seen in the relatively high mobility of those in business and commerce; almost as high as for the professionals. Skilled workers migrated little more than average, as presumably the flourishing agricultural base provided a reasonable demand for blacksmiths, carpenters, builders, and the like. It is more difficult to account for the persistence of nearly four-fifths of the clerical workers, except to note that there were not very many of them in total, and

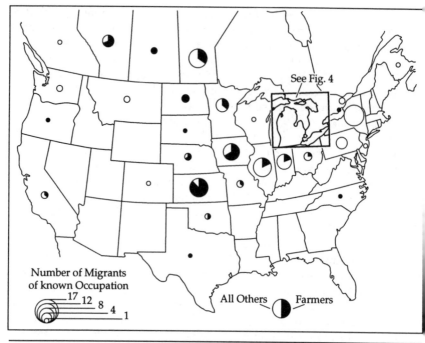

Number of Migrants
of known Occupation

All Others ● Farmers

FIGURE 3 FARMERS AND OTHER MIGRANTS
BY DESTINATION

that most were likely to be humble clerks working for a family business and aware that their lack of skills would give them little hope of bettering themselves elsewhere.[39]

Study of the direction of migration of different occupations reveals some interesting patterns. Migrating farmers and businessmen were least inclined to move out of Ontario. The distribution of farmer-migrants is quite striking: the attraction of the plains and the prairies is obvious, while the eastern parts of the continent are almost entirely avoided (see figures 3 and 4). The Mennonite farmers of Waterloo appeared to have had four objectives, in descending order of importance:

1. to stay where they were;

2. to move into the neighbouring counties to the north or west;

3. to move to central Michigan;

4. to move to the plains or prairies.

Nowhere else seems to have interested them very much. Availability of land was clearly the dominant criterion: it was not there in sufficient quantity in the east or in the mountains; too little was known about the west coast; and the southern states were likely to be unattractive on religious grounds. The slightly lower enthusiasm of those in the business category to

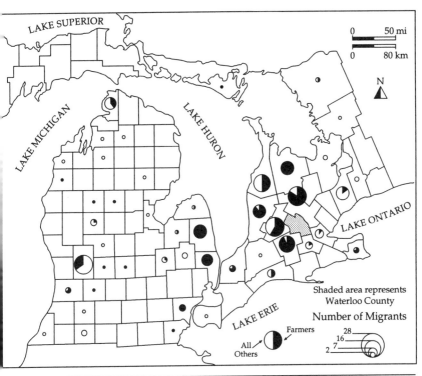

FIGURE 4 *FARMERS AND OTHER MIGRANTS BY DESTINATION: MICHIGAN AND SOUTHWESTERN ONTARIO*

move to the United States may be related to difficulties in setting up capital-based enterprises across the border. On the other hand, professionals and skilled workers both had an above-average tendency to migrate southwards, especially to the eastern and midwestern states.

○

To examine the Waterloo Mennonites as families, a somewhat different arrangement of the data had to be established. Each individual, as isolated in the earlier part of the study, was grouped with his brothers and their father, even if these relatives had been born outside the county.[40] A total of 243 families, composed of 936 adult males, was extracted for study, each family having at least one son born in Waterloo County.

In 21 families, involving 100 individuals, the father himself left the county. In these cases 70 percent of the sons left as well, slightly over half of them ending up at the same destination as their fathers. In 222 families, involving 836 individuals, the father remained in Waterloo County. In this instance, 34 percent of the sons migrated. Migration of the father may thus seem to have been an inducement to family migration, but it is likely that many of the sons would have left as small children, or even have been born in the new location. It may be more significant that nearly a third of the sons of migrating fathers stayed behind.

Of the 222 families whose fathers did not leave, it would seem reasonable to assume that the larger the family, the more likely it was that any member of that family would migrate. An only son would hope to inherit his father's farm, business, or trade, and would be sufficiently aware of that prospect to stay at home or at least in the area. Multiple sons would face the prospect of the farm being subdivided, increasingly difficult as the century progressed, and there would be pressure on at least some of them to leave and find land of their own or jobs elsewhere.[41] In fact, this reasonable assumption is not borne out by the Waterloo Mennonite experience: there is no discernible relationship between size of family and propensity to migrate (see table 3).

There is no obvious explanation for this lack of a measurable relationship. Even given the large size of pioneer farms, there must have been a limit to the extent that they could be divided amongst the numerous Mennonite offspring. Moreover, there were many who had no farms to pass on.[42] A social factor might provide a partial answer. Since the Mennonites *were* so family-conscious, it may be that the larger families felt more secure and were more reliant on each other's moral and practical assistance. This inward family pull may have been enough to counter the economic pressures to move. There must, even so, have been a lot of internal colonization going on, to accommodate these large farming families without subdividing the existing farms to the point of inefficiency.

However, it was still the case that younger sons were likely to have felt more pressure to look out for themselves; especially those from non-farming families and those with long-lived fathers unwilling to retire. Investigation of the relationship between tendency to migrate and the rank of sons in a family shows, unexpectedly, that for smaller families (three sons or fewer) younger sons were *less* likely to migrate than their older brothers. Presumably, in

TABLE 3   *RATE OF MIGRATION BY SIZE OF FAMILY*

Number of Adult Sons in Family	Number of Families	Number of Individuals	Number Migrated	Percentage Migrated
1	19	19	7	37
2	49	98	28	29
3	49	147	44	30
4	30	120	42	35
5	32	160	60	37
6	18	108	34	31
7+	25	184	69	37
Total	222	836	284	34

Source: Eby, *A Biographical History.*

TABLE 4 *RATE OF MIGRATION BY RANK OF SON*
IN FAMILY

Rank of Son	Number at That Rank	Number Migrated	Percentage Migrated
1	197	61	31
2	168	55	33
3	118	40	34
4	74	32	43
5	51	23	45
6	26	10	38
7+	20	10	50

Source: Eby, *A Biographical History.*

these cases the changes of inheritance were seen to be proportionately greater. Overall, if size of family is ignored, there is a definite though far from overwhelming increase in the percentage migrating with increasing rank (see table 4).[43]

○

Direct comparisons between the findings of this paper and those of other nineteenth-century demographic studies must be treated with caution. The data used here concern a distinct population group, the pioneer Pennsylvania German families of Waterloo County, and any conclusions drawn from these data apply to that population group only. Non-pioneer Mennonites in Waterloo, and non-Mennonites among the German-speakers, may have behaved quite differently.[44] Moreover, there are limitations to the data. Dates of migration are rarely available and individuals are traced only up to 1894. Within these limitations, however, the source used provides a picture of almost unparalleled depth of the structure of this distinctive group.

It is clear that, in contrast to most other nineteenth-century populations studied, migration (defined as leaving Waterloo County) was the exception rather than the rule: the persistence rate from 1850 to 1860 was nearly 90 percent. Those who did migrate settled firmly in their new homes; multiple migrations were rare. Preferred destinations for migrants were the lands immediately north and west in Ontario and the central part of Michigan, followed well behind by the midwestern and great plains states, and the prairie provinces. Nowhere else attracted more than a few migrants. Most went to rural areas or to small towns. Occupation had an important influence on both propensity to migrate and direction of migration, but family size did not seem to have any importance in encouraging migration.

The pioneers of Waterloo County and their descendants thus do not, in most aspects, conform to the picture being established for other populations. This is not to cast doubt on earlier findings: "no theory of migration which does not account for the context in which the movement takes place can capture the complexity of the process as it actually exists."[45] The context in this instance is a relatively small, closely-knit group, highly conscious of and cherishing their differences from the larger society within which they found themselves, but of which they did not particularly want to be a part.

The Mennonites today are being swamped by the urbanization and overall growth of population in Waterloo County; the more traditional sects are moving out "in order to preserve their serene and unhurried way of life" to the quieter counties north and west, where many of their forebears had settled.[46] Even in this rapidly-changing, increasingly technological world they strive to maintain their traditional values of co-operation, of family work on the farm, of disdain for worldly goods and modern progress.[47] It is not surprising that in the slower and more isolated world of nineteenth-century Ontario they should have clung so strongly to the area they had made their own.

NOTES

1. Michael B. Katz, *The People of Hamilton, Canada West: Family and Class in a Mid-Nineteenth-Century City* (Cambridge: Harvard University Press, 1975), 119.

2. David Gagan and Herbert Mays, "Historical Demography and Canadian Social History: Families and Land in Peel County, Ontario," *Canadian Historical Review* 54 (1973): 35.

3. Katz, *The People of Hamilton*, 125, 127.

4. Where there is a very strong differentiation of characteristics, minority groups may long retain their separate identities even in urban areas: for example, the former Jewish ghettos of Europe and the current black areas of most cities in the United States. Emrys Jones, *Human Geography* (London: Chatto and Windus, 1969), 206–7.

5. R.A. Murdie, "The Mennonite Communities of Waterloo County," in A.G. McLellan, ed., *The Waterloo County Area: Selected Geographical Essays* (Waterloo: Department of Geography, University of Waterloo, 1971), 22–23.

6. Murdie, "Mennonite Communities," 23.

7. E.R. Officer, "Waterloo County: Some Aspects of Settlement and Economy before 1900," in A.G. McLellan, *The Waterloo County Area*, 13–14.

8. Rev. A.B. Sherk, "The Pennsylvania Germans of Waterloo County, Ontario," *Ontario Historical Society, Papers and Records* 7 (1906): 105.

9. See, for instance, James T. Lemon, *The Best Poor Man's Country: A Geographical Study of Early Southeastern Pennsylvania* (Baltimore and London: Johns Hopkins Press, 1972), 71; G. Elmore Reaman, *The Trail of the Black Walnut* (Toronto: McClelland & Stewart, 1957), 141; E.A. Haldane, "The Historical Geography of Waterloo Township, 1800–1855" (MA thesis, McMaster University, 1963), 42, 45.

10. Reaman, *Black Walnut*, 108. The first Mennonites settled in Waterloo County in the spring of 1800 (Officer, "Waterloo County," 13). By July 1805 some thirty-five families of Pennsylvania Mennonites had arrived (Reaman, *Black Walnut*, 112). By 1835 Waterloo Township, the earliest-settled part of the county, had a total population of under 2800 of whom about 2000 were Mennonites (Haldane, "Waterloo Township," 58–59). By 1861, however, the county population had risen to 38 750, of whom only just over 11 percent professed to being Mennonite (*Census of Canada, 1861*).

11. Ezra E. Eby, *A Biographical History. . .* , 2 vols. (Berlin, ON: 1895–96). Reprinted in one volume with additions, E.D. Weber, ed. (Kitchener, 1971). Henceforth referred to as "Eby."

12. The fact that Eby frequently notes his inability to trace some particular fact or facts about individuals increases the confidence with which one uses the information he has compiled.

13. There was, however, a certain amount of migration by young unmarried females, particularly to go to live with married sisters.

14. Reaman, *Black Walnut*, 212–13.

15. There were several persons listed as "imbecile," "of unsound mind," or "intellectually weak." Presumably this was in part a result of generations of close intermarriage.

16. Throughout this paper, it is the last known destination that is counted. Twelve persons left Waterloo County for a while and returned; they are not counted as migrants. One who left, returned, and then left again, is. Those normally resident in the county who died while on a trip or in a hospital outside the county are not counted as migrants.

17. Katz, *The People of Hamilton*, 119; Gagan and Mays, "Canadian Social History," 37. Mean age of migration at twenty is consistent with table 3.4 of Katz (*The People of Hamilton*, 124), from which it may be calculated (given the approximations necessary due to Katz's grouping of ages) that the average age of a migrant was a little over twenty-one. Eight of Eby's (*A Biographical History*) biographees whose age at migration could be determined averaged twenty-nine years old, but this group included no children. In any case, even if the mean age of migration from Waterloo were as low as ten, the persistence rate would still be 83 percent. If it were thirty, then the rate would be 91 percent.

18. It is unlikely that inclusion of inter-township movements would have made much difference to the persistence rate. Study of a 10 percent random sample (fifty-three individuals) of those listed in volume 1 who never left the county showed that two changed their township of residence twice, but fifty-one never left the township of their birth.

19. "Whatsoever their motivation, one characteristic shared by many migrants has been their propensity to move frequently." Katz, *The People of Hamilton*, 117.

20. Bruce, Grey, Huron, Oxford, Perth, and Wellington counties.

21. According to the manuscript annotation by the editor of the 1971 reprint of Eby, "Generous terms offered the Homesteader attracted many Waterloo County Residents to Michigan from about 1860." Eby, *A Biographical History*, M-5.

22. W.H. Breithaupt, C.E., "First Settlements of Pennsylvania Mennonites in Upper Canada," *Ontario Historical Society, Papers and Records* 23 (1926): 9. It is possible that some of the destinations chosen by these migrants were populated with other Mennonites, not from the pioneer families. This can hardly have applied to more than a few of the wide scatter of places settled by this group.

23. Haldane, "Waterloo Township," 165.

24. Only 16 percent of those born between 1800 and 1829 found employment outside farming, while the figure for those born between 1850 and 1876 is 43 percent.

25. Thirty percent of the migrants born in 1860 or later went to urban areas, compared with only 8 percent of those born before 1840. The dominance of cities in eastern settlement may be seen in that seventeen of the twenty-two migrants to New York State ended up in Buffalo, Rochester, or New York City, and the only migrations to New Jersey, New Brunswick, and eastern Ontario were to urban

areas. It is interesting that the opening of Manitoba to Mennonite settlement in 1874 did not attract the Waterloo pioneer families, none of whom went to the parts of that province set aside for their co-religionists. Significantly, the Manitoba settlement, though of German-speaking Mennonites, was of migrants from Russia who brought with them the common-field agriculture with which they were familiar (John Warkentin, "Mennonite Agricultural Settlements of Southern Manitoba," *Geographical Review* 44 (1959): 342–68). The Waterloo Mennonites, while in Pennsylvania, had adopted the agricultural patterns of the Quakers, who "preferred to live on their own farms, and they wanted their farms to be relatively compact parcels, not scattered fields or strips" (Lemon, *Poor Man's Country*, 219).

26. Katz, *The People of Hamilton*, 114.

27. Ninety-five percent of those born before 1860 married. Details of marriage and migration were analyzed for those in the first volume of Eby (*A Biographical History*) only; family names A to L.

28. The 50 migrants for whom this information is available married at a median age of twenty-three; the 174 persisters at twenty-four.

29. A great deal of interesting data on the marital patterns of the Waterloo Mennonites awaits systematic study. Not only was early marriage the norm; it appears that both sexes tended to remarry fairly soon after the death of a spouse, on many occasions to the sister or brother of the deceased. One man married three sisters in succession; after burying the third he turned to another family for his fourth wife, though whether because he had run out of sisters-in-law, or because he concluded that the first family did not have adequate staying-power is not clear. Only one case of divorce was noted. Wives seem usually to have been two to five years younger than their husbands, even in cases of middle-aged remarriage.

30. In many cases, the wife's maiden name was that of a family listed in Eby (*A Biographical History*), but she herself was not mentioned; presumably she came from a non-pioneer branch of the family. Identification of German names is made difficult by the habit of anglicizing family names (e.g., Baumann to Bowman, Liebengut to Livergood); in many cases forenames proved a better guide to ethnicity.

31. The grouping of occupations closely follows that used in Peter G. Goheen, "Victorian Toronto, 1850 to 1900: Pattern and Process of Growth" (The University of Chicago, Department of Geography, Research Paper No. 127, 1970), with some variations to suit the particular circumstances of this study. It proved impossible satisfactorily to distinguish Goheen's intermediate class of semiskilled worker, and such occupations were allocated to skilled or unskilled as seemed appropriate. Farming was made into a separate category, in recognition of its importance. This classification is also similar to that used to study Toronto Gore, where the categories were "farmers [owners and tenants], unskilled labourers, artisans and mechanics, professional people, and those engaged in commerce." Gagan and Mays, "Canadian Social History," 41.

32. Reaman, *Black Walnut*, 13.

33. Ivan Groh, "History or Fiction," *Waterloo Historical Society, Annual Report* 51 (1963): 54–58.

34. Eby notes that it was said of his paternal grandfather, Bishop Benjamin, that as he was bookish and not very strong as a child: "'Aus 'em Bennie gebts ka Bauer, er muss Schulmaster werre!' 'Bennie will never make a farmer, he must become a schoolteacher.'" Eby, *A Biographical History* 1: 136. The category "professional" includes ministers of religion. Mennonite ministers were elected to their posi-

tions, and rarely had any formal qualifications. However, their election implies that they were seen as superior individuals. Only those who appear to have been full-time ministers are included in this category.

35. Katz, *The People of Hamilton*, 115, 132.

36. Gagan and Mays, "Canadian Social History," 39.

37. Ibid., 41; Katz, *The People of Hamilton*, 115.

38. If teachers and ministers, who may be considered to have special ties of language and religion to the area, are excluded; then of the other professionals no less than 70 percent migrated.

39. Some of the individuals in each category are likely to have migrated as children and not developed their trades or professions until reaching their new homes. There is no reason to suppose that this was any more common in one category of occupation than in any other. Others changed their jobs on migration, though there were few changes of category of occupation. In each case it is the last occupation which is counted, unless it was clearly adopted only towards the end of an individual's working life. Those retired or deceased are listed under their last full-time occupation.

40. Those who died young, had not reached eighteen by 1894, were still at school, or were mentally deficient were again omitted, as were all females and those of whom it was not clear whether they had migrated or not. Since omitting, say, all but one brother in a family of six could cause bias, whenever more than one in four of a set of brothers had to be excluded then the whole family was ignored. The data in this section are derived solely from volume 1 of Eby, *A Biographical History*, family names A to L.

41. The Waterloo Mennonites were accustomed to providing land for each son (Murdie, "Mennonite Communities," 27). The original settlement in Waterloo comprised farms of 448 acres each (Haldane, "Waterloo Township," 36–37). No systematic count was kept of total family size, but those families studied had a mean of nearly 4 adult sons each. Two couples were noted in passing, each with 112 grandchildren.

42. No systematic study was carried out of inheritance patterns, but an analysis was made of twenty-eight families where the father was a retired or deceased farmer, all of whose sons stayed in Waterloo County. In twelve cases (the number of sons ranging from two to seven) *none* succeeded to their fathers' farms, although the majority went into farming. In twelve cases a single son succeeded. In only four instances were there signs of a divided inheritance: two of two brothers sharing, two of three brothers sharing. Even in these cases it is not clear if the farms were actually divided, or if one brother inherited the title while the others worked for him. In two of the cases where no son succeeded, it was a married daughter who took over her father's farm, though in both cases the daughter had brothers who farmed. In so far as any pattern emerges, it seems to have been the practice for the sons to stay with their parents and help with the farm until the sons married, when they would leave to set themselves up on their own land. When the father retired or died, the farm passed to whichever son or sons remained on it at the time: if all had gone, then one might come back if the family farm was better than the one he had at the time. This was when daughters and their husbands had the opportunity to move in. While this pattern is based on rather scanty evidence it would certainly explain why, in the twelve instances cited of a single son succeeding to the family farm, in only two cases was it the eldest son, while in six instances it was the youngest.

43. Some of the younger sons would still have been in their twenties or late teens at the time of Eby's (*A Biographical History*) compilation. This would exaggerate the

tendency of that group to persist. Table 4 therefore includes only those born before 1860. Any one of these still alive at the time Eby was writing would have been at least thirty-four, and well past the most common age of migration.

44. It can be estimated that about 1140 of the biographees studied here were resident in Waterloo County in 1881. At that date there were 5098 professed Mennonites in the county: since the county was evenly divided between the sexes, there were likely to have been about 2550 male Mennonites. The population studied therefore represents about 45 percent of all male Mennonites in Waterloo in 1881.

45. Katz, *The People of Hamilton*, 116.

46. Murdie, "Mennonite Communities," 116.

47. Julius Mage and Robert Murdie, "The Mennonites of Waterloo County," *Canadian Geographical Journal* 80 (1970): 10–19.

IMMIGRATION AND CHARITY
IN THE MONTREAL JEWISH
COMMUNITY BEFORE 1890[*]

GERALD TULCHINSKY

o

Indigency and philanthropy were twin aspects of the social and religious
setting of nineteenth-century Canada. In the absence of publicly funded
relief services, the needs of the "deserving poor" were assumed to be the
responsibility of private charities having religious, ethnic, or workplace
affiliations.[1] While much of the poverty and social distress in Canada
resulted from the seasonal nature of employment in primary occupations,
public works, or shipping, these problems were especially acute among
immigrants arriving at the major ports.[2] Until distressed new arrivals
moved on—willingly or not—they were aided by voluntary associations of
co-religionists, fellow nationals, or brother workers.[3] By the 1840s Montreal
possessed a wide variety of institutions and benevolent associations ministering to the needs of its indigent population. City directories of the time list
the numerous orphanages, magdalene asylums, missions, and hospitals, all
providing "indoor relief," as well as organizations like the national associations of Irishmen, Scotsmen, Englishmen, Germans, Italians, and Jews offering occasional assistance in the form of "outdoor relief."[4]

As one of Canada's major ports and commercial centres, Montreal in
1850 was the home of a small but well-established Jewish community.[5]
Attracted there in the eighteenth century by the city's economic opportunities, the tiny group of former Army commissary officers, merchants, and fur
traders had established in 1768 the *Sherith Israel* (the Remnant of Israel) congregation, also known as the Spanish and Portuguese synagogue to denote
the national origins of some of its founders and the Sephardic order of
prayers followed in its services.[6] By the late 1830s this synagogue was

[*] *Histoire sociale/Social History* 16, 32 (Nov. 1983): 359–80. Reprinted with the permission of the journal.

housed in an impressive new edifice on Chenneville Street.[7] Over the next decade the city's Jewish community increased slowly. By 1851, there were about 150 Jews and, after 1846, a second congregation was formed in Montreal, the *Sha'ar Hashamayim* (Gates of Heaven), also known as the English, German, and Polish congregation. Its members were virtually all recent immigrants who followed the Ashkenazi or German rite and customs.[8] While the distinction between the two synagogues was far from being a nominal one in the 1850s and 1860s, the divisions began to wane subsequently as the new arrivals acquired social prominence and material success, and as the two groups recognized their common interests and responsibilities towards poor immigrant Jews who arrived during the 1870s and 1880s.

By mid-century then, the Spanish and Portuguese were already a venerable, proud, and distinguished community which included prominent merchants, doctors, and lawyers, several of whom also held commissions in the militia, as well as offices in the consular corps, the magistracy, and municipal government.[9] Like their counterparts in the United States, these Sephardic Jews enjoyed a general acceptance in "Society."[10] They were admitted to fraternal orders and lodges, and their Rabbi, Rev. Dr Abraham de Sola, formerly of London, was a distinguished Hebraist who lectured on Hebrew and Oriental Literature at McGill University.[11] Inasmuch as the newly arrived Jews from Britain, Germany, and Poland included successful merchants and manufacturers, they soon acquired roughly the same social standing as the Spanish and Portuguese. Some were admitted to local Masonic lodges and universities and achieved prominence in literary and sports activities.[12] This was especially true of the Jews of British origin who added considerably to the general Anglophile tone of the whole Jewish community. In March 1881, a number of these British Jews formed a Montreal branch of the London-based Anglo-Jewish Association, a prestigious organization channelling political and educational assistance to distressed Jewish communities overseas.[13]

Although Montreal Jewry was generally middle-class and prosperous, the immigrants of the 1840s included some who required charity and who turned, quite naturally, to their fellow Jews for help. In the Jewish tradition, charity was called *tsedakah*, a Hebrew word which translates as "righteousness," implying that in helping the poor the donor is fulfilling a religious duty from which he derives a moral benefit. (In his code of Jewish law and ethics, the medieval scholar, Maimonedes, taught that the noblest form of *tsedakah* is to provide the poor with economic opportunities to help themselves.)[14] But in whatever form this benevolence was expressed, Jews were required to help their brothers and sisters, and in the long history of the Jewish people the tradition of *tsedakah* was often put to the test.[15] How well did the Montreal Jews meet their religious duties towards their fellow Jews during the late nineteenth century? In what respects did their approaches change during the period 1850–90? And how does the experience of the one relief organization that operated throughout that period reflect changes in attitudes among its supporters in the light of the tragedies befalling the Jewish people in Eastern Europe? In short, what does this experience tell us about the internal coherence of a community that was undergoing such rapid and far-reaching expansion and social change in late nineteenth-century urban Canada?

o

As the pace of Jewish immigration from Europe to Britain and America accelerated during the second half of the nineteenth century, the growing need for welfare assistance led to the founding of Jewish benevolent societies in most of the major eastern North American ports. By the late 1840s the Jews of Boston, New York, Philadelphia, Baltimore, Charleston, and Montreal possessed associations to help their poor.[16] When the Montreal Hebrew Philanthropic Society was established in 1847, its immediate task was to provide temporary help for thirty of the new immigrants, mainly German Jews, who had arrived in the city that year, as well as ten others already resident in the city.[17] The Society's officers included a theatre owner, the police chief of Montreal, Rabbi Abraham de Sola, and Moses Hays, an entrepreneur in municipal services.[18] Businessmen Simon Hart, David Moses, and Joseph Lyons constituted a Relief Committee whose purpose was to provide financial assistance.[19] Dr Aaron Hart David, a distinguished local physician, ministered to the health needs of the newly arrived immigrants.[20] These few dozen immigrants, most of whom were apparently in transit to the western United States, created an unprecedented but temporary burden for Montreal Jews. A more serious local problem faced the Hebrew Philanthropic Society: the "undeserving" Jewish poor who were badgering their brethren for handouts. According to a contemporary report on the migration of 1847, "the professed and sturdy beggars, by repeated and pressing importunity, obtained an undue amount of relief" while "the respectable, but decayed, has suffered from a modest unwillingness in forcing his claims upon the attention of his co-religionists." The Society intended therefore "to promote a more just and efficient mode of relief." Drawing on contemporary concepts of scientific charity, their object was to investigate "certain persons professing to be poor Israelites ... [and] use every possible precaution, and institute every possible inquiry to assure itself that the applicants are really what they pretend to be."[21] The undeserving poor would thus be frowned upon while the Society promised to seek the deserving poor "at the bedside of the sick, in the attic, the loft, the hospital, even at the grave to prove that Jewish benevolence, when invoked by the plaintive voice of suffering, is not invoked in vain; that it has no limit, and that mercenaries can erect for it no barrier over which it will not gloriously and triumphantly pass." As the immigrants of 1847 departed or settled in, the Society was left to assist only a few local and transient indigent Jews and occasional donations seem to have been adequate to meet its needs.[22] Perhaps because of the Society's intention to weed out the undeserving poor, over the next few years the organization all but ceased to exist and it apparently was never called upon to implement its goal of genuinely humane charity—real *tsedakah*—proclaimed in its founding declaration.

By the early 1860s, however, a new, larger, and stronger organization which would draw more broadly on the community's resources for efficient charity work seemed to be needed as some Montreal Jews expected that more Jewish immigrants would begin arriving, many of them en route to the United States. At its formation in July 1863, when L.L. Levey invited "the members of the Jewish persuasion to meet ... to consider the desirability of forming some association to assist our needy or unfortunate co-religionists," the new group called itself the Young Men's Hebrew Benevolent Society (hereafter YMHBS or the Society).[23] The founders were drawn from both of the city's congregations, especially after the Society's membership was enlarged in 1869 to include married as well as single men.[24] From the outset, support seems to have been about evenly balanced between the two congregations;[25] both rabbis, Abraham de Sola of the Spanish and Portuguese and Jacob Fass of the English, German, and Polish, who were made honorary members, sat on the relief committee.[26] Even though differing synagogue affiliation resulted in some friction, this rivalry did not seem to affect the dispensation of charity. In fact, though the Spanish and Portuguese Jews remained an important element in the Society's numerical and financial support until the early 1890s, the executive positions were pretty evenly divided between them and members of the other congregation, indicating that in this endeavour, at least, community leaders were willing to share authority and responsibility between old and new arrivals.

During its first decade the relief work of the YMHBS was limited because the number of Jews in the city before 1871 was small. Although the Jewish population of Canada East had grown by 1861 to 572 people, with all but a few dozen of them living in Montreal,[27] over the next ten years the community actually declined in size as many immigrants and some established residents left the city. An upswing in immigration to Canada during the 1870s increased the Montreal Jewish population by 1881 to about 950 and over the next ten years Montreal's Jewry grew to about 2473 people.[28] Many of the new arrivals came from Central and Eastern Europe and needed considerable help. As early as October 1874 the Society felt that it had to bear heavy financial burdens due to "the fact that many families having arrived here from Germany and other adjoining countries in a state of utter destitution."[29] Aid to forty-two families cost only $542 but depleted resources, even occasioning some deficit financing. But the strain was brief and by no means overwhelming.

The sums of money raised and spent on relief were in fact very small, usually between two and five hundred dollars in one year, except for two years in the mid-1870s. From October 1874 to November 1875, $1090 was spent on 103 applicants, an average of $10.58 each, and about the same amount on 153 persons, $7.13 on each, in 1875–76. However, expenditures for an unspecified number of relief cases dropped the following year to $490 and remained at approximately that level until 1882. The funds for these outlays came almost entirely from the members' annual fees or from special contributions requested whenever the treasury was especially low. At that point, collection committees were struck to encourage members to pay up and to collect from other local Jews as well.[30] Occasionally contributions were received from non-Jewish donors, including an annual grant from the Montreal City and District Savings Bank.[31] The Society attempted to augment its finances by planning theatrical performances of various kinds.[32] However, for the most part its members, albeit slowly, paid the costs of relief work.

Although most expenditures were for the alleviation of distress among resident and transient Jews, providing necessities such as food, clothing, coal, and medicines, money was also spent on assisting transients to move on. The Society's relief committee which handled these cases reported briefly to the Society at the quarterly or half-yearly meetings and to the annual general meeting usually held in October, where the committee provided full and detailed reports of all their cases.[33] There was also a visiting committee to determine need while medical assistance was provided by Dr David, and hospital care at the Montreal General.[34]

Notwithstanding the relatively light load of Jewish indigency—and the ancient tradition of *tsedakah*—the extent of the Society's obligations to assist indigent Jews became an issue at one of its earliest meetings. Reflecting current Victorian ideas of charity and perhaps also some members' dilatoriness in paying their annual dues, one prominent member argued in 1863 that the Society "is not based on the principle of granting permanent relief" and therefore "no application [should] receive assistance oftener than once in three months."[35] The same member also tried to limit relief payments to an annual maximum of ten dollars for any single applicant or family group. Most members of the Society recognized that to become committed to "permanent relief" would necessitate the raising of much larger amounts of money. They were clearly unwilling to do this and therefore reiterated their agreement to providing only "temporary" relief, as was laid down in the Society's bylaws.[36]

Rabbi de Sola raised this matter again a year later, in open disagreement with these views. De Sola argued "that in view of the desirableness of affording permanent relief required by the parties hitherto receiving the same from the Society," a special committee be formed to raise enough money to continue that relief. He argued that the Society could not confine itself to alleviating immediate distress because there were growing numbers of indigents whose rehabilitation would take much longer. A decision was made to extend permanent relief to "selected applicants," but it was reversed a short time later "in view of this Society not having been sufficiently supported by some of our co-religionists."[37] Thus the decision to make only limited commitments was reasserted.

o

Over the next decade, however, the problem of long-lasting poverty became a serious one in the Montreal community. In 1876 Moses Gutman called attention to the several families that were annually dependent upon the Society during "our long winters" because of their inability to find employment. He felt that these families should be denied relief altogether if they refused to be moved "to some other place where they might perhaps find friends or relations to assist them or constant work and pay the year round."[38] This view was supported by Rabbi E.M. Myers of the English, German, and Polish Congregation who voiced the opinion that the "Board of Relief should take a decided stand in the matter, and refuse any longer to submit to such regular imposition." He even suggested that "these families were unable to support themselves any longer and should be forced to go away."[39] Precisely how many families were regularly imposing on the Society is not clear, nor were either Gutman or Rabbi Myers prepared to recommend where or how these families could make a more regular income.

In an effort to improve its efficiency in helping immigrants and lessen its own obligations, the Society attempted to establish co-operative contact with other philanthropic organizations in Montreal, not all of whom, however, were friendly towards these overtures.[40] In 1874 Mona Lesser recommended that the YMHBS participate with "all the National and Charitable Societies in this City" in the formation of a "Colonization Society" whose purpose would be to secure a grant from the Dominion government for relieving immigrants landing in Montreal. But the Dominion government, which maintained an Immigration Bureau in Montreal to assist immigrants, was unwilling to oblige while local national or ethnic societies like the St Andrew's Society, the Irish Benevolent Society, and the German Society, were also apparently not interested.

While only partially successful in its efforts to restrict its philanthropic assistance to one-time local and transient indigents, the Society attempted to stem the flow to Canada of what it called "too many destitute and helpless Israelites."[41] In 1875, alarmed by the rumours of a large Jewish migration on its way to Canada, the executive dispatched strong protests to the *London Jewish World* and the *Jewish Chronicle* of London in the hopes of preventing various Jewish organizations, such as the Ladies' Emigration Society, from shunting too many of the European Jews arriving in England out to North America. "Our transatlantic brethren object—and we confess, very properly so. . . , " commented the *Jewish Chronicle* in October 1875, "to being burdened with the poor and unskillful Jews who are assisted to emigrate from Europe to the United States and Canada."[42] But this and other sympathetic comments did not stop the London agencies from continuing to export their problems. Two years later the Montrealers found it necessary to complain again about the London organizations sending to Montreal too many Jews "in a state of destitution and generally incapable of self help."[43] In addition to writing hostile letters to the London Jewish newspapers, the Society sent Rabbi de Sola on a mission to London in 1877 to protest personally on behalf of Montreal Jewry against the London Jewish Emigration Society which was chiefly responsible for sending poor Jews to Canada.[44] While there, he was partly persuaded that "the statements of the immigrants that they had been sent [to Canada] by the Jewish Emigration Society, should not always be accepted." In any event his protests seem to have had the desired effect and for the time being the London migrations ceased abruptly.[45]

During the Jewish influx of the mid-1870s, the emergence of other charities in Montreal resulted in some duplication of relief efforts. The most important of these organizations, the Ladies' Hebrew Benevolent Society, concerned with the welfare of women and children, had, since its formation in 1877, exchanged information with the YMHBS on those people seeking help. However, similar co-operation or agreement to share responsibility for indigents apparently had not been established with any of the other newer charities, most of them self-help associations formed by the immigrants. This resulted in considerable confusion and animosity because of the increasing numbers of overlapping appeals for money to the Jews of Montreal.

Observing this proliferation of effort and perhaps influenced by the success of New York's recently formed United Hebrew Charities, one of the Society's most active early members, Moses Gutman, suggested in 1874 that a similar body be established in Montreal since "the time has now arrived when a more general co-operation is demanded."[46] In his view, "the interest of charity will be best served by this Society merging itself into a more general organization, embracing all the Jews of Montreal as its members." Few people were ready for that. Such action, claimed the members, should be taken "only after mature deliberation" since it "threatened the very existence of the Society."

The objections suggest that the officers of the YMHBS preferred to retain their control. The alteration of the Society into a mass charity organization embracing the entire Montreal Jewish community was an unwelcome prospect at a time when the immigrants were beginning to outnumber the established Jewish residents. These newcomers were more likely to be receivers than givers of philanthropy and they might well have more traditional concepts of what Jewish charity should be. Moreover, the directors and a good number of the Society's members were either Canadian-born or long-time residents of Canada, in comfortable if not well-to-do financial positions. There was little common ground on which they could meet the immigrants: they were not likely to mix socially and their contacts on the economic level would be on an employer–employee basis, usually in the clothing or tobacco industries in which several Jewish families were involved. Nor would they meet in the synagogues, for the immigrants tended to avoid the older congregations with their imposing buildings in the alien west end of the city and dignified services which included sermons in English. Organizations such as the Jewish Literary and Social Union Society founded in 1876 by the McGill graduate and poet Isidore Gordon Ascher, would have been of little interest to these new arrivals from Eastern Europe.[47] And the Montefiore Club for Jewish businessmen had little to do with immigrant Jews. Indeed, the residential patterns of the two groups differed, with the newcomers clustering in a part of the city where they worshipped in tiny makeshift synagogues of their own, prayed in their own fervent manner, and extended *tsedakah* in the traditional way. A brief announcement in the *Gazette* in December 1882 concerning the formation of a new congregation of Jews from Denmark and Russia, reflects their activity: "A charitable society has been organized in connection with the congregation to administer to the sick. Another object of this society is to furnish whatever assistance may be possible to Jewish immigrants in securing employment."[48]

o

The anti-Jewish pogroms that erupted in Russia in 1881 and 1882 resulted in the emigration of tens of thousands of Jews to the United States and Canada. The Jewish communities were then challenged to provide relief on an unprecedented scale. As hundreds of Russian Jewish refugees landed in Montreal, the Young Men's Hebrew Benevolent Society was obliged to become a more diversified philanthropic organization.

Reports began reaching Montreal of the persecution of Jews in Russia as early as May 1881, when the newly formed Anglo-Jewish Association held a public meeting to protest against the murder, rape, arson, and mass expulsions taking place in Kiev.[49] A city-wide organization with support in the Christian community, the Citizens' Committee, and the Jewish Relief Fund, was quickly formed as Montrealers learned of the Russian atrocities. Meanwhile long descriptions of the Russian persecutions and editorials appearing in Montreal newspapers began to arouse considerable sympathy for Russia's Jews and public support for assistance to any refugees who might arrive in Canada. In early February 1882, the *Montreal Gazette* asserted that:

> It is the duty of the Dominion to make proper provision for the hospitable reception of such of them as may land on our shores. . . . The people of their own race and faith, of whom many living amongst us occupy positions of respectability and influence will of course do all that is in their power for the succor of their unfortunate brethren, but it is no less incumbent on Christians of all denominations to give a helping hand, which shall atone, to some extent at least, the brutal usage by those who profess to serve the same master.[50]

The Anglican Bishop of Montreal, William Bennett Bond, a deeply spiritual champion of Evangelicalism, headed the Citizens' Committee. Other members included prominent Montreal businessmen David Morrice, George Hague, Hon. Justice Ferrier, P.E. Grafton, Hugh McLennan, and two local MPs, Mathew Hamilton Gault and Thomas White, as well as a number of Protestant clergymen and professors. The committee solicited subscriptions of over $4600 from the local citizens: contributions came in daily and the *Gazette* kept its readers informed of the latest donations.[51] Assisted by John Redpath Dougall, publisher of the widely circulated temperance newspaper, Montreal *Witness*, the Citizens' Committee called a public meeting at the YMCA on 13 March 1882 to express their indignation over the Russian atrocities, "these inhuman barbarities . . . a foul blot on the name of Christianity, a disgrace to our civilization, and a wound inflicted on our common humanity."[52]

Meanwhile, in order to co-ordinate their efforts to help the expected flood of refugees, all important Jewish charity groups in the city, the YMHBS, the Ladies' Hebrew Benevolent Society, and the Anglo-Jewish Association joined in forming the Jewish Emigration Aid Society (hereafter JEAS).[53] Probably modelled on the similarly named New York society established the preceding year, this committee took on the task of caring for the immigrants, providing food, clothing, housing, furniture, medical aid, jobs, and, if necessary, transportation to other parts of Canada.[54] The fact that its executive and Board of Directors consisted mainly of YMHBS members, most of them drawn from the Jewish immigrants of the 1840s and 1850s, is a strong indication of the recognition the other two associations gave to the experience of the Society in performing this kind of service.[55] They were also taking advantage of the leadership skills of this small but influential élite.

The JEAS barely had time to organize before the first group of 260 Russian refugees who, according to the *Montreal Gazette* "were not particularly distinguished for cleanliness," arrived at Bonaventure station on 16 May 1882.[56] With its own emergency funds and the monies flowing in to Bishop Bond's Citizen's Committee, the JEAS, spearheaded by the venerable Rabbi Abraham de Sola, moved in swiftly to aid them. Within days a large building in Montreal's waterfront area was converted to a dormitory with relief and medical assistance for the refugees, many of whom had to be boarded with poor Jewish families for the interval.[57] The Mansion House Committee of London, organized by that city's major Jewish Societies to assist Russian Jews immigrating to Britain, and to encourage them to continue moving westward, dispatched some of its money to help the Montrealers cope with their new responsibilities. By 21 June, besides the many whom the JEAS had helped as they passed through Montreal to the United States, Ontario, or Manitoba, 180 refugees had been received at the "home" and employment had been found for most of them.[58] Although it was maintained for only a few months, the "home" filled a very important need in the first stages of immigrants' adjustment to Canadian life, because it provided a refuge in which they could convalesce after the terrors of the pogroms. Donations of all kinds poured in to the home from all over Montreal to help the Jewish refugees: clothing, bags of potatoes, groceries, crockery, shoes, fish, fruit, a sewing machine, a telephone from the Bell— and shrouds for the dead.[59]

Once the refugees of 1882 moved on or settled in during the next few months, the JEAS was disbanded and its remaining assets handed over to the YMHBS.[60] Although short-lived, the JEAS represents one of the most significant developments in the history of Canada's Jews in the nineteenth century. It marked the beginning of a general understanding of the need for co-ordinated action by all Jewish philanthropic societies. It was clear to many that the immigrants presented the entire Canadian Jewish community with a common responsibility entailing far-reaching responsibilities. Emergency organizations similar to Montreal's JEAS were set up in Toronto and Winnipeg where both Jews and sympathetic Christians contributed to the relief work.[61] In Montreal indeed the financial contributions of Bishop Bond's Citizens' Committee ($4700) surpassed those of Jews themselves ($4000). This development suggests interesting dimensions of contemporary Christian perceptions of Jews and of Jewish–Christian relationships.

The influx of Jews to Canada during the 1880s increased Canada's Jewish community by 165 percent. It was to some extent a directed immigration based on a belief that, as well as providing refuge from persecution and poverty, Canada offered the possibility of large-scale Jewish agricultural settlement. While Canada's West was generally seen by both Canadian and imperial planners as a new Eden, a land of opportunity for large-scale agricultural development, it was also thought of as a place where Europe's displaced Jews could be settled as farmers.[62] Indeed, many of the Jews who came in 1882 had expressed an interest in taking up farming. In May 1882, London's Mayor, J. Whittaker Ellis, wrote to Louis Davis, President of the Anglo-Jewish Association of Montreal, that "at the suggestion of Sir Alexander Galt [Canada's High Commissioner in Britain], the Mansion House Committee are sending a considerable number of the Russo-Jewish refugees to Canada, the more able-bodied to Winnipeg." He added that "Sir A. Galt had given my committee so glowing an account of the charity and benevolence of the Canadian Jews that I feel sure that this suggestion will meet with your ready acceptance."[63] In fact, Galt strongly supported, if indeed he did not originate, the idea of moving "the agricultural Jews to our North West," as is indicated in a letter he wrote to Baron Rothschild in January 1882.[64]

At that moment a number of Montreal Jews such as John and Hyam Moss, David and Samuel Davis, and Moise Schwob—all prominent manufacturers and merchants—were discussing the formation of an International Colonization Association, with a capital of one million dollars to establish communities of Russian and Polish Jews in the Canadian Northwest. They proposed to begin the project by locating one hundred families in the Territories as early as the following spring.[65] Supported by other influential members of the Montreal community and the local press,[66] the Montreal group sent Lazarus Cohen, a dredging contractor and foundry owner, to Ottawa to discuss the matter with the Minister of Agriculture, John Henry Pope, who assured Cohen of his interest and desire to assist the settlement scheme.[67] Acting on his own initiative in London meanwhile, Galt began sending Jews to Winnipeg, which he viewed as the best starting point for any settlement project.[68] These efforts in 1882–83 resulted in the establishment of the Jewish colony called New Jerusalem, near Moosomin, Saskatchewan,[69] with the assistance of the Mansion House Committee which provided each family with cattle, implements, and food for three years.[70] In this way, the first of several Jewish farming communities in Manitoba and the North West Territories was established. Montreal's Jewish élite was greatly interested in these colonization schemes but only as an auxiliary to foreign Jewish benefactors like Baron de Hirsch and the Rothschilds who initiated the programs and who, it was assumed, would pay the costs.[71]

While the movement of immigrants to the Canadian west and the growth of Jewish agricultural settlements there constitute an interesting aspect of the YMHBS's work during the early 1890s, between 1882 and 1891 its most pressing responsibilities lay in providing assistance to the immigrants who, despite all encouragements to move elsewhere, elected to remain in Montreal. Once the JEAS was disbanded, the YMHBS again was forced to shoulder the main burden of all forms of Jewish relief work, among both immigrants and local long-term indigents in the city just as it had until the spring of 1882.

Even after the experiences of that year, however, or perhaps because they had been so taxing, the Society was still unprepared and, to a great extent, unwilling to accept such a burden. The long-standing reluctance to make major or lasting commitments still prevailed. Although its members were aware that many more immigrants would soon be en route to Montreal they also knew that they would not easily be able to raise sufficient funds in the community. An emergency lasting a few months was manageable although only with help from outside the community. But a continuing flow of more and more impoverished Jews to a community that considered itself already overburdened financially was quite another matter. Without adequate funds, the Society would be unable to meet the obligations which the continuing flood of immigrants thrust upon it during the decade. This prospect, in fact, so depressed some members, once strongly active and anxious to accept office, that they now shied away from taking responsibility. At the annual election of officers in 1883, "a great amount of reluctance [was] shown on the part of members to accept office."[72] During the next three years, the problem was so serious that the executive proposed to retreat altogether and "hand over the affairs of the Society to the Young Men as was heretofore carried on by them."[73] Presumably, the younger members of the community would have more time and energy for these matters than their elders.

So uneasy had the executive become at the prospect of dealing with the numbers, costs, and social problems of the immigrants, that they angrily protested to London's Mansion House Committee which, like its predecessors a few years earlier, was simply dispatching to the United States and Canada many poor European Jews almost as soon as they arrived at the London docks. Resentful of the fact that both Galt and London were imposing on them by sending indigents to Canada,[74] the Society's executive in November 1882 even considered returning to London as many refugees as possible so as to compel the Jewish organization there to recognize Montreal's need for assistance. In a gesture of appeasement, Mansion House replied in March that a $500 grant was on its way to the resentful Montrealers.[75] This seems to have placated them for a few years but, as immigration to Canada increased again later that decade, small sums were clearly not enough. In 1887 the executive recommended that "some measures must be brought to bear, so that this community should not receive more than its share of immigrants."[76] But the London Jews were also under serious pressure. The protests from Montreal were mild in comparison to the objections voiced by London's prestigious Jewish Board of Guardians to continental European Jewish aid committees for sending to London so many refugees.[77] The burdens were so serious that Jewish organizations actually sent refugees back to the continent just as German, Austrian, and French Jews were returning thousands of newcomers back to Russia and Romania.[78] Perhaps because such a solution was too costly, the Montreal Society never resorted to it. But it did continue to complain.

It was not just the prospect of large numbers that alarmed the Society but the manner of their coming. Frequently, immigrants landed with no advance warning, often in groups of two and three hundred at a time. In late September 1886 a large but unspecified number of sick, bewildered, and bedraggled Romanian and South Russian Jews landed on the Montreal docks with no money or food and little clothing. The most pitiful of these cases was that of the young wife of a man who had died aboard ship leaving her with eight children, one of whom was dying in her arms.[79] During the voyage these hapless people were often fleeced of both baggage and money, and some even arrived without knowing whether they were landing at Montreal or New York.[80] In 1888, a group of sixteen people arrived from Hamburg where they had been sold tickets to Montreal instead of to New York where they hoped to go.[81] The Society requested the German Consul in Montreal to see that the port authorities in Hamburg prevented frauds of this kind. The Anglo-Jewish Association in London was also asked to have the British Home Office prevent similar irregularities from occurring at British ports. These complaints, however, apparently had little effect and when the same swindles occurred in Hamburg the following year, the Society lodged protests directly with the Allan Line, whose agents were believed to be responsible, and again with the German Consul in Montreal.[82] Similar frauds were perpetrated on immigrants on the North American side of the ocean as well. The Society felt compelled to protest these conditions for because of them "this society . . . in the end, is the heaviest sufferer."[83]

Notwithstanding the need on occasion to furnish "indoor relief" in the form of housing and food for weeks at a time for particularly piteous cases, the Society mainly supplied "outdoor relief" such as food, clothing, coal, medicine, and Passover *matzos* (unleavened bread). Sums were also spent on transportation to move people to other places; in some years more than one-third of all expenditures were spent on railway tickets.[84] While a few individual members privately assisted some of the immigrants to get jobs—L. Harris seems to have been acting as an employment agent for immigrants—many of the new arrivals could not find work. The *Gazette* in late September 1886 reported that Jewish carpenters, locksmiths, sewing machine operators, mechanics, tinsmiths, tailors, shoemakers, and railway workers were languishing in the dockside immigration sheds: "industrious men anxious for work . . . entirely penniless and . . . subsisting on almost nothing."[85]

In 1883 the Society began experimenting with interest-free loans to a number of immigrants who proposed to operate apple carts on Montreal streets.[86] By February 1884, $556 had been loaned in amounts of $10 to $30 "on security which satisfied the Board"; some nineteen to fifty-six such loans were repaid in sums of between $0.25 and $1.00 per week. Everyone was pleased with the success of this loan policy since it "has worked so advantageously and thereby saved to the Society unlimited expenditure and unnecessary trouble, while at the same time benefiting in a more efficient degree the deserving poor."[87] Inexplicably, however, the Board decided to discontinue the practice the following year, thus ending an interesting and potentially highly beneficial—although limited—method of assisting people.[88] Perhaps the fear of competition, of the Jewish "image" as peddler, or the desire by manufacturers to encourage immigrants to work in their factories might help to explain the termination of this brief experiment.

The Society also made arrangements for the burial of indigents after protracted but unsuccessful attempts to have local synagogues accept responsibility for the burial of Jewish paupers in their own cemeteries. Many years later, the Society was forced to purchase a special burial ground on the outskirts of the city.[89] Even in death, the social barrier remained.

Despite the growing number of problems as Jewish immigration increased during the 1880s, the YMHBS actually reduced its annual relief expenditures. In fact, although early in the decade a fairly consistent relationship existed between total relief expenditures and the amount of assistance per capita (table 1), such outlays declined drastically at the end of the 1880s. In the wake of the refugee migration of 1882, the outlay in 1883 amounted to $1863, which was spent on 205 "cases" involving approximately 600 people, an average of $3.05 each.[90] By 1890, however, the Society spent less than half that amount per person, although expenditures per capita increased significantly the following year.

Aside from soliciting special donations during crises, the organization's finances came entirely from the members' annual dues or from local supporters or "subscribers" who chose to contribute money rather than join the Society. Frequently, total receipts were exceeded by relief outlays which in those days of volunteer work, was the only significant item of expenditure. Besides its initial $500 grant in 1883, London's Mansion House Committee provided more funds in 1884, sending a further grant of $2400 for immigration relief.[91] After 1890, an annual grant of $250 came from the government of Quebec, symbolizing official recognition of the Society's work.[92] Thus the Jewish community of Montreal continued to draw on external sources of funds for aiding Jewish immigrants.

	Total Expenditure $	Individuals Aided N	Per Capita Expenditure $
TABLE 1	RELIEF EXPENDITURES OF YOUNG MEN'S HEBREW BENEVOLENT SOCIETY, MONTREAL, 1883–1891		
Year			
1883	1863	600✧	3.15
1884	1400	—	—
1885	815	239	3.41
1886	699	200	3.45
1887	492	113	4.43
1888	592	180✧	3.26
1889	673	374	1.80
1890	398	245	1.50
1891	1035	433	2.39

Sources: Public Archives of Canada, MG 28, V 86, Baron de Hirsch Institute of Montreal Papers, Minutes, I, 1 Oct. 1889.

✧ Estimated from number of "cases" or families.

o

Membership in the Society was never large during the 1880s. Except for the emergency year of 1882–83 when it grew from 72 to 125, membership increased slowly. Thirty new members joined during 1884. By February 1887 membership had grown to 176, but it levelled off to about 150 by 1891. Although the Society in the 1860s and 1870s probably included a large portion of the heads of Jewish families in Montreal as well as a considerable number of the unmarried young men, in the 1880s it was far less representative of the majority of Montreal's Jewish male population.[93] While the Jewish population of Montreal mushroomed in the 1880s and 1890s, the membership of the YMHBS increased only modestly. Efforts to induce more people to join and support its charitable work were not successful. Circulars proclaiming the Society's work and asking for the Jewish community's support were distributed widely and frequently; members exhorted one another to bring in friends and so enlarge the Society's resources but with little effect.

By 1885, some members of the Montreal Jewish community asserted that they would soon require a permanent "refuge" or "home" of a type already in existence for the city's Roman Catholics and Protestants. That year more extended care was required for four orphans whom the Society had been supporting for several months. After an unsuccessful attempt to place the children in Jewish orphanages in Philadelphia, Baltimore, Rochester, and New York, the Board decided to investigate the possibility of establishing a Jewish "home" which would serve the needs of the entire Canadian Jewish population for an orphanage, refuge for the "aged, infirmed and decrepit," as well as for the inevitable transients. In October 1886 the issue was aired again at a public meeting of Montreal Jews, many of whom opposed establishing such a home, apparently on the grounds that it would encourage indigency and cost too much for the community to maintain. Rabbi Friedlander, spiritual leader of the *Sha'ar Hashamayim* Congregation, was one of the most active participants in the discussion; he stated his belief that immigrants sheltered there "would acquire habits of laziness," while clothing manufacturer David Friedman argued that such a home "would be a shelter for the paupers of America."[94] Others contended that the existence of such an institution would be a "public boon, not only to the Jewish residents of Montreal but of the whole of Canada generally, as the custom of shipping paupers from one city to another will be discontinued."[95] For the time being, the establishment of a Jewish house of refuge failed to receive enough support but the question itself did not disappear. Premises of some kind were required to house transients and such services as a used clothing depot. Moreover, the transients, mostly immigrants from Eastern Europe, also had to adjust to their new environment by learning some English or French. A night school was organized for this purpose in 1890 with the support of a grant from the Quebec provincial government.[96]

On 13 April 1890, the Society's semi-annual meeting discussed an idea that, when pursued successfully, was to enable the association to provide greatly improved social services for the Jewish community of Montreal. Many of the needs of the poorer section of the Jewish population could perhaps be met by an enthusiastic, dynamic, and financially stronger organization aided by the Baron de Hirsch, the Paris-based Jewish railway tycoon and philanthropist, and the organization he had established in 1885, the Jewish Colonization Association (hereafter JCA). It was suggested that the Society apply for part of the $120 000 that the Baron was prepared to donate to American Jewish philanthropies that were aiding immigrants. Although there was some fear that the receipt of this money would attract immigrants to Canada, thus compounding the Society's problems, the Board decided to apply to the Baron.[97] In August he replied that he would send them $20 000 to establish a Jewish house of refuge in Montreal.[98] This was only the beginning of the Baron de Hirsch's generosity to Canadian Jewry through the YMHBS, for in subsequent years both he and the JCA, greatly assisted the Society in helping to settle Jewish immigrants both in Montreal and in other parts of Canada.[99] For a number of years the Society became the agent of the Baron's colonization schemes in the Canadian West while it was also heavily dependent upon his largesse for acquiring and maintaining a house of refuge and, gradually, offering a range of new social services for impoverished Jews in Montreal.

○

Vulnerability and dependency were two of the leading characteristics of Jewish relief work in Montreal during the period from the 1840s to 1890. Firstly, it was clear that the responsibilities of the Society and its more transitory sister associations were a function of the growing numbers of immigrants who were so badly in need of material assistance. Yet, it became evident that this voluntary association, on which the overwhelming portion of that burden fell, and whose resources were inadequate to meet those responsibilities, had no control over the numbers landing in Montreal. Though London's Mansion House Committee sent remittances to the Society to help provide for the immigrants, and acceded temporarily to demands to limit the numbers of East European Jewish refugees coming to Canada, Montreal's Jewish community was highly vulnerable to decisions of these external agencies and, indirectly, to European migration trends over which it had no control. This was a situation in which the Society found it more difficult to operate. As Montreal's primary Jewish philanthropic association, it could not fail for the immediate effect would be widespread distress among the immigrants. This situation made it necessary for the Society to seek substantial outside assistance. Both the nature and source of that aid, almost entirely from the Baron de Hirsch and his agency, the JCA, were to influence the work and character of the YMHBS in the future.

The Montreal Jewish community, tiny, divided, and comprised of people who were for the most part only newly established themselves, was especially ill-prepared to handle the demands of immigration in the 1880s when the city's Jewish population increased by nearly 300 percent. Powerless to stop the flood of people and to cope with their problems, Montreal Jews had to appeal for local non-Jewish assistance as well as for aid from London and Paris. They also considered the aid they were giving to be temporary. Ideas of establishing a permanent refuge or home, with local resources, and of undertaking long-term relief were strongly and successfully resisted. Moreover, the Montreal group expressed keen interest in passing on as many of their immigrant problems as possible to other cities or to the Canadian prairies. The forty-year experience of Jewish philanthropy in Montreal during the late nineteenth century suggests that the tradition of *tsedakah* was not very widespread among Montreal Jews. Instead, what seems to have been demonstrated is the validity of the Yiddish proverb: "If charity cost no money and benevolence caused no heartache, the world would be full of philanthropists."[100]

While this example of Jewish charity indicates some major similarities with the ideas and practices of philanthropy current in the English-speaking world during the late nineteenth century, it also suggests certain subtle differences. For example, the reluctance to establish an institutionalized refuge or to couple philanthropy with religious evangelism or social meliorism indicates an absence of moral and religious reform ideas that underlay much of the philanthropic work of many Roman Catholic and Protestant groups during the same era.[101] North American Jewish charity organizations were not generally inclined to mix religion with philanthropy, not because religion was thought to be unimportant, but because they were behaving more as a national or ethnic organization like the local St Andrew's or St Patrick's societies. Despite the reluctance or inability to respond in the true tradition of *tsedakah*, there was an understanding that Jews were one people in which religion was not the only common denominator. Most Jews understood the truth of the Talmudic admonition that "without bread, there is no Torah" and seem to have believed that it was not religious faith or practice (then almost universally Orthodox) that was at fault, but material circumstances and political forces over which Jews had no control.

From 1847 to 1890, however, Montreal Jewish philanthropy demonstrated several additional characteristics which distinguish it from that organized by New York's Jews. In a masterful study of New York Jewry from 1870 to 1912, Moses Rischin underscores the social and economic divisions between the older German and the newer Russian immigrants.[102] Self-confident, well-to-do (if not wealthy), and practising "enlightened" Reform Judaism, these gentlemen dispensed a detached philanthropy without *tsedakah* to the Russian Jews because, as Germans, they believed themselves to be culturally superior to Russians. Although Montreal at the end of the nineteenth century, unlike New York, had no significant number of wealthy and prestigious German Jews, it did possess a community of prosperous bourgeois who filled the same function. By the 1880s many of the immigrants from the 1840s and 1850s were already well on the road to prosperity. They included tobacco manufacturers, furriers, and growing numbers of clothing contractors and manufacturers whose increasing wealth was

·eflected in the impressive new synagogue they erected on fashionable McGill College Avenue in 1885. The older Spanish and Portuguese congregation built an equally imposing synagogue a few years later on Stanley Street, still farther into Montreal's well-to-do west end. Between these two congregations, as the early history of the YMHBS suggests, a certain cooperation and common middle-class identity—strengthened by some marriages and business associations—seem to have emerged by the end of the 1880s. A similar process of successful upward mobility by immigrant Jews in Toronto about a decade later and of acceptance by that city's older Jewish élite suggests that class rather than national identity was the most important criterion in determining the social structure of the Jewish communities of Canada before 1914.[103] What distinguishes Jewish immigration to Montreal in the 1880s from that of the period 1830–61 was its very size and apparently significant occupational differences. The experience of the city's principal Jewish charity indicates that these realities tended to create two communities. More important still is that the older Montreal Jewry was too ill-prepared, poorly financed, and ineffectively led to confront the problems of the large later migrations. Without aid from non-Jewish Montrealers and, more significantly, from London and Paris, they could not have coped.

Dependency upon outside assistance allowed not only the perpetuation of these two distinct communities but also the attempt by one to control the other. Jewish charity in Montreal during these transitional years was to remain limited and dependent until the Montreal Jewish élite—still using Hirsch money—was forced to recognize larger dimensions of Jewish adjustment in urban Canada.

NOTES

1. On the philosophy underlying charity in the English-speaking world in the nineteenth century, see David Owen, *English Philanthropy, 1600–1900* (Cambridge: Harvard University Press, 1960) and Robert H. Bremner, *American Philanthropy* (Chicago: University of Chicago Press, 1960). Judith Fingard, "The Relief of the Unemployed Poor in St. John, Halifax, and St. John's," *Acadiensis* 5 (Autumn 1975): 32–53, is a perceptive analysis of voluntary social welfare in three Canadian cities. See also Stephen A. Speisman, "Munificent Parsons and Municipal Parsimony: Voluntary vs Public Poor Relief in Nineteenth-Century Toronto," *Ontario History* 65 (March 1973): 33–49; and James Pitsula, "The Emergence of Social Work in Toronto," *Journal of Canadian Studies* 14 (Spring 1979): 35–42. On New Brunswick's experiences with public welfare, see Brereton Greenhous, "Paupers and Poorhouses: The Development of Poor Relief in Early New Brunswick," *Histoire sociale/Social History*, 1 (April 1968): 103–26; and James M. Whalen, "The Nineteenth-Century Almshouse System in Saint John County," *Histoire sociale/Social History*, 7 (April 1971): 5–27; and by the same author, "Social Welfare in New Brunswick, 1784–1900," *Acadiensis* 2 (Autumn 1972): 54–64.

2. Judith Fingard, "The Winter's Tale: The Seasonal Contours of Pre-industrial Poverty in British North America, 1815–1860," *Canadian Historical Association Historical Papers* (1974): 65–94.

3. Gerald E. Hart, "The Halifax Poor Man's Friend Society, 1820–1827: An Early Social Experiment," *Canadian Historical Review* 34 (June 1953): 109–23; John

Irwin Cooper, "The Quebec Ship Labourer's Benevolent Society," *Canadian Historical Review* 30 (Dec. 1949): 336–43.

4. Robert McKay, *The Directory of Montreal* (Montreal, 1850), 384–90; and John Shearer, "The Centennial Story of the St Andrew's Society of Montreal" (unpublished manuscript in possession of the St Andrew's Society of Montreal, 1935), G.R.C. Keep, "The Irish Adjustment in Montreal," *Canadian Historical Review* 31 (March 1950): 39–46; J.I. Cooper, "The Social Structure of Montreal in the 1850's," *Canadian Historical Association Report* (1956): 63–73.

5. Louis Rosenberg, "Some Aspects of the Development of the Canadian Jewish Community," *Publications of the American Jewish Historical Society* 50 (Dec. 1950): 121–42.

6. J. Douglas Borthwick, *History and Biographical Gazeteer of Montreal to the Year 1892* (Montreal, 1893), 475–79; Rabbi Solomon Frank, *Two Centuries in the Life of a Synagogue* (Montreal: Corporation of Spanish and Portuguese Jews, 1970), 28.

7. See Newton Bosworth, *Hochelaga Depicta* (Montreal, 1839); *History of the Corporation of Spanish and Portuguese Jews "She'erith Israel" Montreal, Canada* (Montreal, 1918). See also David Rome, *On the Early Harts—Their Contemporaries*, part 1 (Montreal: Canadian Jewish Congress, National Archives, 1981).

8. Ben Bernstein, *The History of Congregation Shaar Hashamayim, 1846–1946* (Montreal, 1946), 1; and Louis Rosenberg, *Canada's Jews: A Social and Economic Study of the Jews in Canada* (Montreal: Canadian Jewish Congress, Bureau of Social and Economic Research, 1939), 10.

9. Benjamin G. Sack, *History of the Jews in Canada* (Montreal: Harvest House, 1965), 143–52.

10. Ibid., ch. 3. For a recent assessment of the historical evolution of the Sephardic communities in the United States, see Stephen Birmingham, *The Grandees: The Story of America's Sephardic Elite* (New York: Dell, 1972).

11. Carman Miller, "Alexander Abraham de Sola," *Dictionary of Canadian Biography* (Toronto: University of Toronto Press, 1982), 11: 253–56.

12. Gerald J.J. Tulchinsky, *The River Barons: Montreal Businessmen and the Growth of Industry and Transportation, 1837–1853* (Toronto: University of Toronto Press, 1977), 9–34; Arthur D. Hart, ed., *The Jew in Canada: A Complete Record of Canadian Jewry from the Days of the French Regime to the Present Time* (Montreal: Jewish Publications Limited, 1926), 93 and passim; Sack, *Jews in Canada*, 171; *Montreal Gazette*, 22 Dec. 1879, 14 Nov. 1879; John I. Cooper, *History of St. George's Lodge, No. 10 Q.R., 1829–54* (Montreal, 1954), 37–62.

13. *Montreal Gazette*, 29 March 1881; Stuart A. Cohen, *English Zionists and British Jews: The Communal Politics of Anglo-Jewry, 1895–1920* (Princeton: Princeton University Press, 1982), 19–20.

14. A. Cohen, *Everyman's Talmud* (New York: E.P. Dutton, 1949), 219–26. See Philip Birnbaum, ed., *Mishne Torah: Maimonedes' Code of Law and Ethics* (New York: Hebrew Publishing Co., 1974), 158–59.

15. H.H. Ben-Sasson, ed., *A History of the Jewish People* (Cambridge: Harvard University Press, 1976); Mark Zborowski and Elizabeth Herzog, *Life Is With People: The Culture of the Shtetl* (New York: Schocken, 1972), 191–213.

16. See list in Jacques J. Lyons and Abraham De Sola, *A Jewish Calendar For Fifty Years* (New York, 1854), 148–73.

17. *The Occident* 6 (October 1848): 368–70, quoted in Sack, *Jews in Canada*, 139–40; "Baron de Hirsch Institute," in Hart, *The Jew in Canada*, 201–5.

18. Carman Miller, "Moses Judah Hayes (Hays)," *Dictionary of Canadian Biography* (Toronto: University of Toronto Press, 1976), 9: 379–80.

19. Hart, *The Jew in Canada*, 201.

20. Sack, *Jews in Canada*, 131–33. Dr David's brother, Eleazar David, achieved a certain fame and notoriety in early nineteenth-century Montreal society. See Elinor K. Senior, "Eleazar David David," *Dictionary of Canadian Biography* (Toronto: University of Toronto Press, 1982), 11: 234.

21. Sack, *Jews in Canada*, 139–40.

22. *Montreal Gazette*, 8 Jan. 1856.

23. Public Archives of Canada, Baron de Hirsch Institute of Montreal Papers, MG 28, V 86, Minutes, I, 23 July 1863 (hereafter Minutes). The YMHBS was renamed the Baron de Hirsch Institute in 1891. The qualification that members be unmarried was changed in November 1864 to open membership to any unmarried member of the Hebrew faith over 13 years old. In the event of marrying while members, they still retained their membership. Minutes, 27 Nov. 1864.

24. The religious affiliations of most original members can be established from Hart, *The Jew in Canada*; Bernstein, *Congregation Shaar Hashamayim*; and Frank, *Life of a Synagogue*.

25. Minutes, I, 23 July 1863.

26. Minutes, I, 14 April 1867.

27. Rosenberg, *Canada's Jews*, 308.

28. Ibid.

29. Minutes, I, 18 Oct. 1874; *Montreal Gazette*, 7 Jan. 1875.

30. For one such instance see Minutes, I, 17 Nov. 1867.

31. Minutes, I, 25 March 1876.

32. Minutes, I, 4 Jan. 1864, 25 Feb. 1872. See also the *Montreal Gazette*, 4 Feb. and 11 Feb. 1873, for a lengthy description of one of these entertainments.

33. No records of the Relief Committee have survived for this period.

34. Dr David was Dean of Medicine at the University of Bishop's College from 1870 to 1880. The Montreal General Hospital later received a financial contribution from the Society in return for its services. Minutes, I, 1874 ff.

35. Minutes, I, 1863. Levey persisted in his efforts to limit the Society's relief activities by giving notice of a motion in 1868—which he apparently did not push any further—that would have limited relief payments to a maximum of $15 per applicant. Minutes, I, 12 July 1868.

36. Revised by-laws of YMHBS, Art. II, Object, section 1, included in Minutes, I, 13 Aug. 1871.

37. Minutes, I, 1 Feb. 1864.

38. Minutes, I, 25 March 1876.

39. Minutes, I, 25 March 1876.

40. Minutes, I, 14 July 1867.

41. Minutes, I, March 1878.

42. *London Jewish Chronicle*, 22 Oct. 1875; Minutes, I, 14 Nov. 1875.

43. Minutes, I, 4 Nov. 1877.

44. Lloyd Gartner, *The Jewish Immigrant in England 1870–1914* (Detroit: Wayne State University Press, 1960), 49–50.

45. Minutes, I, 17 Nov. 1878.

46. Minutes, I, 1874. Gutman then pointed out that the YMHBS "should be a general one, open to all Israelites in the city."

47. *Montreal Gazette*, 6 March 1876.

48. Ibid., 18 Dec. 1882.

49. Ibid., 27 May 1881.

50. Ibid., 1 Feb. 1882.

51. Ibid., 13 Sept. 1882. From May to August 1882 almost every issue of the *Montreal Gazette* included a list of contributors to the JEAS and the Citizens' Committee. On Archbishop Bond see John I. Cooper, *The Blessed Communion: The Origins and History of the Diocese of Montreal, 1760–1960* (Montreal: Diocese of Montreal, 1960), chs. 12 and 15.

52. *Montreal Gazette*, 16 March, 26 May 1882.

53. Ibid., 14, 22 May 1882.

54. Irving Howe, *World of Our Fathers* (New York: Harcourt Brace Jovanovich, 1976), 47.

55. Besides the four Moss brothers who were garment manufacturers, the Montreal JEAS board included L. Lewis, B. Kortosk, Jacob Ascher, and David Ansell. Ansell became a major figure in Montreal Jewish philanthropic affairs from the 1880s to the early 1900s.

56. *Montreal Gazette*, 16 May 1882.

57. Ibid., 22 May 1882.

58. Ibid., 21 June 1882. Of the 180 persons who had used the home since it was opened, 80, mostly women and children, still remained, 48 of whom had been on their way to Manitoba where "they were most anxious to take up farming, with which they were acquainted."

59. Ibid., 2 June 1882.

60. Ibid., 12 March 1883.

61. Stephen Speisman, *The Jews of Toronto: A History to 1937* (Toronto: McClelland & Stewart, 1979), 58; Simon Belkin, *Through Narrow Gates: A Review of Jewish Immigration, Colonization and Immigrant Aid Work in Canada, 1840–1940* (Montreal: Eagle Publishing Co., 1966), 31.

62. Doug Owram, *Promise of Eden: The Canadian Expansionist Movement and the Idea of the West* (Toronto: University of Toronto Press, 1981); Arthur A. Chiel, "Herman Landau's Canadian Dream," *Canadian Jewish Historical Society Journal* 2 (Fall 1978): 113–20.

63. *Montreal Gazette*, 27 May 1882.

64. The most thorough account of Galt's efforts in 1882 on behalf of Jewish colonization in the Northwest is in Abraham J. Arnold, "Jewish Immigration to Western Canada in the 1880's," *Canadian Jewish Historical Society Journal* 1 (Fall 1977): 82–95. In the early 1890s the Berlin (Jewish) Conference on Emigration considered Canada as a suitable destination for refugee Russians; see Jonathan D. Sarna, "Jewish Immigration to North America: The Canadian Experience, 1870–1900," *Jewish Journal of Sociology* 18 (June 1976): 31–41.

65. *Montreal Gazette*, 18 Jan. 1882.

66. Ibid., 23 Jan. 1882.

67. Ibid., 1 Feb. 1882.

68. On 8 November 1882, the Society requested Galt "to refund to this Society, out of the fund granted for the Winnipeg batch of refugees, under his charge, any sums that may have been expended by the Montreal community to assist such Winnipeg batch." See Minutes, I, 12 Nov. 1882.

69. Abraham J. Arnold, "The Jewish Farm Settlements of Saskatchewan: From 'New Jerusalem' to Edenbridge," *Canadian Jewish Historical Society Journal* 4 (Spring 1980): 25–43; S. Belkin, "Jewish Colonization in Canada," in Hart, *The Jew in Canada*, 483–88; N. Macdonald, *Canada: Immigration and Colonization, 1841–1903* (Toronto: Macmillan, 1966), 220–22.

70. Samuel J. Lee, *Moses of the New World: The Work of Baron de Hirsch* (New York: T. Yoseloff, 1970), 279.

71. *Montreal Gazette,* 16 Aug., 15, 17 Nov. 1884.

72. Minutes, I, 11 Feb. 1883.

73. Minutes, I, 10 Feb. 1884, 22 Feb. 1885, and 14 Feb. 1886.

74. Minutes, I, 12 Nov. 1882.

75. Minutes, I, 11 Feb. 1883.

76. See "Annual Report of the Board of the YMHBS of Montreal, for the Fiscal Year Ending January 1, 1887," in Minutes, I, 13 Feb. 1887; and Gartner, *Jewish Immigrant in England*, 54.

77. See V. Lipman, *A Century of Social Service, 1859–1959: A History of the Jewish Board of Guardians* (London: Routledge and Kegan Paul, 1959).

78. Between 1880 and 1886, the Jewish Board of Guardians sent a total of 12 000 Jews back to Eastern Europe, according to Jay M. Pilzer, "Jews and the Great 'Sweated Labour' Debate: 1888–1892," *Jewish Social Studies* 41 (Summer-Fall 1979): 257–74, esp. 273. The only recorded instance of the Montreal Society's doing the same thing occurred in 1890 when "a young Roumanian who had consumption" was sent back to Hamburg. See Minutes, I, 13 April 1890.

79. *Montreal Gazette,* 22, 24, 29 Sept. 1886.

80. Zasa Szajkowski, "The Jewish Emigration Policy in the Period of the Roumanian 'Exodus,' 1899–1902," *Jewish Social Studies* 13 (Jan. 1951): 47–70; Minutes, I, 13 Feb., 16 Oct. 1887.

81. See Minutes, I, 8 April 1888.

82. Minutes, I, 21 April 1889.

83. Minutes, I, 16 Oct. 1887.

84. Ibid., I, 15 Nov. 1885. "Most of the visitors [transients] after making futile attempts to earn a livelihood here, beseeched to be sent to other parts."

85. *Montreal Gazette,* 24, 29 Sept. 1886.

86. Minutes, I, 11 Nov. 1883.

87. Minutes, I, 10 Feb. 1884.

88. Minutes, I, 22 Feb. 1885.

89. Minutes, 1903, Report of the Baron de Hirsch Institute, 5.

90. The annual reports after 1886 usually included a table indicating the nationality of applicants for relief, the number in each family, and the amount spent on each national group. It is not clear whether "nationality" was determined by

citizenship, most recent previous abode, or place of birth. If it were based on immediate past residence, it is possible that some "English" or "Americans" were really Russians who had previously lived for short periods in London or New York.

91. Minutes, I, 17 May 1885. See also entries for 13 May 1883 and Feb. 1884.

92. Minutes, I, 12 Nov. 1882, 13 April 1890; *Montreal Gazette*, 2, 14, 20 Nov. 1889.

93. According to L. Rosenberg, "The Diamond Jubilee of the United Talmud Torahs of Montreal, 1896–1956" (typescript, Jewish Public Library, Montreal, 1956), there were only about two hundred Jewish families in Montreal in 1881; and, according to Rosenberg (*Canada's Jews*, 20), probably about five hundred in 1891.

94. *Montreal Gazette*, 28 Oct., 1 Nov. 1886.

95. Ibid., 28 Oct. 1886.

96. Ibid., 2, 14, 20 Nov. 1889; Minutes, I, 13 April 1890.

97. Minutes, I, 13 April 1890.

98. Minutes, I, 24 Aug. 1890.

99. The Baron is said to have donated approximately one hundred million dollars to various charities in his lifetime. See Samuel Joseph, *History of the Baron de Hirsch Fund: The Americanization of the Jewish Immigrant* (Philadelphia: Jewish Publication Society, 1935).

100. Hanan J. Ayalti, *Yiddish Proverbs* (New York: Schocken, 1965), 107.

101. See Charles S. Rosenberg, *Religion and the Rise of the American City: The New York City Mission Movement, 1812–1870* (Ithaca: Cornell University Press, 1971).

102. Moses Rischin, *The Promised City: New York's Jews, 1870–1914* (New York: Harper Torchbook, 1970), 74–115.

103. Speisman, *Jews of Toronto*, chs. 5–7.

PEOPLING THE PRAIRIES WITH UKRAINIANS ✧

JOHN C. LEHR

O

Between 1892 and 1914 Ukrainian immigrants from Galicia and Bukovyna settled large tracts of the plains of Western Canada.[1] The immigrants seldom dispersed themselves among settlers of different ethnic backgrounds but settled adjacent to one another on quarter-section homesteads, with the result that extensive areas of agricultural land in the West became almost totally Ukrainian in character. This type of settlement also occurred among other ethnic groups, but it generally arose when the government set aside land for the exclusive settlement of a specific group as in the case of the Mennonites, Icelanders, and Doukhobors.[2] The Ukrainians were not accorded this privilege, yet they established some of the largest bloc settlements in the West. These Ukrainian blocs were remarkable for their extent and were a reflection of a pronounced natural tendency to settle next to relatives and kin.

Ukrainian settlement in Western Canada was also distinct in terms of its location. The Ukrainian pioneers were noted for their avoidance of the open grasslands of the Canadian Prairies and their settlement in the bush country of the northern parkland of the three Prairie provinces. From an agricultural standpoint they took out their homesteads on some of the poorest land opened to settlement in Western Canada. The land they chose was often wooded, stony, sandy, or marshy. In many cases it had been ignored, rejected, or abandoned by more discriminating pioneers who elected to settle on the more open lands to the south, which proved to be exceptionally fertile and admirably suited for the development of commercial wheat farming. For the Ukrainians settlement in the "bush country" of the northern parkland was little short of disastrous and retarded both their economic progress and their assimilation into Canadian society.

✧ Lubomyr Luciuk and Stella Hryniuk, eds., *Canada's Ukrainians: Negotiating an Identity* (Toronto: University of Toronto Press in association with the Ukrainian Canadian Centennial Committee, 1991), 30–52.

This apparently inept environmental appraisal by a people with long-standing agricultural traditions is not easy to explain. So glaring was the discrepancy between the lands settled by Ukrainians and the lands settled by German, English, and American settlers that it gave rise to the accusation that at the time of settlement the Canadian government had discriminated against the Ukrainian immigrants and by controlling access to homesteads had forced them to accept marginal lands on the fringe of the ecumene.[3] This paper traces the process of Ukrainian settlement in Western Canada during the pioneer era. It argues that its geography cannot be explained by the charge of governmental discrimination and was a product of complicated relations between the immigrants, the officers of the Department of the Interior responsible for the settlement of the West, the Ottawa politicians, and the largely anglophile Canadian public.

UKRAINIAN IMMIGRANTS

Over 120 000 Ukrainians came to Canada between 1892 and 1914.[4] Although the character of immigration changed during the twenty-two years of this first phase of Ukrainian settlement in Canada, the vast majority of Ukrainian immigrants throughout this period were peasants whose goal was to secure a homestead.[5] Almost all of them came from the westernmost limits of the Ukrainian ethnic area, the provinces of Galicia and Bukovyna, which until 1918 were part of the Habsburg empire (figure 1). About 5 percent came from Hungarian Transcarpathia. Less than 1 percent came from Greater Ukraine, which then fell under the dominion of the Russian tsarist regime.

FIGURE 1 *GALICIA AND BUKOVYNA*

In the 1890s peasants in Austrian Western Ukraine were emerging from quasi-feudal conditions. Absentee landlords, mainly Austrian or Polish in Galicia and Romanian or German-Austrian in Bukovyna, controlled most of the land. Despite emancipation from serfdom in 1848, the mass of the peasantry remained poor, oppressed, and exploited. Land rents and prices for timber were high, but wages for labour were low. Farms were small and often fragmented. In Galicia almost half of all peasant holdings consisted of fewer than two hectares at a time when about five hectares were necessary to achieve self-sufficiency.[6] Self-sufficient farms, those ranging from five to ten hectares, accounted for only 14.6 percent of all holdings. In Bukovyna the situation was worse. There 16 percent of the peasants were landless, 42 percent had less than two hectares, and 25 percent had less than three hectares.[7] In Transcarpathia one feudal landowner alone held 20 percent of the territory and, according to one historian, kept the Ukrainian peasantry "in virtual serfdom, illiterate, ignorant, and financially dependent."[8] Although it was changing for the better, agricultural technology in most areas of Western Ukraine was backward; farm operations were labour-intensive, and productivity was low.[9] The situation gave little hope for improvement. The Austrian government was content to maintain its Ukrainian territories as economic colonies, captive markets for Austrian manufactured goods. Economic betterment was beyond the reach of the average peasant, for the usurious interest rates charged on mortgages made farm consolidation or expansion difficult.[10]

Social and political repression exacerbated the economic woes of the peasantry. Although Galicia was under Austrian rule, it was under a de facto Polish administration.[11] Polish and German were the languages of administration; Ukrainian was relegated to vernacular status. In Bukovyna and Transcarpathia the situation was similar, for there civil administration was the preserve of Romanian and Hungarian minorities.[12]

Seasonal migration to work on the estates of Prussia or in the oilfields of Boryslav ameliorated the economic situation for some peasants.[13] But by the 1870s Ukrainian peasants were working further afield, in the factories and mines on the eastern seaboard of the United States. For the most part they went as temporary workers, not as settlers, and although many eventually remained, their movement, at least initially, was that of migrants rather than emigrants.[14]

For many peasants such seasonal or short-term movements were a palliative, not a cure. They looked to emigration as a way for their children to escape from a depressing social and economic future. By the late 1880s peasants from Galicia were settling on the frontiers of Brazil; the dawn of the 1890s saw their first tentative steps towards free homesteads in Western Canada.[15]

Most of those who contemplated emigration came from the middle stratum of the peasantry. The wealthy peasants had no pressing economic reason to emigrate, and the poorest peasants could not afford to do so. The peasants who left their homeland in search of a new life were those who feared that the future would see their children's well-being decline and who had sufficient property to raise the fare for a transatlantic journey.

UKRAINIAN IMMIGRATION

The first immigrants from Western Ukraine to Canada were not ethnically Ukrainian. Volksdeutsche (ethnic Germans) from Kryvulia near Belcha Volytsia in Galicia settled at Josephburg, near Edmonton, Alberta, in 1890.[16] Correspondence between Volksdeutsche from Galicia and their former neighbours initiated the mass migration of Ukrainians to Western Canada.[17] The first Ukrainians to migrate to Canada left the village of Nebyliv, in the Kalush district of Galicia, in 1892. Those who immediately took up homesteads did so in Alberta, where they settled adjacent to former neighbours, seeking opportunities for work from established settlers conversant in Ukrainian. For the next four years word about settlement opportunity in Canada diffused slowly from Nebyliv through the Kalush district. The few score Ukrainians who emigrated to Canada in this period were almost all from around Nebyliv, and virtually all gravitated to the solitary Ukrainian settlement at Star, near Josephburg, in Alberta (figure 2).[18]

In light of the considerable migration of Ukrainians to the mines and factories of the United States it is curious that few Ukrainians entering Canada chose to remain in the urban centres. Nevertheless, not all Ukrainians went on the land; Osyp Oleskiv, the Galician educator and agricultural expert who visited Canada in 1895, reported that ten Ukrainian families were living in Winnipeg; all of them were from the Kalush district and had elected to stay in the city and to pursue trades or to work as labourers.[19] For most Ukrainian immigrants the chance to obtain land was the primary lure; most, but by no means all, had no skill in a trade and no experience of living in a

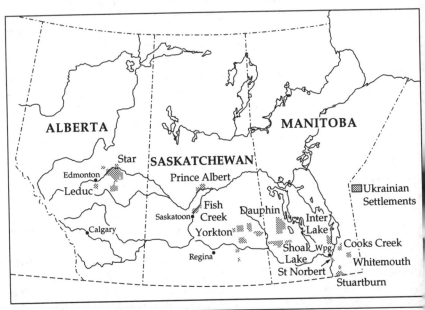

FIGURE 2 *UKRAINIAN SETTLEMENTS IN WESTERN CANADA, CIRCA 1905*

arge city and so had little incentive to remain in any of the cities or towns through which they travelled en route to the frontier.[20]

The Canadian government had no desire to see its settlers remain in urban centres, and immigration officers went to some lengths to discourage them from remaining in Winnipeg even for a short time.[21] The government regarded immigrants who decided to remain in a city as a direct loss to its program for settling the West. Those Ukrainians who took manual jobs in the industrial and mining areas of the East Coast such as Sydney, Nova Scotia, were most likely remigrants from the Pennsylvania mines rather than immigrants from Ukraine.[22] Nevertheless, by 1900 the demand for labour in Canadian industries, and the immigrants' need for capital, led many arrivals to seek work in factories and mines. Many later moved out and took up homesteads, but a proportion remained as urban dwellers.

The choice of the Star area for settlement established a pattern that later arrivals followed with little deviation and ultimately created a distinctive geography of Ukrainian settlement across the Canadian West (see figure 2). Initially the attraction of Star was the Volksdeutsche. Later, it was fellow Ukrainians from Galicia. No less important was the setting of Star in the aspen parkland belt, which the Ukrainian immigrants found well-suited to their needs, since it provided the wood, water, and meadow that they craved.

From a tiny settlement of less than five families in 1893 the Ukrainian settlement in Alberta grew to a modest thirty-eight families at the beginning of 1896.[23] They attracted little attention. The government regarded them as Austrian nationals and hence ethnic Germans.[24] Indeed, their origin came to government notice only in 1895, when Osyp Oleskiv sought information about settlement in Canada.[25]

Oleskiv was concerned about the growing Ukrainian emigration to Brazil. There in the rain forests of Parana Ukrainians were being decimated by disease and reduced to penury. Realizing that emigration was inevitable given the socio-economic situation in Western Ukraine, he hoped to redirect it to more favourable regions.

Early in 1895 Oleskiv published a pamphlet for intending emigrants, *Pro vilni zemli* (About free lands), which reviewed the alternatives open to them.[26] It was based on secondary sources and materials solicited from countries then seeking immigrants. Its message was one of caution, but suggested that Western Canada was the most promising destination. After a subsequent reconnaissance of Western Canada as a guest of the Canadian government in July 1895, Oleskiv threw aside his reservations and in two further pamphlets enthusiastically recommended Canada. *Rolnictwo za Oceanem a Przesiedlna Emigracja* (Agriculture across the ocean and the emigration movement), in Polish, received little attention,[27] but his pamphlet in Ukrainian, *O emigratsii* (On emigration), circulated throughout the Ukrainian areas of Galicia and Bukovyna. Oleskiv hoped to obtain a monopoly on the organization of Ukrainian emigration to Canada, so as to prevent rapacious steamship agents from extorting a profit from naive emigrants. He also wished to ensure that all emigrants were well provided for and were adequately prepared for the rigours of pioneering. He failed to do this, partly because the Canadian government distrusted his motives and refused his request for total jurisdiction in the promotion of Canada in Western Ukraine, but mainly because the success of his publications so spurred emigration to Canada that he was swept aside by the rush of emigrants. Although he organized and dispatched many parties, his major influence lay in popularizing Canada and reinforcing the patterns of decision making that had already been manifested by those who had emigrated before 1896.

In *O emigratsii* Oleskiv purveyed a good deal of practical advice to immigrants. Knowing that most Ukrainian peasants lacked the means and experience to settle on the open prairie, he advised against moving beyond the shelter of the parkland and intimated that soils would be more fertile in wooded areas. He also implored them to follow the example of the Galician Volksdeutsche and Ukrainian settlers already established in the West.[28] Oleskiv stressed the advantages of settling near such settlers along river banks and by freshwater lakes.[29] His advice carried substantial weight with the peasants, who respected him for his integrity and expertise as a professor of agriculture.

Oleskiv's writings and instructions to departing emigrants had the effect of entrenching the pattern of spatial behaviour already manifested in the selection of Star for settlement by those who had emigrated before 1896. In the eyes of the Ukrainian immigrants timber was vital for building, fencing, and fuel. They were anxious to avoid a replication of the circumstances in their homeland, where timber was strictly controlled and often expensive.[30] Their obsession surprised even the government colonization officers, who were aware that settlers of all nationalities wanted some timber on their land: "The Galicians [Ukrainians] are a peculiar people; they will not accept as a gift 160 acres of what we should consider the best land in Manitoba, that is first class wheat growing prairie land; what they want is wood, and they care but little whether the land is heavy soil or light gravel; but each man must have some wood on his place."[31]

But the Ukrainian settlers were concerned with more than the presence of timber. Most of them had little capital and appraised the land from the perspective of the peasant farmer intent on attaining self-sufficiency. Few contemplated entering the market economy immediately. In consequence, the Ukrainian settlers prized aspects of the physical environment that facilitated self-sufficiency. Whereas commercially oriented farmers would try to avoid slough or swamp, the penurious Ukrainians saw in them materials for thatching, water for stock, and fish and game for dietary supplements[32]

The land that best fulfilled the Ukrainians' needs was found in the aspen parkland belt.[33] The best lands along the southern fringe of this belt had been settled before the onset of massive Ukrainian immigration, but large tracts along its northern edge still awaited settlement in the late 1890s.[34] Ukrainian immigrants soon made clear their aversion to settlement on the prairie, and Crown agents acknowledged the wisdom of their predilection for the timbered environments of the northern parkland, but considerable friction arose from the Crown's attempt to modify the pattern of settlement that immediately began to emerge. Left to their own devices, Ukrainian immigrants headed for the existing Ukrainian settlements, hoping to obtain the benefits of a familiar social, religious, and linguistic milieu. Even though in 1896 Crown agents established some Ukrainian settlers on homesteads at Cook's Creek and Stuartburn in southern Manitoba and a few others settled independently on river lots along the Red River at St Norbert close to Winnipeg, the main flow of Ukrainians was to Star in Alberta.[35] This was administratively undesirable. To have large numbers of settlers searching for homesteads within a limited area caused squabbles between settlers and led to chaos. Furthermore, and far more serious, it raised the spectre of the Star colony expanding into a massive ethnically homogeneous settlement—a virtual Canadian Ukraine—in east-central Alberta, a potential development that the government viewed with apprehension, if not alarm.

The government found it difficult to halt or break up the patterns emerging in 1896 and 1897. Under the terms of the Dominion Lands Act all settlers were free to go where they chose in the West, so long as the land they selected had not been alienated under the terms of a land grant or set aside for use as a timber lease or Indian reserve. The function of the Crown officials in the field was intended to be purely advisory. They were responsible for placing immigrants in locations that would facilitate agricultural progress and ensure permanent and successful settlement. They had no authority to order immigrants into specific locations and were thus obliged to achieve their ends by persuasion and accommodation to the wishes of the incoming settlers. Hence, although the government could to some extent channel Ukrainian immigrants, it could not coerce them into specific areas.[36]

This lack of authority immensely complicated the Crown's task of administering the efficient and orderly settlement of Ukrainians. As of 1896 a system had been established whereby the commissioner of immigration organized incoming Ukrainians into parties at Winnipeg and placed them under the guidance of a colonization agent. These parties were then dispatched to various centres in the West, where land guides led them to areas open for homestead settlement.[37] Immigrants with specific destinations were sent wherever they wished to locate, but those without a destination in mind were assigned one by the commissioner.[38]

The success of this system depended upon the co-operation of the immigrants, most of whom were amenable so long as their wishes were accommodated but were not disposed to accept government decisions that would place them in isolated locations away from their fellows or on lands they regarded as unsuited to their requirements. But in the case of the Ukrainians the government was unable to maintain its laissez-faire policy of settlement administration in the West, for the immigration of 1896 had brought the Ukrainians to public notice. By the summer of 1897 they were at the centre of a national debate on the wisdom of the government's policy of encouraging Slavic immigration.[39] Emotions ran high. Clifford Sifton, the minister of the interior, stoutly defended the Ukrainians as good material for pioneer settlement: "I think a stalwart peasant in a sheepskin coat, born on the soil, whose forefathers have been farmers for ten generations, with a stout wife and half a dozen children is good quality. We do not want mechanics from the Clyde—riotous, turbulent and with an insatiable appetite for whiskey. We do not want artisans from the southern towns of England who know absolutely nothing about farming."[40]

Sifton's opponents rejected this view. Through the anglophone Conservative press they vilified the Ukrainians as the scum of Europe—"physical and moral degenerates not fit to be classed as white men."[41] For five years the debate over the merits of Ukrainians raged in the western press. It ceased only when the Conservatives realized in 1902 that it was politically unwise to alienate a segment of the population that was acquiring the franchise.

During this crucial formative period of Ukrainian settlement in Canada the government found its actions in the field subject to the scrutiny of the public and the press. Its critics refrained from demanding the immediate and total cessation of Slavic immigration only long enough to insist that the Slavs be segregated from immigrants from Western Europe, yet be dispersed throughout the West so as to ensure their rapid assimilation into the mainstream of Britannic culture. As the government was painfully aware, the two latter demands were essentially irreconcilable, for segregation implied the growth of massive ethnic bloc settlements, which, even if on the edge of the ecumene, were unacceptable to both the Liberal and the Conservative parties.

The question of bloc settlement was more than a matter of administration. The bureaucrats charged with settling immigrants in the West favoured their placement in bloc settlements for administrative convenience and because settlers located together demanded less governmental aid.[42] But the press saw the issue as one that affected the very nature of the society that was emerging in the West. On 20 July 1897, the *Nor'Wester* launched a sustained vitriolic campaign against the "colony system" of Ukrainian settlement in the West:

> It is a positive misfortune for an enlightened community to be handicapped by having a cargo of these people settled in or near it. Both economically and socially they will lower the standard of citizenship. If they are put in colonies by themselves, they will be still less susceptible to progressive influences; and the districts where the colonies are located will be shunned by desirable immigrants. Not only are they useless economically and repulsive socially, but they will constitute a serious political danger. They are ignorant, priest-ridden and purchasable. In the hands of a practical politician, a few thousand of such votes will decide the political representation of the province. . . . All who are interested in the progress of Manitoba should protest more vigorously against the further importation of such a dangerous element.[43]

The question soon transcended regional interest and became the subject of national debate. The anglophone press manifested a rare unanimity when it insisted that immigrants must not be permitted to dilute the British character of the West through creation of foreign enclaves resistant to assimilation. The only correct policy, editorialized the *Winnipeg Telegram*, was the complete assimilation of all foreigners:

> The Government is making a great mistake in establishing these exclusively foreign colonies. The proper policy is to mix the foreigners up with the rest of the population as much as possible. It is only in that way that they will be assimilated. The colony system tends to perpetuate their own language and peculiar customs. It prevents their observation of improved methods of cultivation and keeps them out of touch with British institutions and ideas.[44]

Most anglophones in the West subscribed to the view that "Canada is British, and Canada is English," and undoubtedly many were sympathetic to the claims of Frank Oliver, the Liberal member of Parliament for Edmonton, who argued that the creation of large blocs of Ukrainian settlers would "lower levels of intelligence and civilization and cause native-born Canadians to leave in favour of the United States."[45] The *Winnipeg Telegram* expressed the fears of many English-speaking settlers:

> It must be thoroughly disheartening to any respectable English speaking settler to find himself surrounded by a colony of Russian serfs [Ukrainians], and to know that, if he remains on his homestead, he is likely to have no other neighbors for himself and his family all his natural life. He has braved all the difficulties of a pioneer in the hope of building up a comfortable home for himself and his children. He has selected for his home the Canadian Northwest because the British Flag flies over it, and because, as a Canadian, an Englishman, an Irishman or a Scotsman, he wants to remain a Britisher among British people. . . .
> The unfortunate settler finds himself hemmed in by a horde of people little better than savages—alien in race, language and religion, whose customs are repellent and whose morals he abhors. Social intercourse is impossible, all hopes of further British settlement in the neighborhood vanishes; he becomes an alien in his own country. There is nothing left for him but a galling life-long exile on British soil equivalent to deportation to a Siberian settlement.[46]

Although the Liberal, staunchly pro-Sifton *Manitoba Free Press* rejected the negative assessment of the Ukrainians, it did not take issue with the assumption that Canadianization of the immigrants was vital for the welfare of the West.[47] The failure of the *Free Press* to support the denunciation of the colony system may be attributable to fear of embarrassing its owner—Clifford Sifton—and the government rather than to any sympathy for the immigrants' preference for settling together.[48]

The controversy surrounding Ukrainian immigration undoubtedly had an impact upon the Crown. It never articulated a formal policy for the guidance of its agents in the field, but the extensive correspondence between James A. Smart, the deputy minister of the interior in Ottawa, and William F. McCreary, the commissioner of immigration in Winnipeg, suggests that the government was apprehensive of adverse public reaction to its actions in the West.[49] At a time when the press was decrying bloc settlement and when some newspapers were labelling the Ukrainians "Sifton's pets," alleging that they received preferential treatment, it was politically imperative that the government's actions refute such charges.[50] This heightened the need to check the growth of large bloc settlements and to place Ukrainian immigrants in locations where they could fend for themselves and be independent of governmental aid.

It was ironic that the most expeditious approach to minimizing immigrant reliance upon governmental assistance in settlement was to allow the settlers to pursue the collective security of the bloc settlement. As noted, it was an approach fraught with political dangers, and one that the Crown could not openly promote. Indeed, from 1897 onwards the Crown made determined efforts to deflect settlers from the largest bloc of Ukrainian settlement at Star, Alberta. It did this by attempting to establish new settlements elsewhere in the West that would serve as attractive alternative destinations for incoming Ukrainians. The Crown's agents in the field were well aware that the complete dispersal of Ukrainian immigrants was impractical. It ran counter to the wishes of the immigrants, and the government lacked the authority and personnel to implement it. There was no enthusiasm for a course of action that would lead to direct confrontation with incoming settlers.

Apart from political considerations, the government colonization officers working in the field were generally well-disposed to the concept of bloc settlement. Planning and administration were greatly simplified when immigrants of the same ethnic background were settled together.[51] Social and religious needs were more easily provided for and co-operation between settlers was usually better than in ethnically mixed areas. There were fewer crises in settlement, fewer cases of destitution requiring government assistance, and a concomitant decrease in the work load of the Crown agents responsible for their welfare. Indeed, in the early days of mass immigration Commissioner McCreary had advocated bloc settlement:

> These people [Ukrainians] at least for the first few years should be settled in colonies; each colony will need an Interpreter who will also act as a Farm Instructor, Purchasing Agent and so forth. They should have in each colony a Priest or spiritual advisor who will also act as Teacher. . . . In each colony there should be reserved by the Crown a piece of land suitable for a Church, Cemetery, School house, Store building and so forth. This piece of land to be devoted to the general interests of the entire colony.[52]

This practical advice was seldom, if ever, followed in full, for expediency and financial constraints dictated otherwise. But colonization officers found that once they had placed Ukrainian settlers in an area opened for settlement they experienced little difficulty in locating further immigrants alongside them. Established settlers attracted their kinfolk and compatriots and enabled them, in the words of the commissioner for immigration, to "drop into their place without a tithe of the trouble hitherto experienced."[53]

CREATION OF NEW SETTLEMENTS

The great difficulty facing the Crown was the creation of new nodes of settlement. No Ukrainians with friends or relatives already settled in the West wanted to miss the opportunity to settle adjacent to them. They were reluctant frontiersmen and hesitated to be the first of their group to settle in a new area. Indeed, much of the time and energy of McCreary and his staff at Winnipeg was devoted to the vexing question of inducing incoming settlers to go to pioneer areas remote from other Ukrainians. McCreary appealed without success for the legal authority to direct immigrants into specific areas as he saw fit.[54] Denied this authority, he harangued, cajoled, and even tricked incoming Ukrainians in a sustained effort to channel them into new areas.[55] At times his procedures contravened the Dominion Lands Act, but in the main they provoked little opposition from Ottawa, the western press, or the Ukrainians themselves.

McCreary strove to settle Ukrainians in areas where the physical environment satisfied their marked predilection for wood, water, and meadows. Prospective sites were also evaluated in terms of their ability to absorb large numbers of immigrants, the opportunities for capital generation through resource development, the availability of off-farm employment, the presence of Ukrainian-conversant Volksdeutsche settlers, and accessibility by railway or all-weather trails.[56]

Since few Ukrainian settlers contemplated the immediate organization of a commercial farming operation, acquisition of prime wheat-growing land was not an overriding concern. The range of the resource base was of greater interest than the quality of one aspect of it. From the standpoint of both the government and the immigrants the lands on the northern fringe of the parkland, usually regarded as of second quality by settlers who were oriented towards commercial farming, afforded the range of resources vital to the penurious settlers bent upon subsistence farming. On such lands capital could be generated by exploiting the non-agricultural resources. By cutting and marketing cordwood new settlers could raise sufficient capital to establish themselves in farming. In most districts with a market for cordwood, an industrious settler could earn 70 cents a day. This was a reasonable return on labour at the turn of the century, when heavy labour on the railway section gangs brought only $1.25 for a ten-hour day, from which the railway companies deducted 75 cents for board, while farm labourers in the Brandon area were receiving a maximum of $15 a month in addition to their board.[57] In the bush country a family could also earn over a dollar a day by digging snakeroot (*Polygana senega*).[58] Other features of the northern parkland that had no commercial potential were prized as aids to survival, and colonization officers encouraged new settlers to supplement their diets with wild fruits, berries, fungi, game, and fish.[59]

Areas of this type adjacent to established Volksdeutsche from Ukraine were always viewed as excellent sites for settlement of Ukrainians. Government agents had high regard for these Ukrainian-conversant Germans, and after several years of settlement most were in a position to employ new immigrants as farm help.[60] The Volksdeutsche, furthermore, played an important psychological role in ameliorating the sense of disloca-tion experienced by the Ukrainian settlers cut off from contact with their countrymen. Oleskiv, too, in *O emigratsii* had advised settlement near "older [Ukrainian] colonists or at least near Germans," arguing that those striking out alone without the benefit of advice from experienced settlers would come to grief.[61]

In evaluating potential sites for settlements the government had to con-sider their accessibility. The logistics of mass settlement demanded that immigrants be carried by rail as close to their destination as possible; it was undesirable to have settlers walking fifty miles or more to reach the area opened for settlement. Colonization trails were cut into areas not reached by the railway, but they were liable to become impassable during wet weather.[62] But uninterrupted access was vital: the government could not afford, either financially or politically, to have angry and often destitute settlers crowding the immigration halls in the major distribution centres of the West.

McCreary was further constrained in his choice of areas for the estab-lishment of new Ukrainian colonies. Areas not yet surveyed could not be opened to settlement. Nor could areas wherein the railway companies were still eligible to select lands under the terms of a land grant.[63] Despite these formidable obstacles, by 1900 the government had managed to create a series of Ukrainian settlements across the northern fringe of the parkland belts, running from Leduc, near Edmonton, to Stuartburn, southeast of Winnipeg (figure 3).[64]

The government attained this only by making determined efforts to minimize immigrant resistance towards pioneering new areas and taking great pains to select lands for new colonies that accommodated the immi-grants' needs: wooded environments offering access to settlements of Volksdeutsche or other nationalities with potential for off-farm employ-ment. When such tactics were adopted with well-led groups which had been exposed to the influence of Oleskiv and which were not determined to join relatives at all costs, the government easily established new nodes of settlement. In 1896, for example, a new settlement was established without difficulty at Stuartburn in southeastern Manitoba. The initial party of set-tlers had been dispatched by Oleskiv. They were well organized, well led by Kyrylo Genik, and had some knowledge of the character of the lands in southeastern Manitoba from the description in *O emigratsii*.[65] Like the gov-ernment officials accompanying them, they hoped to obtain land near the Mennonite reserves, "where stock, food and other necessities, required for a new settler could be had on very reasonable conditions and where employ-ment is plenty at any time of the year."[66]

Although the settlers failed to find sufficient land for a colony along-side the Mennonite reserves, they were favourably impressed by the large tracts of vacant homestead land in the Stuartburn district only forty-eight kilometres from the Mennonite West Reserve and less than thirty kilometres from the East Reserve. The land was officially described as "for the most part of inferior character" and not such as to attract much attention from the Canadian settler, being "to a good extent very rough and hard to clear and

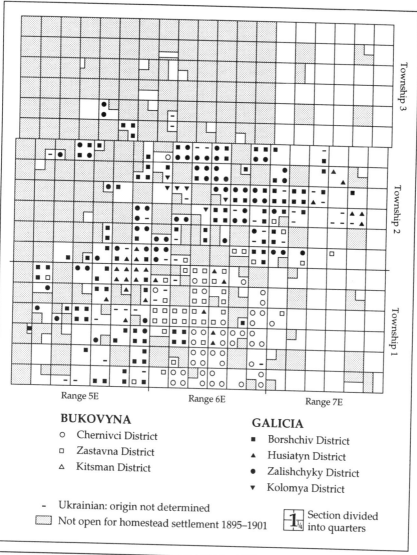

Range 5E Range 6E Range 7E

BUKOVYNA

○ Chernivci District
□ Zastavna District
△ Kitsman District

GALICIA

■ Borshchiv District
▲ Husiatyn District
● Zalishchyky District
▼ Kolomya District

- Ukrainian: origin not determined

▢ Not open for homestead settlement 1895–1901

▦ Section divided into quarters

FIGURE 3 *THE STUARTBURN COLONY BY DISTRICT OF ORIGIN IN 1900*

improve," although it was still thought to be "well adapted for mixed farming."[67] It was eagerly settled by Ukrainian immigrants impressed by the presence of wood and water and the closeness to the Mennonite reserves and the railway at Dominion City.

An attempt to establish a new settlement near Dauphin, Manitoba, early in 1896 ran into difficulties when the colonization road into the area became impassable after the spring thaw. Late in the year some eight Ukrainian families moved into the area, following advice that their leader had solicited from Oleskiv.[68] After the completion of the railway into Dauphin in 1897 the Crown was able to direct more settlers into the district and to establish a solid basis for further expansion. All of these early settlers were induced to go to the Dauphin district by Oleskiv, hence the ease with which the nucleus of settlement was established. Significantly, it was these early settlers sent by Oleskiv who showed the greatest concern for soil quality and who were prepared to strike out into new areas in order to secure lands in a setting reminiscent of their Carpathian highland home.[69]

In 1897 Crown agents also experienced little difficulty in planting a nucleus of eleven families in the Manitoba Interlake district, which appealed to the first Ukrainians to homestead there because it offered good timber, hay meadows, easy access to Winnipeg, and, perhaps, the psychological comfort provided by the nearby long-established Icelandic settlements along the shores of Lake Winnipeg.

COERCION

It was only when colonization officers failed to accommodate the wishes of immigrants and attempted to direct them away from their fellows and into districts which the Crown saw as fine wheat-growing areas that conflict erupted. The most notable example of this occurred in 1898 when the minister of the interior suggested the creation of a Ukrainian settlement at Fish Creek in Saskatchewan. The Crown agents at first disregarded the ministerial instruction to settle the next group of immigrants there, arguing that the immigrants then in their charge "had made up their minds to go to certain parts, and it would have been very difficult to get them to change this decision, in fact, impossible. . . . A large number had friends in the Edmonton district . . . and would go nowhere else."[70] Nevertheless, it was resolved to locate "several families at least of the next large party at that point."[71]

Shortly thereafter a large consignment of Ukrainian immigrants, mostly from Bukovyna, arrived in Winnipeg. Some two years of experience with Ukrainian immigrants had convinced McCreary that "it is simply an impossibility, by persuasion, to get a number of these people to go to a new colony, no matter how favoured, and some ruse has to be played, or lock them in the [railroad] cars." The immigrants were therefore told that they were bound for Edmonton or Dauphin and were dispatched to Fish Creek under the control of Colonization Agent Speers. When they learned of their true destination, open revolt broke out, and all but a few began walking back to Regina. Unable to cope, Speers telegraphed McCreary in Winnipeg:

> Almost distracted with these people, rebellious, act fiendish, will not leave cars, about seventy-five struck off walking [to] Regina, perfectly uncontrollable. Nothing but pandemonium since leaving Regina. Have exhausted all legitimate tactics with no avail. Policeman here assisting situation—eclipses anything hitherto known. Edmonton, Dauphin or die. Will not even go [to] inspect country, have offered liberal inducement, threatened to kill inter-

preter. Under existing circumstances strongly recommend their return Edmonton and few Dauphin and get another consignment people special train leaving this afternoon. Could take them [to] Regina. Answer immediately am simply baffled and defeated— quietest and only method will be their return. Waiting reply. Mostly have money and will pay fare. They are wicked.[72]

Faced with the possibility of an armed revolt by hundreds of Ukrainians determined to walk to where they wished to settle, the government decided to transport the dissidents to Edmonton or Dauphin and drew some consolation from Speer's success in persuading seven families to locate at Fish Creek. In essence it mattered little whether seven or seventy families had been established. The nucleus of a new colony had been set in place, and the Crown could afford to acquiesce to the demands of the notoriously stubborn Bukovynian settlers, whom McCreary described as "an obstreperous, obstinate, rebellious lot [who] all want to go where the others have gone."[73]

It is noteworthy that the triumphant dissidents of the Fish Creek incident congratulated themselves on having settled on the open prairie, saying "Hey, if it wasn't for us stubborn Bukovynians you'd be eating gophers in Siniboia [Assiniboia]." To which the Galicians would respond, "That's why we stuck with you Hutsuls, because Hutsuls know where are the woods and meadows."[74] Woods and meadows settled by their kinfolk exerted a seemingly irresistible pull upon the newly arrived Ukrainian immigrants. It was certainly sufficient to cause them to disregard even the advice of the government agents and interpreters of their own nationality; it caused them to overlook obvious shortcomings in the land upon which they could settle, and it led them to endure years of adversity on lands clearly less promising than others still open to settlement.[75]

RESOURCE APPRAISAL

Although the new immigrants may have lacked the experience of North American conditions necessary to evaluate homestead lands, it is difficult to accept that they could have been oblivious to the shortcomings of the lands they enthusiastically settled in the Interlake and Stuartburn regions of Manitoba and in the Sniatyn area of Alberta. In the former case homesteaders waded waist-deep to their homesteads, while in the latter new immigrants settled eagerly on land described as "mostly covered by water" and "all sand and bush and not fit for farming."[76] That they did so was partially a reflection of the nature of their experiences in the homeland. Certainly the Ukrainian peasants valued resources differently. Equally important was their experience of working tiny fragmented farms in Galicia and Bukovyna. Many assumed that even on an extremely poor homestead they would find a dozen acres of arable land, which, if supplemented by a few acres of meadow or marshland, would permit the kind of farming operation of which they had experience. Some even thought their 160-acre homesteads were too large and tried to achieve denser settlement by requesting permission to subdivide them into 80-acre units.[77]

KINSHIP LINKAGES

The determination to settle alongside others of the same nationality may also have been a major factor in leading Ukrainian settlers to homestead on lands of inferior character. It is important to note that the initial groups of settlers farming the nucleus of colonies selected lands that fulfilled their needs in settlement. If the land was not the "finest wheat growing land," at least it suited their needs. Indeed, it was in the interests of the government that it be so, for it had no wish for the Ukrainians to perform poorly as farmers and have charges that they were poor material for settling the West borne out. The surge in the volume of Ukrainian immigration after 1896 saw a concomitant expansion of settlements. In some instances, this led to a gradual movement of the settlement frontier on to progressively poorer land.

When the first Ukrainians settled in Stuartburn in southeastern Manitoba, they selected a locale endorsed by Oleskiv that promised to be well-suited to their intended purpose of stock rearing.[78] What neither the immigrants, Oleskiv, nor the government agents realized was that the quality of the land declined rapidly as one moved east of the initial area of settlement. In 1896 the first Ukrainian settlers on Township 2, Range 5E, obtained land that was satisfactory to them and, it should be added, to English stock raisers who had moved into the area several years earlier. Subsequently, as immigrants sought land adjacent to their established kinfolk and compatriots, the tide of settlement in the Stuartburn area was funnelled eastwards, away from the fertile Red River clays on to stony beach ridges and areas of poor drainage, marsh, and swamp. Successive newcomers traded off a progressive decline in land quality against the advantages of a familiar social, religious, and linguistic milieu. For many, if not most, of those homesteading in the Stuartburn district, emotional factors clearly determined the decision. Within the colony members of extended families and former neighbours settled together, effectively re-creating elements of their former society in Ukraine. The settlement of Bukovynians in this area showed the extent to which family, village, and regional ties influenced the choice of homestead land within an area of settlement.[79] By 1900 Ukrainian settlers had occupied over five townships (180 square miles) in the Stuartburn area. This area of contiguous settlement was characterized by a marked separation of immigrants in a settlement on the basis of their province of origin and a clustering on the basis of their district and village of origin (see figure 3).

Immigrants from Galicia settled alongside but separately from those from Bukovyna. In part this arose from a natural inclination of all immigrants to seek out the company of those who shared a similar cultural heritage, religion, and outlook.[80] At the time of settlement in Canada the Ukrainians from the two provinces were divided on the basis of religion. Those from Galicia were almost all of the Greek Catholic (Uniate) church; those from Bukovyna of the Green (Russian) Orthodox church. Adherents of each church regarded the other with distrust. The Uniates held the Orthodox as agents of Russian imperialism who were preaching a gospel of Russification and oppression of Ukrainian culture. The Orthodox thought the Uniate clergy was bent on the absorption of Western Ukraine into the Polish sphere.[81] These religious differences, which have political undertones, were heightened by other minor cultural and linguistic differences between the two groups.

This intra-ethnic division was manifested in the pattern of Ukrainian settlement across the West.[82] Wherever the two groups settled in the same locale, they segregated themselves according to province of origin. Though puzzled at first by their determination to avoid mixing, Crown agents willingly accommodated their requests when it became evident that those from Bukovyna were "somewhat different from regular Galicians; their chief difference however, being in their religious persuasion. They do not affiliate and, in fact, are detested by the Galicians."[83]

The attitude of the immigration officials was one of amusement rather than annoyance. One colonization officer reported an incident when he was settling Ukrainians in the Yorkton district of Saskatchewan: "after a little trouble which arose, the Galicians, not wishing to go with the Bukowinians—verily the Jews not wishing to deal with the Samaritans—I assured them that they were all Canadians now under free institutions and they were well satisfied as we agreed to colonize them in different parts of the Township."[84] Thus the actions of Crown agents who were anxious to avoid intra-group conflict contributed to the division of Ukrainian settlements on the basis of the province of origin.

The Stuartburn area is therefore typical of Ukrainian bloc settlements in this regard and illustrates the intensity of old-country groupings in Ukrainian settlement on the Canadian frontier.[85] Among the settlers from both Galicia and Bukovyna who settled in the Stuartburn area there was a further clustering according to the district of origin. For example, settlers from the Zalishchyky district of Galicia settled in two discrete groups, and those from the Chernivtsi and Zastavna districts of Bukovyna showed a strong tendency to cluster in settlement.[86] This extended even to the level of village of origin. Families from the village extended even to the level of village of origin. Families from the village of Bridok in the Zastavna district intermixed with families from the village of Onut, also in the Zastavna district. Settlers from the village of Lukivtsi in the Chernivtsi district of Bukovyna settled alongside them but did not intermix to any great extent (figure 4).

The determination of Ukrainian immigrants to settle alongside their former neighbours and kinfolk was undoubtedly a major factor in perpetuating old-country village and district ties. Eleven of thirty-eight families from Lukivtsi, Chernivtsi district, had the surname Kossawan; several were related to the Kossawans by marriage; three had the surname Zyha, and three Shypot. This is not conclusive evidence of strong kinship ties, but it certainly points in that direction. It is almost impossible to determine kin linkages created through marriage, yet it is probable that such ties played a role comparable to ties of blood in maintaining closely clustered patterns of settlement.[87]

The social structure of Ukrainian pioneer settlements shows that Ukrainian immigrants who sought homesteads were strongly influenced by

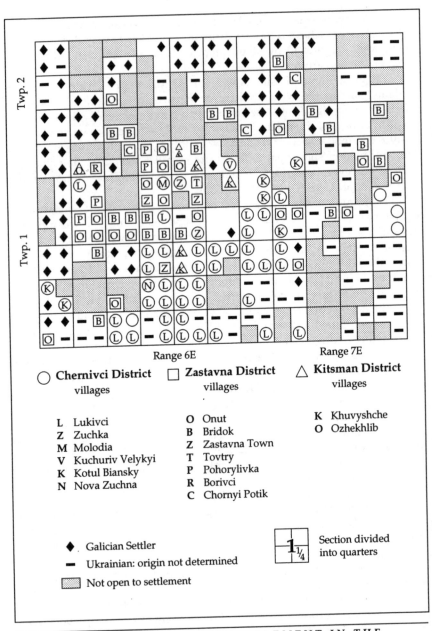

Range 6E   Range 7E

○ **Chernivci District**   □ **Zastavna District**   △ **Kitsman District**
   villages   villages   villages

L Lukivci	O Onut	K Khuvyshche
Z Zuchka	B Bridok	O Ozhekhlib
M Molodia	Z Zastavna Town	
V Kuchuriv Velykyi	T Tovtry	
K Kotul Biansky	P Pohorylivka	
N Nova Zuchna	R Borivci	
	C Chornyi Potik	

♦ Galician Settler

— Ukrainian: origin not determined

▨ Not open to settlement

Section divided into quarters

FIGURE 4 *BUKOVYNIAN SETTLEMENT IN THE STUARTBURN COLONY BY VILLAGE OF ORIGIN*

their determination to attain a familiar linguistic, religious, and social milieu. The consistency in their appraisal of any prospective homestead had an important geographical effect. It led to the re-creation of the geography of Western Ukraine in microcosm across the lands that they settled, perpetuating old-country ties and relationships in the new land. But those ties, so comforting to disoriented and fearful settlers, bound many of them to a life of hardship and penury on land that they would never have settled had they evaluated it on its agricultural merits alone.

In some areas—at Pakan, Alberta, on the southern slopes of the Riding Mountains, or at Stuartburn, Manitoba, for example—the newcomers' determination to settle near friends and kin led them to squat on lands not open to homestead settlement.[88] But squatters ran awesome risks. There was no guarantee that they would ever obtain title to the land on which they had made improvements, no certainty that their improvements lay completely within one quarter-section or that their houses and building did not lie on land found to be a road allowance. And the lands for which such risks were taken were by no means first class; some were even designated as "swamp lands." Such homesteads derived their attraction from their location adjacent to kinfolk and compatriots and not from their agricultural qualities.

CONCLUSION

The Ukrainian immigrants who sought homesteads in the West were remarkably consistent in their behaviour. A desire for timber and a wide resource base, proximity to Volksdeutsche, an emotional affinity for the topography, fear of the open prairie, lack of mobility, and ignorance of alternative areas open to homesteading influenced their decision to locate in a specific area. The willingness of later arrivals to rank cultural factors above economic or environmental ones determined the perpetuation and expansion of settlement. This the immigrants did, according to one official, "regardless of their own welfare."[89] Less desirable sites were occupied because of a perceived superiority of location. The tide of settlement rolled on to marginal lands, and immigrants made formal application to take out homesteads on land they would have probably rejected if their assessment of it had been more dispassionate and based only on its long-term agricultural potential. Thus the Ukrainians came to settle increasingly larger areas of marginal land. They did so not because of incompetence at environmental appraisal, but because they valued the company of their fellows and because the bush country presented a far better prospect for immediate survival than the more fertile prairies. This pattern of Ukrainian settlement in the West was sketched by 1900, cast by 1905, and firmly entrenched by 1914, when the war curtailed immigration from Europe and ended the period of massive frontier settlement in Western Canada. During the following decade Ukrainians remigrating from the industrial centres and the resource frontiers of Canada and others fleeing from the turmoil of war and revolution in Europe extended the margin of settlement but had negligible impact upon the established geography.

With the passing of the frontier, the tastes and inclinations of the Ukrainian settlers veered towards cash flow and entry into the market economy, and the marginal homestead came to be seen as less than satisfactory. As the Ukrainian pioneers assimilated Anglo-Canadian agricultural goals, old-country values declined and social ties were weakened. Resource perception thus came to reflect more clearly the qualities of the land rather than those of the cultural milieu. The passing of old-country values and regional loyalties marked the beginning of a new phase of Ukrainian life in Canada, one dominated by the Canadian-born, in which actions and attitudes revealed an attachment to the values of the New World and a loosening of ties with the Old. It was in this context that the mythology of governmental responsibility for the plight of those Ukrainians struggling to survive on marginal farmsteads found fertile ground.

NOTES

1. Ukrainians were for a long time a subject people, politically fragmented under a variety of alien administrations. By the end of the nineteenth century they replaced the ancient names of *Rus'* and *Rusyn* with *Ukraine* and *Ukrainian*, but in Canada *Ukrainian* was not officially recognized until 1930. Before then, in Canadian governmental correspondence, Ukrainians were described variously according to their national origin as Austrians or Russians, as Ruthenians (the Latin form of Rusyn), or as Galicians and Bukowinians after their provinces of origin. The Canadian government favoured the latter terms before 1914. The practice of expanding the term *Galician* to embrace all Ukrainians regardless of province of origin created further confusion. For a discussion of the problems of the ethnic name see G.W. Simpson, "The Names 'Rus',' 'Russia,' 'Ukraine,' and Their Historical Background," *Slavistica: Proceedings of the Institute of Slavistics of the Ukrainian Free Academy of Science* 10 (1951): 1–24; E.D. Wangenheim, "Problems of Research on Ukrainians in Eastern Canada," in *Slavs in Canada: Proceedings of the First National Conference of Slavs, Banff, Alberta, 1965*, ed. Yar Slavutych (Edmonton: Inter-University Committee on Canadian Slavs, 1966), 1: 44–53; and Vladimir J. Kaye, *Early Ukrainian Settlements in Canada, 1895–1900: Dr Josef Oleskow's Role in the Settlement of the Canadian Northwest* (Toronto: University of Toronto Press for the Ukrainian Canadian Research Foundation, 1964), xxiii–xxvi.

2. Hansgeorg Schlictmann, "Ethnic Themes in Geographical Research in Western Canada," *Canadian Ethnic Studies* 9 (1977): 10–14; C.A. Dawson, *Group Settlement: Ethnic Communities in Western Canada* (Toronto: Macmillan, 1936).

3. This claim is most common in left-wing Ukrainian-Canadian historiography. See, for example, Charles H. Young, *The Ukrainian Canadians: A Study in Assimilation* (Toronto: Thomas Nelson and Sons, 1931), 57; Vera Lysenko, *Men in Sheepskin Coats: A Study in Assimilation* (Toronto: Ryerson Press, 1947), 33; Petro Kravchuk, *Na novii zemli* (Toronto: Tovarystvo obiednanykh ukrainskykh kanadtsiv, 1958), 82–85; William Harasym, "Ukrainian Values in the Canadian Identity" in *Proceedings of the Special Convention of United Ukrainian Canadians* (Winnipeg: Association of United Ukrainian Canadians, 1966), 67; and Helen Potrebenko, *No Streets of Gold* (Vancouver: New Star Books, 1977), 38–39. Some right-wing historians—for example, Michael H. Marunchak, *The Ukrainian Canadians: A History* (Winnipeg: Ukrainian Free Academy of Sciences, 1970), 87—also subscribe to this view.

4. William Darcovich and Paul Yuzyk, eds., *A Statistical Compendium on the Ukrainians in Canada, 1891–1976* (Ottawa: University of Ottawa Press, 1980), 500–2.

5. There have been three major immigrations of Ukrainians into Canada, each having distinct characteristics in terms of the socio-economic character of the immi-

grants, their motives for emigration, and their destinations in Canada. See Vladimir J. Kaye, "Three Phases of Ukrainian Immigration" in *Slavs in Canada*, 1: 36–43.

6. Emily Greene Balch, "Slav Emigration at Its Source," *Charities and the Commons* 16 (May 1906): 179.

7. A.M. Shlepakov, *Ukrainska trudova emihratsiia v SShA i Kanadi: Kinets XIX-pochatok XX st.* (Kiev: Akademiia nauk Ukrainskoi RSR, 1960), 23.

8. Peter F. Sugar, "The Nature of the Non-Germanic Societies under Habsburg Rule," *Slavic Review* 22 (1963): 17; Shlepakov, *Ukrainska trudova emihratsiia*, 29.

9. Stella M. Hryniuk, "A Peasant Society in Transition: Ukrainian Peasants in Five East Galician Countries 1880–1920" (PhD thesis, University of Manitoba, 1985), offers a comprehensive review of conditions in Galicia at the time of emigration. She argues that conditions were not as poor as has often been claimed and that the Galician peasantry was entering a stage of rapid change and improved economic conditions.

10. Henry J.T. Dutkiewicz, "Main Aspects of the Polish Peasant Immigration to North America from Austrian Poland Between the Years 1863 and 1910" (MA thesis, University of Ottawa, 1958), 58.

11. W.L. Scott, "Catholic Ukrainian Canadians," *Dublin Review* 202 (1938): 283; Hans Kohn, "The Viability of the Habsburg Monarchy," *Slavic Review* 22 (1963): 38–39: Nicholas Andrusiak, "The Ukrainian Movement in Galicia," *Slavonic and East European Review* 14 (1935–36): 163–75, 372–79; and Ivan L. Rudnytsky, "The Ukrainians in Galicia under Austrian Rule," *Austrian History Yearbook* 3, pt. 2 (1967): 394–429.

12. Although poor, social and political conditions in the part of Ukraine administered by Austria were far better than those endured under Russian rule. See Ivan L. Rudnytsky, "The Intellectual Origins of Modern Ukraine," *Annals of the Ukrainian Academy of Arts and Sciences in the US* 6 (1958): 1381–405.

13. John Paul Himka, "The Background to Emigration: Ukrainians of Galicia and Bukovyna, 1848–1914" in *A Heritage in Transition: Essays in the History of Ukrainians in Canada*, ed. Manoly R. Lupul (Toronto: McClelland & Stewart, 1982), 16–18.

14. Rudnytsky, "Ukrainians in Galicia," 418; Balch, "Slav Emigration," 177.

15. For a fascinating personal account of migration to Brazil, remigration to Canada, and return to Brazil by an emigrant from Galicia, see Michael Ewanchuk, *Pioneer Settlers: Ukrainians in the Dauphin Area, 1896–1926* (Winnipeg: n.p., 1988), 33–35, 107–15, and 129–32.

16. Iosyf Oleskiv, *O emigratsii* (Lviv: Obshchestvo Mykhaila Kachkovskoho, 1895), 35; and Isidore Goresky, "Early Ukrainian Settlement in Alberta" in *Ukrainians in Alberta* (Edmonton: Ukrainian Pioneers' Association of Alberta, 1975), 17–19.

17. Ivan Pylypiw, "How We Came to Canada" in *Land of Pain, Land of Promise: First Person Accounts by Ukrainian Pioneers, 1891–1914*, ed. and trans. Harry Piniut (Saskatoon: Western Producer Prairie Books, 1978), 27–35. For an assessment of the role of emigration propaganda in generating immigration to Canada, see John C. Lehr, "Propaganda and Belief: Ukrainian Emigrant Views of the Canadian West" in *New Soil—Old Roots: The Ukrainian Experience in Canada*, ed. Jaroslav Rozumnyj (Winnipeg: Ukrainian Academy of Arts and Sciences in Canada, 1983), 1–17.

18. For a popular account of this initial phase see James G. MacGregor, *Vilni Zemli— Free Lands: The Ukrainian Settlement of Alberta* (Toronto: McClelland & Stewart,

1969). A more scholarly treatment is found in Goresky, "Early Ukrainian Settlement," 17–38.

19. Oleskiv, *O emigratsii*, 41. Oleskiv noted that the Ukrainians in Winnipeg did "not live too badly." Some were saving money to buy a farm; others had become accustomed to city life and intended to remain in town.

20. Dr R.H. Mason, Saltcoats, Assiniboia, to James A. Smart, Ottawa, 12 July 1899, Record Group 76, vol. 144, file 34214, pt. 1, National Archives of Canada (hereafter NAC). Mason noted that in the Saltcoats colony he found "several clever carpenters and wagon makers," an expert shoemaker, and "a musician who constructed a very good violin and played selections from Mozart."

21. See, for example, William F. McCreary, Winnipeg, to James A. Smart, Ottawa, 20 May 1897, RG 76, vol. 144, file 34214, pt. 1, NAC.

22. On the Ukrainian community in Sydney, see John Huk, *Strangers in the Land: The Ukrainian Presence in Cape Breton* (Sydney, NS: n.p., 1986).

23. Government of Canada, Records of Homestead Entry for Alberta, 1891–96.

24. This fallacy led the Department of the Interior to engage interpreters proficient in German to deal with "Austrian" immigrants as late as 1897. William F. McCreary, the commissioner of immigration at Winnipeg, went to considerable pains to convince his superiors in Ottawa that interpreters conversant in Ukrainian, not German, were required. William F. McCreary, Winnipeg, to James A. Smart, Ottawa, 24 May 1897, RG 76, vol. 144, file 34214, pt. 1, NAC.

25. Oleskiv's role in the settlement of Ukrainians in Canada has been examined in detail in Kaye, *Early Ukrainian Settlements*. Oleskiv's first letter to the Canadian Department of the Interior was received on 1 April 1895. Dr Joseph Oleskow, Lemberg (Lviv), Austria, to the Department of the Interior, Ottawa, 16 March 1895, translation from the German by Miss Mercer, Department of the Interior, RG 76, vol. 109, file 21103, pt. 1, NAC.

26. Osyp Oleskiv, *Pro vilni zemli* (Lviv: Tovarystvo Prosvita, 1895).

27. Józef Oleskóv, *Rolnictwo za Oceanem a Przesiedlna Emigracja* (Karlsbad: Basilian Fathers, 1896). Accounts of the circumstances surrounding Oleskiv's visit to Western Canada are given in Vladimir J. Kaye, "Dr. Josef Oleskow's Visit to Canada, August–October 1895," *Revue de l'Université d'Ottawa* 32 (1962): 30–44; and Kaye, *Early Ukrainian Settlements*, 3–43.

28. Oleskiv, *O emigratsii*, 39.

29. Ibid., 30–31.

30. Michael Ewanchuk, *Pioneer Profiles: Ukrainian Settlers in Manitoba* (Winnipeg: n.p., 1981), 13; Gus Romaniuk, *Taking Root in Canada: An Autobiography* (Winnipeg: Columbia Press, 1954), 37; Ol'ha Woycenko, *The Ukrainians in Canada* (Winnipeg: Trident Press, 1967), 38; Young, *Ukrainian Canadians*, 55; MacGregor, *Vilni Zemli*, 117; and E. Shlanka, "Krydor Community No. 13, Interviews of Pioneers," April 1944 (typescript), 11, G.W. Simpson papers, Archives of Saskatchewan.

31. William F. McCreary, Winnipeg, to James A. Smart, Ottawa, 14 May 1897, RG 76, vol. 144, file 34214, pt. 1, NAC.

32. S. Dymianiw, ed., *Land of Dreams Come True* (Gorlitz, SK: Ukrainian School Division No. 972, 1955), 11–12.

33. See John C. Lehr, "The Rural Settlement Behaviour of Ukrainian Pioneers in Western Canada, 1891–1914" in *Western Canadian Research in Geography: The Lethbridge Papers*, ed. B.M. Barr, BC Geographical Series, No. 21, Occasional Papers in Geography (Vancouver: Tantalus Research, 1975), 51–66, and "The

Process and Pattern of Ukrainian Rural Settlement in Western Canada, 1891–1914" (PhD thesis, University of Manitoba, 1978), 129–65.

34. T.R. Weir, "Pioneer Settlement of Southwest Manitoba, 1874 to 1901," *Canadian Geographer* 8 (1964): 66–69.

35. Canada, Parliament, Sessional Papers, "Department of the Interior," 1896, Report of E.F. Stephanson, Winnipeg Land Agent, 12–13; J.R. Burpé, Commissioner of Dominion Lands, Winnipeg, Report to the Secretary, Department of the Interior, Ottawa, 27 Aug. 1896, RG 76, vol. 110, file 21103, pt. 2, NAC. For a comprehensive history of the Star bloc settlement see Orest T. Martynowych, *The Ukrainian Bloc Settlement in East Central Alberta, 1890–1930: A History* (Edmonton: Historic Sites Service, Alberta Culture and Multiculturalism, 1985).

36. For a more detailed discussion of the question of coercion in directing immigrants to various locales, see John C. Lehr, "Government Coercion in the Settlement of Ukrainian Immigrants in Western Canada," *Prairie Forum* 8 (1983): 179–94.

37. Frank Pedley, Winnipeg, to CPR Agent, New York, n.d., RG 76, vol. 144, file 34214, pt. 3, NAC; and P. Doyle, Quebec City, to the Secretary, Department of the Interior, Ottawa, 30 May 1898, RG 76, vol. 144, file 34214, pt. 2, NAC.

38. William F. McCreary, Winnipeg, to James A. Smart, Ottawa, 20 May 1898, RG 76, file 34214, pt. 2, NAC.

39. John C. Lehr and D. Wayne Moodie, "The Polemics of Pioneer Settlement: Perspectives on Ukrainian Immigration from the Winnipeg Press, 1896–1905," *Canadian Ethnic Studies* 12 (1980): 88–101.

40. Clifford Sifton, "The Immigrants Canada Wants," *Maclean's Magazine*, 1 April 1922, 16, 33. For a discussion of the government's attitudes towards Ukrainian settlers see John C. Lehr, "Government Perceptions of Ukrainian Immigrants to Western Canada, 1896–1902," *Canadian Ethnic Studies* 19 (1987): 1–12.

41. See, for example, *Winnipeg Telegram*, 7 July and 2 Nov. 1899. The attacks of the *Telegram* appear restrained in comparison with those of other Canadian newspapers. The *Belleville Intelligencer* called the Ukrainians "disgusting creatures" and wondered how "beings having human form could have sunk to such a bestial level"; *Halifax Herald*, 18 March 1899. For even more extreme views see Clive Phillips Wolley, "Mr. Sifton's Anglo-Saxondom," *Anglo-Saxon* 12 (June 1899): 1–4.

42. *Winnipeg Telegram*, 11 June 1898, 1 Aug. 1899, and 14 July 1900; *Kingston News*, 23 June 1899.

43. *Nor'Wester*, 20 July 1897.

44. *Winnipeg Telegram*, 3 Feb. 1899.

45. Ibid., 21 July 1909; *Daily Sun*, (Saint John, NB), 31 July 1899.

46. *Winnipeg Telegram*, 10 Aug. 1899.

47. Lehr and Moodie, "The Polemics of Pioneer Settlement," 93–98.

48. Established in 1872, the *Manitoba Free Press* was connected with Canadian Pacific Railway interests until its purchase in 1898 by Clifford Sifton and a business associate. Ramsay Cook, *The Politics of John W. Dafoe and the Free Press* (Toronto: University of Toronto Press, 1963), 15.

49. RG 76, vol. 144, file 34214, NAC.

50. See, for example, *Nor'Wester*, 10 March 1897 and 21 Jan. 1898; *Winnipeg Telegram*, 9 June 1899.

51. *Manitoba Free Press*, 16 Oct. 1901.

52. William F. McCreary, Winnipeg, to James A. Smart, Ottawa, 13 May 1897, RG 76, vol. 144, file 34214, pt. 1, NAC.

53. Canada, Parliament, Sessional Papers, 1899, "Department of the Interior," 113.

54. William F. McCreary, Winnipeg, to James A. Smart, Ottawa, 26 May 1898, RG 76, vol. 144, file 34214, pt. 2, NAC.

55. William F. McCreary, Winnipeg, to James A. Smart, Ottawa, 18 May 1898, ibid.

56. The many applications for work entered with the Edmonton colonization agent were an important factor in the decision to curtail the growth of the Star settlement by establishing other nodes of Ukrainian settlement. The Strathclair–Shoal Lake area was selected for settlement by Ukrainians partly because of the employment potential of the Riding Mountain Timber Reserve lumbering camps and the opportunity to employ settlers on fire protection work if extra employment was found to be necessary. For an extended discussion of this question see John C. Lehr, "The Government and the Immigrant: Perspectives on Ukrainian Bloc Settlement in the Canadian West," *Canadian Ethnic Studies* 9 (1977): 48–49.

57. D. McIntosh, Roadmaster, CPR, Prince Albert, to William F. McCreary, Winnipeg, 25 July 1898, RG 76, vol. 178, file 60868, pt. 1, NAC; James Mavor, *Report to the Board of Trade on the North-West of Canada with Special Reference to Wheat Production for Export* (London: HMSO, 1904), 57.

58. William F. McCreary, Winnipeg, to James A. Smart, Ottawa, 27 June 1900, RG 76, vol. 144, file 34214, pt. 4, NAC; J.S. Crerar, Yorkton, to William F. McCreary, Winnipeg, 7 July 1900, RG 76, vol. 178, file 60868, pt. 1, NAC; Todor Kutzak, pioneer of the Sirko district, Manitoba, interview with author, 15 Sept. 1975; Peter Humeniuk, *Hardships and Progress of Ukrainian Pioneers: Memoirs from Stuartburn Colony and Other Points* (Steinbach, MB: Derksen Printers, 1979), 56–58.

59. William F. McCreary, Winnipeg, to James A. Smart, Ottawa, 27 June 1900, RG 76, vol. 144, file 34214, pt. 4, NAC; C.W. Speers, Winnipeg to Frank Pedley, Ottawa, 22 May 1899; "Report of Thomas McNutt, Strathclair–Shoal Lake Colonization Scheme," ibid., pt. 3, NAC.

60. Canada, Parliament, Sessional Papers, "Department of the Interior," 1896, 118.

61. Oleskiv, *O emigratsii*, 39.

62. J. Obed Smith, Winnipeg, to the Minister of Public Works, Manitoba, 7 Jan. 1902, RG 76, vol. 238, file 141288 (1), NAC. The map accompanying this letter shows proposed routes for colonization roads to be built in Manitoba during 1902. Over 420 miles of colonization roads were planned for that year in Manitoba alone.

63. Under pressure of circumstances beyond their control, Canadian immigration officials occasionally ignored and sometimes even promoted squatting ahead of the survey, if by doing so they could attain contiguity of group settlement. In some instances the local land guides simply had no surveyed land upon which to locate the settlers under their charge. Petition to Clifford Sifton, Minister of the Interior, Ottawa, from Basil Barawatski et al., Fork River, MB, 2 Jan. 1902; J.A. Mitchell, Pakan, AB, to Frank Oliver, MP, Ottawa, 4 March 1903, John W. Thompson, Minnedosa, MB, to M.E. Darby, Ottawa, 10 Sept. 1902; and D.T. Wilson, Justice of the Peace, Asessippi, MB, to the Minister of the Interior, Ottawa, 24 Dec. 1904, RG 15, B-1a (224) 410595, pts. 2–3, NAC. This practice was not confined to settlement of Ukrainians. In 1901 a Norwegian colony of 40 families was established ahead of the survey in Manitoba's Interlake district. J. Obed Smith, Winnipeg, to Frank Pedley, Ottawa, 5 June 1901, RG 76, vol. 238, file 141288, pt. 1, NAC.

64. Map accompanying memorandum from C.W. Speers, Winnipeg, to E.L. Newcombe, Ottawa, 24 Jan. 1901, RG 76, vol. 238, file 141288, pt. 1, NAC.

65. In *O emigratsii* and *Rolnictwo za Oceanem* Oleskiv may have contributed to an erroneous view of southeastern Manitoba as a settlement location. In 1895 he visited the prairie margins east of Dominion City, MB, but as far as can be ascertained he did not inspect the area as far east as Stuartburn, where the first Ukrainians chose their homesteads. He probably endorsed the area as suitable for settlement on the assumption that the country did not change greatly east of Dominion City. Unfortunately, land quality declines rapidly east of the area viewed by Oleskiv as fertile Red River clays give way to gravelly beach ridges, areas of impeded drainage, and thin stony soils. Oleskiv, *O emigratsii*, 31, *Rolnictwo za Oceanem*, 10. The first party of Ukrainian immigrants to settle in the Stuartburn district assessed the land in late July, at the driest time of the year. Many areas then dry became virtual swamps during the following spring thaw. J.R. Burpé, Secretary to the Commissioner of Dominion Lands, Winnipeg, to the Secretary, Department of the Interior, Ottawa, 30 Nov. 1896, RG 76, vol. 110, file 21103, pt. 2, NAC.

66. John W. Wendelbo, Winnipeg, to H.H. Smith, Winnipeg, 8 Aug. 1896, RG 15, B-1a (224), file 410595, pt. 1, NAC.

67. Canada, Parliament, Sessional Papers, "Department of the Interior," 1900, Report of E.F. Stephanson, Winnipeg Land Agent, 12–13; Hugo Carstens, Winnipeg, to H.H. Smith, Winnipeg, 25 Nov. 1896, RG 76, vol. 110, file 21103, pt. 2, NAC.

68. Canada, Parliament, Sessional Papers, "Department of the Interior," 1900, Report of E.F. Stephanson, Winnipeg Land Agent, 12–13.

69. Kaye, *Early Ukrainian Settlements*, 180–85.

70. Alfred Akherlindh, Winnipeg, to Frank Pedley, Ottawa, 3 May 1898, RG 76, vol. 144, file 34214, pt. 2, NAC.

71. William F. McCreary, Winnipeg, to Frank Pedley, Ottawa, 4 May 1898, RG 76, vol. 144, file 34214, pt. 2, NAC.

72. C.W. Speers, Saskatoon, telegram to William F. McCreary, Winnipeg, 19 May 1898, ibid.

73. William F. McCreary, Winnipeg, to James A. Smart, Ottawa, 20 May 1898, ibid.

74. William A. Czumer, *Recollections about the Life of the First Ukrainian Settlers in Canada*, trans. Louis T. Laychuk (Edmonton: Canadian Institute of Ukrainian Studies, 1981), 38.

75. Ewanchuk, *Pioneer Profiles*, 128; Anne B. Woywitcka, "Homesteader's Woman," *Alberta History* 24 (1976): 20.

76. Wasyl Mihaychuk, "Mihaychuk Family Tree" (typescript), n.p. Stefan Yendik, Frazerwood, MB, interview with author, 12 Nov. 1974. Ewanchuk, *Pioneer Profiles*, 130–31. Declarations of Abandonment, Records of Homestead Entry, SE 1/4 Section 18, Township 57, Range 18, West of the 4' meridian; NE 10, T. 59, R. 17, W. 4; SE 22, T. 59, R. 17, W. 4; NW 30, T. 57, R. 16, W. 4, Provincial Archives of Alberta.

77. Kaye, *Early Ukrainian Settlements*, 139; Ewanchuk, *Pioneer Profiles*, 13; Woycenko, *Ukrainians in Canada*, 39; N. Wagenhoffer, "Some Socio-economic Dynamics in Southeastern Manitoba with Particular Reference to the Farming Communities Within the Local Government Districts of Stuartburn and Piney" (MA thesis, University of Manitoba, 1972), 55.

78. Canada, Parliament, Sessional Papers, "Department of the Interior," 1897, Report of John W. Wendelbo, 127.

79. The role of kinship and "old-country" linkages in determining the new social geography of homestead settlement established by Ukrainian immigrants is dis-

cussed in detail in John C. Lehr, "Kinship and Society in the Ukrainian Pioneer Settlement of the Canadian West," *Canadian Geographer* 24 (1985): 207–19.

80. Donald R. Taft and Richard Robbins, *International Migrations: The Immigrant and the Modern World* (New York: Ronald Press, 1955), 111.

81. Michael Hrushevsky, *A History of Ukraine* (New Haven: Yale University Press, 1941), 469–71.

82. Lehr, "Process and Pattern," 249–85. See also Thomas McNutt, "Galicians and Bukowinians" in *The Story of Saskatchewan and Its People*, ed. John Hawkes (Chicago: S.J. Clarke Publishing, 1924), 731–32; Paul Yuzyk, The *Ukrainians in Manitoba: A Social History* (Toronto: University of Toronto Press, 1953), 42; Kaye, *Early Ukrainian Settlements*, 142, and *Canadians of Recent European Origin: A Survey* (Ottawa: Citizenship Division of the Department of National War Services, 1945), 46; Timothy C. Byrne, "The Ukrainian Community in North Central Alberta" (MA thesis, University of Alberta, 1937), 31; MacGregor, *Vilni Zemli*, 157; Young, *Ukrainian Canadians*, 75; Iuliian Stechyshyn, *Istoriia poselennia ukraintsiv u Kanadi* (Edmonton: Ukrainian Self-Reliance League, 1975), 242–47; Mykhailo Ivanchuk, *Istoriia ukrainskoho poselennia v okolytsi Gimli* (Winnipeg: Trident Press, 1975), 24–28; and Petro Zvarych, "Do pytannia rozvytku i postupu v materiialnii kulturi ukrainskykh poselentsiv u Kanadi" in *Zbirnyk na poshanu Zenona Kuzeli* (Paris: Shevchenko Scientific Society, 1962), 151; Goresky, "Early Ukrainian Settlement in Alberta," 17–38; Joseph M. Lazarenko, "Rusiw Pioneers in Alberta" in *Ukrainians in Alberta*, 38–41; and Alexander Royick, "Ukrainian Settlements in Alberta," *Canadian Slavonic Papers* 10 (1968): 278–97.

83. William F. McCreary, Winnipeg, to James A. Smart, Ottawa, 15 May 1897, RG 76, vol. 144, file 34214, pt. 1, NAC.

84. C.W. Speers, Winnipeg, to William F. McCreary, Winnipeg, 9 July 1897, ibid. See also Thomas McNutt, "Galicians and Bukowinians" in *The Story of Saskatchewan*, 731–32.

85. John C. Lehr, "'The Peculiar People': Ukrainian Settlement of Marginal Lands in Southeastern Manitoba" in *Building Beyond the Homestead*, ed. David C. Jones and Ian MacPherson (Calgary: University of Calgary Press, 1985), 29–46.

86. The data upon which the following discussion of kinship linkages in settlement is based were compiled from Vladimir J. Kaye, *Dictionary of Ukrainian Canadian Biography: Pioneer Settlers of Manitoba 1891–1900* (Toronto: Ukrainian Canadian Research Foundation, 1975), 120–98; and Homestead General Registers, Department of Lands, Government of Manitoba. These data were supplemented by information contained in John Panchuk, *Bukowinian Settlements in Southern Manitoba* (Battle Creek, MI: n.p., 1971), and by field research in southeastern Manitoba.

87. Ties of marriage accounted for the presence and initial close settlement of settlers from Galicia and Bukovyna in the Stuartburn area. Stefan Storeschuk, Gardenton, MB, interview with author, 21 July 1975.

88. Kaye, *Early Ukrainian Settlements*, 273–76.

89. C.W. Speers, Brandon, to Frank Pedley, Ottawa, 4 April 1899, RG 76, vol. 144, file 34214, pt. 3, NAC.

NETWORKS AMONG BRITISH IMMIGRANTS AND ACCOMMODATION TO CANADIAN SOCIETY: WINNIPEG, 1900–1914 ⬦

A. ROSS McCORMACK

O

In recent years historians and sociologists who study migration have abandoned such concepts as "the marginal man" and "uprootedness." Instead they have explained the immigration experience in terms of the mechanisms which immigrants employed as groups to accommodate to new societies. I have argued elsewhere that English immigrants in Canada asserted a group identity based upon shared cultural forms because there were explicit social advantages to such ascription.[1] The same essay postulated the emergence of a pan-British identity in the face of competition from alien ethnic groups. My purpose here is to elaborate the content of that identity. The collective strategy whereby British immigrants accommodated to Canadian society was based upon what scholars have called networks. By the term network, I mean a series of individuals and institutions which is connected by social relationships and which is unbounded so that it may incorporate other individuals and institutions.[2] By the term British, I mean a functional social category subsuming the four national groups which emigrated from England, Scotland, Ulster, and Wales. This essay, which focusses on the British community in Winnipeg between 1900 and 1914, argues that immigrants from the UK used networks which were based in the nuclear family, sustained by chain migration, and elaborated through ethnic institutions, to maximize group advantage in Canada's heterogeneous society.

⬦ *Histoire sociale/Social History* 17, 34 (Nov. 1984): 357–74. Reprinted with the permission of the journal.

Immediately upon arrival, migrants begin to reconstruct their social lives, using both resources that are part of their cultural baggage and part of their new environment.[3] This process is common to migration. The newcomers need a place to live, advice on social and cultural norms, help in finding a job, and assistance in a hundred other ways. To facilitate the process of economic and emotional adaptation, migrants must establish a new set of social relationships. This can have many dimensions ranging from secret fraternities to football clubs. Usually the reconstruction is based on such institutions as the church, benefit societies, and neighbourhoods. The most effective and enduring social affiliation that a migrant can enjoy during the initial period of accommodation is with a kinship network.

British networks grew out of the nuclear family. By filling its traditional role of furnishing both emotional and material support, the family constituted a model for other networks. Because it is a principal mediator of social identity in modern society, immigrants have traditionally used the family as a mechanism to reduce their sense of dislocation and to facilitate their adaptation.[4] Before 1914 the structure of British immigration facilitated this process; men and women entered Canada at a ratio of 3:2. The British established a traditional patriarchal system of family organization in which the husband assumed a dominant and public role and the wife a subordinate and private one.[5] Oral history interviews indicate the woman was assigned all household tasks, even if she held a full-time job, and routine child-rearing responsibilities, except for disciplining which was considered a male prerogative; the man was the principal bread-winner and the family's representative in the community.[6] This structure imposed heavy responsibilities on the wife and mother. An emigration promoter familiar with British communities in Canada told the Dominions Royal Commission that "she is the foundation stone" of the family. And the home she made was central to her husband's and children's emotional adjustment to Canadian society. The home became the focus for the maintenance of British aesthetic cultural forms such as idiom, diet, and values. "I love my home," a London woman told a friend, "and make it as homely and English as I can. I generally get English jams, pickles, sauces, etc. and thus keep up our English taste of food."[7] In this way the home provided immigrants with a congenial and familiar environment insulated from an alien society.

In addition to providing immigrants with emotional support, the nuclear family filled a significant economic role. Both Anderson and Parr have elaborated this interpretation of English family relationships.[8] Among the British working-class it was customary for older children, living at home, to supplement family income through wage-labour. The practice was part of the cultural baggage immigrants took to Canada. Indeed this income supplement mechanism became institutionalized in the migration process. Emigration societies routinely assumed that it would be used to facilitate economic adjustment; the East End Emigration Fund defined the "ideal family" as one composed of "parents under 40, with four children, two of whom are working age." As a matter of policy, the Canadian immigration service discouraged the migration of families with more than two children under twelve.[9]

A majority of the nuclear families travelling as units in this essay's sample of British immigrants appear to have adopted an instrumental strategy to migration.[10] Families with more than one potential wage-earner constituted the larger proportion of those travelling as units. Married couples without dependent children comprised 36 percent of the population. The eldest child of 15 percent of the nuclear families was between 12 and 17 and presumably able to contribute to family income. An additional 6 percent had at least one child over 18. Nonetheless the eldest child of 43 percent of the nuclear families was only 11.[11] A nuclear family's ability to migrate with dependent children may have been related to the extent of support it could expect in Canada. For instance while only 13 percent of families with children went out "on spec," 21 percent of couples without dependants did.[12]

British immigrant families with children of working age clearly exploited their wage-earning potential as need arose. "Everybody out," a Cumberland man told his three adolescent children when the family arrived in Winnipeg, "you have all got to work."[13] Many families appear to have functioned as co-operative economic units with wives, sons, and daughters working in the home, going into domestic service, or joining the labour force. In 1911 a Winnipeg social agency found that in a sample of thirty British families over one-third had, on the average, two children in full-time employment.[14] The obligation to supplement family income apparently remained on children as long as they were part of the household.

Wives, sons, and daughters went to work, Anderson argues, only as a "solution to family poverty."[15] The practice appears to have had the same cause in Canada. Dislocation attendant upon migration produced short-run economic hardship equal to any crisis in the life cycle of a family. The need to repay passage loans, to compete for housing in a tight market, and to re-establish a household placed heavy demands on resources. And when the principal wage-earner's employment was irregular, as it often was in Canada's seasonal economy, supplementary income became essential. Apparently wives and children were equally expected to support the family in these circumstances. A Durham woman who married a Scottish butcher recalls, "if he wasn't working or something, I've gone out to work and I've done a day's work. And I scrubbed floors for one dollar a day." A Belfast machinist who could never secure regular employment from the CPR frequently became dependent upon his children. His daughter remembers, "my brother and I . . . got to work and with what we were earning, although it wasn't much—I had eight dollars a week and I think he had ten—but with that little bit coming in, it always kept things going until Dad would get another spell."[16]

To ensure the integrity of the family, British immigrants practised preferential endogamy. Emigration propaganda emphasized that Canada offered excellent matrimonial prospects for women; the East End Emigration Fund for instance announced that "Winnipeg has three times as many men as women."[17] Once in Canada British immigrants manifested a pronounced tendency to maintain group cohesiveness through intermarriage. The phenomenon is demonstrable through an examination of some 460 marriages in three Anglican parishes in and around Winnipeg in the years between

1903 and 1913.[18] Of the 231 English-born bridegrooms in the parishes, 65 percent married countrywomen; 74 percent of the 200 English brides entered endogamous unions. The operation of networks ensured that in some cases the origins of the bride and groom showed a remarkable propinquity. A West Bromwich woman who immigrated in 1912 met and married a man who had lived "only a busride away" in her home town. On the day the couple was married in Winnipeg their families held a wedding breakfast "at home" in Staffordshire.[19]

For the most part the British did not, of course, migrate to Canada in nuclear families. Twenty-six percent of the sample migrating in 1913 were going out to relatives.[20] These data point to the process of chain migration. The standard definition was provided some years ago by the MacDonalds who described chain migration as a "movement in which prospective migrants learn of opportunities, are provided with transportation, and have initial accommodation and employment arranged *by means of primary social relationships with previous migrants.*"[21] The family remained basic to this process whether it was a divided nuclear family, an extended family, or even a surrogate family. Quantitative data and qualitative evidence indicate that extended families facilitated the migration of more individuals than the other two institutions. Litwack has argued that the extended family is "uniquely suited" to this role because its size expedites the accumulation of capital and its solidarity ensures the provision of reliable information.[22] These were the commodities that prospective immigrants needed most.

Reliable information is essential to rational choice. The need was especially acute in Britain's highly competitive emigration market. In the Canadian trade alone, prospective migrants were faced with a welter of propaganda from railways, steamship companies, passenger agents, and provincial governments. By 1913 federal immigration officials, for instance, were giving one thousand illustrated lectures annually in the United Kingdom.[23] In spite of—perhaps because of—the intensity of Canadian advertising, prospective immigrants relied on information from persons whom they knew and trusted. Letters from friends and relatives in Canada, an emigration society claimed, "do more to enlighten [recipients] and their neighbours as to the reality of the prospects offered than any amount of official information." Because the information sent home within networks was considered authoritative, it was shared. Like other members of emigrant-exporting societies, the British circulated letters from Canada within extended families. The practice cut across class lines; pauper apprentices and public school men alike exchanged information within networks.[24]

Prospective migrants valued the information contained in personal letters from Canada because it was frank, specific, and current. Immigrants offered advice on the various dimensions of migration and settlement—cultural, logistical, economic, and so on. For instance, a Gateshead man, whose luggage had been badly damaged during passage to Winnipeg, sent his wife detailed instructions complete with diagrams on how to pack the family's goods.[25] But information on economic conditions—accurate and up-to-date advice on prices, the availability of housing, and the state of the job market—was most important for those about to leave Britain. Personal knowledge of the prospective migrant allowed individuals in Canada to provide highly specific advice. A Londoner informed a friend that men in his trade "are in great demand. Bricklayers command 4 ½ dollars a day." But in Canada's unstable seasonal economy, shifts in the labour market were rapid. What made information conveyed in personal networks virtually unique was explicit warnings not to migrate. During the recession of 1907–8, an Oxfordshire man, whose brothers were going out sequentially to Manitoba, warned the head of the family that "trade all over Canada just now is bad . . . and there is nothing being done to speak of."[26]

In addition to information, letters to relatives in Britain contained remittances. Anthropologists, such as Philpott and Watson, have demonstrated that emigrant-exporting communities can become virtually dependent on a flow of funds from individuals working overseas.[27] Even though Britain was hardly a remittance economy, there were clearly families who were dependent, in one of several ways, upon the earnings of immigrants in Canada. In 1912 the Winnipeg Board of Trade estimated that a group of some three hundred British men remitted on the average $300 annually to support their wives and children in the United Kingdom.[28] These men, mainly clerks and artisans, may have been somewhat unrepresentative. Still there can be no doubt that substantial funds were flowing from Canada to Britain. Trends in Canadian postal money orders payable in Britain, one of the principal vehicles for remittances, provide a good index of this condition. In 1900 the value of such orders was $929 000; by 1914, after hundreds of thousands of British immigrants had arrived in Canada, the value had risen to $15 430 000. The capacity of immigrants to make remittances depended on the condition of the Canadian labour market. When the economy was booming in 1904, orders payable in Britain averaged $13.21, but five years later, when a severe recession had resulted in widespread unemployment, the average value dropped by more than 20 percent.[29]

Remittances were made, in part, to fulfil customary obligations within the family. Anderson posits a consensual "duty to assist less fortunate kin."[30] Apparently this sense of obligation was part of British cultural baggage. Even though separated by great distances, some immigrants appear to have accepted the responsibility to support aged parents and other dependent relatives at home. Members of Winnipeg's British community took pride in having met such obligations. "Even when my wife come out," a Macclesfield butcher recalls, "we sent a dollar, two home, home to the old people, and we were only making a bit of money." Those who had failed to make remittances offered rationales such as "I never made big money."[31] Relatives in Britain expected immigrants to contribute to family welfare, especially if Canada was perceived positively. One family established "a home allowance" which kin in Manitoba were bound to pay.[32] The strength of customary obligations is demonstrated by remittances to family members whom the immigrant would in all likelihood have never seen again. For instance a Herefordshire machinist settled in Winnipeg made regular and substantial contributions to the maintenance of his invalid brother, whose condition precluded immigration to Canada.[33]

Some remittances were made explicitly to facilitate migration. Apart from supporting a wife and children at home, the first obligation that an immigrant had was to repay loans used to finance his passage. This process replenished family capital and thus allowed other family migrants to travel within the network.[34] Chain migration was even more dependent upon the higher real wages earned in Canada. Immigrants working in the Dominion could accumulate capital more quickly than in Britain; it was then remitted home to finance passages. The benefits could accrue to members of either the immigrant's extended or nuclear family. When a Welshman working for the CPR in Winnipeg learned that his brother was unemployed as a result of a miners' strike, he sent home the best form of relief he could, a steamship ticket. Another Winnipeg CPR employee who immigrated in 1911 wrote his wife in April, "I want to make good money to send and get you out as soon as I can." After a month of frugal living he remitted her passage, even though it was "putting me on my last legs to get you out."[35]

When the prospective migrant became an immigrant, reception by family and friends was highly advantageous. During the nineteenth century, the British working-class family became the principal institution facilitating the migration of rural masses to the new industrial towns. Given this experience, immigrants transferred the mechanism to Canada. Here as in the United Kingdom personal networks provided the aid specific to families. Accommodation, food, personal care, loans, advice, and assistance in finding a job, all afforded the newcomer going out to a family connection a more favourable start than the individual alone in an alien society could make. Immigrants certainly appear to have perceived an advantage. In the sample, 48 percent of the women and 24 percent of the men were migrating in chains.[36] Because individuals tended to travel within available personal networks, the location of family and friends was clearly influential in the spatial distribution of the British.[37] Immigrants appear to have been more likely to settle in a place to which they had been attracted by a family connection than a place to which they had been directed by an emigration society or the state. When a London woman recalled the process by which her family had been established in Winnipeg, she provided a classic description of chain migration: "[friends] talked Harry into coming back with them so that's how he got started. Then, of course, gradually one from the other, like my sister and my other brother came out. Then my married sister with her two children and I came in 1910. That's the way that finally, you know, so many of us got out here." Given her passage by a brother, the respondent nursed her two sisters through confinements and financed the passage of an additional brother and sister to Winnipeg.[38]

Improved communications on the North Atlantic and relatively high wages in Canada made it feasible for a man migrating a year or two in advance of his family to begin accumulating the capital necessary to re-establish a household. Thirty-one percent of the men travelling alone in the sample were married.[39] The reception that these men had appears significant. While only 20 percent were going out to family and friends, 44 percent had to settle for state-arranged employment. An additional 27 percent planned to manage entirely on their own resources, even though only 11 percent of the population as a whole went out "on spec."[40] These data suggest that men migrating in advance of their nuclear families tended to lack access to personal networks. The second phase of the process was demonstrated by the behaviour of women travelling with their children; fully 87 percent were going out to their husbands.[41] The decision for nuclear families to migrate sequentially appears to have been related to the wage-earning potential of children. While only 20 percent of the families going out for reunification had a teenaged child able to work, 69 percent had no child older than 11 years of age.[42] The case of an Ulster tailor was typical. In 1909 he immigrated to Winnipeg, leaving his family in the care of Belfast relatives. "Father came out," one of his daughters remembers, "to see how things were before he brought us over." After eighteen months' work he had accumulated sufficient capital to open a small shop and send for his wife and daughters who ranged in age from two to eight.[43]

Chain migration also appears to have been important for young, unmarried men and women. Twenty-five percent of those in the sample were going out to family and friends.[44] Women appear to have been somewhat more likely to use this mechanism than men. Of the single men and women migrating within personal networks, 58 percent were within the ages of 18 and 29.[45] On the average, women appear to have been somewhat older than the men. The class composition of the cohort going to family and friends appears significant and coincides with Tilly and Brown's assertion that low-status individuals are more likely to travel in personal networks. Nearly 60 percent of the women were domestic servants, while only 20 percent belonged to skilled trades.[46] The men enjoyed only slightly higher status. Forty-six percent of them worked in unskilled occupations and 34 percent in skilled, such as metal or building trades.[47] Their lower status precluded resources adequate to carry them through any sustained period of unemployment. Upon arrival they needed material assistance in the form of accommodation and food from their hosts. And they needed assistance in finding work. Custom in Britain had taught them, Anderson argues, that families were "typically responsible for getting a man a job."[48] The experience of a Kentishman who immigrated in 1910 at the age of 24 was typical. "I just came out to my brother," he recalls. "He was here two years. . . . Anything for my future I'll get advice from him. I relied on him." The confidence was well placed; his brother provided temporary lodging and arranged a job with the CPR.[49]

The reception of family and friends entailed emotional strain and monetary costs. The anxieties attendant upon beginning life in an alien society exacerbated the tension caused by crowding into another household; a good deal of wear and tear on emotions resulted. The process was undoubtedly intensified by a shared awareness that the longer the newcomer remained dependent, the more the increased costs depleted his host's capital. The disadvantages of chain migration for the settled immigrant were demonstrated by the case of a Glasgow woman. In 1912 she financed the passage of her sister, unemployed brother-in-law, and two nieces on the understanding that the family would repay the loan through work in her Winnipeg boarding house. But when relations between her and her brother-in-law became so strained that the family moved out, the Glaswegian lost both her investment and her assured labour supply.[50] Such experience clearly made some individuals reluctant to receive family and friends or at least imposed limits on support. Oral testimony indicates that the settled immigrants appear to have been more inclined to provide material aid to relatives than to friends and to place more constraints on the support given friends. When a Welshman sent for his wife and sons, he warned her to "tell the boys not to spread the news to bring a large crowd with you—there will be no accommodation for them." But even family relationships could be ruthlessly instrumental. In 1905 a Portsmouth woman living with her son and daughter-in-law in Winnipeg lost her sight and thus her ability to contribute to the family economy; she was turned out of the house and deported.[51]

Whatever the disadvantages, however, settled immigrants received family and friends for the same reasons that they made remittances. The propensity to favour family members demonstrated the strong influence of custom. British communities in Canada were sufficiently integrated to help maintain compliance with cultural norms. But scholars have also identified trans-oceanic mechanisms which effectively enforce behavioural standards among migrants.[52] The consensual obligation of a son or daughter to care for an aged parent appears to have resulted in the immigration of a significant number of elderly, and unproductive, individuals. The sample contained 115 people over 60; 62 percent were travelling to join relatives or friends. A Londoner explained that he was bringing out his elderly mother because "she will be all right and end her days in peace with me."[53] Possibly there was another dimension to a settled immigrant's sense of obligation. Those who had already benefited from chain migration may have felt a need to repay the system. In an invitation to a friend, a Londoner who had travelled in a network explained that "I must do to others what others have done for me."[54]

Settled immigrants also received family and friends because the process was, at least potentially, functional for the hosts. The unstable nature of a migrant's life necessitated observance of obligations, especially to family members, because an individual could never be certain when he might need the support of the kinship network. In other words a migrant to Canada could not risk breaking the chain. And networks operated in such a way that real sanctions could be brought against miscreants. Not all migrants remained in Canada permanently; for instance in the decade 1901–11 emigration was almost as high as immigration. This condition was partly a function of sojourning which was well established in the North Atlantic economy, especially in seasonal occupations. Building tradesmen, miners, and even unskilled labourers migrated to Canada to work so long as wages were higher than in Britain. When the Canadian economy slumped, as it periodically did, they went home. Thus an Ulsterwoman, who had married a carpenter from Norfolk, returned with her husband to his family when the recession of 1913 put thousands of building tradesmen out of work.[55]

But even if an immigrant was, more or less, permanently settled in Canada, personal networks continued to provide support in times of need. This condition is demonstrated in the remittances sent from Britain to Canada. Fluctuations in their value indicated how these funds facilitated immigrant adjustment. After increasing at a modest annual rate, the average value of postal money orders sent to this country shot up by 20 percent during the recession of 1908 which caused severe hardship for the British in Canada. When the head of an Oxfordshire family provided special financial aid in 1908, he insisted that the recipients give greater help to their brother.[56]

Personal networks extended beyond the family into neighbourhoods, which provided the base for group institutions. While final conclusions must wait on the availability of quantitative data, qualitative evidence strongly suggests that the British formed spatially discrete communities. Reynolds found substantial levels of residential concentration among Montreal's British population.[57] Similar patterns developed in Winnipeg. In some cases segregation was national-group-specific and in a few even town-specific. But oral testimony indicates that, for the most part, urban settlement integrated English, Scottish, Ulster, and Welsh immigrants. The city's west end, adjacent to the CPR shops, was a British neighbourhood. A London woman whose husband worked for the railway told a friend "we like this place very much; . . . it is all English, Scotch and Irish. It's like being at home."[58] Elmwood, across the Red River from factories where many British artisans worked, also had a distinctive character. The area developed during the massive influx of British immigrants to the West after 1910; apparently as a result, settlement patterns here were somewhat more refined. One street was populated by families from Leicester. A resident recalled that "there was a bunch from the same city as we were. . . . They all came from Leicester. They came one after another." Nearby an Ulsterwoman, whose husband had emigrated from Sheffield, was the "only foreigner" on another English street.[59]

Like the family, the neighbourhood provided immigrants with both material and emotional support. In fact a Scottish woman who lived in Winnipeg's west end before 1914 remembers that her neighbours "were all so friendly; we were all like one family."[60] Even allowing for romantic nostalgia, the perception is informative. British residents of the west end practised various forms of mutuality, such as lending money, donating food and clothing, or providing shelter during family crises. An Ulsterwoman whose father's employment with the CPR was irregular explained that "over the years we had financial [problems]. . . . I suppose the fact those people were around, I suppose that was the only help that, you know, that you got."[61] But networks based on residential segregation apparently had greater cultural importance. The custom of "neighbouring," frequent and informal house visits, characteristic of the British working-class, was common, and this practice tended to insulate immigrants from the larger community and increase group cohesiveness. Women appear to have found the familiar atmosphere of the west end especially congenial. A Lincolnshire immigrant who lived with her Ulster husband in the area recalls "if you went out or went for a walk or went to the shops you always met somebody from the Old Country."[62] In addition the density of British population was adequate to the formation and maintenance of institutions which preserved the immigrant's cultural identity. The west end contained ethnic parishes, benefit societies, and British boarding houses.

Like the neighbourhoods in which they developed, British boarding houses usually integrated individuals from the four national groups, although there were a few town-specific houses. Their exclusive British character was not accidental. Boarding-house keepers recognized that the admission of low-status ethnic groups was bad for business. An English landlord who always respected his lodgers' distaste for "foreigners" admitted that "you kinda select them a little bit you know."[63]

An extension of personal networks, boarding houses functioned as family surrogates for migrants who did not enjoy real kinship support. Although these establishments were unquestionably commercial enterprises, several scholars have argued that the relationships which characterized boarding went much beyond the cash nexus. Lodging provided "a substitute for absent kin."[64] This function appears to have been prevalent in Winnipeg's houses; immigrants who boarded usually used the metaphor of the family to describe their experience. For instance, the term "mother" was frequently applied to landladies. "An Old Country woman" with whom an Englishman lodged acted out her matriarchal role when his family was reunified; he recalls that "she was the one that took my wife—when she came here and she didn't know a soul—took her around to get these bits of things like the fifteen cents store to start a couple of rooms."[65]

In fact boarding houses provided immigrants with support which was in many ways similar to that of the family, though economic assistance was much less important. The latter usually took the form of advice on the labour market, circulated among lodgers or brokered by the landlord. Such assistance was not unimportant, however, since it was essential to successful economic adjustment. A Lancashire man, who arrived in Winnipeg when "times were bad," remembers securing work under the auspices of fellow boarders at an English establishment in the west end.[66] But boarding houses appear to have played a more important role in facilitating cultural adjustment. The emotional support that lodging could afford immigrants who lacked actual kin networks was recognized by family and friends in the UK. A young Ulsterwoman, who "had no people" in Winnipeg, was advised that "the best thing for you to do is to get into a private home with a nice family until you get acquainted with the town." She lived in an Irish-Protestant household until she was married. With their familiar diets, accents, and values, boarding houses provided a tangible link with the native culture. Such security helped overcome the immigrant's sense of dislocation. The British clearly sought out the emotional support afforded by insulation from Canadian society. A Scotsman told a friend that he had taken lodgings with a Cornish landlady in the west end, because "born Canadians are most unpleasant, voices harsh, manners aggressive, dollar greedy beyond anything known in England, despising and defrauding the British-born."[67]

Immigrants' hostels were essentially institutionalized boarding houses. They were certainly no less ethnocentric. Winnipeg had several for both men and women, but for a broad range of social reasons, hostels appear to have been more important in facilitating the adjustment of women.[68] The city's most important hostel was the Girls Home of Welcome. Winnipeg's Anglophilic élite established the Home in 1896 to serve the needs of women travelling alone but assumed from the beginning that those helped would be British. A Scotswoman who stayed at the hostel for several days in 1906 remembers it as an "Old Country place." Indeed it was; in the year she arrived in Winnipeg, 97 percent of the women who passed through the Home were British.[69] This condition was typical of all the Winnipeg hostels.

Much more than boarding houses, hostels consciously attempted to assume the role of surrogate families. Barber believes that a woman's hostel in Toronto, modelled on Winnipeg's, "served as a home away from home."[70] Starting with their names—Welcome Home, Friendly Lodge—hostels adopted a mannered familial relationship with their "girls." The metaphor, and its actualization, was explicit and sustained. Matrons never merely served clients but always "mothered" them. The superintendent of the Friendly Lodge took pride in the fact that she monitored the behaviour of women who had passed through the hostel to jobs in rural Manitoba. The Welcome Home's matron, who received many young women coming out to fiancés, assumed a traditional family responsibility, protection of a daughter's honour. She believed that "parents will be glad to hear" that she did not allow the bride to leave the hostel until after the marriage ceremony.[71]

In fact hostels probably came closer than any other institution to replicating the support families provided to female immigrants. The material benefits were relatively substantial. Because the Welcome Home functioned as an employment bureau for domestics, it could provide British women with passage loans to be repaid in service. Like families the institutions provided free lodging for a short time while immigrants sought work. But the hostels' most important support took the form of finding British women jobs. This function resulted from the patronage of the local élite. The Welcome Home specialized in domestic service "generally with old country people." A Staffordshire woman who was placed by the Home in 1912 remembers offers of employment from several would-be mistresses. Her impression conforms to available data; by the year she passed through the hostel, it had found work for 61 percent of the 17 500 clients it had served since opening.[72]

The emotional support that hostels provided British women apparently approximated that provided by kin networks better than boarding houses. Like family members, matrons met immigrants at railway stations and thus welcomed them at the earliest possible moment. The ambiance of the hostels themselves was probably much the same as that of respectable British boarding houses. But in addition to familiar aesthetic cultural forms, the hostels provided a religious atmosphere which was undoubtedly comforting to many young women. Immigrants who frequented the Winnipeg institutions appear to have drawn emotional support from them. Writing about the Welcome Home a domestic servant reported that she and her friends "all feel as if it is our own home; and it is so nice to go there and meet all the other girls, and hear their troubles and cheer them up, and get cheered."[73]

Churches played an equally important role in the adaptation of many British immigrants to Canadian society. The Anglican and Presbyterian communions were the principal immigrant-receiving churches. The former grew by recruiting Church people from England and members of the Church of Ireland. Canadian Presbyterians accepted their co-religionists from Scotland and Ulster. The process is well illustrated by census data. Between 1901 and 1911 national membership in the Anglican church grew by 53 percent, outstripping that of all other denominations. Only the Presbyterians came close with a growth rate of 32 percent. The two churches flourished most in immigrant-receiving provinces. In 1911 Presbyterians were the largest denomination in Manitoba, and their numbers had grown 59 percent since the previous census. The Anglicans had become the second largest communion in the province by 1911 because of a 93 percent increase in the preceding decade. Both churches enjoyed extraordinary growth in the city of Winnipeg. The Church of England led with an increase approaching 200 percent, while the number of Presbyterians grew by 180 percent.[74]

Because of its composition, the Anglican church assumed a greater responsibility for British immigrants than did other Protestant denominations. The Church gave some material support. Anglican immigration chaplains met members of the Churches of England and Ireland at all Canadian Atlantic ports. Their responsibility was to provide immigrants with lodging, advice on their destination's job market, and letters of introduction to their new bishop.[75] Cities with large Anglican populations had their own immigration chaplains appointed by missionary societies. Winnipeg's chaplain monitored the labour market for emigration societies in England as well as securing various forms of charity and jobs for immigrants.[76] In this latter function he co-operated with parish priests who had access to the patronage of affluent Anglicans. "The ladies at the Church," a Londoner who belonged to a west end parish told a friend, "have been very good in engaging me for sewing, which is done here principally at the home of one's customers."[77]

But Anglican parishes were more useful to immigrants because they mitigated their sense of dislocation. The Church considered itself the natural "centre of Christian reunion" for the English in Canada and took up a mission to bring them into the communion. Reynolds' findings in Montreal and Synge's in Hamilton indicate that many responded.[78] This occurred largely because of the emotional support that the Church's mission provided. A Middlesex woman who did not live in a British neighbourhood recalls with gratitude that when an Anglican priest "found I was English and had only been out here for a while, he visited me frequently."[79] The Church became a social centre for many recent immigrants and promoted group cohesiveness by sponsoring collective activities, such as women's auxiliaries, musical societies, athletic clubs, and youth organizations. The process insulated them from Canadian society. "We went to the Anglican Church right away . . . [because] a lot of our friends were old country people," a Cumberland woman who belonged to a west end parish explains; "you know people sort of get together with their own kind."[80] There was another dimension to Anglican solace. Among protestant denominations, the Church of England was unique in that its liturgy and doctrine were identical to those observed in the United Kingdom; it linked sending and receiving societies in a powerfully emotive way. Because immigrants could practise their religion in the manner they always had, their identification with England was regularly renewed. "When we are at church it seems so much like home," a labourer from the southern countries wrote, "and one feels the new life enter in him, after the toils of the week."[81]

The various societies, clubs, and lodges which British immigrants established had, in part, a similar function. Their ethnocentricity demonstrates how group-specific some networks were. Among others, Winnipeg had a Glasgow Association and a Devonian Society. According to its constitution, one of the principal purposes of the Aberdeen, Banff, and Kincardine Association was to "renew old acquaintances, form new ones, and promote friendly intercourse amongst those who hold a common interest in the three shires." Winnipeg's British societies achieved their shared goal primarily through the sponsorship of recreational activities which maintained aesthetic cultural forms, what the Kentish Association described as its "Reconstruction Policy."[82] The most important vehicle in this process was the regular social evenings which the societies held. "At homes" allowed, indeed demanded, the most explicit exhibition of overt cultural signs; the evening succeeded only if all present indulged in wanton nostalgia. They thrilled to the skirl of the pipes; they wept at evocations of England's green and pleasant land; they savoured warm, dark ale; and they reverted to regional dialects. One of the founders of the Cumberland Association explained the societies' appeal: "I suppose everybody was homesick and wanted to associate with people that they could talk about the old country to."[83]

The clubs and lodges also provided British immigrants with important material support. Another element of cultural baggage, the organizations were modelled on friendly societies, the mutual aid associations which provided British workers with insurance and other benefits.[84] Because immigrants received real aid from clubs and lodges, emigration societies recommended membership to facilitate economic adjustment. The memberships of British societies in Winnipeg cut across class boundaries. Clubs and lodges provided much of their support to immigrants through the patronage of affluent members who had been incorporated into the local élite.

The best example of such ethnocentric philanthropy among Scots was provided by the St Andrew's Society. It had as its principal object "the affording of pecuniary, medical and other relief to such natives of Scotland and their descendants as may from sickness or other causes have fallen into distress." But because the Society was dominated by professionals and businessmen, the relief that it provided to working-class Scots was essentially charity. The Sons of Scotland and several shire associations which were better representative of the city's Scottish community as a whole, functioned more on the model of classic immigrants benefit societies.[85]

The Sons of England was the principal mutual benefit society for Englishmen. By 1929 the organization in Manitoba had 2500 members, most of whom belonged to Winnipeg lodges.[86] Immigrants joined the society partly because of the various forms of insurance—against unemployment, sickness, and death—which it provided. A Birmingham man who belonged to a west end lodge remembers that medical benefits "helped a little" in the days before the national health programs.[87] Even more important, however, was the informal assistance that the Sons of England provided immigrants. The society's constitution enjoined lodges to help "members rendered to economic hardship." The obligation was honoured. A Macclesfield butcher who arrived in Winnipeg during the recession of 1913 remembers that "going through the hard times we'd hear from clubs . . . that so and so didn't have any fuel; we'd vote to send him a ton of coal."[88] Help in finding work was provided on a similarly informal basis. Using a network of members who controlled patronage in private and public corporations, the Sons of England routinely arranged jobs for recent immigrants considered worthy of assistance. "They didn't encourage lazy people," a Londoner who joined the society soon after his arrival in Winnipeg in 1906 recalls; "they found them work. They found them jobs."[89]

Assuming that the acquisition of jobs is essential to the successful economic adjustment of immigrants, the British networks in Winnipeg appear to have been effective. This proposition will be elaborated through a discussion of the hiring practices of two large firms, the CPR and the T. Eaton Co. It would be possible to cite a number of public and private corporations, for instance the CNR, the street railway, or the police department, in fact virtually any Winnipeg employer that offered high-status jobs would do. But the CPR, which provided work primarily for men, and Eaton's, which hired women for the most part, were two of Winnipeg's largest employers.

The T. Eaton Company, the founder of which had emigrated from Ulster, became an important employer of British women. A Cumberland woman who worked in the Winnipeg store believes that "Eaton's was very partial to old-country people. . . . I don't think they ever turned anybody down."[90] Like other Canadian corporations, Eaton's recruited skilled workers in England. When the company began full-scale garment production in 1911, it despatched specifications to the British Women's Emigration Association which supplied several hundred seamstresses and shirt-makers. Brought out with company funds, the women, mainly Londoners, dominated Eaton's factories across the country. In the spring of 1912 one of the Association's field workers reported that "a good many of our girls" were employed by the Company in Winnipeg.[91] But generally personal networks were more important than overseas recruitment in placing women in work. A Glasgow woman recalls that she secured her job "through some friends of my aunts . . . I got into the bindery in Eaton's; . . . by the time I was sixteen I was working in an office."[92] The Company's British face was most manifest in the relatively high-status jobs in the sales departments. Eaton's appears to have believed, as a matter of policy, that its reputation for honesty and reliability in trade would be best preserved by the "respectability" of young women from the United Kingdom. Respondents, several of whom worked for the Company, invariably describe sales clerks as British. A Suffolk woman and old Eatonian remembers "most of them were girls, you know, like myself."[93]

Because of the composition of its work force, the Company developed services designed to serve the needs of immigrant women. An elaborate welfare system provided employees not only with medical care but with emotional support during "trouble of any kind." There was even a Women's Club complete with parlour "where under suitable chaperonage, such members as live in boarding houses may receive their young men friends."[94]

Because the expanding Canadian Pacific Railway required large supplies of skilled workers, especially in the metal trades, the company became an important employer for British artisans. CPR agents in the United Kingdom regularly recruited workers for the Company's great repair shops. But the railway also introduced the innovative policy of using the union which organized metal trade workers in Britain, the Amalgamated Society of Engineers (ASE), as a labour supplier. In 1904 the ASE, one of the few British unions established in Canada, estimated that 30 percent of the artisans in some CPR divisions were union members. But more than brokerage was involved in this condition; the union ordered members who had risen to supervisory positions to discriminate in favour of ASE, which meant British, artisans when hiring.[95] The experience of a machinist, who chose Winnipeg as his destination because of the presence of the CPR shops, demonstrates how the network operated. Upon arrival in Montreal he secured a letter of introduction from that city's ASE secretary which he presented to a shops foreman in Winnipeg who knew him from a previous sojourn. "So I got a start with my old boss, . . . [who] seemed pleased to see me again," the machinist told his brother. "I have been there a week now and am all right so far."[96]

Reynolds explained the British domination of Montreal's CPR shops in terms of "the strategic position of the foremen."[97] In Winnipeg, shops foremen were almost exclusively British artisans who belonged to the ASE. A Glasgow machinist, who worked thirty-eight years for the railway, recalls that "all the foremen that I had came from the Old Country; they got promoted."[98] These men routinely discriminated in favour of British workers when hiring. The Company apparently accepted the custom as an effective means of securing skilled workers. The manner in which a Londoner was hired during the 1908 recession was typical. He recalls "when I was in the freight sheds, I was on the look-out for some chance to get into the engineering department of the CPR and this friend of mine . . . got a friend of his to look out for me and I got into the engineering division."[99]

There is no reason to consider Winnipeg's British community atypical or its institutions unique. Like other immigrants, the British were distributed in Canada by general structural trends. And the social conditions they faced in cities varied little from place to place. Winnipeg's west end could as easily have been Toronto's Cabbagetown; the discriminating employer the latter city's street railway company. Forty years ago Reynolds demonstrated that the British of Hochelaga employed networks to facilitate their economic and cultural adjustment to life in Montreal. Across the country the British very likely used the same mechanisms as their compatriots in Winnipeg to pro-mote their collective self-interest. The group employed networks because they afforded competitive advantage in a heterogeneous society. A Londoner explained the assistance that his "club" gave immigrants in the most elemental terms: "we've got to stick together."[100]

NOTES

1. A. Ross McCormack, "Cloth Caps and Jobs: The Ethnicity of English Immigrants in Canada, 1900–1914," in *Ethnicity, Power and Politics in Canada*, ed. Jorgen Dahlie and Tina Fernando (Toronto: Methuen, 1981), 38–57.

2. Anthropologists have used the concept of networks more effectively than histo-rians. For some excellent examples of its application, see James L. Warson, ed., *Between Two Cultures: Migrants and Minorities in Britain* (Oxford: Oxford University Press, 1977).

3. Raymond Breton, "Institutional Completeness of Ethnic Communities and the Personal Relations of Immigrants," *American Journal of Sociology* 69 (1964): 194.

4. Charles Tilly and C. Harold Brown, "On Uprooting, Kinship and the Auspices of Migration," *International Journal of Comparative Sociology* 8 (1967): 67–75.

5. Michael Anderson, *Family Structure in the Nineteenth Century Lancashire* (Cambridge: Cambridge University Press, 1971); Patricia Branca, *Silent Sisterhood: Middle Class Women in the Victorian Home* (London: Croom Helm, 1973); Leonore Davodoff, Jean L. Esperance, and Howard Newby, "Landscape with Figures: Home and Community in English Society," in *The Rights and Wrongs of Women*, ed. Juliet Mitchell and Ann Oakley (London: Penguin, 1976); Peter N. Stearns, "Working-Class Women in Britain, 1890–1914," in *Suffer and Be Still: Women in the Victorian Age*, ed. Martha Vicinus (Bloomington: Indiana University Press, 1972); and Paul Thompson, *The Edwardians: The Remaking of British Society* (London: Paladin, 1977).

6. Since 1979 University of Winnipeg researchers have been conducting intensive life-history interviews with British immigrants who arrived in the city before 1914. The tapes are on deposit at the University.

7. *Dominions Royal Commission on Natural Resources, Trade and Legislation of Certain Portions of H.M. Dominions*, pt. 1, Migration, pp. 1912–13 (Cd. 6516), 109; *Friendly Leaves*, London (Aug. 1908).

8. Anderson, *Family Structure*, 66–67; and Joy Parr, *Labouring Children: British Immigrant Apprentices to Canada, 1869–1924* (Montreal: McGill-Queen's University Press, 1980), 20–21.

9. *East End Emigration Fund: Report 1905*, 4; and Public Archives of Canada (here-after PAC), Immigration Branch Records, RG 76, 6775-2, Culver to Marquette, 20 Feb. 1908.

10. The sample comprises 6599 persons of record, and their dependants, who immigrated under Salvation Army auspices, mainly in 1913. Their files contain some forty variables and are on deposit at the Salvation Army Archives in Toronto.

11. N = 544.

12. Couples: N = 159; families with children: N = 304. There is a statistically signifi-cant association between couples and migration "on spec" ($x^2 = 3.91$; df = 1; $p = .05$).

13. Interview 1-Wi-79-7.

14. *Imperial Home Reunion Association: Annual Report, 1911,* 6.

15. Anderson, *Family Structure,* 71–76; and Stearns, "Working Class Women," 113–14.

16. Interviews 1-Wi-81-3 and 4-Wi-79-3.

17. *East End Emigration Fund: Report 1905,* 5.

18. The parishes are All Saints, St Andrew's, and St Paul's. The records of the first are housed in the vestry offices while those of the latter two are on deposit at the Public Archives of Manitoba.

19. Interview 1-Wi-79-3.

20. N = 4336.

21. John S. and B.D. MacDonald, "Chain Migration, Ethnic Neighbourhood Formation and Social Networks," *Millbank Memorial Fund Quarterly* 42 (1964): 82. The italics are in the original.

22. Eugene Litwak, "Geographic Mobility and Extended Family Cohesion," *American Sociological Review* 25 (1960): 385–94.

23. Charles Stokes, "Canadianizing Britain," *The Westminster* 22 (1913): 457.

24. *British Women's Emigration Association: Report 1902,* 13; Parr, *Labouring Children,* 72–76; and Patrick A. Dunae, *Gentlemen Emigrants: From the British Public Schools to the Canadian Frontier* (Vancouver: Douglas and McIntyre, 1981), 69.

25. University of Winnipeg Archives, George Leach Papers, Geo. Leach to Lizzie Leach, 28 March 1911.

26. *East End Emigration Fund: Report 1912,* 26, and Oxford University, Bodleian Library, Sydney Marvin Papers, d. 258-179, Herbert Marvin to Sydney Marvin, 31 Oct. 1907.

27. Stuart B. Philpott, "Remittance Obligations, Social Networks and Choice Among Montserration Migrants in Britain," *Man* 3 (1968): 466; and James L. Watson, "Restaurants and Remittances: Chinese Emigrant Workers in London," in *Anthropologists in Cities,* ed. George M. Foster and Robert V. Kemper (Boston: Little, Brown, 1974), 219.

28. *Imperial Home Reunion Association: Annual Report, 1912,* 4.

29. Canada, *Sessional Papers,* 1903-15, no. 24, "Reports of the Postmaster General," appendix C.

30. Anderson, *Family Structure,* 65.

31. Interviews 1-Wi-79-18 and 1-Wi-79-1.

32. Marvin Papers, d. 260-27, John Marvin to Sydney Marvin, 14 Sept. 1908.

33. University of Winnipeg Archives, Nelson Smith Papers, account book.

34. Marvin Papers, d. 256-106, Thomas and John Marvin to Sydney Marvin, 25 June 1905.

35. PAC, RG 76, 34688-1, McCreary to Griffith, 1 June 1898, and Leach Papers, Geo. Leach to Lizzie Leach, 10 April 1911 and 2 May 1911.

36. Women: N = 2672; men: N = 3312.

37. Yona Ginsberg, "Rural–Urban Migration and Social Networks: The Israel Case," *International Journal of Comparation Sociology* 20 (1979): 243.

38. Interview 1-Wi-79-12.

39. N = 2840.

40. N = 777.

41. N = 600.

42. N = 701.

43. Interview 4-Wi-81-2.

44. N = 3333.

45. N = 800.

46. N = 267; Tilly and Brown, "On Uprooting," 143–44.

47. N = 276. For the sample as a whole, 40 percent of the men were unskilled and 40 percent skilled. Similarly the hypothesis appears also to be supported by the status distribution among immigrants travelling "on spec." While 10 percent of unskilled workers came out independently, 40 percent of the professionals migrated outside any network; only skilled building tradesmen, a group that sojourned in the North Atlantic economy, came close to the latter proportion with 33 percent.

48. Anderson, *Family Structure*, 119–20.

49. Interview 1-Wi-79-1.

50. Interview 2-Wi-79-1.

51. PAC, 76, 29501-3, Heath to Heath, 14 Nov. 1897, and 15197, Moffatt, "Report on Deportation," 15 Feb. 1905.

52. Philpott, "Remittance Obligations," 472; and Watson, "Restaurants and Remittances," 219.

53. *Church Emigration Society: Annual Report 1908*, 26.

54. *East End Emigration Fund: Report 1905*, 13.

55. Canadian Immigration and Population Study, *Immigration and Population Statistics* (Ottawa: Manpower and Immigration—Information Canada, 1974), 8; A.K. Cairncross, *Home and Foreign Investment 1870–1911: Studies in Capital Accumulation* (Cambridge: Cambridge University Press, 1953), 210; and interview 4-Wi-79-1.

56. "Reports of the Postmaster General," 1903–15; and Marvin Papers, d. 260-27, John Marvin to Sydney Marvin, 14 Sept. 1908.

57. Lloyd Reynolds, *The British Immigrant: His Social and Economic Adjustment in Canada* (Toronto: Oxford University Press, 1935), 118–22.

58. *Imperial Colonist* (April 1908).

59. Interview 1-Wi-79-10 and Interview 4-Wi-79-2.

60. Interview 2-Wi-79-6.

61. Interview 4-Wi-79-3.

62. Thompson, *The Edwardians*, 123–24; and interview 1-Wi-79-26.

63. Interview 1-Wi-79-1.

64. Robert F. Harney, "Boarding and Belonging," *Urban History Review* 7 (1978): 31; Michael Katz, *The People of Hamilton, Canada West: Family and Class in a Mid-Nineteenth Century City* (Cambridge: Harvard University Press, 1975), 230–32; John Modell and Tamara K. Hareven, "Urbanization and the Malleable Household: An Examination of Boarding and Lodging in American Families," *Journal of Marriage and the Family* 35 (1973): 470. For a qualification of this interpretation, see Sheva Medjyck, "The Importance of Boarding for the Structure of

the Household in the Nineteenth Century: Moncton, New Brunswick and Hamilton, Canada West," *Histoire sociale/Social History* 13 (May 1980): 207–13.

65. Interview 1-Wi-79-18.

66. Interview 1-Wi-79-13.

67. Interview 4-Wi-79-2; and *The Clarion*, 9 Aug. 1907.

68. Marilyn Barber, "The Women Ontario Welcomed: Immigrant Domestics for Ontario Homes, 1870–1930," *Ontario History* 72 (1980): 149–72; and Barbara Roberts, "'A Work of Empire': Canadian Reformers and British Female Immigration," in *A Not Unreasonable Claim: Women and Reform in Canada, 1880s–1920s*, ed. Linda Kealey (Toronto: Women's Press, 1979), 185–201.

69. PAC, RG 76, 33136-1, Gordon to Sifton, 7 Jan. 1897; Interview 2-Wi-79-9; and *Girls' Home of Welcome: Annual Report, 1906*, 3; N = 608.

70. Barber, "Women Welcomed," 158.

71. *Friendly Leaves*, London, (1905); *British Women's Emigration Association: Report 1903*, 16; and *Imperial Colonist* (April 1908).

72. *Girls' Home of Welcome: Annual Report, 1902*, 6; and *Annual Report, 1912*, 10; *Imperial Colonist* (July 1905); and Interview 1-Wi-79-3.

73. *Imperial Colonist* (May 1909), and *Friendly Leaves*, London (Aug. 1908).

74. Canada, *Census, 1901*, vol. 1, table 9; 1911, vol. 2, tables 2 and 5.

75. *Canadian Churchman*, 3 Feb. 1910; and *Church Emigration Society: Annual Report 1909*, 15.

76. *Church Emigration Society: Annual Report 1908*, 15.

77. *Imperial Colonist* (June 1910).

78. *Canadian Churchman* 19 March 1903 and 16 Oct. 1913; Reynolds, *British Immigrant*, 137; and Jane Synge, "Immigrant Communities—British and Continental European—in Early Twentieth Century Hamilton, Canada," *Oral History* 5 (1976): 46.

79. Interview 1-Wi-81-9.

80. Interview 1-Wi-79-7.

81. *Church Immigration Society: Annual Report, 1910*, 21.

82. Aberdeen, Banff and Kincardine Association, *Constitution* (Winnipeg, n.d.); and *The Englishman's Annual Register* (Winnipeg, 1919), 41.

83. Interview 1-Wi-79-7.

84. P.H.J.H. Gosden, *Self-Help: Voluntary Associations in the Nineteenth Century* (London: Batsford, 1973).

85. Public Archives of Manitoba, St Andrew's Society Collection, MG 10, C43, Box 4, *Constitution* (Winnipeg, 1886).

86. Sons of England, *Provincial Directory* (Winnipeg: Stovel Advocate, 1929).

87. Sons of England Benefit Society, *Constitution* (n.p., 1897); and interview 1-Wi-81-2.

88. Interview 1-Wi-79-18.

89. Interview 1-Wi-79-23.

90. William Stephenson, *The Store That Timothy Built* (Toronto, 1969), 63; and interview 1-Wi-79-7.

91. *Friendly Leaves*, London (Dec. 1911); *Imperial Colonist* (Feb. 1912), (April 1912); and *British Women's Emigration Association: Report 1913*, 48.

92. Interview 2-Wi-79-1.

93. Interview 1-Wi-79-12.

94. "The Scribe," *Golden Jubilee 1868–1919: A Book to Commemorate the Fiftieth Anniversary of the T. Eaton Co. Ltd.* (Toronto, 1919), 224–26.

95. *Amalgamated Engineers Journal* (Jan. 1900), (Nov. 1903), and (Feb. 1804).

96. Leach Papers, George Leach to Lizzie Leach, n.d., and 28 March 1911; George Leach to Will Leach, n.d.

97. Reynolds, *British Immigrant*, 104 and 167–68.

98. Interview 1-Wi-79-7.

99. Interview 1-Wi-79-28.

100. Interview 1-Wi-79-23.

THE IDEA OF CHINATOWN:
THE POWER OF PLACE AND
INSTITUTIONAL PRACTICE
IN THE MAKING OF
A RACIAL CATEGORY[*]

KAY J. ANDERSON

o

They come from southern China . . . with customs, habits and modes of life fixed and unalterable, resulting from an ancient and effete civilization. They form, on their arrival, a community within a community, separate and apart, a foreign substance within but not of our body politic, with no love for our laws or institutions; a people that cannot assimilate and become an integral part of our race and nation. With their habits of overcrowding, and an utter disregard for all sanitary laws, they are a continual menace to health. From a moral and social point of view, living as they do without home life, schools or churches, and so nearly approaching a servile class, their effect upon the rest of the community is bad. . . . Upon this point there was entire unanimity.[1]

It would be easy to interpret the words of Royal Commissioners Clute, Munn, and Foley in 1902 as further evidence, if more were needed, of the weight of racial discrimination in British Columbia during the stern years of the late nineteenth and early twentieth centuries. Like many other official utterances at the turn of the century, their words strengthen the claim that the Chinese, because of their distinctiveness, were subjected to many forms of victimization at the hands of a vigourously nativistic white community. Largely in response to that prejudice, overseas Chinese formed Chinatowns, or so a tradition of liberal discrimination studies has held. Chinatown has been a victimized colony of the East in the West.

[*] *Annals of the Association of American Geographers* 77, 4 (1987): 580–98. Reprinted with the permission of Blackwell Publishers.

Neighbourhoods of Chinese settlement in Western societies have been extensively studied throughout the twentieth century. Subjected to hostile receptions, Chinatowns serve as commentaries on the attitudes and behaviour of their host societies.[2] They have also been an entry point to many research questions in sociology and anthropology about cultural transfer overseas and the dynamics of social organization and community stratification in new environments.[3] A recent history of Toronto's Chinatown, for example, examines the transformation from "the homogeneous population of the traditional period" to "the diverse heterogeneous Chinese population today."[4] In social geography, Chinatown has been conceptualized as a launching point in the assimilation of Chinese immigrants, as an urban village pitted against encroaching land uses, as a product of segregation on the basis of race or ethnicity, and as a Chinese architectural form.[5] Chinatown has been viewed as either a ghettoized, minority community or as an "ethnic" community. One geographer summarizes the common social science conceptualization in his words: "Chinatown in North America is characterized by a concentration of Chinese people and economic activities in one or more city blocks which forms a unique component of the urban fabric. It is basically an idiosyncratic oriental community amidst an occidental urban environment."[6]

It is possible, however, to adopt a different point of departure to the study of Chinatown, one that does not rely upon a discrete "Chineseness" as an implicit explanatory principle. "Chinatown" is not "Chinatown" only because the "Chinese," whether by choice or constraint, live there. Rather, one might argue that Chinatown is a social construction with a cultural history and a tradition of imagery and institutional practice that has given it a cognitive and material reality in and for the West. It is, as Ley describes the elements of human apprehension, an object for a subject.[7] For if we do not assume that the term *Chinese* expresses an unproblematic relationship to biological or cultural constants but is in one sense a classification, it becomes apparent that the study of the Chinese and their turf is also a study of our categories, our practices, and our interests. Only secondarily is the study about host society attitudes; primarily it concerns the ideology that shaped the attitudes contained in the opening quotation. This step beyond "white" attitudes is critical because it is not prejudice that has explanatory value but the racial ideology that informs it. Such an argument is not unimportant for the conceptualization of Chinatown. Indeed it requires a more fundamental epistemological critique of the twin ideas of *Chinese* and *Chinatown*, of race and place.

It is not possible to investigate in one brief article the process of the classification of identity and place in the numerous contexts where the race idea has been institutionalized. Rather, my aim here is to argue the case for a new conceptualization of Chinatown as a white European idea with reference to one context, that of Vancouver, British Columbia. There, one of the largest Chinatowns in North America stands to this day, in part as an expression of the cultural abstractions of those who have been in command of "the power of definition," to use Western's valuable phrase.[8] But the thrust of the paper is not limited to the study of ideas. Indeed the significance of "Chinatown" is not simply that it has been a representation perceived in certain ways, but that it has been, like race, an idea with remarkable social force and material effect—one that for more than a century has shaped and justified the practices of powerful institutions toward it and toward people of Chinese origin.

The brevity of a paper also precludes attention to the century-long workings of the race definition process in Vancouver. Such a process has operated from the time Chinatown was reviled as Vancouver's public nuisance, promoted in the mid-1930s as its "Little Corner of the Far East," reconstructed in the 1950s and 1960s as a "slum," and finally under the aegis of multiculturalism courted by the state in the 1970s precisely for its perceived "Chineseness."[9] I thus confine the historical focus to Vancouver's Chinatown in the late nineteenth and early twentieth centuries, when its social definition was sweeping in both cause and effect. I thereby attempt to uncover the broader relationship between place, power, racial discourse, and institutional practice in one British settler society. Such an interpretation of Chinatown might be equally relevant to the making of other racial categories in Vancouver, to "Chinese" and "Chinatowns" in other settings, and to other racially defined people in other settings.

I begin by providing a brief outline of the geographical site of the subject of this paper. Following that sketch, I discuss conceptualization of Chinatown as a Western landscape type and then present empirical material from the Vancouver example.

A SKETCH OF THE SETTLEMENT AT DUPONT STREET, 1886–1900

By the time the City of Vancouver was incorporated in 1886, Chinese settlement in the city was severely proscribed. The senior levels of state had already intervened in the "Chinese question" and ensured that by the mid-1880s, there would be limits on the participation of Chinese-origin people in political life,[10] their access to Crown land,[11] and their employment on public works.[12] In 1885, after the completion of the trans-Canada railway, the federal government in Ottawa took a decisive step by imposing a head tax on Chinese entrants, and in 1903 Wilfrid Laurier's administration raised it to an almost prohibitive level of $500. Thus by the time of Vancouver's first municipal election in May 1886, when sixty Chinese-origin men were chased from the polls and denied the vote,[13] a culture of race was fully respected in separate statutory provisions for "Chinese" by the provincial and federal administrations.

From the late 1850s, when gold was first discovered in British Columbia, people from China lived and worked on Burrard Inlet. Most were men employed in unskilled jobs at the Hastings and Moodyville sawmills, but a minority opened stores to service the mill employees. By 1884, the population of Chinese on the inlet was 114[14] and a number of settlements had been established. One of these was built in the vicinity of Dupont Street where woods and a rocky outcrop afforded protection[15] and where nearby industries on

False Creek offered employment opportunities. Other small settlements of Chinese pioneers existed on the road to New Westminster, in Stanley Park, and the West End.

One such camp on the Brighouse Estate in the West End was particularly provocative to Vancouver's early European residents. Resentment was intense against the labourers who cleared land there at low cost, and on the night of 24 February 1887 some 300 rioters decided to escalate their intimidation strategies. Unimpeded by local police, they raided and destroyed the camps of Chinese labourers; they then attacked the washhouses, stores, shacks, and other structures in the vicinity of Dupont Street.[16] The day after, some ninety Chinese from that area were moved to New Westminster.[17] So lax were the local authorities in controlling the violence that the Smithe administration in Victoria, hardly known for its sympathy to Chinese, annulled Vancouver's judicial powers and dispatched special constables to take charge of what the attorney general described as Vancouver's decline into "mob rule."[18]

In the context of such hostility the Chinese returned to Vancouver and re-established a highly concentrated pattern of residence. Most of those who had fled returned directly to the original Dupont Street settlement, which also attracted many of the West End labourers after they completed the Brighouse Estate contract. It was a swampy district, with an adverse physical quality that paralleled the peripheral legal, political, social, and economic status of the pioneers it housed. Some lived more comfortably than others, however. Labourers mostly resided in wooden shacks, in conditions a Chinese statesman found "distressed and cramped" on his visit in 1903,[19] but merchants usually lived in elevated brick structures on the north and south sides of Dupont Street.

By the turn of the century, the total population of the settlement was 2053 men (of whom 143 were merchants and the rest workers), 27 women (16 of whom were wives of merchants), and 26 children.[20] Family life was the preserve of a small economic and political elite, some members of which established a property base in the area from the 1890s.[21] As W.A. Cumyow, a British Columbia-born court interpreter testified in 1901, "a large proportion of them would bring their families here were it not for the unfriendly reception . . . which creates an unsettled feeling."[22] Such was the marginal turf from which the Chinese launched their contested claim to Canadian life in the twentieth century.

CHINATOWN AS A WESTERN LANDSCAPE TYPE

How was it that the streets of Dupont, Carrall, and Columbia in Vancouver became apprehended as "Chinatown"? Whose term, indeed in one sense whose place was this? No corresponding term—"Anglo town"—existed in local parlance, nor were the residents of the likes of Vancouver's West End known as "Occidentals." Why then was the home of the pioneers known and intelligible as "Chinatown"? Consistent with the prevailing conceptualization of Chinatown as an "ethnic neighbourhood," we might anticipate the response that Chinese people—a racially visible and culturally distinct minority—settled and made their lives there through some combination of push and pull forces. One view, then, might be that the East lives on in the West and Chinatown expresses the values and experiences of its residents.

That people of Chinese origin, like other pioneers to North America, brought with them particular traditions that shaped their activities and choices in the new setting can hardly be disputed. Indeed an important tradition of scholarship has outlined the significance of such traditions for North American Chinatowns as overseas Chinese colonies. Needless to say, Chinese residents were active agents in their own "place making" as were the British-origin residents in Vancouver's Shaughnessy. My decision not to give primary attention to the residents' sense of place then is not to deny them an active role in building their neighbourhood nor of any consciousness they may have had as Chinese. Some merchants from China might have even been eager to limit contact with non-Chinese, just as China had obviated contact with Western "barbarians" over the centuries. Others, given a choice, might have quickly assimilated.

But the multiple reality of place invites another equally important but neglected viewpoint. The phenomenon of "John Chinaman's" overseas home was well-known to late nineteenth-century North Americans of European origin, whatever definitions of place the residents themselves might have held. Regardless of how each of the residents of such settlements defined themselves and each other—whether by class, occupation, ethnicity, region of origin in China, surname, generation, gender, or place of birth—the settlement was apprehended and targeted by European society through that society's cognitive categories. Without needing the acknowledgement or acceptance of the residents, Chinatown's representers constructed in their own minds a boundary between "their" territory and "our" territory.

In his important discussion of "imaginative geographies" such as Europe's "Orient," Edward Said argued that this distinction is one that "helps the mind to intensify its own sense of itself by dramatizing the distance and difference between what is close and what is far away."[23] This process suggests the argument that although North America's Chinese settlements have often been deliberately isolated, "Chinatown" has been an arbitrary classification of space, a regionalization that has belonged to European society. Like race, Chinatown has been a historically specific idea, a social space that has been rooted in the language and ethos of its representers and conferred upon the likes of Vancouver's Dupont Street settlement.

The word "arbitrary" is not unimportant here. "Chinese" have been residentially segregated and socially apprehended in North America on capricious grounds. Such a claim rests on the view that any classification of the world's populations into so-called "races" is arbitrary and imperfect. Despite the biological fact that systematic differences in gene frequencies exist among geographically or culturally isolated inbreeding populations, most contemporary biologists agree that genetic variability between the populations of Asia, Europe, and Africa is considerably less than that within those populations.[24] Apart from the visible characteristics of skin, hair, and bone by which we have been socialized to "see" what is popularly called a difference of "race," there are, as Appiah notes, "few genetic characteristics to be found in the population of England that are not found in similar proportions in Zaire or China."[25] The important point is that because genetic variation is continuous, "radical" difference cannot be conceptualized as absolute. "Racial categories form a continuum of gradual change, not a set of sharply demarcated types,"[26] a point that leads biologists Lewontin, Rose, and Kamin to argue: "Any use of 'racial' categories must take its justification from some other source than biology."[27]

A growing literature in ethnic studies would also suggest that categorizations such as "black," "white," "Oriental," or "Hispanic" are not rooted in an unproblematic difference of ancestral culture or ethnicity either. Frederick Barth began the critique in anthropology over twenty years ago when he claimed "we can assume no simple one-to-one relationship between ethnic units and cultural similarities and differences."[28] There is by now a convincing critique of the tradition of cultural relativism in North American ethnic studies, where ethnicity was accepted as an innate property of culture-bearing groups.[29] According to the more recent argument, ethnic groups are created socially by internal rules of exclusion and inclusion around idioms of actual or perceived common descent such as language and religion. Territory may also be a symbol and resource around which ethnic boundaries are negotiated.[30]

Clearly, there is a distancing in such a perspective from a reified notion of ancestral culture as an external system of values and practices. "Chineseness" is not an entity that is imbibed across generation and context by a person of Chinese origin in Hong Kong, a third generation Chinese-origin resident of Malaysia, a Chinese in mainland China, a person of Chinese descent in South Africa, and a fourth generation "Chinese Canadian" of Vancouver. Of course a subjective sense of ethnic identity can be strong in the absence of binding cultural traditions, but the important point here is that an analytical distinction must be drawn between self (or emic) definitions of identity and those etic classifications that are conferred from without. The former are predicated upon subjective or inclusive processes, whereas the latter are based upon exclusive processes.[31]

Clearly, I do not assume that race and racial categories are discretely given facts with their own descriptive and analytical utility. In itself, "race," and the prejudice it is often ipso facto assumed to inspire, explains nothing. For the purposes of social science, the concept of race must be located strictly in the realm of ideology. Of course other social scientists, including Western in geography,[32] have recognized race as problematic, but there have been few attempts to confront the epistemological implications of this in substantive research.[33] Almost no attention has been given to the process by which racial categories are themselves constructed, institutionalized, and transmitted over time and space. Banton suggests as much in his statement: "Though much has been said about the evils associated with racial classification, there has been little systematic study of the process."[34]

Chinatown has not been incidental to the structuring of this process in the example of the classification "Chinese" or "Oriental." Indeed by situating one such place "in process, in time,"[35] it is possible to demonstrate that as a Western idea and the concrete form Chinatown has been a critical nexus through which a system of racial classification has been continuously constructed. Racial ideology has been materially embedded in space (as we have seen in the earlier sketch) and it is through "place" that it has been given a local referent, become a social fact, and aided its own reproduction.

In itself, the idea of Chinatown would not be so important or enduring but for the fact it has been legitimized by government agents who make cognitive categories stand as the official definition of a people and place. In the Vancouver case, "Chinatown" accrued a certain field of meaning that became the justification for recurring rounds of government practice in the ongoing construction of both the place and the racial category. Indeed the state has played a particularly pivotal role in the making of a symbolic (and material) order around the idiom of race in Western societies. By sanctioning the arbitrary boundaries of insider and outsider and the idea of mainstream society as "white," the levels of the state have both "enforced" and "propagated" a white European hegemony.[36] Such links of the polity to the cultural realm have not been sufficiently explored in the recent literature on the state in capitalist societies.[37] A theoretical discussion of the state and racial ideology is beyond the scope of this paper, however.[38] I wish instead to pursue the theme of the concept of place and to investigate the manner in which one arm of white European hegemony—the civic authorities of Vancouver—sanctioned the racial and spatial categories of the dominant culture in the late nineteenth and early twentieth centuries.

"CHINATOWN" IN INTELLECTUAL CONTEXT: THE AGE OF THE RACE IDEA

Since classical times, Europeans have shared with other cultural traditions a tendency to generalize about the world's different populations.[39] Aristotle, for one, referred to his own "Hellenic race" around 300 BC as "high spirited and intelligent," while "Asiatics" were "inventive" but "wanting in spirit."[40] Indeed well before the birth of capitalism and colonialism, a European worldview made evaluative distinctions of "East" and "West," Christian and heathen, civilized and uncivilized. There was also a classical colour sensitivity that became heightened during the spread of Christianity from the tenth to the thirteenth centuries.[41] In subsequent centuries, European explorers relied upon, reinforced, and extended this early cognitive package. The Portuguese slave traffic in Africa in the fifteenth century[42] and, by 1650, slavery in the American colonies[43] sealed the outlook with the stamp of phenotype, and British imperialism from the late eighteenth century consolidated all the we/they distinctions into an ideological structure of formidable rigidity.

During the nineteenth century a transformation from ethnocentrism to a radical biological determinism took place, facilitated by a major theoretical effort in the new biological sciences. Certainly by the time immigrants from China arrived in British Columbia, the leap from colour to a fundamental difference of "race" had been solidly made by the scientific community of

Britain, North America, and Western Europe. Environmental explanation for human variation had been abandoned, and the focus of scientific atten tion had become fixed upon discrete types. Skull sizes and shapes were out ward signs of innate biological and cultural differences, and a generation o physical anthropologists measured them despite the nagging problem tha features such as skin colour, facial angle, and cranial shape did not co-vary in a systematic way.[44] Nor did Charles Darwin's evolutionary and environ mental theory prompt people to question their beliefs about absolute differ ences.[45] Indeed biologists, social scientists, and the populace at large made their own interpretation of *The Descent of Man*, taking it as confirmation that discrete races of variable "fitness" were governed by impersonal laws and engaged in an inexorable struggle.[46]

The early nineteenth-century discovery of the vast stretch of geologic time seemed to confirm the European view that human history was a kind of natural progression from barbarism to civilization. Like the transforma tion of the earth, the evolution of humanity was a formidably slow process in which savages might become "Caucasians," but the latter were thou sands of years "ahead" of the other races.[47] For all contemporary purposes, the races were immutably separate. "John Chinaman," for example, pos sessed properties that permitted him to achieve only a semicivilized, despotic state. His race was so retarded, claimed Judge J. Gray of the British Columbia Supreme Court, that he could see no reason why "the strong, broad shouldered superior race, superior physically and mentally, sprung from the highest types of the old world and the new world, [should be] expressing a fear of competition with a diminutive, inferior, and compara tively speaking, feminine race."[48] More often, however, the evolutionary doctrine was taken as a warning that the higher "races" were vulnerable to contamination from immigration and "hybridization" with those who would pass along their deficiencies.

According to this nineteenth-century worldview, Vancouver's Dupont Street settlement would be a generically "Chinese" or "Oriental" phenom enon. It would be *their* home, *their* evil—evidence, in itself, of a different capacity for achieving civilization. Even before a "Chinatown" had been identified as such in Vancouver, Secretary of State Chapleau conveyed the connotation of the term: "Their custom of living in quarters of their own— in Chinatowns—is attended with evils, such as the depreciation of property, and owing to their habits of lodging crowded quarters and accumulating filth, is offensive if not likely to breed disease."[49] Clearly, "Chinatown" would be an evaluative classification. Chapleau had formed his opinion from an investigation in California in 1884 when many witnesses referred to Chinatown and told British Columbians what to expect. "The Chinaman seems to be the same everywhere," Chapleau concluded;[50] and his Chinatown was "an ulcer lodged like a piece of wood in the tissues of the human body, which unless treated must cause disease in the places around it and ultimately to the whole body."[51]

With this diagnosis, how did respective Vancouver officials confront the district of pioneers from China? How did they justify the idea of Chinatown and invest it with the authority of some "natural" truth? The rest of the paper is devoted to answering that question and is divided into two sections; the first concerns the image of Chinatown as an unsanitary sink, and the second deals with the perception of Chinatown as a morally aberrant community. These components of the Chinatown idea in Vancouver converged in a public nuisance definition, which, I shall argue, became both a context and justification for the making of the racial category, "Chinese."

THE "CELESTIAL CESSPOOL": SANITARY DIMENSIONS OF THE CHINATOWN IDEA, 1886–1920

Shortly before the anti-Chinese riot of 1887, a reporter for the *Vancouver News* wrote: "The China Town where the Celestials congregate is an eyesore to civilization" and if the city could be "aroused to the necessity of checking the abuse of sanitary laws which is invariably a concomitant of the Chinese, [it] will help materially in preventing the Mongolian settlement from becoming permanent."[52] Four months later, a row of "hateful haunts" on Carrall Street was specifically singled out for the attention of council. There, warned the *News*, "in the nucleus of the pest-producing Chinese quarter . . . strict surveillance by the City will be necessary to prevent the spread of this curse."[53]

True to Chapleau's image of the "ulcer," it was the "ordinary Chinese washhouse scattered over the city"[54] that was an early target of civic concern. For a "race" so dirty, there was certainly plenty of work in the business of cleanliness, and by 1889 as many as ten of the thirteen laundries owned by merchants from China were located outside Dupont Street.[55] One medical health officer found the spread so fearful as to condemn the washhouse "an unmixed evil, an unmitigated nuisance"[56] and from the late nineteenth century, council sought means of keeping the "Chinese" laundry in its proper place.

Important judicial limits hampered the City of Vancouver, however. For one, Vancouver's municipal charter (and ultimately the British North America Act of 1864) did not grant legal competence to council to deny business licences to "particular nationalities or individuals."[57] The city's challenge was to circumvent such legal restrictions on its political will, and in the case of the "Chinese" laundry, numerous indirect strategies were devised. One alderman, for example, arrived at an artful solution. According to his 1893 bylaw, no washhouse or laundry in Vancouver could be erected outside specified spatial limits, "that is to say beyond Dupont Street and 120 feet on Columbia Avenue and Carrall Street, southerly from Hastings."[58]

During the late nineteenth century, an equally vigourous assault was launched in the name of sanitary reform on the wooden shacks of the Dupont Street settlement. In 1890, fear of cholera gripped the city and the local press demanded the city take action against "the people of Dupont Street" given that "in Chinese style . . . they will not fall into line for the purpose of maintaining cleanliness."[59] Fear of contamination from "the degraded humanity from the Orient"[60] was widespread in Vancouver society, and it was customary for letters to the editor to argue that although the "white" race was superior, "Oriental" afflictions would eventually subvert it.

The city fully shared this twist of Darwinist logic and in the mid-1890s—in a significant act of neighbourhood definition—council formally designated "Chinatown" an official entity in the medical health officer rounds and health committee reports.[61] Along with water, sewerage, scavenging, infectious disease, slaughter houses, and pig ranches, Chinatown was listed as a separate category and appointed "a special officer to supervise [it] under the bylaws."[62] One officer reported the following impressions in 1895:

> In my inspections of Chinatown this year, I have not observed any improvement in the cleanliness of the dwellings and surroundings. The former are becoming increasingly dilapidated and filthy and the latter, together with the shores of False Creek, are more and more saturated with manurial refuse and garbage. . . . All the cabins on the foreshore should be condemned and destroyed. In no other way is it possible to abate the nuisance arising from the constant deposition of filth and refuse by the occupants. At present they cannot be other than a standing menace to public health.[63]

In response to this and similar descriptions, four rows of shacks and cottages were destroyed by the city in the latter part of the decade.[64] In 1897, Medical Health Officer Thomas recommended the destruction of more shacks on Dupont Street because "they are dangerous to the health of the city,"[65] and two years later, Health Inspector Marrion served notices under the newly enacted Boarding House Bylaw after a visit by a number of city officials, including Mayor Garden.[66] The bylaw had been passed, without being so framed, as another attempt "to secure better regulation and supervision in the case of Chinese dwelling places."[67]

Marrion adopted a firm stance toward Chinatown from the time of his appointment in 1893. "The Chinese method of living is totally different to that of white people," he claimed in 1902. "The Japs try to obey the laws, but the Chinese are always on the lookout to evade them."[68] The living conditions the health inspector perceived along Dupont Street therefore had little to do with constraints on Chinese family settlement, job and pay discrimination, or the physical condition of the industrial inlet. Rather they were a product of "the difficulty to get Chinese people to adopt sanitary methods. . . . Even where every convenience is provided . . . Chinese are generally dirtier than whites."[69] Though blunt, Marrion's statements were entirely conformist for his day; he spoke not out of irrational prejudice but rather in the accepted vocabulary for discovering and characterizing the district that housed these pioneers to Vancouver. Identity and place were inextricably conflated, and the process of racial classification was corroborated with every official expedition.

Given this nearly universal scheme by which "Chinatown" was comprehended,[70] it was remarkable for a non-Chinese to argue: "It would be extremely difficult, if not impossible, even in the worst Chinese quarter, to parallel the state of affairs revealed amongst some white men in our city not so long ago in some of the cabins behind the Imperial Opera House."[71] Other evidence reveals that the bias of the municipal authorities' attention to sanitary matters in Dupont Street stemmed from their respect for the race idea. For example, the "Chinese" disease-bearing capacity was never borne out by actual disease or epidemic outbreaks recorded in the health inspector's reports or in the local press.[72]

At the same time, a number of Chinese-origin merchants made known their willingness to establish an amenable environment for business and residence. At odds with the typifications projected on the area, some merchants complained to council about the poor condition of Dupont Street and its sidewalks;[73] in 1899, twenty-four firms requested Dupont Street be sprinkled twice daily in the summer and back lanes be repaired;[74] and in 1905, a group of businessmen asked the Board of Works to pave Shanghai Alley.[75] Far from passive victims steeped in some fixed standard of living, or for that matter, hapless victims of "white" prejudice, the entrepreneurial sector of Chinatown effectively used its understanding of civic politics to try to elevate the physical condition and social profile of the neighbourhood. The Lim Dat Company was so dissatisfied with the city's refuse collection in the area that in 1906 it applied for a licence to conduct its own street-cleaning operation.[76]

The local unit of knowledge called "Chinatown" was carried forward in government practice and rhetoric well into the new century. In the same month as the riot of 1907 in Chinatown, Inspector Marrion could describe the neighbourhood in no more original terms than its "fowls, refuse, filth, dead dogs, and offal."[77] Whether or not the image of Chinatown as unsanitary was accurate, the perceptions of image makers intent on characterizing the area as alien were the ones that continued to have consequences.[78] Certainly the city was not prepared to compromise its idea of some essentially "Chinese" Chinatown in the face of challenges to its authority from the courts. Such obstructions served only to provoke new strategies, so assured were city officials of the integrity of their mission. By 1910, for example, a circle of city officials including Mayor Telford and Chief of Police Chamberlain, sought to achieve "full control of conditions in Chinatown." They hoped to "reform" the area with wider powers of bylaw enforcement that would stifle "Chinamen [who] manage to fight bylaws by successful applications for injunctions."[79] Fortunately for the residents, the provincial government was not inclined to concede such powers to the city.

It was not as if other districts in Vancouver, of actual or perceived marginal sanitary status, did not exist. In 1914, Inspector Hynes visited a district in Vancouver's East End that was home to a number of residents from Italy and found conditions "sickening in the extreme;" as "abominable" as the Chinese quarter.[80] But only the Dupont (by this time Pender) Street settlement was publicly known as a social and spatial unit according to putatively immutable "racial" qualities. Even the much-disliked settlement of pioneers from Japan on Powell Street appears to have escaped the crude neighbourhood characterization that gave "Chinatown" its name in

the early decades of this century. In part this can be explained by the widely
held view that, although the Japanese were also a foreign "race," their
homeland was not only a world power of some import in Britain's eyes, but
the Japanese seemed to possess a conception of progress and civilization
more assimilable to the European cultural tradition than was that of Japan's
more mysterious "Oriental" neighbour. (Such a generous view gave way to
extreme forms of discrimination by World War II, however.[81])

The distilled vision that was Vancouver's Chinatown was, for the city, a
pressing mandate, and its actions reinforced both the vision and the reality
of a neighbourhood and a people apart. Almost immediately after the
alleged murder of the wife of a well-known West End railway administrator by her "China-boy" in 1914,[82] Council led the clamour to have Chinese
removed from the schools. Based solely on the fact that the "boy" was educated in the school system, Council stated its "grave apprehension" at

> the prevailing practice of the School Board in permitting children
> and young men of Oriental race to attend our public schools. . . . By
> being indiscriminately thrown into contact with Orientals . . . our
> children are wantonly exposed to Oriental vices at an age when
> revolting incidents may be indelibly stamped upon their minds.
> Furthermore the health of our children is endangered by such close
> association with Oriental children, many of whom hail from habita-
> tions where reasonable sanitation and cleanliness are not only
> despised but utterly disregarded. In some cases, these Orientals
> come into our public school classrooms with their apparel polluted
> with the fumes of noxious drugs and germs of loathsome diseases
> on their persons.[83]

Although Council's request to Victoria for school segregation foundered
on legal obstacles, the city continued to wield its own power tirelessly. In
the following year, the local press described "Chinatown" as no less than
"besieged." "Lined up on this side," wrote the *Sun*,

> is the civic authority led by the medical health officer, the building
> inspector and the chairman of the health committee supported by
> the City aldermen. This great civic force has as its ally the law in
> the form of health bylaws, building regulations, police officers and
> penalties. Arrayed against this seemingly formidable army is the
> wily Oriental with his fondness for defying the civic powers. . . .
> Civic regulations are dust to the Chinaman.[84]

Clearly, the idea of "Chinatown" was being inherited by successive
rounds of officials who adopted the conceptual schemes of their predecessors. The health committee of council described the area as a "propagating
ground for disease" in 1919, and, true to old remedies, an inspection team
was set up to monitor the area despite the fact that still no concrete evidence confirmed that Chinatown was a threat to public health.[85] Within ten
months, the owners of more than twenty lodgings were threatened with
orders to condemn their buildings, including the Chinese Hospital at 106

Pender Street East.[86] Indeed, well into the 1920s the city operated assertively in the idiom of race, indiscriminately raiding Chinatown and harassing residents about bylaw compliance.[87]

In translating racial ideology into official practice, the civic authorities of Vancouver performed an important legitimizing role in the social construction of Chinatown in the late nineteenth and early twentieth centuries. Chinatown was not simply an idea. It had a concrete referent in the form of a concentrated community whose physical presence propped up the vision of identity and place we have been examining. Furthermore, the circumstances of Chinese immigration to Canada probably encouraged objectively poor living conditions in many sectors of the community. In that sense, the material reality of the district justified and fulfilled the prophecy of Chapleau's "Chinatown." But it was the mutually reinforcing ideas of race and place, and their scope and influence in British Columbian culture, that gave the district its coherence as a discrete place in the social consciousness of its representers. In the eyes of successive civic officials, "Chinatown" signified no less than the encounter between "West" and "East"; it distinguished and testified to the vast asymmetry between two "races." As such, Chinatown was not a benign cultural abstraction but a political projection, through which a divisive system of racial classification was being structured and institutionalized.

VICE-TOWN: MORAL DIMENSIONS OF THE CHINATOWN IDEA, 1886–1920

Much as the "West" has defined the "Orient,"[88] Vancouver's "Chinatown" was a collection of essences that seemed to set the Chinese fundamentally apart. Above all, it was nonwhite, non-Christian, uncivilized, and amoral. It was something of a "counter-idea," into which were concentrated qualities thought to be in opposition to the European ingroup.[89] Matters of hygiene were only part of the vocabulary out of which this idea was being constructed. Equally significant and perhaps more effective were moral associations. Because the "Chinese" were inveterate gamblers, "Chinatown" was lawless; as opium addicted, Chinatown was a pestilential den; as evil and inscrutable, Chinatown was a prostitution base where white women were lured as slaves. "Is there harm in the Chinaman?" Reverend Fraser asked a meeting of the Asiatic Exclusion League in 1907. "In this city," he said, "that would be answered with one word, 'Chinatown,' with its wickedness unmentionable."[90]

Two city hardliners, Police Magistrate Alexander and Chief of Police Chamberlain, legitimized a particular vision of Chinatown in their everyday business. As the home of the "racial other,"[91] Chinatown signified many impulses that Europeans feared and attempted to repress in themselves. Indeed, only those aspects of Chinese living that conformed to the categorization "Chinese" were being filtered by members of the governing body of Vancouver, as they were by European communities throughout North America.[92]

Why did the municipal officials of Vancouver reach the conclusic
they did when describing and managing Chinatown? How was it t
Chamberlain and Alexander were concerned with [a] few elements
Chinese living] and not others? The relevance of this question has be
obscured by the familiar prejudice framework for the study of race re
tions. That perspective has tended to explain away such systems of image
and indeed racial categories themselves, in some unproblematic "whit
predisposition toward nonwhites.[93] In particular, the explanatory foc
upon prejudice and discrimination (attitudes and behaviour) has obscur
the deeper process by which classifications have themselves been bu
around the concept of race.

Or again, economic competition was a major rallying point for an
Chinese sentiment in British Columbia, as it was in other areas of Chine
settlement.[94] But it, too, has been less a primary cause of such sentime
than an outcome of the more decisive role that must be accorded collecti
conceptions about the "Chinese" as a category in the European cultural tr
dition. Of course, racial ideology did not alone cause a segregated occup
tional order in British Columbia, and another paper might examine t
relationship between racial ideology and the development of a capital
economy in that province.[95] The point here is that ideological formulatio
have made their own powerful and distinct contribution to such structur
of inequality and must be examined on their own terms.[96] Were it not f
ideas about "race"—myths that were readily exploited by owners of capi
in British Columbia (see the testimony of capitalists in the royal commissi
of 1885) and by the Dominion government during the construction of t
trans-Canada railway[97]—so-called "coolie" labour might not have been
cheap; nor might the entry of labour from China have been considered an
thing but "natural." Certainly there would have been no logical basis
which to charge and penalize the Chinese as a category with collective
undermining the standard of living and the bargaining power of t
"white" worker.

What then were the features of the language, imagery, and rheto
with which the "West" interpreted China in the late eighteenth and nin
teenth centuries? What notions of China (in conjunction with the race ide
prepared the likes of Chamberlain and Alexander to confront Vancouve
Chinatown "intelligently" rather than "blindly"?[98] This is a question tha
can address only briefly here.

"THE HEATHEN CHINEE"

The desire of Westerners to measure China against an idealized vision
themselves dates as far back as the thirteenth century when travelle
imbued with the Greek dualisms of "Europe" and "Asia," "East" ar
"West," "Orientis" and "Occidentis," set out to uncover the unknown
Consistent with the Greek conception of "Asia" as the oldest, richest, ar
most populous of civilizations, medieval travellers such as Marco Polo we
captivated by China's opulent ruler, the abundance of silks, rugs, ar

porcelains, and the splendour and size of Chinese cities. China was the vast, farthest shore of the East, the most marginal, isolated, and ipso facto most Oriental of all of Asia, and it was this romantic view that lingered in the European consciousness for more than three centuries.[100]

By the late seventeenth and certainly by the early eighteenth century, Europe's emerging image of itself as imperial, industrial, enlightened, and progressive provided the benchmark for different perceptions of "the Middle Kingdom." A new construction upon China's antiquity began to be articulated that focussed relationally upon its changelessness, homogeneity, and uniformity—"the despotism of Custom"—as John Stuart Mill wrote in his mid-nineteenth century essay *On Liberty*.[101] With British military power in ascendancy, the European image of China began to darken. The Chinese became "a people of eternal standstill," or as Mr Chapleau put it: "Races change slowly but the stationariness of the Chinese seems phenomenal."[102] In so conceiving China, and more generally "Asia" as a negative—that is, non-European—construct, scholars have argued that Europe was giving force to its own idea of itself.[103]

Miller traces this decline in China's image from the time of its first trade with America in 1785.[104] It was around that time that frustrated traders, diplomats, and missionaries sent home the message of China's resistance to their commercial and evangelical entreaties. From the records of fifty traders to China from 1785 to 1840, Miller identifies the following themes: China's technological and scientific backwardness; its military ineptitude, from which many traders deduced a national cowardice; the venality of the Chinese character, as revealed by their devotion to gambling and their "diabolical cunning"; and their peculiarity, for which one had only to look to their theatre, music, insistence on writing up and down the page, slant eyes, and their propensity for eating birds nests.

The diplomat's memoirs and accounts—from Lord Macartney's in 1792 to the embassy sent by President Jackson in 1892—were more important than were the traders' reports in shaping American public opinion. Despite some nostalgia for Marco Polo's Old Cathay, most memoirs were contemptuous of the backwardness and vice that China's despotism was thought to inspire. Military impotence, infanticide, depravity, and addiction to "pernicious" drugs were all construed as signs of a civilization in decline.

As opinion maker, however, it was the nineteenth century Protestant missionaries, armed with their own press, who commanded the widest audience in America. Unlike the Jesuits, who had seen valuable preparation in Confucianism for Christian teachings, Protestant missionaries to China in the nineteenth century were scathing critics. For them, there could be no more damning evidence against Confucianism than the rampant idolatry, infanticide, slavery in women, polygamy, opium obsession, noonday orgies, treachery, and endemic gambling. So puny was the record of conversions in fact, that some missionaries concluded that the wily Chinese were conscious agents of Satan who deliberately humiliated God with acts of immorality.

DISCOVERING "THE HEATHEN CHINEE"

In February 1912, a newspaper feature on Vancouver's Chinatown began:

> Conditions prevailing in the cities of China are familiar topics of the returned missionary, who will dwell at length upon the awful condition of the slums, the armies of the unwashed, and the prevalence of vice in the shape of opium smoking and gambling, in the empire across the seas. Would you believe that the same condition of affairs is in existence in the city of Vancouver in our Chinatown, which constitutes a considerable quarter on Pender street between Canton and Shanghai alleys?[105]

Yet how else, we might ask, could Pender Street be known?

The plight of the fallen woman disappearing into the clutches of procurors in segregated "Oriental" vice districts was, from the turn of the century, a pressing concern of Vancouver's moral reform groups.[106] Not surprisingly, therefore, anxiety was heightened in Vancouver by the location of the "restricted area" (where prostitution was tolerated by the police right next to the Chinese quarter from the time the city was incorporated. But the reform groups' worst fears were realized in 1906 when prostitutes moved en masse to Shanghai Alley following a Council request for their eviction from the prior location.[107] No police protection like that offered the residents of Mount Pleasant (the area that was expected to receive the dislodged prostitutes) was extended to Chinatown, and for some time it became the new "restricted area" for prostitution in Vancouver. Later, in the face of much local protest about the unhappy combination of prostitutes and "Chinamen" in the one location, the restricted area was moved to other areas in the East End.[108]

Of these various niches where prostitution enjoyed a blind eye in Vancouver, an especially evil construction was cast upon the practice only in "Chinatown." Wrote one indignant citizen about the "almond-eyed law breakers" in 1908: "A regular traffic in women is conducted by the Chinese in Vancouver. The Chinese are the most persistent criminals against the person of any woman of any class in this country . . . all this goes on in a Christian community."[109] Most often, petitions to Council concerning prostitution dwelt on the risk to property values; however in Chinatown, the voice of the nineteenth-century Protestant missionary reverberated. One resident contended: "It is a disgrace to our city to have that *evil* in *that* location."[110]

Stamped with the weight of a typification, Chinatown was intelligible only in terms of a few (unflattering) criteria. Class distinctions paled beneath the more influential racial characterization. Indeed council simply ignored a 1906 petition from the Chinese Board of Trade, which, in protesting the unimpeded movement of prostitutes into Shanghai Alley and Canton Street, reflected concerns not far removed from the most traditional of Christian mission ministers in Chinatown. "We the undersigned (30 merchants and others," the Board wrote, "beg leave to respectfully call your attention to the fact that several of the women of ill repute . . . are moving into Shanghai Alley and Canton Streets. This we consider most undesirable

It is our desire to have our children grow up learning what is best in Western civilization and not to have them forced into daily contact with its worst phases."[111]

Some Chinese merchants mounted a campaign in Vancouver against another perceived vice out of which the non-Chinese concept of place was constructed. In 1908, the merchants' anti-opium league sent a petition to Ottawa asking the federal government to "decisively exercise its authority and powers to prohibit the importation, manufacture and sale of opium into Canada so that the social, physical, and moral condition of both Chinese and Europeans may be vastly improved."[112] But try as some merchants did to counter the idea of Chinatown, the drug that Britain had introduced to China in the 1840s was now a powerful metaphor for neighbourhood definition. In 1889, a newspaper reporter who accompanied Marrion on one of his tours of Chinatown's bachelor shacks, remarked that "the luxury of smoking opium is beyond comprehension in such tight boxes."[113] Another in 1908 noted the fine access that such tight quarters provided to "bargain-rate heaven."[114] And like the construction put upon "white" participation in Chinatown's bawdy houses, the large extent of non-Chinese use of opium that the Minister of Labour, Mackenzie King, uncovered in his 1908 investigation only confirmed the belief that Chinatown was a menace to civilized life.[115] White drug use did not prejudice, but rather validated, the more comforting racial and spatial category.

Once the image of "Chinatown" as an opium den was consolidated, no amount of counter-evidence could acquit it and all manner of accusations could be adduced, especially by politicians, to support the neighbourhood image. By the 1920s, when the race idea was being feverishly exploited in British Columbia, the old opium image fed and was assimilated into an image of Chinatown as a narcotics base and "Chinese" as dangerous drug distributors. In March 1920, for example, an editorial warned: "The traffic in habit-forming drugs centres in Chinatown" and "if the only way to save our children is to abolish Chinatown, then Chinatown must and will go, and quickly."[116]

In the context of rising anti-Chinese sentiment in the House of Commons, Consul General Yip and the Chinese Benevolent Association of Vancouver formed a Self Improvement Committee to try to elevate the reputation of their neighbourhood.[117] Cumyow (by this time president of the Chinese Benevolent Association) also spoke out against the Sun's vendetta, calling attention to "the suggestion of Police Commissioner Buckworth that Chinese vendors are merely conveniently used and that the traffic is controlled by persons other than Chinese."[118] But the irrepressibly anti-Chinese member of Parliament for Vancouver Centre, H. Stevens (also secretary of the Vancouver Moral Reform Association) was not to be deterred, and in a series of speeches in the House of Commons in the early 1920s, he transmitted these most recent charges against Vancouver's Chinatown to the senior level of government. "The basis of the pernicious drug habit on the Pacific Coast is Asiatic," said Stevens in 1921. "We have seen in Vancouver almost innumerable cases of clean, decent, respectable young women from some of the best homes dragged down by the dope traffic and very, very largely through the medium of the opium dens in the Chinese quarter."[119]

A more lurid tale of Chinatown's "snow parties" was told for Parliament in 1922 by L. Ladner of Vancouver South. Within months, the federal authorities amended the Opium and Narcotic Drug Act to provide for the deportation of aliens found guilty of any drug offence.[120] In 1923, the language of race was conferred its most extreme official seal when Canada's door was effectively closed to immigrants from China for twenty-five years.[121] With considerable consequences, then, local definitions of place continuously influenced rounds of legislative activity at all levels of government in the ongoing construction of this category of outsiders.

Known to police for "inveterate" gambling, the "heathen Chinese" was actively pursued by officers of the Vancouver police force from the 1890s to the late 1940s. By that time, the extent of the harassment had become embarrassingly transparent even to the city. Until then, however, it was rare to find a year that the *Chinese Times* and the local press did not report a raid on Chinatown's gambling quarters. Cumyow saw the record as more telling of the enforcement practices of the police than of any intrinsic "Oriental" proclivity to gamble, as he told the royal commission in 1901:

> There is proportionately a large amount of gambling among the Chinese. Some do gamble for large amounts, but more commonly, the play is for amusement only and for small sums to pass the time as this is done in the common room of the boarding house. If a police raid is made and any are caught playing, all are arrested for gambling and looking on. If the same course were pursued in relation to white men, gamblers could be caught in barrooms and of course all who were at the bar would be arrested as onlookers.[122]

Just as the opium den raids vindicated widespread assumptions about the moral laxity of the Chinese, the formidable scrutiny that Chinatown experienced from the city for gambling sprang from the confirmed popular assumptions about a generically addicted "Chinaman." And one vice bred another, as Alderman McIntosh observed in 1915. Gambling and opium in Chinatown required constant civic vigilance he claimed, because they were associated with tuberculosis and slavery in women.[123]

Yet gambling was not restricted to the Pender Street area. One letter to the editor in 1900, appealing for greater control of gambling in the city, said: "Everyone knows that gambling goes on promiscuously all over Vancouver, in clubs, in hotels, in saloons, in rooms connected with saloons and in private houses."[124] But only in "Chinatown," was a neighbourhood image built around both its practice and the attempts of police—confronted by "ingenious Oriental systems of spring doors and getaway rat tunnels"[125]— to suppress it. So perturbed were Chinese merchants by this harassment that in 1905, the Chinese Board of Trade protested:

> The members of our board are law abiding citizens. Many of them have been residents of this country for a number of years and are large holders of real estate, payers of taxes and other civic assess-

ments. The members . . . have been constantly annoyed by what we believe to be an unjustifiable intrusion of certain members of the Vancouver Police Force . . . in the habit of going into our stores and rooms where our families live, showing no warrant whatsoever, nor do they claim any business with us. . . . We are subjected to indignities and discriminating treatment to which no other class would submit and to which [under] *your* laws, we are advised, we are not required to submit.[126]

CONCLUSION

I have argued that "Chinatown" was a social construct that belonged to Vancouver's "white" European society, who, like their contemporaries throughout North America, perceived the district of Chinese settlement according to an influential culture of race. From the vantage point of the European, Chinatown signified all those features that seemed to set the Chinese irrevocably apart—their appearance, lack of Christian faith, opium and gambling addiction, their strange eating habits, and odd graveyard practices. That is, it embodied the white Europeans' sense of difference between immigrants from China and themselves, between the East and the West. This is not to argue that Chinatown was a fiction of the European imagination; nor can there be any denying that gambling, opium use, and unsanitary conditions were present in the district where Chinese settled. The point is that "Chinatown" was a shared characterization—one constructed and distributed by and for Europeans, who, in arbitrarily conferring outsider status on these pioneers to British Columbia, were affirming their own identity and privilege. That they directed that purpose in large part through the medium of Chinatown attests to the importance of place in the making of a system of racial classification.

Studies of the social meaning of place in human geography have too rarely taken measure of the role of powerful agents, such as the state, in defining place. Yet those with the "power of definition" can, in a sense, create "place" by arbitrarily regionalizing the external world. In the example here, Chinatown further became the isolated territory and insensitive representation its beholders understood in part through the legitimizing activities of government. Perhaps not all places are as heavily laden with a cultural and political baggage as "Chinatown." But Chinatown is important in pointing up once again the more general principle that a negotiated social and historical process lies behind the apparently neutral-looking taxonomic systems of census districts.[127] More importantly perhaps, the manipulation of racial ideology by institutions is additional testimony to the fact that a set of power relations may underpin and keep alive our social and spatial categories.

The importance of these "imaginative geographies" cannot be underestimated because, as we have seen, they organize social action and political practices. Indeed the idea and influence of "Chinatown" is further evidence of the growing consensus in human geography that our landscape concepts, as symbolic resources, have a critical structuring role in the making of wider social processes. In the course of its evolution, Chinatown reflected the race definition process, but it also informed and institutionalized it, providing a context and justification for its reproduction. Pender Street has been the home of the overseas Chinese to be sure, but "Chinatown" is a story, which, in disclosing the categories and consequences of white European cultural hegemony, reveals more the insider than it does the outsider.

NOTES

1. Canada, *Report of the Royal Commission on Chinese and Japanese Immigration* (Ottawa: S.E. Dawson, 1902), 278.

2. G. Barth, *Bitter Strength: A History of the Chinese in the United States, 1850–70* (Cambridge: Harvard University Press, 1964); S. Lyman, *Chinese Americans* (New York: Random House, 1974); H. Palmer, *Patterns of Prejudice: A History of Nativism in Alberta* (Toronto: McClelland & Stewart, 1982); C. Price, *The Great White Walls Are Built: Restrictive Immigration to North America and Australia, 1836–1888* (Canberra: Australian National University Press, 1974); P. Roy, "British Columbia's Fear of Asians, 1900–50," *Histoire sociale/Social History* 13, 25 (1980): 161–72; P. Ward, *White Canada Forever: Popular Attitudes and Public Policy Toward Orientals in British Columbia* (Montreal: McGill-Queen's University Press, 1978).

3. L. Crissman, "The Segmentary Structure of Urban Overseas Chinese Communities," *Man* 2, 2 (1967): 185–204; B. Hoe, *Structural Changes of Two Chinese Communities in Alberta, Canada*, National Museum of Man Mercury Series, no. 19 (Ottawa: National Museum of Man, 1976); V. Nee and B. Nee, *Longtime Californ'* (Boston: Houghton Mifflin, 1974); M. Weiss, *Valley City: A Chinese Community in America* (Cambridge, MA: Shenkman, 1974); E. Wickberg, H. Con, G. Johnson, and W.E. Willmott, *From China to Canada: A History of the Chinese Communities in Canada* (Toronto: McClelland & Stewart, 1982); B. Wong, *Chinatown: Economic Adaptation and Ethnic Identity of the Chinese* (New York: Holt, 1982).

4. R. Thompson, "The State and the Ethnic Community: The Changing Social Organization of Toronto's Chinatown" (PhD thesis, University of Michigan, 1979), 361.

5. G. Cho and R. Leigh, "Patterns of Residence of the Chinese in Vancouver" in *Peoples of the Living Land*, ed. J. Minghi, Geographic series, no. 15 (Vancouver: Tantalus, 1972); R. Cybriwsky, "The Community Response to Downtown Redevelopment: The Case of Philadelphia's Chinatown" (paper presented at the Association of American Geographers Conference, Minneapolis, 1986); D. Lai, "Socioeconomic Structures and the Viability of Chinatown" in *Residential and Neighbourhood Studies*, ed. C. Forward, Western Geographical series, no. 5 (Victoria: University of Victoria, 1973); C. Salter, *San Francisco's Chinatown: How Chinese a Town?* (San Francisco: R. & E. Research Associates, 1978).

6. Lai, "Socioeconomic Structures," 101.

7. D. Ley, "Social Geography and the Taken-for-Granted World," *Transactions of the Institute of British Geographers* 2 (1977): 498–512.

8. J. Western, *Outcast Capetown* (Minneapolis: University of Minnesota Press, 1981), 8.

9. K. Anderson "'East' as 'West': Place, State and the Institutionalization of Myth in Vancouver's Chinatown, 1880–1980" (PhD thesis, University of British Columbia, 1986).

10. In 1875, the jurisdictional competence of the province to deny the franchise to people of Chinese origin was affirmed. (British Columbia, *Statutes*, 1875, 35 Vict., c. 26, s. 22).

11. Clause 122 of the Land Act deemed it unlawful "for a commissioner to issue a preemption record of any Crown land, or to sell any portion thereof to any Chinese." (Ibid., 1884, 51 Vict., c. 16).

12. By 1900, an anti-Chinese clause was introduced in government contracts that refused provincial aid to public works contractors who employed "Orientals" (British Columbia, *Journals of the Legislative Assembly*, 1900, 29: 125).

13. A. Morley, *Vancouver: From Milltown to Metropolis* (Vancouver: Mitchell Press, 1961), 73.

14. J. Morton, *In the Sea of Sterile Mountains* (Vancouver: J.J. Douglas, 1977), 144.

15. Q. Yip, *Vancouver's Chinatown* (Vancouver: Pacific Printers, 1936), 11.

16. "Outbreak Against the Chinese," *Vancouver News*, 25 Feb. 1887, 1.

17. "The Chinese Leaving," ibid., 26 Feb. 1887, 1.

18. P. Roy, "The Preservation of Peace in Vancouver: The Aftermath of the Anti-Chinese Riot of 1887," *BC Studies* 31 (1976): 44–59; "Their Drastic Measures," *Vancouver News*, 2 March 1887, 1; "The Robson Regime," ibid., 16 March 1887, 1.

19. L. Ma, "A Chinese Statesman in Canada, 1903: Translated from the Travel Journal of Liang Ch'i-ch'ao," *BC Studies* 59 (1983): 34.

20. *Royal Commission on Chinese and Japanese Immigration*, 13.

21. See P. Yee, "Business Devices from Two Worlds: The Chinese in Early Vancouver," *BC Studies* 62 (1984): 44–67.

22. *Royal Commission on Chinese and Japanese Immigration*, 236.

23. E. Said, *Orientalism* (New York: Vintage Books, 1978), 55.

24. E.g., D. Farish, *Biology: The Human Perspective* (New York: Harper and Row, 1978); R. Lewontin, S. Rose, and L. Kamin, *Not in Our Genes: Biology, Ideology, and Human Nature* (New York: Pantheon, 1984); A. Montagu, *The Concept of Race* (New York: Free Press, 1964).

25. A. Appiah, "The Uncompleted Argument: Du Bois and the Illusion of Race," *Critical Inquiry* 12, 1 (1985): 22.

26. M. Marger, *Race and Ethnic Relations* (Belmont, CA: Wadsworth, 1985), 12.

27. Lewontin, Rose, and Kamin, *Not in Our Genes*, 127.

28. F. Barth, *Ethnic Groups and Ethnic Boundaries: The Social Organization of Cultural Difference* (Boston: Little, Brown, 1969), 14.

29. E.g., P. Jackson, "A Transactional Approach in Puerto Rican Culture," *Review/Revista Interamericana* 11 (1981): 53–68; C. Peach, "The Force of West Indian Island Identity in Britain" in *Geography and Ethnic Pluralism*, ed. C. Clarke, D. Ley, and C. Peach (London: George Allen and Unwin, 1984), 214–30; R. Perrin, "Clio as an Ethnic: The Third Force in Canadian Historiography," *Canadian Historical Review* 64, 4 (1983): 441–67; S. Steinberg, *The Ethnic Myth: Race, Ethnicity, and Class in America* (New York: Atheneum, 1981); G. Watson, "The Reification of Ethnicity and Its Political Consequences in the North," *Canadian Review of Sociology and Anthropology* 18, 4 (1981): 453–69.

30. G. Suttles, *The Social Order of the Slum* (Chicago: University of Chicago Press, 1968).

31. M. Banton, *Ethnic and Racial Competition* (Cambridge: Cambridge University Press, 1983), 104; R. Cohen, "Ethnicity: Problem and Focus in Anthropology," *Annual Review of Anthropology* 7 (1978): 379–403.

32. Western, *Outcast Capetown*.

33. One volume edited by C. Husband—"Race" in *Britain: Continuity and Change* (London: Hutchinson, 1982)—addresses aspects of the culture of race in contemporary Britain. The literature on labeling may be relevant here. For original statements on mental illness, see E. Goffman, *Stigma* (Englewood Cliffs, NJ: Prentice-Hall, 1963), and on crime, see D. Matza, *Becoming Deviant* (Englewood Cliffs, NJ: Prentice-Hall, 1969).

34. M. Banton, *The Idea of Race* (London: Tavistock, 1977), 19.

35. P. Abrams, *Historical Sociology* (Bath: Pitman Press, 1982).

36. The words *enforced* and *propagated* are borrowed from MacLaughlin and Agnew's discussion of the state and socially based hegemonies. J. MacLaughlin and J. Agnew, "Hegemony and the Regional Question: The Political Geography of Regional Industrial Policy in Northern Ireland, 1945–72," *Annals of the Association of American Geographers* 76 (1986): 247–61. On the state's role in South Africa, see G. Pirie, "Race Zoning in South Africa: Board, Court, Parliament, Public," *Political Geography Quarterly* 3 (1984): 207–21, and Western, *Outcast Capetown*.

37. G. Clark and M. Dear, *State Apparatus* (London: Allen and Unwin, 1984); P. Saunders, *Urban Politics: A Sociological Interpretation* (London: Hutchinson, 1979), ch. 4.

38. See Anderson, "'East' as 'West'," ch. 1.

39. See Tuan's figure of traditional Chinese world views with zones of increasing barbarism away from the Chinese court. Y.-F. Tuan, *Topophilia* (Englewood Cliffs, NJ: Prentice-Hall, 1974). On the universality of the categorization process see also P. Berger and T. Luckmann, *The Social Construction of Reality* (Garden City, NY: Doubleday, 1966).

40. A. March, *The Idea of China: Myth and Theory in Geographic Thought* (New York: Praeger, 1974), 23–24.

41. R. Bastide, "Color, Racism, and Christianity," *Daedalus* 96 (1967): 312–27.

42. C. Boxer, *Race Relations in the Portuguese Colonial Empire, 1415–1825* (Oxford: Clarendon Press, 1963).

43. W. Jordan, *White Over Black: American Attitudes Towards the Negro, 1550–181* (Baltimore: Penguin, 1968).

44. N. Stepan, *The Idea of Race in Science: Great Britain, 1800–1960* (London: Macmillan, 1982); S. Gould, *The Mismeasure of Man* (New York: Norton, 1981).

45. In geography, Griffith Taylor's "migration-zone theory" of cultural evolution challenged the assumptions of the day, arguing that environmental pressures were more critical than were biological constants in shaping human destiny. Like Darwin himself, however, Taylor remained locked within the old race science because he assumed that the racial type was the unit upon which evolutionary processes operated. Only by the 1940s did a new theory of heredity enable scientists to integrate Darwin's work into a view of human evolution that emphasized genotypic variation of populations rather than the anatomy of immutable types. See Taylor, *Environment and Race* (London: Oxford University Press, 1927).

46. See G. Jones, *Social Darwinism and English Thought* (Sussex: Harvester Press, 1980).

47. M. Harris, "Race," *International Encyclopedia of the Social Sciences* (New York: Macmillan, 1972), 266.

48. Canada, *Report of the Royal Commission on Chinese Immigration* (Ottawa: Printed by Order of the Commission, 1885), 69.

49. Ibid., 130.

50. *Royal Commission on Chinese Immigration*, 128.

51. Canada, House of Commons, *Debates*, 2 July 1885, 3010.

52. "Progress of the Agitation," *Vancouver News*, 13 Jan. 1887, 2.

53. "Slave Labor," ibid., 1 May 1887, 4.

54. City of Vancouver Archives (hereafter CVA), *City Clerk's In Correspondence*, vol. 6, 4 July 1893, 5275.

55. *Henderson's BC Directory* (Victoria: L.G. Henderson, 1889), 426.

56. CVA, *City Clerk's In Correspondence*, vol. 17, 26 Nov. 1900, 13301.

57. There were other legal limits on the ability of agents within the divided Canadian polity to implement their will. At the provincial level, anti-Chinese legislation that contravened the division of powers laid down by the British North America Act was routinely disallowed by Ottawa. See G. La Forest, *Disallowance and Reservation of the Provincial Legislation* (Ottawa: Department of Justice, 1955). At the municipal level, an important precedent was set in 1888 when M. Fee of Victoria successfully appealed to the Supreme Court of BC the refusal of the City of Victoria to renew his pawnbroker's licence (*R. v. Corporation of Victoria*, [1888] BCR 331).

58. CVA, Office of the City Clerk, *Bylaws*, vol. 1, no. 176, 15 May 1893, 1044–45.

59. "Preserve the Public Health," *Vancouver Daily World*, 30 Aug. 1890, 4.

60. W. McDonald, "The Degraded Oriental," ibid., 23 March 1893, 4.

61. CVA, *Health Committee Minutes*, vol. 2, Chairman's Report, 1899–1906.

62. CVA, *City Clerk's In Correspondence*, vol. 17, 26 Nov. 1900, 13292.

63. Ibid., 13291.

64. Ibid., vol. 10, 15 Aug. 1896, 8522.

65. Ibid., vol. 11, 9 March 1897, 9296.

66. Ibid., vol. 14, 10 Dec. 1899, 10696.

67. Ibid., vol. 17, 26 Nov. 1900, 13299.

68. "Chinese Defy City By-Laws," *Province*, 18 June 1902, 1.

69. *Royal Commission on Chinese and Japanese Immigration*, 14.

70. There are difficulties with reducing majority perceptions to the constant of a singular "white" European viewpoint. The ideas of race and Chinatown enjoyed a popularity, however, that overrode any idiosyncrasies that might have existed in the British, American, and Canadian perceptions. Although no origin classifications are available from the 1891 or 1901 census, early Vancouver society was made up of predominantly British immigrants and their Canadian-born descendants. P. Roy, *Vancouver: An Illustrated History* (Toronto: Lorimer, 1980), 28.

71. "Shall the Chinese Go?" *Vancouver Daily World*, 6 July 1893, 3.

72. The solicitor for the Chinese Board of Trade, A. Taylor, told the commissioners in 1901: "No instance is given of the origin of any contagious disease in the

Chinatown of either city [Vancouver or Victoria]." Using city statistics, he sub mitted "there is no evidence that the presence of the Chinese is in any way menace to health." *Royal Commission on Chinese and Japanese Immigration*, 297.

73. CVA, City of Vancouver, RG2-B1, *Council Minutes* (hereafter *Minutes*), vol. 7, 2 Jan. 1896, 4.

74. CVA, *City Clerk's In Correspondence*, vol. 14, 14 June 1899, 10433.

75. CVA, *Minutes*, vol. 13, 22 May 1905, 395.

76. "To Do Their Own Work," *Province*, 9 Feb. 1906.

77. "Dirty Chinese Are Fined," *Province*, 16 Sept. 1907, 16.

78. Foucault has said that "The problem is not one of drawing the line betwee that in a discourse, which falls under the category of scientificity or truth, an that which comes under some other category, but with seeing historically how effects of truth are produced within discourses that in themselves are neithe true nor false," cited in P. Rabinow, *The Foucault Reader* (New York: Pantheo Books, 1984), 60.

79. "City Powers To Be Widened," *Province*, 27 Jan. 1910, 28; "Dealing with th Chinese," *Times*, 29 Jan. 1910, 18.

80. "Cleaning Up Starts in Foreign Quarters," *Sun*, 31 March 1914, 3.

81. See, e.g., A. Sunahara, *The Politics of Racism: The Uprooting of Japanese Canadian During the Second World War* (Toronto: Lorimer, 1981).

82. "City Acts upon Oriental Agitation," *Province*, 7 April 1914, 3.

83. CVA, *Minutes*, vol. 20, 8 April 1914, 122.

84. "Aldermen and Chinese Having Royal Battle," *Sun*, 24 May 1915, 14.

85. CVA, *Minutes*, vol. 22, 19 May 1919, 488.

86. *Chinese Times*, 24 Jan. 1920.

87. E.g. ibid., 4, 8 March, 5 April 1921.

88. Said, *Orientalism*.

89. See E. Voegelin, "The Growth of the Race Idea," *Review of Politics* 2, 3 (1940) 283–317.

90. "Greed at Bottom of Importation of Orientals," *Province*, 7 Oct. 1907, 2.

91. See H. Gates, "Writing 'Race' and the Difference It Makes," *Critical Inquiry* 12, (1985): 1–20, and other essays in the same volume. The phrase refers to th metaphorical negation of the European in Western language use and is derive from the more general notion that consciousness of the self involves distancin from the Other. R. Laing, *Self and Others* (London: Tavistock, 1961.)

92. That it was more the white European view that was the "same everywhere" and less Chapleau's "Chinaman," see, for example, I. Light, "From Vice Distric to Tourist Attraction: The Moral Career of American Chinatowns, 1880–1940," *Pacific Historical Review* 43 (1974): 367–94; K. Paupst, "A Note on Anti-Chines Sentiment in Toronto Before the First World War," *Canadian Ethnic Studies* 9, 1 (1977): 54–59; C. Salter, "Urban Imagery and the Chinese of Los Angeles," *Urban Review* 1 (1984): 15–20; S. Steiner, *Fusang: The Chinese Who Built Americ* (New York: Harper and Row, 1979), ch. 15. Some of the themes are common to descriptions of other racially defined outgroups such as "blacks" in Americ (e.g., D. Ley, *The Black Inner City as Frontier Outpost*, monograph no. 7 (Washington: Association of American Geographers, 1974), ch. 1, and "Eas Indians" in Canada (e.g., Ley, *A Social Geography of the City*, 268.)

93. Ward, *White Canada Forever*, 169, explains anti-Chinese sentiment in terms of "that psychological tension that *inhered* in the racially plural condition" (emphasis added). In reifying race as something external to the situation under investigation, he treats as an explanation that which itself must be explained. Within the white racism thesis, there are more precise analyses, such as Jordan, *White over Black*, ch. 1, who emphasizes the culture of early English colonists to America in his account of tensions between "blacks" and "whites."

94. E.g., H. Hill, "Anti-Oriental Agitation and the Rise of Working-Class Racism," *Society* 10, 2 (1973): 43–54; P. Roy, "White Canada Forever: Two Generations of Studies," *Canadian Ethnic Studies* 11 (1979): 97–109; A. Saxton, *The Indispensable Enemy: Labor and the Anti-Chinese Movement in California* (Berkeley: University of California Press, 1971).

95. For an attempt to locate racial ideology within the field of capitalist social relations in early British Columbia, see G. Creese, "Immigration Policies and the Creation of an Ethnically Segmented Working Class in British Columbia, 1880–1923," *Alternate Routes* 17 (1984): 1–34. T. Bowsell, "A Split Labor Market Analysis of Discrimination Against Chinese Immigrants, 1850–82," *American Sociological Review* 51 (1986): 352–71, develops the argument of the American context. Split labour market theory emphasizes the economic sources of conflict between groups distinguished by colour under conditions of unequal labour costs. It is less successful in explaining why Chinese labourers were underpaid in the first place.

96. See also J. Prager, "American Racial Ideology as Collective Representation," *Ethnic and Racial Studies* 5, 1 (1982): 99–119.

97. See, E.g., A. Chan, *Gold Mountain* (Vancouver: New Star Books, 1983).

98. C. Geertz, *The Interpretation of Cultures* (New York: Basic Books, 1973), ch. 8.

99. March, *The Idea of China*.

100. R. Dawson, *The Chinese Chameleon: An Analysis of European Conceptions of Chinese Civilization* (London: Oxford University Press, 1967).

101. March, *The Idea of China*, 40–41.

102. *Royal Commission on Chinese Immigration*, 98.

103. Dawson, *The Chinese Chameleon*; D. Hay, *Europe: The Emergence of an Idea* (New York: Harper and Row, 1966); Said, *Orientalism*.

104. S. Miller, *The Unwelcome Immigrant: The American Image of the Chinese, 1785–1882* (Berkeley: University of California Press, 1969).

105. "Vancouver's Chinatown Has Become Plague Spot," *World*, 19 Feb. 1912, 6.

106. Roy, *Vancouver*, 82.

107. CVA, *City Clerk's In Correspondence*, vol. 22, Sept. 1906, 17480.

108. D. Nilsen, "The 'Social Evil': Prostitution in Vancouver 1900–20" (BA hons. essay, History Dept., University of British Columbia, 1976), ch. 3.

109. "In the Sunset Glow," *The Saturday Sunset*, 10 Oct. 1908, 1.

110. Cited in Nilsen, "The 'Social Evil,'" 37.

111. Shum Moon, "Chinese Deny Responsibility," *Province*, 3 Feb. 1908, 16.

112. "Seek to Check Opium Manufacture," *Province*, 3 July 1908, 3.

113. "Unsanitary Chinese," *World*, 28 April 1899, 4.

114. "How Two Lung Lee Goes to Heaven, " *Province*, 26 Sept. 1908, 25.

115. Canada, *Sessional Papers*, 1908, no 36b, 13.

116. "Chinatown—or Drug Traffic?" *Sun*, 22 March 1920, 6.

117. *Chinese Times*, 15 April 1921.

118. W.A. Cumyow, "In Defence of Chinatown," *Sun*, 24 March 1920, 6.

119. House of Commons, *Debates*, 26 April 1921, 2598.

120. Canada, *Statutes*, 1922, 12–13 Geo. V, c. 25.

121. Ibid., 1923, 13–14 Geo. V, c. 38.

122. *Royal Commission on Chinese and Japanese Immigration*, 236.

123. "Urge Enforcement of Health Bylaws" *Province*, 26 Jan. 1915, 5.

124. A Lover of the Truth, "The Curse of Gambling," *Province*, 30 Jan. 1900, 10.

125. "Burrows under Chinatown," *Sun*, 19 June 1915, 10.

126. D. Young, "The Vancouver Police Force, 1886–1914" (BA hons. essay, History Dept., University of British Columbia, 1976), 65.

127. See also Lowman's argument that crime maps may be mental maps reflecting more the images of the city and the activities of control agents than the inherently criminogenic nature of "problem" areas. J. Lowman, "Conceptual Issues in the Geography of Crime: Towards a Geography of Social Control," *Annals of the Association of American Geographers* 76 (1986): 81–94. Ley (1983, 293–94) discusses the labeling practices of institutions. D. Ley, *A Social Geography of the City* (New York: Harper and Row, 1983).

THE PADRONE SYSTEM AND SOJOURNERS IN THE CANADIAN NORTH, 1885–1920[◊]

ROBERT F. HARNEY

o

On 23 January 1904, more than two thousand Italian labourers paraded through the streets of Montreal. They were there to fête Antonio Cordasco, steamship agent, *banchista* (immigrant banker), and director of a labour bureau. Two foremen presented him with a crown "in a shape not unlike that worn by the King of Italy." The crown was later displayed in a glass case along with a souvenir sheet containing eleven columns of Italian names and entitled "In Memory of the Great Parade of January, 1904, in honour of Signor Antonio Cordasco, proclaimed King of the Workers." During February, foremen, *caposquadri*, and *sub-bossi* organized a banquet for Cordasco. Invitations to the banquet bore a seal suspiciously like the Royal Crest of Italy, and Cordasco's "kept" newspaper, the *Corriere del Canada*, reported the occasion in detail.[1]

Four months later, in June and July of 1904, the "King of the Workers" was under investigation by the Deputy Minister of Labour, about to be the centre of a Royal Commission inquiry into fraudulent business practices, and excoriated by officials of the Italian Immigrant Aid Society. What emerges from the reports, testimony, and newspaper accounts about the activity of Cordasco and his competitors in Montreal is not just the picture of an exploitive and dishonest broker[2] but of a man truly in between—willing enough to put his boot into those beneath him, such as the green-horns who depended upon him for jobs, but also forced to tug his forelock and to anticipate the wishes of the English-speaking businessmen and employers whom he served.

[◊] George E. Pozzetta, ed., *Pane e Lavoro: The Italian-American Working Class* (Toronto: Multicultural History Society of Ontario, 1980), 119–37. Reprinted with the permission of the publisher.

Antonio Cordasco, the protagonist of my story, was, in the end, a nearly perfect Italian parody of the "negro king," that peculiarly ugly phenomenon of an ethnic or colonial puppet who serves those who really control the society and the economy.[3] In 1904 his avarice combined with circumstance—a late thaw, high unemployment in the United States, and the alliance of the Montreal Italian Immigrant Aid Society with his chief competitor, Alberto Dini—to expose him to public scrutiny. He proved to be a man whose new crown rested uneasily; he had to threaten and cajole his *sub-bossi*, placate his capitalist overlords, hide from irate workers, and scheme to destroy competitors who aspired to his throne. At the same time, he carried on a complex foreign policy with padroni in other cities and with steamship and emigration agents in Italy and on Italy's borders. Cordasco stood astride a free enterprise system that brought Italian migrant labour into contact with North American job opportunity. His power lay in his control of the communications network between labour and capital, and that was not an easy position from which to carve an empire. Like the "negro king," he had neither the affection of his people, the migrant Italian labourers, nor the trust of his Wasp masters, but he served them both as intermediary and spared them both from dealing directly with the mysterious other.

The commerce of migration which Cordasco had ridden to power had grown up in the last quarter of the nineteenth century. Canadian conditions were particularly suitable for the development of a seasonal guest worker system. The need for manual labour at remote northern work sites, the attitudes of Canadian big business and of European village labourers, the climate, the difficulty of transportation, and the xenophobic immigration policy of the government meant that only a sojourning work force could reconcile the Dominion's needs and the target migrants' self-interest.[4] The three necessary components to such a system of seasonal migrant labour were the capitalist employer, the European worker, and the intermediaries and brokers who controlled the recruitment, transportation, and organization of the labour pool for the employers. All involved saw an advantage in the system. For the Canadian employer—particularly the labour intensive industries such as the railways, the mines, and the smeltering interests—there was constant need for a docile and mobile work force, a force free from the taint of unionism and willing to be shipped to remote northern sites, a work force which tolerated exploitation at those sites in order to make ready cash, and which required no maintenance on the part of the employer during the long winter months.

For the workers, the advantage of this system was that they could operate as target migrants. They had come to North America without their families, not in order to settle, but to earn enough money to change their condition of life in the old country. Their image or myth of Canada, if they had one, was of a very hostile and frozen land whose people were not well disposed toward south Europeans or toward foreign bachelors.[5] The system usually allowed them to reach Canadian job sites for the short work season without undue delay or hardship, and a single season's campaign enabled them to save money to send home; and by staying several seasons they could make a nest-egg so that they might never come back again. However, because of the necessity of arriving with the thaw in time for work and leaving before the St Lawrence froze, or because of dishonest exploitation, target migrants were often trapped for many seasons, their savings dissipated by padroni-run boardinghouses, saloons, and provisioners.

For the intermediaries, of course, the system itself was the source of their income. Without a constant flow of labour, without being able to pose for both the village labourer and the North American capitalist as the only possible go-between, the padrone had no function. In the Canadian situation, they were helped by the problems of national boundaries, the new rigour of Italian laws, the competition between steamship companies, and the worker's lack of knowledge of the northern target. The fact that the North American employers maintained an almost willful ignorance of the work force made it easier for the intermediaries to manipulate the labour supply and to tie job brokerage to the network of migration, which ran all the way from the remote towns of Italy to the remote towns of northern Ontario and British Columbia.

As Italian laws against the excesses of agents and recruitment grew more stringent, the town of Chiasso on the Swiss-Italian border became the centre of the illicit recruitment and flow of Italian workers to North America.[6] Unravelling the *vincolismo* (linkages) of sham immigration societies, travel agencies, steamship companies, and padroni who controlled the flow is beyond the scope of this paper, but it is significant that a major role in this unholy commerce was taken by King Cordasco. Two simple points need to be made. First, in the so-called *commercio di carne umana*, there was as much competition in earning the right to transport human cattle to the slaughter yards of North American industry as there was in running the North American holding pens. For every padroni in Montreal or Boston, there were one or two steamship sub-agents in a town like Chiasso or in the interior of Italy. These agents earned their way by the *senseria*, the bounty paid for each migrant recruited for steamship passage, and although the more responsible or clever among the sub-agents cared whether those they sent to America found work—because their reputation as agents depended on it—they were naturally not as sensitive to the fluctuations in the demand for labour as the North American padroni had to be. This made the sub-agents a sometimes unreliable part of the network for those who faced the more delicate task of maintaining a balance between the labour force and the employer in North America. One agent for Beaver Lines even boasted to the Canadian authorities that in a given year he had recruited more than 6000 passengers from Italy, as well as Syrians and Germans and as many more as anybody might request.[7]

Before we try describing the padroni's activities in Montreal—using Cordasco and also his competitor, Alberto Dini, as models—we have to explain the rapidity of Cordasco's rise to power athwart the lines of communication. The new king of Italian labour does not really seem to have been intelligent enough to control the situation, but by its decision to place the mantle of sole agent on him, the Canadian Pacific Railroad (CPR) turned

a small time hustler into a large padrone broker. Cordasco's power the
derived from his felicitous relationship with one major employer and pa
ticularly with the railway's chief hiring agent, George Burns. It was Burn
who made Cordasco into his "negro king." Burns operated out of an offic
in Windsor Station in Montreal called the Special Services Department o
the Canadian Pacific Railway. Despite that euphemism, its main functio
was the hiring of docile foreign labour, especially Italians, Galicians, an
Chinese for the railway's summer work.

Burns had made up his mind during the strike of 1901 that Cordasc
offered him the easiest and surest means of maintaining an available labou
pool in Montreal. The agent admitted as much on the stand during th
Royal Commission hearings in 1904.

> Question: What means do you take in order to obtain this extra
> Italian labour? Answer: I have engaged that labour entirely through
> Italian labour agents. . . . During the past three years, since the sum-
> mer of 1901 I have dealt almost exclusively through Cordasco.
> Previous to that I had several others engaged, such as Mr. Dini, two
> gentlemen by the name of Schenker, and possibly one or two more.
> Question: But since 1901 you have dealt exclusively with Mr.
> Cordasco? Answer: Yes, I have Your Honour. Question: Was that the
> year you had the strike? Answer: It was. Question: And Cordasco
> got in touch with you during that year? Answer: I think the first
> business I had with Cordasco was in 1901. Question: In connection
> with the strike? Answer: In connection with supplying Italians to
> take the place of track men who went on strike.[8]

Cordasco, working for the Canadian Pacific Railway and Alberto Dini
on behalf of the Grand Trunk Railway, had to negotiate with the agents in
Switzerland who were the immediate recruiters of manpower. A letter to
Dini from the firm of Corecco and Brivio in Bodio, Switzerland, reveals the
means by which North American labour agents and European steamship
agents formed their alliances. The firm in Switzerland was in a covert relationship with both Frederick Ludwig in Chiasso and with Beaver Steamship
Lines, and possibly even with Canadian Pacific Lines, but masqueraded as
representatives of something called Societa Anomina di Emigrazione La
Svizzera.

In fact, Corecco and Brivio had tried to monopolize the Chiasso
Connection and the commerce of migration there. The letter to Dini in 1904
suggested the advantages of a full alliance.

> You do not ignore that a brother of Mr. Schenker, one of those who
> has opened an office in Montreal for the exchange of money in
> order to compete with you, has lately opened an office in Chiasso,
> Switzerland and gets passengers from Italy through the help of
> Schenker who is in Montreal. The latter sends to his brother in
> Chiasso notices and orders for the shipment of men and the brother
> reads the notices to the passengers mentioning the ships they are to

go by. Having acknowledged this action on the part of Schenker we took the liberty of addressing ourselves to you in order to advise you and inform you thereof and to ask if it would be possible for you to do something for us in the matter.[9]

So the steamship agents and immigration agents in Italy or on the Italian borders who needed to protect their bounties sought allies among the padroni while the latter sought safe suppliers of labour. In 1903, only one season after he had gained his lucrative hold over the Canadian Pacific labour supply, Cordasco wrote to the most powerful of the agents in Chiasso, Frederick Ludwig.

By the same mail I am sending you a package of my business cards. I ask you to hand them to the passengers or better to the labourers that you will send directly to me. . . . To satisfy the Italians better here I have opened a banking office of which I send a circular to you from which you can see that I can do all that they request. Awaiting for some *shipment* and to hear from you soon. Yours truly, A. Cordasco.[10]

Cordasco apparently demonstrated both naiveté and lack of finesse in the letter to Ludwig. That gentleman, a smoother, tougher exploiter, wrote back to him within a month. Addressing himself to "Mr. Cordask," he explained that he had not answered "the letter immediately because I wanted to get some information about you." From the tone of the letter, Ludwig felt he had the upper hand in dealing with a padrone *arrivato* like Cordasco. He informed Mr. Cordask that he would "try him out and send passengers to him and see if he acts as an honest man and then he will give his address to most of the migrants going to Montreal." He added, "What I especially recommend to you is not to change your address every moment like a wandering merchant. On your envelope the address is 441 St. James Street and on your business card it is 375, now which of the two is the right address?" Ludwig went on to remark that he had done business with Dini for years and had found him a capable and good business associate. Mr Cordask finally is warned, "We shall see then if you will work with the same conscience and punctuality."

Communication with those in the Old World who put labour on the *via commerciale*—steamship agents, immigration agents, and local notables— was sometimes testy to say the least. We find Cordasco complaining to a man from Udine who has sent him men who were stone cutters not labourers. The stone cutters had expected work as skilled masons or in quarries, but Cordasco claimed that he had distinctly warned the men before they left the old country that everyone should understand that the railway work available in Canada was for labourers, not artisans. A number of these men refused to go to British Columbia to work; they claimed that they were promised free passage on the railway, skilled work, and better wages than those offered them when they arrived in Canada.[11] Caught amidst the promises of the agents in the old country, his own hyperbole in the pages of the *Corriere del Canada*, and the parsimonious approach to migrant labour of Canadian big business, and worker demands, Cordasco's role as a go-between sometimes reduced itself to lying to all parties involved, while walking a very difficult tightrope.

Cordasco's networks ran from Chiasso on the Italian-Swiss border to the various padroni and labour agents in the American "Little Italies" and the major steamship companies. The official report of the Royal Commission listed some of the methods Cordasco used to make contact with the labour supply in Europe. The investigators admitted that they could only infer from the correspondence a conspiracy to mislead workers. Mackenzie King, the chief investigator, had remarked that "there is no business relation existing between himself [Cordasco] and these agents but I think there can be no doubt as to their acting in direct accordance with an understood arrangement which he has with them."[12] King's remark has a resonance similar to that of American investigators at a later time who became convinced that the Mafia existed because they could not find evidence of it.

The memoranda of understanding and letters of agreement that passed between Cordasco and his peers were callous documents reflecting the tenor of the commerce in human flesh. But steamship agents and labour agents of every ethnic background dealt with migrants thus, and the line between the clever use of the free enterprise system and fraud is more discernible to us now than it was then. Also, it is obvious from the testimony of Mr Mortimer Waller that business practices did not change much as one crossed ethnic lines.

> Question: Is there anything else you would like to state in connection with this investigation Mr. Waller? Answer: No sir, I do not think so. I think myself that Englishmen should have as fair a chance of supplying this Italian labour as the Italians themselves. Question: You think that an Englishman should have as good a chance to supply this labour? Answer: Yes. Question: You think that Englishmen have not that chance? Answer: No sir. Question: Why? Answer: The companies like the CPR will not go to anybody but Italians for the men.[13]

Mr. Waller had the same system of registering labourers as Cordasco, and charged approximately the same commission for unskilled workers and foremen.

In his testimony, Dini told the judge, "I have got an employment office, banker is name known to Italians." Earlier in his testimony, he had also pointed out that he was the steamship agent for North German Lloyd's Line, Hamburg–American Anchor Line, and two Italian Lines, including La Veloce. Cordasco, in turn, had extracted a promise from Mr Burns that if he helped find strikebreakers in 1901, the CPR would help him become the agent for their steamship line, Compagnie Générale Transatlantique, and for several others. Like Dini, he referred to himself as a banker and his newspaper announcement to the labourers in 1904 began:

To the army of the pick and shovel Italian laborers, bosses do not show a double face, do not be false but only one. Be true. Have a soldier's courage, apply to the elegant and solid Italian bank of Antonio Cordasco, if you do not want to weep over your misfortunes in the spring when the shipments of men will begin.[14]

Both men described themselves as bankers, perhaps as steamship agents and employment agents, but would not have used the word padrone. They specialized in performing as brokers between labour and capital, as transmitters of remittances and pre-paid tickets, and as travel advisors, while engaging, because of the migrants' dependence on them, in many other businesses.

Cordasco's banking, for example, included lending money to foremen so that they could pay the registration fee of a dollar a head for their work gangs. Often the faith of the workers in the *banchista* was touchingly naive. A letter of 1903 reads, "We the undersigned, signed with a cross mark because we cannot write or read, both of us, we authorize Mr. A. Cordasco to draw our wages for work done in the month of October last, 1903. And we both authorize the Canadian Pacific Railway Company to pay over our wages to Mr. Cordasco at 375 St. James Street." Cordasco himself understood the nature of his *intermediarismo*. An advertisement appearing in *La Patria Italiana* showed a rather charming, if dangerous and old-fashioned, sense of the world *patronato*: "If you want to be respected and protected either on the work or in case of accident or other annoyances which may be easily met, apply personally or address letters or telegrams to Antonio Cordasco."[15] It was protection that the padrone offered, protection against undue delay, protection against fraud by others, protection against all the dangers of an unknown world, of a world where the labourer could not cope for himself because of lack of education, lack of language skills, and lack of time to stand and fight when his cash supply was threatened.

Mr Skinner, Mr Burns' assistant, showed a certain sympathy for Cordasco, for the padrone who had to deal with what Skinner seemed to see as the child-like qualities of the labourers. "He has lots of trouble. He keeps an office with a waiting room, and they are the resorts where these people spend all winter. They come to smoke, he keep all sorts of conveniences for them."[16]

In a strange way, the chief power of the intermediary, just as in the old country, lay in his literacy. Cordasco's clerk on the witness stand mentioned writing over eighty-seven letters a month. When Dini was pressed as to what he actually did when people came to him seeking work, he answered, "I write to several contractors, to employers, to Grand Trunk if they want labourers and if they want them I'll ship them quickly." He was asked how many contractors he represented, and replied, "ten or twenty." "When the contractors want labourers, they have my address, they write or telegraph me, if I have any Italians to send them." So it was their ability to correspond and to communicate with the American employer which made padroni powerful. They played a role no different from that played by the *generetti* of the small towns of the Italian south and northeast, a role in which literacy was a form of capital and the basis of the brokerage system itself. Men who would have been brokers between *signori* and peasantry or between government and peasantry in Europe, found themselves brokers between sojourners and English-speaking employers.[17]

There is no doubt that Cordasco made a profit from both the employer and labourer. That was only fitting since he served both groups. The amount of the profit, however, was outrageous by any standard. At one point, it became clear that Cordasco was buying from his own supplier near Windsor Station and providing most of the canned anchovies (sardines) and bread for labourers at different CPR sites across northern Ontario. He made a 150 percent profit on a can of sardines, the bread was often mouldy, and he clearly made a high profit on it as well. In a single season he cleared $3800 as a provisioner. The figure of a dollar a head for registration of men pales in comparison. Cordasco obviously was not only profiteering but downright grasping. Foremen, testifying against him, pointed out that they had been forced to raise the money for the banquet that had been held in his honour and that some of that money had also mysteriously disappeared into Cordasco's pocket.[18]

If the investigators, the commissioner, and the officials of the Italian Immigrant Aid Society had understood the system a little better, had understood the degree to which the foremen and labourers were also consumers, they would have noticed that the anger of those who came to the stand was not over the fact that they had to pay tribute to Cordasco or that they had to register seasonally for work with him, but that he had not found jobs for them or their gangs that year. The foremen particularly, since they too were men in between, were galled by the fact that they had promised their gangs work, that they had often raised the dollar a head for Cordasco from their men, and then had lost both a season's work, the respect of their workers, and perhaps the possibility of exercising their own petty tyranny and corruption over the work force. One foreman, Michael Tisi, was pressed on the witness stand about the fact that he had paid ten dollars to be foreman of a gang of a hundred men and that each of the men had paid two dollars. He admitted paying that, but he felt that he had no grievance against Cordasco. He answered simply, "They went to work. I'm not complaining about that."[19]

It has always seemed illogical to speak about a large scale broker like Cordasco controlling thousands of men through ties of paesanism, kinship, or even through shared ethnicity. In 1903 the CPR hired over 3500 Italians. Cordasco could not have known them all. They came from all over Italy, from the Veneto to Sicily; few, if any, were his *paesani*, let alone his friends and relatives. It was the *sub-bossi* who organized and controlled the work gangs. Sometimes those gangs were made up of *paesani* but not always. The testimony of the *caposquadri* and foremen partially explains one aspect of the padrone's power. One of the foremen, Sal Mollo, testified to the Commission that his "men don't know him [Cordasco] at all. They know me. When I went there to his bank he would not hear me." Another foreman, Pompeo Bianco, claimed to know all of his gang of 104 men brought from the United States, except for perhaps a dozen.[20]

Sub-bossi boasted that they could move their men to any site at a moment's notice, and one foreman even came from Nova Scotia to Montreal to register his men in case work was found, leaving the gang behind in Nova Scotia. Loyalty to the bosses was functional; it had to do with their ability to operate as secondary intermediaries, in this instance between the men and Cordasco, but usually between the men and the section bosses of the CPR. If that loyalty was sometimes based on regional allegiances, such as the whole gang and the boss being Calabrese or Venetian, it was still not synonymous with paesanism.

From the ranks of these *sub-bossi* however, as well as from other small entrepreneurs, individuals came forth to try to compete with Dini and Cordasco in the lucrative trade in migrants. If Cordasco was the *generone*, then these were the *generetti*, nipping at his heels. Whatever the true basis of loyalty between *sub-bossi* and gangs—Cordasco was able to control thousands of men from his Montreal office without going into the field—it could depend not just on his own immediate employees but on the *sub-bossi* as vassals. As long as Cordasco had the support of his own liege lord, the CPR agent Burns, the *generetti* could not usurp his control of labour.

A significant aspect of the padrone's role—the deftness with which he had to manipulate the labour pool to meet the employer's hiring intentions—was not pursued. No government official wished to have the blame for the large numbers of unemployed Italian migrants loitering about Montreal come to rest squarely on the shoulders of a great institution like the Canadian Pacific Railway. This was so, although the CPR, like other major employers, seemed to be carrying on an immigration policy of its own, favouring unskilled sojourners from southeastern Europe while the Ministry of the Interior tried to recruit agriculturalists from northwestern Europe.[21]

The hearings of the Royal Commission are marred as a source by a pervasive, if latent, nativism. The authorities and the non-Italian witnesses agreed on one thing, which an exchange between Mr Burns and Judge Winchester put flatly: "Burns: But Your Honour must know that in investigating the Italian cases there is great difficulty in getting at the truth. Winchester: I have found that myself."[22] So, whatever the Italian labour bosses were doing, it was being done in a manner strange to the Canadian way. Mr Waller had implied as much when he lamented how Anglo-Saxon labour bureaux had been eased out of the commerce in Italian brawn. Obviously, it was ethnicity itself, the trust, often ill-founded, and the networks it provided, that was the dark alien unknown which troubled all those outside it, from the CPR officials to the judge.

The veil lifted enough in 1904 to see how the padrone ultimately depended on his Anglo-Saxon master, the employer of labourers. Cordasco met with Burns or his assistant Skinner almost daily. No doubt the lines of communication between him and Burns were closer than those between most padroni who served a more varied clientele, but Dini's relation with the various contractors and with the Grand Trunk Railway seem to have been as intense. Much of Cordasco's power over his Italian migrant labourer clientele derived from his right to advertise himself as the only acting agent for the CPR. Although he maintained some independence from Burns and the CPR by being able to pose as the most efficient intermediary for the gathering of Italian labour, his position vis-à-vis the company was not strong. It could withdraw its patronage at any time and turn to his potential competitors or directly to his *caposquadri* and *sub-bossi*.

Burns contributed directly to the expansion of Cordasco's role from that of a minor employment agent into a *banchista*. The commerce of migration led inevitably to a variety of entrepreneurial possibilities and the CPR's agent gave his blessing.

> The way it came about was this. He only had a regular office and was doing a large business but he had no steamship agencies. And of course when these Italians come back from work most of them have a good deal of money which they want to send over to their relatives and friends, some for their wives and children and they buy these steamship pre-paid tickets. Cordasco is desirous of getting a line of these tickets on the different steamship agencies. And he came to me about the matter and I told him he could easily get agencies if he made the proper representation to the agents that were in New York. Question: You recommended him? Answer: I took some steps to get these agencies for him.[23]

So from his castle in Windsor Station, George Burns protected his vassal from both do-gooders and the competition of lesser brokers because the railway found the padrone system efficient and flexible. A delegation from the Italian Immigration Aid Society had approached Burns offering to provide him with Italian labourers directly from Italy through the good offices of the Italian government. Burns replied to them,

> I have taken up the question of the employment of labour with the proper authorities and have to advise you that it is not the intention of this company to change the arrangements of the employment of Italian immigrant labour which have been in effect during the past few years. Our present system has given entire satisfaction so far and I therefore regret I shall be unable to place direct with your Society any specific order for any number of men.[24]

Cordasco's sway over Italian migrant labour was reinforced by the company. For example, at the famous banquet in the padrone's honour, most of the foremen in attendance noted the presence of the chief superintendent of the CPR's Vancouver division. After all, that gentleman would be hiring five or six thousand Italians during the coming spring, and he seemed to be there honouring his friend Cordasco.

In 1904, company support, even though it showed the limits of Cordasco's independence, enabled him to thwart attacks upon his monopoly. That support came in at least four ways. First, at no point in their testimony did Skinner or Burns speak explicitly enough to compromise Cordasco. Second, they maintained throughout his exclusive right to hire Italians for the railway rather than turning to aspiring *sub-bossi*. Third, they had refused to order manpower from Alberto Dini, Cordasco's main competitor. Fourth, Burns did his best to discredit or ignore the Italian Immigration Aid Society. With his overlords to protect him, Cordasco's lines of communication to Ludwig in Chiasso, to Stabili in Boston, to other lesser padroni in Portland, Providence, and Fall River, and to agents in New York and Buffalo were secure. Cordasco seemed as safe as a padrone could be. To raise money for the banquet in his honour he warned any man who hesitated to donate five dollars to the cause that he would publish his photograph upside down on the souvenir sheet. The real threat was that "anyone who refuses to pay will go out of my office," i.e., would be eliminated from the hiring register. In an address to labourers printed in *La Patria Italiana*, Cordasco flaunted his control.

> If you do not want to weep over your misfortune in the spring when the shipment of men will begin you will do business with me. Do not believe that with your dollar that you will be able to get work like your comrades who have been faithful. Those who had signed the book earlier. We will inspect our books, and money orders and our passage ticket books and those who will not have their names in them will in their despair tear out their hair and will call Mr. Cordasco, Lordship Don Antonio, "Let me go to work." "No, never," will be answered to them. "Go to those to whom you have sent your money away. . . . " Forewarned is a forearmed man.[25]

Despite his parody of Christ's monopoly over salvation, Cordasco could not stifle all the competition. The same entrepreneurial spirit that brought so many of the migrants to North America led a certain number of men to see in Cordasco or Dini models for action. One could almost say that an infernal spirit of capitalism had begun to inject itself into his feudal system. Foremen, *sub-bossi*, and *caposquadri* who had been in America for a number of seasons—especially if they spoke English well—must have seen advantage in eliminating Cordasco as intermediary, even if they did not aspire to a brokerage status for themselves. The *sub-bossi* were, much like the *generetti* of the post *Risorgimento*, at once in a feudal and capitalist relationship with the padrone. The *sub-bossi* gave Cordasco his power; he gave them theirs. Each could claim to provide work to those below them. If one of them tried to by-pass Cordasco and deal directly with the employer, Cordasco could only hope that the employer would not take advantage of the situation to undermine him.

As we have seen, George Burns of the CPR did not take advantage of the situation. He found it easier to have one reliable padrone and to turn a blind eye to his corruption and unfair exactions. By 1904, with the help of the company, Cordasco had defeated non-Italian suppliers of labour and had excluded Dini from the CPR system, while he himself cut into Dini's commerce with the Grand Trunk Railway. From the padrone's correspondence, we can see how he used Burns and the sub-contractors' fear of anarchy in the supply system to thwart emerging competitors. Cordasco went so far at one point as to write a letter to Boston, interfering in the recruitment of labourers there and in the competition between the Bianco Stabili Company and Torchia and Company. He warned Messieurs Torchia that there was no point in recruiting people for the CPR in British Columbia because he, Cordasco, was the sole agent for that railway and he would only order manpower through Stabili. He ended his letter thus: "No shipment of men will be recognized but those made through Stabili and Company."[26] Despite the bravado of that letter, Cordasco pestered Burns with complaints about incidents in which sub-contractors along the right-of-way hired workers through Italian foremen rather than through Burns and Cordasco.

Thus far this paper has treated the sojourning worker—with the exception of *sub-bossi* and *caposquadri*—as the commodity in the commerce of migration, delivered by the padrone to the North American employer. Despite moral clichés about supine greenhorns in the clutches of padroni, the thoughtful historian soon sees that the migrants were as much the consumers of the padrone brokerage services as the employers were. The labourers judged Cordasco by only one measure—did he deliver? Did he provide employment for the length of time and at the wages promised, and did he do so without either delay, ancillary expenses, or hassle with North American authorities? If he did, the padroni played his assigned role in the commerce of migration. There was no doubt whatsoever that men sought other intermediaries if a padrone failed them. For example, in March 1904, Cordasco urged Burns to begin hiring for CPR summer projects because he could not hold the men who had registered with him. Many were drifting off with construction bosses and agents of other smaller railways and street railways. The pages of the *Labour Gazette* in the 1900s were studded with accounts of short-lived revolts by Italian work gangs. Almost all of these uprisings occurred because of fraudulent wage promises or attempts to reduce pay; none seems to have been over working conditions.[27]

Employers such as the Canadian Pacific Railway section bosses had the means to resist revolt. When Italians at Crow's Nest Pass in British Columbia refused $1.50 a day, they were simply dismissed and the local labour agent began "filling orders with Galicians from the North."[28] On the other hand, Cordasco had no protection from the caprice or anger of Italian workers; he faced physical attack and verbal abuse. If men he gathered were dismissed or left a job site disgruntled, he could only plead for patience from *sub-bossi* or for patronage from other employers. So the consumer power of the migrants—before they were acclimatized or turned to North American unionism—when it was exercised, was against the padrone, not the employer. In this, as in every aspect of the system, a padrone like Cordasco was the man in between. Not only did he face the anger of workmen and treason from his vassals, but he ran the risk of being seen as an unreliable broker by big business because he supplied troublesome men.

Cordasco then was a nasty man and certainly did not deserve the excess profits he exacted from the migrant labour force, but he did, except perhaps in the spring of 1904, do his job. The sojourners accepted the padrone because they reckoned that he provided them the best alternative in their search for cash; their commitment to the system, like their avoidance of unionism or agricultural work, reflected their desire to return home as quickly as possible with cash and with as little North American encumbrance as possible. When an official of the Commissariat asked Italian labourers in the Niagara Peninsula why they hadn't taken up some of the rich farm lands in that region, the answer was simple: "We have to think about our families in Italy."[29] In 1900 the Canadian consul in Montreal had reported that of all the trapped migrants interviewed there, none had come to Canada to settle. Agricultural work did not bring in the cash which was the goal of the sojourning family member. Some measure both of the padrone's successful delivery of services and of the frame of mind of the Italian Canadian labour force can be found in the fact that Canadian remittances to Italy were the highest per unit for any part of *Italia oltremare* as late as 1908.[30]

Dini testified honestly and simply at one point to the Royal Commission. When pressed to admit that it was the extraordinary competition between agents like him and Cordasco that had led to so many migrants arriving in Montreal that spring, he remarked that that was not so. It was easy enough, he said, to understand why men who earned the equivalent of twenty-five cents a day in their home towns might come to a land where they could make $1.50 a day, and twice that much if they became foremen. All of the commissioners who investigated Canadian conditions later on for the Canadian government concurred on one point: the sojourners were content with their margin of saving and profit. They complained of the cold, of unsanitary and unsafe conditions, and sometimes of a padrone's dishonesty, but, for example, in 1910 Viola found men in the mines at Cobalt saving a dollar a day. Foremen, according to Moroni, made as much as $3.50 a day—ten times the daily wages in southern Italy, and reason enough, if not justification, for Cordasco's surcharge when registering *caposquadri* in 1903 and 1904.[31]

Commissioner Attolico, in 1912, met a Calabrese youth in the bush "at a little station four hours away from Lake Superior."[32] The youngster complained to him about missing his hometown, but he had wintered over in a bunkhouse because he did not want to go to Port Arthur and spend his salary on *madamigella* (the ladies). The boy had already sent 350 lire—the equivalent of a half year's wages in Italy—to his mother back in the *paesello*. He had been in Canada less than three months when Attolico encountered him. He did not mind the deprivation but he kept repeating that, while there were many other Calabrese about, he was the only one from Mammole and had no one for company but God. Since the young Calabrese section hand worked for the Canadian Pacific Railway, he was mistaken if he thought the deity was his only companion. The latter might have heard his prayers, but it was Cordasco or one of his successors who had found him his job, remitted his money to his mother, delivered her letters to him, and would handle prepaid tickets for kinfolk or for his passage home later on. It was a padrone, not God and not the free flow of labour to capital, who had brought a man from the hills of Calabria to the northern Ontario bush.

Protest against the padrone system came more often from social workers, labour leaders, and nativists than it did from the consumers, the migrant labourers. Historians have assumed that this was so because the sojourners knew no better or had no choice. In fact, the system ended when the consumer no longer found it satisfactory. Padronism was callous, exploitive, and often dishonest, but it fulfilled a function for those migrants who chose to come to America, not as permanent immigrants, but in search of cash to improve their condition in the old country. To understand padronism properly and to give all parts of the system—employer, intermediary, and labourer-consumer—their due, we must see it not as a form of ethnic crime, but as part of the commerce of migration.

NOTES

1. The chief source for this essay is the *Royal Commission appointed to inquire into the Immigration of Italian Labourers to Montreal and the alleged Fraudulent Practices of Employment Agencies* (Ottawa, 1905) (hereafter *Royal Commission, 1904*). The Commission produced a 41 page report and 170 pages of testimony.

2. The word "padrone" does not appear in the testimony. Mackenzie King, chief investigator for the Dept. of Labour and future prime minister of Canada, probably knew the word and its connotations from his American experience. I have used the word throughout the paper as a convenient label for the chief intermediaries, but do so on the understanding that the reader has a wary and sophisticated approach to its use. See R.F. Harney, "The Padrone and the Immigrant," *Canadian Review of American Studies* 5 (Fall 1974).

3. The expression was popularized in Canada by André Laurendeau (1912–68), the editor of Montreal's *Le Devoir*. Laurendeau claimed that Quebec was governed by "les rois nègres"—the equivalent of those puppet rulers in Africa through whom the British authorities found it convenient to wield power. The expression in English would probably have the strength of "nigger king" not "negro king."

4. See Joan M. Nelson, *Temporary versus Permanent Cityward Migration: Causes and Consequences* (Migration and Development Group, Massachusetts Institute of Technology, 1976); and R.F. Harney, "Men without Women: Italian Migrants in Canada, 1895–1930," in B. Caroli, R.F. Harney, L. Tomasi, eds., *The Italian Immigrant Woman in North America* (Toronto, 1978). On government immigration policy, see M. Timlin, "Canada's Immigration Policy, 1896–1910," *Canadian Journal of Economics and Political Science* 26 (1963). For popular attitudes toward the immigrant labourers, see E. Bradwin, *The Bunkhouse Man* (New York, 1928), and J.S. Woodsworth, *Strangers within our Gates* (Toronto, 1909). The latter was significant enough to have a *Bollettino* of the Italian Commissariat of Emigration devoted to reviewing its ideas and impact: "Gli stranieri nel Canada giudicati da un canadese (recensione)," *Bollettino* 19 (Anno 1909). See also D.H. Avery, *Canadian Immigration Policy and the Alien Question, 1896–1919: The Anglo-Canadian Perspective* (PhD thesis, University of Western Ontario, 1973).

5. There was apparently little knowledge of Canada in Italy before the mass migration of the 1900s. The only available study of Canada in Italy seems to have been E. Cavalieri, "Il Domino del Canada. Appunti di Viaggio," which appeared first in serial form in *Nuova Antologia* 43: 700–47; 44: 319–53; 44: 665–92. As late as 1914, a *vademecum* for immigrants, *Calendario per Gli Emigranti di Società Umanitaria* (Milan, 1914), although it had accurate descriptions of many parts of the world, showed Niagara Falls on its map of Canada, but not the industrial city of Toronto.

6. For the debate over emigration in Italy and the evolution of Italian laws about protection of emigrants, see F. Manzotti, *La Polemica sull'emigrazione nell'Italia*

unita (Milano, 1969); R. Foerster, *The Italian Emigration of Our Times* (Harvard, 1919).

7. Luigi Gramatica, General Agent (Genoa), to W.T. Preston, London, 7 Jan. 1902, RG 76, vol. 129, *Immigration Branch, 1901,* File 28885, Public Archives of Canada, Ottawa, Canada.

8. Testimony of G. Burns, *Royal Commission, 1904,* 41.

9. Corecco & Brivio to A. Dini, 7 May 1904, *Royal Commission,* 1904, 50.

10. Correspondence between Cordasco and Ludwig, Oct. 1903, *Royal Commission, 1904,* 82.

11. On Ludwig, see Marcus Braun's supporting documents and miscellaneous related correspondence in the National Archives in Washington: RG 85, Immigration Subject Correspondence, File 52320/47 (1903–1904), Immigration and Naturalization, Dept. of Justice (hereafter cited as *Braun Report, 1903*). Cordasco to Antonio Paretti, 26 April 1904, *Royal Commission, 1904,* 82.

12. Report in *Labour Gazette* (June 1906).

13. Testimony of Mortimer Waller, *Royal Commission, 1904,* 48. Waller incidentally charged two dollars to register labourers for work and five dollars for foremen.

14. Notice in *La Patria Italiana, Royal Commission, 1904,* 106.

15. *La Patria Italiana,* 20 Feb. 1904; *Royal Commission, 1904,* 107.

16. Testimony of CPR agent Skinner, *Royal Commission, 1904,* 26.

17. See Harney, "Commerce of Migration," on the concept of the *borghesia mediatrice*; see G. Dore, *La Democrazia italiana e l'emigrazione in America* (Brescia, 1964).

18. Testimony of Pompeo Bianco, foreman, *Royal Commission, 1904,* 163.

19. Testimony of Michele Tisi, foreman, *Royal Commission, 1904,* 33.

20. Testimony of Salvatore Mollo, foreman, *Royal Commission, 1904,* 34; testimony of Pompeo Bianco, foreman, *Royal Commission, 1904,* 29.

21. For the government attitude footnote 4 as well as W.D. Scott, "Immigration and Population," in A. Shortt and A. Doughty, *Canada and its Provinces* (Toronto, 1914), 561. The government's asserted preference for agricultural settlers over migrant workers coincided with Anglo-Saxon racialist hierarchies. The matter has received remarkably little study in Canada. Canadian Pacific records have not generally been open to scholars.

22. Testimony of Burns, *Royal Commission, 1904,* 153. It was Judge Winchester himself, the head of the inquiry, who agreed with Burns that Italian cases were murkier than others.

23. Testimony of Burns, *Royal Commission, 1904,* 41, 61. It is important to note that Burns stressed that Cordasco was sole agent for Italian labour; Cordasco had, in that sense, an ethnic monopoly but not a franchise for hiring all track crews. As Burns pointed out (p. 52), Italian labour had a specific purpose: "The Italians on our line are used to replace those men who have been employed earlier in the season on contracts, and to whom at this time of year, July and August, when the harvest starts, the farmer offers high wages and they jump their jobs, and the work is left behind, and we have to rely on anything we can get."

24. Burns to C. Mariotti, Secretary of the Italian Immigration Aid Society, 16 March 1903, *Royal Commission, 1904,* 3.

25. *La Patria Italiana* advertisement, 20 Feb. 1904, *Royal Commission, 1904.*

26. Cordasco to M. Torchia & Co., 12 March 1904, *Royal Commission, 1904,* 89.

27. See, for example, *Labour Gazette*, Reports of the Local Correspondent, vol. 7 (1906–1907). A systematic look at the various labour incidents would provide a better index of sojourning and the question of worker militance than does concentration on a few articulate leaders or on major confrontations.

28. Burns to Cordasco, *Royal Commission, 1904*, 113. Burns also informed the Italian Immigration Aid Society of this matter.

29. B. Attolico, "L'agricoltura e l'immigrazione nell'Canada," *Bollettino* 5 (Anno 1912), Commissariat of Emigration, Rome, 547.

30. See *Revista di Emigrazione*, Anno 1:6 (Aug. 1908). On a basis of amount per remittance, the figures were Canada, 221 lire; Argentina, 194; United States, 185; Brazil, 168. Sixty-four percent went to the South of Italy and the vast majority of remittances to Italy from Canada came through the postal savings system.

31. Moroni, "Le condizioni attuali," 49.

32. B. Attolico, "Sui campi di lavoro della nuova ferrovia transcontinentale canadese," *Bollettino* 1 (Anno 1913), Commissariat of Emigration, Rome, 7.

SHOVELLING OUT THE "MUTINOUS": POLITICAL DEPORTATION FROM CANADA BEFORE 1936[*]

BARBARA ROBERTS

O

Deportation is not a well-explored topic in Canadian historical writing. A few historians of labour, dissent, or immigration have suggested recently that deportation has served as a method of political repression, a reinforcer of economic exploitation, a de facto guest-worker system, and, moreover, that it has been arbitrarily and unjustly administered. Countering this view, Henry Drystek has recently argued that "deportation was never designed for these specific purposes" but instead served to pacify the nativist middle classes who "lacked the assurance and confidence which would have allowed them to adapt to the emerging urban, industrial society," by providing a cheap substitute for adequate social services, and defusing their fear of the hordes with "different cultural and social values" brought in to please the importers of cheap labour.[1] These few studies have had little impact on the conventional view of deportation as a rare occurrence, as a regrettable but unavoidable necessity arising out of mistakes in selecting or admitting immigrants, or caused by the shortcomings or wickedness of individual immigrants.

We still know very little about the process by which the deportation work of the Department of Immigration was built up from a patchy network of inspection and processing procedures into an ironclad administrative absolutism with slight flexibility, and we know virtually nothing about the civil servants who were responsible for that development. The rare

---

[*] Reprinted with the permission of the editor from *Labour/Le Travail* 18 (Fall 1986): 77–110. © Committee on Canadian Labour History.

sketches that do exist are portraits which hardly inspire confidence: they paint a picture either of incompetent political hacks or of smooth, professional administrators grasping the reins of power, enshrining their racist and conservative prejudices in policy and practice. For example, Malcolm Reid, a Vancouver agent, used illegal and improper tactics against the *Komagata Maru* immigrants in 1914. Top level bureaucrat Frederick Blair played a major part in refusing entry to or deporting Polish Jews around 1920, and held the line against refugees fleeing Nazi persecution in the 1930s, even after realizing these refugees would be killed if they remained in Europe. He and his colleagues likewise had few compunctions about the fate of deported radicals.[2]

Was deportation policy being made and carried out by ordinary Canadians, as Henry Drystek suggests, and were mild-mannered civil servants merely ministering to an atavistic frontier impulse of Canadians?[3] Or were good grey bureaucrats and conscious forerunners of the police state, using ends to justify means, knowingly causing human suffering, and, when necessary, barefacedly lying about what was being done to further the goals of the department or their own careers? Many a career has been made in Canadian government by whitewashing the unthinkable; career bureaucrats in the Department of Immigration are no exception. They may even have had more opportunity than most to practise the art of *raison d'état*. Officials managing Canada's deportation policy whitewashed so well that some historians today find it difficult to understand the true nature of the department's policies and practices.

A critical reading of the internal documents of the department reveals that immigration officials repeatedly violated the letter and the spirit of the law, routinely concealed their activities behind bureaucratic reporting procedures, sometimes falsified statistics, and, when necessary, deliberately and systematically lied to the public and the politicians.[4]

Strong measures may have seemed necessary to discharge their duty and protect the nation. Deportation was the drain through which our immigration refuse was directed, in order to assure that "the river of our national life" would not be unnecessarily "polluted by the turgid streams" of the immigrant, unfit, unemployed, unprofitable, and ungrateful.[5] Deportation served an important economic function for the state, as Drystek and others have pointed out;[6] but it also served a political function. Deportation helped relieve employers, municipalities, and the state from the burdens of poverty, unemployment, and political unrest. Deportation helped the municipalities to shovel out some of their poor (much as emigration had helped English parishes in the mid-nineteenth century), thereby reducing the cost of maintaining them. Deportation got rid of workers when they became useless, surplus, or obstreperous. It helped the state reduce the cost of maintaining some of its non-producing members by deferring these costs to the economies of the countries whence the immigrants had come. It also served the function of political and social control by getting rid of immigrant protesters who challenged the assumption implicit in immigration policy that they were commodities for the use of the powerful.[7]

Deportation became legal (it had long been practised extra-legally) under the Immigration Act of 1907; political deportation was legalized in 1910. The World War I period from 1914 to the early 1920s saw the first deliberate and systematic deportation of agitators, activists, and radicals. These were people who had not necessarily done anything illegal, but who were considered undesirable on the basis of their political beliefs and activities. The threat they posed was not to the common people of Canada, but to the vested interests represented by big business, exploitative employers, and a government acting on behalf of interest groups. The radicals represented a new target group for systematic deportation. Before this, they had been expelled on an individual basis whenever possible; during the war period (and during the Great Depression), they were dealt with as a group. They were designated as undesirable not merely by legislation (as immigrants with tuberculosis or venereal disease were, for example), but by employer blacklists and complaints, by the surveillance networks of the industrial and Dominion police, the militia, and the Royal North West Mounted Police (later the RCMP), and United States intelligence, as well as by a certain anti-labour tradition among immigration officials.[8]

The department did not stay within the law in dealing with these "undesirables." Between 1918 and 1922, for example, about twenty radical groups, including the Industrial Workers of the World (IWW), were made illegal in Canada under the War Measures Act. Before and after that period, it was not legal for the department to debar or deport immigrants simply because they were (or were suspected of being) IWW members. Nonetheless, this was common practice. Political deportations were frequently carried out under other legal headings, such as criminality, or they were accused of becoming a public charge.[9] These cases were in any event concealed in the annual reports of the department by the simple expedient of tabulating political deportations under the normal reporting categories.

The war period offered a unique opportunity for the department to learn how to conceal illegal or unfair practices behind the legal categories through which it reported its deportation work. This period was characterized by a decrease in the number of deportations, and by a sharp increase in the intensity of deportation work.[10] During this period the head office at Ottawa devoted much attention to instructing the local offices in how to build a tight case for each deportation, a case that would stand up to challenges from the courts, from the transportation companies (who had to pay costs for taking away "defective" immigrants they had brought in), from foreign governments, and from interest groups in Canada.

The conditions of the war created new political crimes, and new opportunities to get rid of trouble-makers, opportunities not available in pre-war circumstances. The "interned enemy alien" (these were legal immigrants, not prisoners of war) category, for example, created by the War Measures Act and specific to the war, was used to get rid of some long-term residents who were considered undesirable, but who were not legally deportable.[11] This was especially true for radicals and agitators. Because these people were not, technically speaking, legally deported (they were "repatriated" through the Department of Justice), the procedures used were not subject to the provisions of the Immigration Act, and the cases were not included in deportation statistics. Anyone the department wanted to get rid of, it had merely to intern, even briefly.[12]

Political deportation must be seen in the context of the economic imperatives underlying the development of deportation policies and practices. Drystek points out correctly that deporting "undesirables" was simpler and cheaper than providing adequate social services.[13] When immigrants became unproductive, they were shovelled out. But this is only half of the equation: apparently straightforward economic imperatives were also profoundly political. Agitators and radicals challenged a social and economic order (and a political system) that immigration policy served. Political deportation and economic deportation (although they are in reality not separate or separable) were methods of preserving the status quo. The Department of Immigration set itself up as the protector of the public purse, the public health, the public morals, and increasingly, the public "safety," as these were defined by powerful political and business interests.

Between 1906 and the beginning of World War I, modern deportation practices were developed. The department's work became specified in law and regulation, became systematized, and rationalized. The department constructed a number of systems to seek out and deport individuals and members of undesirable social groups: the insane, infected, diseased, mentally defective, and unemployed, for example. It took on a moral and punitive tone during this period, in response to economic and social conditions that produced large numbers of clients for deportation services. In fact, most deportations were caused by illness, accident, industrial injury, unemployment, and other conditions largely beyond the control of individual immigrants. But the department blamed the victims for their plight; deports became public charges because they were lazy or had bad characters. They deserved to be punished, not just given the reward of a free trip home. This curiously old-fashioned tone contrasted strangely with the distinct bureaucratic modernism of the way the department was beginning to organize and carry out its work. It is probably explained in part by the cost argument; the department needed to prove it was not frivolously sending home those who did not deserve a free trip, and it had to assure that the transportation companies would pay for as much of the cost as possible.[14]

In its endeavour to safeguard the country, the department stretched, ignored, and sometimes flouted its own rules. As the laws and regulations became increasingly complex, the procedures laid out for the department to follow became more minutely defined. Failure to follow legal niceties could bring trouble, such as painful court appearances, losing deports on habeas corpus writs, and the like. The common response of the department in these cases was to tighten up the procedures (and the paperwork) when it had to, and try to get the law changed to legalize what it had already been doing.

The 6 June 1919 amendments to section 41 of the Immigration Act widened the scope for political deportation: anyone who advocated or acted to bring about the overthrow of organized government either in the empire (at the provincial level in Canada, too) or in general or destroy property or promote riot or public disorder, became a prohibited immigrant who could not be legally landed in Canada, no matter how long they had been here. If someone fell under this section at any time after 4 May 1910 (the amendments made actions or affiliations retroactively illegal), they were still a member of the prohibited classes. The sole exceptions were Canadian citizens by birth or naturalization. British-born immigrants could not be naturalized (their Canadian citizenship was automatic after the required period of residence); they were thus subject to this amendment.

The original 1910 version of section 41 had provided for political deportation only for immigrants who had not met domicile requirements. A first set of amendments proposed in the spring of 1919 merely provided that someone undesirable or prohibited on political grounds could never gain domicile. The 6 June amendments removed in addition the protection of citizenship for British subject immigrants. Three days later, amendments to the Citizenship Act made it possible to strip naturalized citizens of their protection. Section 41 was finally restored by Parliament to its pre-6 June 1919 form in 1928, after the Senate had refused on eight separate occasions to pass liberalizing or revoking measures. Its strikingly similar companion law, section 98 of the Criminal Code, remained on the books until 1936, but was not used during the 1920s by a King government dependent on progressive support to stay in office.[15]

The Department of Immigration continued to deport radicals throughout the 1920s, but it was handicapped by the loss of War Measures Act antiradical legislation. Employer groups pressed the department and the government for action against immigrant radicals and activists. The department did its best to oblige, but found section 41 deportations politically and legally risky. Radicals who had gained domicile were less likely to be deported in this period. In 1928, for example, Arvo Vaara was convicted for sedition after he wrote in a *Vapaus* editorial that he did not care if the king recovered from his present serious illness. The Reverend Thomas Jones got a Finnish fellow missionary to translate Vaara's seditious editorials, and took the translations to the *Sudbury Star* for publication. Jones' public-spirited act was personally motivated as well as politically; Vaara and the red Finns hindered Jones' missionary work, and *Vapaus* made fun of missionaries. Worse, *Vapaus* was campaigning to organize a union for northern Ontario miners. The timing was inopportune: two major nickel companies were negotiating a merger, and Queen's Park, ever a friend of the mine owners, would not like any hitches.[16] His tactics were effective: the town was stirred up, the Legion passed resolutions, the local Crown attorney stepped in, and Vaara went to jail. But he was not deported. After the Sam Scarlett fiasco in 1924, when the Department of Justice had given Immigration bad advice about charging Scarlett, then later had been forced to recant and tell Immigration to grant his appeal and release him because there were no legal grounds for his deportation, the department was much more cautious and tended to carry out political deportations under other legal causes.[17]

Legal causes for deportation were published in the Department of Immigration's annual report under five headings. "Public charge" covered those who were non-paying inmates of any publicly funded institution (usually medical or charitable), or who received some form of welfare payment from the public purse. "Criminality" covered those who had served sentences in penal institutions. Domiciled immigrants could not be deported as public charges or for criminality. "Accompanying" referred to members of families who were themselves not necessarily deported or deportable (Canadian citizens by birth, for example), accompanying a deported family head or member. "Medical causes" included those who were ill, injured, or incapacitated in ways that contravened the Immigration Act; these people were usually not self-supporting at the time they had been ordered deported, and might have been non-paying inmates of hospitals and so on. Some may have been self-supporting but had a contagious disease, or were afflicted in some way that might in the future affect their ability to be self-supporting. Causes ranged from industrial accidents, TB, epilepsy, heart disease, varicose veins, VD, retardation, and psychological problems (from raving insanity to masturbation). Most domiciled immigrants could not be deported under this category. "Other causes" referred to various violations of the act, usually related to improper entry, or belonging to some prohibited category.[18] The key to deporting domiciled immigrants under these categories lay in removing their domicile by establishing that they belonged to the prohibited classes and could never have obtained domiciled status.

"Other causes" covered a multitude of sins. A board of inquiry could use section 33 for an immigrant whose entry had been improper (not necessarily knowingly), or section 3 for an immigrant belonging to the prohibited classes on account of medical conditions, political beliefs, activities, or intentions, criminal records, morals, etc., at the time of entry. Many cases falling under sections 3 or 33 could be deported regardless of the number of years of residence subsequent to entry.

The charge of "entry by misrepresentation" was a handy catchall used by the department to deport those who undertook activities at variance with those they stated as intended at the time of entry. For example, Mikolaj Dranuta was brought over under the auspices of the Ukrainian Colonization Board in 1926 to do farm work. Instead, according to an RCMP spy report, he took a job in an Edmonton meat packing plant, joined the Ukrainian Labor Temple and taught in a Ukrainian school, helped to organize cultural activities such as the visit of a dance troupe, and so on. The Mounties described him as a communist, and noted that while he had not made any public speeches ("yet"), he was open about his views. After reviewing the spy report, an immigration official perused Dranuta's photograph (from his CPR Occupational Certificate) and decided on that basis that Dranuta was not the farming or peasant type. "Under the circumstances" wrote the official, the department would take "action . . . with a view to deportation on the ground of entering Canada by misrepresentation."[19]

Despite the relatively liberal climate in 1920s federal politics, a right-wing element continued to flourish. Anti-radical drives were established in several Canadian cities by the end of the 1920s. Police and civic officials as well as provincial politicians, were prominent in such campaigns.[20] At conferences, in groups, and individually, officially and privately, they warned that the "communist menace" was growing, and urged clampdowns and wholesale deportations. In Toronto, regulations were passed in 1929 against public meetings conducted in languages other than English, and disorderly or seditious utterances. Anyone renting a public facility for such a meeting could lose their licence. Police Chief Draper and Mayor McBride promoted police harassment and assault against radicals, for which the radicals frequently found themselves arrested. The "free speech" issue became a cause célèbre; and Toronto remained a hotbed of radical action and repression by the authorities until the mid-1930s.[21]

The 1930 election of a right-wing federal government brought a change in political climate. A senior immigration official spoke for those who saw their chance to get rid of radicals: Western Commissioner of Immigration Gelley argued that to allow the "communistic element" to come into contact with young people was like a farmer allowing potato bugs to multiply until the whole potato patch was endangered. The department must now take some "radical action . . . to stamp out this element from Canadian life."[22] As the cost of relief and the number of local protests over unemployment rose, municipal politicians demanded increased deportation: by the spring of 1931, over seventy city councils had sent resolutions to the federal government. Provincial premiers and other officials wrote urging more action.[23]

In the meantime, municipalities did what they could to deal with the unemployed and contentious:[24] Askeli Panjata was arrested for marching in a Port Arthur, Ontario parade of unemployed workers in November 1930. He was sentenced to three months in prison, then was hastily removed from the local jail to Halifax, "before any of his friends were aware of it." He was deported to Finland in March 1931, in spite of his protests that his life would be in danger there.[25] Hymie Sparaga was arrested in Toronto in January 1931 on the picket line of a garment worker strike, was sentenced to two months in jail, then was deported and, according to Annie Buller, he was later killed by the Nazis.[26] Louis Revay and John Gryciuk were convicted respectively of unlawful assembly and rioting during the 1931 Estevan strike, and were deported.[27] A number of local employers', veterans', and fraternal associations supported such actions; the Bennett papers contain many resolutions and demands for stiffer laws and intensified or automatic deportation of radicals.[28]

In Winnipeg, Mayor Ralph Webb, a staunch supporter of law and order, carried out a one-person campaign, writing regularly to R.B. Bennett demanding action against communists and agitators. In May 1931, Webb sent Bennett the names of fifteen Winnipeggers who had gone to Moscow to study revolutionary organizing, asking that the Immigration Department be told to bar their reentry. In July, Webb wired Minister of Labour Gideon Robertson urging him to press for "deportation of all undesirables" including behind-the-scenes radical activists and administrators.

Such sentiments were not surprising from the influential classes of a city that had survived Canada's strongest attempted Bolshevik revolution (or so they thought) a scant dozen years before. There was a fear in some quarters that such an event might again be in the making. RCMP and provincial police headquarters especially were prone to such alarms, basing their intelligence on typically wild-eyed spy reports. They warned the premier that the local Communist Party was setting up a "fighting group . . . to obtain funds" by "rob[bing] banks and stores," and reported that the CP had insinuated many of its important members into municipal and other government positions, to gain protection against the authorities.[29]

In fact, the powers-that-be had reason for concern. The Communist Party was planning a nationwide protest and recruiting drive among the unemployed in 1931. Since the 1920s, Communists and other radicals had been involved in activities which deeply alarmed the government and business community of Canada: organizing industrial unions, building left wing groups within existing unions, organizing the unemployed, leading militant strikes, and conducting successful public campaigns, such as the one that collected 100 000 signatures on a petition for unemployment insurance, a five-day work week, and a $35 weekly minimum wage for both women and men workers.[30]

The Bennett government was determined to stamp out "communism" (radicalism and social protest). Bennett began meeting with police and other officials early in 1931 to plan the campaign.[31] He revived section 98 of the Criminal Code, lying virtually unused throughout the King years, and the government used it to go after the Communist Party. The CP was declared an illegal organization in Canada on 11 August 1931, under section 98 of the Criminal Code.[32]

Police signalled this campaign by raiding the offices of the party and the homes of three of its leaders, the offices of the Workers' Unity League, and the official paper, *The Worker*, on 11 and 12 August 1931. The raids had been planned by the Ontario Conservative government with the enthusiastic co-operation of the OPP, the RCMP, and Toronto's "red squad."[33] It was an attempt to cut off the CP's head. Bennett called it his iron heel policy.[34]

The actions resulted in the arrest of eight party members and officials, all were charged with being members of an unlawful organization, and with seditious conspiracy.[35] The eight were tried by jury in Toronto. The Crown's method of presenting evidence was to become a precedent for the numerous prosecutions that followed. Rather than arguing that these individuals advocated force or violence, it argued that as communists, they were under the direction of the Communist International, which advocated revolutionary violence. The views or actions of the individuals were not germane; all that was necessary was to show that a person was a member of the CP, which was obliged to follow Comintern policy. The Crown's case rested primarily on Comintern policy documents and publications, and on the testimony of a Mountie spy who had been an undercover member of the party for ten years. Sergeant Leopold's statements were used to establish the subordination of the Canadian CP to discipline from abroad, and the seditious nature of the organization. All eight men were convicted. All save Tomo Cacic were sentenced to five years' imprisonment.[36] On appeal, in February 1932 the seditious conspiracy charges were dropped, but the section 98 charges stood. All eight were supposed to be deported, but in the end, only Cacic was.[37]

Thus the Communist Party's status as an illegal organization was confirmed; all its members were chargeable under section 98. Such an outcome had been the hope of the authorities,[38] and it was particularly pleasing to immigration officials. Now the only evidence needed for political deportation was to prove that the immigrant was a member of a communist organization. Naturalized citizenship was no sure defence against deportation. The department routinely sent names of prospective deports to the Citizenship Branch of Secretary of State to see if naturalization certificates could be revoked. Stripped of citizenship, an immigrant could revert to being a member of the prohibited classes, unable to gain domicile no matter how long in Canada, because persons of that class could never legally enter.[39]

Pending the appeal, Immigration Department officials had been routinely exploring various avenues to expedite the deportation of radicals. They received names from the RCMP and other sources, investigated the immigration status of the prospective deports, and set in motion the appropriate machinery. By the fall of 1931, intensified political deportation had become federal policy. In October, the minister of justice hosted a special meeting to discuss the need to increase deportation. It was attended by the minister of national defence, the commissioner of immigration, the military chief of general staff, and the RCMP commissioner. They decided to use the RCMP barracks in Halifax to house the expected deports.[40]

Although it is impossible to be sure how many political deportations were carried out during the Depression, it is possible to verify that they were numerous. The evidence suggests a conservative estimate of at least several hundred during the 1930s (and perhaps a somewhat lesser number in the 1914–22 period). They were usually carried out under public charge, criminality, or other legal categories, and they were not explicitly acknowledged as political deportations in the public documents of the department, such as the annual reports. Internal documents are somewhat more revealing.[41] Department files, memos, and correspondence contain names and discussions of cases of radicals. Whatever the details of individual cases, it is clear that such practices were routine and widespread.[42]

Another source of information on individual cases is the *Canadian Labor Defender*, the organ of the Canadian Labor Defense League, which cites numerous instances of deportations for political activities.[43] Also informative are oral history interviews with people who participated in the events of the time. Satu Repo's interview of Einar Nordstrom, a Lakehead radical, provides details not only about department practices, but also about community responses. By late 1932, deportation had become so common, according to Nordstrom, that ethnic associations had developed the custom of holding dances and other fundraisers to pay a tailor to make a suit of clothes for the person to wear on the trip home.[44]

Some cases, such as Sophie Sheinen's, were widely publicized in radical circles. She was ill-treated in jail and lost nearly thirty-five pounds in six months; she was ill and spitting blood.[45] By September 1932 protests against her deportation were gaining Bennett's attention. He sought advice from Immigration Department officials, who told him that Sheinen had been "mutinous" in jail. Her claims of ill health were simply a device to avoid deportation, they said; she had been examined by a doctor and pronounced "fit to travel." As was their policy, they ignored protests and deported her in September 1932.[46]

Another typical pattern was exemplified in the experience of Sam Langley. He was an activist in northern Ontario who was deported to England on 23 December 1931. He had been ordered deported previously after a 1929 jail sentence for a free speech demonstration, on charges of vagrancy (the disorderly conduct subsection)—part of a whole series of arrests by Toronto police beginning in February and continuing on into the summer. Protests averted his deportation at that time, but by 1931 the political climate had changed. He was picked up in Port Arthur at 5 PM, and was on the train to Halifax by 9 PM that same evening, to be deported under the reactivated 1929 order.[47]

John Ferris of Sault Ste Marie, a young man during the Depression, recalled pressures exerted against radicals. Women canvassing for the Canadian Labor Defense League, for example, were arrested, then released without charges being heard. These cases were merely adjourned and left hanging so they could be picked up long after if needed. Ferris remembers numerous cases where radicals were picked up and deported—sometimes so fast that friends did not even know they were gone. Most of these cases involved non-British immigrants. The Sault Ste Marie city council, like others, had passed a resolution to "deport all known Reds." "Reds" was synonymous with "activists," in their view.[48]

Cases were often built on personal impressions of officials about the attitudes of the accused; the immigrants were not privy to and could not refute this material. Sam Kluchmik's experiences in Canada were representative of many who ended up on relief in the 1930s. He had entered as a farm worker in 1928, but quit in disgust at the wages (75¢ a day). In the ensuing years he worked seasonally in railway construction. More often than not unemployed, he lived "on the charity of friends" through most of 1930 and 1931. By October 1931 he was sufficiently desperate to apply for relief, and when the deportation complaint was recorded he had received a total of $101.50 in beds, meals, and clothing, in exchange for which he had worked a number of weeks on the Grassmere ditch. He was reported for deportation by J.D. Fraser, superintendent of the City of Winnipeg Relief Department in June 1932.[49]

At his deportation hearing he said quite clearly that he was prepared to accept any kind of work, including farm work; he hoped to get hired for the harvest. Nonetheless, he was ordered deported as a public charge. He appealed. The regional Immigration Department official contacted Ottawa about the appeal, and said that the chair of the board of inquiry had found that Kluchnik was "surly and gave the impression of one who belonged to one of the 'Red' organizations of this country, although he denied this. The Chairman of the Board is of the opinion that Canada would be well rid of the appellant."

The next step in the proceedings was to get the steamship company to pay the costs of deportation. If an immigrant were proven to be "defective," the transportation company who brought them in was liable to remove them at its own expense. To the steamship company, Commissioner Joliffe wrote that Kluchnik "refuses to accept farm work." The transcript of the board of inquiry reveals that Kluchnik made no such statement, nor could anything he said be so interpreted. But an internal memo to the commissioner of immigration and the deputy minister had claimed that Kluchnik

> had not fulfilled the conditions of entry to Canada and apparently has no intentions of doing so. While he claims to be anxious to remain in this country he does not desire to take farm work and in the opinion of the examining officer he is a surly individual and gave the impression of being a Red although he denies this.

However, Sam Kluchnik's deportation was not effected; by the time the order got back to Winnipeg, he had found farm work. He was lucky; by now there had been such an outcry against deporting the unemployed that the department had begun suspending deportation orders against those who had been on the dole but had found work by the time their orders were ready. Should they go on relief again, the orders would be activated and carried out; otherwise, they would remain suspended.[50] Kluchnik remained under suspended sentence of deportation for more than twenty years.[51] Kluchnik's case shows that department statistics on incidence and causes of deportation cannot be taken at face value.[52]

There were several easy ways to deport radicals. "Criminal conviction" was a handy catchall, greatly aided by police harassment. "Vagrancy" was a common criminal charge against radicals, used with increased frequency during periods of repression. John Ferris recalls that in Sault Ste Marie, activists in unemployed workers' movements were picked up and charged with vagrancy because they were "without substantial means of support."[53] The real actions for which radicals were deported varied. Arvi Johannes Tielinen, Thomas Gidson Pollari, Viljo Adolf Piispa, and Jaako Emil Makynen were convicted (along with several others) of taking part in an unlawful assembly after they had marched in a parade at Timmins, and deported in 1932.[54] Of thirty-four people convicted of unlawful assembly for a similar parade in May 1932, eight were deported.[55] Those deported for organizing or participating in relief strikes or demonstrations included Matti Hautamaki of Port Arthur, Leontie Karpenkower of The Pas, and W. Jacobson of Vancouver.[56] Deportation for any cause except section 41, that is, under any category not overtly political, was considered so problemfree, so automatic, by the department, that it did not normally bother to hire lawyers for the boards of inquiry. There was little likelihood of any successful challenge, even by the courts.[57] The department processed tens of thousands of deportations without any interference whatsoever during the 1930s. Most were carried out under "public charge" although many were in fact political deportations, such as those of Winnipeg Poles reputedly "members of organizations connected with the Communist movement."[58]

In May 1932 the authorities carried out another showcase "red raid" of leaders in cities and towns all across Canada. Victims were quickly sent to Halifax for hearings and deportation.[59] As details of the proceedings became known, there were widespread protests. There was good reason.

Questioning of the immigration minister in the House of Commons by Woodsworth and others revealed an arbitrariness and a disregard for due process all too typical of deportation methods. Gordon evaded questions concerning the nature of the charges and the whereabouts, date, and nature of the hearings. Cornered, he excused the hurried removal of the men by saying that when immigration officials were sure that an immigrant was illegally in the country, they frequently chose the "nearest most convenient port" for deportation as the site of the hearing.[60]

Feeble on the face of it, subsequent revelations suggested Gordon was trying to cover up star chamber tactics. One of the arrested men, Orton Wade, was a Canadian citizen by birth, under no circumstances deportable, and not accountable to the Department of Immigration for any reason. He sued the deputy minister and others for false arrest and imprisonment. His case was dismissed by Winnipeg's Court of Queen's Bench, but heard by the Manitoba Court of Appeal. The hearing produced a number of scandalous revelations for which the department was roundly criticized by the bench and the public. For example, Deputy Minister Egan had signed the warrant for Wade's arrest five months before it was used, but had made no effort to verify that Wade was subject to the Immigration Department's authority. Nor did he think it reasonable to do so. If the department verified particulars before issuing warrants, it would never get its work done, he said. Egan's response was as revealing as his apparent imperturbability. He defended the department's actions on the grounds that they were perfectly routine and normal procedures used in a "great number" of instances. Thus, if there were anything wrong in the Wade case, by implication, it was wrong in most deportation cases. And indeed it was. A victory in this case would have put a serious crimp in the department's activities.

Wade's treatment after arrest "amounted to a denial of justice . . . actuated by motives which are not permitted by the law," said Justice Dennistoun. Further, even if Wade had been deportable, there was no excuse for his removal from Winnipeg (close to the United States border, thus the nearest port for his deportation) to Halifax. Justice Trueman compared the department's conduct to "parallel high handed proceedings" of 1667 when Clarendon shipped off various of his opponents to islands and other remote outposts so they could not have the protection of the law. Wade lost the case by a narrow 3-to-2 decision, one judge ruling against him solely on a technicality.

Orton Wade got away only because he was Canadian-born. The remaining "Halifax Ten," as they came to be known, lost their appeal before the Nova Scotia Supreme Court.[61] Although the justices agreed that the department had not acted in complete conformity to the law, in the end they dismissed the appeal, as did the minister of immigration in December.[62] Despite much agitation and a veritable flood of letters, petitions, telegrams, and other documents attempting to avert the deportations or alter the destinations, as soon as arrangements for documents and transportation were completed, the men were shipped out.

All too often, neither human life nor British liberties appear to have been a concern. We get rare glimpses of the bureaucrats' punitive and reactionary attitudes in private correspondence. In a little joke to the RCMP director of intelligence in 1931, Assistant Immigration Commissioner Munroe hoped political deports would "appreciate the laws and conditions which prevail [in their own countries] better than those which we have in Canada and which they decry so violently." RCMP Commissioner Starnes complained that two Yugoslav radicals had escaped in Germany during their deportation, obtained clothes and false passports, and fled to the USSR. If they had gone to Yugoslavia, it would have meant their deaths, he admitted. The response of the Immigration Department was to tighten procedures to prevent more escapes.[63]

Publicly the department denied it was deporting people to prison or death. Concerning an "alleged danger to those men following deportation," it wired the Canadian Labor Defense League, "they will unquestionably have the full protection of the laws of their native countries to which they are being returned."[64] When victims of red raids were awaiting disposal, the department received massive protests about the dangers awaiting the men in native countries now under repressive governments. Arvo Vaara and Martin Parker, for example, were to be sent back to Finland, where the Whites had been in power for more than a decade (which they had initiated with concentration camps and executions for Reds) and were busily carrying out anti-radical campaigns of their own through the agency of fascist thugs.[65] Immediately after receiving strong warnings of dangers to Vaara and Parker in Finland, and pleas to let them go to the Soviet Union instead, the department ordered extra guards and arranged particularly tight security to insure their delivery to Finland. Similar examples abound in department records.[66] The kindest thing that can be said about the department officials is that they did not take such warnings seriously, even those given by the RCMP. They hid behind the law, which said that deportation sent immigrants back whence they came; if they felt any reluctance about this choice, it is nowhere in the records. As Minister of Justice Guthrie of the Bennett government said about protests of political deportations, he got too many to acknowledge. "I merely hand them over to the Mounted Police in order that a record may be kept of the names and addresses of the people who sign them and I make this statement so that the petitioners may know what I do with them."[67]

By 1934, public opinion was beginning to change. It was no longer merely the communists who objected to mass deportation, the curtailment of civil liberties, and section 98. King had found it expedient to oppose the worst of Bennett's iron heel policies. He had promised that if elected he would repeal section 98, and, by implication, stop the abuses.[68] The CCF, whatever support it mustered, also opposed mass deportation and section 98 as violations of civil liberties and common decency.[69]

Many people who had been untroubled by the summary deportation of radicals were not so sanguine about wholesale deportation of the unemployed. Challenges in the courts had combined with public opinion to cause the Department of Immigration to become slightly more circumspect in its activities. By 1933, the department had to tighten up on irregular or illegal practices. As the commissioner of immigration noted in a directive, the courts were increasingly reviewing deportation cases upon habeas corpus applications by the prospective deports. When courts found procedural irregularities, they were empowered to order the release of the appellant. Any departure from strict legality, if detected and challenged, had the potential to destroy a case and lead to "an adverse decision with embarrassing consequences and complications."[70]

The excesses of some local authorities had also begun to come under fire. The Toronto Police Red Squad had been under criticism for some time, because of its heavy-handed and arbitrary actions: beating up suspects, seizing papers, almost at Red Squad leader Nursey's whim. Whims were no substitute for good judgement or legality. Lawyers and judges began to express concern. In the fall of 1933, the Toronto Police Commission (its two most rabid members had retired) told the Red Squad that henceforth they could only raid meetings that were clearly in violation of the law.[71] That cooled down Toronto considerably.

After 1934, the worst was over. That year was a turning point. The most spectacular event was the arrest and trial for sedition of A.E. Smith, the head of the CLDL. It all began with a play called *Eight Men Speak*, put on by the CLDL in Toronto in December 1933, which castigated prison conditions, the shooting of the Estevan strikers, and the attempted shooting of Tim Buck, allegedly on orders from high authority. The play was quickly closed by Toronto police. Bennett was furious about the play. He hated Smith and had been seeking a way to silence him. Two weeks later Smith publicly accused Bennett of giving the order to shoot Buck.[72] Bennett ordered Smith charged with sedition.

This time Bennett and his minions had gone too far. They were criticized in the press, and support for Smith came also from mainstream labour and church groups. Then the trial revealed that the Crown had no case against Smith and he was found innocent. If he was not guilty, other sedition cases were cast into doubt. A few months later, all the remaining Kingston Communist prisoners from the August 1931 red raids were set free, except Tim Buck, who was held until November. Bennett had backed down.[73]

The Department of Immigration still carried on. It scoured the jails periodically to find those "convicted as a result of identifying themselves with riots, or disturbances of a communistic nature."[74] But when the country-wide crackdown against reds lessened, so did the supply of radicals in the jails who could be deported for their political activities. When King repealed section 98 early in 1936, the authorities lost their strongest weapon for political deportation. Immigration still had all its apparatus intact; it merely had to return to a more discreet style of operation, relying on other methods and other charges for deporting immigrants it judged undesirable.

Deportation ultimately depended on a network of referrals from criminal justice, relief, medical, and political authorities. When such referrals became inexpedient, deportation diminished. There were limits to what could be accomplished by administrative fiat from the top down. The limits had been reached. After 1935, deportation declined to "normal" levels.[75]

Cui bono? The stated ideal of Canadian immigration policy was to attract a permanent agricultural population. Behind this ideal, thinly concealed and little denied, lay a more-or-less Wakefieldian system.[76] These permanent settlers would often be forced into wage labour, either in the short term to accumulate the capital ("cash stake") to start farming their own land, or in the long term to supplement inadequate farm earnings.[77] Hidden behind that bitter but still palatable modification of the ideal lay yet another reality: a massive system of importing industrial workers who could hardly claim to be farmers, even potentially. As Donald Avery has shown, Canada's immigration policy promoted the recruitment of a large body of unskilled industrial workers who would function (and likely remain) as an industrial proletariat.[78] Yet whether the immigrants were assumed to go straight to their prairie homesteads, to detour briefly or intermittently into wage labour, or to be permanently absorbed into the industrial wage sector of the economy, one thing was clear: they were supposed to remain here and become Canadians. Even the severest critics of Canadian immigration policy tended to accept the claim that Canada was trying to attract a permanent population. Attempts by corporate interests to import large numbers of contract workers for temporary work were refused. Scott and other departmental officials "time after time refused to allow industrial workers into the country on temporary permits."[79] Industrial workers who entered came on the same legal terms as the highly prized and politically palatable legitimate agriculturalists: as landed immigrants who could become citizens after three or five years.

The government was uncomfortable about the reality of the immigrant industrial proletariat that lay behind the myth of the immigrant independent agricultural producer. But this "reality" was in fact little more than another part of the myth that disguised a politically devastating truth: that "many of the Europeans who came to Canada were in effect guest-workers, who met the needs of Canadian industry and agriculture and then went home.[80]

Agriculture's seasonality makes it easy to detect the stream of migrant harvester labour thinly concealed within the flow of those who were ostensibly and legally permanent settlers. Yet other industries were equally, if not more, dependent on this type of work force. This was particularly true of lumbering, mining, and railway construction. The department was not particularly pleased about this. As Avery points out, "by 1913, Immigration officials were concerned that Canada was becoming increasingly committed to a guest-worker form of immigration." But there was little the department could do. These industries wanted "an expendable labour force [that] takes its problems away when it is re-exported," as the United States Senate's Dillingham Commission on immigration had put it in 1910. All the department could do was to refuse to issue temporary work permits.[81] This was not a problem for the employers: as long as there was a flow of cheap immigrant labour, it made little difference whether they were legally guest-workers or landed immigrants. In fact, the landed status offered a number of advantages to the employer, in part because it was unregulated.

Canada's concealed guest-worker system offered significant economic and political advantages to employers and to the state. As Michael Burawoy has pointed out, one of the invariable characteristics of a migrant work force is that the functions of maintenance and reproduction take place in different locations. In a migrant labour system, the costs of renewing the work force are passed on completely or partially to the sending economy or state. The employer of migrant labour is "neither responsible politically nor accountable financially to the external political and economic systems," that is, to the sending countries.[82] The receiving, or using, country has greatly reduced costs for social services partly because the families of workers remain in the sending country, where whatever available educational, medical, and other social services will be paid for. These reproductive costs— that is, the cost associated with family formation, child-rearing, and labour market training—are thus of no concern to the receiving employers or government. Migrant labour is cheap not only in terms of the lower wages paid to the migrant worker, but in terms of other costs incurred in maintaining the work force. Migrant workers can be kept in camps, fed en masse, and provided with minimal welfare services. Moreover, if these workers are injured, incapacitated, or incapable, neither the employer nor the state is obliged to take care of them over the long term. Because under this system these workers have no claim on the resources of the receiving country or the employer, they can be sent back "home" when their usefulness is at an end.[83]

Burawoy is discussing migrant miners in South Africa and farm workers in California. Yet many of the points he raises describe remarkably well a number of aspects of Canadian immigration in the period discussed here. In Canada there was a parallel system of occupational segregation and subordination based on ethnicity; many workers were housed and fed in isolated camps, often at very low standards.[84] Sojourners who came to Canada in boom times might succeed in realizing their dream to return home rich— but for many, possibly a majority in times of economic depression, the dream could turn suddenly to ashes. The pre-World War I railway workers are a case in point: thousands of them were trapped by depression, imprisoned in internment camps during the war, and released to the big companies when the demand for their labour again became acute.

Unless immigrants lived here continuously long enough to get domicile, and better, attain citizenship, they could be deported if they ceased to be productive members of the work force or otherwise got into trouble. This deportation could take place legally and formally, under the auspices of the department, or it could take place informally and outside the legal framework. For instance, an immigrant thrown out of work might apply to a municipality for some form of poor relief. The administration would then report the immigrant to the Department of Immigration, setting in motion the legal deportation process. Alternatively, the municipality might refuse to grant relief. In many cases, this left the immigrant with little alternative but to effect his or her own do-it-yourself deportation, by leaving. This method was even cheaper for the municipality (and Ottawa), and was favoured in times of economic distress. Nonetheless, department records show 28 097 people formally deported between (fiscal years ending) 1930 and 1935.[85]

In eighteenth-century Britain,[86] and in parts of the United States in the twentieth century, poor relief was given to agricultural and other workers to hold them until their labour was needed, at which time the relief was cut off and they were forced to take the available jobs.[87] In Canada it was not necessary to use poor relief grants to maintain a readily available supply of cheap labour. Immigration took care of this, particularly after World War I when inflow was directly adjusted to the labour requirements of certain large employers. Deportation was one of the mechanisms that maintained a balance between the need for cheap (and docile) labour in times of economic expansion, and the desire to cut welfare costs (and political unrest) in times of economic contraction. Those who were superfluous to demand or useless to production, those who upset the system or threatened its smooth working, could, if they were immigrants (and they often were), be gotten rid of. Deportation deferred some of the costs of maintaining and reproducing the labour force onto the sending country and economy. Deportation was an unnoticed but important way not only to keep the stream of immigration pure, but, more to the point, to keep profits high and problems few. One of the most significant features of an industrial economy is the need for a large supply of mobile labour. Canadian immigration policy made sure that getting that labour supply was not a problem. Deportation helped to assure that getting rid of it was not a problem either. Deportation, both formal and informal, helped to create a hidden system of migrant labour that functioned much like a "guest-worker" system, even though the stated policy was that immigrants were to be permanent settlers.[88] It was a concealed but necessary regulator of the balance between labour demand and labour supply, which was in itself a critical determinant of Canadian immigration policy and practice between 1900 and 1935.

There was little check on the Department of Immigration's deportation activities. International legal authority C.F. Fraser, comparing deportation in Britain, Northern Ireland, Canada, South Africa, Australia, and New Zealand, concluded in 1940 that the Canadian practices were the most arbitrary, that the power of Canadian officials, unchecked by an apathetic judiciary, had grown dangerously, had gone beyond its legislative authority, and continued to increase.[89] Parliament was consistently uninformed or misinformed about the department's deportation activities, and judicial review was severely limited by the Immigration Act.[90] Neither Parliament nor the courts chose to test the limits set upon their sphere of inquiry. It was Parliament which passed the laws relating to deportation, but it neither made those laws, nor knew, nor controlled how they were carried out. Fraser commented,

> the most notable feature of deportation cases in Canada is the apparent desire to get agitators of any sort out of the country at all costs. . . . [T]he executive branch of the government, in its haste to carry out this policy . . . displayed a marked disregard for the niceties of procedure.[91]

Deportation officials operated in disregard of the law and beyond the control of Parliament.[92] C.D. Fraser concluded that "later cases indicated a premeditated intent to deprive the alien of his right to judicial protection."[93]

Immigration officials lied to conceal their activities, broke their own laws, and consistently abused their power. To argue that they merely reflected the prevailing views of the Canadian public is naive: the conceal-ment of deportation policy and practice meant that the public had virtually no idea of what was being done in its name. Drystek edges close to a class analysis when he specifies (however one might question the characteriza-tions) interest groups: the middle classes are nativists, the employers want cheap labour, the farmers want seasonal workers and harvesters—a labour force with a high turnover, not requiring services or demanding rights. But he denies that deportation was intended to function as a means of social control, or that it maintained a concealed migrant labour system.[94] For him, department bureaucrats may have been cheapskates, but if they served the interests of the dominant classes, that was due to innocence or coincidence.

The weight of the evidence suggests strongly that they were not only cheapskates, but dishonest and malevolent as well. Most of this appears systemic rather than individual in cause; these bureaucrats, it could be argued, were just doing their jobs, which virtually required them to break the law when its very substantial leeway proved inadequate, to lie about or misconstrue the statements of immigrants at their deportation hearings, and the policies and practices of their department. Although it is little more than speculation to discuss their motives, the question of individual responsibil-ity is moot here. There is no evidence in the departmental papers to suggest that the top Immigration Department bureaucrats saw their actions as dis-honest or hypocritical, although there is much to indicate that they were anxious to avoid public exposure, scandal, and court cases relating to proce-dural "irregularities" or substandard conditions. Yet the law gave them arbitrary powers which went beyond and contravened British traditions of justice and fair play; deports, as critics observed, had not even the legal rights of criminals, and the courts were expressly forbidden to interfere as long as the department followed its legally proper, if arbitrary, procedures (or was not caught violating them). In this setting, it was easy to overstep the boundaries, to move from actions which kept the letter but violated the spirit of the law, to actions which violated the letter, to those which were simply beyond the law. One suspects that they would not have thought their actions wrong or dishonest, and if they had, would have believed that the ends justified the means.

But there was a logic of capitalist necessity operating here that was prior to the caveats of liberal democracy, and a social imperative that went beyond individual judgements about right and wrong, or individual British liberties. As Winnipeg Senator McMeans asked rhetorically during Senate debate, arguing against the repeal of section 41, "Do you think that any man of a good character would be accused of sedition and deported?" Insofar as deportation law, policy, and practice were concerned, the right to British lib-erties was based on a social contract, and could be forfeited when individu-als broke that social contract by becoming unemployed, sick, radical, or in some other way a threat to the social order or a liability on the public. While the "deportation policy of the Canadian government" may not have been designed exclusively to "control radicals and to expel surplus labour,"[95] these intentions were well served by its initial and subsequent development over the years, and were consistently among its most important functions.

NOTES

1. Donald Avery, *"Dangerous Foreigners": European Immigrant Workers and Labour Radicalism in Canada* (Toronto, 1979); B. Roberts, "Shovelling out the Unemployed: Winnipeg City Council and Deportation, 1930–35," *Manitoba History* 5 (1983): 12–24; Shin Imai, "Deportation in the Depression," *Queen's Law Journal* 7 (1981): 66–94; B. Roberts, "Purely Administrative Proceedings: The Management of Canadian Deportation, 1900–1935" (PhD thesis, University of Ottawa, 1980); B. Roberts, *Deportation from Canada* (forthcoming); Henry Drystek, "The Simplest and Cheapest Mode of Dealing with Them: Deportation from Canada before World War II," *Histoire sociale/Social History* 14 (1982): 407–41.

2. Hugh Johnston describes "Conservative party hack" and former elementary school teacher Malcolm Reid, the Vancouver immigration agent who was appointed in 1911, thanks to Tory MP H.H. Stevens, for whom Reid served as a mouthpiece and agent. Johnston describes Reid as racist, consistently willing to violate the law, court orders, and departmental regulations, and in concert with his master Stevens, the embodiment of "local prejudice pure and simple." Judged incompetent after his mishandling of the *Komagata Maru* situation, he was finally kicked upstairs and ended his days harassing his colleagues. H.J.M. Johnston, *The Voyage of the Komagata Maru* (Bombay 1979), 19–20, 49–52, 68, 129, 152 n12. *None Is Too Many* exactly describes the immigration mentality of the 1930s, exemplified in Frederick C. Blair. He had joined the department by the turn of the century; in 1905 he became an immigration officer and moved up rapidly. After a spell as secretary, he became acting deputy minister from 1921 to 1923, and in 1936 director (equivalent to deputy minister in rank). Irving Abella and Harold Troper, *None Is Too Many: Canada and the Jews of Europe, 1933–1948* (Toronto, 1982), 7–9.

3. Drystek, "Simplest and Cheapest," 440.

4. On cooked statistics and deliberate lies, see B. Roberts, "Shovelling out the Unemployed," "Purely Administrative Proceedings," and *Deportation from Canada*.

5. Dr J. Halpenny of Winnipeg, writing in the October 1919 issue of *The Canadian Journal of Mental Hygiene*, cited by W.G. Smith, *A Study in Canadian Immigration* (Toronto, 1920), 226. On early deportation policy see Public Archives of Canada (hereafter PAC), RG76, file 837, McNicholls to Immigration, 3 Sept. 1895, and Lowe's testimony before the Select Standing Committee on Immigration and Colonization, 1877 Session, cited in Boardman to Fortier, 19 Oct. 1894. Unless otherwise indicated, all RG and MG files refer to the PAC.

6. Drystek, "Simplest and Cheapest," passim; for a fuller discussion see Avery, *"Dangerous Foreigners,"* ch. 1, and Roberts, "Purely Administrative Proceedings," ch. 12, and *Deportation from Canada*, chs. 1 and 8.

7. On the poor law and provisions for removal, see George Nicholls, *A History of the Scotch Poor Law in Connexion with the Condition of the People* (London, 1856); Dorothy George, *London Life Before the Eighteenth Century* (Evanston, IL, 1925; 1964 reprint); Pat Thane, "Women and the Poor Law in Victorian and Edwardian England," *History Workshop Journal* 6 (1978): 29–51; "Poor Laws Report," *Westminster Review*, 1834, in *Poverty in the Victorian Age: Debates on the Issue from Nineteenth Century Critical Journals*, vol. 2, *English Poor Laws, 1834–70*, ed. A.W. Coats (London, 1973). On the similarities between English poor law and deportation, see Roberts, "Purely Administrative Proceedings," 440–44. On useless, surplus, and obstreperous workers, see Avery, *"Dangerous Foreigners,"* 12–13 and passim, and Roberts, "Shovelling out the Unemployed," and *Deportation from Canada*, esp. chs. 5 and 7 on political deportation.

8. For surveillance, see J.S. Woodsworth's 1922 comments in the House of Commons, cited by Lorne Brown and Caroline Brown, *An Unauthorized History of the RCMP* (Toronto, 1978), 52–53, 56–57. The RCMP files contain lengthy and detailed examples of surveillance networks: see RG18 B2(c), file 16/6, and file 17/2. Mountie officers in charge summarized secret spy reports and other intelligence and sent monthly reports on labour and radical activities. The 1919 annual report of the RCMP discusses the role of the Mounties in helping the Immigration Department deal with the red menace. The Borden papers also contain examples of surveillance activities and networks. See, for example, a confidential memo from Percy Reid, immigration chief inspector, to Immigration Minister Calder. Reid had obtained information about various radical individuals and organizations from Pinkerton's, the Dominion police, the CPR police, the United States Immigration Department, as well as from Canadian Immigration: MG26 H1(a), vol. 112, OC559 61050-2. Political deportations depended on information from these and like sources (such as various industrial police and private security agencies). See RG24, files 363-47-1, 3568, and 2656 for weekly intelligence reports and periodic preparations for rumoured armed red uprisings. Militia officials recommended deportation for troublemakers: RG24, vol. 2544, file 2051, Mr and Mrs Joseph Knight, Edmonton radicals whose names appear a number of times in surveillance files, "the most dangerous of the [OBU] group . . . should certainly be deported," 25 March 1919. During the Winnipeg General Strike, Col Godson, provost marshal in Calgary, had urged that the only method to deal with all alien enemies and revolutionists was to pass legislation for massive deportations, take "drastic action" by having "these men . . . quietly deported without any fuss or bother, simply just put across the border without public trial or advertisement": RG24 363-47-1, 4 June 1919. RG24 C1, file C2101, the IWW file, contains surveillance and deportation references, such as the case of John Nelson of Port Arthur, a Finnish immigrant arrested for possession of prohibited literature: "Nelson has been under surveillance. . . . [H]e is the leader of the Lumber Workers Industrial Union at Pt. Arthur . . . a branch of the IWW. Nelson is a dangerous agitator and at the conclusion of his trial . . . I propose to take action . . . [to bring about his] deportation," wrote RCMP Commissioner Perry to Comptroller McLean, 25 Oct. 1919.

9. See Roberts, "Purely Administrative Proceedings," ch. 4, passim, for examples of illegalities and of political deportation under other legal headings. The files of Immigration, Justice, the RCMP, the World War I press censor, and the militia reveal the background work carried out to identify and investigate political activists so they could be deported under various causes. They also provide a sprinkling of names of political deports not found in the few Immigration Department records of admittedly and overt political deportations. Whatever headings were used, the department's files contain numerous references to political deportations during the World War I era; for example, see RG76, files 817510, 917093, 563236, 961162, 267931, and 884866. Some of the Immigration Department's annual reports do discuss political deportations, although they do not include them as such in their statistics: for such discussions, see *Annual Reports*, 1924 (for 1922–23), Western Division report; 1921, Pacific Division report of BC activities for 1919–20 describes the deportation of 14 (of 22 arrested) members of the Russian Workers' Union; 1920, describing political deportation work at Montreal for 1918–19. For legalities, see Leslie Katz, "Some Legal Consequences of the Winnipeg General Strike of 1919," *Manitoba Law Journal* 4 (1970): 39–53; and Kenneth McNaught, "Political Trials and the Canadian Political Tradition," *University of Toronto Law Journal* 24 (1974): 149–69. See also Ernest Cashmore, "The Social Organization of Canadian Immigration Law," *Canadian Journal of Sociology* 3 (1978): 409–29.

10. See B. Roberts, "Purely Administrative Proceedings," ch. 2, "Lying with Statistics," or *Deportation from Canada*, ch. 3, for a critical analysis of the published statistical reports of the department. According to Drystek, "The deportation of criminals was a much more straight-forward matter. Between 1902 and 1939 just over thirty percent of the persons deported were returned for criminal activity." Drystek, "Simplest and Cheapest," 440. But scrutiny of public reports shows that criminality did not emerge as an important cause for deportation until 1908–09, when it almost doubled. In 1920–21 it was the most significant single cause for deportation. In the nine-year period after 1916, criminality accounted for one-half to one-third of all deportations. Were there recurring crime waves among immigrants? Or was there an increasing propensity to convict immigrants of such crimes as vagrancy, watching and besetting (picketing), nuisance, or obstruction of police, as well as a number of "enemy alien" infractions invented during World War I? Crime is not merely a legal, but also a socio-political category; criminality statistics are a better reflection of social control than of real crime. On this see Jason Ditton, *Controlology: Beyond the New Criminology* (London, 1979), esp. ch. 2, "Crime Waves or Control Waves? A Recipe for Atheistic Statisticians." On the necessity to consider where the categories of criminality statistics come from, rather than just count "crime," see John Kitsuse and Aaron Cicourel's classic "A Note on the Uses of Official Statistics," *Social Problems* 11 (1963): 131–39, reprinted in *An Introduction to Deviance*, ed. William Filstead (New York, 1972). On the use of criminal justice to control surplus population that can't be absorbed into the political economy, see Richard Quinney, *Class, State, and Crime: On the Theory and Practice of Criminal Justice* (New York, 1977), 131–39. On the ONDA (drug laws), see Elizabeth Cormack, "The Origins of Canadian Drug Legislation" in *The New Criminologies in Canada: State, Crime, and Control*, ed. Thomas Fleming (Toronto, 1985), esp. 83. Criminality deportations rise sharply in periods of repression, such as around World War I and during the 1930s. Roberts, "Purely Administrative Proceedings," 78–85.

11. RG76, file 912971, Scott to Director of Internment Operations, 25 April 1919, 7 May 1919; Director to Scott, 16 May 1919; Scott to Director, 15 May 1919, 17 May 1919; on attempts to ship out mental patients and other ill people with the interned enemy aliens, see ibid., Superintendent of Verdun Asylum to Secretary of Immigration, 17 Nov. 1919, and Secretary Blair to Commandant of Vernon Internment Camp, 11 Oct. 1919. On wartime internment, see Desmond Morton, "Sir William Otter and Internment Operations in Canada during the First World War," *Canadian Historical Review* 14 (1974): 32–58.

12. RG76, file 912971, Scott to Director of Internment Operations, 17 May 1919, 26 Aug. 1919; RG76, file 563236, Deputy Minister of Justice to Blair, 12 Oct. 1919. See also Press Censor Records, RG6 A12, vol. 10, file 1431, correspondence between Acting Registrar of Enemy Aliens [Dominion Police] Captain J.N. Carter, Sherwood of the Dominion Police, and Mulvey of Secretary of State, May and June 1918, passim, for discussion of the seizure of the Ukrainian Social Democratic Party's press; the USDP had printed anti-conscription pamphlets in Ukrainian for Montreal and in English for Ottawa branches. The authorities eventually followed Carter's recommendation that the type be melted down, all objectionable material be destroyed, and the remainder of the property seized by the landlord in lieu of rent. Carter arranged to have Immigration investigate press head John Hyndei (aka T. Hynda) "with a view to having him deported after the war." Carter discovered that Hyndei had once been a corporal in the Austrian army, had in his possession objectionable printed material, was receiving a prohibited newspaper (*Nardona Wola*) at a post office box, had an order to print a theatrical notice of an anti-conscription play planned by the Ukrainians, and, moreover, was reputed to have an appointment with the secretary of the Russian consulate. Any of these would have sufficed; many were deported on lesser grounds after the war through the simple expediency of being interned, even briefly, during the war. One of many examples is Blair's step-by-step

instruction to a Department of Immigration agent faced with a shaky case against suspected OBU member Nicklas Babyn, concluding, "I think, however, if it is desired to get rid of him, the best plan is to have him interned and then his deportation is very simple" and would take place "as a matter of course and without any further examination or difficulty," RG76 961162, 18 Dec. 1919.

13. Although he attributes this choice to Canadians' lack of self assurance and the confidence necessary to provide social services for immigrants, rather than deport them, Drystek, "Simplest and Cheapest," 44. For a more critical discussion of the issue, see Michael Katz, "Origins of the Institutional State," *Marxist Perspectives* 1 (1978): 6–22.

14. On making transportation companies pay for deportations of "defective" immigrants, see Roberts, "Purely Administrative Proceedings," 103–07.

15. Immigration files on subversives, especially RG76 917093 and 961162 show that existing legal limits forced Immigration to look for technical violations of unrelated regulations, to stretch the law to its limit, or to act illegally; by the fall of 1918 the Department of Justice was developing amendments: RG76, file 917093, Scott to Deputy Minister of Justice, 6 and 9 Sept. 1919. The authorities were determined to get rid of the radicals not only in Winnipeg but also in other cities on the apparent verge of strikes, revolts, or revolution. On the amendments of section 41, to the Citizenship Act, and section 98, see Roberts, "Purely Administrative Proceedings," ch. 1, passim. See also J.B. Mackenzie, "Section 98, Criminal Code, and Freedom of Expression in Canada," *Queen's Law Journal* 1 (1972): 469–83. Militia records, notably those found in RG24, file 363-47-1, passim, contain a series of telegrams between Andrews, the lawyer for the Citizens' Committee, and Meighen, and from Meighen and Minister of Immigration Calder to Andrews, Robertson, and other officials (such as Manitoba attorney-general Thomas Johnson), and military reports, all of which were sent in code by the military, which trace the development of the June 1919 legislation, its intent, and its proposed and actual application. Pressure for denaturalization legislation (and toughened sedition legislation) came from Andrews and Senator H.W. Laud, General Ketchen, RCMP Commissioner Perry, and other officials and Citizens' Committee members. The government had intended the section 41 amendment to be even more sweeping; see Andrews' (and Perry's) complaint that they had been led to believe that the amendment would allow them to "deport any undesirable save Canadian-born stop anything less than this is absolutely useless and will not meet situation." Andrews to Meighen, 6 June 1919. Andrews was given authority over local Immigration Department and RCMP officials; Calder instructed Colonel Starnes and immigration officials on the scene that they were to act to initiate deportation of prominent strikers on Andrews' say-so (with Robertson's approval). Drystek's discussion of the Winnipeg General Strike deportations, attempted and accomplished, mentions the internment at Kapuskasing of 12 Bloody Saturday "rioters," ordered by Starnes after Magistrate Macdonald had urged internment and deportation of many of the 31 men brought before him; 10 of the 12 were deported by means of "prisoner of war repatriations," without boards of inquiry being held or normal procedures followed, or records of these actions appearing in the Immigration Department annual reports. But this relatively picayune purge was not what Robertson and the Citizens' Committee had in mind when they planned to carry out mass round-ups and deportations of strikers. Robertson wired Meighen: "we therefore propose and are preparing to make the necessary arrangements to as quietly as possible accomplish this. . . . Our plan will probably be to remove a considerable number directly to a train" destined for Kapuskasing Internment Camp, and any "necessary Board of Inquiry to deal with individual cases at leisure can then be arranged." RG24, file 363-47-1, Robertson to Meighen, 13 June 1919. These round-ups, initially intended to also include about a hundred activists from across the country, in fact went awry in Winnipeg and dwindled

to the arrests and imprisonment at Stony Mountain Penitentiary (necessary because there were no other secure places to hold them, explained Andrews) of 10 strike leaders which Avery describes, *"Dangerous Foreigners,"* 84–85. The strategy was to arrest them for seditious conspiracy, but to substitute deportation for criminal proceedings as soon as the necessary legalities were completed. (As carried out, the arrests and imprisonment were illegal.) Kapuskasing was to be used as a prison, not as a substitute for normal deportation procedures.

16. Lita Rose Betcherman, *The Little Band* (Ottawa, 1983), 29–33. Vaara was not Jones' only target. See RG76, file 95027, Joliffe to Starnes, 23 April 1930, re Jones's letter informing on Hannes Sula, another red Finn returning to Sudbury after a visit to the USSR. Joliffe ordered his officers to take "any action possible under the circumstances." On other 1920s intended or completed political deportations see Roberts, "Purely Administrative Proceedings," chs. 4 and 5, and *Deportation from Canada,* ch. 5.

17. It even denied it had carried out any deportations under the 6 June 1919 version of section 41—a falsehood, as the internal records reveal: Roberts, "Purely Administrative Proceedings," 152–72. See also then-Minister of Labour Gideon Robertson's Senate speech claiming that large numbers had been deported under its provisions: Senate *Debates,* 1920, 388–89, 417, 422. His claims were never challenged, even in the internal records of the department, perhaps because they were accurate, as records cited throughout these notes suggest.

18. RG76, file 563236, department memo requested by High Commissioner for Canada Ferguson, London, 4 March 1931. The deportation of Winnipeg striker Oscar Schoppelrei was an example of the use of this legal heading. For militia records on Schoppelrei, who was a military bandsman of the 10th Garrison Detachment, and had been under surveillance for some time, see RG24 363-47-1, WGS situation report, 14 June 1919, and GOC to Adjutant-General, Ottawa, 17 June 1919. For records of the boards of inquiry and trials of the four non-British strike leaders, see RCMP Records, RG18 H1, vol. 4–5, July 1919, passim. A Mountie officer sent regular reports to Commissioner Perry about Almazoff's court trial; other Winnipeg activists' trials are reported in vol. 7, including those of Fred Dixon and George Armstrong, see Dec. 1919. But whether political deportation took place invisibly, by way of internment and "repatriation," or overtly under section 41 or other antiradical legislation, or was concealed under various unrelated technicalities, the most cursory crosschecking of evidence in Immigration Department files alone, not to mention RCMP, militia, Borden papers, and other labour and left non-governmental sources, shows that deportation was intended to be a systematically employed method of social control and that it was used as such, albeit not as widely and successfully as the more extreme anti-dissent elements inside and outside government had hoped. I am puzzled by Drystek's understanding that because Schoppelrei's deportation was carried out under the heading of "illegal entry," it was actually for that cause, e.g., not a political deportation, and that despite Drystek's discussion of the law and the examples of attempted political deportations he cites for the 1910s and 1920s, he nevertheless asserts in his conclusion that the small number of overtly political deportations of Communists listed in a few specific Immigration Department files in the 1930s "indicates that there was no concerted effort to deport radicals;" see Drystek, "Cheapest and Simplest," 422–27, 440–41.

19. RG76, file 274485, memo for Mr Joliffe, 23 July 1927. Three-page RCMP spy report included. Similar cases are discussed passim.

20. Michiel Horn, "Keeping Canada Canadian: Anticommunism in Toronto, 1928–29," *Canada: An Historical Magazine* 3 (1975): 35–37, and "Free Speech Within the Law: The Letter of the 68 Toronto Professors, 1931," *Ontario History* 72 (1980): 27–48; the *Canadian Labor Defender* (hereafter *CLD*), passim, describes many such campaigns. Weisbord's brief account of the 1931 sedition trials in

Montreal is illuminating; see Merrily Weisbord, *The Strangest Dream* (Toronto, 1983), 35–37. She notes the deportation of one of the Montreal sedition prisoners, David Chalmers, to Scotland after he served his one-year prison term at Bordeaux, 39. His case is discussed in RG76, file 513057, C Division, Commander to Commander, RCMP Ottawa, 8 Sept. 1932; his Canadian-born co-defendants could not be deported.

21. Horn, "Free Speech"; *CLD*, ibid.

22. RG76, file 95027, Winnipeg Commissioner of Immigration Gelley to Commissioner of Immigration Joliffe, 25 June 1931.

23. City of Winnipeg Archives, Winnipeg City Council Papers, file 15141, Sudbury City Clerk to Winnipeg City Clerk, 1 May 1931; B. Roberts, "Shovelling out the Unemployed"; Lyle Dick, "Deportation under the Immigration Act and the Canadian Criminal Code, 1919–1936" (MA thesis, University of Manitoba, 1978), 118.

24. See Roberts, "Shovelling out the Unemployed."

25. For Panjata see *Canadian Forum* 11 (1931): 284–85.

26. For Hymie Sparaga, see *CLD*, Jan. 1931 and May 1931; *Canadian Forum* 11 (1931): 284; Louise Watson, *She Never Was Afraid: The Biography of Annie Buller* (Toronto, 1976), 111.

27. Stanley Hanson, "Estevan 1931" in *On Strike*, ed. Irving Abella (Toronto, 1974), 57. Gryciuk and Revay are on the RG26 list (see 41 below).

28. MG26K, Bennett papers, file C-650, "Communists, 1931, S98," Webb to Bennett, 29 May 1931; Webb to Robertson, 9 July 1931, cited by Michiel Horn, ed., *The Dirty Thirties* (Toronto, 1972), 457–58. The Bennett papers are an excellent source of examples.

29. Henry Trachtenberg, "The Winnipeg Jewish Community and Politics: The Interwar Years, 1919–1939," *Manitoba Historical and Scientific Society Transactions* 35 (1978/79–1979/80), 115–53.

30. In 1930 the absolute minimum upon which a worker's family could live with some degree of health and decency, although certainly not in comfort, was $20 weekly. This figure is based on unpublished research by F.D. Millar, and his "Real Incomes in Manitoba" (unpublished manuscript); see also B. Roberts, "Social Policy, Female Dependence and the Living Wage" (paper presented to the Canadian Women's Studies Association, Learned Societies, 9 June 1982, Ottawa); and Roberts and Millar, "Living with Less" (Western Association of Sociology and Anthropology, Regina 1984). For an account of organizing activities, see J. Petryshyn, "R.B. Bennett and the Communists," *Journal of Canadian Studies* 9 (1974): 45–48, and "Class Conflict and Civil Liberties: The Origins and Activities of the Canadian Labor Defense League, 1925–1940," *Labour/Le Travailleur* 10 (1982): 39–63. See also Weisbord, *The Strangest Dream*, 10–48.

31. Betcherman, *Little Band*, 159.

32. William Beeching and Phyllis Clarke, eds., *Yours in the Struggle: The Reminiscences of Tim Buck* (Toronto, 1977), 161. Ian Angus claims the CP itself was partly to blame for not responding effectively in court; it had lost most of its members and isolated itself from the broader left movement, and the Buck group was so focussed on sectarianism, adventurism, and a suicidal clash with the authorities (which they called revolutionary) that it almost invited persecution. On internal splits within the party during the 1930s, see Ian Angus, *Canadian Bolsheviks: The Early Years of the Communist Party of Canada* (Montreal, 1981).

33. Ron Adams, "The 1931 Arrest and Trial of the Leaders of the Communist Party of Canada," Canadian Historical Association, 1977; Betcherman, *Little Band*, chs.

15–17, is the best published account, especially when read with Buck, *Yours in the Struggle*. Public Archives of Ontario (hereafter PAO), Attorney-General's Department, RG74, series D-1-1, file 3188/1931, Justice Minister Guthrie to Ontario Attorney-General Colonel Price, 18 March 1931, and 1 April 1931. See Betcherman's detailed account of the role Bennett played in the months of planning, *Little Band*, 159–70.

34. Petryshyn, "Bennett and the Communists."

35. The 8 were: Tim Buck (age 40, married, 3 children, British-born, here since 1912), chief official of the CP in Canada; Sam Carr (age 31, of Ukrainian origin, immigrated in 1924), in charge of the party's organizational work; Malcolm Bruce (age 50, born in PEI), editor of *The Worker* and on the party executive; Matthew Popovitch (age 41, Ukrainian-born, in Canada since 1911), was former editor of *Robochny Narod* and a leader in several organizations, such as the Ukrainian Labor Farmer Temple Association; John Boychuk (age 39, married with 1 child, Ukrainian origin, immigrated in 1913), was a long-time organizer and official Ukrainian representative on the Central Executive Committee; Tom Ewan (age 40, widower with 4 children, in Canada since leaving Scotland in 1911), was national secretary of the Workers' Unity League; Amos Hill (age 33, married, 1 child, Finnish-born immigrant to Canada in 1912), was active in various Finnish organizations; and Tomo Cacic (age 35, Croatian, in Canada since 1924), was active in various ethnic branches. For biographical sketches see *CLD*, Dec. 1931, 4–5; William Rodney, *Soldiers of the International* (Toronto, 1968), 161–70; Anthony Rasporich, "Tomo Cacic: Rebel Without a Country," *Canadian Ethnic Studies* 10 (1978): 86–94; and RG76, files 513173, pt. 2, and 513057. Petryshyn, "Bennett;" Betcherman, *Little Band*; Buck, *Yours in the Struggle*. Weisbord describes the problems with the indictment, which Chief Justice Rose refused to accept as initially written. He did not accept the view that mere membership in an illegal organization was an offence as provided in section 98; he believed the accused had to be an officer of the organization and commit the illegal actions laid out in the section, to be indictable. The prosecutors had to negotiate with Department of Justice officials in Ottawa, and eventually change the wording of the indictment; see her discussion, *The Strangest Dream*, 36–39.

36. Frank Scott, "The Trial of the Toronto Communists," *Queen's Quarterly* 39 (1932): 512–27; Adams, "1931 Trial," and Betcherman, *Little Band*, have details. The transcript can be found in *Rex v. Buck* et al., Ontario Court of Appeals, Mulock CJO, *Dominion Law Reports* (1932) 3.

37. Petryshyn, "Bennett," 45; Rasporich, "Cacic." As the Immigration Branch records show, the government's initial hopes that all could be deported were dispelled by subsequent investigations, each of which shortened the list of those who might come under the deportation provisions of the Immigration Act. See RG76, file 513109, Assistant Commissioner of Immigration, memo, 13 Nov. 1931, RCMP to Immigration, 7 Dec. and 12 Dec. 1931, Commissioner Joliffe to Mr Fraser, 31 Jan. 1933. In August 1932, the assistant commissioner of immigration wrote to his colleague, "You will remember there was a question as to whether we would take action against those men under Section 41 of our Regulations and the information contained above would indicate that the majority of those concerned are either Canadian-born, British subjects with Canadian domicile [thus citizens], or have the protection of their Canadian naturalization certificates" which the Secretary of State did not wish to cancel. Although he considered calling a deportation board of inquiry for each of these regardless, Cacic was in any event to be tried; ibid., 27 Aug. 1932. That winter Immigration notified the RCMP it would hold deportation hearings under section 41 for Carr, Popovitch, and Cacic; ibid., 28 Nov. 1932. The assistant commissioner of immigration wrote to the minister only a few weeks later that only Carr and Cacic were eligible for deportation. Curiously, no mention was made of Carr's revoked citizenship certificate; the memo said only that "while he has resided in Canada over five

years, his conviction under Section 98 of the Criminal Code brings him within the purview of Section 41 of the immigration Act," ibid., 8 Feb. 1933. Carr was duly tried and ordered deported to Russia, but plans were brought up short when the British Foreign Office wrote to the Office of the High Commissioner for Canada pointing out that Carr had lost his Russian citizenship by emigrating after 1917 and becoming a British subject, so he could not be readmitted to the USSR, and in any case he had still been a British subject on 13 Dec. 1932, when Immigration had asked the British Foreign Office to negotiate with the Soviet authorities; ibid., 17 July 1933. Immigration hastily cancelled Carr's deportation; ibid., 2 Aug. 1933. Details of the Cacic case, and copies of thousands of requests to halt his deportation, are in RG76, file 513173-2, passim. Although the bulk of RG76, file 513057 is concerned with the deportation of CP members from later raids and arrests, it does contain some material on the department's procedures in the Cacic case and the attempted Popovitch and Carr deportations (see especially Commissioner of Immigration to RCMP, 7 Jan. 1933, naming Cacic and Carr as the only remaining two of the Buck group subject to deportation due to others' Canadian citizenship). The authorities had Buck under surveillance since the early 1920s, and there is some evidence that they had long been desiring his deportation, despite his Canadian citizenship, which they hoped to cancel. See RG76, file 513173-3, passim, and especially Commissioner of Immigration to RCMP Commissioner, 5 May 1927.

38. Dick, "Deportation," 124–25, citing Sedgewick to Price, 17 Oct. 1931, "it would establish the unlawfulness of the association, and future proceedings could be taken against those who are mere members of the association, as was always intended." Ontario A-G papers, file 3188/1931. On actions against "mere members," see, for example, Gordon Hak, "The Communists and the Unemployed in the Prince George District, 1930–1935," *BC Studies* 68 (1985–86): 45–61; Hak describes political deportations on 52 and 54. See also Glen Makahonuk, "The Saskatoon Relief Camp Workers' Riot of May 8, 1933: An Expression of Class Conflict," *Saskatchewan History* 37 (1984): 55–72.

39. RG76, file 563235, memo from the Assistant Deputy Minister, 26 June 1931; see also Shin Imai, "Deportation in the Depression"; he points out that in the fiscal year ending March 1932, there were 239 certificates revoked, a rate 6 times greater than average. Imai overlooks the use of sections 3 and 33 to negate domicile and thus render long-time residents deportable. (Even if every revocation did not end in deportation, this figure supports the view that 1930s political deportations were numerous.) He also mistakenly claims the department did not resort to illegalities: on this see B. Roberts, "Purely Administrative Proceedings," and "Shovelling out the Unemployed;" RG76, file 513157, Joliffe to Mulvey, 18 Nov. 1931, Mulvey to Joliffe, 24 Nov. 1931; RG76, file 513057, RCMP Commissioner J.H. MacBrien to Joliffe, 16 Nov. 1931. Bennett had appointed MacBrien to succeed Starnes. According to Sawatsky, MacBrien was "an even greater anti-Communist fanatic" than Starnes: John Sawatsky, *Men in the Shadows: The RCMP Security Service* (Toronto, 1980), 65. RG76, file 513057, department memo, 19 Nov. 1931. Radicals were not infrequently warned not to apply, or rejected for citizenship in the 1930s. See "Branded as a Communist in 1930s," *Toronto Globe*, 17 June 1974, 8, about Nick Urkewich, who was told by the RCMP not to apply, after a 1932 strike in Crow's Nest Pass; when he finally did apply in 1972, he was rejected, presumably on the basis of his involvement in left and other labour causes in the 1930s. Others in the area were in a similar situation and it took intervention by their MP to get citizenship, after 40 years. See also comments on citizenship refusal by Shin Imai, "Deportation," 70–71.

40. Brown and Brown, *Unauthorized History of the RCMP*, 64, citing McNaughton papers, vol. 10, file 46, secret memo of Chief of General Staff to Adjutant General, 14 Oct. 1931.

41. There are only a few memos in the Immigration Department files listing the names of agitators deported under the 1930s' S98-S41 legislation. One lists 82 names; it is found in RG26, vol. 16, "Deportation of Communist Agitators, 1931–1937." A second is a list of 35 names compiled to have citizenship status checked and naturalization certificates revoked, in order to effect deportation (note Imai's figures above); this is found in RG76, file 513057, Mulvey to Joliffe, 24 Nov. 1931, and gives names that do not appear on the list of 82. A third list gives 26 names of alleged communists, some of which are not included on the first two lists; this is in RG76, file 513116 (Arvo Vaara): see memo, Immigration to RCMP, 21 Nov. 1931. A fourth file concerned with political deportation includes 13 of the 23 immigrants arrested in Rouyn and ordered deported for participating in a May Day demonstration in 1932: file 513057, memo for file, 17 June 1932. Other files mention single or a few individuals by name, for example, RG76, file 513173. Labour and left sources supply names and some numbers. For example, the *Canadian Labor Defender*, Jan.–Feb. 1933 gives a figure of 59 deported militants from its own circles for 1932 alone. Between January 1932 and April 1935 this journal names over 80 of the group's activists being deported, and discusses many more cases without giving individuals' names. Although crosschecking is tedious and inconclusive, it is possible. However, most radical deportations took place under grounds other than section 41, so they do not appear as such in the Immigration Department files. Sources other than Immigration provide a glimpse of the depth, breadth, and intentionality of political deportation. For example, RG24, file C-2380, documents the widespread RCMP surveillance of labour and political groups in various cities (unemployed groups under surveillance are more numerous in the latter decade but by no means absent from the early 1920s records); numbers of the activists who are named in the 1920s surveillance files were deported in the 1930s under various charges not necessarily overtly political, although these documents make it clear that these were indeed political deportations, and neither isolated nor rare events. As Shin Imai says, referring also to unemployed deportations (and his unfamiliarity with many of the RG sources causes him to understate the case), "deportation was used in the Depression to carry out the most massive repression in Canada's history": "Deportation," 90. I am beginning to compile a data base and would be pleased to receive information about cases.

42. "Deportation Abuses," *Winnipeg Tribune*, 26 Oct. 1931.

43. See Oscar Ryan, *Deported! Canadian Labor Defence League* (Toronto n.d. [1932]), 10, and RG26, vol. 16.

44. Satu Repo, "Lakehead in the 1930s—A Labour Militant Remembers," *This Magazine* 13 (1979): 40–45. Mauri Jalava's interviews with Sudbury Finns revealed that deportations were a strongly feared feature of Finnish life in Canada during the Depression. By the early 1930s many Finns still did not have citizenship, and others were refused when they applied, so any contact with the authorities could prove dangerous. Political persecution could take place even if no laws were broken: translators for companies hiring Finns were often anti-radical informers. From discussions about his research with Mauri Jalava, 27 July 1981. At the time he was researching an MA thesis on left-wing Finns in Sudbury for Laurentian University.

45. See "They're Killing Sophie in Jail," *CLD*, June 1932; see also *CLD*, Dec. 1931, Nov. 1932; she is on the RG26 list.

46. RG76, file 244957, Secretary of Immigration to Prime Minister's Secretary, 6 Oct. 1932; see also Ryan, *Deported!*; RG26, vol. 16; *CLD*, Nov. 1932.

47. *CLD*, Jan. 1932; RG26, vol. 16; see also Betcherman, *Little Band*, 44–50. Essentially the same thing happened to Joseph Farley, who had been arrested and jailed with Langley and 4 others in 1929. The old order was activated and used to

deport him after he completed a 10-month sentence in Lethbridge. He was sent back to England in December 1931.

48. Personal communication, 19 Aug. 1981.

49. Roberts, "Shovelling out the Unemployed."

50. Ibid., for reaction to the deportation of the unemployed.

51. In December 1949 he hired a Winnipeg law firm to try to get his passport. The Department of Immigration investigated the request. Their records show that since 1932 Kluchnik had worked in farming, construction, and had finally gone into mining. By 1949 he had a family, owned a home and other property, and had savings. The local immigration official declared himself ready to quash the outstanding deportation order, but the RCMP demurred. In a confidential memo, Special Branch replied "We have no alternative but to say that he is 'Not Clear For Security' on the grounds of 'A.'" On this basis, the Department of Immigration decided to retain the deportation order, although Kluchnik had never done anything to warrant its use. RG76, file 530021, including Board of Inquiry transcript, 21 July 1932.

52. Drystek, "Simplest and Cheapest," 435, repeats a number of questionable department claims on 1930s public charge cases. For example, the department claimed that over 40 percent had requested deportation. Further 28 percent of those ordered deported had refused available work, he states. For other examples of questionable claims and lies, see Roberts, "Shovelling out the Unemployed," Roberts, "Purely Administrative Proceedings," and Roberts, *Deportation from Canada*.

53. John Ferris interview, 19 Aug. 1981.

54. RG76, file 513057, memo for file, 17 June 1932; names on RG26, vol. 16 list.

55. RG76, file 513057, memo to Joliffe, 17 June 1932; *CLD*, Nov. 1932; 8 names appear on the RG26 list, for the Rouyn deports: Mathias Ruhinski, Lauri Renko, Emile Suorsa, Kalle Simola (all domiciled Finns); Steve Garich, Mitar Mrdic, Steve Pavletich (Yugoslavs, Pavletich domiciled), and Byll Semergo (Pole, here since 1913). For Timmins, the following were listed: Arvi Tielinen, Thomas Pollare (aka Tom Blaren), Viljo Piispa, Emil Maki (Makynen) (all Finns, none domiciled). RG76, file 513057, memos, 17 June 1932.

56. *CLD*, Jan. 1931, Jan. 1932, May 1933; Hautamakki is on the RG26 list; so is Karpenkower, whose case is mentioned in *CLD*, Sept. 1931. Jacobsen is on the RG26 list, and is mentioned in the *CLD*, Feb. 1931. The fruit of CP organizing drives, these 1932 hunger marches were usually the occasion for police violence.

57. See, for example, the discussion of the need to hire legal counsel for the department if the Poles had been charged under section 41; RG76, file 817510. Winnipeg to Ottawa, 3 Sept. 1931.

58. RG76, file 563236, Winnipeg Commissioner to Ottawa, 5 Sept. 1931, Ottawa to Winnipeg, 2 Oct. 1931; RG76, file 817510, Winnipeg Commissioner to Ottawa, 3 Sept. 1931; RG76, file 563236, Ottawa to Winnipeg, 6 Nov. 1931. The Poles had refused to sign passport applications, but the department ingeniously found their photographs and other necessary documentation on their entry cards, as they had come in under the Railway Agreements, a series of 1920s agreements permitting the transportation companies to bring in agricultural immigrants.

59. RG76, file 513111, warrant to search Dan Chomicki's residence.

60. House of Commons *Debates*, 6 May 1932, 2658–59.

61. Account taken from case comment by Frank Scott, "Immigration Act: False Arrest, Illegal Treatment of Arrested Person," *Canadian Bar Review* 14 (1936): 62–67; see also *Wade v. Egan, et al.*, Manitoba Court of Appeal, Prendergast CJM,

Canadian Criminal Cases, 193, vol. 54. The Halifax agent pointed out the danger of using only section 41 in such cases, suggesting that section 3 be used as well or instead. Under section 3, when membership in the prohibited classes was established, persons were illegally in the country, no matter how long they had resided here. RG76, file 513057, personal to Munroe, 9 June 1932. See also RG76, file 513057, 6 May 1932.

62. RG26, vol. 172, file 3-10-111, "Communist Name Cases . . . Robinson, Reid, Carr etc.," Memo from V.J. LaChance, Chief, Bureau of Records, on Parket et al. appeals, 15 Oct. 1932. See also *Arvo Vaara and others v. the King, Canadian Law Reports*, Supreme Court of Canada (1932): 37–43; RG76, file 513116 on Vaara and others, RG76, file 513111 on Chomicki (Holmes) and others; and RG76, file 513057, R.B. Curry to Brother Stanislaus, 24 Feb. 1966.

63. RG76, file 513057, 1 Dec. 1932, 3 Dec. 1932, Immigration to RCMP, 15 Dec. 1932.

64. Ibid., Minister Gordon to CLDL, 17 Dec. 1932.

65. A. Upton, *The Communist Parties of Scandinavia and Finland* (London, 1973). He points out that in 1918 about 20 000 Reds were killed directly or died in prison camps as a result of repression by the Whites, 119. By the late 1920s communists in Finland were being arrested for political activities. By 1930, fascist vigilantes were terrorizing communists, with the approval of the government. In October 1930 anti-communist laws were passed and during the 1930s there was very little communist or communist front activity in Finland: it was simply unsafe, see 153–55, 178–93. For a brief mention of the anti-communist regime in Hungary, see N. Dreiszinger et al., *Struggle and Hope: The Hungarian Canadian Experience* (Toronto, 1982), 16–18. See also file 95027, Starnes to Joliffe, 15 Aug. 1930. See also Becky Buhay, "Bennett's Answer to the Unemployed: Deportation," *Canadian Labor Defender* (hereafter *CLD*), June 1931, especially her comment about Don Evanov of Toronto and the consequences of his deportation to Bulgaria. There is a further mention of Evanov in "Facing Bulgarian Gallows," *CLD*, July 1931. See as well discussion of the case of Peter Zepkar, a Croat arrested in a Ft Frances lumberworkers' strike in January 1934 and ordered deported to Yugoslavia: *CLD*, Oct.–Nov. 1934. Other cases include Ted Merino of Vancouver, ordered deported to Japan, *CLD*, Jan. 1935, and Nick Stitch of Port Arthur ordered deported to Hungary, *CLD*, April 1935.

66. The department went to great lengths to assure his deportation; they held a second board of inquiry, every step detailed by Department of Justice instructions, to be sure the courts did not free him. They organized a secret route and extra guards to make sure his friends did not free him. See RG76, file 513173-2 for case records; see also RG76, file 513109, passim, 1932–33.

67. RG76, file 513057, Ottawa to London office, 20 Dec. 1932; House of Commons Debates, 14 Feb. 1933, 2101-2.

68. Petryshyn, "Class Conflict," 50–53; Justice Minister Guthrie's comment that in the repeal campaign the "CLDL had managed to build up a huge protest movement with even the churches committing themselves."

69. See the Regina Manifesto, section 12, "Freedom," in Kenneth McNaught, *A Prophet in Politics: A Biography of J.S. Woodsworth* (Toronto, 1959).

70. RG76, file 563236, Ottawa to Winnipeg Commissioner, 1 April 1933. See Roberts, "Shovelling out the Unemployed," on opposition to wholesale deportation of the unemployed.

71. Betcherman, *Little Band*, 124.

72. Justice Minister Guthrie gave credence to such accusations when he said that the 11 shots had been fired at Buck "to frighten him": *Winnipeg Free Press*, 27 June 1934, cited by Betcherman, *Little Band*, 215.

73. Petryshyn, "Class Conflict," 53–59; see also Buck, *Yours in the Struggle*, 247–48.

74. RG76, file 513057, Division Commissioner of Immigration at Vancouver to Commissioner at Ottawa, 11 Feb. 1935; Ottawa to Vancouver, 19 Feb. 1935.

75. For a discussion of "normal" levels of deportation, and the difficulty in determining patterns and incidence of deportation from published official statistics, see B. Roberts, *Deportation from Canada*, ch. 3; on the 1930s, see chs. 7 and 8.

76. See E. Gibbon Wakefield, *Letters from Sydney and Other Writings* (London, 1929). Gary Teeple, "Land, Labour and Capital in Pre-Confederation Canada" in *Capitalism and the National Question in Canada* (Toronto, 1972); see also the British House of Commons, *Report on Agricultural Settlements in British Colonies*, 1906, British Parliamentary Papers (2978), 86: 533.

77. See S.D. Clark, *The Position of the French-Speaking Population in the Northern Industrial Community* (report presented to the Royal Commission on Bilingualism and Biculturalism, 1966), for an analysis of the latter system at work. For an African comparison, see Bernard Magubane, "The 'Native Reserves' (Bantustans) and the Role of Migrant Labor System in the Political Economy of South Africa" in *The World as a Company Town: Multinational Corporations and Social Change*, ed. A. Idris-Soven and M. Vaughan (The Hague, 1978), 263. Magubane says that the South African system of intense exploitation of Africans as migrant workers developed because mine owners could not get a large and certain supply of imported cheap migrant workers. See also, George Haythorne, *Labor in Canadian Agriculture* (Cambridge, MA, 1960); he was then assistant deputy minister of labour in Canada. See also his "Harvest Labor in Western Canada: An Episode in Economic Planning," *Quarterly Journal of Economics* 47 (Aug. 1933).

78. Donald Avery, "Canadian Immigration Policy and the 'Foreign' Navvy, 1896–1916," Canadian Historical Association *Historical Papers* (1972), and "*Dangerous Foreigners*," 9.

79. Ibid., 12.

80. Ibid. See also Robert Harney, "Men Without Women: Italian Immigrants in Canada, 1885–1930" in *The Italian Immigrant Woman in North America* (Toronto, 1978), 82. As Harney points out, these men came "intending brief sojourns, usually hoping for a summer's work in the railway, timbering and mining camps of the Canadian North." For harvesters, see George Haythorne, "Harvest Labor," 536–37. The majority of harvesters were Canadian, but others constituted an important reserve, and the idea was that some would stay on and settle. In 1928, 90 percent of the British workers imported (in a particularly disastrous scheme involving unemployed industrial workers) returned home after the harvest was in.

81. Avery, "*Dangerous Foreigners*," 9, 12, 29–32.

82. Michael Burawoy, "The Functions and Reproduction of Migrant Labour: Comparative Material from South Africa and the United States," *American Journal of Sociology* 81 (1976): 1050–87.

83. Ibid., passim. See also S. Castles and G. Kosack, *Immigrant Workers and Class Structure in Western Europe* (London, 1973). Also on the advantages to employers of "non-citizen" and undocumented workers, see Robert Thomas, "Citizenship and Gender in Work Organisation: Some Considerations for Theories of the Labor Process," *American Journal of Sociology* 88, Marxist Inquiries supplement (1982): S86–S112. For a blatant example of this system in action in Canada, see my discussions of deportation of the unemployed during periods of depression, especially, but not exclusively, the 1930s, when tens of thousands whose labour was not needed were shovelled out under various legal headings: B. Roberts, "Shovelling out the Unemployed," "Purely Administrative Proceedings," chs. 2

and 6, and *Deportation from Canada*, chs. 1 and 8. In some instances, as Burawoy points out, migrant workers may end up becoming domestic workers, may change from migrant to immigrant with a consequent improvement in status in terms of political rights (and access to resources available to landed immigrants or citizens), although not necessarily an immediate economic improvement (such as higher wages). On becoming immigrants, see Burawoy, "Migrant Labour," 1076; citing Castles and Kosack, *Immigrant Workers*, ch. 2: "in contrast to all other European countries, Britain has until recently awarded full citizenship rights to immigrants from other parts of the Commonwealth. Whereas immigrants to France, Germany, and Switzerland have tended to assume the status of immigrants, in Britain they become part of the domestic labour force." In Canada, immigrants tended to do somewhat different jobs than Canadians so it is difficult to prove they were worse off by showing wage discrimination, etc., although it is a given that as a group, immigrants from non-preferred countries did the hard dirty work, often at wages that Canadians avoided. (This is analogous to the debate about the extent of contemporary discrimination.) It is difficult to argue that becoming domiciled (to take a legal indicator) or sending for/acquiring a family (to take another widely used indicator)— becoming an immigrant instead of a migrant (sojourner), to use Burawoy's terms—brought with it a real economic improvement. The Canadian case may offer evidence for the debate about the relationship between political and economic status in migrant/immigrant labour systems. See Burawoy, "Migrant Labour," on this, 1076.

84. Ibid., 1052–63. See also P.C. Lloyd, *Africa in Social Change: Changing Traditional Societies in the Modern World* (Harmondsworth, 1967), 94, "Migration does not create a wealthier category of men in the village." See also Y.M. Ivanov, *Agrarian Reforms and Hired Labour in Africa* (Moscow, 1979), 10–32. In Canada, see Edmund Bradwin, *The Bunkhouse Man: A Study of Work and Pay in the Camps of Canada, 1903–1914* (Toronto, 1972); see also, I. Abella and D. Millar, *The Canadian Worker in the Twentieth Century* (Toronto, 1978).

85. On informal deportation, Donald Avery, personal communication, 4 Feb. 1980. On the use of departmental statistics to determine the incidence and patterns of deportation, see Roberts, *Deportation from Canada*, ch. 3.

86. E.P. Thompson, *The Making of the English Working Class* (Harmondsworth, 1968), 243–44.

87. Burawoy, "Migrant Labour," 1069.

88. Avery, personal communication, 4 Feb. 1980.

89. C.F. Fraser, *Control of Aliens in the British Commonwealth of Nations* (London, 1940), 104, 106, 111, 114.

90. *In re: Munshi Singh*, 1914, cited by Fraser, ibid., 100.

91. Ibid., 114. Compare this to Drystek's conclusion that "there was no concerted effort to deport radicals." Drystek, "Cheapest and Simplest," 441. On the development of deportation law and Parliament's role, see Roberts, "Purely Administrative Proceedings," ch. 1 and *Deportation from Canada*, ch. 2.

92. See Roberts, "Purely Administrative Proceedings," 458–59 on the illegal admissions systems developed and operated by the department after 1910. See Report of the Select Standing Committee on Agriculture and Colonization, Minutes of Proceedings and Evidence and report, Appendix Number Eight of Select Committee, *Sessional Papers*, House of Commons, 1928. There is no indication that Parliament was disturbed by Egan's revelations. On this see Blair Fraser, "The Built-in Lie Behind our Search for Immigrants," *Maclean's*, 19 June 1965, 11–13, 48–50. He says, "Canadian immigration policies and practice are a monument to Canadian hypocrisy."

93. C.F. Fraser, *Control of Aliens*, 114.

94. Drystek, "Cheapest and Simplest," 440–41.

95. See John Duncan Cameron, "The Law Relating to Immigration to Canada. Volume II. From Confederation to the Present" (PhD thesis, University of Toronto, 1943), 577–80 on arbitrary powers, on court interference. The arbitrary nature of immigration law was admitted by supporters such as Cameron, as well as critics. Cameron was born in Minnedosa, Manitoba in 1882, received his BA from the University of Manitoba in 1909, his LLB there in 1933, his MA from University of Toronto in 1935, and the PhD from that institution in 1945. He was a practising lawyer for more than 20 years when he wrote the dissertation and certainly was not an adversary of the immigration system: he was superintendent of immigration and colonization for the CPR in Ontario, 1933–34, and was European colonization manager for the CPR beginning in 1944. For McMeans' remarks, see Senate *Debates*, 15 June 1926, 244. On deportation law, and attempts to change it, see Roberts, "Purely Administrative Proceedings," ch. 1, and *Deportation from Canada*, ch. 2. The quote is from Drystek's abstract, "Cheapest and Simplest," 407, and see also his conclusions and n126, 441.

RELUCTANT HOSTS: ANGLO-CANADIAN VIEWS OF MULTICULTURALISM IN THE TWENTIETH CENTURY[*]

HOWARD PALMER

INTRODUCTION

The way in which Anglo-Canadians have reacted to immigration during the twentieth century has not simply been a function of the numbers of immigrants or the state of the nation's economy. The immigration of significant numbers of non-British and non-French people raised fundamental questions about the type of society which would emerge in English-speaking Canada; hence, considerable public debate has always surrounded the issue of immigration in Canada. The questions which have repeatedly been raised include the following: Were the values and institutions of Anglo-Canadian society modelled exclusively on a British mould and should immigrants be compelled to conform to that mould? Or, would a distinctive identity emerge from the biological and cultural mingling of Anglo-Canadians with new immigrant groups? Would cultural pluralism itself give English-speaking Canada a distinctive identity? These three questions reflect the three theories of assimilation which have dominated the twentieth-century debate over immigrant adjustment.

The assimilation theory which achieved early public acceptance was Anglo-conformity. This view demanded that immigrants renounce their ancestral culture and traditions in favour of the behaviour and values of Anglo-Canadians. Although predominant prior to World War II, Anglo-conformity fell into disrepute and was replaced in the popular mind by the "melting pot" theory of assimilation. This view envisaged a biological

[*] From *Multiculturalism as State Policy*, Canadian Consultative Council of Multiculturalism (Ottawa: Department of Secretary of State for Canada, 1976).

merging of settled communities with new immigrant groups and a blending of their cultures into a new Canadian type. Currently, a third theory o
assimilation—"cultural pluralism" or "multiculturalism"—is vying for public acceptance. This view postulates the preservation of some aspects o
immigrant culture and communal life within the context of Canadian citizenship and political and economic integration into Canadian society.[1]

All three of these views have been expressed throughout the twentieth
century debate over immigration; as has been suggested, however, the relative popularity or influence of each has varied throughout this long public
debate. The term "multiculturalism" was coined during the days of the
Royal Commission on Bilingualism and Biculturalism as a reaction against
what appeared to be the neglect of the "other ethnic groups" in the terms o
reference and deliberation of the Royal Commission. Since multiculturalism
is such a recent word, and since I am an historian, I do not intend to concentrate exclusively on Anglo-Canadian attitudes toward the multicultura
movement or government multicultural policies. Rather, I will attempt to
discuss the ways in which non-British and non-French immigrants and ethnic minorities have been viewed by Anglo-Canadians throughout the twentieth century.[2]

The pages that follow will explore the contours of the public controversy
prompted by immigration and suggest how this controversy has been influenced by changing economic, political, social, and intellectual conditions.
The impact of issues which have, historically, been of national concern, will
be assessed. For example, how have views toward immigration and assimilation been affected by Canadian nationalism and by English–French tensions? How have the ethnic minorities themselves—their class positions,
their regional distributions, their proportionate numbers within the population as a whole—affected public opinion? What has been the impact of
major catastrophic events such as economic depression and war? How have
changing intellectual assumptions such as concepts of race, been translated
into public opinion and policy?

Common sense suggests and recent studies confirm the close interrela-
tionship of attitudes toward immigration and attitudes toward multiculturalism.[3] In discussing Anglo-Canadian attitudes toward ethnic pluralism, I
have therefore been drawn into a discussion of immigration. Changing attitudes toward pluralism must be discussed against the backdrop of the three
main waves of immigration which have come to Canada since the turn of
the century. The first main wave occurred between 1896 and 1914; the second during the 1920s and the third during the post World War II period.[4]
As well as dealing with specific time periods, I have also found it necessary
to deal with the question of attitudes toward specific ethnic groups as well
as attitudes toward immigration and ethnic pluralism in general, since general attitudes were usually expressed within the context of debate over
admitting a particular immigrant group to the country and what role that
particular group would play in Canadian life.

Throughout the paper, I have discussed the attitudes of Anglo-
Canadians as revealed in government legislation in addition to opinions
expressed in the usual avenues of public debate, such as political speeches,

newspaper editorials or letters to the editor, scholarly articles, resolutions of pressure groups, and (for the more recent period) public opinion polls. An analysis of legislation at the provincial level concerning ethnic minorities would appear to be one of the most reliable gauges of public opinion, particularly for the pre-World War II period, before the days of scientific public opinion polls. By including a discussion of federal policy toward immigration and ethnic minorities, I am not assuming that only Canadians of Anglo-Celtic origin had an impact on these policies. However, except for the last ten years, Anglo-Canadians have had the predominant role in determining these policies. This is made evident not only by analyzing Anglo-Canadian predominance in federal cabinets during most of the twentieth century, but also by observing that French Canadians have been unhappy with federal immigration policy for most of this time.[5] Had they exercised more influence on federal policies, one assumes that they would not have been as critical. One other reason for the focus on federal policies is simply that in English-speaking Canada, immigration has been considered primarily a matter for federal concern and jurisdiction, and Anglo-Canadian attitudes have been expressed within the context of national debates over immigration policies.

Despite its apparent length to the contrary, this paper does not attempt to consider all aspects of Anglo-Canadian attitudes toward ethnic diversity. There is no attempt to discuss the accuracy of Anglo-Canadians' view of the assimilation process. In other words, I have not attempted to deal with the sociological reality of what happens to immigrant groups in English-speaking Canada and whether Canada can in fact be characterized as a melting pot, a mosaic, or something else.[6] I have only discussed the actual levels of assimilation among minority groups to the extent that it helps to explain Anglo-Canadians' views about what they think *should* happen to ethnic minorities. Nor have I attempted a full catalogue of the discriminatory legislation which has been enacted against the "other ethnic groups." I have only discussed pieces of discriminatory legislation to the extent that they reveal prevailing attitudes in a particular period.

I have not analyzed in any depth regional or class differences among Anglo-Canadians. There is, however, considerable evidence that people of lower socioeconomic status have held the most negative attitudes toward immigration and ethnic minorities, both in terms of the past and present day.[7]

My research has also neglected attitudes toward immigration and ethnic minorities among Anglo-Canadians in Quebec and in the Maritimes. In Quebec, the question of French–English relations has of course been the primary group relations question for Anglo-Canadians. With the notable exception of Stephen Leacock, Anglo-Canadians in Quebec do not seem to have concerned themselves to any significant degree with the issue of immigration or the place of "other ethnic groups" in Canadian society. The views which have been expressed do not suggest any significant differences from Anglo-Canadian views in other parts of the country. There is certainly a need for more research on these questions. In the Maritimes the issues of immigration and multiculturalism have certainly not been as salient as in Ontario or the West. There is some research however on Maritimers' attitudes toward the blacks, the most visible and the most oppressed of the non-British, non-French, and non-native minorities in the Maritimes. The research suggests that attitudes toward the "other ethnic groups" differ little from attitudes in other parts of English-speaking Canada. The blacks may have encountered slightly more discrimination in the Maritimes than in other parts of Canada,[8] but this stems from their concentration in relatively large numbers in certain parts of Nova Scotia. Levels of prejudice differed little in different regions,[9]—it was simply a question of which group served as the focal point of prejudice. Anti-Hutterite sentiment was strongest in Alberta and Manitoba; anti-Eastern European sentiment was strongest in Saskatchewan, and anti-Oriental and anti-Doukhobor sentiment was strongest in British Columbia. In the latter part of the paper, I will return to the question of regional differences in attitudes toward multiculturalism.

In discussing their attitudes, I have also treated "Anglo-Celts" as an undifferentiated group, at least in terms of their ethnic background. Canadians of English, Scots, Welsh, or Irish descent did not always think of themselves as an undifferentiated group. They could and did have differences of opinion among themselves when it came to their own ethnic identity. But when it came to the other ethnic groups, the Anglo-celts closed ranks.[10]

There has been a recent burgeoning of historical and sociological research on Anglo-Canadian attitudes toward ethnic minorities. Much of this research contradicts the view which has been propagated during the last ten years by Anglo-Canadian historians[11] and politicians that Anglo-Canadians have always adopted the "mosaic" as opposed to the American "melting pot" approach. Much of this rhetoric has simply been wishful thinking. Perhaps immigrant groups did not "melt" as much in Canada as in the United States, but this is not because Anglo-Canadians were more anxious to encourage the cultural survival of ethnic minorities. There has been a long history of racism and discrimination against ethnic minorities in English-speaking Canada, along with strong pressures for conformity to "WASP"[12] ways. In this paper I have attempted to summarize and synthesize much of this recent research. This is done not so much to beat the beleaguered "WASP" over the head; Anglo-Canadians have been no worse, and perhaps slightly better in their treatment of immigrant minorities than other major immigrant receiving countries such as the United States or Australia. I proceed rather from the assumption, as historians must, that if we are to understand current attitudes we need to understand their historical roots.

THE "SETTLEMENT" PERIOD AND THE PREDOMINANCE OF ANGLO-CONFORMITY: 1867–1920

Among the several objectives of the architects of the Canadian confederation in 1867, none was more important than the effort to accommodate the needs of the two main cultural communities. There was virtually no recognition of ethnic diversity aside from the British–French duality. This is, of course, somewhat understandable since at the time of confederation, only

8 percent of the population of 3.5 million were of non-British[13] or non-French ethnic origin. There were, however, significant numbers of people of German and Dutch origin, well-established black and Jewish communities, as well as a few adventurers and entrepreneurs from most European ethnic groups now in Canada. The proportion of people of other than British, French, or native origin in Canada remained small until nearly the turn of the century; the United States proved more attractive for most European emigrants. In fact it was attractive for many Canadians as well, and the Dominion barely maintained its population. But with the closing of the American frontier which coincided with improving economic conditions in Canada and an active immigration promotion campaign by Wilfrid Laurier's Liberal government, many immigrants began to come to the newly opened land of Western Canada in the late 1890s.[14] Immigration policy gave preference to farmers, and most non-British immigrants came to farm in Western Canada. However, some immigrants ended up working in mines, laying railway track, or drifting into the urban working class.[15] During the first main wave of immigration between 1896 and 1914, three million immigrants, including large numbers of British labourers, American farmers, and Eastern European peasants, came to Canada. Within the period of 1901 to 1911, Canada's population rocketed by 43 percent and the percentage of immigrants in the country as a whole topped 22 percent. In 1911, people of non-British and non-French origin formed 34 percent of the population of Manitoba, 40 percent of the population of Saskatchewan, and 33 percent of the population of Alberta.

Throughout the period of this first large influx of non-British, non-French immigrants (indeed up until World War II), Anglo-conformity was the predominant ideology of assimilation in English-speaking Canada.[16] For better or for worse, there were few proponents of either the melting pot or of cultural pluralism (contrary to the flood of recent political speeches and scholarly articles on ethnicity in Canada which assume that the "mosaic" approach has always been predominant). Proponents of Anglo-conformity argued that it was the obligation of new arrivals to conform to the values and institutions of Canadian society—which were already fixed. During this period when scarcely anyone questioned the verities of God, King, and country, there was virtually no thought given to the possibility that "WASP" values might not be the apex of civilization which all men should strive for.

Since at this time the British Empire was at its height, and the belief in "progress" and Anglo-Saxon and white superiority was taken for granted throughout the English-speaking world, a group's desirability as potential immigrants varied almost directly with its members' physical and cultural distance from London (England, not Ontario) and the degree to which their skin pigmentation conformed to Anglo-Saxon white. Anglo-Canadians regarded British and American immigrants as the most desirable.[17] Next came Northern and Western Europeans who were regarded as culturally similar and hence assimilable. They were followed by Central and Eastern Europeans, who in the eyes of Clifford Sifton and immigration agents, had a slight edge on Jews and Southern Europeans, because they were more inclined to go to and remain on the land. These groups were followed in the ethnic pecking order by the "strange" religious sects, the Hutterites, Mennonites, and Doukhobors, who were invariably lumped together by public officials and the general public despite significant religious and cultural differences between them. Last, but not least (certainly not least in the eyes of those British Columbians and their sympathizers elsewhere in the country who lay awake nights worrying about the "Asiatic" hordes), were the Asian immigrants—the Chinese, Japanese, and East Indians (the latter of whom were dubbed "Hindoos," despite the fact that most were Sikhs). Running somewhere close to last were black immigrants, who did not really arise as an issue because of the lack of aspiring candidates, except in 1911, when American blacks were turned back at the border by immigration officials because they allegedly could not adapt to the cold winters in Canada; a curious about face for a department which was reassuring other American immigrants that Canadian winters were relatively mild.[18]

As might be expected, prevailing assumptions about the relative assimilability of these different groups were quickly transformed into public debate over whether immigrants whose assimilability was problematic should be allowed into the country. During the first wave of immigration, considerable opposition developed to the entry of Central, Southern, and Eastern European immigrants, Orientals, and to the three pacifist sects. Opposition to these groups came from a variety of sources, for a variety of reasons. But one of the most pervasive fears of opinion leaders was that Central, Southern, and Eastern Europeans and Orientals would wash away Anglo-Saxon traditions of self-government in a sea of illiteracy and inexperience with "free institutions."[19] Many English-Canadian intellectuals, like many American writers at the time, thought that North America's greatness was ensured so long as its Anglo-Saxon character was preserved. Writers emphasized an Anglo-Saxon tradition of political freedom and self-government and the "white man's" mission to spread Anglo-Saxon blessings.[20] Many intellectuals and some politicians viewed Orientals and Central Southern and Eastern European immigrants as a threat to this tradition and concluded that since they could not be assimilated they would have to be excluded. The introduction in Canada of a head tax on Chinese immigrants, a "gentlemen's agreement" with Japan which restricted the number of Japanese immigrants, the passing of orders-in-council which restricted immigration from India, the gradual introduction of restrictive immigration laws in 1906, 1910, and 1919 relative to European immigration, and the tightening of naturalization laws was based in considerable part on the assumptions of Anglo-conformity—immigrants who were culturally or racially inferior and incapable of being assimilated either culturally or biologically, would have to be excluded.[21] Those who rose to the immigrants' defence argued almost entirely from economic grounds: immigration from non-British sources was needed to aid in economic development, not because it might add anything to Canada's social or cultural life.

Although the trend toward restrictionism during the early 1900s seemed to indicate a government trend toward Anglo-conformity in response to public pressure, for the most part between 1867 and 1945, there was no explicit federal government policy with regard to the role of non-British and non-French ethnic groups in Canadian society. It was generally assumed, however, that immigrants would eventually be assimilated into either English-Canadian or French-Canadian society. A recent careful study of Clifford Sifton's attitudes toward immigrant groups in Canadian society concludes Sifton assumed that Central and Eastern Europeans "would be 'nationalized' in the long run through their experience on the land."[22] The federal government's concern was tied to the economic consequences of immigration, while schools, the primary agents of assimilation, were under provincial jurisdiction. The federal government had encouraged Mennonites and Icelanders to settle in blocks in Manitoba during the 1870s and had given them special concessions (including local autonomy for both and military exemptions for the Mennonites) to entice them to stay in Canada rather than move to the United States.[23] But this was not because of any conscious desire to make Canada a cultural mosaic, nor was it out of any belief in the value of cultural diversity (although politicians sometimes gave lip service to pluralism). Block settlements, by providing social and economic stability, were simply a way of getting immigrants to settle in the West and remain there.[24] The government policy was pragmatic and concerned primarily with economic growth and "nation building"; there was little rhetoric in immigration propaganda picturing Canada as a home for oppressed minorities who would be able to pursue their identities in Canada.

Provincial governments were faced with the problems of assimilation more directly than the federal government since the provinces maintained jurisdiction over the educational systems. The whole question of the varying attitudes of provincial authorities toward assimilation is much too complex to outline in this article; suffice it to say that with some notable exceptions (like the bilingual school system in Manitoba between 1896 and 1916, and the school system which was established for Hutterites in Alberta), Anglo-conformity was the predominant aim of the public school system and was an underlying theme in the textbooks.

Anglo-conformity was most pronounced during World War I as nationalism precipitated insistent hostility to "hyphenated Canadianism" and demanded an unswerving loyalty. For many Anglo-Canadians during the war, loyalty and cultural and linguistic uniformity were synonymous. During the war, western provincial governments acted to abolish the bilingual schools which had previously been allowed.[25] The formation of the Union party of Conservatives and Liberals during the first World War was an attempt to create an Anglo-Saxon party, dedicated to "unhyphenated Canadianism" and the winning of the war; even if this meant trampling on the rights of immigrants through press censorship and the imposition of the War Time Elections Act which disfranchised "enemy aliens" who had become Canadian citizens after 21 March 1902.[26] Various voluntary associations like the YMCA, Imperial Order Daughters of the Empire (IODE), National Council of Women, Canadian Girls in Training, Girl Guides, Big Brothers and Big Sisters Organizations, and Frontier College, as well as the major Protestant denominations also intensified their efforts to

"Canadianize" the immigrants, particularly at the close of the war when immigrant support for radical organizations brought on anti-radical nativist fears of the "menace of the alien."[27] The pressures for conformity were certainly real, even if English-Canadians could not always agree completely on the exact nature of the norm to which immigrants were to be assimilated.

One could give innumerable quotes from newspaper editorials, political speeches, scholarly articles, or resolutions of patriotic, business, or labour groups to show the Anglo-Canadian belief in Anglo-conformity in the pre-1920 period. Let me briefly cite one. Perhaps I should introduce the editorial reaction of Calgary's satirical journalist, Bob Edwards, to the arrival of the German-speaking pacifist Hutterites in Alberta in 1918 with the title "The Worst of Bob Edwards." In reacting to the arrival in Alberta of 1000 Hutterites, out of a total number of 1700 in the world, Edwards wrote "God knows how many are coming here from the States, but it is said the particular brotherhood which has been wished on Alberta has two million members . . . who are coming to Canada."[28] In Bold type the *Eye Opener* thundered, "BUT WHY SHOULD THEY WANT TO IMPOSE SUCH A BUNCH OF GERMAN CATTLE ON US? That gets our goat. WHY?"[29] Does one need to add that Edwards did not see the Hutterites as adding anything worthwhile to Canadian society?

All the major books on immigration prior to 1920, including J.S. Woodsworth's *Strangers Within Our Gates*, J.T.M. Anderson's *The Education of the New Canadian*, Ralph Connor's *The Foreigner*, Alfred Fitzpatrick's *Handbook for New Canadians*, C.A. Magrath's *Canada's Growth and Some Problems Affecting It*, C.B. Sissons, *Bilingual Schools in Canada*, and W.G. Smith, *A Study in Canadian Immigration*, were based on the assumptions of Anglo-conformity. To lump all these books together is of course to oversimplify since they approached the question of immigration with varying degrees of nativism (or anti-foreign sentiment), and humanitarianism. Nor were all of the voluntary organizations' attempted "Canadianization" work among immigrants motivated solely by the fear that immigrants would undermine the cultural homogeneity of English-speaking Canada. Many of these writers and organizations saw their work with the immigrants as a means of fighting social problems and helping immigrants achieve a basic level of political, social, and economic integration into Canadian society. But it cannot be denied that their basic assumption was that of Anglo-conformity. Cultural diversity was either positively dangerous, or was something that would disappear with time, and with the help of Anglo-Canadians.

Perhaps it should be emphasized that the individuals advocating Anglo-conformity were not just the reactionaries of their day. Protestant Social Gospellers, (including J.S. Woodsworth, later one of the founders of the Cooperative Commonwealth Federation (CCF)) who played such a prominent role in virtually all the reform movements of the pre-World War I period (including women's rights, temperance, and labour, farm, and penal reform) believed that immigrants needed to be assimilated to Anglo-Canadian Protestant values as part of the effort to establish a truly Christian society in English-speaking Canada.[30] Women's groups pushing for the franchise argued that certainly they deserved the vote if "ignorant foreigners" had it, and joined in the campaign to Canadianize the immigrants who "must be educated to high standards or our whole national life will be lowered by their presence among us."[31]

But there was a central contradiction in Anglo-Canadian attitudes toward ethnic minorities. Non-Anglo-Saxon immigrants were needed to open the West and to do the heavy jobs of industry. This meant not only the introduction of culturally distinctive groups, but groups which would occupy the lower rungs of the socioeconomic system. The pre-1920 period was the period of the formation of, and the most acute expression of what was later called the "vertical mosaic." Anglo-Canadians were not used to the idea of cultural diversity, nor the degree of class stratification which developed during this period of rapid settlement and industrialization. The answer to all the problems of social diversity which the immigrants posed was assimilation. The difficulty however with achieving this goal of assimilation was not only the large numbers of immigrants, or the fact that not all (or even a majority) of them wanted to be assimilated. One of the major factors preventing assimilation was discrimination by the Anglo-Canadian majority.

The basic contradiction, then, of Anglo-Canadian attitudes as expressed through the "Canadianization" drives was the tension between the twin motives of humanitarianism and nativism—between the desire to include non-British immigrants within a community and eliminate cultural differences and the desire to stay as far away from them as possible because of their presumed "undesirability." This contradiction was graphically revealed at the national conference of the IODE in 1919. The women passed one resolution advocating a "Canadianization campaign" to "propagate British ideals and institutions," to "banish old world points of view, old world prejudices, old world rivalries and suspicion" and to make new Canadians "100 percent British in language, thought, feeling and impulse." Yet they also passed another resolution protesting "foreigners" taking British names.[32]

It does not appear that this was simply a case of the Anglo-Canadian majority being divided between those who wanted to pursue a strategy of assimilation, and those who wanted to pursue a strategy of subordination and segregation. Certainly there was some division along these lines, but as suggested by the IODE resolutions, discrimination and Anglo-conformity were often simply two different sides of the same coin—the coin being the assumption of the inferiority of non-Anglo-Saxons.

What developed throughout English-speaking Canada during this period was a vicious circle of discrimination. Non-Anglo-Saxons were discriminated against because they were not assimilated, either culturally or socially, but one of the reasons they were not assimilated was because of discrimination against them. As one researcher noted in a 1917 report on "Social Conditions in Rural Communities in the Prairie Provinces," the group "clannishness" of immigrants which was so widely deplored by the public was caused as much by the prejudice of the "English" as it was by the groups' desire to remain different.[33]

There is no need to catalogue here the extensive patterns of social, economic, and political discrimination against non-Anglo-Saxons.[34] Patterns of discrimination paralleled preferences of immigrant sources with Northern and Western Europeans encountering relatively little discrimination, Central and Southern Europeans and Jews encountering more discrimination, and non-whites encountering an all pervasive pattern of discrimination which extended to almost all aspects of their lives. Discrimination was one of the main factors which led to the transference (with only a few exceptions) of the same ethnic "pecking order" which existed in immigration policy to the place each group occupied in the "vertical mosaic," with the British (especially the Scots) on top, and so on down to the Chinese and blacks who occupied the most menial jobs.[35] Non-British and non-French groups not only had very little economic power; they also would not even significantly occupy the middle echelons of politics, education, or the civil service until after World War II.

The ethnic stereotypes which developed for Eastern European and Oriental groups emphasized their peasant origins. These stereotypes played a role in determining the job opportunities for new immigrants and functioned to disparage those who would climb out of their place. Opprobrious names such as "Wops," "Bohunks," and especially "foreigner" indicated class as well as ethnic origin and these terms were used as weapons in the struggle for status. The very word "ethnic" carried, for many people, such an aura of opprobrium that food and folklore were regarded by most Anglo-Canadians as not only "foreign," but "backward" and lower class. Folklorist Carole Henderson has aptly described the views of Anglo-Canadians toward folklore (views which continue to the present day): "Except for members of some delimited regional and usually ethnic, subcultures such as Newfoundlanders or Nova Scotian Scots, most Anglo-Canadians simply fail to identify folklore with themselves, and tend to consider such materials to be the . . . unimportant possessions of the strange, foreign or 'backward people in their midst.'"[36]

THE 1920S AND THE EMERGENCE OF "MELTING POT" IDEAS

The 1920s brought the second main wave of non-British and non-French immigrants to Canada and saw the emergence of the second ideology of assimilation, the "melting pot." During the early 1920s both Canada and the United States had acted to further restrict immigration from Southern, Central, and Eastern Europe and from the Orient. Chinese were virtually excluded from Canada, and Central, Southern, and Eastern Europeans were classified among the "non-preferred" and restricted category of immigrants. But by the mid-1920s several powerful sectors of Canadian society, including transportation companies, boards of trade, newspapers, and politicians of various political persuasions, as well as ethnic groups, applied pressure on the King government to open the immigration doors.[37] These groups believed that only a limited immigration could be expected from the "preferred" countries and that probably only Central and Eastern Europeans would do the rugged work of clearing marginal land. The railways continued to seek immigrants to guarantee revenue for their steamship lines, traffic for their railways, and settlers for their land. With improving economic conditions in the mid-twenties, the Federal government responded to this pressure and changed its policy with respect to immigrants from Central and Eastern Europe.

While continuing to emphasize its efforts to secure British immigrants, in September 1925, the Liberal government of Mackenzie King entered into the "Railways Agreement" with the CPR and CNR which brought an increased number of Central and Eastern Europeans. The Government authorized the railways to encourage potential immigrants of the "non-preferred" countries to emigrate to Canada and to settle as "agriculturalists, agricultural workers and domestic servants."[38]

Through this agreement, the railways brought to Canada 165 000 Central and Eastern Europeans and 20 000 Mennonites. They represented a variety of ethnic groups and a diversity of reasons for emigrating. Most of the Ukrainian immigrants were political refugees. Poles, Slovaks, and Hungarians were escaping poor economic conditions. German-Russians and Mennonites were fleeing civil war, economic disaster, and the spectre of cultural annihilation in Russia.[39] Often they chose Canada since they could no longer get into the United States because of its quota system and the Canadian route was the only way they could get to North America. With this new wave of immigration, the proportion of the Canadian population that was not of British, French, or native origin, rose to more than 18 percent by 1931.

In responding to this new wave of immigration, many opinion leaders held to an earlier belief that Canada should be patterned exclusively on the British model, and continued to advocate Anglo-conformity. In national periodicals and newspapers during the 1920s, the emphasis which was placed on the need to attract British immigrants was related to this assumption that Anglo-conformity was essential to the successful development of Canadian society. "Foreign" immigrants had to be assimilated and there needed to be enough Britishers to maintain "Anglo-Saxon" traditions.[40] R.B. Bennett, later to become the Conservative prime minister during the early 1930s, attacked melting pot ideas in the House of Commons and argued "These people [continental Europeans] have made excellent settlers: . . . but it cannot be that we must draw upon them to shape our civilization. We must still maintain that measure of British civilization which will enable us to assimilate these people to British institutions, rather than assimilate our civilization to theirs."[41]

The influx of new immigrants from Central and Eastern Europe during the mid and late twenties also aroused protests from a number of nativist organizations such as the Ku Klux Klan, The Native Sons of Canada, and The Orange Order who were convinced that Canada should "remain Anglo-Saxon."[42] Nativist sentiment in Western Canada was most pronounced in Saskatchewan where one of its leading spokesmen was George Exton Lloyd, an Anglican bishop and one of the founders of the Barr colony at Lloydminster.

In a torrent of newspaper articles and speeches, Lloyd repeated the warning that Canada was in danger of becoming a "mongrel" nation: "The essential question before Canadians today is this: Shall Canada develop as a British nation with the empire, or will she drift apart by the introduction of so much alien blood that her British instincts will be paralyzed?"[43] According to Lloyd, Canada had but two alternatives: it could either be a homogeneous nation or a heterogeneous one. The heterogeneous or "melting pot" idea had not worked in the United States (as evidenced by large numbers of unassimilated immigrants at the outbreak of World War I), and could not, he argued, work in Canada. With Lloyd, as with other individuals and organizations promoting Anglo-conformity at this time, one gets the distinctive feeling that they were on the defensive. Like other English-speaking Canadians who had a strong attachment to Britain and the Empire, Lloyd saw a threat to Canada's "British" identity, not only in the increasing numbers of "continental" immigrants, but also in the declining status of things British as Canadians moved toward a North American based nationalism which did not include loyalty to the British Empire as its primary article of faith.[44]

During the late 1920s, a new view of assimilation, the melting pot, developed greater prominence. This view of assimilation, which arose partly as a means of defending immigrants against nativist attacks from people like Lloyd, envisioned a biological merging of Anglo-Canadians with immigrants and a blending of their cultures into a new Canadian type. Whereas Lloyd and other other nativists that since immigrants could not conform to Anglo-Canadian ideals they should be excluded, a new generation of writers argued that assimilation was indeed occurring, but to a new Canadian type.[45] Since assimilation was occurring, nativist fears were unwarranted. Indeed, immigrants would make some valuable cultural contributions to Canada during the process of assimilation. Although these writers did not all use the "melting pot" symbol when discussing their view of assimilation, one can lump their ideas together under the rubric of the "melting pot" because they did envisage the emergence of a new society which would contain "contributions" from the various immigrant groups.

Most of these writers who defended "continental" European immigration did not seriously question the desirability of assimilation. Robert England, a writer and educator who worked for the CNR had read widely enough in anthropological sources to be influenced by the cultural relativism of Franz Boas and other anthropologists and did in his writing question the desirability of assimilation.[46] But most of these writers were concerned primarily with attempting to promote tolerance toward ethnic minorities by encouraging their assimilation, and many became involved in programs to facilitate this assimilation.

Advocates of Anglo-conformity and the melting pot both believed that uniformity was ultimately necessary for unity, but they differed on what should provide the basis of that uniformity. Advocates of the melting pot, unlike the promoters of Anglo-conformity, saw assimilation as a relatively slow process, and saw some cultural advantages in the mixing that would occur.

There was not, however, always a clear distinction between Anglo-conformity and the melting pot. Rhetoric indicating that immigrants might have something more to offer Canada than their physical labour was sometimes only a thinly veiled version of Anglo-conformity; the melting pot often turned out to be an Anglo-Saxon melting pot. For example John Blue, a prominent Edmonton promoter and historian, wrote in his history of Alberta in 1924 that the fears about foreign immigration destroying Canadian laws and institutions had proved groundless. "There is enough Anglo-Saxon blood in Alberta to dilute the foreign blood and complete the process of assimilation to the mutual advantage of both elements."[47]

There were a variety of reasons for the development of melting pot ideas during the 1920s.[48] The growth during the 1920s of an autonomous Canadian nationalism helped the spread of melting pot ideas. Some English-Canadian opinion leaders began to discuss the need for conformity to an exclusively Canadian norm rather than a "British" norm. One of the arguments that John W. Dafoe, the influential editor of the *Winnipeg Free Press* and J.S. Ewart, a constitutional lawyer, used in support of their view of Canadian nationalism was that non-British immigrants could not be expected to feel loyalty to the British Empire.[49]

Melting pot advocates tended to be people who had some personal experience with immigrants, and recognized both the intense pride that immigrants had in their cultural backgrounds as well as the rich cultural sources of those traditions. But they also lived in a time when recognition of ethnicity meant mostly "WASP" use of ethnicity as a basis of discrimination or exploitation. It was also a time when some ethnic groups were still close enough to their rural peasant roots that ethnic solidarity was often not conducive to upward mobility. The view of most melting pot advocates that the disappearance of ethnicity as a basis of social organization would increase the mobility opportunities of the second generation was based on a sound grasp of the realities of the day. The life-long campaign of John Diefenbaker for "unhyphenated Canadianism" and "one Canada" grew out of this experience with ethnicity as something that could be used to hinder opportunities, and was consistent with his emphasis on human rights, rather than group rights.[50] Perhaps the greater acceptance in Canada during the 1920s of melting pot ideas may have been part of the growing popularity of American ideas and influences. This suggestion must be made tentatively since in the United States during the 1920s, there was widespread criticism of melting pot ideas.[51]

THE 1930s

Although immigration was severely cut back during the depression of the 1930s, the role of ethnic minorities in English-speaking Canada continued to be a major public concern. Paradoxically, although the depression witnessed the high point of discrimination against non-Anglo-Saxons, it was also during the 1930s that the first major advocates of cultural pluralism in English-speaking Canada began to be heard.

The depression affected non-Anglo-Saxon immigrants more than most other groups in the society. These immigrants because of their language problems and lack of specialized skills, were concentrated in the most insecure and therefore most vulnerable segments of the economy. Since immigrants were the last hired and the first fired, a large proportion were forced onto relief. Government officials were gravely concerned about the way immigrants seemed to complicate the relief problem. Calls by some officials for deportation as the solution to the relief problem were heeded by the federal government; sections 40 and 41 of the Immigration Act (still essentially the same act as the one which existed in 1919) provided for deportation of non-Canadian citizens on relief and government officials took advantage of the law to reduce their relief rolls.

While there was some continuing concern over the assimilation of non-British and non-French immigrants during the 1930s, most Anglo-Canadians were more concerned about protecting their jobs.[52]

Prior to the depression, most Anglo-Saxons were content to have the "foreigners" do all the heavy work of construction, and the dirty work of the janitors and street sweepers. But as the economy slowed down, these jobs became attractive. Whereas the pre-depression attitude was "let the foreigners do the dirty work," the depression attitude became "how come these foreigners have all of our jobs?" The 1930s also saw the high point of anti-semitism in English-speaking Canada, as the patterns of discrimination which had hindered the desires of second generation Jews for entry into the professions, were extended into a vicious and virulent anti-semitism by fascist groups.[53]

Barry Broadfoot's book, *Ten Lost Years*, also makes it very clear that discrimination and prejudice flourished during the depression. In the transcripts of his interviews with the "survivors" of the depression, one is struck by the all-pervasiveness of derogatory ethnic epithets in interviewees' recollections of their contact with immigrants. One does not read of Italians, Chinese, or Poles. One reads of "Dagos," "Wops," "Chinks," "Polacks," "Hunyaks."[54] One "survivor" of the depression, waxing philosophical, gives explicit expression to the prevailing attitudes of the time. He compares how the depression affected people from R.B. Bennett down to "the lowest of the low," "some bohunk smelling of garlic and not knowing a word of English."[55] Another "survivor" recalls that her boy had great difficulty finding work during the depression, and went berserk because of the blow to his self-esteem when the only job he could find was "working with a bunch of Chinks."[56]

The vicious circle of discrimination became perhaps even more vicious during the 1930s as non-Anglo-Saxons' political response to the depression further poisoned attitudes toward them. The discrimination and unemployment which non-Anglo-Saxons faced was an important factor in promoting the support of many for radical political solutions to the depression, in either communist or fascist movements. Indeed the vast majority of the support for the communists throughout Canada, and for the fascists in Western Canada came from non-Anglo-Saxons.[57] Ethnic support for these two movements, and the conflict between left and right within most Central and Eastern European groups and the Finns was seen as further evidence of the undesirability of non-Anglo-Saxons. The existence of fascist and communist movements in Canada was not of course due simply to the presence of immigrants bringing "old world" ideas. The leaders in both movements were predominantly of British origin,[58] and their "ethnic" support came more from immigrants reacting to depression conditions than from immigrants bringing to Canada "old world" ideas. But the depression gave further support to the notion of non-Anglo-Saxons being unstable politically; one more proof along with immigrant drinking, garlic eating, and the legendary violence at Slavic weddings, that non-Anglo-Saxons were in dire need of baptism by assimilation. Deporting immigrant radicals was seen as one alternative to assimilation and the federal government did not hesitate to use this weapon.[59]

The relationship in the public mind between ethnicity, lower social class origins, and political "unsoundness" explains why during the late 1920s so many second generation non-Anglo-Saxons who were anxious to improve their lot economically made deliberate attempts to hide their ethnic background, such as changing their names. Ethnic ties were clearly disadvantageous for those non-Anglo-Saxons seeking economic security or social acceptance. The experience of the second generation in English-speaking Canada was similar to the second generation experience as described by a historian writing about ethnic groups in the United States. "Culturally estranged from their parents by their American education, and wanting nothing so much as to become and to be accepted as Americans, many second generation immigrants made deliberate efforts to rid themselves of their heritage. The adoption of American clothes, speech, and interests, often accompanied by the shedding of an exotic surname, were all part of a process whereby antecedents were repudiated as a means of improving status."[60]

Despite the continuing dominance of the old stereotypes concerning non-Anglo-Saxons and the continuing dominance of assimilationist assumptions, the 1930s also saw the emergence of the first full blown pluralist ideas in somewhat ambiguous form in John Murray Gibbon's book, *The Canadian Mosaic*, and in the writings of Watson Kirkconnell, then an English professor at the University of Manitoba. These writers were much more familiar than earlier writers with the historical backgrounds of the ethnic groups coming to Canada, and they were influenced by a liberalism which rejected the assumptions of Anglo-Saxon superiority. Gibbon, a publicity agent for the Canadian Pacific Railway, wrote his book as an expansion of a series of CBC radio talks on the different ethnic groups of Canada. He traced the history of each group and related their "contributions" to Canadian society. Although he was concerned with the preservation of folk arts and music, he also went out of his way to alleviate fears of unassimilability by discussing individuals' assimilation as well as the "cement" of common institutions which bound the Canadian mosaic together. Perhaps from our perspective we would raise questions about the depth of Gibbon's pluralism; however his book was certainly a departure from the earlier books like *Strangers Within Our Gates*, which took as their starting point the assumption of Anglo-Saxon superiority. Although Gibbon was not the first writer to use the mosaic symbol, he was the first to attempt to explore its meaning in any significant way.

Kirkconnell was an essayist, poet, and prolific translator of European verse from a number of European languages. His writing on ethnic groups was based on a different approach than Gibbon's. He tried to promote tolerance toward "European Canadians" by sympathetically portraying the cultural background of the countries where the immigrants originated and by demonstrating the cultural creativity of European immigrants in Canada through translating and publishing their creative writing.[61] In his writing he attacked the assumptions of Anglo-conformity, and advocated a multicultural society which would allow immigrants to maintain pride in their past.

> it would be tragic if there should be a clumsy stripping-away of all those spiritual associations with the past that help to give depth and beauty to life. . . . If . . . we accept with Wilhelm von Humboldt "the absolute and essential importance of human development in its richest diversity," then we shall welcome every opportunity to save for our country every previous element of individuality that is available.[62]

Kirkconnell was not advocating complete separation of ethnic groups so that they might be preserved. He believed that assimilation needed to occur in the realm of political and economic values and institutions but he hoped that some of the conservative values and folk-culture of immigrants could be preserved.

Kirkconnell did not ignore the political differences within ethnic groups. Indeed, with the outbreak of World War II he wrote a book in which he attempted to expose and combat both fascist and communist elements in different ethnic groups.[63] But he was also active in attempts to bring various other factions of Eastern European groups together in order to alleviate public criticism of divisions within ethnic groups.[64]

These advocates of pluralism believed that ethnic diversity was not incompatible with national unity. Unity need not mean uniformity. They believed that recognition of the cultural contributions of non-Anglo-Saxon groups would heighten the groups' feeling that they belonged to Canada and thus strengthen Canadian unity. But Gibbon and Kirkconnell were voices crying in the wilderness—a wilderness of discrimination and racism.

THE SECOND WORLD WAR AND POSTWAR IMMIGRATION: 1940–1960

The war period and early postwar period was a transitional time with respect to attitudes toward immigration and ethnicity. Although the war brought renewed hostility toward enemy aliens, a number of developments during the war eventually worked to undermine ethnic prejudice. During the arrival of the third wave of immigration in the late 1940s and 1950s, many prewar prejudices lingered, and ethnic minorities encountered considerable pressures for conformity. But economic prosperity and changing intellectual and social assumptions diminished nativism and prejudice, and helped pave the way for a growing acceptance of pluralism by the 1960s. The war period itself hardly seemed conducive to ethnic tolerance or pluralism. Patriotic groups mushroomed and many turned their concerned attention to the loyalty of "enemy aliens." Germans, Italians, and the three pacifist sects—Hutterites, Mennonites, and Doukhobors—all encountered a great deal of discrimination.[65] The Japanese, however, encountered the most hostility. The irrational build up of hostility toward the Japanese in British Columbia and their forced relocation to other parts of Canada[66] indicated Anglo-Canadians' continuing racism, their complete ignorance of a group long established in Canada, and a continued willingness on the part of government to respond to public bigotry and violate the civil rights of ethnic minorities who were regarded as second class citizens.[67]

Nevertheless, a number of developments during the war period worked to undermine nativism in the long run. Groups like the Chinese and Ukrainians who had previously encountered serious problems in social acceptance, won a new respectability by their support for the war cause. The channels for mobility which the army provided and the involvement of all levels of society in wartime industries undermined certain social barriers.[68] Some ethnic prejudices were overcome by the experience many young English-speaking Canadians had of widening their parochial outlooks by exposure to European conditions. The revulsion against Hitler and Nazism also eventually extended to a revulsion against Hitler's concept of a superior race and any public expression of anti-semitism. The heightened sense of Canadian nationalism which the war helped produce stimulated hostility toward "enemy aliens," but it also helped undermine the definition of English-speaking Canada as "British." This helped undermine Anglo-conformity and cleared the way for a less rigid definition in the postwar era of what it meant to be a Canadian. This shifting focus of national identity was symbolized in the introduction of the new Canadian citizenship act of 1946. Economic development during the war also laid the basis for the postwar prosperity which helped ease ethnic tensions.

The outbreak of World War II also found the federal government beginning to concern itself with the adjustment and acceptance of Canada's ethnic minorities. The Nationalities Branch of the Department of National War Services was established in 1942 to encourage and assure "ethnic" participation in the war effort. By helping to establish national "umbrella" organizations for groups like the Ukrainians and Poles, the branch was able to alleviate some of the public criticism about factionalism within ethnic groups, and some of the concern about "ethnic" support for the war.

The third main wave of immigration commenced after the second World War with the influx of refugees from war-torn Europe and thousands of German, Dutch, and British immigrants seeking better economic opportunities. The 1950s and 1960s also brought a growing number of immigrants from Mediterranean countries—Portugal, Greece, and particularly Italy. Between 1945 and 1961, 2 100 000 immigrants came to Canada, helping to increase the proportion of people of "other ethnic groups" origin to 25 percent by 1961.

The immigrants who were involved in this wave of immigration were still predominantly European. This reflected the continuing assimilationist and racist basis of postwar immigration policy which included a discriminatory clause giving preference to those of British and French origin and virtually excluding Asians and West Indians (although laws restricting the entry of relatives of Chinese in Canada were relaxed). Prime Minister Mackenzie King probably spoke for the majority of Anglo-Canadians in his 1947 speech outlining the federal government's postwar immigration policy when he stated that immigration should be limited to those groups that could be "absorbed."[69] As he stated, "There will, I am sure, be general agreement with the view that the people of Canada do not wish, as a result of mass immigration, to make a fundamental alteration in the character of our population."[70] While King's statement was concerned primarily with justifying the exclusion of non-whites, it is clear from his emphasis on immigrant absorption that he continued to underline the importance of "assimilability" in immigration policy. He was no more interested in having a multicultural society than he was in having a multiracial society.[71]

Despite King's assurances that postwar immigration would not change the character of Canada's population, the size of the postwar influx to the expanding industrial centres of Ontario, particularly to Toronto, brought significant changes in the society or urban Ontario. Although between 1941 and 1961 the proportion of people of other than British or French origin in the Prairie provinces increased by only four or five percentage points, and did not increase in British Columbia at all, the proportion in Ontario increased by 12 percent from 18 percent in 1941 to 30 percent in 1961.[72] All of these changes were, of course, accompanied by a decline in the proportion of the population of British origin. While H. Troper and R. Harney have shown us the relative degree of diversity which existed in pre-World War II Toronto in their book *Immigrants*, the observations by W.L. Morton on the impact of postwar immigrants on Toronto are not far wrong. "Toronto was transformed from a staid and complacent British city, essentially sober and provincial, into a varied and vivacious cosmopolitan metropolis, on many of whose streets the flat Canadian English accent is lost in the lively rhythms of other less inhibited tongues."[73]

For a variety of reasons, much less nativist opposition developed to this third wave of immigration than to the previous waves of Central and Eastern European immigration. The majority of English-speaking Canadians were favourable to immigration:[74] earlier arrivals had accustomed English-Canadians to diversity, the war had enabled some previously unaccepted groups to prove their loyalty, and the tie between immigration and economic growth was firmly cemented in the public mind.[75] Another important factor in the acceptance of this wave of immigrants was the large proportion of educated and skilled among the postwar immigrants.[76] In a break with prewar immigration policy, Canada began to seek out skilled industrial and urban-oriented immigrants capable of assisting Canada's industrial expansion and capable of "integrating" more rapidly than rural immigrants. The settler "in a sheepskin coat" destined for the land, was replaced by the immigrant with a slide-rule, bound for the city. There were also, of course, many city bound immigrants who came with the proverbial strong backs, and who occupied the lower rungs of the socioeconomic system, but urban residential concentrations of Italians, Portuguese, or Greeks did not arouse the same degree of Anglo-Canadian concern as the rural block settlements had in Western Canada.[77] Although both the early rural settlements of Central and Eastern Europeans, and the postwar urban concentrations of Southern Europeans were characterized by occupational concentration, residential segregation, strong kinship ties, a multiplicity of ethnic organizations, and a strong church presence, urban immigrants were simply unable to achieve the same degree of isolation, self-sufficiency, or "institutional completeness" as earlier rural immigrants in "bloc settlements" on the prairies had done.

The 1950s and 1960s were marked not only by a greater acceptance of immigrants than in the prewar period, but also by a growing tolerance toward established minority groups in English-speaking Canada.[78] Probably the most important factor in accounting for the relative tolerance of the postwar era was the undermining of the intellectual assumptions and social respectability of Anglo-Saxon racism. This resulted from a variety of factors, including not only the postwar revulsion against racism in the aftermath of Hitler's treatment of the Jews, but the decline of Great Britain as a world power, and the cultural relativism taught by modern sociology and anthropology. Canadian awareness of the problems arising from racial discrimination was also stimulated by exposure to the civil rights movement in the United States. The growing concern with human rights throughout North America was encouraged by both the federal and provincial governments and by various voluntary organizations.

The prosperity of the postwar years also contributed to more relaxed inter-ethnic attitudes. Relatively high wages and economic security in urban areas removed the fear of competition. Prosperity also laid the basis for rising educational levels, which would have a great impact on the level of tolerance in urban areas. The striking upward socioeconomic mobility of the second and third generation non-Anglo-Saxons in both the professions and business was facilitated by prosperity, thus helping to break down the earlier fairly rigid relationship between class and ethnicity.

However, growing tolerance was still dependent on whether or not particular groups conformed to prevailing middle-class behaviour. The greater acceptance of postwar central and eastern Europeans as compared to prewar immigrants from this area was partly related to the fact that they were more highly educated and not as culturally distinctive as the earlier immigrants. The declining proportion of "foreign-born" in the Prairie provinces also lessened the visibility of non-Anglo-Saxons. The growing acceptance of Mennonites, Central and Eastern Europeans, and Japanese was dependent on their conformity to middle-class norms.[79]

Although the symbol of the "mosaic" came increasingly to be used in English-speaking Canada to express Canada's diversity, and despite the growing interest in ethnic food and folklore, one most conclude that general attitudes in English-speaking Canada were closer to the melting pot than to pluralism. After-dinner speakers and politicians may have paid lip-service to the mosaic, but it was like praising an elderly relative who was quietly passing away.

Despite the fact that old assumptions regarding conformity remained, the 1950s saw the breakdown of the vicious circles of discrimination which had developed prior to the war. Economic, social, and political mobility of non-Anglo-Saxons[80] and (at least in the Prairie provinces) growing assimilation worked together to break down traditional stereotypes and undermine previous rationalizations for discrimination.

World War II and the immediate postwar period served, then, as a watershed in terms of Canadian attitudes toward ethnic diversity. A variety of social, intellectual, and economic factors worked to break down ethnic prejudices, leading eventually to a more liberalized immigration policy and an increased acceptance of cultural diversity. The third wave of immigration led in turn to a greater proportion of people of non-British, non-French origin in the population, whose presence (both physically and politically) was increasingly felt, and who brought to Canada a number of immigrant intellectuals who could articulate the values of cultural pluralism. This period also brought greater government intervention in social policy, and the federal government began to play a substantial role in shaping attitudes toward ethnic diversity.

THE DEBATE OVER MULTICULTURALISM: 1960–1975

Multiculturalism as an idea, a movement, and a government policy developed during the 1960s and early 1970s in response to a variety of social, political, and intellectual currents and pressures, both national and international. As might be expected, given the prevailing assumptions about conformity during the 1950s as well as Anglo-Canadians' long history of racism, multiculturalism has not met with universal acceptance in English-speaking Canada. Melting pot advocates have rallied to oppose it for a variety of reasons, and some Anglo-Canadian advocates of a bicultural Canada have joined French-Canadian opponents of multiculturalism. Even among Anglo-Canadian supporters of cultural pluralism, there is a good deal of debate over the meaning of multiculturalism. Aside from the opinion leaders who have been publicly debating multiculturalism, what do recent sociological studies reveal about general Anglo-Canadian attitudes toward it? And what does the debate over the Green Paper on Immigration reveal about contemporary attitudes toward non-white ethnic minorities and multiculturalism?

Unlike the 1920s or the post-World War II period, changes in immigration policy were not among the most important factors in determining changes in attitudes toward ethnic diversity among Anglo-Canadians. International pressures for ethnic tolerance and human rights and the continuing need for skilled workers at a time when immigration from Europe was declining led in 1962 and 1967 to the introduction of new immigration regulations which eliminated the old racial biases in immigration laws and made it possible for significant numbers of non-whites from the "third world" (particularly from Hong Kong, India, and the West Indies) to enter Canada. These changes in immigration laws were not made in response to pressure from Anglo-Canadians for more liberalized laws; public opinion polls in 1959 and 1971 indicated that if anything, they were becoming more negative in their view of the desirability of immigration than they had been in the immediate postwar period.[81] Whether or not the new influx of immigrants from the "third world" would eventually have an impact on Anglo-Canadians' attitudes toward ethnic diversity is a question to which we shall return shortly.

The growing acceptance of pluralist ideas during the 1960s in English-speaking Canada did not stem from changes in immigration policy. It developed rather from the impact of French-Canadian nationalism and the Pearson government's setting up of a Royal Commission on Bilingualism and Biculturalism, the increased awareness of the way in which ethnicity could provide a basis for personal identity in an impersonal mass society which was unsure of its own values, the increased awareness of the value of cultural diversity in a technological and affluent society, and the upsurge of English-Canadian nationalism with its need to distinguish Canada from the United States by asserting the existence of a Canadian "mosaic" in opposition to the American melting pot.

The Royal Commission on Bilingualism and Biculturalism of the 1960s did much to convince English-speaking Canadians that full-fledged recognition of French-Canadian cultural and linguistic rights was desirable, but it also paved the way for multiculturalism.[82] The Royal Commission proved significant impetus to the development of multiculturalism because of the "ethnic" backlash against the Commission, whose terms of reference seemed to place non-British and non-French groups into the category of second class citizens. The term "multiculturalism" itself arose as a response to the attempt by the Royal Commission to define Canada as "bicultural." French-Canadian nationalism also served as a spur to the development of "ethnic" consciousness and ethnic pressure group mobilization, and the hearings of the Royal Commission provided a forum for ethnic minorities to articulate their place in Canadian society.

The Commission hearings were not particularly conducive to convincing Anglo-Canadians that multiculturalism was desirable. But they were instructive for Anglo-Canadian politicians since they made plain that many non-Anglo-Saxons (whose economic and political power was growing) were not willing to let themselves be defined out of existence by "biculturalism." The public debate surrounding the work of the Royal Commission also necessarily raised the question: if it is valuable for French Canadians to maintain their distinctive culture and identity, why not other groups? Just as in the past, there were some Anglo-Canadians who argued against granting any additional status to the French language and culture since it would lead to demands by other groups, but the argument was just as often turned in a pluralist direction. Book IV of the Royal Commission's Report on the "other ethnic groups," which was commissioned as something of an afterthought by the commission, made a persuasive case for the value of ethnic minorities maintaining their identity, although it did so within the framework of biculturalism: ethnic minorities maintaining their cultural identity within the context of two dominant societies, Anglophone and Francophone.

In response to Book IV of the Royal Commission, in October 1971, the federal government announced its multicultural policy, which has continued to provoke considerable debate to the present day. It is impossible at this time to attempt to assess the role of Anglo-Canadians in the introduction of this policy. But the introduction of a multicultural policy by the federal government (and by the provinces of Ontario, Manitoba, Saskatchewan, and Alberta) has provided a forum for debate on the value and meaning of multiculturalism. This debate gives us a fairly good idea of how some influential Anglo-Canadian opinion leaders view multiculturalism.

What we now have in English-speaking Canada is a debate between proponents of assimilation vs proponents of multiculturalism, between proponents of biculturalism and multiculturalism, and between different proponents of multiculturalism. The debate between assimilationists and pluralists occurs on a variety of levels. Assimilationists such as sociologist John Porter, one of the most vocal critics of multiculturalism, argue that the policy will only serve to perpetuate the "vertical mosaic" in which class lines coincide with ethnic lines by preserving conservative values which are detrimental to the social and economic mobility of individuals from minority ethnic groups and diverting energy from economic advancement to group maintenance.[83] Pluralists argue, on the contrary, that multiculturalism, if successful, will raise the self-concept of low status groups, break down discriminatory attitudes, and hence facilitate the mobility of the "other ethnic groups."

Assimilationists are also concerned about the stress that some pluralists place on group maintenance and belonging as opposed to individual self-development,[84] while the latter often argue that ethnicity can provide a liberating rather than a constricting context for identity.[85] One variation of the assimilationists' concern for individualism is the view that multiculturalism will foster the alleged authoritarian values of ethnic minorities. This view served as the point of departure for Douglas Fisher and others who were interviewed on a 1974 "Up Canada" CBC program,[86] and is the basis for one definition of multiculturalism which I have heard, "Fascists dancing in their church basements."

Assimilationists like Charles Lynch argue that multiculturalism will perpetuate old world hatreds,[87] while pluralists argue that the public recognition of Canada's ethnic minorities will heighten their feeling that they belong in Canada. Some assimilationists (continuing in the path well-trodden by the anti-Japanese bigots of the Second World War period) seem to believe that one cannot make a distinction between national loyalties and attachment to cultural traditions, while pluralists generally argue that such a distinction is possible.[88] Perhaps the assimilationists' basic fear is, then, that multiculturalism will lead to a fragmentation of Canadian society. Pluralists are also concerned about Canadian identity and unity, but see pluralism as the essence of Canadian identity, and believe that positive action is necessary to preserve cultural pluralism since throughout the world it is being eroded by the impact of technology, mass communications, and urbanization. Some of these assimilationist arguments have a familiar ring from the past, with their emphasis on the need for cultural uniformity and the need to enlighten the poor backward ethnic and bring them "progress."

The differences of opinion between assimilationists and pluralists are profound and are perhaps even more extensive than indicated here. They are partly differences which can and should be subject to objective research, but they are also partly differences of philosophy and values. John Higham has so aptly described the same difference of opinion in the United States, "Integration [assimilation] in its modern form expresses the universalism of the enlightenment. Pluralism rests on the premises of romantic thought. From this fundamental distinction others flow. In the United States both integrationists and pluralists claim to be the true champions of democracy; but democracy means different things to them. . . . The democracy of integration is an equality of individuals; pluralist democracy is an equality of groups."[89]

The second major group of critics of multiculturalism in English-speaking Canada have been those who have argued that multiculturalism threatens to undo the work of the Royal Commission on Bilingualism and Biculturalism (B & B Commission).[90] They oppose multiculturalism for both sociological and political reasons. Joining with French-Canadian critics of multiculturalism like Claude Ryan and Guy Rocher, they argue that multiculturalism is a distortion of the realities of Canadian life, because there are two main cultures, tied to the two main language groups. In their opinion, it is contradictory to have a policy of official bilingualism along with multiculturalism, because language and culture are inseparable. Multiculturalism is viewed as being not only sociologically mistaken, but politically dangerous, since it detracts from the status of French Canadians. These fears that multiculturalism will endanger the status of French Canada may not be justified,[91] but they are nonetheless real. According to a lead editorial in the *Journal of Canadian Studies* in 1971, multiculturalism is "dangerous" because it will endanger the achievements of biculturalism, and lead only to increased demands by the proponents of "One Canada" for conformity by everyone, including French Canadians.[92] Some of these critics of multiculturalism, like Gertrude Laing, a former Royal Commissioner for the B&B Commission, and now chair of the Canada Council, do not oppose, or they even support, ethnic groups maintaining their own cultural identity and language if they so desire, but they do not feel it either realistic or desirable that such a policy be labelled "multiculturalism."

A third debate is now in progress among pluralists over the meaning of multiculturalism. Does an emphasis on cultural preservation reinforce conservative images and alienate ethnic youth, or is an emphasis on tradition necessary to serve as the basis of ethnic solidarity, and to provide that sense of deep historical roots which we need in a technological age? Does multiculturalism, with its emphasis on cultural preservation, have anything to offer new immigrant groups who are concerned primarily with economic and social adjustment?

Another crucial question is to what extent should government be involved in promoting pluralism? Does government involvement in providing funds for groups accentuate competition and friction both within and between groups, or will it bring different groups together in common projects working for common goals, knowing that the larger Canadian public is interested in their cultural life? Will a government emphasis on "sharing" of cultures, make it more difficult for groups to maintain their cultures and hence have less to share? Is the federal multicultural policy serious about attempting to overcome social and economic inequalities between ethnic groups and make the Canadian mosaic less vertical, or is multiculturalism simply a means of "containing" the demands of ethnic minorities without envisaging basic changes in the power structure of Canadian society?[93] Given a set of desirable pluralist goals, to what extent can government action have a significant impact on the maintenance of cultural and linguistic diversity and the overcoming of social and economic inequalities?

Another contentious issue among supporters of pluralism is the degree to which language maintenance is necessary to have a viable multicultural policy. Some supporters of multiculturalism accept the arguments of the B&B Commission that language and culture are inseparable but pursue the argument to conclude that if Canada is to be a multicultural society it must also in some ways be a multilingual society. Others see language maintenance as less essential for the survival of ethnic groups.

Perhaps the most perceptive analyst in English-speaking Canada of multiculturalism is Toronto sociologist Jean Burnet, formerly a researcher for the Royal Commission on Bilingualism and Biculturalism. Her analysis is too complex and sophisticated to classify her as an opponent or defender of multiculturalism.[94] She agrees with many of those critics of multiculturalism who were involved with the B&B Commission, that multiculturalism is a misleading term. But she has also given persuasive rebuttals to critics of multiculturalism like John Porter and Guy Rocher. According to Professor Burnet, the term "multiculturalism" is inaccurate since most ethnic minorities do not preserve complete cultures; what they preserve is a sense of identity. Folkdance, handicrafts, even language are symbols of group identity rather than elements of a complete culture. The support advocated for the languages and arts of "other ethnic groups" will facilitate their retention as symbols of ethnic identity but not as parts of living, complete cultures. Therefore, a distinction should be made between cultural and ethnic group, since it can be argued that while cultural differences have been waning, there has been no diminution and perhaps even an accentuation of ethnic awareness. Federal government policy is aimed at supporting ethnic *groups*, not cultures. According to her view, Canada is multi-ethnic rather than multicultural.

In her view the question of whether or not multiculturalism is a viable policy depends on how one defines multiculturalism.

> Multiculturalism within a bilingual framework can work, if it is interpreted as is intended—that is, as encouraging those members of ethnic groups who want to do so to maintain a proud sense of the contribution of their own group to Canadian society. Interpreted in this way, it becomes something very North American: voluntary

marginal differentiation among peoples who are equal participants in the society. If it is interpreted in a second way—as enabling various peoples to transfer foreign cultures and language as living wholes into a new place and time—multiculturalism is doomed.[95]

Aside from the scholars and journalists, how does the "average" Anglo-Canadian feel about multiculturalism? A recent sociological survey, based on a national sample, conducted by a team of social psychologists in the summer of 1974, gives us some indication of contemporary attitudes in English-speaking Canada toward multiculturalism. The first conclusion of the study was that knowledge of the federal multicultural policy was minimal. In the country as a whole only 19.3 percent of the population knew about the policy, and only 16.9 percent of people of Anglo-Celtic background knew about it. This general ignorance about the multicultural policy was mitigated however by the fact that 89 percent of the Anglo-Celts believed that assimilation was not the official government policy.[96] The general perception was that cultural diversity was permitted, but not encouraged by the government.

The authors of the study asked a series of questions like "Canada would be a better place if members of ethnic groups would keep their own way of life alive," in order to elicit attitudes toward the general idea of multiculturalism. From the response to the questions, the authors concluded: "A multicultural ideology is not rejected by the sample as a whole; rather there is a fair degree of uncertainty about such an ideology with a mild acceptance being apparent."[97]

Acceptance of multiculturalism also varied in different parts of the country, with the greatest acceptance of multiculturalism in Ontario and the Prairies, and the least acceptance in Quebec. The regional responses are not surprising, since they show that multiculturalism as an idea is most accepted where multiculturalism is a reality.[98] These findings are paralleled by regional differences in evaluating six specific ethnic groups. The study found that in general, with the exception of attitudes toward Indians, minority groups were given the most positive evaluation in areas where they were most concentrated. Ukrainians and Germans were regarded most favourably on the Prairies, and Italians and Jews were viewed most positively in Ontario. The Chinese proved a minor exception—Chinese were rated highest in the Prairies followed closely by British Columbia.[99] Immigrants "in general" received their most favourable evaluations in British Columbia and Ontario, the two regions with the highest concentrations of immigrants. All groups with the exception of Indians, received their most negative evaluations in the Maritimes and Quebec.

In terms of ethnic background, the authors found the greatest acceptance of multiculturalism among people of Anglo-Celtic background, followed by people of non-British or non-French background, with the least acceptance among French Canadians. The finding that people of Anglo-Celtic background are the most favourable of the three groups toward multiculturalism is intriguing and requires some explanation. Comparing their attitudes with French Canadians it is apparent that Anglo-Canadians, unlike French Canadians, do not feel that their own culture is under any serious threat so are less concerned about the consequences of pluralism.[100] The fact that Anglo-Celts are more positive toward multiculturalism than "ethnics" themselves is a rather surprising finding. The differences between the two groups are not great however,[101] so too much should not be made of them. The findings concerning the attitudes of ethnic minorities themselves are not however consistent with the findings of the recent Non-Official Languages Study (NOL study) which was also commissioned by the Department of the Secretary of State. The NOL Study (which deserves more public exposure and discussion) found that for ten ethnic groups in five of Canada's major urban areas, there was a fairly strong degree of support for the maintenance of ethnic identity and non-official languages.[102] Perhaps the differences stem from the way the sample was drawn. The Non-Official Languages Study included only some of the largest ethnic groups in the major metropolitan centres, and interviews were conducted in the non-official languages as well as in English or French. The Majority Attitudes Study included a representative sample from across the country, and interviews were conducted only in English and French. This suggests, not surprisingly, that people from smaller ethnic groups, in non-metropolitan areas, who are not fluent in an official language, are not as positive in their attitudes toward multiculturalism as those included in the NOL study.

Questions were also asked in the Majority Attitudes Study concerning attitudes toward specific federal multicultural programs. The authors concluded "overall, although extant programs are reacted to with some moderate degree of favour, those items concerned with the public use of third languages were clearly unacceptable, particularly in public schools and on public broadcasting."[103]

In order to tap respondents' degree of commitment to multiculturalism, they were asked whether they would vote for a political candidate who supported multiculturalism, try to convince other people that the program was a good one, and be willing to pay taxes to support such a program. The authors concluded in this area, attitudes "are considerably less positive than for previous issues, with means for all groups falling below the mid-point of the scale. In particular, those behaviours involving the greatest commitment [convincing others, paying taxes] are least positive."[104]

What we find then among Anglo-Canadians is somewhat limited support for multiculturalism. Unlike any previous period in the past, there is no widespread fear that multiculturalism would destroy "our Canadian way of life"[105] and there is a positive feeling that multiculturalism will make Canada "richer in culture." Anglo-Canadians are not sure however that "social harmony will improve in Canada" with a multicultural policy.[106] Support for multiculturalism includes support for the maintenance of ethnic groups in Canadian society, the encouragement of ethnic folklore, and an increased public awareness of Canada's diversity, but it does not in general include approval for the public support of non-official languages. This study, as well as others[107] suggests a continuing hostility to the languages of "other ethnic groups" and the feeling that people who use non-official languages in public are not really "Canadian." There is no widespread public understanding of the importance of language maintenance to many ethnic groups. Given the general lack of awareness of the federal multicultural policy, the luke-warm support for multiculturalism as an idea, and the unwillingness to take any positive action in support of multiculturalism, one must conclude that the prevailing Anglo-Canadian attitude toward it is one of indifference. The majority of respondents agreed to the statement "if members of ethnic groups want to keep their own culture, they should keep it to themselves and not bother other people in this country." Unfortunately it would appear that the prevailing attitude toward multiculturalism in English-speaking Canada is the one outlined by sociologist Jim Frideres in his summary of the findings of the research presented at a recent conference on "Multiculturalism and Third World Immigrants":

> Those of "English" group membership adhere to the policy of multiculturalism but only to the extent that the "different" ethnic groups nominally display their ethnicity. This means that these . . . groups should speak English in public and accept the anglo way of life in all respects when in public. However, in the private confines of one's house and on holidays, these groups can speak their native language, wear their "traditional" clothes and paint their Easter eggs.[108]

It is difficult to say whether these findings are consistent with the seemingly positive response to events such as Metro Caravan in Toronto and similar happenings in other cities. Certainly there are many Anglo-Canadians who (given the growing appreciation of the values of community and folk traditions) respect the folk traditions and close-knit solidarity among some ethnic minorities. Indeed, some may even be envious of these traditions. I have been told several times recently of classroom discussions of ethnicity in which students rather reluctantly reported that their ethnic origin was "just British."

While it is not surprising, one of the disturbing findings of the Majority Attitudes Study (confirming a number of other recent studies)[109] is that the ethnic pecking order, which has had such a long history in Canada's immigration policy and class system, is still part of the mental framework of many Anglo-Canadians. Anglo-Canadians evaluated themselves as being more "important," "clean," "likeable," "wealthy," and "interesting" than other minority ethnic groups. (Although they were willing to concede that some other groups were more "hardworking.")[110] Anglo-Canadians also had more favourable attitudes toward Northern European groups than toward Southern Europeans or non-whites. This pecking order also continues to be reflected in patterns of social and economic discrimination with Northern Europeans encountering the least amount of discrimination and non-whites encountering the most.[111]

What does the Green Paper on Immigration and the debate surrounding it reveal about contemporary Anglo-celtic attitudes? Has there been a recent growth of re-emergence of racist sentiments in English-speaking Canada in response to the influx of non-white immigrants? Did the Green Paper debate, by focussing attention on the growing number of non-whites, contribute to the development of racist sentiments among Anglo-Canadians?[112] Has the Green Paper debate made immigrants scapegoats for the government's inability to solve Canada's social and economic problems? Was the Green Paper itself racist, and was it an attempt to respond to the political pressures of racist groups? Are the fears that are expressed about non-white immigrants based primarily on racist assumptions about their physical or cultural undesirability? Are they based on assimilationst fears that the new immigrants will congregate together, speaking their own language and remaining outside the mainstream of Canadian life? Or are they based on simple ethnocentric reactions to cultural differences? Does the growing restrictionist mood toward immigration in English-speaking Canada[113] indicate the development of racist ideas, or does it indicate instead changing attitudes toward population growth in Canada and a belief that Canada no longer needs as many immigrants, whatever their colour?[114]

It is difficult to provide answers to these questions since research is scanty, research findings are somewhat contradictory,[115] and we are still too close to the events to see overall patterns. However, one fact is clear. Although the Green Paper debate has revealed the persistence of racist sentiments in English-speaking Canada, it has also indicated that these racist sentiments are not as powerful as in the past. During the public hearings on the Green Paper, for the first time in any major national public debate on immigration policy, racists were clearly on the defensive. Groups wanting to restrict non-whites had to answer not only to noisy left-wing groups, but more significantly to a parliamentary committee which included two non-whites, as well as several members for whom any hint of racism was anathema. Groups who opposed the entry into Canada of immigrants who would not immediately assimilate also had to contend with the father of Canada's multicultural movement, Senator Paul Yuzyk.

If the Green Paper debate has revealed the persistence of racist ideas in English-speaking Canada, what implications does this have for multiculturalism, and for a federal multicultural policy? Does it suggest that Anglo-Canadians are willing to tolerate a multicultural society, as long as it is not also a multiracial society? The debate over the Green Paper has raised serious questions in the minds of leaders of Third World groups, as well as political leaders concerned with multiculturalism, over whether at this point in time, an emphasis on cultural maintenance by non-white groups might increase their visibility and hence make them more likely targets for racist attacks. Should the emphasis at present be on human rights and overcoming discrimination as opposed to cultural maintenance, or is one of the best ways to overcome prejudice the "sharing of cultures" approach? One thing is certain. The Green Paper debate has made it painfully clear that we need a federal human rights initiative and a multicultural policy which will move as quickly as possible to introduce measures to help improve Anglo-Canadians' understanding of Canada's ethnic minorities and their aspirations, with particular emphasis on our "visible" minorities.

CONCLUSION

The interpretation which one places on these findings and developments depends in part on whether one is an optimist or a pessimist, whether, to use a metaphor, one sees the glass as being half full, or half empty. There are strong strains of racism in Canada today; indeed there are many Anglo-Canadians who do not even like the idea of a multicultural society, let alone a multiracial society. But the strains of racism, discrimination, and the pressures toward conformity for non-British and non-French groups are certainly less powerful then they were even twenty years ago, to say nothing of what they were seventy-five years ago.

The ethnic "hierarchy of desirability" or pecking order still exists in the preferred social relationships of most Anglo-Canadians. But it has been abolished (at least *de jour*) from our immigration laws, it is more difficult to maintain in our class system because discrimination in jobs and housing has been made illegal by human rights legislation, and even in personal relationships, the "hierarchy" is not as rigidly held as in the past.[116] The Anglo-Canadian may not be willing to have a black or Asian marry his daughter, but whereas his father did not want Chinese in the country, he would not be unwilling to have someone of Chinese descent next door. Legal discrimination against ethnic minorities, such as the laws which prevented Orientals, Doukhobors, Hutterites, Mennonites, and "enemy aliens" from voting at different periods of time, or the laws restricting landholding by Orientals and Hutterites, or the access of Orientals to professions, has been abolished.

The vertical mosaic still exists in the class system. But it has been breaking down—one could cite numerous striking examples of "ethnics" in the media, and civil service, the professions, and especially politics to provide evidence of the fact. While non-Anglo-Saxons may not have broken into the Canadian economic establishment in any significant way,[117] entry into the "establishment" is becoming increasingly based on merit rather than family connections. It strikes me as significant that it is a postwar immigrant, Peter Newman, who is describing and interpreting the "establishment" to English-speaking Canada.

One could cite many other examples of major changes in attitudes. Political parties no longer strain to see who can be most anti-Oriental as a way of getting votes; they vie instead for that elusive commodity, the "ethnic vote." Social workers who are involved in helping immigrants adjust to Canadian society and scholars studying immigrants and ethnic minorities no longer assume assimilation as the inevitable and desirable goal for Canadian society; most operate instead from pluralist assumptions. Prominent Anglican bishops no longer rail against the evils of "dirty, ignorant, garlic-smelling foreigners."[118] We no longer try to deport immigrants who are unemployed. While the use of ethnic slurs has not disappeared, it is not accepted as a matter of course. (Indeed, one of the few ethnic slurs still acceptable is the acronym "WASP.") Most Anglo-Canadians now look back with regret and guilt on the relocation of Japanese-Canadians. Canada has in the postwar period, established an international reputation for its liberal treatment of refugees. In the last eight years, we have had a significant influx of non-white immigrants without serious racial confrontation. Last, but not least, we have a government supported multicultural policy which has garnered the support of many Anglo-Canadians, and the support of politicians of all political parties. The policy has not always met our expectations and a great deal remains to be done. But perhaps we should not be too harsh in our judgment of a policy which is so new, and which is working against one of the oldest and most persistent of human vices: ethnic and racial prejudice.

NOTES

1. For a discussion of these three ideologies of assimilation in the United States, see Milton Gordon, *Assimilation in American Life* (New York, 1964).

2. Some might object that this view of multiculturalism coincides too closely with the pragmatic political view that multiculturalism is a short-term policy intended to pacify or, if you will, "respond" to the needs of "immigrant" groups and has little to do with the place in confederation of Canadians of Anglo-celtic, French, or native origin. The question as to whether or not Anglo-Canadians, French-Canadians, and native peoples should or should not be considered part of a national multicultural policy has long been hotly debated. In not including Anglo-Canadian attitudes toward French-Canadians or native peoples, I am not attempting to give credence to the view that multiculturalism does not, or was not intended to deal with them. Government policy aside, Canada is a multicultural country and Anglo-Canadians, French-Canadians, and native peoples, as well as the "other ethnic groups" form very important parts. However, the attitudes of Anglo-Canadians toward French-Canadians and Native groups are simply too complex and, for the historian, cover too great a time span, to deal with in a paper of this length. I have, however, where possible, attempted to discuss how Anglo-Canadian attitudes toward French-Canadians influenced their attitudes toward the "other ethnic groups." This view of multiculturalism as a question concerned primarily with the role of "other ethnic groups" in Canadian society is, I believe, the prevailing view among Anglo-Canadians themselves (with the exception perhaps of some Scots).

3. G.S. Paul, "Immigrant Composition and Multiculturalism: An Empirical Analysis" (paper presented at conference on Multiculturalism and Third World Immigrants in Canada, Edmonton, Sept. 1975). By selecting certain types of immigrants, immigration policy has also determined to a considerable degree the class position, regional concentration, and ethnic composition of the immigrants who have come to Canada. These three factors—place in the class system, regional distribution, and ethnic composition—have all played very important roles in determining Anglo-Canadian attitudes toward multiculturalism.

4. Some might argue that the post-1967 influx of third world immigrants constitutes a fourth wave of immigration, but I have rather arbitrarily included the whole post-World War II period as the third wave of immigration.

5. William Peterson, *Planned Migration* (Berkeley, 1955), 127–37; Claudette Begin-Wolff, "L'Opinion Publique Québécois Face à l'Immigration, 1906–1913" (MA thesis, Université de Montréal, 1970).

6. For a discussion of these issues, see H. Palmer, *Land of the Second Chance: A History of Ethnic Groups in Southern Alberta* (Lethbridge, 1972), 257–59.

7. John Berry et al., "Majority Attitudes Study: The Acceptance of Multiculturalism in Canada" (Department of the Secretary of State, 1975), 74; Nancy Tienhaara, "Canadian Views on Immigration and Population" (Ottawa, 1974), 26–27; H. Palmer, "Nativism and Ethnic Tolerance in Alberta: 1920–1972," (PhD diss., York University, 1973), 367.

8. Robin Winks, *The Blacks in Canada* (New Haven, 1971); Frances Henry, *Forgotten Canadians: The Blacks of Nova Scotia* (Don Mills, ON, 1973).

9. This statement is based on a comparison of attitudes as portrayed in the following sources in addition to other studies cited in this paper. C.H. Young, H. Reid, and W.A. Carrothers, *Japanese Canadians* (Toronto, 1938); Patricia Roy, "The Oriental 'Menace' in British Columbia," in Susan Trofimenkoff, ed., *The Twenties in Western Canada* (Ottawa, 1972), 243–58; John Norris, *Strangers Entertained* (Vancouver, 1971); W.E. Calderwood, "The Rise and Fall of the Ku Klux Klan in Saskatchewan" (MA thesis, University of Saskatchewan); Morris Mott, "Nativism in Winnipeg, 1916–1922" (MA thesis, University of Manitoba, 1970); T. Peterson, "Ethnic and Class Politics in Manitoba," in Martin Robin, ed., *Canadian Provincial Politics* (Scarborough, ON, 1972), 69–116; John Bennett, *Hutterian Brethren* (Stanford, CA, 1967); Victor Peters, *All Things Common* (Minneapolis, 1965); G. Woodcock and I. Avakumovic, *The Doukhobors* (Toronto, 1968); Paul Yuzyk, *The Ukrainians in Manitoba* (Toronto, 1953); Victor Turek, *Poles in Manitoba* (Toronto, 1961).

10. I can find little evidence for the hypothesis that the minority groups from the British Isles—the Irish, Scots, and Welsh—had any more sympathy than people of English origin for the aspirations of the "other ethnic groups." One wonders, however, if perhaps Anglo-Canadian Catholics have been more sympathetic than Anglo-Canadian Protestants to the aspirations of the Catholic minorities from central and southern Europe. These questions require further research. When it came to their attitudes toward the immigration of Central, Southern, and Eastern Europeans and Orientals, Anglo-Canadians were as often as not joined by Canadians of German and Scandinavian origin. When it came to their attitudes toward multiculturalism generally, Anglo-celts were again joined by these same two groups in promoting the assimilation of all ethnic minorities. Ken O'Bryan et al., "Non-Official Languages: A Study in Canadian Multiculturalism" (Department of the Secretary of State, 1975); J.T. Torson, *Wanted: A Single Canada* (Toronto, 1972); Jorgen Dahlie, "Scandinavian Experiences on the Prairie, 1890–1920" (Western Canadian Studies Conference, March 1975).

11. L.G. Thomas, "The Umbrella and the Mosaic: The French–English Presence and the Settlement of the Canadian Prairie West," in J.A. Carroll ed., *Reflections of Western Historians* (Tuscon, AZ, 1969), 135–52; Allan Smith, "Metaphor and Nationality in North America," *Canadian Historical Review* 51, 3 (Sept. 1970).

12. "WASP" stands of course for white, Anglo-Saxon Protestant. Since it is more familiar, I have used it in preference to the more accurate "WACP"—white Anglo-Celtic Protestant.

13. The Canadian census has consistently classed the Irish as part of the "British" group.

14. Palmer, *Land of the Second Chance*; Norman Macdonald, *Canada Immigration and Colonization, 1841–1903* (Toronto, 1967); Harold Troper, *Only Farmers Need Apply* (Toronto, 1972).

15. Donald Avery, "Canadian Immigration Policy and the Foreign Navvy," *Canadian Historical Association Reports* (1972); Edmund Bradwin, *Bunkhouse Man* (New York, 1928); H. Troper and R. Harney, *Immigrants* (Toronto, 1975).

16. Donald Avery, "Canadian Immigration Policy, 1896–1919: The Anglo-Canadian Perspective" (PhD diss., University of Western Ontario, 1973).

Cornelius Jaenan, "Federal Policy Vis-à-Vis Ethnic Groups" (unpublished paper, 1971); Palmer, "Nativism and Ethnic Tolerance in Alberta, 1880–1920" (MA thesis, University of Alberta, 1971); Palmer, "Nativism and Ethnic Tolerance in Alberta, 1920–1972."

17. H. Palmer, "Nativism and Ethnic Tolerance in Alberta, 1880–1920", chs. 1 and 2; H. Troper, *Only Farmers Need Apply* ; D.J. Hall, "Clifford Sifton: Immigration and Settlement Policy, 1896–1905" (unpublished paper delivered to Western Canadian Studies Conference, 1975).

18. H. Troper, "The Creek Negroes of Oklahoma and Canadian Immigration, 1909–11," *Canadian Historical Review* (Sept. 1972): 272–88.

19. Rev. George Bryce, "Past and Future of Our Race," *Proceedings* (Canadian Club of Toronto, 1911), 6–7; C.A. Magrath, *Canada's Growth and Problems Affecting It* (Ottawa, 1910); Goldwin Smith in *Weekly Sun*, 1 Feb. 1899, 17 Sept. 1902, 23 Sept. 1903, 18 May 1904, 16 Aug. 1905; W.A. Griesbach, *I Remember* (Toronto, 1946), 214–17, 220–21.

20. Carl Berger, *Sense of Power* (Toronto, 1970), 117–88.

21. Morton, *In A Sea of Sterile Mountains* (Vancouver, 1974); W.P. Ward, "The Oriental Immigrant and Canada's Protestant Clergy, 1858–1925," *B.C. Studies* (Summer 1974): 40–55; Ted Ferguson, *A White Man's Country* (Toronto, 1975).

22. D.J. Hall, "Clifford Sifton: Immigration and Settlement Policy: 1896–1905," 35.

23. W.L. Morton, *Manitoba, A History* (Toronto, 1957), 161, 162.

24. J.B. Hedges, *Building the Canadian West* (New York, 1939); Frank Epp, *Mennonites in Canada, 1786–1920* (Toronto, 1974).

25. Cornelius J. Jaenen, "Ruthenian Schools in Western Canada 1897–1919," *Paedagogica Historica, International Journal of the History of Education* 10, 3 (1970): 517–41. Donald Avery, "Canadian Immigration Policy," 374–420.

26. Avery, "Canadian Immigration Policy," 408.

27. Kate Foster, *Our Canadian Mosaic* (Toronto, 1926); J.T.M. Anderson, *The Education of the New Canadian* (Toronto, 1918); C.B. Sissons, *Bi-Lingual Schools in Canada* (Toronto, 1917); W.G. Smith, *Building the Nation* (Toronto, 1922). For a discussion of some of the concrete activities involved in these "Canadianization" programs, see Troper and Harney, *Immigrants*, ch. 4.

28. *Calgary Eye-Opener*, 5 Oct. 1918.

29. Ibid.

30. J.S. Woodsworth, *Strangers Within Our Gates* (Winnipeg, 1909); Marilyn Barber, "Nationalism, Nativism and the Social Gospel: The Protestant Church Response to Foreign Immigrants in Western Canada, 1897–1914," in Richard Allen, ed., *The Social Gospel in Canada* (Ottawa, 1975), 186–226.

31. Quoted in Barbara Nicholson, "Feminism in the Prairie Provinces to 1916" (MA thesis, University of Calgary, 1974), 71. For the views of womens' groups on immigration and the role of immigrants in Canadian society, see 83–85, 86, 114, 121, 133, 165–69, 186–87.

32. Reported in *Lethbridge Herald*, 29 May 1919.

33. J.S. Woodsworth, *Social Conditions in Rural Communities in the Prairie Provinces* (Winnipeg, 1917), 38.

34. For a fairly extensive chronicling of patterns of discrimination against a number of minority groups see Morris Davis and J.F. Krauter, *The Other Canadians* (Toronto, 1971).

35. For an analysis of the various causes of ethnic stratification (settlement patterns, time of arrival, immigrant and ethnic occupations, ethnic values, language barriers, and discrimination and exploitation) see Book 4, *Report of the Royal Commission on Bilingualism and Biculturalism* (Ottawa, 1969), ch. 2.

36. Carole Henderson, "The Ethnicity Factor in Anglo-Canadian Folkloristics," *Canadian Ethnic Studies* 7, 2 (1975).

37. *Canadian Annual Review, 1923,* 264–65; *Canadian Annual Review, 1924–25,* 190–92.

38. *Canada Year Book, 1941,* 733.

39. Olha Woycenko, *The Ukrainians in Canada* (Winnipeg, 1967); Victor Turek, *Poles in Manitoba* (Toronto, 1967), 43; J.M. Kirschbaum, *Slovaks in Canada* (Toronto, 1967), 101; Edmund Heier, "A Study of German Lutheran and Catholic Immigrants in Canada formerly residing in Czarist and Soviet Russia," (MA thesis, University of British Columbia, 1955), ch. 3.

40. R.B. Bennett, House of Commons *Debates,* 7 June 1929, pp. 3925–27.

41. Ibid.

42. H. Palmer, "Nativism in Alberta, 1925–1930," *Canadian Historical Association Reports* (1974): 191–99.

43. G.E. Lloyd, "National Building," *Banff Crag and Canyon,* 17 Aug. 1928.

44. A.R.M. Lower, *Canadians in the Making* (Don Mills, ON, 1958), chs. 22, 27.

45. J.S. Woodsworth, "Nation Building," *University Magazine* (1917): 85–99. F.W. Baumgartner, "Central European Immigration," *Queen's Quarterly* 37 (Winter 1930): 183–92; Walter Murray, "Continental Europeans in Western Canada," *Queen's Quarterly* 38 (Winter 1931); P.M. Bryce, *The Value of the Continental Immigrant to Canada* (Ottawa, 1928); E.L. Chicanot, "Homesteading the Citizen: Canadian Festivals Promote Cultural Exchange," *Commonwealth* (May 1929): 94–95; E.K. Chicanot, "Moulding a Nation," *Dalhousie Review* 9, 2 (July 1929): 232–37; J.H. Haslam, "Canadianization of the Immigrant Settler," *Annals* (May 1923): 45–49; E.H. Oliver, "The Settlement of Saskatchewan to 1914," *Transactions of the Royal Society* (1926): 63–87; Agnes Laut, "Comparing the Canadian and American Melting Pots," *Current Opinion* 70 (April 1921): 458–62; Kate Foster, *Our Canadian Mosaic* (Toronto, 1926). Robert England, "Continental Europeans in Western Canada," *Queen's Quarterly* 38 (Winter 1931).

46. Robert England, *The Central European Immigrant in Canada* (Toronto, 1929).

47. John Blue, *Alberta Past and Present* (Chicago, 1924), 210.

48. There were some advocates of the melting pot prior to 1920, but the idea did not gain widespread acceptance until the 1920s. See Palmer, "Nativism and Ethnic Tolerance in Alberta, 1880–1920," ch. 1; Marilyn Barber, "Nationalism, Nativism, and the Social Gospel."

49. Douglas Cole, "John S. Ewart and Canadian Nationalism," *Canadian Historical Association Reports* (1969), 66.

50. John Diefenbaker, *One Canada* (Toronto, 1975), 140, 141, 218–19, 274.

51. John Higham, *Strangers in the Land,* 2nd ed. (New York, 1967), chs. 10, 11.

52. Palmer, "Nativism and Ethnic Tolerance in Alberta, 1920–1972," ch. 3.

53. James Gray, *The Roar of the Twenties* (Toronto, 1975), ch. 11; Lita-Rose Betcherman, *The Swastika and the Maple Leaf* (Don Mills, ON, 1975).

54. Barry Broadfoot, *Ten Lost Years* (Toronto, 1973), 25, 70, 76, 132, 156–64, 186, 279.

55. Ibid., 132.

56. Ibid., 186.

57. Ivan Avakumovic, *The Communist Party in Canada: A History* (Toronto, 1975), 66–67; Lita Rose Betcherman, *The Swastika and the Maple Leaf*, ch. 5.

58. Ibid.

59. Palmer, "Nativism and Ethnic Tolerance in Alberta, 1920–1972," ch. 3.

60. M.A. Jones, *American Immigration* (Chicago, 1960), 298. For fictional treatments of the second generations' repudiation of the ethnic past in an attempt to become accepted see John Marlyn, *Under the Ribs of Death* (Toronto, 1951) and Magdalena Eggleston, *Mountain Shadows* (New York, 1955), 122. See also *Change of Name* (Toronto: Canadian Institute of Cultural Research, 1965).

61. Watson Kirkconnell, *The European Heritage, A Synopsis of European Cultural Achievement* (London, 1930); and by the same author, *Canadian Overtones* (Winnipeg, 1935). For a complete listing of Kirkconnell's work, see the list in his memoirs, *A Slice of Canada* (Toronto, 1967), 374–75. For an assessment of his work see J.R.C. Perkin, ed., *The Undoing of Babel* (Toronto, 1975).

62. Kirkconnell, *Canadian Overtones*, preface.

63. Watson Kirkconnell, *Canada, Europe and Hitler* (Toronto, 1939).

64. Kirkconnell, *A Slice of Canada*.

65. Palmer, *Land of the Second Chance*, 43–48, 99, 207. A. Spada, *The Italians in Canada* (Montreal, 1969), ch. 8.

66. Forrest Laviolette, *Canadian Japanese and World War II* (Toronto, 1948).

67. J.W. Pickersgill and D.F. Forster, *The Mackenzie King Record*, vol. 4, *1947–48* (Toronto, 1970), 234–35.

68. See Robin Winks, *The Blacks in Canada*, 423, for a discussion of how World War II was instrumental in improving the status of blacks in Canada.

69. W.L. Mackenzie King, House of Commons *Debates*, 1 May 1947, pp. 2644–46.

70. Ibid.

71. Although immigration policy and prevailing Anglo-Canadian attitudes emphasized the need for "assimilable" immigrants, the federal government's policy concerning the role of immigrants and ethnic groups in Canadian society was not strictly assimilationist during the 1950s. The Citizenship Branch, the postwar successor to the Nationalities Branch of the Department of National War Services, concerned itself with the linguistic, social, and cultural adjustment of immigrants to life in Canada and their acceptance by Canadians. The branch defined its objective as that of achieving the "integration" of immigrants and ethnic groups. This could mean either the melting pot or cultural pluralist approach, depending on which government was in power or which civil servant was interpreting the policy. Most often, however, "integration" approached the cultural pluralist ideal; it envisioned the retention of the immigrants' cultural identity, coupled with full participation at all levels of Canadian economic and political life. Palmer, "Nativism and Ethnic Tolerance in Alberta: 1920–1972," 288–92.

72. Between 1941 and 1961, the proportion of people of non-British, non-French origin showed the following increases: Manitoba—from 43 to 48 percent; Saskatchewan—from 45 to 50 percent; Alberta—from 44 to 49 percent. British Columbia remained at 37 percent. *Census of Canada, 1941* and *1961*.

73. W.L. Morton, "The Historical Phenomenon of Minorities: The Canadian Experience" (paper presented at International Congress of Historical Sciences, August 1975), 26.

74. Nancy Tienhaara, *Canadian Views on Immigration and Population* (Ottawa, 1975), 19. Several qualifications should be made, however, to this picture of the growing acceptance of immigrants in the postwar period. Attitudes toward immigration varied in different regions of English-speaking Canada in the postwar period (though no region was consistently more favourable or unfavourable in its attitudes). Attitudes varied by age and sex with women generally more negative toward immigration. Education played a very important factor in determining attitudes with more highly educated people more favourable toward immigration. Occupation was also important in determining attitudes with unskilled labour and the unemployed more negative in their attitude toward immigration. Attitudes also became slightly more restrictive during the 1950s than they had been in the immediate postwar period. Tienhaara, *Canadian Views on Immigration and Population*, 20–36.

75. William Petersen, *Planned Migration: The Social Determinants of the Dutch-Canadian Movement* (Berkeley, 1955). For a full discussion of postwar immigration policy see Freda Hawkins, *Canada and Immigration* (Montreal, 1972).

76. Royal Commission on Bilingualism and Biculturalism, Book 4, *The Cultural Contribution of the Other Ethnic Groups* (Ottawa, 1970), 29.

77. Anthony Richmond, *Ethnic Residential Segregation in Metropolitan Toronto* (Toronto, Institute for Behavioural Research, York University, 1972).

78. Palmer, "Nativism and Ethnic Tolerance in Alberta, 1920–1972," chs. 5–6.

79. Palmer, *Land of the Second Chance*, chs. 6, 7, 8.

80. Palmer, "Nativism and Ethnic Tolerance in Alberta," ch. 5.

81. Tienhaara, *Canadian Views on Immigration and Population*, ch. 2.

82. For a detailed discussion and documentation of the impact of the Royal Commission on the development of pluralist ideas see Palmer, "Nativism in Alberta," ch. 6.

83. John Porter, "Dilemmas and Contradictions of a Multi-Ethnic Society," *Transactions of the Royal Society of Canada* 10, 4 (1972): 193–205. In his article, "Ethnic Pluralism in Canadian Perspective" in *Ethnicity: Theory and Experience*, ed. Nathan Glazer and D.P. Moynihan (Cambridge, MA, 1975), 267–304, Porter gives a comprehensive statement of his opposition to multiculturalism, which he sees as "regressive," and attempts to refute some of the arguments for multiculturalism.

84. Porter, ibid.

85. For recent discussion on these issues within an American context see Murray Friedman, ed., *Overcoming Middle-Class Rage* (Philadelphia, 1971); Michael Novak, *The Rise of the Unmeltable Ethnics* (Macmillan, 1972); Andrew M. Greeley, "The Rediscovery of Diversity," *Antioch Review* (Fall 1971): 343–65; Harold R. Issacs, "The New Pluralists," *Commentary* (March 1972): 68–73, and the articles by John Highman, Michael Novak, and Gunnar Myrdal in *Center Magazine* (July–August 1974).

86. An informal analysis which I conducted of grants given under the multicultural program suggests that left-wing ethnic groups have not been excluded from the grants program, although some extreme right-wing ethnic groups have.

87. *Montreal Gazette*, 9 Oct. 1971.

88. Federal Government's Response to Book 4 of the *Report of the Royal Commission on Bilingualism and Biculturalism* (Oct. 1971), 3.

89. John Higham, "Integration vs. Pluralism: Another American Dilemma," *Center Magazine* (Oct.–Nov. 1974): 67–68. W.L. Morton also points to the dilemma of individual vs group rights in his discussion of minorities in Canadian society.

W.L. Morton, "The Historical Phenomenon of Minorities: The Canadian Experience," 44.

90. *Toronto Star*, 16 Oct. 1971; 13 June 1972.

91. For one point of view, see Palmer, "Canada: Bicultural or Multicultural?" *Canadian Ethnic Studies* (June 1971): 113–14.

92. Ralph Heintzman, "In the Bosom of a Single State," *Journal of Canadian Studies* (Nov. 1971): 1–2, 63–64.

93. A.K. Davis, "The Politics of Multiculturalism and Third-World Communities in Canada: A Dialectical View" (paper presented to Conference on Multiculturalism and Third World Immigrants, Edmonton, Sept. 1975).

94. Jean Burnet, "Ethnic Relations and Ethnic Policies in Canadian Society" (paper delivered at the Ninth International Congress of Anthropological and Ethnological Sciences, Chicago, 1973); and "The Policy of Multiculturalism within a Bilingual Framework: An Interpretation," in A. Wolfgang, *The Education of Immigrant Children* (Toronto, 1975); "Multiculturalism, immigration and racism: a comment on the Canadian Immigration and Population Study," *Canadian Ethnic Studies* 7, 1 (1975); "The Definition of Multiculturalism in a Bilingual Framework" (paper presented at Conference on Multiculturalism and Third World Immigrants, Edmonton, Sept. 1975).

95. Jean Burnet, "The Policy of Multiculturalism within a Bilingual Framework." It seems to me her view that sociologically speaking Canada is multi-ethnic rather than multicultural is basically accurate, although perhaps it does not adequately take into account the rural subcultures of Hutterites, Ukrainians, and Doukhobors, nor the urban subcultures of the new immigrants from China, Italy, Portugal, and Greece. It must also be realized that in calling Canada multicultural, the federal government, and various provincial governments, are not trying to make a definitive sociological analysis of Canadian society. Politicians are operating within a historical framework of a political and constitutional dialogue about Canada. Once Canada had been defined as bicultural, its redefinition as multicultural was inevitable, if the "other ethnic groups" were to be given recognition.

96. John Berry et al., "Majority Attitudes Study," Interim Report (Jan. 1975), ch. 8.

97. Ibid., 87.

98. Two other studies, done in Edmonton and Toronto, indicate a fairly strong support for multiculturalism in these cities. The Toronto study conducted in 1970 found that 68 percent of the total population and 62 percent of those of British origin favoured a multicultural society while a 1974 Edmonton study found that 61 percent of the total population supported multiculturalism. Anthony Richmond, *Ethnic Residential Segregation in Metropolitan Toronto*, table 4.7; Gurbachan Paul, "Immigrant Composition and Multiculturalism."

99. Berry, "Majority Attitudes Study," ch. 5.

100. For a detailed analysis of French-Canadian attitudes, see ibid., 94–96.

101. On a scale of 7 with 7 being the most positive toward multiculturalism, the Anglo-celtic score was 4.68, English-speaking ethnic minorities scored 4.62, French-speaking ethnic minorities scored 4.31, and French-Canadians 3.98. Berry, "Majority Attitudes Study," 74.

102. Ken O'Bryan et al., "Non-Official Languages: A Study in Canadian Multiculturalism" (Ottawa, Department of the Secretary of State, 1975).

103. Berry "Majority Attitudes Study," 80.

104. Ibid., 87.

105. Quotes in this paragraph taken from questions used in the survey.

106. Berry, "Majority Attitudes Study," 76.

107. J.S. Frideres, "Prejudice and Discrimination in Western Canada: First and Third World Immigrants" (paper presented to conference on Multiculturalism and Third World Immigrants, Edmonton, Sept. 1975).

108. J.S. Frideres, "Multiculturalism and Third World Immigrants: A Report on a National Conference," *Canadian Ethnic Studies*, 7, 2 (1975): 105–13.

109. Marlene Mackie, "Ethnic Stereotypes and Prejudice: Alberta Indians, Hutterites and Ukrainians," *Canadian Ethnic Studies* 6 (1974): 48. Leo Driedger and Jacob Peters, "Ethnic Identity and Social Distance: A Comparison of Ethnic Groups" (paper presented to 1974 meetings of the Canadian Association of Sociology and Anthropology, Toronto, Aug. 1974), table 1.

110. Berry "Majority Attitudes Study," ch. 5.

111. Richmond, *Ethnic Residential Segregation in Metropolitan Toronto*; Jim Frideres, "Prejudice and Discrimination in Western Canada"; Jim Frideres, "Discrimination in Western Canada," *Race* 25, 2 (1973): 213–22.

112. Richmond, "The Green Paper: Reflections on the Canadian Immigration and Population Study"; and Warren Kalbach, "The National Conference on Canadian Immigration and the Green Paper in Retrospect" in *Canadian Ethnic Studies* 7, 1.

113. Tienhaara, *Canadian Views on Immigration and Population*, ch. 2.

114. Certainly not all current opposition to immigration stems from racist motives. See for example the articles, Lorna Marsden, "Population Issues in the Immigration Debate" and C.F. Bently, "Immigration Increases Food Costs" in *Canadian Ethnic Studies* 7, 1.

115. Berry's *Majority Attitudes Study* suggests relatively little concern about non-white immigration, while studies by Paul and Frideres suggest a good deal of concern. Paul, "Immigrant Composition and Multiculturalism"; Frideres, "Prejudice and Discrimination in Western Canada."

116. Frideres, "Prejudice and Discrimination in Western Canada," table 4; Anthony Richmond, "Black and Asian Immigrants in Britain and Canada: Experiences of Prejudice and Discrimination" (paper presented at a conference on Multiculturalism and Third World Immigrants in Canada, Edmonton, Sept. 1975), table 8. Palmer, "Nativism and Ethnic Tolerance in Alberta: 1920–1972," 360–72.

117. Peter Newman, *The Canadian Establishment* (Toronto, 1975); Merrijoy Kelner, "Ethnic Penetration into Toronto's Elite Structure," *Canadian Review of Sociology and Anthropology* 7: 128–37; Wallace Clement, *The Canadian Corporate Elite: An Analysis of Economic Power* (Toronto, 1975), 237–38.

118. Bishop G.E. Lloyd, quoted in *Manitoba Free Press*, 18 July 1928.

THE SKILLED EMIGRANT AND HER KIN: GENDER, CULTURE, AND LABOUR RECRUITMENT✧

JOY PARR

o

Emigration is generally understood as a gendered process, beginning for men with a solitary experiment in distant lands, for women with a long interlude between two worlds while they wait for word that it is safe to follow. For men the journey is seen as a response to international differentials in the labour market, for women as a way to begin or consolidate a married life. Emigration usually seems to cast men in active roles and women in adaptive roles, men being part of a structured system, and women living out the consequences of subjective choices.[1] These characterizations probably miss the mark, even for emigration within marriage. As descriptions of female migration outside marriage (and probably also within it for all but women of independent wealth), these depictions omit several essentials.

⸰ Single female emigrants have not been uncommon historically. Typically they left home in early adulthood, at a marriageable age, although, as Charlotte Macdonald reminds us, the fact that emigration and marriage have similar locations in many life cycles does not establish that young women, any more than young men, left home in order to marry. Most working-class women understood that marriage, either before or after emigration, would not end their experience with wage work. Female emigrants had their eye on the job market, both short and long term.[2] In Canada even young women recruited for their domestic skills often remained for many years in the labour force before marriage.[3] In the twentieth century, emigration frequently has been a flight from marriage rather than a strategy to pursue it, a way either to evade or escape conjugality.[4] ⸰

✧ *Canadian Historical Review* 68, 4 (Dec. 1987): 529–51. Reprinted by permission of University of Toronto Press Incorporated. The author is grateful to Shula Marks, Alice Kessler-Harris, and the members of the Queen's University seminar in National and International Development for thoughtful commentaries on this paper.

Emigration is a sex-selective process experienced differently by women and men. It is also part of a wider social existence in which gender is perceptible only as it is confounded by time, class, and place. Emigration can be the product of sex imbalances; it also forms them, both in the old country and the new. By its sex-selectivity, emigration creates social groupings in which women and men are present in radically unequal numbers. Gill Burke describes the two such communities created by miners' emigration from nineteenth-century Cornwall—the women's world of the Cornish villages, the male society of overseas mining territories.[5] As large emigrant flows alter the economies at both source and destination, they also change the demography and create communities in which same-sex bonds are especially important. Sometimes this heightened homosociability is an unintended and unwanted consequence of the move. In other instances it may be an integral part of the decision to emigrate for both the emigrants and the non-emigrating kin.[6] Emigration has offered a release from domestic tensions as well as an escape from economic deprivation. For skilled wage-earning women, anomalies in both the factory and the family circle, the recruiter's promise of a "Golden Land"[7] suggested new lives in more than a material sense.

This paper considers the relationships among gender solidarities, wage work, and the reconstitution of family in a community to which many women emigrated when preference or circumstance led them to lives without men. It deals with the particular case of approximately 700 British hosiery workers, principally from the East Midlands, whom Penman's Company, then the largest Canadian knit-goods firm, assisted to emigrate to Paris, Ontario, population 4000,[8] between 1907 and 1928. This is a study of the reasons for their emigration, their relationships with the networks of female kin who followed them to Canada, and the reasoning and rituals that characterized the women's culture forged by life-long mill work in one Canadian hosiery community. It is about female British wage workers whom Canadian managers sought out and whose emigration they financed. It examines the life these women thought they were choosing when they accepted an offer to go to a community where their future in the work force was much more certain than their prospects as wives.

The Penman's emigrants were selected because they were accomplished hosiery workers. The contradictions between being female and being financially independent did not exist for the recruiter while he was recruiting them. Rather, he assiduously searched out skilled female wage earners for the very combination of attributes that complicated their lives at home. He was looking for female wage earners simply because they were wage earners, promising steady long-term employment; but his offer presented these emigrants with a social possibility as alluring as the expected hike in pay.

The period was one of considerable British emigration to Canada. Although government advertising was directed towards agriculturalists and domestic servants, and the Canadian Manufacturers' Association more frequently sought out male industrial workers for its members, the recruitment of female factory operatives did occur. The British Women's

Emigration Association sponsored a factory scheme from 1904, publicizing requests from Canadian employers, principally in textiles and garment manufacture, among Girls' Clubs in industrial cities, and arranging for the extension of assisted passages to young women who decided to go abroad.[9] Penman's used Canadian Manufacturers' Association representatives and hired their own recruiters to work through the commercial emigration bureaux associated with shipping offices, advertising in the local press and labour exchanges for experienced help.[10]

The knit-goods industry in Canada grew rapidly between 1907 and 1928. Labourers building two new transcontinental railways and opening mines in the Rockies and the northern shield wore Penman's underwear and sweaters. Wartime contracts followed the completion of the railways, and the postwar fashion for knitwear prolonged strong demand until the late 1920s. Paris was a small town in a prosperous agricultural district and, even in the nineteenth century, the mill's demand for female labour had exceeded the local supply. As the firm grew after a major financial reorganization in 1906, the labour shortage became acute.

Raw recruits could be found nearer to hand than Leicestershire. "Skilled and experienced workers, those able to earn the highest wages" were what the firm specified in British advertisements. The demand was greatest for operators with machine-specific skills on equipment traditionally run by women. Penman's purchased knitting and looping machines from Midlands builders, and on occasion arranged for both mechanics and operatives who knew a new technology to come to Canada with the equipment. More generally, the firm wanted that combination of judgment and dexterity that allowed a worker simultaneously to maximize volume of production and quality, to make the most efficient use of the equipment, and to generate the fewest possible seconds. The smallest flaw, of no significance in woven fabric, easily spread the length of a knitted garment. A firm selling under trade mark needed operatives who knew the machines they were running well enough to diagnose imperfections, and a cadre of meticulous inspectors and menders who reliably detected and stabilized seconds. A male Penman's manager called these "limited skills," comparing the specific expertise of the female immigrants with the all-round knowledge of the trade he had gained in a Midlands technical apprenticeship. (Might he, in considering males, have said specialized?) The healthy profitability of the firm, however, depended on these limited proficiencies, depended upon them sufficiently to justify the inconvenience of offshore recruitment and the risk of extending prepaid passages. The Midlands was considered a reservoir of such skill, with a population so long engaged in the trade that "expert hosiery production [had become] an instinct."[11]

The East Midlands hosiery was not experiencing the gradual sectoral extinction that had expelled earlier agricultural and mining immigrants to the Canadas and other colonies. Relative to the woven cloth trade, in fact, the knit-goods industry fared relatively well in the first third of this century. There were, however, certain general and gender-specific economic reasons for Midlands hosiery workers to consider emigration. When Penman's began their Nottinghamshire and Leicestershire recruiting in

1907–09, times were slack in the British trade. It was in the spring of 1910, in the wake of these hard times, that Canadian agents had their greatest pre-war success in encouraging hosiery workers to consider Canada. This activity was not well regarded by Midlands hosiery manufacturers, who wondered in print about the improbability of British hosiery hands departing "old England for the land of the maple leaf—and snow" and who suggested suspiciously that "whoever has succeeded in persuading so many workpeople to leave these shores must be given credit for a rare fund of tact, energy and persistence," given the "extreme briskness of the English hosiery trade." When Penman's recruiters used the Leicester and Nottingham labour exchanges to secure a contingent of 130 female hosiery emigrants in 1910, the editor of the *Hosiery Trade Journal* protested that the exchanges "were certainly not intended to find skilled labour for competitors even though they may be colonials."[12] The deportation of one of the May 1910 parties, after a week's detention in Quebec, was widely publicized as a cautionary tale for "poor knitting folk" who might be tempted to break up their homes and hazard their fortunes to colonial "red-tapism."[13] The warnings went largely unheeded. Penman's June and July 1910 parties proceeded to Canada without incident.

After the war there was a brief fillip in the British industry, and then, beginning in 1921, a stretch of years in which union officials reported "uncertainty in the trade," "bad trade," and then a "general slump." Unemployment in the hosiery averaged 8200 in 1923 and 6700 in 1927. Many of these redundancies were caused by productivity-enhancing technological changes and were unlikely to be reduced even when demand recovered. Heightening external tariffs in Germany and Canada, among other jurisdictions, limited Britain's traditionally vigorous export markets for knit goods. In this sense, the emigration to Canada was part of a new international division of labour.[14]

Within the new regime, women's prospects in particular were better in Canada than in Britain. As the number of jobs in British knit-goods firms was reduced, the hosiery unions moved, cautiously but deliberately, to protect men's jobs to the detriment of women's and to redraw gender divisions in the industry so as to favour men. In Canada, because the hosiery industry was not unionized until the late 1940s, as well as for many other reasons,[15] jobs in knitting, countering, and shading, which remained or were becoming increasingly men's work in the Midlands, were open to women. Besides more jobs, Canadian recruiters could promise, and deliver, better paying and more steady work. Travellers between Paris and the Midlands reported women's wages 50 percent higher in Canada in both 1908 and 1923.[16] Because capital in the Canadian industry was highly concentrated, Penman's and the small number of companion firms with which it colluded in the market could work to inventory rather than to order, running their plants at a reasonably steady rate year round. The promise of regular work was especially inviting to employees of small Midlands firms, which had always produced seasonally and which, in the 1920s, quickly assimilated the advantages of the new Unemployment Insurance Act, "using the people whilst it was necessary and then giving them their cards."[17]

Many Midlands immigrants came to Paris independently, using their own savings or tickets sent back to them by kin already established in town. The first English hosiery workers arrived in the 1870s, soon after the small Penman's partnership began factory production. Others came with state support, having declared their intention to farm, and then reached Paris by way of Saskatchewan or Alberta, some directed to the town by their children who found the picture of Penman's mills in their primary school geography book. There were a few mill families in town headed by male spinners or mechanics who had been to Australia, New England, the American West, and back to England again before they settled on Paris.[18] The core of the mill-worker community in town, however, consisted of the 700 persons assisted by the firm to emigrate in the twenty years after 1907, along with their kin.[19]

Of the assisted emigrants, at least three-quarters were female, four-fifths of them unmarried.[20] In Britain they were given tickets covering their rail fares and their transatlantic passage and, in some cases, small cash advances. They travelled in parties, accompanied by a Penman's agent. On arrival in Paris they were required to sign a contract agreeing to repay the sum advanced at a rate of 50 cents per week while earning less than $6.00 per week and $1.00 per week while earning more, the unpaid sum "at all times constituting first lien" on their wages, the whole unpaid balance becoming due immediately should they leave the company's employ. Most immigrants arrived owing Penman's about $60 in 1910 and $110 in 1928, sums that throughout the period took between twelve and eighteen months to repay.[21]

Contract labour schemes such as this were usually failures in both the settler dominions and the United States. Workers simply decamped, leaving their ticket stubs behind them, to find jobs where their wages would be their own. In Paris, by contrast, most assisted immigrants faithfully repaid their loans. It was the Depression of the 1930s rather than defaulting debtors that caused the firm to discontinue overseas recruitment. One in four of the "imported help" left before the loan was entirely repaid, but in most cases the sum remaining on the firm's books was small.[22] The majority stayed for the rest of their lives in town, for most of their years as employees of the mill.

It was not a keen sense of contract that kept them. As Philip Corrigan has noted from Marx, there are "chains" in capitalism apart from the law.[23] The distinction between bound and free labour is to be found in the "conditions of work" and in the social relations that accompanied it. For migrants, as Colin Newbury has argued, the distinction lies between those "allowed to enjoy a measure of vertical mobility and participation in the organization of a political economy, and those whose entry into such economies was partial, peripheral and without political influence."[24]

In a sense the Penman's immigrants, as skilled female wage earners, had no place to go. Among the emigrant parties, those who began at the Paris mills as lower-paid workers were most likely to quit before their loans were repaid, partly because they were discharging the debt at a much slower rate but also because they had much less to leave (see table 1). Those who found other jobs in town quickly confronted the loyalty and hierarchy among local capitalists, and had their wages at their new employment docked for remission to the "masters of the mill." Having arrived without savings, set down in a small community in a strange country, even those without ties in town and willing to take any job were likely to linger through most of the repayment schedule accumulating the cash and information with which to make a move. For skilled workers, leaving was less attractive. They were unlikely to be able to get good hosiery work and to evade their debt. The fraternity among the few Canadian knit-goods manufacturers was close, and those who, in applying for new jobs, had to explain themselves to new employers found their obligation to Penman's followed them.[25] More importantly, they would be leaving behind a range of other advantages that, as skilled female wage earners, they were less likely to secure elsewhere. Paris was a place where they were at the centre of the local economy, where community social relations were organized around wage-earning women, where they were not an anomaly.

Penman's recruiters went to the East Midlands not only because it was a reservoir of skill in the hosiery trade but also because, particularly in Leicestershire, there was an accepted tradition of life-long female wage work, a tradition that was lacking in the surrounding Ontario community. In searching out women such as Miss Florrie Morris, born 1895, emigrated to Paris 1912, retired from Penman's in 1970 at the age of seventy-five, and Mrs Annie Smith, born 1890, emigrated to Paris 1913, retired from Penman's at the age of seventy-nine in 1969, managers were seeking both skill and stability in their work force. Overseas recruitment was a way to overcome what Charlotte Erickson has called the "social obstacles" that existed locally to the labour system the firm wished to sustain. In this conjuncture was a social setting that female mill workers made their own. Florrie Morris and Annie Smith were exceptional in their length of service at the mills, and exceptions to the common Canadian story about the passing of an adult woman's days and years, but they were not as life-long wage workers considered oddities in Paris by either the community or the firm. That acceptance, and the range of possibilities of which it was a part,

TABLE 1   *PENMAN'S IMPORTED HELP:*
REPAYMENT OR DEFAULT ON LOANS
BY EARNING LEVELS

Earnings Level◇	Repaid	Defaulted	Total
Low	100	82	182
(row %)	(54.9)	(45.0)	(52)
(col %)	(40)	(82)	
High	150	18	168
(row %)	(89.2)	(10.7)	(48)
(col %)	(60)	(18)	
Total	250	100	350
(%)	(71.4)	(28.6)	

◇ Low earnings levels were those of less than $6.00 per week. High levels were $6.00 per week or more. Those earning more than $6.00 repaid twice as much per week on their passage debts as those earning less.

drew several skilled female immigrants back to Paris from confinement on the margins of the mainstream economy in larger centres (and also to discharge the debts that remained unlapsed on Penman's books).[26]

The Midlands tradition of life-long female wage work was as anxious and self-denying as it was persistent. There are enough affirmations in the record that married women's employment should not exist to convince a careful scholar that indeed it did not.[27] As female seamers and menders were brought from domestic workshops into the factories in the 1890s, industrialists argued against mothers' wage work "on moral and humanitarian grounds" that children were thereby "persistently neglected" and "very, very poorly cared for." Yet they continued to employ wives during all but the first month after childbirth—"on business grounds . . . some of them are the best workers we have, and we should be sorry to lose them." Unionists worried that married women with husbands at work would undercut the wages of single women and men.[28] But both the oral history and the wage-book evidence is clear. Large numbers of married women were employed in the East Midlands hosiery industry through the first half of this century.[29] In 1919 "hundreds" of these workers struck in Hinckley, "determined their custom continue of going in at 9 AM instead of 8," presumably so as to have time for their home duties before reporting for wage work. Male union officials were both individually conflicted and organizationally divided on the issue of married women's employment. Although they recognized that question as one to be handled "very delicately" since "married women had the same rights as members" as all others in the union, they worked steadily to shift the boundaries between men's and women's work in favour of men. There are examples of women themselves, while largely supporting their households, struggling to maintain for their children the illusion of the husband as breadwinner.[30]

A wage-earning woman existed in the thralls of an awkward and unsatisfactory negotiation, not only to retain the right to work and to be employed on schedules that made wage earning tenable, but also to reconcile social ideology with her own experience. In other communities, women were employed for a time in their teens and twenties and perhaps returned to the labour force later in life when their children were grown, so that wage work was scripted to a safe place as a contingency, to be pursued only when it would not collide with primary obligations as mother and wife.[31] Where the labour force tradition was different, where daughters followed mothers in patterns of life-long wage work in the presence of a patriarchal culture that declared these patterns pathogenic, a safe place was more difficult to secure. The antipathies between female wage work and heterosexual conjugality called for a different resolution. There are signs of these negotiations in textile towns: the later age at marriage, the greater incidence of nonmarriage, the commercial provision of food preparation and laundry services elsewhere labelled wives' work, and the more intense networks for labour exchanges among households.

These struggles to reconcile material sustenance and domestic satisfaction pose questions about consciousness of gender and the experience of security in same- and cross-gender connections. Like Ross and Rapp's parsing of the relationships of inheritance patterns through nuptiality to sexuality, these indications take us towards an emerging social possibility.[32] Could it not be that, for some, wage work came to be understood as the continuity, and marriage the contingency in the unfolding of an adult woman's life?

Were this the case, how would one come to acknowledge it as a social existence rather than as a personal happenstance? There must have been many routes through which this process of "self-discovery" as a group developed, and as many paths at which it was blocked. For Penman's mill households emigration was a section in one of the open routes. Midland women workers were coming from wage work to wage work, making the decision to emigrate based on the gains they could achieve as wage workers. The emigrant group was dominated by widows with families, veterans of troubled marriages, women alone, single women with children, and pairs of women friends. For many, marriage was not an active post-emigration consideration. Emigration by congregating numbers of women who were living without men clarified this cultural alternative. They came with common experience of wage work and the domestic dilemmas female employment engendered to a women's town, a place where the prevailing wage form did not require a male breadwinner or give precedence to households which included men, where the numerical dominance of female wage earners offered a certain psychic and physical protection, a shelter for a woman-centred culture.

Among widows the domestic provocations for emigration were most plain. For older women whose spouses had died, especially those with several daughters, emigration was a way to keep the family solvent and together. Mary Cavan and a female cousin came to Paris in 1912 and returned to Glasgow in 1914 to fetch her widowed mother, a younger sister, and one of her two brothers. Maud Chappell, her three sisters, and widowed mother arrived in Paris in 1913. All but Maud had worked previously in lace and box-making in Nottingham. Her first week in Canada, fifteen-year-old Maud began her twenty-nine-year career in the mill. Anne Hedley and her sister were urged to emigrate by their mother when their coal-miner father died, so that they could make a home together rather than live separately in domestic service. Each of these households became the nucleus of a spreading mill family in Paris, bound together by strong female kin ties. In each of these cases, and characteristic of Midlands families in town, links with male siblings attenuated. There were brothers in the Cavan, Chappell, and Hedley emigrant groups, but all left town and lost close connection with the family circle. On several occasions it fell to daughters to assume their brothers' passage debts as family obligations when sons lost patience with their widowed mother's choice of destination overseas.

Atypically of chain migrations, males among the Paris emigrants were frequently the last rather than the first in kin groups to go abroad, reluctantly following the initiative of female family members. Betty Shaw's widowed mother, a lacemaker, went to Paris alone in 1913, leaving two-year-old

Betty in the care of her grandparents and returning later to persuade them to join her overseas. Betty's grandfather, a coal miner, did a youngster's work as chore-boy in the mills in Paris, but the earnings of several skilled women in the household carried them through until 1949, when, to a woman, they were fired as militants in a long local strike.[33] Their husbands' deaths made widows consider emigration to a place where they and their children might be self-supporting. The widow's initiative gave her household independence, drawing daughters together, but frequently cast sons and male kin in dependent roles.

For women in troubled marriages, as for widows, emigration to skilled work overseas offered an opportunity to overcome the wrecked promises of conjugality. Edith Elliott's grandmother summoned all her children and shepherded them to Paris; as Elliott recalled, "the whole family came out, except the father and he stayed back because he worked in the coal mines over there and they came here." The Elliott family became prominent in the mill community, proprietors of a large boardinghouse, where grandmother Elliott might supervise her daughters' courtships with lodgers and arrange for aunts to initiate their nieces into the better jobs at the mill. Hilda Sharp's mother had come to Canada at the urging of female kin already established in Paris. Her husband had been invalided after the South African War; she may have seen the move as a way to reduce the domestic tensions arising from his limited earnings. The household prospered in Paris, turning its female members' domestic and hosiery skills into accumulations of real estate, earning the respect of the mill community as boardinghouse keepers and midwives. Mr Sharp, however, saw none of this, having early returned to his old job in Ilkeston. Ida Pelton's father stayed with her mother in Paris, but emigration consolidated a change in their household relationships. Her father's family had come to Paris at the turn of the century from Bulwell, Notts. He stayed behind, employed by an uncle in a declining trade:

> in those days they had horses not cars, and they had funerals and weddings and they had all the outfits for them, that's what he did. My Dad had to go to war and he was in Germany a year after the war ended and when he was away my Mother had read in the paper where people like us, we could come to Canada . . . so she told my Dad this when he came home and . . . it was all fixed for us to come.

Ida's mother earned good money as a mender at Penman's; Ida became a looper, a job that paid high piece rates. Together they managed, pooling their earnings and sharing domestic labour, although none of Ida's three brothers stayed in town, and neither her father nor husband was regularly employed. For Ida and her mother, as for many others, Paris offered a certain refuge to those for whom the scripted plan of stable marriage to a male breadwinner had gone awry.[34]

Within the mill community the intertwining of emotional and economic reasons for emigration was commonly experienced and understood. Emigration offered a resolution to domestic tensions which poverty, legality, and convention made otherwise unresolvable. Among women, so long as there was no harm done to others, an accepting discretion surrounded the paternity of youngsters and the mortal and marital state or whereabouts of spouses. A line between discretion and the countenancing of deception was, however, maintained by group scrutiny. Sam Horsley, a Midlands knitter active in the mill community but exceptional in town as a mature unattached male, found himself vexed by "false stories being circulated around town that I am a married man, and have left a wife and children in England"; to counter the rumours, he posted a $100 reward in the local paper in 1926 to "be paid to anyone bringing forward the slightest evidence that these stories are true," and threatened action "against any person making such false statements." In the case of Margaret Etherington, the local gossip turned out to be true. Etherington had emigrated from a textile town in Yorkshire to work in the local flannel factory. She declared herself a widow and in December 1923 married Bert Raynes, a knitter mechanic at the hosiery mill. Something seven years later made Raynes enlist the aid of the local police in Paris to inquire into her past. Word came back from the chief constable in Burnley that her husband, Frank Etherington, was alive in Earby, Yorkshire. He had commenced divorce proceedings twelve years previously, "but being short of money was unable to go forward with the case." Raynes chose to resolve the matter by full disclosure, declaiming in the press, "she is still his wife and I give this notice that the public may know that I have no lawful wife."[35]

In most early-twentieth-century communities the respectability of young unmarried women was closely scrutinized, female factory workers with, perhaps, more public flourish than any others. The majority of the Penman's assisted emigrants were single women; few travelled abroad by themselves. Most came with friends or female kin, many to join relatives already established in Paris.

For single mothers with children the demographics in town were sheltering. In 1936 more than a quarter of Penman's female employees lived in single-headed households, the majority of which included children. Ann Wilson had been a winder in Nottingham. In a slack season she and a woman with whom she worked in the hosiery encountered a Penman's recruiter and decided to emigrate, Ann bringing with her Gordon, her pre-school-aged son. They set up housekeeping together and worked side by side in the knitting mill. In time Ann's friend's daughter joined them. The community had developed housing forms, work schedules, and child-care arrangements that accommodated wage-earning mothers. Among others whose household form was similar, at a distance from past personal events, widows, deserted wives, and single mothers shared the dilemmas of wage work and childrearing outside conjugality. Frances Randall, a child born out of wedlock in Bulwell, came to Paris at the age of fourteen to join her maternal kin in a community where, although her early circumstances were known, they distinguished her less than they might have in the town of her birth.[36]

Emigration and the help of female kin did not resolve all the problems of being single and alone. In December 1919 Christina Addison joined her sister, Mrs Ireland, in the comfortable boardinghouse she ran on Elm Street near the Grand River and took a job in the mill. Her family noted her melancholy but could not assuage it. In April she rose one morning, instructed the postmaster to destroy all further correspondence, walked to the mill race, set her hat by the dam, and jumped to her death. But the community of single women was large in town; in 1936, 28 percent of Penman's women workers entered middle age unmarried, and the female society of the boardinghouses smoothed the emigrant transition. The acceptance that women should live as well as work together, organizing community events and convening festive gatherings in their homes, extended through the Penman's Pleasure Club and the company-owned YWCA to the churches, the Maids and Daughters of England, and the Ladies Auxiliary of the British Empire Service League. All-female households composed of sisters and friends were among the most vigorous social centres in the mill community, and their members unself-consciously claimed the scrupulous and attentive acknowledgment their domestic milestones were due. When the local paper reported in May 1935 that a "friendship of seventeen years had been severed" by the death of Miss Susan Baldwin in the house she shared with Lottie Trueman on Yeo Street, the editors were obliged to publish a correction noting that the two women "had been friends for 35 years, and came to Canada together 23 years ago, during seventeen of which Miss Baldwin was an invalid." Susan Baldwin was survived by five sisters in England but had remained through years of heart trouble in her Canadian home with her friend.[37]

It was rare for single emigrants to wed within their first eighteen months in Canada. Paris was probably not the easiest place in which to find a spouse, if one were looking, there being relatively few jobs to attract or keep unattached men in town. However, combining wage work with marriage was common in the community. In 1936, 40 percent of Penman's female employees were wives.[38] Among the skilled emigrant women who had come to Canada as wage earners and commanded the highest piece rates as knitters, loopers, shaders, and finishers, continuing on at the mill after marriage was especially common. Coping with employment, marriage, and motherhood simultaneously rather than sequentially required adaptations in domestic gender divisions and household boundaries that the Midlands emigrants shared with couples in the mill community generally.[39] But there were some ways of signalling symbolically the rules that must govern marriage between wage-earning spouses that were unique to the East Midlands emigrants.[40]

Most intriguing of these rituals were the mock weddings which Sallie Westwood describes as continuing in Leicester to this day. The Midlands origins of the mock wedding are unclear. Today in Leicester factories where men's and women's occupations are strictly segregated and men command the best-paying manufacturing and mechanical jobs, mock weddings are women's rituals. Brides are to wear pornographic costumes designed by female co-workers and are left by their women friends tied to the factory fence in a frightening public display of bondage, as "a celebration of their own oppression in marriage." The rites mark changes in a women's intimate life, acknowledging that she now will be sexually available to her husband and that, in accord with the appropriate power relationships of marriage, her sexuality will be "crucially mediated by men." These bridal rituals take place on the shop floor and around the factory gate, but they are not about the particular imminent dilemmas of wage-earning wives.[41]

As practised among the East Midlands emigrants in Paris in the 1920s and 1930s, mock weddings had very different functions. As pantomimes of gender roles, they ridiculed conventions of patriarchal hierarchy within marriage; as celebrations among co-workers who would continue to be employed together, they warned the couple that the intense commitment they were about to make to each other must be exclusively domestic and not privilege their relationship on the shop floor.

It was in the mixed-gender knitting, spinning, and cutting rooms, and when both spouses worked in the mill, that mock weddings were most common. On these elaborately costumed occasions, sex and age roles were reversed, the bride being a senior male skilled worker or foreman, the clergyman a young girl, the groom an older married woman, the best man one of her peers. The games were raucous parodies of domestic life. Sam Horsley, the machinist who a decade earlier had taken to the press to refute rumours concerning his own marital state, organized a mock wedding in 1937 at the home of a male co-worker in the shadow of the hosiery mill. Horsley himself was the bride, "charmingly dressed in black and pink velvet, carrying a bouquet of roses and sweet peas." Mrs Crump from the finishing room "took the part of the groom dressed in evening suit and top hat." Mrs Alice Russell, a sixty-year-old winder, was the bridesmaid,

> dressed in pink and silver lace, carrying a spray of forget-me-nots. The flower girl was Miss Williamson and the best man Miss Raycraft. The ceremony was ably performed by Miss F. McLaughlin. After the service Mr. J. Raycraft and Mr. S. Horsley rendered the beautiful duet "Love's Sweet Dream" accompanied on the guitar by Miss M. Williamson. . . . Mr. C. Williams executed an old fashioned clog dance to "Bye Bye Blues."[42]

The workplace parity between male and female co-workers in mixed departments (the bride in this case, Violet Jones, was a skilled burson knitter) carried over into sociability. The ritual affirmed that these conventions must influence marital politics as well if the bride were to continue effectively in her job. The inversion of the mock wedding played upon the suppleness of gender boundaries. The common laughter affirmed that equality among co-workers did not imply sameness in marital partners.

Because most women from Midlands emigrant families worked in the mills after they were married and for many years after they had children as well, the politics of mill and domestic life were interdependent and intertwined. When Jean Elliott, the granddaughter of a woman who had brought her family from Nottinghamshire, married her foreman in 1938, the mock wedding took place in their department in the hosiery mill. Here the significance of the role reversals was especially marked. Co-workers used the occasion to emphasize that nepotism must not intrude after the marriage, prejudicing the fair distribution of work in the room. The topic of mock weddings came up in this interview while we were talking about work-place tensions, rather than marriage:

John: She was just another worker there; I could love her up at home but not at work. If there was a choice of a good bag for this one and a bad one for that one, she would get the bad one.

Edith: Wasn't that nice.

Then John came to the question of mock weddings:

John: You couldn't play favourites—people would be looking for that type of thing. They had a mock wedding for us—the whole mill up to the department, over a hundred people. It was something I tell you, the old pot that goes under the bed, they had that all tied up in ribbons and I know I blushed too. I wish we had pictures of it but we didn't.

The mock wedding had achieved its purpose, reminding the foreman of his vulnerability before shopfloor consensus and of the limits on his authority as both husband and boss.[43]

o

The lives of the female skilled workers and their kin in Paris were formed by a series of common transatlantic experiences passed down as family lore and neighbourhood reminiscence to daughters and granddaughters. The women from the East Midlands were recruited for their work-place proficiencies with hosiery machinery and knitted fabric and their community traditions of life-long female wage work. In English hosiery districts these traditions were embattled. They were fortified by manufacturers' preferences for experienced, lower-waged women employees and long-standing community acceptance of the jointly constituted household rather than the individually garnered, male-breadwinner wage. They were challenged by the male-dominated hosiery unions who claimed wage-earning wives were complicit in pay cuts and who feared long-serving female employees as competitors with men for the declining pool of skilled jobs in the knit-goods industry. For all parties to the convention, life-long female wage work existed in awkward contradiction to the prevailing social ideology governing gender roles. For skilled women workers, emigration mitigated these conflicts by offering steady and well-paid employment and anonymous distance from the domestic tensions their English circumstances had conditioned. Emigration brought together women experienced in wage work, selected because of their workplace skills, and congregated them in a community where their prospects as wage earners were brighter than their likely fortunes as wives. Among the female emigrants and their kin, the economic and emotional reasons for leaving Britain were recounted as of a piece. Emigration, by offering women in one generation a way to evade or escape conjugality, opened a social possibility that wage work rather than marriage would be the continuity in an adult woman's life. In the community in which women were at both a numerical and an economic advantage, life after emigration was characterized by stronger bonds between women, weakened links with male kin, a more comfortable social acknowledgement of variously constituted female-headed households, and a greater willingness, at least within the emigrant community, to use group pressure to reinforce marital relations that would facilitate life-long female wage work.

NOTES

1. Sheila Allen, *New Minorities, Old Conflicts: Asian and West Indian Migrants in Britain* (New York, 1971), 29; Mirjana Morokvasic, "Why Women Emigrate? Towards Understanding of the Sex-Selectivity of the Migratory Movements of Labour," *Studi Emigrazione* 20 (June 1983): 133; Elizabeth Ewen, *Immigrant Women in the Land of Dollars* (New York, 1985), ch. 3.

2. Charlotte J. Macdonald, "Ellen Silk and Her Sisters: Female Emigration to the New World" in London Feminist History Group, *The Sexual Dynamics of History* (London, 1983), 82–85.

3. Varpu Lindström Best, "'I Won't Be A Slave': Finnish Domestics in Canada" and Marilyn Barber, "Sunny Ontario for British Girls" in *Looking Into My Sister's Eyes: An Exploration in Women's History*, ed. Jean Burnet (Toronto, 1986), 36, 44–50, 55–71.

4. Annie Phizacklea makes this point, based on the unpublished work of Mirjana Morokvasic, in her introduction to *One Way Ticket: Migration and Female Labour* (London, 1983), 7.

5. Charlotte Macdonald in "Ellen Silk" argues for closer study of communities characterized by sex imbalances, 81. Gill Burke's "The Cornish Diaspora of the Nineteenth Century" in *International Labour Migration: Historical Perspectives*, ed. Shula Marks and Peter Richardson (London, 1984), 57–75, describes such communities.

6. This seems to be the case for many of the non-migrant wives of Turkish emigrants to northern Europe described by Lenie Brouwer and Marijke Priester, "Living In Between: Turkish Women in their Homeland and the Netherlands" in *One Way Ticket*, 113–30.

7. In the context of British immigration to Canada in the first quarter of this century, this term is most closely associated with the illustrated book for popular audiences by Arthur Copping, *The Golden Land* (London, 1911). It is a phrase frequently used by Penman's emigrants when they remembered their encounters with recruiters.

8. *Census of Canada*, 1911, 1921.

9. Fawcett Library, British Women's Emigration Association, vol. 3, "Factory Scheme Subcommittee," Jan.–Nov. 1904; *Imperial Colonist*, "History of the Factory Workers' Fund," Oct. 1905; Nov. 1906; July 1909; May 1910; Nov. 1911, 404; Dec. 1919, 424.

10. *Hosiery Trade Journal* (hereafter *HTJ*), June 1907, 223. *The Leicester Mercury* through the spring of 1908 ran a specific advertising section, "Emigration," directly following the "Hosiery Hands Wanted" listings. I am grateful to Dr Ian

Keil, Department of Economic History, University of Loughborough, for arranging for me to have access to the department's collection of Leicestershire newspapers. See also *HTJ*, April 1910, 137.

11. *Imperial Colonist*, July 1904, 75; Sept. 1904; May 1910; *HTJ*, April 1910, 137, 158; *Canadian Textile Journal*, "Immigration of Skilled Workmen," Jan. 1917, 3; Richard Gurnham, *A History of the Trade Union Movement in the Hosiery and Knitwear Industry, 1776–1976* (Leicester, 1976), 112; Nottingham Local Studies Library, Oral History Collection, Interview A19, a male knitter born in 1919. I am grateful to Judy Kingscott, Oral History Co-ordinator, for assistance in using this collection. The quote from the Penman's technical expert is in Paris Industrial History Project (hereafter PIHP), Charles Harrison, 11. The names cited are the pseudonyms assigned on the transcripts. On the "instinctual knowledge" of Midlands hosiery workers see H. Wignall, "The Economics of the Hosiery Industry," *HTJ*, April 1936, 42. Of the female immigrants from whom data on earnings were available, 147 of 267 were earning wages sufficiently high from the day they began work in Canada to repay their fares at the maximum rate. Paris Historical Society (hereafter PHS), Penman's Imported Help Books, 3 vols.

The definition of skill is problematical. Royden Harrison has suggested that skill be considered as an "active relationship" among "a hard won set of judgments and dexterities," their "worth" as defined by their "scarcity," and the "organizational prowess" of those who hold them to maintain for themselves a social ascription as skilled. Harrison, "Introduction," in Royden Harrison and Jonathon Zeitlin, *Divisions of Labour* (Brighton, 1985), 1, 8–9. The female emigrants meet only the first two of these criteria. In neither the Midlands nor Ontario were they organized to claim equal standing with male mechanics. See Joy Parr, "Disaggregating the Sexual Division of Labour: A Transatlantic Case Study, Comparative Studies in Society and History" (forthcoming). Craig Heron and Robert Storey have argued against too strenuous an assumption of deskilling following mechanization; they note that machine operators, while lacking the "all-round knowledge of the whole production process" assumed of craftsmen, by "care, attention and familiarity" with the equipment produced at premium levels which made employers loathe to lose them. Introduction in Heron and Storey, eds. *On the Job: Confronting the Labour Process in Canada* (Montreal, 1986), 14–15. John Benson argues similarly in "Work" in *The Working Class in England* (London, 1985), 78. Heron and Storey call such workers "semi-skilled" using the artisan as a reference point. In the context of twentieth-century workplaces, specialized skill seems to me a more apt characterization of both the competence and the market power such workers could claim.

12. *HTJ*, June 1907, 223; "Nottingham News," 158, and "Editorial," 137, in *HTJ*, April 1910; May 1910, 206.

13. *HTJ*, "Notes and News," July 1910, 302; Aug. 1910, 350. The party from Derbyshire and Nottingham was detained and then deported because the Penman's agent had not arrived with sufficient funds to meet the £5 in hand requirement for entry of each non-agricultural immigrant. This regulation was an attempt by the Laurier Liberal government to appease its organized labour constituency that was concerned that immigrants were becoming public dependants and undercutting wages.

14. United Kingdom, Board of Trade, *Working Party on the Hosiery*, 1946, 9; *HTJ*, May 1909, 202; April 1910, 136. For statistics on 1920s unemployment in the industry see *HTJ*, March 1928, 94, following the Hosiery Trade Enquiry; also *HTJ*, May 1926, 96, and June 1926, 46; Leicestershire Record Office (hereafter LRO), National Union of Hosiery and Knitwear Workers (hereafter NUHKW), Leicester DE 1655/2/7, secretary's half-yearly report, S. Bassford, 9 May 1925; DE 1655/2/8, secretary's half-yearly report, H. Moulden, July 1928; Hinckley DE 1655/3/3, 1 Feb. 1921; Loughborough DE 1655/7/1 27 Aug. 1923, 30 Aug. 1928;

NLSL Oral History Collection, interview A19 9–10. F.A. Wells, *Hosiery and Knitwear Industry* (Newton Abbott, 1972), 169, but he bases his discussion on production figures. Union officials were reporting on declines in employment which accompanied technological change. Technological change in the hosiery industry is discussed in more detail in Parr "Disaggregating the Sexual Division of Labour." See also an interesting series of papers by Harriet Bradley, including "Technological Change, Management Strategies, and the Development of Gender-based Job Segregation in the Labour Process," and "Gender: Authority and the Division of Labour in the Workplace," Department of Sociology, University of Durham. On overseas tariffs see *HTJ*, July 1926, "British Hosiery Trades Future," 34; LRO, NUHKW, DE 1655/2/7 9 May 1925.

15. The difference in the arrays of sex labels for hosiery jobs in the East Midlands and Ontario is analyzed in detail in "Disaggregating the Sexual Division of Labour."

16. H.W. Hill, a Midlands hosiery expert who visited Canada frequently, reported a 50 percent wage differential in 1908. *HTJ*, March 1908, "Hosiery Trade in Canada," 122; George Wooler, a Midlands emigrant to Paris in 1910, reported the same spread during an extended visit home in 1923. *Paris* (Ont.) *Star*, 15 Aug. 1923.

17. On seasonality in the Nottingham trade see F.A. Wells, "Nottingham Industries" in *A Century of Nottingham History*, ed. J.D. Chambers (Nottingham, 1952), 34. Jeremy Crump made the same point for Leicester in his paper, "Leisure and Non-work in Leicester," given at History Workshop 16, Nov. 1984, in Leicester. The promise of "steady" work was prominent in publicity directed towards female industrial emigrants from early in the century. See *Imperial Colonist*, Sept. 1904, "Report of Miss Vernon," 101, and *Imperial Colonist*, Nov. 1906, similarly. The quote linking seasonality and the Unemployment Insurance Act is from NLSL, Oral History Collection, transcript A17a, Reginald Smith.

18. There were numerous local newspaper reports on Midlands emigrants to Paris in the 1880s. See *Paris* (Ont.) *Star*, 8 Feb. 1934, Golden wedding announcement of Mr and Mrs T. Bishop; 25 April 1935 obituary for Mrs Robert Etherington; 25 July 1936 obituary for Thomas Watson English. For accounts of peripatetic skilled emigrants see Charles Harrison, Ida Glass, PIHP; for agricultural immigrants, Ida Pelton, Jean Hubbard, Elwood Bain, May Phillips, Doris Ashley, Lottie Keen, PIHP; *Paris* (Ont.) *Star*, 23 Aug. 1922, obituary for George Edward Taylor; on skilled male workers see Charles Harrison, Thomas Blaney, Horace Timpson, PIHP.

19. Registers for the assisted emigration are incomplete. The Paris Historical Society has "Imported Help" books for 13 of the 20 years in which recruitment is known to have taken place, including World War I but excluding 1907–08 and 1919–23. The indexes in these registers list 442 names, but the volumes are in poor condition and only 378 collection sheets recording biweekly repayments remain. From oral evidence it seems reasonable to assume that at least as many immigrants arrived in the 7 years for which records are gone as in those 13 for which the registers remain, hence the estimate of approximately 700. The statistics that follow are based on the 378 emigrants for whom repayment schedules exist in the Paris Historical Society collection.

20. Names in the registers appear in two forms, initials and last name alone, or full Christian name and surname preceded by "Miss" or "Mrs." All those listed by initial only were assumed to be men, a convention that biases the test against the assumption that most assisted emigrants were women, as several identified by initial were later discovered in the personnel files to be female. By this convention, 285 of the 378 emigrants for whom repayment schedules exist were

assumed to be female; 227 of these were identified as "Miss" rather than "Mrs," or 80 percent of the 285.

21. PHS, Imported Help Books. Ticket vouchers and copies of several contracts are interleaved with the registers. The sum extended and the date the loan was made appear on each repayment schedule.

22. One hundred (27.1 percent) of the 369 immigrants for whom clear schedules exist defaulted before the full debt was repaid.

23. Philip Corrigan, "Feudal Relics or Capitalist Monuments? Notes on the Sociology of Unfree Labour," *Sociology* 11 (1977): 450, citing Karl Marx, *Capital* (London, 1967), 1: 641.

24. Colin Newbury, "The Imperial Workplace: Competitive and Coerced Labour Systems in New Zealand, Northern Nigeria and Australian New Guinea" in *International Labour Migration*, 226.

25. PHS, Imported Help Books. Clara Fox, emigrated 30 March 1910, had the balance of her debt collected by Mr Isaacs at the Canadian Hotel, Paris. Miss G. Eley, emigrated January 1912, repaid her passage through her employer at the New Royal Hotel. The T. Eaton Company, Toronto, docked the wages of Mrs Morley, emigrated from Ilkeston, July 1912, at the rate of $3 per month. The Ellis Company, Hamilton, collected Penman's loan from Mrs Pemberton, emigrated October 1910, for a year after she left Paris.

26. PHS, Penman's Imported Help Books, F.A. Morris, 32; Mrs Albert Smith, 186. The work history data come from the personnel cards in the Penman's Archives, Cambridge, Ontario. I am grateful to Fred Bemrose and Gordon Parsons for helping me to locate and use these records. Charlotte Erickson, "Why Did Contract Labour Not Work in the Nineteenth Century United States?" in *International Labour Migration*, 35. Among female emigrants who left and later returned to Paris, see PHS, Imported Help Books, May Barker, emigrated September 1913, left Paris December 1914, returned and balance paid September 1919; Lily Russell, emigrated August 1912, left Paris May 1913 for Hamilton, returned December 1914, debt discharged June 1915. Olive Cavan, Alice Russell, PIHP.

27. See Sandra Taylor, "The Effect of Marriage on Job Possibilities for Women and 'the Ideology of the Home: Nottingham 1890–1930," *Oral History* 5 (1977): 46–61.

28. Royal Commission on Labour 1892 [c. 6795-VI], 36, pt 2, Second Report of the Minutes of Evidence, Group C, vol. 2, testimony of B.C. Wates, president, Leicester Chamber of Commerce, questioned by A.J. Mundella, 533, and James Holmes, Midlands Counties Hosiery Federation, questioned by Mundella, 541.

29. Note the Essex Oral History interview with Mrs Randall, born 1910, whose mother, a knitter, did not work after marriage. Randall herself, however, was employed as a winder and knitter throughout her married life. Essex tape no. 157 in Nottingham Local Studies Library. See also NLSL, Oral History Collection, A53, interview with Mrs Fretwell, born Shaw 1883, an over-locker and mender.

  Few hosiery wage books remain, but two collections in the Leicestershire Record Office are of interest. The Jersey Wage Books, 1924–26, for Samuel Davis and Sons, Hinckley, show more than a third of employees as married, DE 2544/30. The J. Lewin and Company records, 1865–1937, also include wage books. The 1946 Board of Trade, *Working Party on the Hosiery*, found that "the hosiery industry retains a large proportion of its women employees after marriage. This applies more particularly to the long-established centres of Leicester and Hinckley," 95.

30. LRO, NUHKW, Leicester Trades, DE 1655/2/7, minutes of 17 May 1919; Hinckley minutes on meeting of the Hosiery Federation on the married woman question, DE 1655 3/3, 22 June 1921. On the devices through which a Nottingham chevenner's husband who was irregularly employed maintained his familial standing as breadwinner see Thea Thompson, *Edwardian Childhoods* (London, 1981), 69, 71, 74.

31. The best discussion of this process of negotiation and resolution is Sarah Eisenstein, *Give Us Bread, But Give Us Roses* (London, 1983), esp. 47–52.

32. Diana Gittins, *Fair Sex: Family Size and Structure, 1900–1939* (London, 1982); Gittins, "Marital Status, Work and Kinship, 1850–1930" in *Labour and Love*, ed. Jane Lewis (Oxford, 1986); Patricia Connelly and Martha MacDonald, "Women's Work: Domestic and Wage Labour in a Nova Scotia Community," *Studies in Political Economy* 10 (Winter 1983); Ellen Ross and Rayna Rapp, "Sex and Society: A Research Note from Social History and Anthropology" in *Powers of Desire: The Politics of Sexuality*, ed. Ann Snitow, Christine Stansell, and Sharon Thompson (New York, 1983), 56, 68, 117.

33. Mary Cavan, Anne Hedley, Maud Chappell, Betty Shaw, Frances Randall, PIHP; *Paris* (Ont.) *Star*, 17 Dec. 1936, obituary for Rebecca Fisher, PHS, Imported Help Books: Olive Adcock emigrated 30 March 1910; Mrs Fanny Adcock, Doris Adcock, Albert Adcock emigrated 17 Oct. 1910; Violet Kelford and Gladys Kelford paying for Rupert Kelford, emigrated 19 July 1912. Annie, Eunice, and Lillian Woods repaid the debt of their father, Thomas Woods, emigrated 20 Sept. 1912.

34. Edith Elliott, Ida Pelton, May Phillips, PIHP, Paris Public Library, Historical Perspectives, Hilda Sharp Scott.

35. *Paris* (Ont.) *Star*, 13 Jan. 1926, advertisement signed S.G.W. Horsley; 17 April 1930, letter from Bert Raynes.

36. Lillian Watson, Frances Randall, PIHP. The statistics are for the Penman's work force as a whole rather than the immigrant group separately. They were derived by linking the firm's personnel records, now in the Penman's Archives with the municipal tax rolls, housed in the Town Hall, Paris. These rolls list all adult household members, the numbers of school-aged children, and household size. Of the women located in the tax rolls in 1936, 47 of 170 were living in single-headed households; 30 of these households included children.

37. The Addison suicide is reported in the *Paris* (Ont.) *Star*, 14 April 1920. The obituary for Susan Baldwin appeared in 30 May 1935 and the correction 6 June 1935. For instances of women's households as centres for community social activities see ibid., 12 Sept. 1923, Lily Cotton and her sisters; 26 Dec. 1923 and 10 Aug. 1927, the Misses Barlow; obituary for Alexandrine Patterson, 6 April 1933. Ida Glass, PIHP. The activities of the Maids and Daughters of England and the Pleasure Club were regularly reported in the local paper through the 1920s. Of the 94 single women located in the personnel files as employed in 1936, 26, or 27.7 percent, were older than age 36.

38. PHS, Imported Help Books. Only 26 of the 227 single women for whom passage repayment schedules remain married before their debts to the firm were extinguished. Of the 168 women traced in the personnel records as employed in 1936, 68 were married.

39. The adaptations of households to life-long wage work among women are treated in detail in my "Rethinking Work and Kinship in a Canadian Hosiery Town, 1910–1950," *Feminist Studies* 13 (Spring 1987): 137–62.

40. I am grateful to H.V. Nelles of York University, Toronto, for alerting me to the clear group limits on this practice within the mill community.

41. Sallie Westwood, *All Day Every Day: Factory and Family in the Making of Women's Lives* (London, 1984), 111–19. The characterization of the costumes as pornographic is on page 117; the interpretation of the brides' rites, 118–19.

42. *Paris* (Ont.) *Star*, 29 April 1937; see similarly, 31 Aug. 1939, 8 Aug. 1935, 2 March 1927. In the latter report Mrs Bert Raynes, soon to be denounced as a bigamist, was the bridegroom.

43. Edith Elliott, PIHP.

A SECRET POLICY, SECRETLY ADMINISTERED♦

REG WHITAKER

o

Even before the Second World War had come to an end, security screening of potential immigrants to Canada had begun. In early 1945, the Department of External Affairs and the Immigration Branch, assisted by the RCMP (which had earlier prepared contingency plans to round up and deport all refugees in Canada at war's end), began to regularize the status of those European refugees who had entered Canada during the war, including the civilian internees who had been dumped into Canadian custody by Britain early in the war. An order-in-council of October 1945 cleared the way for 3500 wartime refugees to become landed immigrants. Well before the end of the war, Canada was already engaged in liaison with British and American intelligence agencies in planning for security screening of prospective immigrants from among the hordes of displaced persons and others in Europe who would be seeking admission to Canada in the aftermath of war. Early in 1945, Supt. Charles Rivett-Carnac, a security specialist in the RCMP who was to be the force's chief representative during the Gouzenko investigation, travelled to Britain to confer with MI5 (the counter-intelligence unit).[1]

In the summer of 1946, the newly created Security Panel noted that Parliament had recently amended the Immigration Act without prohibiting the entry of undesirable immigrants "other than by departmental administrative action." In other words, from the beginning the decision had been made to minimize public and parliamentary scrutiny and rely squarely on administrative discretion. The panel followed up on this by enlisting the services of the RCMP to join the teams of civilians sent to Europe to interview prospective immigrants from among the displaced persons; their job

♦ Reprinted with permission from *Double Standard: The Secret History of Canadian Immigration* by Reg Whitaker, published by Lester & Orpen Dennys c/o Key Porter Books Limited, Toronto, Ontario. Copyright © 1987 Reg Whitaker.

would be security screening and liaison with local security police, beginning with the UK passport control office. "The first two members of the Canadian immigration team to arrive in Germany in 1947 were RCMP officers, responsible for the political screening of refugees."[2]

The immigration teams faced a daunting challenge in the displaced persons' camps. Conditions were chaotic, all sorts of people from ex-Nazis to Jewish survivors of the Holocaust were jumbled together; the "truth" about what people had done over the war years was often as evanescent as the tattered "documentation" clutched in their hands; and over all there hung an air of desperation, a hunger to simply get out and start a new life elsewhere. Living out of suitcases, hitching rides, facing the daily sea of faces of the hopeful, the shattered, and the mendacious, the immigration officers either coped or failed. The turnover rate among officers was high. The administrative raw material was perhaps not promising.

The problems started at the top with a weak and ineffectual minister, J.A. Glen, whose "next to useless" performance in his portfolio drew the withering contempt of his boss, Prime Minister Mackenzie King, and the ire of the powerful minister of trade and commerce, C.D. Howe, who was concerned about securing a more aggressive immigration program to promote postwar economic growth. On the other hand, the new deputy minister was Hugh Keenleyside, a cultured man of liberal and progressive views with long experience in External Affairs, giving him some international perspective on the refugee question. Keenleyside had a mandate to clean house and make immigration a priority in his multipurpose department (which also included mines, resources, and Indian affairs). The task was not simple, however.[3]

As Keenleyside later recalled, the immigration service had been plagued by widespread corruption. In the process of selection of the displaced persons, there were "occasional reports of rough behaviour, mistreatment of women, and poor operational practices." Among the applicants, he also recalls, there was the widespread belief that "even the simplest and most proper requests had to be lubricated with monetary and other more personal favours." The temptations for misbehaviour were there, but the rewards for those who persevered in their duties were high, for here were new Canadians in the making out of the disasters of war—more than 120 000 of them by 1951 transported out of Europe and onto Canadian shores. This, said Keenleyside, was "as remarkable a performance as anything that is to be found in the history of immigration to Canada."[4]

No doubt it was a remarkable performance, yet the raw figures miss some of the darker shadings. Canada was highly selective in choosing from among the displaced persons. They were in effect skimming the cream of the camps in view of Canada's economic needs. As John Holmes, an old External Affairs hand and historian of Canada's postwar foreign policies, has put it, "In the light of the oratory accompanying the victory over Nazi bestiality and the revelations from Belsen, Canadian policy seems incredibly calculating." But the selectivity did not end with the potential value of the immigrant to the Canadian economy. Ethnic discrimination was central to the process. The exercise of prejudice against Jews, the worst victims of the Fascists, was matched by a favourable attitude towards certain more "Nordic" ethnic groups. And in the security screening process, with its notable right-wing bias, a record of discrimination on political or ideological grounds can be found.[5]

That the selection of displaced persons was itself a Cold War issue became apparent as early as 1946 when hearings before the Senate Committee on Immigration and Labour on the European refugees were the scene of bitter recriminations between ideologically opposed delegations from both the Ukrainian and the Polish communities, which were clearly divided between pro- and anti-Soviet elements. The pro-Soviet Ukrainians and Poles echoed the Soviet line expressed in international forums: it was the duty of all displaced persons from Eastern Europe to return home. A left-wing Ukrainian brief asserted that the "so-called 'displaced persons'" either were war criminals and Nazi collaborators or were "free to return to their homelands": in both cases, repatriation was the answer. Anti-Soviet spokesmen stressed that their homelands were now tyrannies, and those who refused to return were political refugees. This was certainly the view of the overwhelming majority of the displaced persons from the East themselves, who not only opposed repatriation in the most desperate manner, but most often cited opposition to communism as the main reason for their stand.[6]

The pro-Soviet Poles (who quickly lost any influence within the Canadian Polish community once the reality of Soviet domination in Poland had become apparent) were reacting at the 1946 hearings to the government's willingness to admit some 4000 Polish army veterans who had been placed under British military command after the fall of Poland in 1939. Admitting them seemed reasonable enough, given their service on the Allied side. Cabinet stipulated that the veterans be security-screened to prevent the entry of "subversives." It turned out that this screening was intended, however, to prevent Jewish veterans from entering along with their Christian comrades; so successful was this screening that of the first 1700 admitted, there was only a single, token Jew. "Security screening" could be a coat of many colours.[7]

The RCMP established its overseas headquarters in London, which was the early collection point for applications from displaced persons and others who sought entry to Canada. By the time the London office began fully functioning in early 1947, it had become apparent to the civil servants in Ottawa that security screening was creating a problem of its own: an administrative bottleneck that threatened to seriously embarrass the government as it tried to carry out its stated policy with regard to immigration. With sponsored applications for relatives already numbering more than 10 000, and with departmental estimates reaching as high as 30 000 to 50 000 within a year or two, the RCMP had made it known that it could clear only twenty-five to thirty applications a day, or about 800 a month. Since the government was withholding approval pending security clearance, "it will be seen," wrote the director of the Immigration Branch, "that an ever increasing backlog would be created and that there would be very serious criticism both in Parliament and from the public."[8]

The Security Panel was put to work on the problem. When the suggestion was made that screening of sponsored relatives be discontinued, Rivett-Carnac of the RCMP bristled: "Any screening system," he asserted, "to be effective must be total. To undertake vetting in principle or under any partial system would mean that a great number of persons would be admitted to Canada without vetting and a very real danger exists of many undesirables entering this country." Since the problem was associated with the slowness of the RCMP in the first place, the insistence on a "total" screening system (whatever that might mean) must have caused some quiet irritation among the bureaucrats. Nor could the RCMP promise more manpower.

The problem bounced back and forth between Cabinet and the Security Panel. Finally the panel narrowed the options down to two. The major security problems, it was argued, were posed by emigrants from countries within the Soviet sphere of influence, on the assumption that these included planted agents; thus, one solution would be to restrict screening to applicants from those countries alone. For now, however, Cabinet chose the second option as a temporary solution: to reduce screening of sponsored applicants to spot-checking of about 20 percent as chosen by the RCMP. Those who were not from Eastern Europe were placed under a "fourteen-day procedure"—if nothing adverse was received by Immigration from the RCMP within fourteen days after the police had passed the applications, visas were authorized. Screening in these cases continued, even though the applicants had gone on to Canada: they could, of course, always be deported later.[9]

A second problem arose during 1947 with regard to sponsored applicants. A number of cases arose in which the sponsored relatives of Canadian citizens were discovered by the RCMP to have left-wing or "communistic" tendencies. It was out of the question that such persons be admitted, but the problem lay in what to tell their sponsors in Canada. In a memorandum to Cabinet, the minister suggested two options. The first was to reject the application and give no reason—an option described as "impracticable and not satisfactory." The second was to inform the sponsor that admission was not in the public interest and to refuse any further explanation, the "inevitable result" of which would be a "demand for additional information." In the event, Cabinet decided that the latter possibility was more alarming than following an "impracticable and not satisfactory" course; here began the policy, cited ever since as a precedent, of refusing to give notice that security was the ground for rejection. The Cabinet Committee on Immigration Policy also decided that "left-wing tendencies" as claimed by the RCMP should be accepted in all cases by the department as sufficient justification for a negative decision, and that the grounds for rejection were not to be reported to the civilians, merely the fact of rejection. It followed from this that an applicant rejected on security grounds by an RCMP officer could not appeal, although appeal procedures were available to those rejected by civilian visa officers. Moreover, the Immigration Branch and the RCMP agreed to an elaborate subterfuge whereby RCMP agents were never to be identified as such, but would pose as civilian immigration officers instead. The logic of administrative discretion was taking over.[10]

Although a new legislative authority was needed to support Canada's new approach to immigration in the postwar world, it was not until 1952 that a new Immigration Act would pass Parliament. In the spring of 1947, however, Prime Minister Mackenzie King made a major statement on immigration in the House of Commons that was to serve as the government's public articulation of its policies. The statement was drafted by Gordon Robertson and J.W. Pickersgill in the Prime Minister's Office and somewhat amended by King himself. Although no explicit reference was made to security, the statement strongly reiterated that immigration was a matter of domestic policy and that Canada was within its rights in selecting "with care" only those immigrants it wanted. This point may have been related more to the question of ethnicity—in particular, the government's stated intention to prevent any large-scale immigration from Asia—but it applied to the question of political suitability as well. Above all there was a strong statement of the principle that would-be immigrants have no fundamental human right to enter Canada, nor do immigrants have a right to Canadian citizenship once they are living in Canada. Immigration to Canada and Canadian naturalization were privileges, not rights. It was on this basis that a security system that emphasized virtually complete administrative discretion, with no judicial or independent review and no recognition of natural justice for the individuals affected, could operate quietly with little public notice.[11]

By the spring of 1948 the RCMP reported that some 22 000 out of 33 538 applications had been screened, leaving a backlog of some 11 000. Fewer than 400 had been rejected, a number that the RCMP commissioner admitted "seemed small." He promised to do better if only Treasury Board would give him more staff and a bigger budget. (By the last quarter of 1948 the rejections were running at over 100 per month, or a rate of about 4 percent.) At the same time, the commissioner struck another, more controversial note when he drew the Security Panel's attention to the failure of the International Refugee Organization (IRO, responsible for the administration of the displaced persons' camps) to co-operate in the screening of displaced persons, a failure he attributed to the "infiltration of Communists and sympathizers" into that organization.[12]

This charge, which appears strange in light of the nature of the IRO ("From the beginning," wrote one careful contemporary observer, "the IRO was entirely an instrument of the West, and from first to last the opposition of the Soviet bloc to the IRO was bitter and uncompromising"), had an unanticipated result when it was picked up immediately by Col. Laval Fortier, associate commissioner of the Overseas Immigration Service and later the deputy minister of the Department of Citizenship and Immigration in the 1950s. Fortier, fresh from visiting the headquarters of the IRO, claimed that "there was a good deal of evidence to support the contention that communistic elements were trying to introduce undesirables into the immigration system" through infiltration of the IRO. On the basis of an eight-week trip to Europe, he painted an alarming picture of a continent ripe for communist take-over and an IRO riddled with "Communist propagandists" not only in the field but in key positions in the organization. Their object was to infiltrate trained communist agents into Canada. "It is impossible for me to bring concrete evidence on communist activities," he admitted, "but this was not the purpose of my trip overseas."[13]

The government was receiving many such alarming reports during 1948 from its officials abroad. The vice-consul in Shanghai, for instance, reported that 20 000 refugees from the USSR in that city were mostly criminals or "very active Communist agitators" and refused to accept any applications for immigration from them. The press in Canada and the US was whipping up hysteria about subversives and saboteurs among the displaced persons.[14] Fortier, however, went one step too far when he suggested that the RCMP security officers in Europe were not sufficiently trained in counter-espionage to offer effective resistance to this communist offensive and demanded a "total re-organization of our security screening and a total change of the officers now employed on the security work." The deputy minister passed on Fortier's report to the RCMP commissioner for his comments, along with the suggestion that it "is admittedly based on opinion rather than ascertained fact" and "probably greatly exaggerates the problem." Commissioner S.T. Wood was more than happy to take the hint. His men had been ordered to conduct neither an intelligence nor a counter-intelligence operation in Europe, but to ascertain the political sympathies of applicants for immigration. The methods were scarcely infallible, but "in the chaotic condition which exists in Europe today . . . it would be impossible to raise a fine enough screen without the use of security forces, the cost of which would be prohibitive." With appropriately injured innocence, Wood—a venerable and seasoned anti-communist of the purest stripe—wrote, "It would appear that Mr. Fortier is under the misapprehension that our men are not particularly interested in the detection of Communists. I may say that this is our primary interest . . . and all members of our security details are fully aware of this fact."[15]

Fortier clearly erred in attacking the RCMP on these grounds. Rare it was for the RCMP to be accused of softness towards communism; the charge was so absurd that Fortier undermined himself. There appears to be no other example in the government records of a civil servant raising such a charge against the police. Indeed, the criticism was generally in the other direction.

To look into the charge of communist infiltration of the IRO, which was echoed by the RCMP, a high-level mission was dispatched to Geneva in the person of Dana Wilgress, former Canadian ambassador to Moscow. Wilgress carefully selected a group of "trustworthy" English-speaking officials of the organization and raised the issue in private. In a lengthy report to the Department of External Affairs, he concluded that this Red Scare had "little justification"; significantly, American officials had dismissed the charges as exaggerated.[16]

Communists were not the only prohibited class, but they did hold pride of place. In a confidential memorandum sent to visa posts by immigration headquarters early in 1949, thirteen categories were listed, as follows:

a) Communist, known or strongly suspected. Communist agitator or suspected Communist agent

b) Member of SS or German Wehrmacht. Found to bear mark of SS Blood Group (non-Germans) and non-German SS prior to Jan. 1, 1943, or who joined voluntarily later
c) Member of Nazi party
d) Criminal (known or suspected)
e) Professional gambler
f) Prostitute
g) Black Market Racketeer
h) Evasive and untruthful under interrogation
i) Failure to produce recognizable and acceptable documents as to time of entry and residence in Germany
j) False presentation; use of false or fictitious name
k) Collaborators presently residing in previously occupied territory
l) Member of the Italian Fascist Party or the Mafia
m) Trotskyite or member of other revolutionary organization

These categories were of course purely administrative, with no specific basis in legislation (other than the general category of "undesirable"). Later, under the Immigration Act of 1952, general instructions were issued to visa officers indicating that "'security screening' means the examination of prospective immigrants and/or of their histories by the RCMP or other authorized agency of Government to determine whether, if admitted to Canada, such immigrants may be inimical to the democratic way of life and of government as such is generally understood in Canada." The specific interpretation of those "inimical to the democratic way of life" was indicated in this list of categories, which was strictly secret. The memorandum reiterated what was by now standard procedure: security grounds for rejection should never be disclosed to applicants, or to other than "senior officers." Even the memorandum itself, readers were advised, "should be kept under lock so that no one will have access to it."[17]

The strong emphasis on communism as the main criterion for security rejection, especially in contrast to Nazism and wartime collaboration, is evidenced by a statistical review prepared by the Department of Citizenship and Immigration (where the Immigration Branch had been located since 1950) in the spring of 1951. In fact, the general criteria for security rejection did turn up a large number of rejections for non-communist political categories, but these were treated very differently when subject to review. While only 20 percent of all rejections were for the category of communist, in only 2 percent of these cases were reviews carried out, and a scant one in five of those reviewed was actually reversed. On the other hand, the prohibited category for enemy soldiers and former SS men accounted for 40 percent of rejections, but of these 50 percent were reviewed and over two-thirds were reversed. Similarly, former membership in the Nazi party accounted for 25 percent of rejections, but of these over a third were reviewed, and 95 percent of those reviewed were reversed. Former collaborators fared less well, although they accounted for only 10 percent of rejections. Communism was not the only target of the screening process, but non-communists fared much better upon review. Moreover, the efforts made in the early 1950s to streamline the system and relieve pressure on the RCMP were entirely directed to lifting the restrictions on former Nazis, Fascists, and wartime collaborators. No responsible public official ever appears to have suggested lifting restrictions on communists.[18]

Yet there was also a fundamental contradiction inherent in the security screening process as an integral—while secret—part of Canadian public policy on immigration. The contradiction manifested itself in a continual tension between departmental officials, with their mandate to bring immigrants in large numbers to Canada, and the RCMP, with its mandate to filter applicants carefully and therefore slowly. As the director of the Immigration Branch indicated in a memorandum to the deputy minister early in 1951, it was government policy, as clearly enunciated in an order-in-council, to stimulate immigration. This had resulted in a marked increase of interest in Canada on the part of prospective immigrants, yet despite the department's "streamlined" procedures, this interest had yet to result in increased arrivals. "Unfortunately," he explained, "the present security procedure has hindered, and, as presently constituted, will continue to hinder the implementation programme."[19]

Since virtually all applicants (except British subjects, American citizens, and the wives, children, and elderly family relatives of naturalized Canadians) had to be screened, each had to be personally interrogated and enquiries made among local police and local sources of data. The London security section was "in essence the focal point of all security screening," taking referrals by officers in the field from all other points. Yet London, with limited access to facilities shared with the British, could process only thirty-five cases per day. "A backlog is building up which, as the immigration programme becomes intensified, will be even greater, with most serious effects." He pointedly went on to suggest that "consideration of the principles involved in security screening might be justified, when it is considered that since security screening was instituted, approximately 220 000 immigrants who required security screening have come forward and of the total number examined only 4146 were rejected on security grounds." An opportunity existed: "To take advantage of the extremely great current interest in immigration, a review of the principles of security screening should be instituted as soon as possible."[20]

A new Immigration Act was already in the policy pipeline, enabling various interested parties to present their views on the security screening question. The RCMP lobbied for a sweeping extension of its discretionary powers of exclusion as well as deportation. The more liberal minds in the senior civil service, especially Norman Robertson and Gordon Robertson, were able to undermine these arguments effectively. But when the act was passed, broader legislative authority was given to prevent the entry into Canada of persons associated "at any time" with any group about which there were "reasonable grounds for believing" that they advocated or promoted "subversion by force or other means of democratic government, institutions or processes, as they are understood in Canada," or were "likely to engage in or advocate" subversion. Moreover, persons "likely to engage in espionage, sabotage or any other subversive activity" were also to be barred. This broad legislative writ offered little restraint on specific decisions made under its authority.[21]

Discretion to bar persons "likely to advocate . . . subversion of democratic government, institutions or processes, as they are understood in Canada," offers a defence lawyer's nightmare. But in the absence of any clear right to judicial appeals, in the absence of any right of rejected applicants to be given the reasons for their rejection, and in the absence of any right to counsel for applicants outside Canada or at ports of entry, there would rarely be defence lawyers to concern themselves with this problem. Further, in the case of landed immigrants facing deportation proceedings, the state's invocation of "national security" considerations could effectively override any appeal process. Finally, specific criteria for applying these very general terms—it was not even spelled out that communists were the main embodiment of those forces of subversion to be barred—were not part of the legislation but secret administrative categories, never to be publicly divulged. And "subversion" is a notoriously difficult word to define in legal terms; when the legislation spoke of "subversion by force or other means" it appeared to imply broadly that certain kinds of lawful political activity directed towards change could bar someone from Canada, the criteria being left entirely to administrative discretion. Indeed, the entire act gave immense scope to administrative discretion, which was the real core of the security process.

Freda Hawkins, in her major study of immigration policy, cites "two fundamental defects" in the 1952 Immigration Act that have had "far-reaching consequences in Canadian immigration. . . . The first was the degree of uncontrolled discretionary power vested by the Act in the Minister of Citizenship and Immigration and his officials." Ministerial discretion was such as to give him "potentially the last word on every individual case," including the power to "confirm or quash . . . or substitute his decision" for the decision of any appeal board that might be set up under the act. Ministerial permits for entry for twelve months could be extended indefinitely. "He had, in fact, total authority over admissions, and total authority in relation to deportations over those immigrants who were not yet Canadian citizens and did not yet have Canadian domicile." In the latter case, there was no recourse in law. Section 39 read:

> No court and no judge or officer thereof has jurisdiction to review, quash, reverse, restrain or otherwise interfere with any proceeding, decision or order [that] the Minister, Deputy Minister, Director, Immigration Appeal Board, Special Inquiry Officer or immigration officer had made or given under the authority and in accordance with the provisions of this Act relating to the detention or deportation of any person, upon any ground whatsoever, unless such person is a Canadian citizen or has Canadian domicile.[22]

A perhaps unexpected result of this enormous discretionary power vested in the minister was that mountains of files on individual cases descended upon the hapless politician—along with enormous pressures from private citizens seeking redress or special considerations on behalf of their relatives, not to speak of pressures from the major organizations representing the various ethnic groups. In addition the act also devolved substantial powers upon departmental officers, with an unfavourable public image of an irresponsible and arbitrary bureaucracy as the result.

There was one significant court challenge to the 1952 Immigration Act. Criticizing the broadness and imprecision of the grounds for deportation, the Supreme Court in 1956 ruled that the government had exceeded its powers in delegating decisions on admissibility and deportation of both immigrants and visitors. The administrative basis of immigration selection was briefly called into question, but within a few months the government had drawn up new regulations that conformed to the court decision without significantly undermining the discretionary element in the legislation.[23]

It was during the passage of the 1952 Immigration Act that another element of Cold War repression was put in place: discrimination against homosexuals on the grounds, among others, that sexual "deviants" constituted a security risk to the state. Interestingly, there appears to have been no concern among Canadian officials about denying homosexuals entry into Canada; there is no record of the matter ever having been raised at the Security Panel. According to Philip Girard, who has addressed the introduction of the prohibition against homosexuals in the 1952 legislation, the pressure appears to have come from the RCMP and, indirectly, from the American security establishment, which had decisively linked communism and homosexuality in its collective mind as part of a complex of Cold War subversion. The clause prohibiting homosexuals was rushed through Parliament with no discussion whatsoever and, it would appear, to little or no effect in the administration of the immigration program. It was certainly unclear just what criteria security officers were to employ in detecting homosexuals among the applicants for entry. Later in the 1950s the RCMP would launch a veritable reign of terror against homosexuals in the public service, but the 1952 Immigration Act is the first example of legislative action in this area. Characteristically, however, both its passage and its implementation were shrouded in silence.[24]

The Immigration Act of 1952 was the sole legislative authority for immigration control for fourteen years. With its strong emphasis on administrative discretion, on the power of the state and the insignificance of the individual in the face of the state, it was an appropriate legislative vehicle for a security screening process that worked out of sight and, as much as was possible, out of mind. Hawkins' considered verdict on this legislation may serve as its fitting epitaph. It created, she writes, "a negative climate in immigration, a climate of suspicion. ... The 1952 Immigration Act was a discouraging document."[25]

Administrative discretion was at the core of citizenship policy as well in this period. Parliament had passed the Canadian Citizenship Act in 1946. Until that time there had been no Canadian citizenship, at least technically; there had been only British subjects in Canada. The passage of citizenship legislation gave Parliament the opportunity to define the rights and obligations of citizenship and the necessary qualifications for admission to citizenship for those who had been born Canadian. The latter were not clearly spelled out. In fact, Canadian practice since at least the First World War had been to disqualify applicants for naturalization, as the acquisition of citizenship was then known, on political grounds. The RCMP had been an integral part of this screening process from the beginning, even though it never had any formal mandate for this activity. Nor did the act make any explicit provision for security screening, which was carried out instead under the provision for ministerial discretion to approve or disapprove applications, and under a section of the act that required that an applicant for citizenship be "of good character." By 1951 the procedures had become formalized, with the establishment of an interdepartmental committee to review cases of citizenship rejections on national security grounds.[26]

By enacting a Citizenship Act, the Parliament of Canada was defining the nature of Canadian citizenship.[27] Although Canada was ostensibly a liberal pluralist democracy, governmental practice had for some time defined certain political beliefs and associations as falling outside the acceptable bounds of the political community and thus as grounds for rejection of applications for citizenship—although these beliefs and associations were not, in fact, illegal. Moreover, the government did not spell out these criteria for rejection in the citizenship law. Once again, in matters of national security, administrative secrecy and discretion were the order of the day, at whatever cost to the formal principles upon which the country was supposed to operate.

o

Secrecy seems to be endemic to the process of security screening in immigration not only in Canada, but in other countries accepting immigrants in the postwar world. As Freda Hawkins comments:

> All the major receiving countries have practised a great deal of private administrative discretion. Security problems, exaggerated in the first place by Cold War difficulties and Cold War psychology, have involved considerable secrecy. Political pressures from all quarters have added to a sensitivity and desire for privacy on the part of governments. . . . Since immigration involves the direct action of one government upon the citizens of another, there is always something slightly surreptitious about it and departments of external affairs have avoided close association with it or have kept it well apart from considerations of foreign policy.[28]

Secrecy, like a good coat of paint, can cover a multitude of sins. Even the chronic overload of security work could be turned by the RCMP into an excuse for more secrecy. By the end of March 1949 the backlog of security clearances in Europe had reached 13 000, and the RCMP had concluded that the screening program had become "partially ineffective" through over-loading and other problems. The whole procedure was sent to be reviewed by the Security Panel. Here the RCMP managed to refocus the entire discussion by complaining that the secrecy surrounding the screening process was not effective enough to allow the police to safeguard their sources of information. MPs or the minister, they complained, had been giving to the sponsors of rejected applicants "information from the highest levels which embarrasses the Police in respect to their relations with the U.K. and U.S. security services." Such leaks should be plugged, the panel agreed, and a Cabinet directive was later issued reiterating that "under no circumstances should the reason for withholding permission to enter Canada be attributed to security investigations." Security was in fact so tight around the screening process that very little publicity, good or bad, seems to have been generated in these early years: certainly there was little enough discussion either in the press or in Parliament. This did nothing to relieve the RCMP of the basic pressure of numbers. By 1950 there were between 2000 and 3000 applications requiring security clearance each month, of which about 3 percent were eventually rejected.[29]

Secrecy was itself zealously guarded. When it was pointed out that "security" was sometimes stamped on forms, this was quickly rectified with the invention of the code phrase "Stage B," which in 1952 replaced "security" on all documentation. Similarly no mention was ever made officially of the fact that "Stage B" officers were actually RCMP personnel since, as one embassy pointed out, "anyone even slightly acquainted with Canada would be able to guess the nature of the connection between that Force and our immigration procedures." Visa officers were instructed that the term "Stage B" was "not to be used in unclassified messages in context with other comments or terms such as 'screening,' 'screened,' 'R.C.M.P.,' 'clearance,' 'security,' etc., which might lead to knowledge of its true meaning."[30]

The grotesque lengths to which security precautions could be taken can be glimpsed in one witless administrative excess in the early 1950s. When non-immigrants seeking visas to visit Canada were to be refused on security grounds, an elaborate system of ink dots placed under certain vowels in code on the applications was devised. ("The dots," intoned the instructions, "shall be carefully applied, not in a conspicuous manner, and not in the presence of the person under examination.") Within a few years the system had, inevitably, self-destructed. A British businessman was detained at the Montreal airport because a dot had appeared under the first "a" in his visa application. A security check on the enraged traveller revealed nothing: the dot was just an errant ink spot. The department privately admitted that there had been enough such cases to cause "considerable embarrassment" and dropped its schoolboy spy device.[31]

It was, of course, only a transparent subterfuge that security was not involved in particular cases. The deputy minister of immigration pointed out that "in public statements, we have always affirmed that immigrants to Canada are always security screened." In 1953 Peter Dwyer on the Security Panel recommended to Cabinet that where delays were caused by security screening of sponsored cases, the Canadian sponsors might be told that "arrangements for security screening are not as yet complete." Dwyer commented quite reasonably that "the fact of security screening for immigrants is well known and there seems no better way to explain the delays that are now and will in future be occurring." His advice seems not to have been taken.[32]

The theory appeared to be that security screening was acknowledged, and even pointed to with pride, in general, but that it was to be denied in particular cases. The instructions for security screening procedures issued to all visa officers (known as "Chapter 7") were quite explicit on this point. When applicants were rejected, "the only statement authorized in such cases is that the person concerned is unable to comply with Canadian immigration requirements." In 1955 one proviso was added: "When an order for deportation is issued for reasons of security, such information may be divulged only to the person ordered deported (or at the inquiry in the presence of his solicitor) and this only in cases where the RCMP have indicated their consent." The foreword to Chapter 7 contained this interesting, if somewhat tortuous, formulation:

> The security of Canada is the vital and legitimate concern of every resident of Canada; notwithstanding this, security procedures can remain in successful operation only when the responsible officers treat all security matters as strictly confidential. This places immigration officers in a position of trust which demands the utmost reserve and tact in dealing with the public. It is expected that every officer will realize the significance of the instructions herein, and carry them out with a full sense of the necessity for implicit compliance.[33]

The bureaucrats soldiered on with the pretence that what was acknowledged in general was not to be acknowledged in particular. In 1954 the *Winnipeg Free Press* questioned Laval Fortier, the deputy minister of immigration, as to why rejected applicants were given no reasons. "If rejected applicants were allowed to know why they were rejected that would be a very wrong thing for the protection of the country," he offered. Then he added: "I'm afraid I can't say why!" Yet the same deputy minister admitted to the minister that in "recent years" MPs, senators, and a "few persons considered trustworthy" were sometimes advised of security grounds for rejections in particular cases, but only by the minister and deputy minister, never by officials below that rank. An unexpected result of this practice was that "strong representations" were made by "various influential organizations and individuals" on behalf of rejected applicants, which "results in both the Minister and the Deputy Minister having to give much of their time to these cases."

Yet when the deputy minister suggested as an alternative that security grounds be given as a reason for rejection and that representations be referred to a special tribunal that would consider all the facts in the case, conduct an in-camera hearing, and render a final decision, the RCMP set up a classic bureaucratic smokescreen. It would be necessary, the RCMP commissioner argued, for his men to "approach all their contacts in the various countries and advise them of the new procedure. . . . This was absolutely essential in order to determine whether their contacts would still be prepared to cooperate under the new system. He pointed out this would take some time to complete and while he would arrange to start enquiries immediately he could not guarantee" the outcome. The initiative, needless to say, fizzled out.[34]

The police stood fast, on the grounds of protecting their sources. This was the same justification they had invoked to protect the government's security screening of its own employees from any appeal procedure, but in the matter of immigration screening they had what in the climate of the time amounted to an unanswerable defence: the threat of non-co-operation from their counterparts in allied and friendly countries. At the same time an inevitable moral ambiguity is attached to this argument. To what extent was it really only self-serving, in that their own mistakes and their own sometimes dubious methods could be protected from scrutiny and criticism? Abraham Lincoln said of doctors that they were the only profession able to bury their mistakes. The RCMP was the only bureaucratic agency able to do the same with relative impunity, and it was zealous in maintaining that privilege.

In a situation in which the police held certain trump cards, the ability of the minister of immigration to assert civilian control was crucial. Two Liberal ministers headed the Department of Citizenship and Immigration before the St Laurent government was defeated in 1957. The first was Walter Harris, who served for four and a half years. Harris was a successful businessman from Ontario, a war veteran, and a genuine power in the St Laurent Cabinet who was very close to the prime minister. He had, in short, considerable clout as a minister, but there is little evidence that he used it to establish civilian control over the RCMP's growing sphere of autonomous activity within his department's operations. Harris was a very conservative Liberal (later, as finance minister, he would be anathematized by the Tories as "Six-Buck Harris" for his niggardly increase in the old age pension), and his conduct of the department was unimaginative, if competent. For the most part, Harris left the RCMP alone.

The same could not be said for his successor, the indefatigable Grit partisan and backroom boy Jack (J.W.) Pickersgill. Having come up through the Prime Minister's Office under Mackenzie King and into the supposedly non-partisan job of clerk of the Privy Council, the one-time Manitoban was parachuted in 1953 into the outports of Newfoundland, where he became an unlikely MP from Canada's newest province. Soon he succeeded Harris as minister of citizenship and immigration. His animated, mobile features and puckish sense of humour quickly made him one of the best known of St Laurent's ministers. But the public image did not always give a clear picture of his abilities as administrator of the department, which were considerable. Pickersgill was an intelligent and able politician whose zest for machiavellian partisanship masked a liberal conscience, which found expression from time to time in initiatives in immigration policy—and sometimes brought him into direct conflict with the RCMP and with the Ottawa security establishment that ranged itself beside the police. When confrontations occurred, Pickersgill did not hesitate to stand fast. As we shall see, Pickersgill was one of the few politicians who had the courage to stand up to the RCMP and convince his Cabinet colleagues to back him. The deputy minister for the decade of the 1950s was Col. Laval Fortier, one of the very small number of French Canadians who succeeded in reaching the deputy ministerial level in Ottawa before the days of bilingualism and biculturalism. Pickersgill recalled Fortier fondly: "Fortier was no yes-man and was direct and forthright in his advice. Whether I took his advice or not, and I sometimes did not, he carried out decisions promptly and effectively and was just as forthright the next time."[35] Fortier reflected, as did the prime minister, the very strong anti-communist views that French-Canadian Catholics tended to hold in this era. The only real clash he seems to have had with the RCMP was his somewhat quixotic attack on them for being insufficiently alert to the communist menace, as described earlier.

Pickersgill was no less anti-communist, but he did take a broader, more enlightened view of how to pursue anti-communism within an immigration program that had other, more important objectives. Fortier did not impede his minister's policy making in this area. Thus the degree of control exercised over the activities of the RCMP in the St Laurent years derived from Pickersgill as minister, not from the permanent civil service in the department. This was as it should be; an active and assertive minister was no doubt the only force capable of keeping the RCMP within bounds.

Despite a degree of civilian control in Ottawa, tension persisted between the RCMP officers and the civilian officials in the field. It derived from what the chief of a special government immigration mission to Europe in the mid-1950s described as the "absolute responsibility" held by the security officers and their tendency in difficult cases to apply the benefit of the doubt against the applicant. The civilians were often less severe in their judgements and resented the lack of recourse when the RCMP ruled that an applicant had "not passed Stage B," especially when they suspected that the basis for rejection might be political judgement or even moral disapproval of character or behaviour based only loosely upon any statutory authority. Criminal records were one source of conflict; officials sometimes complained that much time was wasted by security officers zealously searching out evidence of minor offences committed twenty or more years earlier. An exasperated civilian declared in an internal memorandum in 1955: "We are a nation of immigrants and I am sure that our forefathers never had to submit to such controls when they decided to migrate." The tensions surfaced in other ways. One visa post reported that it routinely destroyed anonymous letters regarding applicants without passing them on to the RCMP man, as a matter of principle—anonymous information was subject to abuse—but the RCMP felt that anonymous letters "helped to open up avenues of investigation which might ordinarily be neglected, and in this way have proved a very material aid." As usual, the RCMP won.[36]

As late as the mid-1960s, Freda Hawkins commented after interviews conducted on a tour of visa posts in Europe that she could find no particular evidence of strong political bias among the departmental employees, but the same was not true of the RCMP security officers attached to the posts:

It is interesting to note, however, that immigration officers considered themselves to be a good deal more politically sophisticated than the RCMP (Stage B) officers who conducted the security screening at each post, and interviews with some of these officers, with rare exceptions, certainly confirmed this. Immigration officers were very critical at that point of the security screening process in relation to political unreliability. They felt that it was out of date and did not reflect a very intelligent approach to the problems of former membership in the Communist party in some countries.[37]

The RCMP also kept very close tabs upon any potential sources of publicity over immigration security within Canada. For instance, the RCMP gave forewarning to Immigration in 1954 that a Vancouver newspaper was planning to probe the screening of Chinese immigrants and was considering sending an investigative reporter to Hong Kong. Yet publicity did get out, and little of it was favourable. Organized labour was one source of hostile criticism. In 1956 a delegation from the Canadian Congress of Labour met with Walter Harris to raise complaints about immigration security screening. The labour representatives cited cases of mistaken identity and examples of persons barred who had no record of subversive behaviour. The minister was unimpressed, stating that agents of subversion had undertaken peaceful means and had attempted to destroy the faith of democratic peoples in the processes of democratic government. None the less, subversion by peaceful means, just like subversion by force, requires counter-action, even though he realized that such counter-action would have to be taken on more intangible, indefinite grounds than the definite grounds presented by forceful subversion.[38]

Two years later, the newly formed Canadian Labour Congress (CLC) complained that while the government had been "highly successful in screening potential communists" it had shown "far less circumspection in admitting people with 'fascist' tendencies." "Many new Canadians," the CLC pointedly added, "showed no understanding of or respect for democratic trade union organizations." The CLC also criticized the lack of civil rights for applicants as contrary to natural justice and, in good Cold War fashion, declared that "disregard of those rights will certainly not help us in our struggle against world-Communism" and was "a very poor advertisement for Western democracy." Criticism of the arbitrary and authoritarian exercise of power under the security system was also echoed by the Canadian Bar Association, which argued that the right to be given reasons for rejection and the right to cross-examine sources of hostile information "seem to be self-evident but most people would be amazed to find that no such procedure is followed."[39]

The Canadian Labour Congress had expressed the vain hope that trade unionists might be represented at "some stage" of the screening process, but an earlier experience in the late 1940s with union consultation had already run aground over the presence of communists among Canadian trade unionists. The government had sought the assistance of trade union representatives in selecting skilled workers from among displaced persons.

An almost comic exchange of letters between the deputy minister of labour and the international representative for Canada of the International Fur and Leather Workers Union (IFLWU) revealed a problem. The IFLWU had nominated Muni Taub, a communist activist who, not surprisingly, was rejected by the government. A second representative was nominated and in turn rejected "by reason of doubt on the same grounds." The union then put forward a third name. The deputy minister wrote to the international representative asking for more information, explaining somewhat guilelessly, "You can take it as a fact that no one will be sent overseas to select displaced persons if he is a Communist. One of the duties is to ensure that displaced persons selected for admission to Canada are not Communists, and obviously it is my duty not to recommend a man who is himself a Communist."[40]

The irony is that he was addressing these words to Robert Haddow, a communist activist in a communist-led union. The RCMP informed the deputy minister that according to its files the third man nominated had in 1933 appeared in the role of Tim Buck in a play produced by the Progressive Arts Club of Toronto, "a Communist controlled organization" (the RCMP files were certainly complete). The deputy minister was warned that the IFLWU was "very badly infiltrated by the Communist element" and that any name put forward by this union "can be viewed with a great deal of suspicion." And so the charade ended.[41]

Despite the growing criticism from without, a growing perception within the government that the security component of immigration posed both administrative and morale problems (in 1955 both the Treasury Board and the Civil Service Commission turned their attention to the administrative difficulties), and the recurrent bottlenecks created in the flow of immigration, the RCMP successfully persuaded the Security Panel that "it did not appear possible to make any recommendations which would substantially improve the present system."[42]

Simply put, the RCMP had posed two stark alternatives: "It is either a question of continuing with our present arrangement or dropping security screening of immigrants altogether." Although this Hobson's choice had been posed within the context of an *obiter dictum* that immigration security was one of the "two duties the Force has which cause us more trouble than all our other work combined," the police showed little inclination to divest themselves of this trouble. Indeed, by the mid-1950s they were rejecting immigration applications on security grounds in greater numbers than ever before. Throughout 1954, for instance, the rejection rate was 4.6 percent, almost double that of a few years earlier—and this despite the elimination of a number of formerly prohibited categories of Germans and former collaborators.

One of the undoubted benefits that the RCMP derived from its immigration role was the opportunity it offered for liaison with the police, and especially the security services, of friendly foreign governments. Immigration work enabled the Canadians to develop contacts and plug into a world-wide network of anti-communist security forces. This was supposed to be a reciprocal relationship, but the Canadian security and intelligence corps had rather less to offer than its big brothers in Washington and London. "In principle," according to confidential External Affairs instructions to its posts abroad in 1949, "our understanding with both United Kingdom and United States services is that the exchange of information will be reciprocal, although in practice it is recognized that our contribution will be very small."[43]

For a security service that had been limited to a domestic role, this was a positive asset, offering a kind of window on the world. But there were serious questions about some of the company it was keeping. British and American security and intelligence agencies were, of course, heavily relied upon, with few qualms—although American co-operation presented special complexities at times, which will be discussed shortly. Local security police in friendly democratic European countries such as France, Italy, West Germany, and the Scandinavian countries presented only rare problems along with a degree of assistance and liaison that was much appreciated by the RCMP.

But if there was no question of any co-operation with the police in the communist countries, there was little reluctance to engage some dubious elements in repressive dictatorships that happened to proclaim their strong anti-communism. Spain, Portugal, and Turkey—three of the most brutally undemocratic regimes in the West at that time—were judged to have "more or less efficient police services," liaison with whom was left to the RCMP's discretion. Israel, on the other hand, for reasons that will be discussed later, was judged with much less indulgence. Latin American countries presented some problems, although the Security Panel believed that in the case of "the more stable countries" the police forces were "not inefficient." The FBI and the CIA, of course, kept close tabs on left-wingers in Latin America, although the RCMP worried a little about reliance on American agencies leading to "an interpretation that immigration to Canada is dependent upon U.S. approval." Contact in Latin America was made with the FBI, with British intelligence, and with local police forces, again at the RCMP's discretion.[44]

In Germany the Allied intelligence agencies had access to the Berlin Documentation Center, a veritable cornucopia of Nazi intelligence on German citizens, including more than 20 million individual files dating back to the 1930s. The centre was, and continues to be, an excellent source for discovering war criminals, because of the Nazi regime's meticulous documentation of its bureaucrats; it was of signal assistance in uncovering the murderous past of Albert Helmut Rauca, the postwar immigrant to Canada deported to West Germany in 1983 as a war criminal. Thirty-seven Germans were employed full-time by British intelligence perusing these voluminous files, and Canada drew indirectly upon their services for screening immigration applicants.

In 1952 the Canadian government was forced to begin paying $24 000 a year for the use of these facilities, as well as $5000 for access to the Hamburg central registry of police records. But the government believed, according to the Security Panel, that continued access to these centres was "essential to the success of the immigrant screening programme." The essential thrust of the screening program was to be against communists rather than against former Nazis, making it unclear just what purpose the Berlin facility was being used for. Was Nazi intelligence being relied upon to detect "communists"? The question had occurred to West German authorities, as evidenced by a report by the Canadian ambassador to Bonn of a conversation with an official of the German foreign ministry: the latter "wanted to know whether our Immigration people used the Berlin (Nazi) Document Center as a basis for information regarding Communist sympathies of a prospective immigrant. (He did not think Nazi documents were reliable on this point.)" It seems that the German official received no answer.[45]

The RCMP did rely to a considerable degree on the American Counter-Intelligence Corps (CIC) in West Germany. The CIC in turn co-operated with some ex-Nazis, who were, in exchange, protected for their anti-communist intelligence. Among the more notorious of these was Reinhard Gehlen, a former Wehrmacht general in charge of military intelligence on the eastern front who assembled, under American auspices, an organization that carried out offensive operations within the Soviet bloc. At hearings in 1984 of the Deschênes commission investigating the possible presence in Canada of war criminals, former RCMP commissioner William Kelly averred that Gehlen was a "very hardened anti-Communist" with whom the RCMP did not work since it wished to avoid any association with offensive operations behind the Iron Curtain. At the same time he admitted that the RCMP relied upon the CIC, which in turn was "very interested in ascertaining if there were Communists within Germany and they actually favoured the Galland [sic] Organization as a source of their information." In short, the RCMP appeared quite happy to accept information from ultra-rightist ex-Nazi sources, so long as it was first laundered through the Americans.[46]

Close liaison with the Americans may have offered many advantages to the RCMP—which was thereby connected, in however junior a capacity, with the leading edge of the Western security and intelligence front in the Cold War—but the relationship brought its discomforts as well. Willing enough to accept the necessity of a subordinate role abroad, the Mounties still bristled when the Americans moved onto their turf. In the late 1940s the US Immigration and Naturalization Service began gathering information in Canada concerning the political background of Canadians visiting the United States. In 1949 the RCMP secured what it thought was an understanding with US officials that such enquiries would be directed through it alone. Instead the Americans conducted their own investigations on Canadian soil and in the process often bypassed the RCMP to consult municipal police sources. According to an angry commissioner, "a situation occasionally arose where Canadian citizens seeking to enter the U.S.A. were dealt with unfairly on the basis of unreliable information provided by a municipal police force. This was sometimes attributed wrongly to the R.C.M. Police and caused embarrassment. In addition, the municipal police forces would sometimes pass on sensitive information which in the opinion of the R.C.M. Police should not be given." External Affairs was similarly outraged, and in 1953 the Security Panel asked External to inform the Americans that henceforth the RCMP was to be considered the "sole source of security information in Canada"; the Panel added the rather elastic proviso that "information would be provided only on those Canadian citizens who either desired permanent or extended residence in the U.S.A., or about whom doubts existed on the part of the U.S. authorities."[47]

Two years later the RCMP complained to the minister of justice of the "trouble" this arrangement caused the force, mainly in the form of bad publicity when Canadians were barred at the US border or, on occasion, summarily deported as undesirables. If the RCMP took full responsibility for liaison with the Americans, it could scarcely escape the odium of providing the information upon which McCarthy-era America made decisions that appeared to many Canadians as arbitrary and illiberal. As the commissioner explained, passing on criminal information (as the RCMP had been doing since the 1930s) was one thing, but passing on information from the subversion files was quite another: "Information from our subversive files does lead to misunderstanding as from its very nature it is frequently indefinite and, furthermore, it cannot be made known or displayed to the Canadian applicant for entry into the United States in the same manner as can a criminal record." In other words, the RCMP was hoisted on its own petard of secrecy, and the commissioner was reduced to admitting: "I do not know how we can improve our present policy to any significant extent." Thirty years later the problem of Americans barring Canadians on security grounds remains—author Farley Mowat's 1984 experience was a well-publicized example—as does Canadian complicity in the process.[48]

On balance, however, the RCMP found that the international connections opened up by immigration security screening were an asset (as did its counterparts in Australia in the same era), and this gave the RCMP a vested interest in perpetuating the screening process, as well as an excuse for continuing to shroud its business in the utmost secrecy.[49] But if the RCMP constituted a powerful pressure group from within, it should not be thought that the policy lacked strong support from other quarters. First, it was plain to all that the United States government would not have tolerated a Canadian immigration security policy that was significantly less rigid in its Cold War logic than that of the United States itself—after all, there was the world's longest undefended border to consider. Secondly, there were influential domestic pressures as well. The bulk of the early postwar European immigration effort was directed to admitting unskilled and, later, skilled labourers. Canadian employers wanted no radical foreign agitators to organize discontent among an immigrant work-force that they expected to accept relatively low wage levels. While there is little evidence of direct pressure by employers on the state, it is clear from reading the business press of the era that Canadian capital expected its government to screen out potentially dangerous elements and indeed was reasonably grateful that this had been done.[50]

Above all there was the pervasive Red Scare atmosphere of the time, kept alive by the press and by opposition politicians who could be expected to pounce upon any examples of government laxity at the immigration controls. This was a point nicely made by Gordon Robertson in the Privy Council Office when Peter Dwyer, formerly of British intelligence and now freshly installed as the senior permanent official on the Security Panel, with a mandate to review policy, looked at the screening process in 1952 and suggested what seemed to him to be a more logical course. Why not, Dwyer mused, concentrate on screening only those applicants whose skills would destine them for industries engaged in the kind of defence-related activity that would require security screening on the shop floor? Why bother with the rest, most of whom could not conceivably brush up against the national interest in their humble day-to-day activities? "I feel," he wrote to Clerk of the Privy Council Norman Robertson, "that an immigrant's profession (and hence the probability or improbability of his access to Canadian secrets) should condition that degree of examination which he is to be given." The logic was impeccable, but Dwyer had failed to grasp the political aspect. Gordon Robertson—an accomplished mandarin who served successfully under six prime ministers, with an ongoing interest over the years in security matters—shrewdly noted in a marginal comment on Dwyer's memo: "Govt. immigration would be attacked if Communists were let in, whether they would do harm or not. Must be a certain amount of general precaution for political reasons."[51]

The government thus believed that public opinion demanded stiff controls. Is there evidence of this? Given the secrecy surrounding the security process, it is not surprising that little evidence was gathered of public opinion in the matter. However, one Gallup poll in 1955 asked if respondents would approve or disapprove of European families moving to their neighbourhoods. Thirty-seven percent disapproved of the idea. Of this category, 3.1 percent gave as their reason (in an open-ended question) "better screening needed." A year and a half later, of respondents indicating disapproval of "Canada's immigration policy" (36 percent of the sample), 7.7 percent gave "not enough screening" as their reason. One can speculate that those who formed the larger percentages, who approved of immigration policy, were satisfied with the results of the screening process or had no views about it.[52]

The security mania of the Cold War years sometimes affected Canada's international obligations in regard to immigration. The abortive attempt in the late 1940s to question the bona fides of the IRO on the grounds of alleged communism has been discussed. There were two other examples of more serious difficulty with international obligations.

The first episode had to do with refugees. In 1951 the Office of the United Nations High Commissioner for Refugees was established in Geneva, and the UN Convention Relating to the Status of Refugees provided an agreed-upon international definition of refugee status and of the obligations of signatory nations to refugees. Despite the widespread expectations that Canada would sign this convention, it did not do so. For seventeen years, the Department of External Affairs attempted to gain Canadian approval but was blocked by the immigration bureaucracy. Behind Immigration stood the RCMP, because the real reason for Canada's refusal to sign was the belief that the convention would restrict Canada's right to deport refugees on security grounds. It was not until 1969 that Canada finally signed the convention. Gerald Dirks comments:

> Canada at last had become formally associated with the vast majority of countries beyond the developing world by acceding to the Convention Relating to the Status of Refugees. Close to a generation had passed, however, since the Canadian representative at Geneva had first argued strongly for this country's ratification of the international agreement.[53]

The second example had to do with the successor body to the IRO, the Intergovernmental Committee for European Migration (ICEM), established in 1952. Canada joined the ICEM at the outset for reasons that, according to an interdepartmental committee on immigration, were strongly anti-Communist: "The political stability of such countries as the German Federal Republic, Italy and Greece are menaced by a continuation of social conditions which facilitate the spread of communist ideology. If those countries are helped to become more economically viable, by being relieved of some of their excess population, they should be in a better position to resist the appeal of international communism."[54]

It was ironic, then, that Cold War attitudes made Canada increasingly negative towards ICEM. By 1953, the Department of Citizenship and Immigration was demanding that Canada get out of ICEM altogether. The core of opposition was concern with ICEM's desire to process and screen refugees itself; Canada tended to see this as an infringement of its sovereignty and a potential security threat. In 1955 Cabinet considered the question of withdrawal. Some ministers were worried about pressures being brought through ICEM to admit refugees from the Soviet bloc who had not been screened according to Canadian standards. On the other hand, there was also concern that withdrawal might cause "a bad reaction amongst Slavic groups in Canada whose kin were assisted by the organization." Notice was given that Canada intended to withdraw by 1957. By that time, however, External Affairs persuaded Cabinet that the ill will generated among the NATO allies by such a move would not be worth the benefits of withdrawal, and so Canada remained for a few more years, until 1962, when a Conservative government ended formal membership in the international body.[55]

NOTES

1. Irving Abella and Harold Troper, *None Is Too Many: Canada and the Jews of Europe, 1933–1948* (Toronto, 1983), 200; Gerald Dirks, *Canada's Refugee Policy: Indifference or Optimism?* (Montreal, 1977), 124. Public Archives of Canada (hereafter PAC), Department of External Affairs (hereafter DEA), A12, vol. 2116 f.AR41812, H. Wrong to V. Massey, 10 March 1945. Rivett-Carnac was back in London on a similar mission in 1947 with Paris, Brussels, and the Hague added to his itinerary (PAC, DEA, A12, vol. 2116 f.AR41812, L.B. Pearson to Massey, 5 June 1947).

2. Privy Council Office Records (hereafter PCO) RG2 Accession No. 83-84, f. R-100-M (1946–47), Security Panel Minutes, 19 Aug. 1946. PCO 18, vol. 103 f. S-100-1 (v.2), A.L. Jolliffe confidential memo, 5 July 1946; Secretary of Security Panel to J.A. Glen, 23 Sept. 1946; ibid., vol. 82 f.I-50 (1945–46), 13 June 1946. Dirks, *Canada's Refugee Policy*, 145.

3. Abella and Troper, *None Is Too Many*, 239–40. J.L. Granatstein writes that Keenleyside had been passed over for the post of permanent head of External Affairs at the end of 1940 because he "had blotted his copybook in the Prime Minister's view by supporting the Japanese Canadians too enthusiastically" (*The Ottawa Men* (Toronto, 1982), 95).

4. Hugh Keenleyside, *Memoirs*, vol. 2, *On the Bridge of Time* (Toronto, 1982), 298–301.

5. John Holmes, *The Shaping of Peace: Canada and the Search for World Order, 1943–1957* (Toronto, 1979), 1: 100. Freda Hawkins, *Canada and Immigration: Public Policy and Public Concern* (Montreal, 1972), 238–40. Abella and Troper, *None Is Too Many*, 190–285. Leonard Dinnerstein, *America and the Survivors of the Holocaust* (New York, 1982), has much interesting material on the American experience in processing displaced persons, especially on the slipshod and discriminatory security screening (192–96).

6. Brief from the Association of United Ukrainian Canadians, 7 June 1947, reprinted in Bohdan S. Kordan and Lubomyr Y. Luciuk, eds., *A Delicate and Difficult Question: Documents in the History of Ukrainians in Canada, 1899–1962* (Kingston, 1986), 149–51; John Kolasky, *The Shattered Illusion: The History of Ukrainian Pro-Communist Organizations in Canada* (Toronto, 1979), 88–101; "Report of the Repatriation Poll of Displaced Persons in UNRRA Assembly Centers in Germany for the Period 1–14 May 1946: Analysis of Negative Votes," May 1946, reprinted in Yury Boshyk, ed., *Ukraine During World War II: History and Its Aftermath* (Edmonton, 1986), 209–19.

7. B. Heydenhorn, "The Left in Canadian Polonia," *Polyphony* 6, 2 (1984): 57–58; Dirks, *Canada's Refugee Policy*, 132, 141–42; Abella and Troper, *None Is Too Many*, 218.

8. PAC, Immigration Branch, Department of Mines and Resources (hereafter IB), vol. 800 f.547-1 (pt. 1), A.L. Jolliffe "for file," 24 Jan. 1947, and Jolliffe to J.A. Glen, 27 Jan. 1947.

9. PAC, William Lyon Mackenzie King Papers, Memoranda and Notes series (hereafter WLMK/M&N), vol. 419, Cabinet Conclusions, 29 Jan. and 5 Feb. 1947, vol. 420, Cabinet Document No. 387 "Security examination of prospective immigrants," 4 Feb. 1947. PCO Acc. No. 83-84, f.S-100-M (1946–47). IB, vol. 960 f.SF-S-129(1). "A brief résumé of the arrangements for security examination of immigrants," Jan. 1967. Note that the figures in the text refer only to applicants, not to spouses and dependent children, so the total numbers of persons involved were actually much higher. The reference to criticism from the public should be placed in context: Gallup polls conducted in the late 1940s indicated that Canadians believed, by a three-to-one margin, that Canada needed a much larger population. In 1947, 51 percent agreed that Canada needed more immigrants, while only 30 percent disagreed. Thus, serious backlogs in immigration processing would almost certainly have roused popular displeasure with government performance. See Nancy Tienhaara, *Canadian Views on Immigration and Population: An Analysis of Post-War Gallup Polls* (Ottawa, 1974), 8–9, 18.

10. WLMK/M&N, vol. 419, Cabinet Conclusions, 5 March 1947; vol. 420, Cabinet Document No. 405, J.A. Glen "Security Screening for Immigrants," n.d. PAC, Louis St Laurent Papers (hereafter LSTL), vol. 225 f.I-17 (1937–54), meeting of Cabinet Committee on Immigration Policy (hereafter CCIP), 27 May 1947. IB,

vol. 800 f.547-1(1), C.E.S. Smith to Deputy Minister, 15 Oct. 1948; L.H. Nicholson to L. Fortier, 12 Nov. 1948; S.T. Wood to A.L. Jolliffe, 3 July 1948; and Jolliffe to Wood, 5 July 1948; joint declaration of 12 July 1948. A Cabinet directive in 1949 declared that the disclosure of any information regarding security rejections resulted in "serious embarrassment to the immigration authorities and to the police" and concluded that "under no circumstances" should a rejection be attributed to security reasons. PCO vol. 139 f.C-20-7 (1947–54), Circular No. 14, 28 Oct. 1949.

11. House of Commons, *Debates*, 1 May 1947; Hawkins, *Canada and Immigration*, 91–95; J.W. Pickersgill and D.F. Forster, eds., *The Mackenzie King Record*, vol. 4, *1947–1948* (Toronto, 1970), 33–36.

12. PCO 18, vol. 103 f.S-100-M, Security Panel Minutes, 2 April 1948; vol. 189 f.S-100-1(1) (1949–50), F.W.T. Lucas to A.D.F. Heeney, 26 Jan. 1949.

13. Malcolm J. Proudfoot, *European Refugees*, 1939–52 (London, 1957), 401. PCO Acc. No. 83-84 f.S-100 (1946–49), G.C. Crean to Secretary, Security Panel, 14 April 1948; C&I, vol. 164 f.3-18-17(1), L. Fortier to A.L. Jolliffe, 22 April 1948. In the fall of 1949, only 2.5 percent of the staff of the IRO were nationals of communist-bloc countries; by contrast, Canadians alone accounted for 2.7 percent, and the British and Americans together for just under half the total (L.W. Holborn, *The IRO: A Specialized Agency of the United Nations* (New York, 1956), 100, adapted from table).

14. United States National Archives, Washington, DC, RG84, State Department Records, vol. 710 f.1948–49 59A543, US State Department, Nanking, to US Ambassador, Ottawa, 10 March 1948. IB, vol. 801 f.547-5-54, Vice-consul, Shanghai to DEA, 18 Aug. 1948. On 16 March 1948 the readers of *The Windsor Star* learned that "seasoned veterans of Red revolution in many lands are entering Canada secretly to lead a nationwide offensive of sabotage and terror scheduled for the immediate future." Even a handful of agents among the DPs could "be more dangerous than their weight in T-N-T" (Don Cameron, "Loopholes in Law Admit Europe's Red Saboteurs"). Cameron particularly cited the dangers of communism among Jewish refugees whose admission was advocated by Joseph Salsberg—a Communist MPP in Ontario. See also *The Chicago Tribune*, 3 Sept. 1948, "Canada Moves to Halt Influx of Reds as DPs"; and *The Detroit Free Press*, 3 Sept. 1948, "Canada Wary of DPs." The minister of labour, on the other hand, hastened to assure reporters after visiting Europe that "these people don't want Communism, they have seen too much . . . they should be a great bulwark against Communism spreading in this country," *Labour Gazette* 48 (1948): 1343.

15. C&I, vol. 164 f.3-18-17(1), H. Keenleyside to S.T. Wood, 28 April 1948; and Wood to Keenleyside, 10 May 1948 (Wood's letter has been heavily censored under the Access to Information Act). Fortier may have been operating on a hidden agenda. For one thing, his trip to Europe and his charges of communist infiltration followed the embarrassing disclosure in the media that IRO officials had revealed an anti-Semitic bias practised by Canadian immigration agents in selecting prospective immigrants from the refugee camps (Abella and Troper, *None Is Too Many*, 254–55). Perhaps Fortier considered that the best defence was an offence. The IRO was much more liberal about finding homes for Jewish survivors of the Holocaust than were immigration officials in countries like Canada where anti-Semitism still reigned. Pro-Jewish sentiment was often characterized in this era as "communistic."

16. C&I, vol. 169 f.3-32-1(1), L.D. Wilgress to L.B. Pearson, 14 May 1948.

17. PCO 18, vol. 189 f.S-100-1(2), "Screening of applicants for admission to Canada," 20 Nov. 1948; IB, vol. 166 f.3-25-11(2), memo from Associate Commissioner to the Commissioner for Immigration, 7 Feb. 1949. In the evidence given by former RCMP commissioner William Kelly before the Deschênes Commission of

Inquiry on War Criminals, references are made to a document that appears to be an office consolidation of the various categories dating from the early 1950s, which I have not been able to obtain (transcript, Commission of Inquiry on War Criminals, hearing of 8 May 1985 (thanks to Ms Alti Rodal of the commission's research staff for making this transcript available)). IB 83-84/347, box 5 f.SF-S-118(1), "Chapter 7: Security screening procedure," 7.01(b).

18. "Evolution of Policy and Procedures: Security Screening," documents submitted to the Commission of Inquiry on War Criminals by the Department of Manpower and Immigration, 1985 (hereafter EPP), W.H. Hickman to P.T. Baldwin, 17 May 1951, and C.E.S. Smith to the Deputy Minister, 18 May 1951.

19. IB, vol. 800 f.547-1(1), "Security Screening," 7 Feb. 1951; PC 2856.

20. Ibid.

21. 1 Eliz. II c.42: note especially "prohibited classes" 5(l), 5(m), and 5(n).

22. Hawkins, *Canada and Immigration*, 102–3.

23. *Attorney General of Canada v. Brent*, [1956] SCR 318; PC 1956-785; J.W. Pickersgill, *My Years with Louis St. Laurent: A Political Memoir* (Toronto, 1975), 240.

24. Philip Girard, "From Subversion to Liberation: Homosexuals and the Immigration Act 1952–1977" (draft paper). Thanks to Professor Girard for making this paper available and for sharing his ideas.

25. Hawkins, *Canada and Immigration*, 105.

26. Statutes of Canada 1946, c.15, s.10(1)(d). Commission of Inquiry Concerning Certain Activities of the RCMP, *Second Report* (Ottawa, 1981), 2: 829–33.

27. See the interesting essays by R. Kenneth Carty and W. Peter Ward, "The Making of a Canadian Political Citizenship," in *National Politics and Community in Canada* (Vancouver, 1986), 65–79; and Alan Cairns and Cynthia Williams, "Constitutionalism, Citizenship and Society in Canada: An Overview," in *Constitutionalism, Citizenship and Society in Canada*, vol. 33 of the studies of the Royal Commission on the Economic Union and Development Prospects for Canada (Toronto, 1985), 1–50.

28. Hawkins, *Canada and Immigration*, 30.

29. PCO Acc. No. 83-84, f.S-100-M (1946–47), Security Panel meeting, 5 April 1949, RCMP memo "Security screening of immigrants—present problems," SP-40, 31 March 1949. PCO 16, vol. 17, Cabinet Conclusions, 24 Aug. 1949, Security Panel Report (Cabinet Document No. 1022), 29 Sept. 1949, citing the danger of compromising "counterespionage activities" if security grounds for rejection were to be disclosed. PCO 18, vol. 189 f.S-100-1(2), R.A.S. McNeil to E.F. Gaskell, 11 July 1950.

30. C&I, vol. 803 f.547-5-645, H. Allard to Director of Immigration, 15 Dec. 1952; Belgrade Embassy to Secretary of State for External Affairs, 29 Nov. 1952; IB 83-84/347, box 5 f.SF-S-118(1), "Chapter 7: Security screening procedure," 7.05(d)(2).

31. C&I, vol. 894 f.591-I(5), C.E.S. Smith to Deputy Minister, 25 March 1952; f.591-1(7), Operations Division to posts abroad, 17 April 1956.

32. C&I, vol. 119 f.3-25-15, L. Fortier to the Minister, 26 Feb. 1953; P.M. Dwyer, draft memorandum to Cabinet, "Immigration security policy," 23 Feb. 1953.

33. IB 83-84/347, box 5 f.SF-S-118(1), "Chapter 7: Security screening procedure," 7.01(b)(i) and (iii) and 7.00(c) and (d).

34. *Winnipeg Free Press*, "Pickersgill to Get Bar Committee's Immigration Data," 3 Sept. 1954. C&I, vol. 166 f.3-25-11(2), Fortier to Pickersgill, 17 Jan. 1955; vol. 167 f.3-25-11-13(1), Minutes of meeting on security, 6 Dec. 1954. As late as 1956 the

deputy minister was writing to such eminently respectable organizations as the Canadian Council of Churches, the Canadian Jewish Congress, and the Canadian Christian Council for Resettlement of Refugees, reviewing reasons for rejections on criminal, medical, and occupational grounds, but scrupulously avoiding any mention of security (vol. 110, f.3-24-12(1), L. Fortier to J.W. Pickersgill, 1 Feb. 1956).

35. Pickersgill, *My Years with Louis St. Laurent*, 231.

36. EPP, J.R. Robillard to C.S.A. Ritchie, 22 April 1955. IB, vol. 800 f.547-1(3), K.W.N. Hall to C.E.S. Smith, 9 Aug. 1955, admitting that "visa officers have had a very legitimate complaint in that certain very minor offences, which could under no circumstances be considered as serious in this country, have been included in the [forms] forwarded by our Security Officers"; vol. 801 f.547-5-513, Robillard to Chief, Operations Division, 30 Sept. 1955; vol. 802 f.547-5-575, A.M. Mont to Officer-in-Charge, 13 Oct. 1955; R. Brunet to Director of Immigration, 20 Oct. 1955; G.R. Benoit to Brunet, 28 Oct. 1955.

37. Hawkins, *Canada and Immigration*, 282–83.

38. IB, vol. 800 f.547-1(1), "Meeting on immigration matters," 22 Jan. 1954. This meeting is reported at greater length by Alvin Finkel, "Canadian Immigration Policy and the Cold War, 1945–1980," *Journal of Canadian Studies* 21, 3 (Fall 1986): 58–60.

39. C&I, vol. 168 f.3-25-13(1), L.H. Nicholson to L. Fortier, 15 March 1954; vol. 103 f.3-18-14(1), Report to the Annual Meeting of the Canadian Bar Association, 9 July 1954. IB, vol. 800 f.547-1(3), Undersecretary of State for External Affairs to Fortier, 24 June 1955. LSTL, vol. 236 f. "Immigration (1952–56)," Canadian Labour Congress to Government of Canada, 15 Dec. 1956. Jack Pickersgill in his memoirs claims that the bar association complaints were entirely attributable to one law firm specializing in Chinese immigration, whose interest was in gaining ministerial backing in specific cases in exchange for calling off its "agitation" (*My Years with Louis St. Laurent*, 233–36). Be this as it may, the bar association's case was certainly not lacking in substance on its own merits.

40. PAC, Department of Labour Records (hereafter DL), vol. 835 f.1-28-1(1), A. MacNamara to R. Haddow, 4 June 1948; Haddow to MacNamara, 5 June 1948; S.T. Wood to MacNamara, 8 June 1948. My thanks to Gary Marcuse for drawing this correspondence to my attention.

41. DL, S.T. Wood to MacNamara, 8 June 1948.

42. C&I, vol. 166 f.3-25-11(2), J.J. Deutsch to L. Fortier, 13 June 1955; draft report on European immigration activities of Canadian government, Dec. 1955; vol. 164 f.3-18-17(1), L.H. Nicholson to S. Garson, 7 April 1955 (this letter has been censored under the Access to Information Act).

43. Secretary of State for External Affairs, "Summary of instructions sent out on April 22, 1948," 1 Nov. 1949.

44. C&I, vol. 119 f.3-25-15, Security Panel Document No. 151 "Immigration security policy," 25 Feb. 1953; draft memorandum to Cabinet, "Immigration security policy," 23 Feb. 1953; Security Panel Minutes, 2 March 1953; L. Fortier, memorandum for the Minister, 3 March 1953. Even the motives of friendly local police authorities might sometimes be doubted, as former commissioner William Kelly was later to recall in regard to the West Germans, whom the RCMP suspected of discouraging the outflow of skilled labour in the 1950s (see Deschênes Commission of Inquiry on War Criminals, transcript, 935-6).

45. PCO 1952, f.S-100-5-B, G.A. Sincennes to Officer-in-Charge, Security Section, London, 18 Dec. 1951; Secretary of State for External Affairs to Washington Embassy, 20 March and 25 April 1952. IB, vol. 153 f.1-18-14, K.W.N. Hall to E.F.

Gaskell, 2 Feb. 1952. DEA, f.50207-A-40, Security Panel Minutes, 11 March 1952. EPP, T.C. Davis, "Immigration security arrangements," 6 March 1952. Sol. Littman, *War Criminal on Trial: The Rauca Case* (Toronto, 1983).

46. Deschênes commission, transcript, 943-5, 972. Information on Gehlen and the CIC can be found in John Loftus, *The Belarus Secret* (New York, 1982). On the flagrant collaboration of the CIC with Nazi war criminals see Magnus Linklater, Isabel Hilton, and Neal Ascherson, *The Fourth Reich: Klaus Barbie and the Neo-Fascist Connection* (London, 1985).

47. C&I, vol. 153 f.1-18-7(1), Security Panel minutes, 20 Nov. 1953.

48. C&I, vol. 164 f.3-18-17(1), L.H. Nicholson to S. Garson, 7 April 1955. Ironically, the very discussion of the question by the RCMP commissioner in the 1955 document has been so heavily censored under the Access to Information Act at the RCMP's insistence that is impossible to know what, if anything, was actually done about it thirty years ago. For some examples of Canadians who have been barred by the United States, see Reg Whitaker, *Double Standard: The Secret History of Canadian Immigration* (Toronto, 1987), ch. 7.

49. This is a point made by Richard Hall, *The Secret State: Australia's Spy Industry* (North Melbourne, 1978), 67.

50. See, for instance, Ronald Williams, "How to Keep Red Hands off Our New Canadians," *The Financial Post*, 12 March 1949. A study of opinion surveys regarding immigration notes that since 1949 "business executives and professionals are found at the favourable end" of a continuum of occupational categories regarding the need for more immigration (Tienhaara, *Canadian Views on Immigration and Population*, 26–27). British immigrants were exempted altogether from screening, and in the early 1950s they represented a large proportion of those skilled trades that were often employed in defence industries. Some defence contractors were reluctant to employ British workers on the grounds of political unreliability since all defence industries were required to screen employees with access to secret work (see Whitaker, *Double Standard*, ch. 8).

51. PCO Acc. No. 83, box 16 f.S-100-5, P.M. Dwyer to N.A. Robertson, 7 March 1952, and Dwyer to L. Fortier, 20 March 1952.

52. Tienhaara, *Canadian Views on Immigration and Population*, 64–65.

53. Dirks, *Canada's Refugee Policy*, 180–82.

54. Ibid., 186–89; Hawkins, *Canada and Immigration*, 18–20.

55. PCO 16, Cabinet Conclusions, 5 May and 15 June 1955.

FROM CONTADINA TO WORKER: SOUTHERN ITALIAN IMMIGRANT WORKING WOMEN IN TORONTO, 1947-62 ◇

FRANCA IACOVETTA

○

On Thursday, 16 November 1956, Maria R. and her daughter arrived in Toronto from her peasant farm in Abruzzi.[1] She was met at Union Station by her husband Eneo, who had left her a year previously for work in Toronto. After eating dinner with relatives, she was ushered into her new home—a basement flat in a Calabrian's house. Next day, Maria and Eneo, who took the day off from his Royal York Hotel janitorial job, went to Honest Ed's discount department store to shop for household necessities, including an espresso coffee-maker and pots for cooking spaghetti. To Marie's delight, next morning the Santa Claus Parade passed by their Dupont Street home. At seven o'clock Monday morning, Maria went directly to work at a nearby laundry where a sister-in-law had secured her a job as a steampress operator at thirty-seven dollars a week. For twenty years Maria worked at many such low-skilled jobs—sewing, cooking, tending a grocery store, and as a cashier—until 1976 when she finally withdrew from the work force to care for her dying husband.[2]

Women played an important role in the immigration of southern Italian peasant families to post-World War II Toronto. Within the patriarchal framework of the family, Italian women performed demanding roles as immigrants, workers, wives, and mothers. Their active commitment to the family helped bridge the move from Old World to New as women's labour, both paid and unpaid, continued to help ensure the survival and material well-being of their families. The transition from *contadina* (peasant) to

---

◇ Jean Burnet, ed., *Looking into My Sister's Eyes: An Exploration in Women's History* (Toronto: Multicultural History Society of Ontario, 1986), 195–222. Reprinted with the permission of the publisher.

worker did not require a fundamental break in the values of women long accustomed to contributing many hours of hard labour to the family. As workers, though, they confronted new forms of economic exploitation and new rhythms of work and life imposed by industrial capitalism. Women at home similarly performed important economic and social functions and endured the alienating and racist aspects of urban industrial life. Bolstered by networks of kinfolk and *paesani* (co-villagers) and the persistence of traditional social forms, women not only endured such hardships but displayed a remarkable capacity to incorporate their new experiences as working-class women into traditionally rooted notions of familial and motherly responsibility.

This article will consider three aspects of southern Italian women's role in postwar immigration: Old-World conditions, chain migration, and early living and working conditions in Toronto. Based on documentary research and interviews, the conclusions presented here are tentative and exploratory. While the essay focuses on women's activities and perceptions, an attempt also has been made to provide the structural contexts—political, economic, social, and familial—in which those experiences took place.

Following the long interruption caused by government restrictions, the Great Depression, and the Second World War, Italian immigration resumed on a major scale once again in the late forties and fifties. Millions of temporary and permanent emigrants travelled to continental Europe, North and South America, and Australia. Between 1951 and 1961 overseas emigrants numbered over one million; 250 000, or 25 percent of them, settled in Canada. A target city after 1951, Metropolitan Toronto alone attracted some 90 000, or 40 percent, of the total Italian immigration to Canada in this period.[3]

Women and children comprised a substantial proportion of the influx. Over 81 000 women aged fifteen and over arrived in Canada from 1951–61. Between 25 000 and 30 000 women, many with children, settled in Toronto. Young, married women sponsored by their husbands and families predominated.[4] After 1952, for example, "dependent" women and children accounted for between 40 and 54 percent of the annual wave of Italians into the country. In a typical year, 1958, dependent women alone comprised almost 35 percent (or 6064) of the total adult population (17 381). And they made up over 70 percent of the number of total adult females (8515).[5] Most women were former peasants from the Mezzogiorno—the southern agricultural regions of Abruzzi-Molise, Basilicata, Campagnia, Puglia, and Calabria. Peasants from the south accounted for nearly 60 percent of the total Italian immigration to Canada in this period.[6]

As southern European Catholics, these women were the target of nativist hostilities. Anticipating the postwar influx of non-British immigrants, the Anglican church in 1941 depicted Southern Europeans as "amenable to the fallacies of dictatorship, less versed in the tradition and art of democratic government," and better suited to the hot climate and fragile political structures of Latin America.[7] The British Dominions Emigration Society dismissed northern Italians as communists and southerners as unsatisfactory settlers.[8] Provincial officials, who worried about increasing numbers of Jews and Catholics entering Protestant Ontario, co-operated with manufacturers in recruiting skilled tradesmen exclusively from Great Britain.[9] Even federal immigration officials who did recruit from Italy focused on the inferiority of southern Italians, whom they portrayed as backward and slovenly, and they worried that these peasants significantly outnumbered their more "industrious" northern compatriots. "The Italian South peasant," one official wrote, "is not the type we are looking for in Canada. His standard of living, his way of life, even his civilization seems so different that I doubt if he could ever become an asset to our country."[10]

Immigration officials interested in recruiting Italian male labourers did not expect the married peasant woman to work and so they paid no attention to her. (By contrast, they welcomed some 16 000 females, mostly single northerners, who arrived as trained domestics, hairdressers, and seamstresses.[11]) A 1950 reciprocal agreement between Canada and Italy that removed customs duties on bridal trousseaus entering either country at least recognized women's role in setting up a home in the new society. But it also reflected notions about married women's prescribed roles as wife and mother and reinforced the assumption that married southern Italian women were dependent upon their men and could make no real contribution to Canadian society.[12]

o

Contrary to contemporary assumptions that women were little more than part of the male newcomer's cultural baggage—a view some male scholars have also adopted—southern Italian women were active agents in family migration. A consideration of their role must begin with life in the Old World.

Southern peasants did not come from a background of isolated, closed villages, nor were they completely self-sufficient subsistence farmers isolated from a market economy and ignorant of the world beyond their village. Typically, southern Italians resided in hilltop agro-towns or villages (paese) situated in the region's mountainous terrain. Daily, the town's peasants (contadini) and agricultural labourers (braccianti) walked long distances to the scattered fields and landed estates below. With populations that numbered in the thousands, towns were characterized by complex social structures and class divisions evident in the presence of gentry, middle men, and professional notaries as well as bureaucrats, artisans, peasants, agricultural labourers and the unemployed poor.[13] One woman, Assunta C., for instance, described her home town of San Paulino in Campagnia as maintaining various commercial and retail and food services, blacksmith and tailor shops, and a train station. People located in village fragments and hamlets had access to larger urban centres.[14]

Various long-term factors produced Italy's infamous "southern problem" and made life brutal for its residents. The heat and aridity of summer, followed by heavy but sporadic winter downpours, resulted in poor irrigation and soil erosion. Though more southerly areas also grew fruits, olives, nuts, and poor-quality wine, peasants relied heavily upon wheat and other grain crops. Hilly and mountainous terrain precluded mechanization and encouraged traditional labour-intensive farming techniques that relied upon an ox or cow, a few simple tools, and brute strength.

Another serious handicap was the highly fragmented nature of peasant holdings. Outside the latifundia, gentry-controlled estates were divided into small tenancies rented or sold to peasants who simultaneously might own, rent, and even share-crop numerous small and widely scattered plots of questionable soil quality. This further discouraged mechanization or intensive cultivation and reinforced undercapitalized and labour intensive methods of farming. The region's "natural" poverty was exacerbated by decades of political neglect as successive governments failed to provide irrigation, develop industry, and institute land reforms; and it contrasted sharply with the industrialized and agriculturally more prosperous North.[15]

Though tied to underproductive plots, *i contadini* were also part of a larger market economy; they engaged in regional trade networks and participated in a cash economy on a local, national, and international scale. Peasants had economic and social connections to the surrounding regions and urban centres where they exchanged money for goods and services. Maria L., who came from a village in Molise too small to sustain artisan or retail activity, noted how family members frequently visited the nearby town to buy shoes and tools or call for the doctor. The women I interviewed said that their families had regularly sold surplus wheat, eggs, and vegetables to co-villagers and residents in nearby villages who came to their home. A woman from the Vasto-Giardi area near Campobasso in Molise, Assunta Ca., sold eggs door to door in her village. And women also purchased linens and cloths from travelling merchants.[16]

The very poverty of the South, which made total subsistence impossible for peasants, compelled families to pursue economic strategies that drew them further into a cash economy. Peasant families effectively supplemented meagre farm incomes by sending out members, usually men, on temporary sojourns as wage workers. Hiring themselves out as day labourers on the landed estates (*giornalieri*), many men found seasonal work in the local or regional economy. Other men, such as the fathers of Maria R. and Vincenza, found outside employment as seasonal woods workers.[17] Others sought jobs in agriculture, railway construction, and in the building trades either on the Continent or overseas. These activities and the cash remittances families received brought them into contact with highly industrialized economies around the world—a pattern which intensified during the decade following the Second World War.[18]

Although scholars debate definitions of the nuclear and extended family, they agree that the family is the most important economic and social unit to peasants and that it provided the basis of peasant solidarity in the South. Familial allegiances were sufficiently strong to exclude membership in other institutions and (apart from some exceptional cases of peasant protests and experiments in peasant communism) communal or collectivist associations. Even the celebration of local feasts took on familial forms.[19]

As the basic mode of production and social organization, the peasant family relied upon the maximum labour power of every member of the household, and each person was expected to sacrifice individual needs and contribute to the family's survival. Women interviewed described typical work days by focusing on how every member performed a necessary task. Some, such as Julia, recalled how the relentless work of farming was made more enjoyable by the camaraderie of family and kinfolk: "we worked so very hard . . . we get up at the crack of dawn to go to work in the *campagnia* [fields] but we singing . . . happy because we're together."[20] Beyond the privileged sphere of close family, members of the extended *familiari*—cousins, aunts, uncles, and in-laws—also shared this mutual trust and help when it did not interfere with the priorities of the family. (In practice, however, conflicts often occurred.) Nevertheless, such status was denied to all others except *i compari*—non-relatives who gained admittance to the *familiari* through the ritual kinship of godparenthood (*comparagio*). Extreme familialism in the South also involved a distrust of others and constant gossiping about others' misfortune, though people did share a spirit of loyalty to their native village or town and its residents (*campanelismo*).[21]

With respect to women, the literature focuses on the twin themes of sexual segregation and subordination. The patriarchal organization of the southern Italian family and society and the cultural mores of the South did impose heavy restrictions on the choices and behaviour of women. As women interviewed remarked, "honourable" women did not accompany men from outside the household in public unless chaperoned. During local dances, Sunday afternoon visits in the piazza, and at religious festivities, young adults socialized under the watchful eyes of their elders. The very concept of familial *onore* (honour) so valued by Italians rested in large part upon the sexual purity of wives, daughters, and sisters and men's success in guarding the virtue of their women and in playing the predominant role of family bread-winner. Linked to prevailing notions of male self-esteem and dominance, an almost obsessive fear that women might engage in pre- and extra-marital sex and thereby bring shame to their entire family was central to women's oppression in southern Italy. Constant supervision of their activities was the inevitable result.[22]

Male privilege was exercised widely within the public sphere. Men were freer to socialize and lead the religious and social feasts celebrated within the village. Considered the family's chief decision-maker, the male head acted as the family's representative in its dealings with the outside world. This included making annual rental payments to absentee landlords, journeying out of the region in search of work, or acting as the main marriage negotiator for children—a task that carried a highly visible profile. Assunta C.'s father, for example, spent two weeks consulting people, including the local cleric and doctor, before granting final approval to his daughter's prospective husband.[23]

Nevertheless, a model of male dominance/female submission is ultimately too simplistic to account for the experiences of peasant women in the Mezzogiorno. It ignores the complexity of gender relations in Italy and serves to underestimate the importance of female labour to peasant family production. The dictates of the household economy regularly drew women outside of the home to participate in agricultural production. Though the supposed "natural" link between women and domestic labour persisted, women's work roles included domestic and farm duties. And both involved back-breaking efforts.[24]

Domestic responsibilities included cooking, cleaning, and child care, as well as weaving, sewing clothes, and, especially during the winter slack period, producing embroidered linens and crocheted tablecloths for bridal trousseaus. Such labours were time consuming and arduous. As Maria L. explained, doing laundry involved fetching water from the town well to boil and then soaking the items for an hour before carrying them to a nearby stream where they were rinsed and laid out on the rocks to dry. Cooking over open wood stoves was hot and dirty work, and the stoves required constant maintenance and cleaning.[25]

Women and girls also farmed—clearing the plots, sowing and planting, hoeing, and sharing in the overall work of the summer grain harvest, a project that drew on help from kinfolk and neighbours. At home, women might supervise the threshing and perform the winnowing process. During the autumn ploughing, women transported manure from barns to the various field plots. Though the actual task of breaking the ground usually involved several men equipped with basic hand tools and an ox or cow, women also performed this exhausting work. All season long, they travelled back and forth between the town and the fields, carrying food and supplies in baskets on their heads. Female members helped in other ways as well. They grew vegetable gardens, fed the animals, and herded them into grazing areas scattered among the family fields. Women made cheese from goat and sheep milk and often sold the surplus locally. In southern regions, women and children picked olives, nuts, and fruits growing on their land, or they picked for large landowners in exchange for a portion of the produce. Girls and boys in coastal towns brought home smelts and other small fish. Women made vegetable and fruit preserves and prepared meats, and they helped collect fuel wood from communal lands. Young women might be sent to the local seamstress to learn pattern-making and sewing or train as a hairdresser. Though there were few non-agricultural job opportunities, some families sent single daughters away to work in domestic service or in garment, textile, and silk factories of the region. There, they lived in chaperoned boardinghouses and regularly sent their wages home. Particularly in the latifundia regions, increasing numbers of "peasant" women after the war engaged in part-time agricultural wage labour.[26]

Distinctions between women's and men's work roles were often blurred—a vital point frequently ignored by scholars. When large numbers of men from the South were conscripted into the Italian army during World War II, for example, women ran the family farms. Similarly, wives, sisters, and daughters, compensated whenever men worked in the paid labour force.[27] It was also linked to the size and character of households. When there were several women in one household, younger females were released from domestic work for field work or, as in Pina's case, a seamstress apprenticeship in town. As a single women, Maria R. often worked in the fields with her parents, grandfather, and brother since her grandmother stayed home and took charge of daily house chores. Assunta C. noted life after marriage was actually easier because she no longer divided her time between work and field duties; she now stayed at home while her husband and in-laws farmed. By contrast, Dalinda, who lived alone with her husband, performed all the domestic labours herself and shared the field work with her husband.[28]

Nor can we assume that patriarchal structures and values in effect to subordinate women meant that they were passive victims with no basis for exercising power. Scholars have stressed the importance of men's public role and have made much of women's tendency to act modestly in mixed company and to claim to outsiders that they speak and act in their husband's or father's name. This can be very misleading, for it is within the private sphere that women could wield the most influence over their families. They made effective use of their capacity to argue, nag, manipulate, disrupt normal routine, and generally make life miserable for men in order to achieve certain demands.[29]

In *Women of the Shadows*, a grim look at postwar southern Italian women, Ann Cornelisen captured the public/private dynamic in her description of a married woman who had been supporting her elderly parents. When asked who made the family's decisions, the woman claimed she consulted with her parents. But when Cornelisen confronted her with the fact she did not usually confer with her parents, she responded: "The Commandments say honour thy father and thy mother, don't they? No reason to let any one know what happens inside the family." Another woman endured months of verbal and physical assault from her husband before convincing him to work in Germany in order to raise funds for their son's hospital care. In fact, she even secured the necessary work permit.[30] Mothers also acted as their children's mediators, as did Julia's mother who sent instructions to her husband in Argentina in 1955 to grant formal approval to their daughter's marriage plans because *she* favoured it.[31]

Far from Ann Bravo's model of lonely, isolated peasant women with a truncated self-identity, women's close identification with their family did not preclude bonds of friendship with other women.[32] Joint labour projects between households permitted women to work together and, during breaks, to chat and gossip. Women performed many chores—such as laundry and shelling beans—outside the house in the company of other women. Within households, in-laws collectivized domestic and field labour and often became close friends. Not all women were natural allies; they could be suspicious of, and cruel to, each other.[33] But there were also numerous opportunities for women to establish friendships and many did so. With the exception of Maria S., whose father had discouraged friendships, all the women interviewed had confided in close women friends back home and most had chosen long-time girlfriends to be their children's godmothers.[34] As the family's social convener arranging visits, meals, and gifts between kinfolk and *paesani*, women placed themselves at the centre of wide networks of family, kin, and friends.[35] Men were also subjected to community sanctions should they squander the family resources or prove to be inadequate providers, and at home husbands frequently conceded to women's demands.[36] Though gender relations reflected patriarchal precepts, they were far more complex than has hitherto been acknowledged. Even victims of abuse refused to be totally submissive wives.

○

No longer compelled by fascist policies to remain in their home region, Italians after the war escaped worsening conditions in the South—the further pulverization of land-holdings, rising unemployment, inadequate housing, sanitation and drinking water, and extensive malnutrition and disease. Attracted to the city's boom economy and pulled by the dynamic of chain migration, many of them arrived in Toronto.[37] The poorest residents of the Mezzogiorno—landless agricultural labourers and the unemployed urban poor—did not figure prominently among the influx, however. Rather peasants, who had owned, rented, or share-cropped various plots of land, sold their surplus crops and perhaps accumulated savings, predominated. They comprised 75 percent of adult Italian immigrants to Canada during the 1950s.[38] All the women interviewed came from such families and each stressed how her family, though poor, was considerably better off than the *braccianti* and unemployed. Assunta C. recalled how poor and malnourished women in town used to beg for the water in which she had boiled beans so they could feed their babies. Assunta Ca.'s husband had even lent money to relatives and friends.[39] Far from a strategy to deal with abject poverty, emigration served to offset the dwindling opportunities of peasants, especially newly married couples, to improve property holdings. In this way, they avoided loss of status and obtained family property elsewhere.[40]

Women were often denied a formal voice in the decision of the family to emigrate largely because migration was linked to men's work opportunities, a pattern reinforced by immigration policies in Canada and elsewhere. By making use of informal mechanisms of persuasion, they nonetheless sought to influence the timing and target of migration. Desperate to marry and leave war-torn Fossocessia, Molise, Maria S. persuaded an initially very hostile fiancé that, after their marriage in 1948, they should join her married sister in Toronto.[41] Against her parent's wishes, a spirited Iolanda, who was a hairdresser apprentice from Miamo, Abruzzi, joined two brothers in Toronto in 1956.[42] Other women could not negotiate their own future. The parents of a large southern Calabrian family in Rocella Ionica sent Pina, two sisters, and a brother to Toronto in order to raise money for their butcher shop and the father's medical bills.[43]

On the other hand, many married women shared with their husbands the desire to immigrate to Toronto. They believed in the "dream of America" and were convinced that several years of hard work would secure wealth and a comfortable life for them. Assunta C. recalled how she had always been impressed by the sojourners who had returned to the home town wealthier men. Others received encouraging letters from friends and family and travelled to join them.[44]

Immigration occurred in a comparatively ragged fashion, and led by young, married men who benefited from kinfolk-arranged sponsorship and accommodation, the process frequently involved the temporary fragmentation of families. Nicolletta met her husband during his periodic visits home to Pescara while working in Belgium coal-mines from 1951–54. Soon after they married in 1954, her husband returned to Belgium and in 1956 a pregnant Nicolletta joined him. Upon receiving news a male cousin had sponsored her husband to Canada, the family returned home, and her husband left immediately for Toronto. In 1961 after her husband had sponsored his father and youngest sister, Nicolletta and daughter finally arrived in Toronto.[45]

Although after 1951 it became more common for women to accompany their men to Toronto, many women continued to stay behind while husbands explored opportunities overseas. Significantly, women were familiar with economic strategies that involved the temporary breakup of the family unit but which secured its long-term survival. Many had experienced the absence of fathers and brothers who had emigrated temporarily outside of Italy and had served in the war.[46] Even so, loneliness and hardship ensued, especially for women whose marriage and separation followed closely together. This also led to a further blurring of traditional gender-linked work roles. With only occasional help from her father and brother, Dalinda ran the farm in Vasto-Giardi, Molise, for two years while rearing two small children, including a son born just two days before her husband's departure in 1951 for a Quebec farm. Immediately after their marriage in Mountarro, Calabria, Vincenza's husband left for several years to work in agricultural and railway repair jobs in Switzerland. He made two brief visits in two years but respected his familial obligations by sending money home regularly. He returned home only to accompany a brother to Toronto; one year later, he called for his wife and child. Initially opposed to joining her husband permanently in Toronto, Julia eventually gave in because she felt responsible for her daughter's unhappiness: "my little girl she call 'daddy, daddy' every day . . . she say, 'mommy why we don't go see daddy; mommy, mommy she's a devil, she not let me see my daddy.' Oh, she make me cry every day."[47]

Travelling alone, with female kin or husbands, southern Italian women benefited from family-linked chain migration which acted as a buffer against the alienating features of immigration. A ticket was financed in a variety of ways—a father's savings, money sent home by a husband, cash raised from a woman's sale of household furniture, and the Canadian government's Assisted Passage Loan Scheme. Women experienced their first direct confrontation with government bureaucracy when they visited the crowded consulate in Rome for processing and medical examinations. Six months later, they embarked upon the two-week sea voyage and the train ride from Halifax to Toronto's Union Station.

Women's reaction to leaving home and to the trip varied. Some cried; others felt optimistic about prospects in Canada. While some enjoyed the food and dancing aboard ship, others feared their children might fall overboard or disturb passengers by crying in the cabin at night. At Halifax, they feared being separated from their children. When Dalinda arrived on a cold November day in 1953, she was embarrassed by her lightly clad sons and feared she might be considered a bad mother. The train ride through Eastern Canada evoked concern as the scattered wood-frame houses resembled more the poverty of home than the expected wealth of the New World. But Toronto brought familiar faces and relief, and women settled with their men in the growing southern Italian enclaves in the city's east and west ends and within College Street's Little Italy.[48]

o

At home and at work, southern Italian immigrant women contributed to the welfare of their working-class families now struggling to survive in Toronto. Their domestic activities and their participation in the paid labour force will be discussed separately.

In order to understand women's domestic duties, a discussion of immigrant households is necessary. They consisted primarily of two types: an extended familial arrangement in which one or more relatives owned the house and other residents paid rent, or a flat rented from non-kin or even non-Italian landlords who normally resided on the main floor. Given their intense clannishness, fewer emotional benefits could be derived by newcomers who rented separate quarters from strangers. Women resented daily infractions of their privacy, and mothers were highly protective of their children. "With the children is very hard to live in . . . another people's house," explained Vincenza. "You have to live in freedom . . . other people they get too frustrated for the children . . . is not fair." She detested three years spent in a tiny third-floor flat near Christie and Bloor streets: "I was think it was gonna be different. I was living worse than over there [Italy]. I live in a third floor . . . two kids after six months . . . and a kitchen in the basement. . . . I wanna go back home. But the money was gone, the furniture was sell, nothing was left." Julia, however, so resented her landlord's complaints regarding water and electricity bills and her child's ruining the hardwood floors that she made her husband move to better quarters within a month of her arrival in Toronto.[49]

By contrast, the *familiari* set-up held greater opportunities for social bonding between kinfolk. A central feature of Italian immigration was the remarkable extent to which family, kin, and *paesani* boarded together temporarily and the high turnover rate of boarders within any particular household. Boarding served an economic and psycho-cultural function for newcomers; it provided boarders with cheap rents, homeowners with savings to put towards mortgage payments, and everyone with an opportunity to engage in "fellow-feeling-ness."[50] It held practical advantages as couples passed on household and baby things, and the group took on labour-intensive projects such as wine-making and the annual slaughter of a pig. Women preferred this arrangement, and several commented on how remarkably rare serious outbursts were in a household containing up to twenty people. A Molisana woman, Ada, who lived for several years in a crowded Dupont Street house, even claimed those early years were special times when *parenti* united during hard times. "We cared more for each other then than now," she added.[51]

Far from huddling indiscriminately, the dynamics of these crowded households reflected a deep-seated sense of propriety and were largely organized according to nuclear families. At supper, for instance, families sharing a kitchen ate at different or overlapping times as each woman, who alone was responsible for her family's meals, awaited her husband's arrival from work before heating her pot of water for pasta. Individual families shared private quarters and while several women might be entrusted to do the grocery shopping, each family paid for its share of the supplies.[52]

Whatever the household structure, women at home performed crucial economic roles. Like other working-class women, they stretched limited resources and found ways to cut costs and earn extra cash. To the benefit of industrial capitalism, woman's labours daily replenished the male bread-winner and fed, clothed, and raised children. In extended households, they served extra menfolk who were unmarried or had not yet called for their wives, as well as elderly parents and in-laws. Maria S., who stayed home to raise three children, divided her days between doing her housework, which included gardening and sewing, and helping her sick married sister who lived nearby.[53] Since some households lacked refrigerators until the late fifties or early sixties, women purchased daily perishables such as milk and bread. Without washing-machines and often with access only to hot-plates located in otherwise unfinished basements, basic chores were time-consuming and arduous.[54]

Women cut living costs by growing vegetable gardens and grape vines and by preserving fruits and vegetables. With pride Assunta C. recalled how she had produced most of the family's food: "I did everything, toma-toes for sauce, pickles, olives. I did pears, peaches, apricots, everything we eat. We bought the meat from the store and I make sausages and pros-ciutto." Maria S. saved money by shopping at a large farmer's market at the city limits. Others earned additional cash by taking in boarders or extra washing and many baby-sat for working relatives—all of which increased domestic chores.[55]

Moreover, the wife frequently acted as the family's financial manager, allocating funds for groceries, furniture, and clothing, paying bills, and depositing savings in the bank or putting them towards mortgage pay-ments. Several women described how at the end of each week their hus-bands would hand over their pay cheques. In Maria S.'s words, "My husband bring the money home and give it to me and he say, 'You know what you're doing, take care of the money.' . . . I tried save money, and I did. After three years we buy a house." Women considered this task to be of the utmost importance. Though men later usurped this role when finances and investments grew more complex, it also suggests that women's influ-ence at home, especially during the critical early years, was considerable. Certainly, when families were merely surviving men relied upon women's resourcefulness to help make ends meet.[56]

Extended households also let women collectivize housekeeping and exchange confidences. Women who were at home all day—one nursing a newborn, another sewing clothes, and another unemployed—frequently shared domestic chores. For over a year Vincenza lived with a sister-in-law and their children while their husbands worked out of town on a mushroom farm. She baby-sat the children while her in-law worked as a hospital chambermaid, and each night they shared the cooking and clean-up duties. Similarly, three single working sisters daily shared cooking and cleaning tasks, and on week-ends they rotated laundry, shopping, and housekeeping.[57]

Many women also made friends with non-related Italian and even non-Italian women in their neighbourhood. Maria S. and her sister befriended several Ukrainian and Jewish women in their neighbourhood. In spring and summer they spent hours outside talking, and they made a point of celebrating each other's birthday. At home with her own and her cousin's children, Assunta C. spent afternoons with a neighbour who also baby-sat children. Each would alternate working in her garden or house while the other supervised the children.[58]

Whether at home or in the factory, urban industrial life evoked anxiety and fear in women who no longer enjoyed the protection of the *paese*. Several women recalled the fear of going out alone at night, the mocking looks of native Torontonians, and even the experience of being robbed in their own homes.[59] Daily they confronted prejudice. Maria S. recalled crying all the way home after being laughed out of a department store one day in 1949 when she could not make herself understood by the saleswomen. (She had wanted to purchase socks and work pants for her plasterer husband.) Interestingly, this incident spurred her on to learn English. While returning from a week-end visit with relatives in New York City, a misunderstanding at the border resulted in the jailing of Pina and her sister for ten days in Buffalo until an American aunt hired an Italian-speaking lawyer who cleared up the confusion.[60]

Mothers also feared for their children's safety at school where outbursts regularly occurred between Anglo-Saxon and Italian schoolmates, especially boys. They worried about being called poor mothers by doctors, school nurses, and teachers. When school authorities sent home a girl suspected of having lice, her family became totally distraught and immediately took her to the hospital. Maria L., who gave birth to a premature son the morning after she arrived in Toronto, was afraid to leave him in the hospital for fear he would die. As she noted, the comfort traditionally provided by the village midwife had been abruptly cut off and impersonal institutions put in her place.[61]

Women's anxieties were well founded, for racism permeated postwar Toronto society. Fearing the loss of the city's British and Protestant character, native Torontonians could be very cruel to the new Jewish and Catholic immigrants of the 1940s and 1950s.[62] Women worried about police harassing their men as they congregated outside churches or clubs to chat with *paesani* as they had at home. Though some noted the kindness of certain strangers, they resented being stared at while riding the streetcars, or being treated like ignorant children.[63] Racism could run deep. In a 1954 letter to Ontario Premier Leslie Frost, a Toronto Orangeman wrote: "In regards to the Immigration to this country of so many Italians the place around here is literally crawling with these ignorant almost black people . . . [and] so many landing in this country with TB disease." While he saved his worst criticism for young Italian men suspected of being "armed with knives and . . . continually holding up people and especially ladies near parks and dark alleys," the writer expressed total distaste for foreign-speaking Catholic men and women and called for a stop to immigration from a Vatican-controlled and disease-infested Italy.[64]

Many southern Italian women contributed to their family's finances by entering the paid labour force. They were part of the dramatic postwar increase of women in general, including married women, who entered the Canadian work force. In 1961 almost 11 percent of over a million working women in Canada were European-born, of whom Italian-born women comprised over 17 percent. Some 15 percent of the over 100 000 working women in Ontario were European-born with the Italian-born making up 20 percent of the total. In Toronto 16 990 Italian women made up 7 percent of the 1961 female labour force. Working women, most of whom were probably postwar immigrants, accounted for 30–38 percent of the total Italian adult female population in Canada as well as Ontario in 1961; for Toronto this was nearly 40 percent. And these statistics do not take into account money raised by women at home.[65]

While Canadian-born women swelled the ranks of white-collar work, immigrant women provided cheap, unskilled, and semi-skilled female labour, suggesting that female migration from Europe after the war helped Canadian employers keep down labour costs. With the approval of employers who considered them hard-working and docile, Italian women in Toronto took on low-skilled, low paying jobs normally offered to immigrant women lacking English-language and other marketable skills beyond some domestic training. These included garment piece-work at home, operating steampresses, sewing and novelty-making machines, packaging, bottling and labelling, cafeteria work, and domestic service.[66]

Manufacturing and domestic service were the largest employers of European-born women in Canada and Ontario in 1961. Almost 57 percent of over 32 000 Italian women workers in Canada were in manufacturing, particularly clothing (50 percent), food and beverage (11 percent), textiles (12 percent), leather goods (6.2 percent), and unskilled factory work (6.6 percent). In service, where 28 percent of the total were located, nearly 76 percent of them were domestic servants. For Ontario, over 20 000 Italian women workers were similarly concentrated in manufacturing (50 percent) and service (31 percent). In the former category, they included leather cutters and sewers (38 percent), tailoresses (22 percent), food processing workers (14 percent), and unskilled factory workers (10 percent). Over 61 percent of the personal service workers were housekeepers, waitresses, and cooks; 38 percent were laundresses and dry-cleaners.[67]

Whether a woman worked outside the home depended on various factors such as a husband's attitude, child-bearing, availability of baby-sitters, and work opportunities. Alone, with menfolk, or in groups of female kin, women in search of work headed for the garment and light manufacturing areas of the city, where they went door to door asking for jobs. It took Pina four months of searching with her brother, who worked nights as a bowling alley janitor, before she found work packaging men's socks in a Spadina garment factory. Following an unsuccessful two-month search, Dalinda sewed children's clothes at home for five cents a garment until a cousin landed her a factory job several months later. Many women benefited from kin-networking at the work place as earlier employed women would arrange positions for incoming relatives.[68] Scholars have stressed how these occupational enclaves eased men's concerns about women working outside the home by providing traditional checks on female behaviour,[69] but the women themselves preferred to emphasize the utility of kinship ties and the camaraderie of the work place. Several said they would have worked wherever they found suitable jobs, and some, such as Ada and Maria L., found work for a time in ethnically mixed work places.[70]

Italian women's paid labour was part of a well-articulated working-class family strategy for success, one most often measured in terms of home ownership. Female wages helped support families through periods of seasonal male unemployment, especially for the men in construction and public works or out of town on farms, in mines, or on government building projects. Women's earnings paid for daily living expenses, such as groceries, clothing, and household necessities, while men's pay cheques went into savings deposits and toward buying houses and other investments. Characterized by low wages and high turnover, their work experience also reflected the gender inequalities of the postwar occupational structure. Predictably, the desire of capital for cheap workers and of immigrant working-class families for additional earnings were inextricably linked.[71]

Like many unskilled male and female workers, Italian women worked long hours at either monotonous or hazardous jobs that were physically demanding. Women employed in the drapery and clothing factories endured poor ventilation and high humidity, as well as speed-ups and close supervision. Women assembling items in plastics factories put up with dust and foul-smelling fumes. Laundry work required much sorting and carrying, and steampresses made the work place almost unbearable in summer. Italian women in factories also confronted the new time and work discipline of industrial capitalism and the impersonal relations between employers and workers. On the other hand, the daily experience of the work place, where Italian women learned to speak English from co-workers and sometimes forged friendships with non-*paese* and non-Italian women, may also have had a broadening impact on women hitherto confined to the household. By contrast, domestic workers cleaning house for middle-class clients toiled in total isolation from the rest of the working women.[72]

During the fifties and early sixties, Italian women workers did not express an articulated political response to their exploitation as female workers. This was linked to their low status as cheap and unskilled labour and to the barriers of language and ethnicity erected between women in the work place. Another major factor was the isolation of domestic workers. Household duties also kept women away from organizing meetings, and many were unsure about union organizers who visited their shops. Since joining a local might endanger their jobs, they feared compromising their main goal of helping the family's finances. Moreover, southern Italians were concentrated in industries characterized by high concentrations of unskilled female workers and high labour turnover rates. As a result, relatively few joined unions.[73]

Familial priorities, especially the duties of newly married women to bear and raise children, helped shape the timing and rhythm of women's participation in the labour force. Some women, such as Virginia, a trained seamstress from Pescara, Abruzzi, who worked for three years in a Spadina Street bathing-suit factory until she had her first child, never returned to work after starting families. Others, such as Assunta C., did not work until all their children reached school-age. Ten years after her arrival in Toronto in 1959 Assunta C. found work in a crest-making factory. Having worked for several years, Vincenza withdrew from the labour force for six years between 1960–66 to rear her children before returning to domestic service.[74]

Significant numbers of Italian women, however, regularly moved in and out of the labour force. They moved from one type of factory work to another, and from factory work to service jobs such as cafeteria and chamber-maid work as well as fruit and vegetable picking. Frequently women left jobs as a protest against poor working conditions and pay. Ada quit work as a shirt packager after losing some overtime hours, but in only a few weeks she secured work as a bow-machine operator for a factory producing wrapping and party accessories. Husbands sometimes urged their wives to quit. In 1963 Maria L. quit work as a Royal York Hotel chambermaid to appease her husband who disliked her cleaning up for strangers and working on Sundays, even though his father and sister also worked at the hotel. Several years earlier, however, Maria had spontaneously quit her job in a Woolworth's cafeteria when management shifted her into a more stressful job in inventory. That time her husband had immediately approved of her quitting, even though he had found her the job in the first place.[75]

Most often, women left work temporarily to fulfill family obligations—having children, tending to a family crisis, or resettling the family in a new home. Shortly after Angella immigrated with her parents in 1958, for example, she worked as a seamstress in a Spadina Street bathing-suit factory and continued to work there for two years following her marriage in 1959. One year later, she left to have a child and then returned in 1962 to similar work at a sportswear and leather factory on College Street. Three years later she left to have her second child and then returned to the same job two years later. Following the family's move to Willowdale, a Toronto suburb, she secured work in a local plastics factory, which she left in 1971 to have her third child only to return six months later. In 1973 she suffered a slipped disc at work, which kept her out of the labour force for ten years.[76]

When baby-sitting could not be provided by female kinfolk or *paesane*, many Italian women put off work until a sister, in-law, or cousin became available to watch the children. (These relatives might themselves be recent immigrants or new mothers.) Mothers who hired landladies or neighbours often felt uneasy about leaving their children with "strangers" unconnected to them by links of kin or village. Maria L. recalled how each morning she hated leaving her crying and clinging son with the landlady downstairs. Suspecting that her son was being neglected by the baby-sitter, who had young children of her own, Maria stopped working for over a year (with her husband's approval) until her mother's arrival in the city in 1959 gave her the confidence to re-enter the work-force. Opting for a different solution, Julia and Vincenza worked as domestic servants while they had pre-school youngsters and brought the children to their clients' homes.[77]

Nor did outside work reduce the burden of housekeeping. Although men performed certain tasks, such as stoking the coal furnace, shovelling snow, and perhaps watching children briefly while their wives shopped or cleaned, working women were responsible for the household chores, even during periods of male unemployment. Indeed, other women often watched the children while their mothers performed domestic tasks. This double burden hung heavily on the shoulders of Maria L., who for over a year combined full-time work as a steampress operator with caring for a son, a husband, and his father and two brothers. "Oh poor me," she recalled, "full-time work . . . wash, clean, cook. . . . I did all that! I was really just a girl, nineteen years old and thin, thin like a stick. I had four men, a baby. I was with no washing-machine. I would go down to the laundry tub. . . . Then I had to cook and I had to work. And it was not only me." Julia probably voiced the frustration of many working women when she said: "Of course he should help in the house. My back I hurt it at work, it hurts to wash the floor, pick up the clothes. But what you gonna do? Can't have a fight every day about it so I do it. But no it's not right!"[78]

Notwithstanding the obstacles to unionization, assumptions regarding Italian women's alleged docility and their outright hostility to unionization may be exaggerated. At a time when female militancy in the work place was not pronounced, it is not surprising that Italian immigrant women did not become politicized during the 1950s. Nor is there any reason to assume they should have felt any sense of working-class solidarity with their Canadian-born sisters, especially white-collar workers. Some women explained that for years the topic of unionization had never come up in the work place. Employers no doubt also took advantage of ethnic and cultural divisions among new arrivals.

In contrast to Italian women radicalized by their participation in the wartime Resistance movement—women who became socialists and communists and who, by the early 1960s, spearheaded Italy's modern feminist movement with the creation of Unione Donne Italiane—most southern peasant women who came to Toronto had little if any prior experience with industrial work and the traditions of worker protest.[79] (There were communists in the South. They included former landless *braccianti* who benefited from land reforms initiated under Italy's postwar reconstruction program as well as peasants, though probably none of the latter came to Canada.) But as peasants long resentful of the exploitation they had suffered at the hands of landowners and local élites, Italian women perhaps understood instinctively the exploitative relations between employers and workers, and many were truly angered by the injustices they suffered as working immigrant women. Even Julia, an anti-unionist, dismissed what she considered ruling-class rhetoric that portrayed Canada as a land of limitless opportunity. "Why feel grateful?" she said. "We really suffered for what we got. I have four back operations. I have to leave my kids alone and work.... And we don't live like kings and queens. I work hard for what I got." Moreover, increasing numbers of women grew to support unionization over the years not only because higher wages further helped their families but because they identified improved working conditions and health benefits won during the sixties and early seventies with a recognition of their labour and with self-respect. In Dalinda's words, "Sure we should get more money, we work hard for it, we leave our kids, come home tired, do the dirty jobs."[80]

The entry of southern Italian peasant women into Toronto's postwar labour force reflected a pattern of continuity, for women had been important contributors to the peasant family economy in the Mezzogiorno. Traditional values that stressed the obligation of all family members to contribute to the family's well-being eased the transition into Toronto's industrial economy. Since women's work was already justified in terms of peasant survival, no dramatic change in values was needed to allow these immigrant women to work outside the home. Women themselves argued that they were accustomed to working long and hard for the family. "I went to work to help out the family," was a common response. Given the scarcity of resources accessible to southern Italian immigrant families newly arrived in Toronto during the forties and fifties, additional wages earned by women, including those at home, amounted to an effective familialist response.[81]

To a remarkable degree southern Italian families preserved traditional cultural forms and familial arrangements and thereby resisted disintegration. Problems confronted by working women were often handled effectively within the context of family and kinship networks. Even so, women's entry into an urban, industrial work force did not occur without considerable strain and difficult adjustments, especially for married women. These strains reflected a dialectical process by which southern Italian peasants became transformed into working-class families. Their familial and collectivist behaviour was not simply the expression of traditional peasant culture; it also reflected their new economic position as working-class families coping with conditions of scarcity and restriction under industrial capitalism. This held particular significance for working Italian women, a fact ignored by scholars who view Italian immigrant women exclusively in terms of family and home. How demands of family and work conflicted with but also complemented each other also requires consideration.[82]

Motivated by a commitment to family, southern Italian women linked their self-identification as women and mothers to the paid and unpaid labour they performed for the benefit of parents, husbands, and children. Whether at home or at work, they took on dirty and difficult jobs and cut costs wherever possible. In the process they developed a conception of feminine respectability that was rooted in both their peasant and immigrant working-class experiences, and that expressed the pride of women who saw themselves as indispensable to their family. Stripped of notions of reserved femininity and delicate demeanour, it also contrasted sharply with postwar middle-class models of womanhood.[83] While the nature of their labour was largely transformed when they entered Toronto's industrial economy, southern Italian women's paid and unpaid work remained critical to the daily survival of their newly arrived families in postwar Toronto.

NOTES

1. I would like to thank Ruth Frager, Margaret Hobbs, Daphne Read, Janice Newton, Janet Patterson, Ian Radforth, and Joan Sangster for their comments on earlier drafts of this paper. And many thanks to the women I interviewed, whose real names I used not only with their approval but at their insistence.

2. Interview with Maria Rotolo.

3. Samuel Sidlofsky, "Post-War Immigrants in the Changing Metropolis with Special Reference to Toronto's Italian Population" (PhD dissertation, University of Toronto, 1969), ch. 1; Franc Sturino, "Family and Kin Cohesion among South Italian Immigrants in Toronto" in *The Italian Immigrant Woman in North America*, ed. Betty Boyd Caroli, Robert F. Harney, and Lydio F. Tomasi (Toronto, 1978); A.T. Bouscaren, *European Economic Migrations* (The Hague, 1969).

4. Sidlofsky, "Post-War Immigrants," 97–110; Sturino, "Family and Kin," 288–90; Freda Hawkins, *Canada and Immigration: Public Policy and Public Concern* (Montreal, 1972), 47–47; Jeremy Boissevain, *The Italians of Montreal: Social Adjustment in a Plural Society* (Ottawa, 1970), 10.

5. Department of Citizenship and Immigration, *Annual Report*, 1950–62, tables indicating dependants and intended employment, my calculations.

6. "White Paper, Canadian Immigration Policy," 1966, cited in Hawkins, *Canada and Immigration*, 9–10; Sturino, "Family and Kin," 291; Sidlofsky, "Post-War Immigrants," 97–101. See also Istituto Centrale di Statistica, *Annuario Italiano* (Rome, 1951–60).

7. Public Archives of Ontario (hereafter PAO), Ontario, Department of Planning and Development, Immigration Branch Files (hereafter IBF), "The Bulletin Council for Social Service," no. 104, Church of England of Canada, 15 Oct. 1941, 15–19. I would like to thank Donald McCloud at the PAO for making these materials available to me.

8. PAO, IBF, E.H. Gurton, Canadian Manager, British Dominions Emigration Society, Montreal, to Ontario Immigration Branch, 1 June 1951, 2b.

9. A departmental memo to the minister responsible for Immigration, William Griesinger, was critical of the federal government for not attracting more British immigrants and advised him that Ontario must secure federal help in its effort to maintain a racial and religious balance in the province, "preferably one British to four others. . . . [A]ny preference to British is given simply because they are our greatest source of skilled help and a minimum readjustment [sic] to our way of life." PAO, IBF, F.W. Stanley to William Griesinger, 28 Nov. 1950; see also Griesinger to Stanley, 30 Oct. 1950; *Telegram* (Toronto), 27 Dec. 1950 (clipping); see also files on the 1951 plan to recruit British tradesmen for Ontario manufacturers.

10. Public Archives of Canada (hereafter PAC), Immigration Branch Records (hereafter IR), vol. 131, Laval Fortier to acting Commissioner of Immigration Overseas, 4 Oct. 1949.

11. Department of Citizenship and Immigration, *Annual Report*, 1950–61, tables on intended occupation, my calculations.

12. PAC, IR, vol. 131, Department of External Affairs Statement, 29 March 1950; A.D.P. Heeney Memo, 30 March 1950; House of Commons, *Debates*, 28 March 1950, 1208.

13. Rudolf Vecoli, "Contadini in Chicago: A Critique of the Uprooted," *Journal of American History* 51 (1964); Robert Foerster, *The Italian Emigration of Our Times* (Cambridge, 1919); Rudolph Bell, *Fate and Honour, Family and Village: Demographic and Cultural Change in Rural Italy Since 1800* (Chicago, 1979).

14. Interview with Assunta Capozzi and Maria Lombardi.

15. Bell, *Fate and Honour*, 123–48; J.P. Cole, *Italy: An Introductory Geography* (New York, 1964); Alan B. Mountjoy, *The Mezzogiorno* (London, 1973).

16. Interview with Maria Lombardi and Assunta Carmosino; also interviews with Maria Rotolo, Assunta Capozzi, Maria Sangenesi, Maria Carmosino, and Dalinda Vincenza Cerulli.

17. Interviews with Maria Rotolo and Vincenza Cerulli.

18. Interviews with Salvatore and Josephine D'Agostino and Julia Toscano. See also Robert F. Harney, "Men Without Women: Italian Migrants in Canada, 1885 to 1930" in *Italian Immigrant Women*; his "Montreal's King of Italian Labour: A Case Study of Padronism," *Labour/Le Travailleur* 4 (1979); Bruno Ramirez, "Workers Without a 'Cause': Italian Immigrant Labour in Montreal, 1880–1930" (paper presented to the Canadian Historical Association, Annual Meeting, 1983).

19. On South Italian peasants, general monographs include: Edward Banfield, *The Moral Order of a Backward Society* (Illinois, 1958); Jan Brogger, *Montavarese: A Study of Peasant Society and Culture in Southern Italy* (Oslo, 1971); Constance Cronin, *The Sting of Change: Sicilians in Sicily and Australia* (Chicago, 1970); John Davis, *Land and Family in Pisticci* (London, 1973); Joseph Lopreato, *Peasants No More! Social Class and Social Change in an Underdeveloped Society* (San Francisco, 1967).

20. Interview with Julia Toscano.

21. Vecoli, "Contadini"; Bell, *Fate and Honour*, 2–3, 72–76; Leonard W. Moss and Stephen C. Cappannaro, "Patterns of Kinship, Comparaggio and Community in a South Italian Village," *Anthropological Quarterly* 33 (1960).

22. See Brogger, *Montavarese*, 106–20; Cronin, *Sting of Change*, ch. 4; Bell, *Fate and Honour*, 90, 120–23; Ann Cornelisen, *Women of the Shadows: A Study of the Wives and Mothers of Southern Italy* (New York, 1970); Virginia Yans-McLaughlin, "Patterns of Work and Family Organization: Buffalo's Italians" in *The Family in History: Interdisciplinary Essays*, ed. Theodore R. Rabb and Robert I. Rotberg, and her *Family and Community: Italian Immigrants in Buffalo, 1880–1930*, 180–217. Also interviews with Ada Carmosino, Maria Lombardi, Maria Carmosino, Dalinda Lombardi-Iacovetta, and others.

23. Interview with Assunta Capozzi.

24. Interviews. Also, Ann Bravo, "Solidarity and Loneliness: Piedmontese Peasant Women at the Turn of the Century," *International Journal of Oral History* 3 (June 1982); Brogger, *Montavarese*, 41–50, 106–09; Miriam Cohen, "Italian-American Women in New York City, 1900–1950: Work and School" (paper presented to the American Studies Association, San Antonio, Texas, 1975); Cornelisen, *Women of the Shadows*, 71–129; Columba Furio, "The Cultural Background of the Italian Immigrant Woman and Its Impact on Her Unionization in the New York City Garment Industry" in *Pane e Lavoro: The Italian American Working Class*, ed.

George E. Pozetta; Donna Gabaccia, "Sicilian Women and the 'Marriage Market': 1860–1920" (paper and discussion at the Sixth Berkshire Conference on the History of Women, June 1984); Simonetta Piccone Stella, *Ragazze del sud* (Rome, 1979).

25. Interview with Marie Lombardi, Assunta Capozzi, Dalinda Lombardi-Iacovetta.

26. Interviews. Yans-McLaughlin, *Family and Community*, 26–27; Bell, *Fate and Honour*, 130–33; Sydney Tarrow, *Peasant Communism in Southern Italy* (New Haven, 1967). On an earlier period, see also Louise A. Tilly and Joan Scott, *Women, Work, and Family* (New York, 1978).

27. Interviews with Julia Toscano, Maria Sangenesi, Ada Carmosino, Maria Carmosino, and Josephine D'Agostino.

28. Interviews with Josephine D'Agostino, Marie Rotolo, Assunta Capozzi, and Dalinda Lombardi-Iacovetta.

29. Brogger, *Montavarese*, 41–109; Bell, *Fate and Honour*, 120–28. On men's role in feasts, see, for example, Enrico Cumbo, "The Feats of the Madonna del Monte," *Polyphony* 5, 2 (Fall/Winter 1983). See also Ernestine Friedl, "The Position of Women: Appearance and Reality," *Anthropological Quarterly* 40 (1967).

30. Cornelisen, *Women of the Shadows*, 222–24, 57–93; see also Vincenza Scarpaci, "La Contadina, The Plaything of the Middle-Class Woman Historian," Occasional Papers on Ethnic and Immigration Studies, Multicultural History Society of Ontario (Toronto, 1972); and her "Angella Bambace and the International Ladies Garment Workers Union: the Search for an Elusive Activist" in Pozetta, *Pane e Lavoro*.

31. Cronin, *Sting of Change*, 78; interview with Julia Toscano.

32. Bravo, "Peasant Women."

33. See especially Cornelisen, *Women of the Shadows*; Bell, *Fate and Honour*; Banfield, *Backward Society*. See also Sydel Silverman, "Agricultural Organization, Social Structure, and Values in Italy: Amoral Familialism Reconsidered," *American Anthropologist* 70 (Feb. 1968).

34. Interviews with Maria Sangenesi, Dalinda Lombardi-Iacovetta, Maria Lombardi, Ada Carmosino, Maria Rotolo, Assunta Capozzi.

35. Interviews; Gabaccia "Sicilian Women." Most studies deal with Italian women almost exclusively in terms of family and home. See for example, Vaneeta D'Andrea, "The Social Role Identity of Italian-American Women: An Analysis of Familial and Comparison of Familial and Religious Expectations" (paper presented to the American Italian Association, 1980); Harriet Perry, "The Metonymic Definition of the Female and Concept of Honour Among Italian Immigrant Families in Toronto" in *Italian Immigrant Women*. At the Columbus Centre in Toronto, Samuel Bailey recently described Italian women in prewar Argentina, New York, and Toronto as living in insular worlds defined by the particular block on which they resided with their children and families. By contrast, men identified more easily with the larger ethnic community. The implication is that women stayed at home and played no role in the ambience of the ethnic enclave.

36. Harney, "Men Without Women."

37. Mountjoy, *Mezzogiorno*, 32–36; Tarrow, *Peasant Communism*. See also Carlo Levi, *Christ Stopped at Eboli* (New York, 1946). On chain migration, see J.S. MacDonald, "Italy's Rural Structure and Migration," *Occidente* 12, 5 (Sept. 1956); J.S. MacDonald and L.D. MacDonald, "Chain Migration, Ethnic Neighborhood Formation and Social Networks," *Millbank Memorial Fund Quarterly* 13 (1964);

Harvey Choldin, "Kinship Networks in the Migration Process," *International Migration Review* 7 (Summer 1973). On Toronto, see, Sidlofsky, "Immigrants"; Sturino, "Family and Kin"; his "Contours of Postwar Italian Immigration to Toronto," *Polyphony* 6, 1 (Spring/Summer 1984).

38. Hawkins, *Canada and Immigration*, 47–48. See also "White Paper," 9–10.

39. Interview with Assunta Capozzi and Assunta Carmosino.

40. On an earlier period, see: Joseph Barton, *Peasants and Strangers: Italians, Rumanians and Slovaks in an American City, 1890–1930*; John Bodnar, "Immigration and Modernization: The Case of Slavic Peasants in Industrial America," *Journal of Social History* 10 (Fall 1976); Yans-McLaughlin, *Family and Community*, 33–36; Harney and Scarpaci, eds., *Little Italies in North America* (Toronto, 1983). See also John Baxevanis, "The Decision to Migrate" in his *Economy and Population Movements in the Peloponnesos of Greece* (Athens, 1972), 60–75.

41. Interview with Maria Sangenesi.

42. Iolanda Marano interviewed by Pina Stanghieri.

43. Interview with Josephine D'Agostino.

44. Interviews with Maria Carmosino, Maria Lombardi, Assunta Capozzi, Vincenza Cerulli, Dalinda Lombardi-Iacovetta.

45. Nicoletta DeThomasis interviewed by Rosemary DeThomasis.

46. Julia Toscano's father, for example, spent her entire girlhood outside the country— in Albany from 1936–38, Germany 1938–39, and Argentina for six years after the war. For a discussion of the impact of men's immigration on home life in Italy see: Harney, "Without Women"; N. Douglas, *Old Calabria* (New York, 1928).

47. Interview with Dalinda Lombardi-Iacovetta, Vincenza Cerulli, and Julia Toscano.

48. Interviews. On postwar settlement, see Sidlofsky, "Immigrants"; Sturino, "Family and Kin" and his "Postwar Immigration."

49. Interview with Vincenza Cerulli and Julia Toscano. Also with Josephine D'Agostino.

50. Harney, "Boarding and Belonging," *Urban History Review* 2 (Oct. 1978). On the importance of kin and boarding for an earlier period see also: Michael Anderson, *Family Structure in Nineteenth Century Lancashire* (Cambridge, 1971); John Modell and Tamara K. Hareven, "Urbanization and the Malleable Household: An Examination of Boarding and Lodging in American Families" in *Family and Kin in Urban Communities, 1700–1930*, ed. T. Hareven (New York, 1977); and her "Family Time and Industrial Time: Family and Work in a Planned Corporate Town, 1900–1924," ibid.

51. Interviews with Ada Carmosino, Maria Rotolo, Maria Lombardi, Maria Sangenesi, Maria Carmosino, Dalinda Lombardi-Iacovetta.

52. Ibid.

53. Interview with Maria Sangenesi. See also *Canadian Ethnic Studies*, special issue on Ethnicity and Femininity, 1981.

54. Interview with Dalinda Lombardi-Iacovetta, Maria Lombardi, Ada Carmosino, Maria Rotolo, Josephine D'Agostino. All of them obtained appliances several years after their arrival.

55. Interview with Assunta Capozzi and Maria Sangenesi; also with Assunta Carmosino. See also labour force statistics indicating Italian-born women who took in washing, boarders, and children. Canada, *Census 1951*. Others, of course, went unrecorded (tables on Canada and Ontario).

56. Of course, working women might also perform this role. Interview with Maria Sangenesi, Maria Rotolo, Vincenza Cerulli, Maria Lombardi, Ada Carmosino, Julia Toscano, and Josephine D'Agostino.

57. Interviews with Ada Carmosino, Maria Lombardi, Dalinda Lombardi-Iacovetta; also with Vincenza Cerulli and Josephine D'Agostino.

58. Interview with Maria Sangenesi and Assunta Capozzi.

59. Dalinda Lombardi-Iacovetta was robbed one day in 1953 while she was at home with her two children doing garment piece-work. The thief, who came to the door, armed with a knife, got away with two weeks' pay—twenty dollars.

60. Interview with Maria Sangenesi and Josephine D'Agostino.

61. Interview with Maria Lombardi (Maria reported on the story above, in which a cousin by marriage was involved); also with Dalinda Lombardi-Iacovetta, Maria Rotolo, Ada Carmosino. Also, in conversation with several Italian-born men who attended elementary and secondary school in Toronto during the 1950s. All stressed backyard brawls in which they engaged and the embarrassment of being put behind in school grade level because of language difficulties.

62. See, for example, *Debates*, 13 June 1950; Margot Gibb-Clarke, *Globe and Mail*, 20 Oct. 1984, 18; Sturino, "Postwar Immigration to Toronto" (paper given to the Columbus Centre, 1984).

63. Interviews. Also interviews with Salvatore D'Agostino, Camilo Schiuli, and Salvatore Carmosino.

64. PAO, IBF, F.J. Love to Premier Leslie Frost, 1 Sept. 1954. See also response; H.K. Warrander to J.L. Love, 2 Sept. 1954. Following an explanation that the Ontario government carried out "a very small selective type of immigration programme . . . [having] to do only immigrants from the United Kingdom," it added: "Other immigrants . . . are dealt with by the Federal Government departments and I am therefore sorry to say that we have no control over that type of immigrant or whether or not he comes here in a healthy condition."

65. Canada, *Census* 1951. The figures for Toronto were provided by Statistics Canada researchers. On postwar women and work see: Pat Armstrong and Hugh Armstrong, *The Double Ghetto* (Toronto, 1978); Julie White, *Women and Unions* (Ottawa, 1980).

66. Ibid. See also Sheila McLeod Arnopolous, *Problems of Immigrant Women in the Canadian Labour Force* (Ottawa, 1979); Laura C. Johnson with Robert C. Johnson, *The Seam Allowance: Industrial Home Sewing in Canada* (Toronto, 1982); Monica Boyd, "The Status of Immigrant Women in Canada" in *Women in Canada*, ed. Marylee Stephenson (Don Mills, ON, 1977); Anthony Richmond, *Immigrants and Ethnic Groups in Metropolitan Toronto* (Toronto, 1967). For useful theoretical discussions of immigrant and migrant women see: "Why Do Women Migrate? Towards Understanding of the Sex-Selectivity in the Migratory Movements of Labour," *Studie Emigrazione* 20 (June 1983); Annie Phizacklea, ed., *One Way Ticket*.

67. Canada, *Census* 1951, my calculations.

68. Interviews with Josephine D'Agostino, Dalinda Lombardi-Iacovetta, Maria Rotolo; also with Maria Lombardi, Maria Carmosino, Vincenza Cerulli, Julia Toscano, Ada Carmosino.

69. See, for example, Yans-McLaughlin, *Family and Community*; Sturino, "Postwar Immigrants."

70. Interviews especially with Maria Lombardi and Ada Carmosino.

71. Interviews; Bettina Bradbury made this argument for an earlier period on working-class families in Montreal. See her "The Fragmented Family: Family Strategies in

the Face of Death, Illness and Poverty, Montreal, 1860–1885" in *Childhood and Family in Canadian History*, ed. Joy Parr (Toronto, 1982).

72. Interviews. Studies on working women in Canada include Ruth Frager, "No Proper Deal: Women Workers and the Canadian Labour Movement, 1870–1930" in *Union Sisters: Women in the Labour Movement*, ed. Lynda Briskin and Linda Yanz (Toronto, 1984); Joan Sangster, "The 1907 Bell Telephone Strike; Organizing Women Workers," *Labour/Le Travailleur* (1978); Wayne Roberts, *Honest Womanhood* (Toronto, 1976).

73. White, *Women and Unions*.

74. Virginia interviewed by Tina D'Accunto; interview with Assunta Capozzi and Vincenza Cerulli.

75. Interview with Ada Carmosino and Maria Lombardi.

76. Angella interviewed by Tina D'Accunto; similar patterns emerged for Dalinda Lombardi-Iacovetta, Maria Rotolo, Maria Carmosino, Maria Lombardi.

77. Interview with Maria Lombardi, Julia Toscano, and Vincenza Cerulli; also with Dalinda Lombardi-Iacovetta, Maria Rotolo, and Assunta Carmosino.

78. Interview with Maria Lombardi and Julia Toscano.

79. Judith Adler Hellman, "The Italian Communists, the Women's Question, and the Challenge of Feminism," *Studies in Political Economy* 13 (Spring 1985); M. Jane Slaughter, "Women's Politics and Women's Culture: The Case of Women in the Italian Resistance" (paper presented to the Sixth Berkshire Conference on the History of Women, June 1984); Margherita Repetto Alaia, "The Unione Donne Italiane: Women's Liberation and the Italian Workers' Movement, 1945–1980" (paper presented to the Sixth Berkshire Conference on the History of Women, June 1984). On the South see, for example, Jane Kramer, *Unsettling Europe* (New York, 1972); P.A. Allum, "The South and National Politics, 1945–50" in *The Rebirth of Italy 1943–50*, ed. J.S. Woolf (New York, 1973).

80. Interview with Julia Toscano and Dalinda Lombardi-Iacovetta.

81. On an earlier period see Scott and Tilly, *Women, Work, and Family*.

82. Bodnar, "Modernization and Immigration."

83. See, for example, Betty Frieden, *The Feminine Mystique* (Harmondsworth, 1965).

FURTHER READINGS

○

ABBREVIATIONS

AHR   *Alberta Historical Review*
BCS   *BC Studies*
CES   *Canadian Ethnic Studies*
CHA   Canadian Historical Association
CHR   *Canadian Historical Review*
CIHA   Canadian Italian Historical Association
HS/SH   *Histoire sociale/Social History*
HSSM   *Historical and Scientific Society of Manitoba*
JCS   *Journal of Canadian Studies*
L/T   *Labour/Le Travail*
MHSO   Multicultural History Society of Ontario
OH   *Ontario History*
SH   *Saskatchewan History*

GENERAL

Avery, Donald. *"Dangerous Foreigners": European Immigrant Workers and Labour Radicalism in Canada, 1896–1932.* Toronto: McClelland & Stewart, 1979.

Behiels, Michael D. *Quebec and the Question of Immigration: From Ethnocentrism to Ethnic Pluralism, 1900–1985.* Ottawa: CHA, 1991.

Bradwin, Edmund. "Some Ethnic Groupings Among Campmen." *The Bunkhouse Man: A Study of Work and Pay in the Camps of Canada, 1903–1914.* Ed. Edmund Bradwin. Toronto: University of Toronto Press, 1972, 91–112.

Burnet, Jean R., and Howard Palmer. *"Coming Canadians": An Introduction to a History of Canada's Peoples.* Toronto: McClelland & Stewart, 1988.

Carrigan, D. Owen. "The Immigrant Experience in Halifax 1881–1931." *CES* 20, 3 (1988): 28–41.

Craig, Terrence L. "F.P. Grove and the 'Alien' Immigrant in the West." *JCS* 20, 2 (1985): 92–100.

Dirks, Gerald. *Canada's Refugee Policy: Indifference or Opportunism?* Montreal: McGill-Queen's University Press, 1977.

Dreisziger, N. Fred. "Watson Kirkconnell and the Cultural Credibility Gap Between Immigrants and the Native-Born in Canada." *Ethnic Canadians: Culture and Education.* Ed. Martin Kovacs. Regina: Canadian Plains Research Center, 1978, 87–96.

Emery, G.N. "The Methodist Church and the 'European Foreigners' of Winnipeg, the All Peoples Mission, 1889–1914." *HSSM*, 3rd Ser., 28 (1971–72): 85–100.

Finkel, Alvin. "Canadian Immigration Policy and the Cold War, 1945–1980." *JCS* 21, 3 (1986): 53–70.

Harney, Robert F. "Ethnicity and Neighbourhoods." *Gathering Place: Peoples and Neighborhoods of Toronto, 1834–1945*. Ed. Robert F. Harney. Toronto: MHSO, 1985, 1–24.

———, and H. Troper. *Immigrants: A Portrait of the Urban Experience, 1890–1930*. Toronto: Van Nostrand Reinhold, 1975.

Hawkins, Freda. *Canada and Immigration: Public Policy and Public Concern*. Montreal: McGill-Queen's University Press, 1972, 1978.

———. *Critical Years in Immigration: Canada and Australia Compared*. Montreal: McGill-Queen's University Press, 1989.

Johnson, Stanley. *A History of Emigration from the United Kingdom to North America, 1769–1912*. London: George Routledge & Sons, 1913.

Knowles, Valerie. *Strangers at Our Gates: Canadian Immigration and Immigration Policy, 1540–1940*. Toronto: Dundurn Press, 1992.

Macdonald, Norman. *Canada: Immigration and Colonization, 1843–1903*. Toronto: Macmillan, 1966.

Malarek, Victor. *Heaven's Gate: Canada's Immigration Fiasco*. Toronto: Macmillan, 1987.

Matas, David, and Ilena Simon. *Closing the Doors: The Failure of Refugee Protection*. Toronto: Summerhill Press, 1989.

Neary, Peter. "Canadian Immigration Policy and the Newfoundlanders, 1912–1939." *Acadiensis* 11, 2 (Spring 1982): 69–83.

Palmer, Howard. "Canadian Immigration and Ethnic History in the 1970s and 1980s." *JCS* 17, 1 (Spring 1982): 35–50.

———. "Ethnic Relations and the Paranoid Style: Nativism, Nationalism, and Populism in Alberta, 1945–50." *CES* 23, 3 (1991): 7–31.

———. *Ethnicity and Politics in Canada Since Confederation*. Ottawa: CHA, 1991.

———. *Patterns of Prejudice: A History of Nativism in Alberta*. Toronto: McClelland & Stewart, 1982.

Rodel, Alti. "Nazi War Criminals in Canada: The Historical and Policy Setting from the 1940s to the Present." Report prepared for the Commission of Inquiry on War Criminals, Sept. 1986.

Scott, Stanley. "A Profusion of Issues: Immigrant Labourers, the World War, and the Cominco Strike of 1917." *L/T* 2 (1977): 54–78.

Sears, Alan. "Immigration and Social Policy." *Studies in Political Economy* 33 (Autumn 1990): 91–112.

Shack, Sybil. "The Immigrant Child in the Manitoba Schools in the Early Twentieth Century." *HSSM*, 3rd. ser., 30 (1973–74): 17–32.

Whitaker, Reg. *Canadian Immigration Policy Since Confederation*. Ottawa: CHA, 1991.

Woodsworth, J.S. *Strangers Within Our Gates: Or Coming Canadians*. Ed. Michael Bliss. Toronto: University of Toronto Press, 1972 [1909].

BRITISH ISLES

ENGLISH AND WELSH

Avery, Donald H. "British-born 'Radicals' in North America, 1900–41: The Case of Sam Scarlett." *CES* 10, 2 (1978): 65–85.

Barber, Marilyn, and P.A. Buckner, eds. *Immigrant Domestic Servants in Canada.* Ottawa: CHA, 1991.

Cherwinski, W.J.C. "Misfits, Malcontents and Malingerers: The British Harvester Movement of 1928." *The Developing West: Essays on Canadian History in Honor of Lewis H. Thomas.* Ed. John E. Foster. Edmonton: University of Alberta Press, 1983, 271–302.

Excerpt from "Settling on Canada's Free Land [issued 1912]: Advice to English Emigrants in 1912." *SH* 32, 1 (1979): 35.

Fedorowich, Kent. "The Migration of British Ex-Servicemen to Canada and the Role of the Naval and Military Emigration League, 1899–1914." *HS/SH* 25, 49 (May 1992): 75–99.

Foster, Keith. "The Barr Colonists: Their Arrival and Impact on the Canadian North-West." *SH* 35, 3 (1982): 81–100.

Glynn, Desmond. "'Exporting Outcast London': Assisted Emigration to Canada, 1886–1914." *HS/SH* 15, 29 (May 1982): 209–38.

Godkin, James Easton. "The Yeomanry Veterans of Elizabethtown." *OH* 62, 4 (1971): 243–64.

Harris, Richard. "Canada's All Right: The Lives and Loyalties of Immigrant Families in a Toronto Suburb, 1900–1945." *Canadian Geographer/Le Géographe Canadien* 36, 1 (Spring 1992): 13–30.

———. "A Working-Class Suburb for Immigrants: Toronto 1909–1913." *Geographical Review* 81, 3 (1991): 318–32.

Hopkins, Elizabeth. "A Prison-House for Prosperity: The Immigrant Experience of the Nineteenth-Century Upper-Class British Woman." *Looking into My Sister's Eyes: An Exploration in Women's History.* Ed. Jean Burnet. Toronto: MHSO, 1986, 7–19.

Johnson, J. Keith. "The Chelsea Pensioners in Upper Canada." *OH* 53 (1961): 273–89.

Maclennan, Gordon. "A Contribution to the Ethnohistory of Saskatchewan's Patagonian Welsh Settlement." *CES* 7, 2 (1975): 57–72.

Martin, Ged. "British Attitudes to Prairie Settlement." *AHR* 22, 1 (Winter 1974): 1–11.

McCormack, A. Ross. "British Working-Class Immigrants and Canadian Radicalism: The Case of Arthur Puttee." *CES* 10, 2 (1978): 22–37.

Roberts, Barbara. "'A Work of Empire': Canadian Reformers and British Female Immigration." *A Not Unreasonable Claim: Women and Reform in Canada, 1880s–1920s.* Ed. Linda Kealey. Toronto: Women's Press, 1979, 185–201.

Rodwell, Lloyd W. "Homestead Venture, 1883–1892: An Ayrshire Man's Letters Home." *SH* 15, 1 (1962): 30–36.

Rowell, Gladys M. "Memories of an English Settler, Pt. 1." *AHR* 29, 2 (Spring 1981): 12–19.

———. "Memories of an English Settler, Pt. 2." *AHR* 30, 2 (Spring 1982): 30–36.

Thomas, Lewis H. "From Pampas to the Prairies: The Welsh Migration of 1902." *SH* 24, 1 (1971): 1–12.

SCOTS

Bumsted, J.M. *The Scots in Canada*. Ottawa: CHA, 1982.

Gibson, John G. "Piper John Mackay and Roderick McLennan: A Tale of Two Immigrants and Their Incomplete Genealogy." *Nova Scotia Historical Review* 2, 2 (1982): 69–82.

McLean, Marianne. *The People of Glengarry: Highlanders in Transition, 1745–1820*. Montreal: McGill-Queen's University Press, 1991.

Moore, Christopher. "The Disposition to Settle: The Royal Highland Emigrants and Loyalist Settlement in Upper Canada, 1784." *OH* 76, 4 (1984): 306–25.

Reid, Richard Gavin. "From the Old Land to the New (Pt. 1)." *AHR* 5, 1 (Winter 1957): 3–9.

———. "From the Old Land to the New (Pt. 2)." *AHR* 5, 2 (Spring 1957): 15–21.

Stuart, Kent. "The Scottish Crofter Colony, Saltcoats, 1889–1904." *SH* 24 (1971): 41–50.

Talman, James J. "Three Scottish-Canadian Newspaper Editor Poets." *CHR* 28, 2 (1947): 166–77.

Wade, Jill. "The 'Gigantic Scheme': Crofter Immigration and Deep Sea Fisheries Development for BC, 1887–1893." *BCS* 53 (Spring 1982): 28–44.

Wallace, Malcolm. "Pioneers of the Scotch Settlement on the Shore of Lake St Clair." *OH* 41, 4 (1949): 173–200.

IRISH

Akenson, Donald H. "An Agnostic View of the Historiography of the Irish-Americans." *L/T* 14 (Fall 1984): 123–59.

———. *Being Had: Historians, Evidence and the Irish in North America*. Port Credit, ON: P.D. Meany Publishers, 1985.

Cottrell, Michael. "St Patrick's Day Parades in Nineteenth-Century Toronto: A Study of Immigrant Adjustment and Elite Control." *HS/SH* 25, 49 (May 1992): 57–73.

De Brou, David. "The Rose, the Shamrock and the Cabbage: The Battle for Irish Voters in Upper-Town Quebec, 1827–1836." *HS/SH* 24, 48 (Nov. 1991): 305–34.

Elliott, Bruce S. *Irish Migrants in the Canadas: A New Approach*. Montreal: McGill-Queen's University Press, 1988.

———. "Regionalized Immigration and Settlement Patterns of the Irish in Upper Canada." *The Untold Story: The Irish in Canada*. Vol. 1. Ed. Robert O'Driscoll and Lorna Reynolds. Toronto: Celtic Arts of Canada, 1988, 309–18.

Gwyn, Julian. "The Irish in the Napanee River Valley: Camden East Township, 1851–1881." *The Untold Story: The Irish in Canada*. Vol. 1. Ed. Robert O'Driscoll and Lorna Reynolds. Toronto: Celtic Arts of Canada, 1988, 355–377.

Houston, Cecil J., and William J. Smyth. "Irish Emigrants to Canada: Whence They Came." *The Untold Story: The Irish in Canada*. Vol. 1. Ed. Robert O'Driscoll and Lorna Reynolds. Toronto: Celtic Arts of Canada, 1988, 27–35.

Johnson, J.K. "Colonel James FitzGibbon and the Suppression of Irish Riots in Upper Canada." *OH* 58, 3 (1966): 139–56.

Keep, G.R.C. "The Irish Adjustment in Montreal." *CHR* 31, 1 (1950): 39–46.

Laighin, Padraic. "Grosse-Île: The Holocaust Revisited." *The Untold Story: The Irish in Canada*. Vol. 1. Ed. Robert O'Driscoll and Lorna Reynolds. Toronto: Celtic Arts of Canada, 1988, 75–101.

Mannion, John J. "Irish Settlements in Eastern Canada: A Study of Cultural Transfer and Adaptation." *University of Toronto, Department of Geography Research Publications*. University of Toronto Press, 1974.

McGowan, Mark G. "The De-Greening of the Irish: Toronto's Irish-Catholic Press, Imperialism, and the Forging of a New Identity, 1887–1914." *CHA Historical Papers* (1989): 118–45.

Nicolson, Murray W. "Peasants in an Urban Society: The Irish Catholics in Victorian Toronto." *Gathering Place: Peoples and Neighborhoods of Toronto, 1834–1945*. Ed. Robert F. Harney. Toronto: MHSO, 1985, 47–73.

Pammett, H.T. "Assisted Emigration from Ireland to Upper Canada Under Peter Robinson." *OH* 31 (1936): 178–214.

Parr, G.J. "The Welcome and the Wake: Attitudes in Canada West Towards the Irish Famine Migration." *OH* 66, 2 (1974): 101–14.

Senior, H. "Ogle Gowan, Orangeism, and the Immigrant Question, 1830–1833." *OH* 66, 4 (1974): 193–210.

Toner, Peter M. "Occupation and Ethnicity: The Irish in New Brunswick." *CES* 20, 3 (1988): 155–65.

———. "The Origins of the New Brunswick Irish, 1851." *JCS* 23, 1/2 (1988): 104–19.

Woodham-Smith, Cecil. *The Great Hunger: Ireland 1845–1849*. New York: Harper & Row, 1962.

CHINA

Armentrout Ma, L. Eve. "A Chinese Statesman in Canada—1903: Translated from the Travel Journal of Liang Ch'i-ch'ao." *BCS* 59 (Autumn 1983): 28–43.

Barbeau, Marius. "Asiatic Migrations into America." *CHR* 13, 4 (1932): 403–17.

Chan, Anthony B. *Gold Mountain: The Chinese in the New World*. Vancouver: New Star, 1982.

Chuen-Yan, David Lai. "Chinese Attempts to Discourage Emigration to Canada: Some Findings from the Chinese Archives in Victoria." *BCS* 18 (Summer 1973): 33–49.

————. "Contribution of the Zhigongtang in Canada to the Huanghuagang Uprising in Canton, 1911." *CES* 14, 3 (1982): 95–104.

————. "The Demographic Structure of a Canadian Chinatown in the Mid-Twentieth Century." *CES* 11, 2 (1979): 49–62.

Day, Patricia. "A Choice Between Evils: The Chinese and the Construction of the Canadian Pacific Railway in British Columbia." *The CPR West: The Iron Road and the Making of a Nation*. Ed. Hugh A. Dempsey. Vancouver: Douglas & McIntyre, 1984, 13–34.

Li, Peter S. *The Chinese in Canada*. Toronto: Oxford University Press, 1988.

Nipp, Dora. "'But Women Did Come': Working Chinese Women in the Interwar Years." *Looking into My Sister's Eyes: An Exploration in Women's History*. Ed. Jean Burnet. Toronto: MHSO, 1986, 179–94.

————. "The Chinese in Toronto." *Gathering Place: Peoples and Neighborhoods of Toronto, 1834–1945*. Ed. Robert F. Harney. Toronto: MHSO, 1985, 147–75.

Roy, Patricia E. *A White Man's Province: British Columbia Politicians and Chinese and Japanese Immigrants, 1858–1914*. Vancouver: University of British Columbia Press, 1989.

Tan, Jin, and Patricia E. Roy. *The Chinese in Canada*. Ottawa: CHA, 1985.

Ward, W. Peter. White *Canada Forever: Popular Attitudes and Public Policy Towards Orientals in British Columbia*. Montreal: McGill-Queen's University Press, 1978.

Wickberg, Edgar, ed. *From China to Canada: A History of the Chinese Communities in Canada*. Toronto: McClelland & Stewart, 1982.

Yee, Paul. "Business Devices from Two Worlds: The Chinese in Early Vancouver." *BCS* 62 (Sept. 1984): 44–67.

————. "Sam Kee: A Chinese Business in Early Vancouver." *BCS* 69–70 (Spring/Summer 1986): 70–96.

EASTERN EUROPE

HUNGARIANS

Dojcsak, G.V. "The Mysterious Count Esterhazy." *SH* 26 (1973): 63–72.

Dreisziger, N. Fred, ed. *Struggle and Hope: The Hungarian Canadian Experience*. Toronto: McClelland & Stewart, 1982.

Kovacs, Martin L. "The Hungarian School Question." *Ethnic Canadians: Culture and Education*. Ed. Martin Kovacs. Regina: Canadian Plains Research Center, 1978, 333–58.

ESTONIANS

Aun, Karl. *The Political Refugees: A History of the Estonians in Canada*. Toronto: McClelland & Stewart, 1985.

Kovamess Kitching, Juta. "Sir John Pitka and His Estonian Colony in British Columbia." *CES* 23, 1 (1991): 103–18.

Palmer, Howard, and Tamara Palmer. "Estonians in Alberta." *AHR* 31, 3 (Summer 1983): 22–34.

LITHUANIANS

Danys, Milda. *DP: Lithuanian Immigration to Canada after the Second World War.* Toronto: MHSO, 1986.

POLES

Avery, D.H., and J.F. Fedorowicz. *The Poles in Canada.* Ottawa: CHA, 1982.

Baker, Richard P. "The Adaptation of Polish Immigrants to Toronto: The Solitary Wave." *CES* 21, 3 (1989): 74–90.

Greening, W.E. *Sir Casimir Gzowski: A Biography.* Toronto: Burns and MacEachern, 1959.

Heydenkorn, Benedykt, ed. *Memoirs of Polish Immigrants in Canada.* Toronto: Canadian Polish Research Institute, 1979.

Kojder, Apolonja. "Women and the Polish Alliance of Canada." *Looking into My Sister's Eyes: An Exploration in Women's History.* Ed. Jean Burnet. Toronto: MHSO, 1986, 91–105.

Matejko, Joanna, ed. *Polish Settlers in Alberta: Reminiscences and Biographies.* Toronto: Polish Alliance Press, 1979.

Prymak, Thomas M. "Recent Scholarship on Polyethnic Emigration from the Republic of Poland to Canada Between the Wars." *CES* 23, 1 (1991): 58–70.

Radecki, Henry. *Ethnic Organizational Dynamics: The Polish Group in Canada.* Waterloo: Wilfrid Laurier University Press, 1979.

———, and Benedykt Heydenkorn. *A Member of a Distinguished Family: The Polish Group in Canada.* Toronto: McClelland & Stewart, 1976.

Shadrodi, Zofia. "The Polish Community in Toronto in the Early Twentieth Century." *Gathering Place: Peoples and Neighborhoods of Toronto, 1834–1945.* Ed. Robert F. Harney. Toronto: MHSO, 1985, 243–55.

Stachniak, Eva. "Canadian Reflections: The Image of Canada in the Polish Ethnic Press (1908–89)." *CES* 23, 1 (1991): 40–57.

Stone, Daniel. "Winnipeg's Polish Language Newspapers and Their Attitude Toward Jews and Ukrainians Between the Two World Wars." *CES* 21, 2 (1989): 27–37.

Turek, Victor. "Poles among the De Meuron Soldiers." *HSSM*, 3rd ser., 9 (1954): 53–68.

———. *The Poles of Manitoba.* Toronto: Polish Research Institute in Canada, 1967.

UKRAINIANS

Darcovitch, William, and Paul Yuzyk, eds. *A Statistical Compendium on the Ukrainians in Canada, 1891–1976.* Ottawa: University of Ottawa Press, 1980.

Hryniuk, Stella, and Neil McDonald. "The Schooling Experience of Ukrainians in Manitoba 1896–1916." *Schools in the West: Essays in Canadian Educational History.* Ed. Nancy M. Sheehan, J. Donald Wilson, and David C. Jones. Calgary: Detselig, 1986.

Isajiw, Wsevolod W., and Norbert J. Hartmann. "Changes in the Occupational Structure of Ukrainians in Canada: A Methodology for the Study of

Changes in Ethnic Studies." *Social and Cultural Change in Canada*. Vol. 1. Ed. W.E. Mann. Toronto: Copp Clark, 1970, 96–112.

Kelebay, Yarema G. "Three Fragments of the Ukrainian Community in Montreal, 1899–1970: A Hartzian Approach." *CES* 12, 2 (1980): 74–89.

Kolasky, John. *The Shattered Illusion: The History of Ukrainian Pro-Communist Organizations in Canada*. Toronto: Peter Martin Associates, 1979.

Kordan, Bolidan."The Intelligentsia and the Development of Ukrainian Ethnic Consciousness in Canada: A Prolegomenon to Research." *CES* 17, 1 (1985): 22–33.

Luciuk, Lubomyr. "Trouble All Around: Ukrainian Canadians and Their Encounter with Ukrainian Refugees of Europe, 1943–1951." *CES* 21, 3 (1989): 37–54.

———, and Stella Hryniuk, eds. *Canada's Ukrainians: Negotiating an Identity*. Toronto: University of Toronto Press in Association with the Ukrainian Centennial Committee, 1991.

Martynowych, Otest T. *Ukrainians in Canada: The Formative Period, 1891–1924*. Edmonton: Canadian Institute of Ukrainian Studies, 1991.

McGowan, Mark. "A Watchful Eye: The Catholic Church Extension Society and Ukrainian Catholic Immigrants, 1908–1930." *Canadian Protestant and Catholic Missions, 1820s–1960s*. New York: P. Lang, 1988, 221–43.

Swyripa, Frances. *Wedded to the Cause: Ukrainian Canadian Women and Ethnic Identity, 1891–1991*. Toronto: University of Toronto Press, 1993.

Yaworsky-Sokolsky, Zoriana. "The Beginnings of Ukrainian Settlement in Toronto, 1891–1939." *Gathering Place: Peoples and Neighborhoods of Toronto, 1834–1945*. Ed. Robert F. Harney. Toronto: MHSO, 1985, 279–302.

Yuzyk, Paul. *The Ukrainian Greek Orthodox Church of Canada, 1918–1951*. Ottawa: University of Ottawa Press, 1981.

WEST INDIES

Clarke, Austin. *The Bigger Light*. Boston: Little, Brown, 1975.

———. *The Meeting Place*. Toronto: Macmillan, 1967.

———. *Storm of Fortune*. Boston: Little, Brown, 1973.

Henry, Frances. "The West Indian Domestic Scheme in Canada." *Social and Economic Studies* 17, 1 (March 1968): 83–91.

Silvera, Makeda. *Silenced: Talks with Working Class Caribbean Women about Their Lives and Struggles as Domestic Workers in Canada*. Toronto: Sister Vision Press, 1989.

Walker, James W. St G. *The West Indians in Canada*. Ottawa: CHA, 1984.

BLACKS

Cooper, Afua. "The Search for Mary Bibb, Black Woman Teacher in Nineteenth-Century Canada West." *OH* 83, 1 (March 1991): 19–54.

Hill, Dan. "The Blacks in Toronto." *Gathering Place: Peoples and Neighborhoods of Toronto, 1834–1945*. Ed. Robert F. Harney. Toronto: MHSO, 1985, 75–105.

———. "Negros in Toronto, 1793–1865." *OH* 55, 2 (1963): 73–91.

Palmer, Howard, and Tamara Palmer. "Urban Blacks in Alberta." *AHR* 29, 3 (Summer 1981): 8–18.

Pease, William H., and Jane H. Pease. "Opposition to the Founding of the Elgin Settlement." *CHR* 38, 3 (Sept. 1957): 202–18.

Walker, James W. St G. "Black Society in Loyalist Nova Scotia: The Growth of a Separate Identity, 1793–91." *The Black Loyalists: The Search for a Promised Land in Nova Scotia and Sierra Leone, 1783–1870.* Ed. James W. St G. Walker. Toronto: University of Toronto Press, 1992, 64–93.

———. "Freedom Denied: The Bondage of Dependence, 1783–91." *The Black Loyalists: The Search for a Promised Land in Nova Scotia and Sierra Leone, 1783–1870.* Ed. James W. St G. Walker. Toronto: University of Toronto Press, 1992, 40–63.

———. "Land and Settlement in Nova Scotia: The Establishment of a Free Black Community, 1783–91." *The Black Loyalists: The Search for a Promised Land in Nova Scotia and Sierra Leone, 1783–1870.* Ed. James W. St G. Walker. Toronto: University of Toronto Press, 1992, 18–39.

———. *Racial Discrimination in Canada: The Black Experience.* Ottawa: CHA, 1985.

Winks, Robin W., ed. *The Blacks in Canada: A History.* Montreal: McGill-Queen's University Press, 1971, 24–60.

GERMANY

Bassler, Gerhard P. "Silent or Silenced Co-Founders of Canada?: Reflections on the History of German Canadians." *CES* 22, 1 (1990): 38–46.

Bell, W.P. *The Foreign Protestants and the Settlement of Nova Scotia: The History of a Piece of Arrested British Colonial Policy in the Eighteenth Century.* Toronto: University of Toronto Press, 1961.

Epp, Frank H. *Mennonites in Canada, 1786–1920: The History of a Separate People.* Toronto: Macmillan, 1974.

———. *Mennonites in Canada, 1920–1940: A People's Struggle for Survival.* Toronto: Macmillan, 1982.

———, and Marlene G. Epp. "The Diverse Roles of Ontario Mennonite Women." *Looking into My Sister's Eyes: An Exploration in Women's History.* Ed. Jean Burnet. Toronto: MHSO, 1986, 223–42.

Grenke, Art. "The German Community of Winnipeg and the English-Canadian Response to World War I." *CES* 20, 1 (1988): 21–44.

Kalbfleisch, H.K. *The History of the Pioneer German Language Press of Ontario, 1835–1918.* Toronto: University of Toronto Press, 1968.

Keyserlingk, Robert. "The Canadian Government's Attitude Toward Germans and German Canadians in World War II." *CES* 16, 1 (1984): 16–28.

Lehmann, Heinz. *The German Canadians 1750–1937: Immigration, Settlement and Culture.* Ed. and trans. Gerhart Bassler. St John's: Jesperson Press, 1986.

Loewen, Royden. "Ethnic Farmers and the 'Outside' World: Mennonites in Manitoba and Nebraska, 1874–1900." *Journal of the CHA* 1 (1990): 195–213.

———. "'The Children, the Cows, My Dear Man and My Sister': The Transplanted Lives of Mennonite Farm Women, 1874–1890." *CHR* 73, 3 (Sept. 1992): 344–73.

McLaughlin, K.M. *The Germans in Canada.* Ottawa: CHA, 1985.

Patterson, Nancy-Lou. "Mennonite Folk Art of Waterloo County." *OH* 60, 3 (1968): 81–104.

Wagner, Jonathon F. *Brothers Beyond the Sea: National Socialism in Canada.* Waterloo: Wilfrid Laurier University Press, 1981.

JAPAN

Adachi, Ken. *The Enemy That Never Was: A History of the Japanese Canadians.* Toronto: McClelland & Stewart, 1976.

Cohn, Werner. "The Persecution of Japanese Canadians and the Political Left in BC, Dec. 1941–March 1942." *BCS* 68 (Winter 1985–86): 3–22.

Dahlie, Jorgen. "The Japanese in BC: Lost Opportunity? Some Aspects of the Education of Minorities." *BCS* 8 (Winter 1970–71): 3–16.

Daniels, Roger. "The Japanese Experience in North America: An Essay in Comparative Racism." *CES* 9, 2 (1977): 91–100.

Iino, Masako. "Japan's Reaction to the Vancouver Riot of 1907." *BCS* 60 (Winter 1983–84): 28–47.

Iwaasa, David B. "The Japanese in Southern Alberta, 1941–45." *AHR* 24, 3 (Summer 1976): 5–19.

Kobayash, Audrey. "Emigration to Canada and Development of the Residential Landscape in a Japanese Village: The Paradox of the Sojourner." *CES* 16, 3 (1984): 111–31.

Roy, Patricia E. "Educating the 'East': BC and the Oriental Question in the Interwar Years." *BCS* 18 (Summer 1973): 50–69.

Sunahara, M. Ann. "Historical Leadership Trends Among Japanese Canadians: 1940–1950." *CES* 11, 1 (1979): 1–16.

Ward, Peter. "British Columbia and the Japanese Evacuation." *Interpreting Canada's Past. Vol. 2. After Confederation.* Ed. J.M. Bumstead. Toronto: Oxford University Press, 1986, 315–32.

———. *The Japanese in Canada.* Ottawa: CHA, 1982.

———. "The Oriental Immigrant and Canada's Protestant Clergy, 1855–1925." *BCS* 22, (Summer 1974): 40–55.

JEWS

Abella, Irving, and Harold Troper. *None Is Too Many: Canada and the Jews of Europe.* Toronto: Lester and Orpen Dennys, 1982.

Anctif, Pierre. *Le Rendez-vous manqué: les Juifs de Montréal face au Québec de l'entre-deux-guerres.* Quebec: Institut Québécois de Recherche sur la Culture, 1988.

Arnold, A.R. "The Contribution of the Jews to the Opening and Development of the West." *HSSM*, 3rd ser., 25 (1968–69): 23–37.

Brown, Michael. *Jew or Juif? Jews, French-Canadians and Anglo-Canadians, 1759–1914.* Philadelphia: Jewish Publication Society, 1987.

Draper, Paula, and Janice B. Karlinsky. "Abraham's Daughters: Women, Charity and Power in the Canadian Jewish Community." *Looking into My Sister's Eyes: An Exploration in Women's History.* Ed. Jean Burnet. Toronto: MHSO, 1986, 75–90.

Frager, Ruth. *Sweatshop Strife: Class, Ethnicity and Gender in the Jewish Labour Movement of Toronto, 1900–1939.* Toronto: University of Toronto Press, 1992.

Gruneir, R. "The Hebrew–Christian Mission in Toronto." *CES* 9, 1 (1977): 18–28.

Hayes, Saul, "Canadian Jewish Culture: Some Observations." *Queen's Quarterly* 84, 1 (1977): 80–88.

Rasporich, A.W. "Early Twentieth-Century Jewish Farm Settlements in Saskatchewan: A Utopian Perspective." *SH* 42, 1 (1989): 28–40.

Robinson, Ira. "The Kosher Meat War and the Jewish Community Council of Montreal, 1922–1925." *CES* 22, 2 (1990): 41–53.

Speisman, Stephen A., "St John's Shtetl: The Ward in 1911." *Gathering Place: Peoples and Neighborhoods of Toronto, 1834–1945.* Ed. Robert F. Harney. Toronto: MHSO, 1985, 107–20.

Swerdlow, Max. *Brother Max: Labour Organizer and Educator.* St John's: Committee on Canadian Labour History, 1990.

Trachtenberg, Henry. "Opportunism, Humanitarianism, and Revulsion: The 'Old Clo Move' Comes to Manitoba, 1882–83." *CES* 22, 2 (1990): 1–18.

Tulchinsky, Gerald. *Taking Root: The Origins of the Canadian Jewish Community.* Toronto: Lester Publishing, 1992.

Vigod, Bernard L. *The Jews in Canada.* Ottawa: CHA, 1984.

MIDDLE EAST

Abu-Laban, Baha. *An Olive Branch on the Family Tree: The Arabs in Canada.* Toronto: McClelland & Stewart, 1980.

Jabbra, Nancy, and Joseph Jabbra. *Voyagers to a Rocky Shore: The Lebanese and Syrians of Nova Scotia.* Halifax: Institute of Public Affairs, Dalhousie University, 1984.

Johnson, Gilbert. "The Syrians in Western Canada." *SH* 12, 1 (1959): 31–32.

Kaprielian, Isabel. "Creating and Sustaining an Ethnocultural Heritage in Ontario: The Case of Armenian Women Refugees." *Looking into My Sister's Eyes: An Exploration in Women's History.* Ed. Jean Burnet. Toronto: MHSO, 1986, 139–53.

Salloum, Habeeb. "Reminiscences: The Urbanization of an Arab Homesteading Family." *SH* 42, 2 (1989): 79–84.

NORTHERN EUROPE

FINNS

Kostiainen, Auvo. "Contacts Between the Finnish Labour Movements in the US and Canada." *Finnish Diaspora I: Canada, South America, America, Africa, Australia and Sweden.* Ed. Michael G. Karnie. Toronto: MHSO, 1981, 33–48.

Laine, Edward. "Finnish Canadian Radicalism and Canadian Politics: The First 40 Years, 1900–1940." *Ethnicity, Power and Politics in Canada.* Ed. Jorgen Dahlie and Tissa Fernando. Toronto: Methuen, 1981, 94–112.

Lindström-Best, Varpu. *Defiant Sisters: A Social History of Finnish Immigrant Women in Canada.* Toronto: MHSO, 1988.

———. *The Finns in Canada.* Ottawa: CHA, 1985.

———. "I Won't Be a Slave! Finnish Domestics in Canada." *Looking into My Sister's Eyes: An Exploration in Women's History.* Ed. Jean Burnet. Toronto: MHSO, 1986, 33–53.

———. "The Unbreachable Gulf: The Division of the Finnish Community in Toronto, 1902–1913." *Finnish Diaspora I: Canada, South America, America, Africa, Australia and Sweden.* Ed. Michael G. Karnie. Toronto: MHSO, 1981, 11–18.

Sangster, Joan. "Finnish Women in Ontario, 1890–1930." *Polyphony* 3, 2 (Fall 1981): 46–54.

Wilson, J. Donald. "The Canadian Sojourn of a Finnish-American Radical." *CES* 16, 2 (1984): 102–15.

———. "Matti Kurikka and A.B. Mäkela: Socialist Thought Among Finns in Canada 1900–1932." *CES* 10, 2 (1978): 9–21.

NORWEGIANS

Dahlie, Jorgen. "From Ringsaker to Instow: A Norwegian Radical's Saskatchewan Odyssey." *Ethnic Canadians: Culture and Education.* Ed. Martin Kovacs. Regina: Canadian Plains Research Center, 1978, 97–108.

———. "Scandinavian Experiences on the Prairies, 1890–1920: The Frederiksens of Nokomis." *The Settlement of the West.* Ed. Howard Palmer. Calgary: Comprint Publishing, 1977, 102–13.

———. "Socialist and Farmer: Ole Hjelt and the Norwegian Radical Voice in Canada, 1908–1928." *CES* 10, 2 (1978): 55–64.

Loken, Gulbrand. *From Fjord to Frontier: A History of the Norwegians in Canada.* Toronto: McClelland & Stewart, 1980.

DANES

Dahlie, Jorgen. "Letters Home from a Danish Family on the Prairies." *CES* 8, 2 (1976): 93–95.

ICELANDERS

The Icelandic Canadian. (Quarterly journal published in Winnipeg).

Kristjansen, William. *The Icelandic People of Manitoba* (Winnipeg: n.p., 1965).

Matthieson, John. "Icelanders." *Canadian Encyclopedia.* Vol. 2 (Edmonton: Hurtig, 1985).

Salverson, Laura. *Confessions of an Immigrant's Daughter.* Toronto: University of Toronto Press, 1981.

SOUTHEAST ASIA

Buchignani, N. "A Review of the Historical and Sociological Literature on East Indians in Canada." *CES* 9, 1 (1977): 86–108.

Dossa, Parin. "Woman's Space/Time: An Anthropological Perspective on Ismaili Immigrant Women in Calgary and Vancouver." *CES* 20, 1 (1988): 45–65.

Goa, David J., Harold C. Coward, and Ronald Neufeldt. "Hindus in Alberta: A Study in Religion Continuity and Change." *CES* 16, 1 (1984): 96–113.

Johnston, Hugh J.M. *The East Indians in Canada.* Ottawa: CHA, 1984.

———. *The Voyage of the Komagato Maru: The Sikh Challenge to Canada's Colour Bar.* Delhi: Oxford University Press, 1979.

Smith, M.W. "Sikh Settlers in Canada." *Asia and the Americas* (Aug. 1944).

SOUTHEASTERN EUROPE

GREEK

Chimbos, Peter D. *The Canadian Odyssey: The Greek Experience in Canada.* Toronto: McClelland & Stewart, 1980.

Douramakou-Petroleka, Lia. "The Elusive Community: Greek Settlement in Toronto, 1900–1940." *Gathering Place: Peoples and Neighborhoods of Toronto, 1834–1945.* Ed. Robert F. Harney. Toronto: MHSO, 1985, 257–78.

Polyzoi, Eleoussa. "Greek Immigrant Women from Asia Minor in Prewar Toronto: The Formative Years." *Looking into My Sister's Eyes: An Exploration in Women's History.* Ed. Jean Burnet. Toronto: MHSO, 1986, 107–24.

CROATIAN

Cloutier-Wojciechowska, Cecile. "Alain Horic—le poète croate du Québec." *CES* 4, 1–2 (1972): 25–33.

Rasporich, Anthony. "A Croatian Family on the Frontier." *CES* 8, 2 (1976): 95–102.

———. *For a Better Life: A History of the Croatians in Canada.* Toronto: McClelland & Stewart, 1982.

———. "Tomo Cacic: Rebel Without a Country." *CES* 10, 2 (1978): 86–94.

MACEDONIAN

Petroff, Lillian. "Contributers to Ethnic Cohesion: Macedonian Women of Toronto to 1940." *Looking into My Sister's Eyes: An Exploration in Women's History.* Ed. Jean Burnet. Toronto: MHSO, 1986, 125–38.

———. "Macedonians: From Village to City." *CES* 9, 1 (1977): 29–41.

———. "Sojourner and Settler: The Macedonian Presence in the City, 1903–1940." *Gathering Place: Peoples and Neighborhoods of Toronto, 1834–1945*. Ed. Robert F. Harney. Toronto: MHSO, 1985, 177–203.

ROUMANIAN

Woywitka, Anne B. "A Roumanian Pioneer." *AHR* 21, 4 (Fall 1973): 20–27.

SOUTHERN EUROPE

ITALIANS

Dubinsky, Karen, and Franca Iacovetta. "Murder, Womanly Virtue, and Motherhood: The Case of Angelina Napolitano, 1911–1922." *CHR* 72, 4 (1991): 505–31.

Feltracco, Anna Marie. "More than Love and Pasta: A Case Study of Italian Immigrant Women's Social Organization—The Italian Immigrant Aid Society's Ladies Auxiliary." MA thesis, University of Western Ontario, 1989.

Gobaccio, Donna R. *From Sicily to Elizabeth Street: Housing and Social Change Among Italian Immigrants: 1880–1930*. Albany: State University of New York Press, 1984.

Gualtieri, Antonio Roberto. "La Favilla and Italian Ethnicity in Canada." *CES* 23, 3 (1991): 60–68.

Harney, R.F. "Ambiente and Social Class in North American Little Italies." *Canadian Review of Studies in Nationalism* 2, 1 (Fall 1974): 208–24.

———. "Boarding and Belonging: Thoughts on Sojourner Institutions." *Urban History Review* 2 (1978): 8–37.

———. "The Commerce of Migration." *CES* 8, 1 (1977): 42–53.

———. "Men Without Women: Italian Migrants in Canada, 1885–1930." *CES* 11, 1 (1979): 29–47.

———. "Montreal's King of Italian Labour: A Case Study of Padronism." *L/T* 4 (1979): 57–84.

———. "The Padrone and the Immigrant." *Canadian Review of American Studies* 5, 2 (Fall 1974): 101–18.

———, and J. Vincenza Scarpas. *Little Italies in North America*. Toronto: MHSO, 1981.

Iacovetta, Franca. "Primitive Villagers and Uneducated Girls." *Canadian Woman Studies* 7, 4 (Winter 1986): 14–18.

———. *Such Hardworking People: Italian Immigrants in Postwar Toronto*. Montreal: McGill-Queen's University Press, 1992.

Perin, Roberto. "Making Good Fascists and Good Canadians: Consular Propaganda and the Italian Community in Montreal in the 1930s." *Minorities and Mother Country Imagery*. Ed. Gerald Gold. St John's: Institute of Social and Economic Research, 1984, 136–58.

Potestio, John. "The 'Memoirs' of Giovanni Veltri: A Contadino Turned Railway Builder." *The Italian Immigrant Experience*. Ed. John Potestio and Antonio Pucci. Thunder Bay: CIHA, 1988, 119–30.

Pucci, Antonio. "Thunder Bay's Italian Community, 1880s–1940s." *The Italian Immigrant Experience*. Ed. John Potestio and Antonio Pucci. Thunder Bay: CIHA, 1988, 79–102.

Ramirez, Bruno. "Brief Encounters: Italian Immigrant Workers and the CPR, 1900–1930." *L/T* 17 (Spring 1986): 9–27.

———, and Michael DelBalso. *The Italians of Montreal: From Sojourning to Settlement, 1900–1921*. Montreal: Association di Cultura Popolare Italo-Quebecchese, 1980.

Sturino, Frank. *Forging the Chain: A Case Study of Italian Immigration to North America 1880–1930*. Toronto: MHSO, 1990.

———. "The Italian Immigration to Canada and the Farm Labour System Through the 1920s." *The Italian Immigrant Experience*. Ed. John Potestio and Antonio Pucci. Thunder Bay: CIHA, 1988, 61–77.

Zucchi, John E. *Italians in Toronto: Development of a National Identity 1875–1935*. Montreal: McGill-Queen's University Press, 1988.

PORTUGUESE

Anderson, Grace M. "Spearhead Anchorages and Initiation of Networks, With Special Reference to the Portuguese Case." *Ethnic Canadians: Culture and Education*. Ed. Martin Kovacs. Regina: Canadian Plains Research Center, 1978, 381–87.

Higgs, David. *The Portuguese in Canada*. Ottawa: CHA, 1982.

Pereira Munzer, Rosa. "Immigration, Familism and In-Group Competition: A Study of the Portuguese in the South Okanagan." *CES* 13, 2 (1981): 98–111.

WESTERN EUROPEANS

Choquette, Leslie Phyllis. "French Emigration to Canada in the Seventeenth and Eighteenth Centuries." PhD thesis, Harvard University, 1988.

Ganzevoort, Herman. *A Bittersweet Land: The Dutch Experience in Canada, 1890–1980*. Toronto: McClelland & Stewart, 1988.

———. "Dempsey–Tunney and the Emigraton Question: Dutch Immigrant Correspondents in 1920s Canada." *CES* 20, 1 (1988): 140–52.

Jaenen, Cornelius J. *The Belgians in Canada*. Ottawa: CHA, 1991.

Lamontagne, Leopold. "Kingston's French Heritage." *OH* 45, 3 (1953): 109–21.

Luethy, Ivor C.E. "General Sir Frederick Haldimand: A Swiss Governor-General of Canada 1777–1784." *CES* 3, 1 (1971): 63–75.

Weatherford, John. "The Vicomte de Vaux: Would-be Canadian." *OH* 47, 2 (1955): 49–57.